Handbook of Research on the Empirical Aspects of Strategic Trade Negotiations and Management

Nuno Crespo
ISCTE - Instituto Universitário de Lisboa, Portugal

Nadia Simoes
ISCTE - Instituto Universitário de Lisboa, Portugal

IGI Global
PUBLISHER of TIMELY KNOWLEDGE

A volume in the Advances in Finance, Accounting, and Economics (AFAE) Book Series

Published in the United States of America by
IGI Global
Business Science Reference (an imprint of IGI Global)
701 E. Chocolate Avenue
Hershey PA, USA 17033
Tel: 717-533-8845
Fax: 717-533-8661
E-mail: cust@igi-global.com
Web site: http://www.igi-global.com

Library of Congress Cataloging-in-Publication Data

Names: Crespo, Nuno, editor. | Simoes, Nadia, 1979- editor.
Title: Handbook of research on the empirical aspects of strategic trade negotiations and management / Nuno Crespo, and Nadia Simoes, editors.
Description: Hershey : Business Science Reference, 2021. | Includes bibliographical references and index. | Summary: "This book discusses the importance that international trade plays in the world economy by providing and spotlighting the most important methods used to evaluate the multiple dimensions of trade"-- Provided by publisher.
Identifiers: LCCN 2020047960 (print) | LCCN 2020047961 (ebook) | ISBN 9781799875680 (hardcover) | ISBN 9781799875697 (ebook)
Subjects: LCSH: International trade. | Foreign trade regulation.. | Negotiation in business.
Classification: LCC HF1379 .H36546 2021 (print) | LCC HF1379 (ebook) | DDC 382--dc23
LC record available at https://lccn.loc.gov/2020047960
LC ebook record available at https://lccn.loc.gov/2020047961

This book is published in the IGI Global book series Advances in Finance, Accounting, and Economics (AFAE) (ISSN: 2327-5677; eISSN: 2327-5685)

British Cataloguing in Publication Data
A Cataloguing in Publication record for this book is available from the British Library.

All work contributed to this book is new, previously-unpublished material. The views expressed in this book are those of the authors, but not necessarily of the publisher.

For electronic access to this publication, please contact: eresources@igi-global.com.

Advances in Finance, Accounting, and Economics (AFAE) Book Series

Ahmed Driouchi
Al Akhawayn University, Morocco

ISSN:2327-5677
EISSN:2327-5685

Mission

In our changing economic and business environment, it is important to consider the financial changes occurring internationally as well as within individual organizations and business environments. Understanding these changes as well as the factors that influence them is crucial in preparing for our financial future and ensuring economic sustainability and growth.

The **Advances in Finance, Accounting, and Economics (AFAE)** book series aims to publish comprehensive and informative titles in all areas of economics and economic theory, finance, and accounting to assist in advancing the available knowledge and providing for further research development in these dynamic fields.

Coverage

- Field Research
- Economic Indices and Quantitative Economic Methods
- Internet Banking
- Accounting information systems
- Fiscal Policy
- Entrepreneurship in Accounting and Finance
- Taxes
- Wages and Employment
- Interest Rates and Annuities
- Economic Policy

IGI Global is currently accepting manuscripts for publication within this series. To submit a proposal for a volume in this series, please contact our Acquisition Editors at Acquisitions@igi-global.com or visit: http://www.igi-global.com/publish/.

The Advances in Finance, Accounting, and Economics (AFAE) Book Series (ISSN 2327-5677) is published by IGI Global, 701 E. Chocolate Avenue, Hershey, PA 17033-1240, USA, www.igi-global.com. This series is composed of titles available for purchase individually; each title is edited to be contextually exclusive from any other title within the series. For pricing and ordering information please visit http://www.igi-global.com/book-series/advances-finance-accounting-economics/73685. Postmaster: Send all address changes to above address.

Titles in this Series

For a list of additional titles in this series, please visit:
http://www.igi-global.com/book-series/advances-finance-accounting-economics/73685

Handbook of Research on Islamic Social Finance and Economic Recovery After a Global Health Crisis
Salina Kassim (Institute of Islamic Banking and Finance, International Islamic University Malaysia, Malaysia) Anwar Hasan Abdullah Othman (Institute of Islamic Banking and Finance, International Islamic University Malaysia, Malaysia) and Razali Haron (Institute of Islamic Banking and Finance, International Islamic University Malaysia, Malaysia)
Business Science Reference • © 2021 • 410pp • H/C (ISBN: 9781799868118) • US $295.00

Money Laundering and Terrorism Financing in Global Financial Systems
Abdul Rafay (University of Management and Technology, Pakistan)
Business Science Reference • © 2021 • 374pp • H/C (ISBN: 9781799887584) • US $215.00

Financial Management and Risk Analysis Strategies for Business Sustainability
Joaquín Enríquez-Díaz (University of A Coruña, Spain) Laura Castro-Santos (University of A Coruña, Spain) and Félix Puime-Guillén (University of A Coruña, Spain)
Business Science Reference • © 2021 • 320pp • H/C (ISBN: 9781799876342) • US $215.00

Theory of Shocks, COVID-19, and Normative Fundamentals for Policy Responses
Olga Ivanovna Pilipenko (The Russian Presidential Academy of National Economy and Public Administration, Russia) Zoya Andreevna Pilipenko (Bank of Russia, Russia) and Andrey Igorevich Pilipenko (The Russian Presidential Academy of National Economy and Public Administration, Russia)
Business Science Reference • © 2021 • 396pp • H/C (ISBN: 9781799843092) • US $195.00

Handbook of Research on Theory and Practice of Financial Crimes
Abdul Rafay (University of Management and Technology, Pakistan)
Business Science Reference • © 2021 • 650pp • H/C (ISBN: 9781799855675) • US $345.00

Comparative Research on Earnings Management, Corporate Governance, and Economic Value
Elisabete S. Vieira (University of Aveiro, Portugal) Mara Madaleno (University of Aveiro, Portugal) and Graça Azevedo (University of Aveiro, Portugal)
Business Science Reference • © 2021 • 433pp • H/C (ISBN: 9781799875963) • US $215.00

Examining the Intersection of Circular Economy, Forestry, and International Trade
Badri Narayanan Gopalakrishnan (University of Washington, USA) Taranjeet Duggal (Amity University, India) and Tavishi Tewary (Jaipuria Institute of Management Noida, India)
Business Science Reference • © 2021 • 266pp • H/C (ISBN: 9781799849902) • US $195.00

IGI Global
PUBLISHER of TIMELY KNOWLEDGE

701 East Chocolate Avenue, Hershey, PA 17033, USA
Tel: 717-533-8845 x100 • Fax: 717-533-8661
E-Mail: cust@igi-global.com • www.igi-global.com

List of Contributors

Table of Contents

Detailed Table of Contents

This chapter aims to shed light on the trends of sectoral trade globalization. This component of trade globalization is often neglected. An accurate evaluation of sectoral trade requires the analysis of the interdependencies of countries and the consideration of distance as a central dimension of trade globalization. As such, sectoral trade globalization is one aspect of a more complex and multi-dimensional phenomenon. Data show that sectoral trade globalization has increased significantly over the last 50 years irrespective of the characteristics of individual sectors. One relevant insight is that the level of trade globalization is on average still different for high-tech sectors compared to low-tech and medium-low-tech sectors even though the former could increase their bilateral trade relationships over time. Even though protectionist tendencies as well as the COVID-19 pandemic have led to a vivid discussion about the return to more local or regional production schemes, digitalization processes could still have the potential to further integrate countries' trade networks.

With the apparent demise of globalization, many states are turning to regional solutions to achieve trade and development goals while institutional structure is fundamental to the strategic and managerial operations of such associations. This study seeks to understand the strategic costs and benefits, as well as the management opportunities and challenges, of a regional institution that maintains an informal structure while specifically examining the relationship between informal regional structure and member (national) resilience. This investigation develops a resilience framework and tests it against a unique structural form, the Pacific Alliance (Chile, Colombia, Mexico, and Peru), which operates without incorporation as a legal entity, without a centralized budget, and without a secretariat. This study reasons that an informal regional institution supports national resilience through an adaptation strategy but not an adaptability strategy and concludes that an informal regional model appears to support continual national development through the adoption of member 'best practice'.

The goal of this study is to investigate the potential effects of international trade on per-capita CO2 emissions among trade partners. To achieve this purpose, the Group of Seven (G7) countries and each of their developing trade-partner countries with the highest trade volume have been selected as the sample. The stochastic convergence methodology has been employed using Augmented Dickey Fuller (ADF), Phillips-Perron (PP), and Enders-Lee Fourier unit root tests in order to test for convergence or divergence. Various results have been obtained from the unit root tests. These results suggest international trade to have no general or common effects on per capita CO2 emissions.

This study investigates the impacts of exchange rate regime (ERR) choice, economic, institutional, and demographic factors on the budget deficit. The recent literature states that fiscal discipline is affected by the ERR preferences in open economies. In this study, the effect of de facto ERR preferences on fiscal discipline were analyzed between 1995 and 2016 for 76 countries classified into income groups. The estimates by Feasible Generalized Least Squares and Panel Corrected Standard Errors estimators show that flexible ERRs provide much more fiscal discipline. The findings highlight the importance of institutional quality, demographic factors, and inflation to ensure fiscal discipline. A country with a high level of trade openness is more vulnerable to exchange rate shocks, which leads to uncertainty in the fiscal policy. The results confirm that ERR preferences affect countries' fiscal disciplines differently, depending on the countries' characteristics.

The theme of regional centrality, more commonly known as accessibility, has been increasingly invoked in recent years, mainly due to a clearer understanding that proximity to the markets is a key determinant of the location of firms. This chapter improves the most standard accessibility index using a decomposition method that allows considering the influence of (1) internal and external factors and (2) economic and geographical aspects. Each component identified has a specific interpretation and allows the identification of policy recommendations, such as the development of the transport and communication networks and active interventions to attract investment. The baseline decomposition method is adjusted in order to incorporate differences in spatial terms among the regional units considered. In order to illustrate the proposed methodology, the authors consider 171 countries. Results lead to the conclusion that the centrality level of the countries analyzed derives from different sources. Therefore, different countries may require different policy interventions to improve their centrality.

This chapter analyses the participation of the agricultural G-20 coalition within the Doha Round of the World Trade Organization. The strategies, modes of operation, as well as the internal and external articulations of the group from its inception during the run-up to the Cancun Ministerial to its dissolution in 2008 are the object of scrutiny. Based on documental analysis of cables from the achieves of the Brazilian Ministry of Foreign Affairs and interviews conducted with stakeholders in the negotiation process, the chapter engages with the contextual circumstances and central factors which both permitted the rise of the G-20 within the negotiation process, but eventually also led to its disintegration.

Trade diversification patterns help explain the level of utilization of trade opportunities by countries, mainly the least developed. Empirical analyses show an inverse U relationship between trade diversification and level of development. Trade diversification measures used do not take into account differences in complexity of exports, and complexity indices only consider products with comparative advantages. This study seeks to cover both gaps by analyzing the differences in the determinants of trade diversification, considering the complexity of products exported by 19 Western Hemisphere countries from 1962 to 2017. The results show that after controlling for economic complexity, the inverted U relationship disappears. Development of financial markets positively affects the complexity of trade diversification in the long term, while the terms of trade that have a negative effect on trade diversification does not affect the complexity-corrected indices. In the short term, transaction costs and trade openness appear to have a significant effect.

The geostrategic approach refers to China's method to rise as global power through worldwide trade expansion and the development of its military and naval capabilities. It creates clusters of countries interlinked as China's trade partners, thus being assets to its global ascent. China's importance in global trade is a function of its partners' behavior embracing its trade mechanism. The edges connecting nodes are multidirectional, implying that countries are as much interested in their China-induced interlinkages as they are in their partnership with China. This results in China's centrality, a quality gained from being dominant in trade partnerships in terms of numbers and significance. This chapter examines the approach, process, and historical, geographic, and behavioral components that China uses in its ascent as central node in the international trade network. It explores how underlying dimensions making China's national character conjointly devise its behavior in global trade.

The upcoming decades are expected to be marked by the rise and consolidation of the People's Republic of China, PRC, as the world's first economy, dethroning the U.S. and altering global economic geopolitics. The Dragon Age will mark the 21st century, with all the consequences that can come from it. This chapter analyzes the changes that are already underway and that prepare China to be the world's great economy. The departure point will be the examination of China's economic situation. Following, the authors move on to analyzing the Belt and Road Investment, the Chinese mega investment that aims to connect China to Europe inspired by the ancient Silk Road, making a geoeconomic analysis of the main world markets and how China has long prepared this economic rise and implicates a political and military ascension statement.

As in any international business relation, factors such as political, economic, social, technological, and legal dimensions are expected to significantly impact trade activities. Social factors include the cultural aspects of exports and imports along with the differences among foreign markets. Culture poses to be complementary to FDI and exports. Cultural components include food, language, clothing, values, traditions, and beliefs, which differ from region to region across the world. When the countries are culturally different, investing and trading becomes a risk. Hence, in today's scenario, it is very important for the organizations to understand cultural differences in order to compete with their competitors. Understanding these cultural differences owes the opportunity to make or break the success of a foreign trade opportunity. The global businesses need to adhere to the demands and perceptions of different cultures in the countries when they purchase different products.

This chapter attempts to analyze trade effects of India's liberalization with the Association of Southeast Asian Nations and five Asia-Pacific countries (ASEAN Plus Five), Bay of Bengal Initiative for Multi-Sectoral Technical and Economic Cooperation (BIMSTEC), European Union (EU), India-Japan-Australia trilateral framework, and Southern African Customs Union (SACU). It also tries to look at how they can create new opportunities for trade among the member countries. The authors sort out which of the above-recorded arrangements will be the most welfare upgrading for India. The chapter attempts to comprehend whether India ought to pull out for the occasions to be essential for value-chains in the areas. Maximum gains occur when India liberalizes with all, that is, liberalizes multilaterally followed by ASEAN 10, RCEP, Indo Pacific, CPTPP, MENA, EU 27, 54 nations African FTA, GCC, among others. Services and investment liberalization would bring further dividends to India.

This chapter aims to look at various existing international economic cooperation groups and analyze the impact of India liberalizing with each of them using the GTAP model. This chapter aims to discuss each of these economic groups composition and identify the key sectors they are specialized in. Further, they analyze the product aggregations in which India and these groups would benefit if we liberalize with them. This chapter looks at different linear and nonlinear methods while performing the simulations and compares them. The chapter looks at the different scenarios with (1) India reducing tariff by 10%, (2) both Indian and the economic group reducing tariff by 10%, (3) both reducing the tariffs to 0%. The chapter then further looks at the impact of each cooperation liberalizing with India in terms of terms of trade (ToT), trade balance, and import and export quantities. Thus, this chapter attempts to get some insights into what product aggregates would be beneficial for India and the economic groups and therefore build a roadmap for the same.

The current challenge for the survival and growth of international businesses is the appropriation of innovation in all its senses. This chapter attempts to analyze the contextual framework of international entrepreneurship and the importance of the entrepreneur's profile that influences the potential to generate innovative environments in relation to success in doing business abroad. This analysis aims to answer the questions of strategic thinking that can be a critical factor in business competitiveness and contribute to its success.

Entrepreneurship has emerged as a key vector, introducing dynamism in stagnant markets, through technological change, innovation, and process restructuring. However, despite all the potential benefits, this is a very arduous and uncertain process, to the extent that many of the companies created end up failing in the first five years of activity. This chapter aims to study the entrepreneur as an individual, focusing on the analysis of their personal characteristics and their impact on the growth of the new created firm. A mixed methodology was developed to test which personal characteristics impact growth. A questionnaire was carried out on a sample of 87 Portuguese entrepreneurs and, additionally, 10 interviews were held with the purpose of complementing the information of the collected data with a qualitative approach and a more personal perspective. Finally, the results revealed that there are certain characteristics that enhance and influence the growth of startups, the most crucial being leadership, the need for achievement, proactivity, and resilience and adaptability.

Preface

International trade is a key dimension of the world economy, accounting for more than 30% of world GDP (a very strong increase since 1960). It is a critical factor in raising living standards, increasing employment, and providing a larger variety of goods to the consumers around the world. Despite the strong focus that international trade questions have received in theoretical terms, the empirical aspects of trade are less clear and justify further research.

This gap in the literature was the key motivation to produce this Handbook of Research. It aims to contribute to this area by putting together a group of studies produced by international experts with the objective of shedding light on some of the most important methods and themes used/considered to evaluate multiple dimensions of trade.

Given the importance of the topic, the research developed in the 18 chapters that integrate this Handbook are a significant contribution to understand key dynamics of a globalized world. The *Handbook of Research on the Empirical Aspects of Strategic Trade Negotiations and Management* is a valuable resource to a vast audience, including scholars, students, government officials, policy makers, and managers. Moreover, it is important to stress that, since trade has a myriad of direct and indirect effects, it touches several fields of research, including economics, management, finance, international relations, political science, and sociology, among others, potentiating even more the universe of readers.

Chapter 1, by Nuno Crespo, Nicole Palan, and Nadia Simoes, provides an in-depth empirical analysis of key trends of sectoral trade globalization. This is an important and less studied topic since the focus of the studies is usually concentrated on the evaluation of globalization in overall terms. The authors make use of several measures to conduct their empirical evaluation and explore interdependence and distance as central dimensions of the phenomenon. A vast period – 50 years – is taken as reference, allowing to obtain a clear and detailed perspective on the evolution of sectoral trade globalization. The evidence produced shows that trade globalization has increased significantly in that period (1967-2016), irrespective of the specific characteristics of the individual sectors, although, of course, important differences emerge regarding the pace of the evolution in districting groups of sectors. The authors conclude their analysis with a discussion about the potential impact of the current COVID-19 pandemic on the world trade flows.

Chapter 2, authored by Larry Crump, analyses the advantages, disadvantages, management opportunities, and challenges of regional institutions with an informal structure. In more concrete terms, this chapter considers the case of the Pacific Alliance (Chile, Colombia, Mexico, and Peru) and evaluates the relationship between informal regional structure and national resilience. Based on a detailed and solid empirical exercise, the study concludes that informal regional institutions provide strategic benefits by contributing to member (national) resilience. Additionally, the analysis conducted in this chapter allows to investigate if this effect occurs through an adaptation strategy and/or an adaptability (transformational) strategy. The conclusions obtained are important to policy action, namely because they allow to establish key principles to define policies for building informal regional institutions.

Chapter 3 was prepared by Furkan Yıldız. It aims to discuss and test the effects of international trade on CO2 emissions among trade partners. This is obtained considering the G7 countries and each of their developing trade-partner countries with the highest trade volume as reference. A stochastic convergence methodology was applied using Augmented Dickey Fuller (ADF), Phillips-Perron (PP), and Enders-Lee Fourier unit root tests. The empirical evidence indicates that international trade does not have general/common effects on per capita CO2 emissions. Several specific results were derived for different pairs of countries, providing a more comprehensive understanding of the impacts under analysis.

Based on the idea – advanced by recent literature – that fiscal discipline is affected by the exchange rate regime (EER) preferences in open economies, Chapter 4, by Mustafa Kiziltan, puts the focus on the study of the impact of the exchange rate regime choice, economic, institutional, and demographic factors on budget deficit. A group of 76 economies (classified into income groups) was studied along a period of more than 20 years. The empirical results presented in this chapter allow us to conclude that flexible exchange rate regimes assure more fiscal discipline. This evidence has significant implications for policy-makers since it highlights the relevance of several factors to ensure fiscal discipline. These include, for example, institutional quality, demographic factors, and inflation. Thus, the impact of EER preferences on fiscal discipline depends on the characteristics of each country. In this context, the study stresses that a high level of trade openness makes the country more vulnerable to exchange rate shocks, leading to uncertainty in fiscal policy.

Chapter 5 is authored by Maria Paula Fontoura, Nuno Crespo, and Nadia Simoes, and is dedicated to the measurement of regional centrality, adopting a world-level perspective. This is a vital issue because accessibility is a critical determinant of firm location. The authors discuss the importance of centrality for international economic trade and propose two methods to decompose the level of centrality exhibited by each region/country into several components with economic interpretation. More specifically, the decomposition methods suggested by the authors allows to take into account the influence of: (i) internal and external factors; (ii) economic and geographical aspects. Four components are identified and, from each of them emerge specific and concrete guidelines for policy action. The chapter presents abundant evidence for a total of 171 countries, concerning not only their overall level of centrality but also regarding the respective sources, allowing to know the weak and strong points of each country in what concerns centrality. It is interesting to emphasize that the methods discussed in this chapter are valid and can easily be extended to other levels of geographical analysis.

Niels Søndergaard is the author of Chapter 6. In this interesting chapter, it is analyzed the participation of the agricultural G-20 coalition within the Doha Round of the World Trade Organization. The chapter makes a detailed evaluation of important aspects such as the strategies, the modes of operation, and the (internal and external) articulations of the group from its inception during the run-up to the Cancun Ministerial to its dissolution, in 2008. The conclusions of this study are based on a detailed documental analysis and on interviews with stakeholders in the negotiation process, providing an interesting perspective about the contextual conditions and factors that allowed the rise of the G-20. This analysis is extremely interesting and useful since the outcome of trade negotiations can shape the links that are formed between national economies and global markets.

Chapter 7 of this Handbook deals with the topic of economic complexity and trade diversity, being authored by Jorge Falcón Gómez and Fernando Martín Mayoral. International trade opens to the countries important opportunities to expand markets and, thus, seize scale economies. However, these opportunities are not well explored by many developing countries, making this topic an important aspect of public policy. While empirical studies suggest the existence of an inverse U relationship between trade diversification and level of development, the most commonly used trade diversification measures do not take into account differences in complexity of exports and complexity indices only consider products with comparative advantages. This chapter aims to overcome these shortcomings of the literature. It evaluates the determinants of trade diversification taking the complexity of products into account. The period between 1962 and 2017 is considered as reference. An important conclusion from this study is that, when economic complexity is considered, the inverted U relationship mentioned by previous studies is no longer valid.

Chapter 8 is devoted to the analysis of the geostrategic approach followed by China in order to increase its worldwide influence. This study, produced by Guy Maurille Massamba, concentrates on the method adopted by China to increase its global power, not only through international trade but also through the development of military capacity. In what regards international trade, the study emphasizes the growing centrality of China, which is caused by the increase importance of China in terms of trade partnerships and their significance. This chapter is an important contribution to understand the circumstances that are vital for the ascendant of China as a central player in the global trade network. These include, for example, historical, geographic, and behavior components. Based on the analysis conducted in this study, the author concludes with a group of key policy recommendations.

Chapter 9 is still concentrated on the central role of China in international trade and, in a broader sense, in terms of economic and political influence in the 21st century. In this chapter, elaborated by Maria João Tomás, abundant evidence is analyzed in order to demonstrate the economic emergence of China in the last years. The central argument of the chapter is that China has been preparing its way to become the world leader in the next years. Several strategies that have been adopted by this country are discussed and it is shown why we will assist in the next decades to the consolidation of China as the world's first economy. This process already made (and will continue to make) significant modifications in terms of the world geopolitics. The author also provides an interesting discussion about the way the different economies (or groups of economies) are reacting to the emergence of China.

Chapter 10, authored by Anusha Thakur, puts the focus on the analysis of the importance of the cultural dimension on trade. Culture includes several components, such as food, language, clothing, values, traditions, and beliefs, which differ from region to region. The existence of remarkable differences between origin and destination countries is a barrier to trade and investment. Therefore, the purpose of this chapter is to understand in more detail the differences among three key areas at the world-level: Europe (evaluated through the specific case of UK), Asia-Pacific (captured through the case of Japan), and North America (analyzed through the specific case of U.S.A.). The study makes use of the Hofstede's six dimensions of culture in order to conduct its empirical research and complements the discussion with an analysis of the cultural challenges raised by globalization.

Chapter 11 is authored by Somesh Kumar Mathur and Naman Agrawal. The goal of this chapter is to assess the effects caused by trade liberalization of India with specific groups of economies. The simulations produced in the study allow us to retain several key conclusions. The most important results is the fact that maximum gains occurs when India liberalizes with all these groups, that is, when it liberalizes multilaterally.

Chapter 12 is authored by José Vargas-Hernández. The main goal of the chapter is to analyze the implications of regionalism in North America region on Mexican exports and, more specifically, on the agricultural exports of the region of Sinaloa. The study evaluates the turbulence experienced in the last years, namely with the possibility, raised by Trump administration, of exit by the U.S.A., and discusses the advantages and disadvantages of renegotiation.

The next chapter – Chapter 13, prepared by Iulia Monica Dumitrescu – is a survey covering three key areas. First, it analyses the most important trends of the world economy over the last decades. In this context, the author discusses important dimensions, such as globalization, regionalization, international agreements, and the emergence of new economic poles in international arena. Second, the chapter presents a comprehensive overview of some critical determinants of specialization. To that end, the main body of theories of international trade are covered and their main implications are emphasized. Finally, still with the objective of providing a survey of the main determinants of specialization, the chapter reviews some groups of factors, including demographic change, advances in technology, investment, and energy and natural resources.

Chapter 14 is dedicated to the empirical study of the Greenfield FDI determinants in MENA region (Middle East and North Africa). The authors of this chapter are Youssra Ben Romdhane Loukil, Souhaila Kammoun, and Imen Ouerghi. The importance of this study is high because it allows us to retain some important conclusions regarding a geographical area characterized by recent important political and economic transformations. Beyond the investigation of the determinants of Greenfield FDI in this region (taking inflation, trade freedom, and investment freedom as macroeconomic variables and political instability as an institutional variable), this chapter aims to identify which environmental sector may affect this mode of foreign investment in MENA region. The period between 2010 and 2018 is assumed as reference and a total of 13 countries are included in the empirical exercise. The results support the idea that trade openness stimulates foreign investment in MENA region. Additionally, the evidence emphasizes the fact that the lack of inflation control may disrupt the inflow of Greenfield FDI (because it expresses the economic stability/instability of the countries). A final key conclusion is that there is a positive relationship between Greenfield FDI and environmental sectors. Adequate guidelines for policy intervention are also derived from the analysis.

Somesh Kumar Mathur and Sachin Angural are the authors of chapter 15. This chapter makes use of GTAP (which is a powerful Computable General Equilibrium model) to investigate the potential impact of a liberalization process between India and several major economic groups. The study starts with the characterization of each of these groups from an economic point of view and, based on that, it identifies the products in which India and these groups would benefit in case of a real liberalization process. Three scenarios were tested and compared, namely: (i) a reduction of 10% of the tariffs applied by India; (ii) a similar reduction but now applied by both India and the economic group under analysis in each specific case; (iii) the complete elimination of tariffs between the two economies/groups. As the tittle of the chapter makes clear, the objective of the authors is to propose a roadmap to this process of liberalization between India and other economies.

Chapter 16, from José Vargas-Hernández and Mario Guadalupe Zazueta-Félix, provides an interesting discussion about the characteristics of the entrepreneur, seen as a critical element for the success of international businesses. In fact, there is a vast literature emphasizing not only the importance of innovation but also the fundamental role of the leader for the success of the firm. The study builds an analytical relationship between entrepreneurial profiles and other critical factors, like strategic thinking, innovative environments, and competitive forces. Beyond a discussion in more general terms, a differentiation element of this study is the fact that it discusses the specific case of entrepreneurship in the gastronomic sector through the consideration of a case study. In a final section, this chapter produces some recommendations and highlights some key aspects that should be kept in mind when considering the role of the entrepreneur in international businesses.

Chapter 17 is also dedicated to the role of the entrepreneur and was elaborated by Vítor Ferreira and Tomás Luís. In specific terms, this study aims to evaluate the impact of the entrepreneur personal characteristics on new firm growth. This chapter makes two critical contributions. First, it provides an extensive survey of the main characteristics of the entrepreneur that can be founded in the literature. Some of the characteristics discussed include motivation, intention, need for achievement, locus of control, leadership, commitment and determination, risk propensity, proactivity, tolerance of ambiguity and uncertainty, spirit of opportunity, innovative spirit, confidence, and resilience and adaptability. Complementing this survey, the second contribution of this chapter is the empirical test of the relevance of these factors. Based on a questionnaire applied to Portuguese entrepreneurs and interviews (with the purpose of complementing the information of the collected data with a qualitative approach), the evidence reveal that leadership, the need for achievement, proactivity, resilience, and adaptability are among the characteristics with more impact on the growth of the startups analyzed.

The final chapter of this Handbook – Chapter 18 – is authored by Mikail Kar. The focus of this chapter is a critical element for the firms – pricing strategy. The chapter examines pricing methods and price indices and evaluates the determination of the pricing method commonly used in a market based on the causality relationship between the producer and consumer price indices. The study emphasizes the importance of supply factors (costs of production), demand factors (wiliness to pay of the consumers), and competition in the identification of the price.

Nuno Crespo
ISCTE – Instituto Universitário de Lisboa, Portugal

Nadia Simoes
ISCTE – Instituto Universitário de Lisboa, Portugal

Chapter 1
Sectoral Trade Globalization

Nuno Crespo
https://orcid.org/0000-0002-6546-6325
ISCTE – Instituto Universitário de Lisboa, Portugal

Nicole Palan
Graz Schumpeter Centre, University of Graz, Graz, Austria

Nadia Simoes
https://orcid.org/0000-0002-4334-4482
ISCTE – Instituto Universitário de Lisboa, Portugal

ABSTRACT

This chapter aims to shed light on the trends of sectoral trade globalization. This component of trade globalization is often neglected. An accurate evaluation of sectoral trade requires the analysis of the interdependencies of countries and the consideration of distance as a central dimension of trade globalization. As such, sectoral trade globalization is one aspect of a more complex and multi-dimensional phenomenon. Data show that sectoral trade globalization has increased significantly over the last 50 years irrespective of the characteristics of individual sectors. One relevant insight is that the level of trade globalization is on average still different for high-tech sectors compared to low-tech and medium-low-tech sectors even though the former could increase their bilateral trade relationships over time. Even though protectionist tendencies as well as the COVID-19 pandemic have led to a vivid discussion about the return to more local or regional production schemes, digitalization processes could still have the potential to further integrate countries' trade networks.

INTRODUCTION

Trade globalization is one of the most critical issues in international economics analysis and one of the most studied topics in applied research along the last years. During the 1970s, containerization has helped to increase the possibilities of international trade for many goods that before were not cost-efficient to transport over long distances. In the 1980s already, Naisbitt (1982) and Levitt (1983) analyze the evolu-

DOI: 10.4018/978-1-7998-7568-0.ch001

tion from national firms to companies that are proper global market players. The period from the early 1990s to the Great Recession in 2009, is often referred to as the Golden Era of globalization as advances in information and communication technologies, automation and digitalization processes as well as the decline in tariffs and quotas reduced trade costs worldwide and integrated China into the global network (Levinson, 2006). Thus, all this together had a great boost on globalization, and therefore this era is also referred to as hyper-globalization (Subramanian & Kessler, 2014). Empirical studies on economic globalization most often refer to trade volume and the effects of trade globalization on nation states, identifying the winners and losers of globalization (Gunter & Wilcher, 2020).

Nevertheless, one aspect that has received much less attention is sectoral trade globalization. Most research at the sectoral level does not involve questions as to how many countries are involved in the production and trade network but rather deals with questions related to global value chains and the possible gains and threats of these global value chains for domestic jobs. However, due to not only nationalistic tendencies, protectionism, trade war between the US and China but also, more recently, to Covid-19 (with a new and vivid discussion about jobs and re-nationalization), the robustness of the trade network has been called into question. All this debate have brought the topic of trade globalization into the public debate, demanding more scientific research about the past and projections about the future. The Economist (2019) referred to this new situation as "slowbalization". Bordo (2017) points to the fact that truly global supply chains as well as completely global firms have become more ineffective over the last decade as the losses in income lead to lower consumption, producing a dampening effect on trade volume.

In this context of analysis, it is important to make the distinction between internationalization and globalization. Whereas the former has the nation state as the main reference point for analysis (Scholte, 2008), the interdependencies of countries need to be at the heart of any study that aim to deal properly with trade globalization in order to shed more light on the trade relations between countries and the role of countries within the global trade network.

In this chapter, the authors aim to address the sectoral component of trade globalization. In order to provide a more depth understanding of the developments of this phenomenon, we not only present evidence for 147 sectors but also discuss in more detail the case of two selected sectors (or groups of sectors). It is important to stress that these sectors are well-chosen examples to highlight important characteristics in the progress of trade globalization. Therefore, the results in these sectors do not necessarily resemble the development of other sectors with the same industry characteristics.

Background

Globalization has been one of the most important topics in international economics analysis over the last decades, with critical implications both for academic research and policy making. The debate on this theme covers a wide set of issues, ranging from its definition to its measurement or its economic, social, political, and cultural implications. Globalization is a complex and multi-dimensional concept. In this chapter, we are interested in its economic facet and, more specifically, in the single most important of its sub-dimensions: trade globalization. More precisely, the focus of the present chapter is the evaluation of sectoral trade globalization, which has so far been neglected in many empirical and theoretical discussions.

In this section, the authors aim to provide a short overview of the existing literature in what regards the conceptualization and the empirical quantification of the phenomenon.

Let us start with the most basic aspect in this context: the concept of globalization. This is a major issue because, in our perspective, the metrics used to evaluate the phenomenon should emerge from the key characteristics that are noticeable from the most important definitions. A vast group of definitions of globalization are suggested in the literature. Al-Rodhan and Stoudmann (2006), for example, summarize a total of 114 definitions. From our perspective, at least three critical elements should be retained from those definitions.

The first element – and perhaps the most critical one – is the idea of interdependence between countries. This is explicit, for example, in the words of Goldberg and Pavcnik (2007, p.41): "globalization is a broad concept casually used to describe a variety of phenomena that reflect increased economic interdependence of countries". Following the same reasoning, another definition of globalization affirms that "contemporary globalisation is defined as the intensification of cross-national interactions that promote the establishment of trans-national structures and the global integration of cultural, economic, ecological, political, technological and social processes on global, supra-national, national, regional and local levels" (Rennen & Martens, 2003, p. 143).

A second element pointed out in several definitions of the globalization phenomenon is the importance of considering distance in its measurement. The reduction of several key components of trade costs (such as freight costs, tariffs and customs duties, just to mention a few examples) has a dramatic impact on the increase of international economic flows. These factors have led to a debate on the progressive death of distance. In this context, while some authors argue that, at least in some domains, we already live in a "global village", other authors find evidence supporting the idea that distance is still an obstacle to international economic flows, and more specifically to trade (Christopherson et al., 2008; Disdier & Head, 2008). From this discussion, we should retain the idea that a proper measurement of the globalization concept (and trade globalization in more specific terms) requires the inclusion of distance as a relevant dimension. However, it is scarcely considered in the empirical analyses, being the study of Vujakovic (2010) an important exception.

Finally, the most consensual idea emerging from the several definitions of globalization is that it corresponds to an intensification of the world flows. Regarding trade globalization, this means that a central dimension of the phenomenon is the (rapid) increase in the volume of world trade.

This group of three dimensions derived from several definitions of globalization are the pillars for the empirical framework of analysis that will be adopted in the next section. In our perspective, the most important merit of the approach developed in this study is the fact that it overcomes three critical shortcomings of the empirical exercises conducted so far. Let us discuss this aspect in more detail concerning the specific case of trade globalization.

A first problem of the dominant measures of globalization – the multidimensional indexes – is that none of them covers all the dimensions identified as important in the definitions of globalization – interdependence, distance, and volume. This applies for example to the widely diffused KOF Globalisation Index (Dreher, 2006; Gygli et al., 2019) but also to several other measurement proposals such as the Foreign Policy/A.T. Kearney Index (A.T. Kearney, 2001, 2007), the Maastricht Globalization Index (Figge & Martens, 2014; Martens & Zywietz, 2006), the New Globalization Index (Vujakovic, 2010), among others. Additionally, also another interesting approach – the network analysis (Arribas et al., 2009; Arribas et al., 2020; De Benedictis et al., 2014; De Lombaerde et al., 2019) – lacks the consideration of all relevant dimensions. For example, in the framework developed by Arribas et al. (2009), the objective is the quantification of the gap between the current level of globalization and the level that corresponds to a "perfect international integration" (the maximum value that globalization – defined as a bounded reality – can assume).

Another important problem of the most common approaches used to quantify globalization (including the simplest one – the degree of openness) is the fact that they measure globalization at the country level. However, as argued by Figge and Martens (2014), this is not the adequate geographical level to analyse the concept of globalization. Palan et al. (2020) consider that this approach evaluates better the concept of internationalization. Thus, instead of a value for each country, a proper measure of globalization, evaluating a truly global phenomenon, should give us only one value for the world in a given year.

Finally, it is important to emphasize that most of the empirical exercises aiming to trace the evolution of globalization along the last years/decades have adopted an overall/macro perspective instead of following a micro/sectoral level analysis. This is a shortcoming because both approaches have important merits and can be seen as useful complements. In fact, an increased international division of labour and the emergence of global value chains, offering to many developing countries new opportunities to integrate into the global trade network, call for a stronger focus on the sectoral evaluation of the globalization phenomenon (Simoes et al., 2020; Stehrer et al., 2011).

MAIN FOCUS OF THE CHAPTER

Issues, Controversies, Problems

As discussed in the previous section, the term "globalization" is complex and hard to capture in full detail. The same problem occurs with one of its key components – trade globalization. Taking the discussion produced in that section as background, in this section the authors introduce some new metrics to quantify sectoral trade globalization. These metrics are defined in the context of a framework of analysis containing three dimensions: number of trade flows, distance, and volume of trade.

The first dimension – number of trade flows – captures, in its simplest way, the importance of interdependence as a key component of the trade globalization phenomenon. Considering the full list of countries as potential exporters and the same group of countries as potential importers, the authors calculate the percentage of bilateral relations with a positive trade flow in the total number of bilateral relations (i.e., the number of elements of each matrix). In order to define the existence of a given trade flow, it is necessary to identify a threshold separating the existing from the non-existing flows. Regarding this issue, it could be interesting for future research to test the definition of alternative values for that threshold. However, in the current study, the authors retain the simplest case, considering that a trade flow exists if there is trade between those countries, regardless of the exact value assumed by the flow.

The second dimension included in the analysis of sectoral trade globalization is distance. This aspect is important because there is an interesting discussion in the literature concerning the difference between the concepts of globalization and regionalization. While the first term assumes – as the word itself suggests – a truly global nature, regionalization corresponds to a more geographically confined phenomenon, in which the countries open to trade but a high percentage of their trade flows are established with relatively close countries. In fact, as emphasized for example by Baldwin and Lopez-Gonzalez (2015), the reduction of trade costs did not imply the full elimination of distance as a barrier to trade as time involved in trade relationships still matters. Thus, it is important to assess whether, along the period considered, trade takes place between countries furthest from each other as proper globalization would imply.

Finally, the third dimension of trade globalization included in the empirical analysis conducted in the present study is volume of trade. This is the most obvious dimension of trade globalization. There are many empirical studies aiming to capture the evolution of the volume of trade at the world level (see for instance, Catão & Obstfeld, 2019). However, almost all of them deal with overall trade. Assuming a complementary perspective, this study puts the focus of analysis on the sectoral volume of trade as a component of the trade globalization phenomenon.

After these initial considerations concerning the dimensions included in the framework of analysis, the authors now introduce the new metrics that will be used to obtain the empirical evidence explored in the upcoming sections.

Let the exporting country be defined by $i(i=1,2,\dots,I)$ and the importing country by $j(j=1,2,\dots,J)$. The trade flow between countries i and j in year t is represented as z_{ijt}.. In turn, when the evaluation is done at the sectoral level, the generic element of the matrix of bilateral trade is represented by z_{ijpt}. Since the countries do not trade with themselves, the total number of elements of each matrix of trades $I*(J-1)$.

The strategy developed by the authors to capture, in empirical terms, the level of trade globalization involves the definition of three measures, defined in gradual terms. Thus, the first measure only includes one dimension of trade globalization – number of trade flows. Next, a second measure takes into account the dimension already considered in the first metric and adds distance as another dimension of analysis. Finally, the third measure includes number of flows, distance, and volume of trade. Each of the measures used for the sectoral evaluation are explained bellow, being important to stress that the overall measures can be obtained in a similar way but using as source of information the overall trade matrix instead of the sectoral matrixes.

The first sectoral trade globalization index (*STGI*) is as follows:

$$STGI[1]_{pt} = \frac{\sum_{i=1}^{I}\sum_{j=1}^{J} b_{ijpt}}{I*(J-1)} \tag{1}$$

where:

$$b_{ijpt} = \begin{cases} 1\, if\ z_{ijpt} > 0 \\ 0\, if\ z_{ijpt} = 0 \end{cases} \tag{2}$$

i.e., b_{ijpt} is a dummy variable that takes value 1 if the bilateral trade flow from i to j exists in sector p in year t.

This first measure of sectoral globalization ranges between 0 and 1. It takes the minimum value if there is no trade in this sector in this year. The maximum value of $STGI[1]_{pt}$ occurs when there is positive sectoral trade in all bilateral relations. Regarding the level of trade globalization, a higher value of the index means, therefore, that globalization – evaluated through the first dimension of the framework considered in this study – is in a more advanced stage in that sector.

The second measure of sectoral trade globalization includes the number of trade flows and distance as relevant dimensions. Thus, the index takes $STGI[1]_{pt}$ as departure point but gives a lower weight to trade flows between closer countries. This index – $STGI[2]_{pt}$ – captures, at the sectoral level, the percentage of the total distance among all the country pairs considered in the analysis in which there is trade. It is obtained dividing the sum of the distance between all country pairs with positive trade by the sum of distance between all pairs, regardless the existence of trade. $STGI[2]_{pt}$ is calculated as:

$$STGI[2]_{pt} = \frac{\sum_{i=1}^{I}\sum_{j=1}^{J} D_{ijt} * b_{ijpt}}{\sum_{i=1}^{I}\sum_{j=1}^{J} D_{ijt}}. \quad (3)$$

D_{ijt} represents the distance between countries i and j. As occurred with $STGI[1]_{pt}$, this index also ranges between 0 and 1. The maximum value corresponds to the case in which there is trade between all country pairs. From the two indexes already introduced, it is possible to obtain a more detailed perspective concerning the sectoral globalization phenomenon. An in-depth analysis of the data using these indicators will allows us to identify which of the dimensions – number of trade flows or distance – prevail in the explanation of a given evolution. Additionally, and perhaps even more important, the interpretation of $STGI[2]_{pt}$ is critical since it corresponds to the bounded dimensions of trade globalization included in the evaluation. The comparison of the current values vis-à-vis the upper limit that can be reached (i.e., $STGI[2]_{pt}=1$) provides very useful information about how far we are from that threshold of "full globalization".

The last measure that we consider in this study is $STGI[3]_{pt}$. This measure includes information about the three dimensions of sectoral trade globalization – number of flows, distance and volume of trade. To obtain this measure, we first compare the total volume of trade in the sector p in year t with the volume of trade in a specific year assumed as reference (which in the current case is the first year of the period considered in the analysis):

$$F_{pt}^{*} = \frac{\sum_{i=1}^{I}\sum_{j=1}^{J} z_{ijpt}}{\sum_{i=1}^{I}\sum_{j=1}^{J} z_{ijp,t-1}}. \quad (4)$$

Based on this, we calculate:

$$F_{pt} = F_{p,t-1} * F_{pt}^{*}. \quad (5)$$

Since the period under consideration starts in 1967, $F_{p,1967} = 1$.

Finally, $STGI[3]_{pt}$ is obtained as follows:

$$STGI[3]_{pt} = STGI[2]_{pt} * F_{pt}. \quad (6)$$

Obviously, since this index includes volume of trade as one of its dimensions, it is unbounded and therefore it is not possible to define the upper limit of this measure.

Data

For the empirical exercise developed in this chapter, the authors use data from Chelem (CEPII). A period of 50 years is covered: 1967-2016. As explained above, the focus of the analysis is the identification of sectoral differences in terms of trade globalization. To that end, the authors consider evidence for the manufacturing sectors at the ISIC 4 digit-level.[2] Additionally, overall bilateral trade is also considered.

In order to calculate some of the measures of sectoral trade globalization, we also use information about bilateral distances. These are retrieved from CEPII. The same source is used to obtain the deflators required to calculate information in real terms.

As political changes in Europe in the beginning of the 1990s lead to the emergence of new counties, the empirical analysis must be split into two sub-periods: the first sub-period ranges between 1967 and 1990 while the second runs from 1994 to 2016. Only this allows us to take properly into account the change in the number of countries due to the disintegration processes in Czechoslovakia, the URSS, and Yugoslavia. Therefore, the total number of countries increases from 72 in the first sub-period to 84 countries in the second one (Table A.2 contains the full list of countries included in the sample). It is important to stress that the panel under consideration in the current study represents world trade very well. Despite the fact that for a large number of countries no data are available, these countries account for no more than around 4 per cent of world trade. Thus, 96 per cent of world trade is covered in this study.

To develop the empirical assessment, a significant amount of data is used. In overall terms, more than 40 million bilateral trade flows are considered. This information includes, for each year, 147 matrixes with sectoral evidence at the bilateral level and an additional matrix containing bilateral trade flows in overall terms.

In the period 1967-1990 (i.e., the first sub-period), each matrix reports data for bilateral trade among the 72 countries considered (I=J=72). Thus, the total number of elements of each matrix in this sub-period is 5,112. Regarding the sub-period starting in 1994, I=J=84. Therefore, each matrix for this sub-period contains 6,972 elements.

Key Evidence

Taking the measures introduced in the previous section as reference, the authors move now to the empirical exercise aiming to characterize the contours of sectoral trade globalization along the period 1967-2016. Due to the reasons already explained, the evaluation will consider two sub-periods: 1967-1990 and 1994-2016.

The current section is divided into three sub-sections covering the following aspects:

- A short picture of trade globalization in overall terms;
- Evidence for each category of a given taxonomy of sectors;
- Evidence at the sectoral level.

In this last case, we not only provide results for each of the 147 sectors but also discuss in more detail the case of two specific sectors: textiles, and motor vehicles. The main goal of such exercise is to get a deeper understanding of individual sector characteristics as well the role of the institutional environment in trade globalization.

Overall Evidence

The main purpose of the current chapter is the analysis of trade globalization at the sectoral level. Before that discussion, a brief overview of the key trends emerging from the overall matrixes of trade is provided in this section.

The results obtained for the three indexes used in this study are shown in Table 1. Since in this case we are discussing the overall evidence, we designate the indexes as *TGI* instead of *STGI*. The values highlighted correspond to years in which the level of trade globalization decreased. Considering the results for *TGI*[1], it is obvious that the level of trade globalization was already remarkably high at the beginning of the period under scrutiny. Even more important, along the fifty years of analysis, there is a consistent upward trend in that level. In fact, slight reductions in the level of trade globalization were detected in only four years, occurring three of them in the first sub-period, namely 1971, 1983, and 1985, and only one in a more recent year (2012). As a consequence of this evolution, in the last year, the level of trade globalization almost reaches its upper limit (i.e., *TGI*[1]=1): the value of *TGI*[1] for 2016 was 0.99. A second important result emerging from the evidence for *TGI*[1] is the fact that the annual average growth rate was significantly higher in the first sub-period. Taking this evidence together, we verify a progressive increase in the level of integration of the different countries in the world trade web, including the less developed countries.

The second index – *TGI*[2] – combines the influence of number of trade flows and distance. Thus, this evidence allows us to verify whether distance is still an active barrier to trade or if, on the contrary, as argued by some authors, the "world is flat" (Friedman, 2005) and distance is not an obstacle anymore (Simoes et al., 2020). In the beginning of the period, the values for the indexes *TGI*[1] and *TGI*[2] point towards an overrepresentation of trade flows occurring between geographically close countries. The difference between the two measures remained along the entire period but its magnitude suffered a strong reduction. In short, we can conclude that the importance of distance as a barrier to trade is now significantly lower than fifty years ago.

A final aspect that must be mentioned regarding the evolution of overall trade globalization is the remarkable increase of trade volume. This is not new, of course. There is a vast empirical literature showing the tremendous growth that occurred along the last decades in terms of volume of world trade and presenting several explanations for that evolution, namely the reduction of several key components of trade costs. While this upward trend is even clearer after mid-1980s, it is already evident before that moment. The most important exception occurred during the Great Recession of the last decade, being 2009 the year with the biggest reduction in what concerns the overall volume of trade. It is important to highlight that, different from what occurs with *TGI*[1] and *TGI*[2], this last index – *TGI*[3] – does not have an upper limit because volume of trade is an unbounded dimension of trade globalization. Interesting enough, the evidence emerging from the results for this measure clearly shows that trade globalization is still increasing at a fast pace and that this evolution occurs, in recent years, above all because of the growth in the volume of trade since the other two dimensions are very close to their upper limit.

Taxonomies of Sectors According to Technological Levels

In the previous sub-section, the authors summarized the key trends regarding the level of overall trade globalization. We now give a step forward and start discussing trade globalization at a more disaggregated level. The authors first consider a sectoral taxonomy, which groups the sectors according to the

Table 1. Overall evidence

Year	*TGI*[1]	*TGI*[2]	*TGI*[3]	Year	*TGI*[1]	*TGI*[2]	*TGI*[3]
1968	0.8353	0.7864	0.8633	1994	0.9284	0.9135	4.0314
1969	0.8439	0.7988	0.9229	1995	0.9369	0.9233	4.4619
1970	0.8572	0.8138	1.0048	1996	0.9410	0.9287	4.6671
1971	0.8543	0.8124	1.0253	1997	0.9455	0.9313	5.1763
1972	0.8601	0.8185	1.1297	1998	0.9495	0.9385	5.3978
1973	0.8740	0.8361	1.3667	1999	0.9525	0.9419	5.7010
1974	0.8803	0.8438	1.6781	2000	0.9607	0.9505	6.8531
1975	0.8846	0.8492	1.6004	2001	0.9659	0.9569	6.8142
1976	0.8901	0.8558	1.7558	2002	0.9676	0.9589	7.0842
1977	0.8912	0.8575	1.8396	2003	0.9690	0.9605	7.6805
1978	0.8981	0.8654	1.9063	2004	0.9745	0.9670	8.7795
1979	0.9045	0.8773	2.1974	2005	0.9753	0.9673	9.5502
1980	0.9045	0.8784	2.3417	2006	0.9785	0.9716	10.6275
1981	0.9061	0.8819	2.3690	2007	0.9788	0.9714	11.2269
1982	0.9098	0.8831	2.3114	2008	0.9809	0.9751	11.6491
1983	0.9063	0.8756	2.3436	2009	0.9834	0.9792	9.6216
1984	0.9100	0.8814	2.6295	2010	0.9864	0.9818	11.3157
1985	0.9092	0.8820	2.7143	2011	0.9884	0.9848	12.3435
1986	0.9173	0.8949	2.6119	2012	0.9871	0.9832	12.5003
1987	0.9229	0.9021	2.7700	2013	0.9891	0.9857	12.6411
1988	0.9294	0.9077	2.9496	2014	0.9892	0.9860	12.9010
1989	0.9329	0.9140	3.2431	2015	0.9897	0.9868	12.7951
1990	0.9374	0.9211	3.4105	2016	0.9902	0.9874	12.8743

Note: The values highlighted correspond to years in which the index decreased.

intensity of R&D activities they incorporate. This taxonomy considers four categories: high-technology, medium-high technology, medium-low technology, and low technology.[1] The results for each of the three measures considered are presented in Tables 2 and 3 for the two sub-periods, respectively.

In generic terms, two central conclusions emerge from the evidence presented in these tables. The first conclusion is the existence of a strong increase in the level of trade globalization. This result is valid for all the categories of sectors. A second result concerns the high value reached at the end of the period. Taking *STGI*[1] as reference, we can see that low-technology sectors are those with the highest levels of trade globalization at the beginning of the first sub-period of analysis whereas the opposite occurs with the high-technology sectors. However, taking the whole period into consideration, we observe that the gap of this last group vis-à-vis the group of low-technology sectors is significantly smaller at the end of the period.

Comparing the different indexes, the biggest differences among sectors are evident when the analysis is conducted in terms of volume of trade, i.e., when *STGI*[3] is assumed as the reference measure. More specifically, it is evident a very strong increase of trade volume in the case of high-technology sectors.

Table 2. Trade globalization in groups of sectors according to the intensity of R&D activities (1968-1990)

Year	*STGI*[1]				*STGI*[2]				*STGI*[3]			
	Low tech	Medium-low lech	Medium-high tech	High tech	Low tech	Medium-low lech	Medium-high tech	High tech	Low tech	Medium-low lech	Medium-high tech	High tech
1968	0.7369	0.6442	0.6125	0.5248	0.6675	0.5647	0.5307	0.4442	0.7222	0.6307	0.6060	0.5153
1969	0.7398	0.6585	0.6250	0.5315	0.6733	0.5819	0.5469	0.4516	0.7754	0.7056	0.6927	0.5822
1970	0.7494	0.6671	0.6471	0.5528	0.6853	0.5877	0.5667	0.4782	0.8267	0.7745	0.7499	0.6876
1971	0.7549	0.6776	0.6495	0.5604	0.6917	0.6058	0.5768	0.4859	0.8784	0.7751	0.8154	0.7232
1972	0.7592	0.6856	0.6651	0.5743	0.6960	0.6162	0.5914	0.5017	0.9898	0.8292	0.8904	0.8122
1973	0.7774	0.7072	0.6872	0.5951	0.7179	0.6437	0.6205	0.5244	1.2145	1.0538	1.0593	0.9870
1974	0.7782	0.7197	0.6968	0.6139	0.7142	0.6583	0.6328	0.5444	1.2932	1.4252	1.3121	1.1617
1975	0.7817	0.7175	0.6913	0.6250	0.7218	0.6548	0.6258	0.5569	1.1809	1.2315	1.2716	1.1468
1976	0.7878	0.7242	0.7044	0.6369	0.7333	0.6601	0.6437	0.5709	1.3167	1.3651	1.4376	1.3188
1977	0.7885	0.7336	0.7150	0.6438	0.7333	0.6709	0.6532	0.5778	1.3928	1.4638	1.5247	1.3899
1978	0.8065	0.7447	0.7259	0.6610	0.7558	0.6838	0.6635	0.5994	1.5050	1.5474	1.6055	1.5807
1979	0.8155	0.7598	0.7430	0.6719	0.7680	0.7034	0.6874	0.6148	1.6894	1.8908	1.8466	1.8136
1980	0.8183	0.7604	0.7414	0.6811	0.7735	0.7063	0.6845	0.6227	1.7262	2.0688	1.8902	2.0526
1981	0.8163	0.7598	0.7383	0.6854	0.7707	0.7066	0.6811	0.6268	1.7398	2.0147	1.9262	2.1796
1982	0.8198	0.7594	0.7478	0.6849	0.7780	0.7044	0.6906	0.6221	1.6824	1.9805	1.9050	2.1507
1983	0.8138	0.7549	0.7484	0.6833	0.7638	0.6967	0.6905	0.6174	1.7135	2.0039	1.9325	2.2914
1984	0.8194	0.7613	0.7600	0.6919	0.7691	0.7001	0.6965	0.6286	1.9363	2.2328	2.1924	2.7187
1985	0.8192	0.7612	0.7580	0.6962	0.7712	0.7028	0.6985	0.6344	1.9820	2.2550	2.3637	2.9177
1986	0.8286	0.7729	0.7696	0.7042	0.7880	0.7193	0.7153	0.6449	2.1222	2.0205	2.3762	3.0540
1987	0.8333	0.7913	0.7885	0.7126	0.7904	0.7405	0.7379	0.6552	2.3571	2.1326	2.5472	3.3496
1988	0.8425	0.8067	0.8040	0.7255	0.8004	0.7586	0.7574	0.6736	2.5423	2.4806	2.7963	3.9523
1989	0.8513	0.8179	0.8101	0.7379	0.8102	0.7718	0.7673	0.6835	2.7783	2.7880	3.0218	4.5498
1990	0.8644	0.8284	0.8212	0.7484	0.8300	0.7851	0.7829	0.6961	3.0414	2.9012	3.1815	5.0320

The growth rate for this group of sectors is clearly faster than the comparable evolution for the other categories of sectors.

Evidence at the Sectoral Level

Results for the 147 Sectors

As mentioned above, an important difference between the first two indexes – *STGI*[1] and *STGI*[2]– and the last one (*STGI*[3]) is the fact the *STGI*[1] and *STGI*[2] are bounded by definition, ranging between 0 and 1 and allowing to compare the actual level of trade globalization with the upper limit.

We start the analysis at the sectoral level presenting some simple descriptive evidence for the bounded dimensions. Table 4 shows the average values for both indexes in six selected years – three from the first sub-period (1968, 1976, and 1986) and three from the second one (1996, 2006, and 2016) – as well as the maximum and minimum values.

Starting with the evolution of the average values, we verify a very significant increase during the entire period with a consistent increase in all years presented in Table 4. This is true for both indexes.

Table 3. Trade globalization in groups of sectors according to the intensity of R&D activities (1994-2016)

Year	G1				G2				G3			
	Low tech	Medium-low lech	Medium-high tech	High tech	Low tech	Medium-low lech	Medium-high tech	High tech	Low tech	Medium-low lech	Medium-high tech	High tech
1994	0.8530	0.8209	0.8166	0.7385	0.8251	0.7791	0.7766	0.6901	3.2353	3.2811	3.7558	6.7451
1995	0.8622	0.8338	0.8272	0.7520	0.8379	0.7975	0.7886	0.7082	3.6642	3.7458	4.2791	7.9060
1996	0.8682	0.8421	0.8392	0.7638	0.8442	0.8069	0.8027	0.7210	3.7183	3.8172	4.5874	8.7590
1997	0.8810	0.8524	0.8439	0.7768	0.8594	0.8168	0.8095	0.7342	4.1692	4.2559	5.1237	10.5667
1998	0.8797	0.8576	0.8524	0.7866	0.8552	0.8208	0.8203	0.7450	4.2243	4.3546	5.3757	11.9179
1999	0.8850	0.8622	0.8623	0.7953	0.8648	0.8269	0.8294	0.7560	4.5247	4.6467	5.6745	13.2200
2000	0.9042	0.8804	0.8759	0.8194	0.8845	0.8464	0.8475	0.7800	5.5753	5.7302	6.5659	16.6556
2001	0.9125	0.8888	0.8880	0.8315	0.8954	0.8603	0.8626	0.7940	5.4781	5.6531	6.7130	16.5205
2002	0.9128	0.8917	0.8906	0.8372	0.8953	0.8624	0.8653	0.8013	5.7267	5.9247	6.9797	17.4153
2003	0.9190	0.8943	0.8966	0.8528	0.9006	0.8636	0.8723	0.8204	6.2866	6.4747	7.4463	19.6615
2004	0.9309	0.9055	0.9104	0.8636	0.9140	0.8788	0.8883	0.8312	7.5632	7.8104	8.5634	23.3267
2005	0.9357	0.9168	0.9165	0.8718	0.9215	0.8913	0.8956	0.8419	8.5532	8.8854	9.3275	25.9208
2006	0.9380	0.9191	0.9192	0.8825	0.9253	0.8964	0.8997	0.8569	10.0018	10.4069	10.3951	29.4470
2007	0.9403	0.9280	0.9279	0.8894	0.9281	0.9071	0.9088	0.8603	11.0379	11.5870	11.5070	29.7023
2008	0.9458	0.9290	0.9393	0.8970	0.9338	0.9109	0.9237	0.8727	11.9050	12.4729	11.9562	29.3740
2009	0.9479	0.9284	0.9379	0.9019	0.9383	0.9101	0.9216	0.8754	8.9498	9.3236	9.3299	25.9837
2010	0.9509	0.9350	0.9431	0.9040	0.9412	0.9161	0.9297	0.8779	11.0005	11.5000	11.4286	31.2898
2011	0.9547	0.9418	0.9419	0.9101	0.9458	0.9273	0.9283	0.8916	12.5603	13.2266	12.7094	31.8640
2012	0.9557	0.9438	0.9431	0.9118	0.9460	0.9289	0.9285	0.8909	12.7487	13.4451	12.9601	32.9692
2013	0.9603	0.9413	0.9466	0.9158	0.9508	0.9248	0.9342	0.8954	12.8399	13.4135	13.1723	33.7713
2014	0.9590	0.9455	0.9462	0.9161	0.9489	0.9311	0.9344	0.8928	12.7141	13.3993	13.5931	34.9174
2015	0.9611	0.9475	0.9508	0.9185	0.9536	0.9329	0.9398	0.9001	11.8424	12.4432	13.8910	37.3552
2016	0.9614	0.9461	0.9522	0.9214	0.9519	0.9313	0.9407	0.9023	11.5325	12.1185	14.1045	38.8144

Regarding *STGI*[1], the evolution is remarkable in both sub-periods, changing from 0.2182 in 1968 to 0.3178 (first sub-period) and from 0.3579 in 1996 to 0.5088 in 2016 (second sub-period). The evolution of *STGI*[2] is similar. At the beginning of the period (1968), the level of *STGI*[2] is slight lower than *STGI*[1], illustrating the negative impact of distance, as discussed above for the case of overall trade. This gap vis-à-vis *STGI*[1] remains roughly stable along the entire period, ranging between 5 and 6 p.p. At the end of the period, the average level of sectoral trade globalization evaluated through *STGI*[2] is 0.4501.

It is also interesting to analyse the evidence for the maximum and minimum values. The key message emerging is consistent with the information for the average values. In fact, a significant increase is also clear, showing once again that the increase in trade globalization is a transversal trend. For example, while the sector with the highest level of trade globalization in 1968, evaluated through *STGI*[1], reaches a score of 0.4677, close to the end of the first sub-period the maximum value of the same index reaches 0.5826. A similar trend is detected in the most recent sub-period. At the end of that sub-period, the sector with the highest score in *STGI*[1] – Plastics products – reaches 0.8493. Taking into account that we are producing the evaluation at the sectoral level, this value is quite remarkable and shows that sectoral globalization is already deep, at least when the number of positive trade flows is assumed as the measure. The evolution for *STGI*[2] is not significantly different from *STGI*[1], being interesting to

Table 4. Bounded trade globalization indexes by sectors – Descriptive evidence

	1968	1976	1986	1996	2006	2016
STGI[1]						
Average	0.2182	0.2742	0.3178	0.3579	0.4553	0.5088
Minimum	0.0002	0.0002	0.0000	0.0036	0.0040	0.0037
Maximum	0.4677	0.5231	0.5826	0.6398	0.7847	0.8493
STGI[2]						
Average	0.1610	0.2121	0.2545	0.2988	0.3955	0.4501
Minimum	0.0000	0.0000	0.0000	0.0022	0.0025	0.0032
Maximum	0.3929	0.4477	0.5045	0.5838	0.7423	0.8115

note however that the gap between *STGI*[2] and *STGI*[1] diminishes along the period: it is around 7-8 p.p. at the beginning and no more than around 3 p.p. at the end of the period.

Table 5 complements the information presented in Table 4 showing, for the two indexes that only incorporate bounded dimensions of trade globalization – *STGI*[1] and *STGI*[2] – the top 5 of sectors with the highest values. Considering the last year as example, the sectors belonging to the top 5 are the same for both indexes (with only a small difference in the ranking, namely regarding the sectors appearing in the fourth and fifth positions): plastics products; other fabricated metal products; wearing apparels, except fur; other general purpose machinery; instruments for measuring.

The detailed analysis of the evidence for each of the 147 sectors included in the empirical exercise conducted in the current study is impossible to do in the context of a single chapter. However, in order to give full information about the key trends registered in each of those sectors, Tables 9-12 in Appendix 1 present the values for the three indexes of sectoral globalization for the first and last year of analysis. Providing a complementary interpretation of the evidence, Table 6 presents for four sub-periods (1968-1976, 1976-1986, 1996-2006, and 2006-2016) the number of sectors with an increase in the level of trade globalization. The basic idea emerging from this Table is the confirmation of the increase in sectoral trade globalization as a trend common to a vast majority of sectors and consistent along the time. Considering all the changes evaluated, the number of sectors showing an increase in trade globalization is higher than 140 (out of 147) in all sub-periods for the case of *STGI*[1] and *STGI*[2]. The same occurs in two of the four variations analysed in the case of *STGI*[3].

Textile Sector

As outlined in Table 5, the textile sector – consisting of the sub-sectors fabrics and wearing apparel – is one of the most globalized sectors in this sample throughout the whole investigation period. The underlying reason can be traced back to the fact that major parts of the production process involve only low levels of skill and are low-tech, requiring only little investment in capital. Thus, firms can easily be set up in countries in which low wages are the main competitive advantage. Opportunities in automation, digitalization and the decline in trade costs fostered international competition from low wage countries and posed problems for jobs in industrialized, high-wage countries, leading to a finer division of labour and increased trade volumes. Yet, not all parts of textile production were transferred to low-wage countries as R&D in innovative materials, design and marketing activities remain in high-wage countries

Table 5. Most globalized sectors

	1968	1976	1986	1996	2006	2016
STGI[1]						
1	Prepared text. fibres; fabrics	Prepared text. fibres; fabrics	Basic chemicals, exc. fertil.	Wearing apparel, except fur	Plastics products	Plastics products
2	Basic chemicals, exc. fertil.	Other fabricated metal prod.	Prepared text. fibres; fabrics	Other fabricated metal prod.	Wearing apparel, except fur	Other fabricated metal prod.
3	Cereals and other crops n.e.c.	Basic chemicals, exc. fertil.	Other fabricated metal prod.	Plastics products	Other fabricated metal prod.	Wearing apparel, except fur
4	Other fabricated metal prod.	Cereals and other crops n.e.c.	Wearing apparel, except fur	Basic chemicals, exc. fertil.	Oth. general purpose machinery	Oth. general purpose machinery
5	Fruit, beverage & spice crops	Wearing apparel, except fur	Cereals and other crops n.e.c.	Prepared text. fibres; fabrics	Office and computing machinery	Instruments for measuring
STGI[2]						
1	Prepared text. fibres; fabrics	Prepared text. fibres; fabrics	Basic chemicals, exc. fertil.	Wearing apparel, except fur	Wearing apparel, except fur	Plastics products
2	Basic chemicals, exc. fertil.	Basic chemicals, exc. fertil.	Prepared text. fibres; fabrics	Other fabricated metal prod.	Plastics products	Other fabricated metal prod.
3	Fruit, beverage & spice crops	Other fabricated metal prod.	Other fabricated metal prod.	Plastics products	Other fabricated metal prod.	Wearing apparel, except fur
4	Cereals and other crops n.e.c.	Cereals and other crops n.e.c.	Cereals and other crops n.e.c.	Prepared text. fibres; fabrics	Office and computing machinery	Instruments for measuring
5	Other fabricated metal prod.	Fruit, beverage & spice crops	Instruments for measuring	Basic chemicals, exc. fertil.	Oth. general purpose machinery	Oth. general purpose machinery

leading to the establishment of a global textile value chain (Gereffi & Memedovic, 2003). The increases in trade volume are yet not only driven by the finer division of international labour and the abolishment of quota and tariffs; this trend is also driven by the recent phenomenon of "fast fashion" or "throwaway fashion" (Bhardwaj & Fairhurst, 2010). The need to react fast to changes of consumer wants and bring "hot" seasonal products as well as the latest consumer trends to the consumers in a short amount of time can be a game changer in a sector that, for decades, was dominated by pure low-wage competitiveness. The closeness of supplier firms to consumer markets plays now a more vital role and therefore there is a competitive advantage for firms in countries like Morocco and Turkey, which are able to produce high-quality garments with the needed degree of flexibility and speed in a fashion environment where time and the advantage of being closer to the European core is becoming an important asset (Tokatli, 2008).

Table 6. Changes in globalization indexes

Number of sectors	1968-1976	1976-86	1996-2006	2006-2016
Δ*STGI*[1]>0	143	141	145	140
Δ*STGI*[2]>0	143	141	145	141
Δ*STGI*[3]>0	143	137	143	127

Turning to our data, we can show that the fabrics sector was the single most globalized sector in the 1960s – regarding the number of countries involved in trade but also taking into account the distance between countries in these bilateral trade relations as well as the absolute volume of trade (see Table 7). Another sector that also belong to the larger family of textile sectors is wearing apparel. This sector was also among the most globalized sectors in the late 1960s, being in line with empirical studies that report the textile sector as often being "the gate of choice" for developing and emerging countries to enter the global trade network (Gereffi, 1998; Kim et al., 2006). The reason can be captured rather easily: as outlined above, major parts of the textile sector are labour-intensive and require only low skills and machines. Therefore, this sector can be set up in many developing countries rather easily – especially for countries that are scarce of capital and skilled labour. Whereas the textile sector expanded from Western European countries and the US to Japan in the 1950s and 1960s, in a second wave, production was taken up in Hong Kong, Taiwan and South Korea in the late 1970s and early 1980s. The third wave involved a reallocation of production to Mainland China after the country decided to open up for international investors and international firms. Also, other Southeast Asian countries, mainly Indonesia, Malaysia, the Philippines, Sri Lanka and Thailand could benefit from their comparative cost advantages (Gereffi, 1998). These restructuring processes that lead to large increases of production in India and China accompanied massive declines in production of Western European high-wage countries. These developments moreover favoured a finer division of labour that can also be measured by increased intermediate trade along global value chains, that do not necessarily involve more countries in international trade relations but increase trade volume tremendously (Schütz & Palan, 2016).

Table 7 gives a more detailed picture on the development of the respective sectoral trade globalization measures for the two textile sectors.

Table 7. Globalization indexes in the textile sector

	1968 *STGI*[1]	**1976 *STGI*[1]**	**1986 *STGI*[1]**	**1968 *STGI*[2]**	**1976 *STGI*[2]**	**1986 *STGI*[2]**	**1968 *STGI*[3]**	**1976 *STGI*[3]**	**1986 *STGI*[3]**
Fabrics	0.4677	0.5231	0.5608	0.3929	0.4477	0.4966	0.4247	0.6825	1.0958
Wearing Apparel	0.3910	0.4799	0.5307	0.3064	0.4007	0.4478	0.3642	0.4478	2.3887
	1996 *STGI*[1]	**2006 *STGI*[1].**	**2016 *STGI*[1]**	**1996 *STGI*[2]**	**2006 *STGI*[2]**	**2016 *STGI*[2]**	**1996 *STGI*[3]**	**2006 *STGI*[3]**	**2016 *STGI*[3]**
Fabrics	0.5970	0.6439	0.6585	5426	0.5902	0.6028	1.7098	2.2467	2.5982
Wearing Apparel	0.6398	0.7844	0.8368	0.5838	0.7423	0.8018	8.3286	21.0579	23.7423

Fabrics was the most globalized sector in 1968, with *STGI*[1] = 0.4677, whereas the mean value was 0.2182 (and the standard deviation is 0.1078). The value of *STGI*[1] steadily increased until 2016 and so did *STGI*[2]. Moreover, the data show almost a steady convergence of *STGI*[2] towards *STGI*[1], indicating that distance became less relevant in this sector. However, in 2016 the value for *STGI*[1] was 0.6585 and for *STGI*[2] was 0.6028, indicating that complete trade globalization is far from being reached. Regarding the inclusion of trade volume in the analysis, the results indicate a remarkable growth trend in the first part of the investigation period, which even accelerated in the second half.

Regarding the sector of wearing apparel, it is interesting to stress that the level of sectoral trade globalization was below the levels of the fabrics sector for *STGI*[1] and *STGI*[2] throughout the first observation period. Only the volume of trade had overtaken the values of fabrics in 1986. Turning to the developments since the 1990s, which coincides with the gradual opening of the sector towards unrestricted trade flows, the development in the apparel sector is much more dynamic than in the fabrics sector, becoming one of the most globalized sectors at the end of the investigation period.

Altogether, the textile sector shows to be a highly globally integrated sector as expected from its low-wage and low-skill characteristic, whereas high-skill and high-tech niches remain in industrialized countries. Concerning the outlook of this sector, the textile industry has been dramatically affected by the recent worldwide Covid-19 pandemic with collapsing worldwide demand. Moreover, major players in advanced economies had seen distortionary effects as shipping from China became to a halt even before the crisis hit Europe and the US. This could lead to a decline not only in *STGI*[3] but also in the number of countries that are involved in value chains as well as to a decline in the average number of countries that every single country trades with.

Motor Vehicles

In contrast to the developments in the textile sectors are those in the sector of motor vehicles. Globalization has played an important role in this sector as well but at a quite different pattern. Whereas the producers in the textile sector are more dispersed, the automotive industry is heavily concentrated regarding the firm structure – quite a small number of firms dominate the market. As Sturgeon et al. (2008) describe, the eleven leading companies in automobiles are also geographically concentrated in only three countries: Germany, Japan and the US (it should however be noted that China is becoming more and more important over the last couple of years). One further component of this high degree of concentration is that also the sub-contractors are highly geographically concentrated. Therefore, one should rather speak of a high degree of internationalization rather than a high degree of globalization in the case of motor vehicles as trade relationships between firms occur only between a rather limited number of countries. Also, this degree of geographical concentration can be observed for decades: while seven countries accounted for around 80 per cent of global automobile production in 1975, in 2005 eleven countries account for this share (Sturgeon et al., 2008).

Regarding trade volume, the global trend towards higher volume is remarkable. This can be explained by the opening of new markets, above all of China and India with their huge population, low motorization levels and the increased demand for automobiles of the growing middle class as well as the finer division of international value chains (Sturgeon et al., 2008; Sturgeon & Van Biesebroeck, 2011). Yet, compared to other sectors – such as the textile sector – trade volume has remained lower as major producers are in few countries only and because suppliers hardly trade with one another.

Turning to our data as displaced in table 8, the results for the various globalization indicators show the motor vehicles sector as an over proportionally globalized sector in the first sub-period. Whereas *STGI*[1], *STGI*[2] and *STGI*[3] increased over time, they did so at a slower pace compared to many other sectors such that, by 2016, it was an under proportionally globalized sector with regard to trade volume. In more detail, the following can be observed. Regarding *STGI*[1], the motor vehicles sector was among the top 15 most globalized sectors and even among the top 10 sectors with respect to trade volume. In 1986, however, it was only among the top 40 of all sectors regarding *STGI*[1] and ranked only place 66 in 2016 for the number of countries. Measuring trade globalization with the help of trade volume, this sector only ranked place 73 out of 147 in 2016. From 1968 to 2016, the levels of *STGI*[2] also slightly converged towards *STGI*[1]. However, there are years where the gap between *STGI*[1] and *STGI*[2] widens.

Altogether, this means that whereas the automobile sector has become more globalized over time, other sectors in the sample have even become more so, again implying that trade concentration has shaped this sector over time.

Table 8. Globalization indexes in the motor vehicles sector

	1968 *STGI*[1]	1976 *STGI*[1]	1986 *STGI*[1]	1968 *STGI*[2]	1976 *STGI*[2]	1986 *STGI*[2]	1968 *STGI*[3]	1976 *STGI*[3]	1986 *STGI*[3]
Motor Vehicles	0.3572	0.4102	0.4153	0.2601	0.3191	0.3200	0.3239	0.7913	1.2745
	1996 *STGI*[1]	**2006 *STGI*[1]**	**2016 *STGI*[1]**	**1996 *STGI*[2]**	**2006 *STGI*[2]**	**2016 *STGI*[2]**	**1996 *STGI*[3]**	**2006 *STGI*[3]**	**2016 *STGI*[3]**
Motor Vehicles	0.4578	0.5369	0.5671	0.3623	0.4471	0.4767	2.0940	4.5527	6.1205

FUTURE RESEARCH DIRECTIONS

The ongoing and still unresolved trade war between China and the US, the increased protectionist movements in other industrialized countries as well as increased concerns about the impact of hyper-globalization on climate change have raised questions whether the peak of globalization has already been reached. Future research could thus focus on issues raised in this context as well as regarding the short- and long-term restructuring processes that the Covid-19 pandemic has on global value chains, trade volume. It is possible that trade relations will not be equally affected across sectors alike as some sectors rely more on regional trade networks whereas others rely on a larger number of countries and can thus be seen as proper global sectors. It needs to be studied to which extent global production networks become more inefficient and to which extent specialization gains and dividing production internationally can still lead to major benefits for firms and consumers worldwide. Uncertainty due to supply shocks as well as costs associated to the impact on the climate have to be studied more extensively. Moreover, the increased reliance on just-in-time production has proven to be associated with problems during the ongoing pandemic. The lessons learnt could be that regional production should pay off.

CONCLUSION

The objective of this study was to investigate the key trends in trade globalization along the last decades, with special emphasis to what happens at the sectoral level. To that end, we make use of a framework of analysis composed by three critical dimensions: interdependence, distance, and volume of trade. These dimensions are selected aiming to assure a direct link between the definitions of globalization and the measures used to quantify this concept. From the empirical analysis developed in the previous sections, some important results should be retained. Starting with the overall evidence, it is important to highlight two fundamental aspects. First, when evaluated through *TGI*[1] and *TGI*[2], trade globalization was already high at the beginning of the time period selected – with values of 0.8353 and 0.7864, respectively – and are very close to its upper limit (1) in 2016. This means that, in what concerns the two bounded dimensions of trade globalization, the phenomenon is reaching its maximum limit. Second, showing that this topic is complex and requires a multidimensional approach, the evolution of trade volume is remarkable along the entire period (and even clearer after mid-1980s) and does not show any stabilizing trend.

Aiming a more disaggregated perspective, we have also provided evidence for groups of sectors organized according with the intensity of R&D activities they incorporate. These results reveal that the generic trend detected for overall trade is also true for all the four categories considered. Nevertheless, the initial level of trade globalization is higher for the case of low-technology sectors. When the focus is on the evolution of trade volume, the strongest increase occurs in the case of high-technology sectors.

A final step of the empirical exercise conducted in this chapter was the evaluation at the sectoral level, which was done though two complementary approaches: (i) a broad perspective of the evolution of each of the 147 sectors includes in the analysis; (ii) a more detailed evaluation and discussion of two selected cases. Concerning the first element, the evidence makes clear that the increase in trade globalization is a consistent (along the time) and transversal trend, common to a vast majority of sectors. As a result, the average value for each of the measures significantly increase during the fifty years under scrutiny. Taking *STGI*[2] as example, the average value increased from 0.1616 in 1968 to 0.4501 in 2016. However, the discussion of the case studies chosen demonstrates that the evolution of trade globalization is sector-specific. Whereas there are sectors where trade occurs globally as in the textile sector, other sectors tend to rely more heavily on regional trade networks. Moreover, there are sectors that are shaped by a small number of suppliers only, which dominate the nature of global trade.

Taking a last look at the more recent developments, it has to be noted that the Covid-19 pandemic has shown that the free movement of people and goods can come to a halt very quickly with major impact on short-run (and maybe medium to long-term trends) in globalization. Additionally it should be kept in mind that even if the disease had affected only China, leading only to a national lockdown in China, still global value chains and international trade would have slowed down dramatically in many sectors as China is a major source for intermediate products. About 25 per cent of intermediate inputs used in high-tech exports such as pharmaceuticals or motor vehicles in Japan, South Korea and the US come from China (Javorcik, 2020). The reliance in other sectors is even higher: about 75 per cent of blood thinners imported by Italy come from China, 60 per cent of antibiotic components imported by Japan come from China (Javorcik, 2020). The shares for other advanced economies also range between 40 and 50 per cent, which has led to heavy debates on reshoring production.

Regarding the production of medical equipment, the ongoing pandemic moreover made clear that national governments are willing to pursue strategies that opposes globalization: the "sicken thy neighbour" strategy as countries decided to restrict or fully ban the export of critical devices. By March, 21 (2020), fifty-four countries had implemented export curbs on medical supplies (Evenett, 2020). Ilzetzki and Reichardt (2020) however highlight the problems of this kind of policy: to increase production, this takes time and cannot be done efficiently soon enough for national states. This is even truer for countries that have no special expertise in the production of the required items. Additionally, production in a globalized world often relied on international cooperation and division of labour. If know-how is not shared along international value chains and every country falls back on its own, in the end many countries can be worse off. A globalized world with plenty opportunities to trade and the possibility to choose from a large set of suppliers thus offers possibilities in risk sharing that are often overlooked or undervalued when assessing the benefits of globalization. Baldwin and Evenett (2020) argue that globalization should thus be rather understood as a *"massive risk mitigation device"*.

As the latest estimates by the OECD (2020a) show, re-shoring and a higher degree of localized production need not necessarily lead to a lower degree of uncertainty or instability compared to a more globally integrated trade world, however. This is due to the fact that if countries choose to produce more locally and try to avoid being too dependent on many other foreign suppliers when disruptions in one of these few trading partners occur, it is even harder to find substitutes. Moreover, there are many sectors for which total autarchy in production is predicted to be hardly achievable as not all production stages can be carried out domestically. Additionally, intermediate inputs are not always available domestically. This is especially true for the following sectors: pharmaceuticals, electronics, motor vehicles, and medical devises (OECD, 2020b; Van Tongeren, 2020). Even though the current pandemic showed the risks of global value chains, it should be kept in mind that trade helps to locate production where it is most efficient, being beneficial also for consumers as there is a wider variety of goods at lower prices available. The gains from international trade should thus be not forgotten. However, the problems associated with just-in-time production as well as with the high reliability of medical equipment or pharmaceuticals on a few producers only, must be re-evaluated and should be seen as a warning sign also for other sectors that rely too much on just-in-time production or on a small number of suppliers only.

ACKNOWLEDGMENT

This research was supported by the Styrian Government for the Project "(Un)Divided Inequalities in the Digital Revolution: Regions, Labor Markets and Policy Responses; and the Fundação para a Ciência e a Tecnologia [grant number UIDB/00315/2020].

REFERENCES

Al-Rodhan, N. R., & Stoudmann, G. (2006). Definitions of globalization: A comprehensive overview and a proposed definition. *Program on the Geopolitical Implications of Globalization and Transnational Security*, *6*, 1–21.

Arribas, I., Bensassi, S., & Tortosa-Ausina, E. (2020). Trade integration in the European Union: Openness, interconnectedness, and distance. *The North American Journal of Economics and Finance*, *52*, 101167. doi:10.1016/j.najef.2020.101167

Arribas, I., Pérez, F., & Tortosa-Ausina, E. (2009). Measuring globalization of international trade: Theory and evidence. *World Development*, *37*(1), 127–145. doi:10.1016/j.worlddev.2008.03.009

A.T. Kearney/Foreign Policy. (2001). Measuring globalization. *Foreign Policy*, *122*, 56–65.

Baldwin, R., & Evenett, S. J. (2020). *Covid-19 and trade policy: Why turning inward won't work*. CEPR Press.

Baldwin, R., & Lopez-Gonzalez, J. (2015). Supply-chain trade: A portrait of global patterns and several testable hypotheses. *World Economy*, *38*(11), 1682–1721. doi:10.1111/twec.12189

Bhardwaj, V., & Fairhurst, A. (2010). Fast fashion: Response to changes in the fashion industry. *International Review of Retail, Distribution and Consumer Research*, *20*(1), 165–173. doi:10.1080/09593960903498300

Bordo, M. (2017). *The second era of globalization is not yet over: An historical perspective*. NBER Working Paper No. 23786.

Catão, L., & Obstfeld, M. (2019). Introduction. In L. Catão & M. Obstfeld (Eds.), *Meeting Globalization's Challenges: Policies to make Trade Work for All*. Princeton University Press. doi:10.2307/j.ctvh1dr13.6

Christopherson, S., Garretsen, H., & Martin, R. (2008). The world is not flat: Putting globalization in its place. *Cambridge Journal of Regions, Economy and Society*, *1*(3), 343–349. doi:10.1093/cjres/rsn023

De Benedictis, L., Nenci, S., Santoni, G., Tajoli, L., & Vicarelli, C. (2014). Network analysis of world trade using the BACI-CEPII Dataset. *Global Economy Journal*, *14*(03n04), 287–343. doi:10.1515/gej-2014-0032

De Lombaerde, P., Iapadre, L., McCranie, A., & Tajoli, L. (2019). Using network analysis to study globalization, regionalization, and multi-polarity - Introduction to special section. *Network Science*, *6*(4), 494–516. doi:10.1017/nws.2018.25

Disdier, A., & Head, K. (2008). The puzzling persistence of the distance effect on bilateral trade. *The Review of Economics and Statistics*, *90*(1), 37–48. doi:10.1162/rest.90.1.37

Dreher, A. (2006). Does globalization affect growth? Evidence from a New Index of Globalization. *Applied Economics*, *38*(10), 1091–1110. doi:10.1080/00036840500392078

Evenett, S. (2020). Sicken thy neighbour: The initial trade policy response to Covid-19. *World Economy*, *43*(4), 828–839. doi:10.1111/twec.12954

Figge, L., & Martens, P. (2014). Globalisation continues: The Maastricht Globalisation Index revisited and updated. *Globalizations*, *11*(6), 875–893. doi:10.1080/14747731.2014.887389

Friedman, T. (2005). *The world is flat: A brief history of the globalised world in the 21st century*. Allen Lane-Penguin Books.

Gereffi, G. (1998). Commodity chains and regional divisions of labour in East Asia. In E. M. Kim (Ed.), *The Four Asian Tigers: Economic development and the global political economy* (pp. 93–124). Academic Press.

Gereffi, G., & Memedovic, O. (2003). *The global apparel value chain: What prospects for upgrading by developing countries. Sectoral Studies Series*. United Nations Industrial Development Organization.

Goldberg, P., & Pavcnik, N. (2007). Distributional effects of globalization in developing countries. *Journal of Economic Literature*, *45*(1), 39–82. doi:10.1257/jel.45.1.39

Gunter, B. G., & Wilcher, B. (2020). Three decades of globalisation: Which countries won, which lost? *World Economy*, *43*(4), 1076–1102. doi:10.1111/twec.12915

Gygli, S., Haelg, F., Potrafke, N., & Sturm, J. (2019). The KOF Globalisation Index–Revisited. *The Review of International Organizations*, *14*(3), 543–574. doi:10.100711558-019-09344-2

Ilzetzki, E., & Reichardt, H. (2020). *Ramping up ventilator production: Lessons from WWII.* VoxEU. https://voxeu.org/article/ramping-ventilator-production-lessons-wwii

Javorcik, B. (2020). Global supply chains will not be the same in the post Covid-19 World. In R. Baldwin & S. J. Evenett (Eds.), *Covid-19 and trade policy: Why turning inward won't work* (pp. 111–116). CEPR Press.

Kearney, A. T. (2007). *The Globalization Index 2007.* Accessed on: https://foreignpolicy.com/2009/10/12/the-globalization-index-2007/

Kim, J.-O., Traore, M. K., & Warfield, C. (2006). The textile and apparel industry in developing countries. *Textile Progress, 38*(3), 1–64. doi:10.1533/tepr.2006.0003

Levinson, M. (2006). *The box: How the shipping container made the world smaller and the world economy bigger*. Princeton University Press.

Levitt, T. (1983). The globalization of markets. *Harvard Business Review*, (May-June), 92–102.

Martens, P., & Zywietz, D. (2006). Rethinking globalization: A modified Globalization Index. *Journal of International Development, 18*(3), 331–350. doi:10.1002/jid.1223

Naisbitt, J. (1982). *Megatrends: Ten new directions transforming our lives.* Warner Books.

OECD. (2020a). *Shocks, risks and global value chains: Insights from the OECD METRO model.* http://www.oecd.org/trade/documents/shocks-risks-gvc-insights-oecd-metro-model.pdf

OECD. (2020b). *Trade interdependencies in Covid-19 goods.* http://oecd.org/coronavirus/policy-responses/trade-interdependencies-in-covid-19-goods-79aaa1d6/

Palan, N., Simoes, N., & Crespo, N. (2020). Measuring fifty years of trade globalization. *World Economy*, twec.13016. doi:10.1111/twec.13016

Rennen, W., & Martens, P. (2003). The globalisation timeline. *Integrated Assessment, 4*(3), 137–144. doi:10.1076/iaij.4.3.137.23768

Scholte, J. (2008). Defining globalisation. *World Economy, 31*, 1471–1502.

Schütz, M., & Palan, N. (2016). Restructuring of the international clothing and textile trade network: The Role of Italy and Portugal. *Journal of Economic Structures, 5*(1), 1–29. doi:10.118640008-016-0046-7

Simoes, N., Palan, N., & Crespo, N. (2020). Is the world flat or not (yet)? Trade globalization and digitalization. In Y. Bayar (Ed.), *Institutional, economic, and social impacts of globalization and liberalization*. IGI Global.

Stehrer, R., Ali-Yrkkö, J., Hanzl-Weiss, D., Foster, N., Rouvinen, P., Seppälä, T., Stöllinger, R., & Ylä-Anttila, P. (2011). *Trade in intermediate products and EU manufacturing supply chains.* WIIW Research Report No. 369. The Vienna Institute for International Economic Studies.

Sturgeon, T., & Van Biesebroeck, J. (2011). Global value chains in the automotive industry: An enhanced role for developing countries? *International Journal of Technological Learning Innovation and Development, 4*(1/2/3), 181–205. doi:10.1504/IJTLID.2011.041904

Sturgeon, T., Van Biesebroeck, J., & Gereffi, G. (2008). Value chains, networks, and clusters: Reframing the global automotive industry. *Journal of Economic Geography*, *8*(3), 297–321. doi:10.1093/jeg/lbn007

Subramanian, A., & Kessler, M. (2014). The hyperglobalization of trade and its future. In F. Allen, J. R. Behrman, N. Birdsall, S. Fardoust, D. Rodrik, A. Steer, & A. Subramanian (Eds.), *Towards a better global economy: Policy implications for citizens worldwide in the 21st century*. Oxford University Press. doi:10.1093/acprof:oso/9780198723455.003.0004

The Economist. (2019). *Slowbalisation. The steam has gone out of globalisation*. https://www.economist.com/leaders/2019/01/24/the-steam-has-gone-out-of-globalisation

Tokatli, N. (2008). Global sourcing: Insights from the global clothing industry – the case of Zara, a fast fashion retailer. *Journal of Economic Geography*, *8*(1), 21–38. doi:10.1093/jeg/lbm035

Tokatli, N. (2008). Global sourcing: Insights from the global clothing industry – The case of Zara, a fast fashion retailer. *Journal of Economic Geography*, *8*(1), 21–38. doi:10.1093/jeg/lbm035

Van Tongeren, F. (2020). *Shocks, risks and global value chains in a Covid-19 world*. https://oecdecoscope.blog/2020/08/25/shocks-risks-and-global-value-chains-in-a-covid-19-world

Vujakovic, P. (2010). *How to Measure Globalization? A New Globalization Index (NGI)*. FIW Working Paper No. 46.

ENDNOTE

1 For further details on the link between ISIC at 4 digit and the four categories of sectors according to technological levels see http://www.cepii.fr/%5C/anglaisgraph/bdd/chelem/internatrade/itpresent.htm.

APPENDIX 1

Table 9. Globalization indexes at the sector level

ISIC sector 4 digit code	Designation	Year: 1968			Year: 2016		
		STGI[1]	*STGI*[2]	*STGI*[3]	*STGI*[1]	*STGI*[2]	*STGI*[3]
0111	Cereals and other crops n.e.c.	0,4321	0,3492	0,3170	0,6728	0,6212	1,7987
0112	Vegetables, horticult. spec.	0,2750	0,1954	0,2026	0,5655	0,5039	4,2625
0113	Fruit, beverage & spice crops	0,4100	0,3497	0,3566	0,6572	0,6118	3,3041
0121	Cattle; dairy farming	0,1829	0,1306	0,1323	0,2226	0,1573	0,1469
0122	Other animals; oth. animal pr.	0,3447	0,2735	0,2878	0,5152	0,4518	1,4621
0150	Hunting, trapping; game	0,0151	0,0113	0,0146	0,0087	0,0093	0,0090
02000	Forestry, logging & rel. act.	0,3550	0,2850	0,3164	0,5459	0,4858	0,9475
0500	Fish, prod. of fish hatcheries	0,1633	0,1235	0,1126	0,4280	0,3818	24,7898
1010	Hard coal	0,0636	0,0307	0,0317	0,1510	0,1070	0,6524
1020	Lignite	0,0141	0,0061	0,0053	0,0443	0,0220	0,1736
1030	Peat	0,0295	0,0133	0,0110	0,1496	0,0878	0,4523
1110	Crude petroleum & natural gas	0,0988	0,0524	0,0544	0,1401	0,0980	0,9779
1200	Uranium and thorium ores	0,0039	0,0034	0,0036	0,0037	0,0032	0,0147
1310	Iron ores	0,0518	0,0303	0,0326	0,0928	0,0686	0,4798
1320	N.ferr. metal ores, exc. nucl.	0,1455	0,1079	0,1238	0,2509	0,2204	2,0466
1410	Stone, sand and clay	0,1982	0,1258	0,1335	0,4600	0,3716	2,9130
1421	Chemical & fertilizer minerals	0,1849	0,1189	0,1250	0,3389	0,2783	0,4344
1422	Salt	0,0739	0,0449	0,0487	0,3368	0,2516	1,6534
1429	Mining and quarrying pr. Nec	0,2115	0,1445	0,1571	0,4006	0,3366	3,6523
1511	Meat and meat products	0,3327	0,2601	0,2624	0,4561	0,3834	1,4840
1512	Preserved fish & fish products	0,3191	0,2571	0,2701	0,5534	0,5180	7,2298
1513	Preserved fruit and vegetables	0,3635	0,2869	0,3041	0,6582	0,5985	6,2265
1514	Vegetable & animal oils & fats	0,3042	0,2388	0,2335	0,5762	0,5180	4,1284
1520	Manufactured dairy products	0,2398	0,1818	0,1771	0,4515	0,3620	1,6429
1531	Manufactured grain mill prod.	0,1753	0,1316	0,1305	0,5346	0,4578	2,7897
1532	Starches and starch products	0,1939	0,1469	0,1561	0,4291	0,3652	2,6529
1533	Prepared animal feeds	0,1195	0,0799	0,0981	0,4465	0,3738	8,7431
1541	Bakery products	0,1551	0,1007	0,1133	0,5307	0,4410	12,7718
1542	Manufactured sugar	0,1150	0,0710	0,0724	0,3391	0,2680	0,8268
1543	Manuf. cocoa, chocolate, sugar	0,2306	0,1630	0,1878	0,5909	0,5165	6,3010
1544	Macaroni, couscous and similar	0,0732	0,0501	0,0574	0,3744	0,2985	15,1893
1549	Other manuf. food prod. n.e.c.	0,2643	0,2053	0,2243	0,7120	0,6571	20,1761
1551	Spirits; ethyl alcohol	0,2299	0,1702	0,2039	0,4530	0,3850	2,3850
15552	Wines	0,1974	0,1416	0,1469	0,4320	0,3711	2,6067
1553	Malt liquors and malt	0,1338	0,0899	0,0933	0,3749	0,3030	3,8188
1554	Soft drinks; mineral waters	0,0910	0,0496	0,0536	0,5087	0,4214	36,5307
1600	Tobacco products	0,1553	0,1051	0,1268	0,3655	0,2884	2,8469
1711	Prepared text. fibres; fabrics	0,4677	0,3929	0,4247	0,6585	0,6028	2,5982
1721	Made-up text. art. exc. appar.	0,3560	0,2784	0,2787	0,7365	0,6776	18,7885
1722	Carpets and rugs	0,2473	0,1733	0,2150	0,5069	0,4216	3,3344
1723	Cordage, rope, twine & netting	0,1993	0,1459	0,1306	0,5240	0,4562	3,3115
1729	Other textiles n.e.c.	0,2993	0,2251	0,2596	0,6668	0,5995	8,3829
1730	Knitted fabrics & articles	0,2093	0,1461	0,1769	0,7501	0,7050	47,4614
1810	Wearing apparel, except fur	0,3910	0,3064	0,3642	0,8368	0,8018	23,7423

APPENDIX 2

Table 10. Globalization indexes at the sector level (cont.)

ISIC sector 4 digit code	Designation	Year: 1968			Year: 2016		
		STGI[1]	*STGI*[2]	*STGI*[3]	*STGI*[1]	*STGI*[2]	*STGI*[3]
1820	Fur; articles of fur	0,1921	0,1368	0,1735	0,3447	0,2780	2,1941
1911	Tanned & dressed leather pr.	0,2169	0,1676	0,1944	0,4257	0,3663	2,0961
1912	Luggage, handbags, saddlery	0,2641	0,1957	0,2297	0,7215	0,6710	44,9896
1920	Footwear	0,2680	0,1978	0,2415	0,6991	0,6318	22,6371
2010	Sawmilled and planed woods	0,2310	0,1635	0,1829	0,4981	0,4118	1,6462
2021	Plywood, particle board & oth.	0,2404	0,1689	0,1979	0,4854	0,3885	2,9839
2022	Builders' carpentry & joinery	0,1201	0,0668	0,0709	0,4329	0,3281	10,5098
2023	Wooden containers	0,1076	0,0611	0,0464	0,4657	0,3703	2,9771
2029	Other pr. of wood, cork, straw	0,3196	0,2455	0,2773	0,6370	0,5690	5,6795
2101	Pulp, paper and paperboard	0,3022	0,2228	0,2381	0,6269	0,5568	2,5659
2102	Corrugated paper & paperboard	0,2064	0,1413	0,1589	0,6189	0,5432	10,9068
2109	Oth art. of paper & paperboard	0,2950	0,2197	0,2533	0,6880	0,6234	6,4180
2211	Books,brochures, musical books	0,2964	0,2264	0,2480	0,6789	0,6200	2,5249
2212	Newspapers journals periodic.	0,1714	0,1157	0,1236	0,3211	0,2471	0,4815
2213	Recorded media	0,1898	0,1307	0,1552	0,0053	0,0045	0,0001
2219	Other publishing	0,1764	0,1269	0,1370	0,5664	0,4960	6,8146
2221	Printed products	0,2606	0,1883	0,2143	0,7159	0,6544	6,8787
2222	Service act. rel. to printing	0,0004	0,0001	0,0001	0,2615	0,1881	129681
2310	Manufactured coke oven prod.	0,0737	0,0374	0,0396	0,0987	0,0562	0,1714
2320	Refined petroleum products	0,2523	0,1701	0,1909	0,5793	0,4821	8,4572
2330	Processed nuclear fuels	0,0782	0,0490	0,0395	0,1928	0,1453	2,9748
2411	Basic chemicals, exc. fertil.	0,4396	0,3613	0,4154	0,7546	0,7103	10,0403
2412	Fertilizers & nitrogen comp.	0,1841	0,1306	0,1395	0,4472	0,3647	2,4538
2413	Plastics and synthetic rubber	0,3173	0,2376	0,2762	0,6608	0,5994	8,6459
2421	Pesticides, oth agro-chem. pr.	0,1989	0,1444	0,1565	0,4548	0,3877	5,6873
2422	Paints, printing ink & mastics	0,2349	0,1609	0,1775	0,6089	0,5324	8,0503
2423	Pharmaceuticals	0,3959	0,3172	0,3672	0,7385	0,6923	27,2948
2424	Soap and detergents, perfumes	0,2694	0,1939	0,2197	0,7388	0,6789	19,8001
2429	Other chemical products n.e.c.	0,3670	0,2901	0,3277	0,8085	0,7683	15,1810
2430	Man-made fibres	0,2128	0,1499	0,1920	0,4392	0,3670	1,7751
2511	Rubber tyres and tubes	0,2576	0,1834	0,2149	0,5558	0,4972	9,9943
2519	Other rubber products	0,3412	0,2819	0,2915	0,7762	0,7351	8,1884
2520	Plastics products	0,3169	0,2417	0,2909	0,8493	0,8115	62,7587
2610	Glass and glass products	0,3230	0,2401	0,2664	0,7179	0,6598	8,5441
2691	N-struct. n-refract. Ceramic	0,2821	0,2118	0,2247	0,6331	0,5683	6,2408
2692	Refractory ceramic products	0,1673	0,1088	0,1167	0,3917	0,3096	2,0377
2693	Struct. n-refract. ceramic pr.	0,1311	0,0833	0,0973	0,3766	0,2852	4,4253
2694	Cement, lime and plaster	0,1256	0,0782	0,0737	0,2899	0,2019	2,2529
2695	Art. concrete, cement, plaster	0,1291	0,0765	0,0797	0,4240	0,3323	5,5076
2696	Cut stones	0,1123	0,0727	0,0835	0,4099	0,3305	10,8292
2699	Oth. non-metallic mineral pr.	0,2666	0,1866	0,2101	0,6096	0,5456	6,7439
2710	Manuf. basic iron and steel	0,3599	0,2641	0,2828	0,7203	0,6661	3,9544
2720	Manuf. basic non-ferr. metals	0,3738	0,2881	0,3411	0,6890	0,6260	6,4192

Table 11. Globalization indexes at the sector level (cont.)

ISIC sector 4 digit code	Designation	Year: 1968			Year: 2016		
		STGI[1]	*STGI*[2]	*STGI*[3]	*STGI*[1]	*STGI*[2]	*STGI*[3]
2811	Structural metal products	0,2019	0,1350	0,1559	0,5898	0,4951	11,5041
2812	Tanks, reservoirs & containers	0,1800	0,1169	0,1231	0,4729	0,3756	3,9214
2813	Steam generators	0,1371	0,0887	0,1112	0,3250	0,2529	1,9812
2893	Cutlery, hand tools & hardware	0,3764	0,2961	0,3179	0,7652	0,7191	8,7011
2899	Other fabricated metal prod.	0,4206	0,3338	0,3662	0,8392	0,8036	15,0128
2911	Engines, exc. vehicle engines	0,1203	0,0792	0,1031	0,4611	0,3967	12,7042
2912	Pumps, taps and valves	0,3279	0,2447	0,2670	0,7856	0,7452	14,2719
2913	Bearings, gears	0,2968	0,2298	0,2367	0,6991	0,6607	9,2868
2914	Ovens, furnaces and burners	0,1528	0,0984	0,0976	0,4739	0,4010	3,4284
2915	Lifting and handling equipment	0,2762	0,1972	0,2124	0,6489	0,5873	6,4502
2919	Oth. general purpose machinery	0,3326	0,2506	0,2720	0,8141	0,7776	12,5908
2921	Agric. and forestry machinery	0,2402	0,1715	0,1725	0,5578	0,4928	2,2486
2922	Machine-tools	0,3392	0,2583	0,2723	0,6787	0,6180	4,1847
2923	Machinery for metallurgy	0,1279	0,0870	0,0971	0,3042	0,2464	1,0383
2924	Machinery for mining & constr.	0,2580	0,1835	0,2105	0,6615	0,6160	6,0325
2925	Machinery for food processing	0,2117	0,1524	0,1496	0,5701	0,5098	4,7960
2926	Machinery for textile prod.	0,2926	0,2196	0,2529	0,5488	0,4914	1,4000
2927	Weapons and ammunition	0,1839	0,1362	0,1425	0,3263	0,2626	2,5587
2929	Oth. special purpose machinery	0,3263	0,2511	0,2678	0,7348	0,6895	8,2608
2930	Domestic appliances n.e.c.	0,3009	0,2224	0,2603	0,6856	0,6127	15,2360
3000	Office and computing machinery	0,2889	0,2280	0,2368	0,7821	0,7353	33,5211
3110	Electric motors and generators	0,3153	0,2328	0,2555	0,7629	0,7131	21,2197
3120	Electricity distrib. apparatus	0,2913	0,2185	0,2383	0,7945	0,7514	22,6309
3130	Insulated wire and cable	0,2160	0,1506	0,1570	0,7090	0,6544	22,4770
3140	Accumulators and primary cells	0,2134	0,1600	0,1805	0,6107	0,5448	28,1111
3150	Electric lamps & lighting eq.	0,2919	0,2224	0,2480	0,6911	0,6268	22,6431
3190	Other electrical equipment	0,2696	0,2035	0,2340	0,7631	0,7191	32,6368
3210	Electronic valves and tubes	0,2191	0,1589	0,1944	0,7169	0,6689	107,0670
3220	TV & radio transmitters & tel.	0,2770	0,2104	0,2346	0,7534	0,7023	81,8330
3230	TV & radio receivers, record.	0,2725	0,1981	0,2507	0,7205	0,6683	21,4856
3311	Medical & surgical equip.	0,2819	0,2210	0,2488	0,7375	0,6949	46,9221
3312	Instruments for measuring	0,3404	0,2629	0,2782	0,8141	0,7784	13,5066
3313	Indust. process control equip.	0,0004	0,0001	0,0001	0,5688	0,5169	9600000
3320	Optical instr. & photo equip.	0,2997	0,2332	0,2577	0,6545	0,5961	14,9093
3330	Watches and clocks	0,2144	0,1713	0,1822	0,5687	0,5052	3,5452
3410	Motor vehicles	0,3572	0,2601	0,3239	0,5671	0,4767	6,1205
3420	Bodies for motor vehicles	0,1694	0,1111	0,1222	0,5000	0,4070	7,9283
3430	Parts for motor vehicles	0,2684	0,1963	0,2388	0,7712	0,7314	17,2799
3511	Building & repairing of ships	0,1858	0,1241	0,1316	0,2959	0,2416	0,9983
3512	Build. repair. pleasure boats	0,0010	0,0004	0,0004	0,3005	0,2389	22895,7
3520	Railway & tramway locomotives	0,1356	0,0914	0,0874	0,3425	0,2663	1,6929
3530	Aircraft and spacecraft	0,1831	0,1251	0,1660	0,5343	0,4743	6,0123
3591	Motorcycles	0,1432	0,0971	0,1087	0,4498	0,4056	6,6523

Table 12. Globalization indexes at the sector level (cont.)

ISIC sector 4 digit code	Designation	Year: 1968			Year: 2016		
		STGI[1]	*STGI*[2]	*STGI*[3]	*STGI*[1]	*STGI*[2]	*STGI*[3]
3592	Bicycles and invalid carriages	0,1483	0,1037	0,1287	0,4974	0,4410	13,7250
3599	Other transport equipment	0,0018	0,0016	0,0016	0,3847	0,3081	62083,2
3610	Furniture	0,2883	0,2091	0,2569	0,7372	0,6748	47,5942
3691	Jewellery and related articles	0,2586	0,2113	0,2588	0,4960	0,4465	4,5526
3692	Musical instruments	0,2044	0,1509	0,1506	0,4676	0,4308	2,7840
3693	Sports goods	0,2326	0,1773	0,2000	0,6287	0,5757	19,5259
3694	Games and toys	0,2711	0,2144	0,2532	0,6480	0,5902	19,2362
3699	Other miscell. manuf. articles	0,3920	0,3156	0,3362	0,7936	0,7464	10,0612
3710	Recycled metal waste & scrap	0,0211	0,0104	0,0092	0,0265	0,0155	0,0781
3720	Recycled n-metal waste & scrap	0,0002	0,0000	0,0000	0,1873	0,1382	533382
4010	Electricity	0,0174	0,0040	0,0043	0,0412	0,0067	0,1643
4020	Manufactured gas	0,0078	0,0042	0,0026	0,0215	0,0078	0,0009
7421	Architec., engineer., consult.	0,0906	0,0535	0,0529	0,1766	0,1347	0,2350
7494	Photographic products	0,1203	0,0792	0,0931	0,1635	0,1190	1,1540
9211	Motion picture and video	0,2473	0,1759	0,1837	0,0651	0,0527	0,0010
9214	Dramatic arts, music and other	0,2220	0,1694	0,1866	0,4651	0,4173	4,9565
9302	Hairdressing & oth. beauty pr.	0,0293	0,0203	0,0126	0,0389	0,0329	0,0518

List of Countries in the Sample

Sub-Period 1967-1990:

- Albania
- Algeria
- Argentina
- Australia
- Austria
- Bangladesh
- Belgium
- Bolivia
- Brazil
- Brunei Darussalam
- Bulgaria
- Cameroon
- Canada
- Chile
- China
- Colombia

- Cote d'Ivoire
- Cyprus
- Denmark
- Ecuador
- Egypt
- Finland
- Former Czechoslovakia
- Former USSR
- Former Yugoslavia
- France
- Gabon
- Germany
- Greece
- Hong Kong
- Hungary
- Iceland
- India
- Indonesia
- Ireland
- Israel
- Italy
- Japan
- Kenya
- Libyan Arab Jamahiriya
- Luxembourg
- Malaysia
- Malta
- Mexico
- Morocco
- Netherlands
- New Zealand
- Nigeria
- Norway
- Pakistan
- Paraguay
- Peru
- Philippines
- Poland
- Portugal
- Romania
- Saudi Arabia
- Singapore
- South Korea

- Spain
- Sri Lanka
- Sweden
- Switzerland
- Taiwan
- Thailand
- Tunisia
- Turkey
- United Kingdom
- United States
- Uruguay
- Venezuela
- Viet Nam

Sub-Period 1994-2016:

Countries included in the previous sub-period minus Former Czechoslovakia, Former USSR, Former Yugoslavia plus:

- Belarus
- Bosnia and Herzegovina
- Croatia
- Czech Republic
- Estonia
- Kazakhstan
- Kyrgyzstan
- Latvia
- Lithuania
- Macedonia
- Russian Federation
- Serbia and Montenegro
- Slovakia
- Slovenia
- Ukraine

Chapter 2
Informal Regional Institutions and National Resilience:
The Case of the Pacific Alliance

Larry Crump
Griffith University, Australia

ABSTRACT

With the apparent demise of globalization, many states are turning to regional solutions to achieve trade and development goals while institutional structure is fundamental to the strategic and managerial operations of such associations. This study seeks to understand the strategic costs and benefits, as well as the management opportunities and challenges, of a regional institution that maintains an informal structure while specifically examining the relationship between informal regional structure and member (national) resilience. This investigation develops a resilience framework and tests it against a unique structural form, the Pacific Alliance (Chile, Colombia, Mexico, and Peru), which operates without incorporation as a legal entity, without a centralized budget, and without a secretariat. This study reasons that an informal regional institution supports national resilience through an adaptation strategy but not an adaptability strategy and concludes that an informal regional model appears to support continual national development through the adoption of member 'best practice'.

INTRODUCTION

The demise of globalization is a prominent theme within the study of contemporary multilateral trade negotiation – a discussion that may have begun after the 1999 debacle that was the World Trade Organization (WTO) Seattle Ministerial (Odell, 2007). Failure to conclude the WTO Development Agenda (i.e. The Doha Round) contributes to this view (Martin & Mercurio, 2017), as does the substantial increase in bilateral free trade agreements that began at the turn of the century (Crump, 2006), along with the 2008 global financial crisis (Crump & Downie, 2018) and America's recent withdrawal from global leadership (Crump, 2019). The inability of the EU to turn its substantial internal political dynamics into some

DOI: 10.4018/978-1-7998-7568-0.ch002

kind of global leadership and China's inability to present a viable global vision complicates matters, as does continual U.S. - China tension.

In response, some studies argue that regional engagement and regional institutions are likely alternatives to globalization (Enderwick & Buckley, 2020; Moller, 2021; Wang & Sun, 2020), while no study has seriously examined regional structure type from a strategic and managerial perspective. This chapter sheds light on this question from the perspective of developing countries generally and from a Latin American view specifically.

Many developing countries are guided by European success in regionalizing through institution building. Consider the Andean Community, a formal regional association established in 1969 that includes Bolivia, Colombia, Ecuador and Peru. The Andean Community has sought to emulate the EU institutional model by establishing a Presidential Council with a secretariat in Lima, a parliament in Bogota and a Court of Justice in Quito (Atkins, 2018; Comunidad Andina, 2020; Mattli, 1999; Phelan, 2015). While these internal institutions provide the Andean Community with stability, they are expensive to operate and, equally importantly, contribute to a loss of member control as internal institutions develop their own agenda and momentum.

A strategic and managerial perspective requires some consideration of the costs and benefits of association control by members, but also compels an examination of an association's functional requirements under conditions of scarce resources. As such, a strategic managerial approach involves an examination of the costs and benefits that emanate from institutional type. What tangible benefit is achieved by replicating an EU institutional model in Latin America, or in any region with a preponderance of developing countries, and at what cost? Answers to such questions are fundamental to this study, but they require a broader understanding of Latin America regionalization before alternative regional structural types are examined.

This study begins by seeking to understand regionalization and regional institutions in a Latin American context, which leads directly to an examination of resilience and the construction of a national resilience framework. Second, regional type or regional arrangement is defined through a formalization continuum. Third, these two theoretical structures (a resilience framework and a regional formalization continuum) support the development of this study's primary proposition: that informal regional institutions provide strategic benefits by contributing to member (national) resilience through an adaptation strategy and an adaptability (transformational) strategy. Fourth, the study empirically examines the primary proposition by utilizing the Alianza del Pacifico – the Pacific Alliance (Chile, Colombia, Mexico, and Peru) – in investigating its structure and operations in the context of the resilience framework. Fifth, the study concludes that an informal regional institution can support national resilience through an adaptation strategy, but not an adaptability strategy. Sixth, this empirical exercise derives principles that establish policies for building informal regional institutions – a policy framework that supports continual change and development at the state level through the adoption of member 'best practice'.

REGIONALIZATION: LATIN AMERICA

Regional integration is an enduring theme within trade and development studies with Latin America appearing prominently (Evans & Stallings, 2016). The contemporary literature on Latin American regionalism explores two major themes primarily: phases of regional development and levels of regional resilience. The former has examined the recent shift from 'new regionalism' to post-neoliberal regionalism (Briceño-Ruiz & Morales, 2017; Carranza, 2014; Grugel & Riggirozzi, 2019; Riggirozzi & Tussie, 2012) and the latter seeks to build a framework to evaluate regional performance. This chapter is concerned with the latter theme, while 'resilience' is often identified in the literature as a possible measure of regional performance.

A paradox of Latin American regional integration — resilience despite repeated failed attempts— has been observed repeatedly (Dabene, 2009; Montecinos, 1996; Rivarola Puntigliano & Briceño-Ruiz, 2013). The link between resilience and success and failure, and the evaluation of regional performance, are not embraced fully. Some studies question if it is misleading to analyze regionalism in terms of success and failure (Dabene, 2012), but others see value in utilizing resilience to examine regional performance (Carranza, 2014, 2017; Riggirozzi & Tussie, 2012; Rivarola Puntigliano & Briceño-Ruiz, 2013). Such issues are fundamental to the strategic management of regional institutions and the trade negotiations they promote.

The validity of such an evaluation, however, depends in-part on the level of analysis and the tools for distinguishing costs from benefits, and success from failure. The Latin American regional literature does not often specify the level of analysis, although prior citations suggest a systems-level analysis. Resilience at a systems or macro-level will include every Latin American regional institution or a defined portion of that system – a question that is beyond the parameters of this study. At a micro-level, a second approach could examine the resilience of a single regional institution, or a comparative study of two or more. A third level of analysis, which is the focus of the current study, investigates the relationship between an institution and its members and if or how an institution supports member (national) resilience. Strengthening or weakening member resilience is but one perspective of regional success or failure with its accompanying costs and benefits.

The Latin American literature on regionalization offers tools to evaluate the type or degree of regional resilience by defining failure as an inability of a regional institution to achieve its objectives, as stated in the founding documents (Carranza, 2014). This instrument is too blunt, however, as circumstances change over time. Goals that were once perceived as achievable may no longer be so, while often more useful goals appear. Goal-shifting can actually demonstrate resilience by turning a cost into a benefit. Defining regional success and failure requires a refined instrument—for example, recognizing that failure is not the absence of success and success in not the absence of failure (Gomez-Mera, 2013).

A more refined evaluative tool of regional success or failure includes a three-part framework: strong resilience, weak resilience, and decline or collapse (Carranza, 2017). This framework requires greater specificity, including detailed criteria, to be operationalized for evaluative purposes. 'Resilience is a slippery concept. Future research on post-neoliberal regionalism in Latin America will have to operationalize the concept of resilience and decline' (Carranza, 2014, p. 170).

Two questions are central in utilizing resilience to measure the success and failure, cost and benefit, of a regional project: 'What factors govern how resilient a given project is likely to be under changing political and economic conditions? … Second, what factors, structural and agential, enable or constrain how transformative a given regionalism is (or can be) with respect to the powers of the actors, the policies and the institutions encompassed by it?' (Riggirozzi & Tussie, 2012, p. 185). Such guidance has utility. This is a useful foundation, as it offers guidance for building tools to operationalize resilience. A framework that defines key concepts and identifies sources of resilience may further operationalize resilience.

RESILIENCE

As a concept, resilience grew from multiple and multidisciplinary paths first in psychology and then in ecology and engineering (Bourbeau, 2018). Initially, psychology focused on 'bouncing back' through interaction between an individual and their social environment. Ecology first examined a return to equilibrium, which brought in Economics, but Ecology moved beyond the constraints of equilibrium theory by considering socio-ecological systems and management. This latter approach eventually considered resilience as the capacity for both adjustment and transformation, and recognized the important role that homogeneous agents, heterogeneous agents and social relations play in supporting such processes (Bourbeau, 2018; Hall & Lamont, 2013; Pendall et al., 2010; Pike et al., 2010).

Resilience is more than a system-level capacity to respond to disturbance, while maintaining the same structure and functions: It 'is also about the opportunities that disturbance opens up in terms of recombination of evolved structures and processes, renewal of the system and emergence of new trajectories' (Folke, 2006: 259). Resilience is the capacity of groups, organizations, communities, nations and regionals to sustain and advance their wellbeing in the face of challenges by securing favorable outcomes under new circumstances and, if need be, by new means (Hall & Lamont, 2013, p. 13).

'Adaptation and adaptability', as paired concepts, offer utility for understanding resilience. 'Adaptation' is the uneven ways that strong and tightly-connected agents respond, cope with and shape movement toward preconceived paths. 'Adaptability' is the capacity of free but loosely-connected agents in interpreting, framing, and effecting multiple trajectories over time. Adaptability is likely to include transformational qualities and temporal, normative, political and policy tensions that can only be resolved at a national level through power relations that frame the kind of resilience desired. Resilience includes a systems ability to continually adapt to changing environmental conditions, while being forced to shift to adaptability to modify fundamental structures only when adaptive processes fail.

Resources support resilience and serve as a replacement for resilience. The less system-level resilience the greater the dependence on resources. But resources, as a resilience strategy, has limits as resources may be more relevant to an adaptation strategy, while political engagement may be more relevant to an adaptability strategy.

Resilience is a 'beloved' concept in many disciplines, although accompanied by controversy at the national-level. Some studies express skepticism toward governments that identify individual resilience as the solution to social problems (Hall & Lamont, 2013). Other studies argue that resilience is best understood as a neoliberal form of governmentality that emphasizes individual responsibility for adaptation (Joseph, 2013, 2018). This is more likely in extreme neoliberal states but even in these nations, governments do not abandon their citizen to the whims of global uncertainty. Nevertheless, resilience does provide a convenient excuse for an uncaring government.

In addition to the underlying national philosophy, it is useful to consider sources of national resilience. Here it becomes clear how managerial concept and practices play an instrumental role in achieving resilience.

The extant literature identifies economic resources, institutional structures, networks, social hierarchies and cultural repertories as primary sources of resilience (Hall & Lamont, 2013). Specifically, structures with bottom-up processes that are actively supported from the top-down contribute to resilience when each exert control on the other (Allen et al., 2014). Institutional structures also support resilience when perceived as legitimate and infused with meaning that serve collective ends, while including actors that

Table 1. National resilience framework

Resilience defined
• **Outcome:** National government that is able to facilitate, sustain and advance national wellbeing when confronted with adverse circumstances to secure favorable ends. • **Process:** Adaptability (transformation) and/or adaptation in response to adverse natural, political, economic and/or social circumstances that involve complex local, national and/or international systems, which are dynamically organized across space and time. • **Adaptability and adaptation:** Resilient processes aimed at achieving different outcomes, although each seeks a strategic alignment between the current system and its natural, political, economic and/or social environment. Complementary and contrasting strategies that are in tension with each other (i.e., cohesive, internally connected systems contribute to a mastery of adaptation but inhibit movement toward adaptability). • **Adaptation process–outcome:** Capacity to respond and shape movement toward preconceived paths in the short run so the current system continues to function effectively, usually through social actors that share strong and tightly-connected unity. • **Adaptability process–outcome:** Capacity to depart from the current path by interpreting, framing and effecting new trajectories to transform the current system, usually through social actors that are free but loosely-connected.
Sources of resilience
• **Leadership:** An ability to establish sufficient centralization to provide control and direction, and sufficient decentralization to achieve creativity and flexibility by imposing meaning, strategy and policy to guide actors in taking relevant action supported by ongoing learning that is converted into behavioral routine. • **Structure:** Hierarchical order (top-down and bottom-up processes that exert control on each other) infused with meaningful purpose, perceived as legitimate and serving collective ends, endowed with actors motivated and constrained by norms supporting the institution. • **Collaboration**: Planning and the implementation of innovation with sufficient economic resources to support the coordination of multiple actors vertically and horizontally via open cooperative processes. • **Homogeneous actors and cohesion:** Social relations, networks and cultural repertories endowed with solidarity, unanimity, social connectedness and innovation (more relevant to adaptation). • **Heterogeneous actors and friction:** Social relations able to manage some tension, while investigating multiple frames, scripts, and models of evaluation that cultivate productive disagreement, recombination and innovation (more relevant to adaptability).

Source: (Author)

are motivated and constrained by norms that support the institution (Swidler, 2013) with processes that encode knowledge into learning to establish routine (Ancelovici, 2013).

Leadership is a key source of resilience. Leader autonomy and centralization matter insofar as each facilitates the implementation and institutionalization of innovation by imposing a particular strategy via collaborative processes (Ancelovici, 2013; Wolfe, 2010), which can be conducted through the vertically and horizontally coordination of multiple actors (Pendall et al., 2010). Leadership, within a resilience framework, aims at encouraging sufficient decentralization to achieve creativity and sufficient centralization to secure control.

System-level heterogeneity and homogeneity are also important. Heterogeneity matters insofar as it feeds friction and collective reflexivity (Ancelovici, 2013). Homogeneity has also been found to contribute to resilience (Keating et al., 2013), as do other forms of social connectedness such as the structure of social relations (Hall & Lamont, 2013). The relationship between heterogeneity, homogeneity and resilience is not completely clear when the role of social cohesion is considered. It may be that social cohesion is most relevant to adaptation and heterogeneity is most relevant to adaptability. Here is a question seeking an answer. Nevertheless, the question of how to maintain the vitality of existing institutions and build new ones has never been more urgent (Swidler, 2013). Table 1 offers a comprehensive National Resilience Framework based on this literature review.

In summary, a resilient regional institution includes hierarchical structures endowed with sufficient economic resources and heterogeneous but cohesive actors that collaborate, and are both motivated and constrained by norms grounded in meaning with autonomous-centralized leaders that foster planning, learning and implementation of innovation. This framework will be used to test the primary proposition: Regional institutions contribute to member resilience through an adaptation strategy and an adaptability (transformational) strategy.

REGIONAL INSTITUTIONS

'Institution' as a concept, is well established in various social science literatures but it is too inflexible to illustrate regional type, while 'regional arrangement' as a concept, offers the required flexibility. Regional arrangements appear in many structural forms although each include six key dimensions: membership, scope, centralization, control, flexibility and vitality (Abbott & Snidal, 1998; Gray, 2018; Koremenos et al., 2001). Formalization, as a concept, can aggregate such dimensions and 'degree of formalization' assists to distinguish the structure of each regional arrangement. A continuum, based on degree of formalization, can be built through five structural variables: (1) nation or union, (2) incorporation present or absent, (3) centralized budget present or absent, (4) complex internal institutions (secretariat, congress, etc.) present or absent, and (5) binding or voluntary member commitment. Figure 1 provides a description and an example of the most formalized regional arrangement at the right and then moves left, toward the least formalized arrangement.

Federation is neither a regional arrangement nor institution, but 'federating' can formalize a regional arrangement into a nation. For example, consider the United States. Separate states or territories joined together in a regional arrangement that eventually evolved into a single nation. Both Texas and California relinquished their sovereignty and joined the U.S. project around 175 years ago (U.S., 2020). On the other hand, the European Union (EU) has established complex internal institutions that allow the EU to speak with a single voice in many venues but is a union not a nation (Europa, 2020).

Regional arrangements, known as associations or institutions, formalized through a treaty that establish a legal entity, a centralized budget, complex internal institutions (e.g., secretariat) and binding commitments is the most common form. Latin America includes many regional associations although Figure 1 only has space for one (Comunidad Andina, 2020). This is followed by the voluntary regional association, which is also a formal legal entity via treaty and includes a centralized budget and complex internal institutions, but members voluntarily adopt commitments. The Asia-Pacific Economic Cooperation (APEC) is an example of a voluntary regional association (APEC, 2020).

For the purposes of this study, the least formalized regional association is referred to as an 'informal regional institution' or association. This regional arrangement may exist through a treaty but operates without incorporating as a legal entity, without a centralized budget and without complex internal institutions or sub-units (i.e., without a secretariat, congress). The Pacific Alliance (Chile, Colombia, Mexico and Peru) is an example of an informal regional institution (Alianza del Pacifico, 2020).

The author concludes that regional arrangements evolve into nations or unions, or are formal associations that are legal entities with centralized budgets and complex internal sub-units operating with or without binding member commitments. This analytical examination also distinguishes formal and informal regional arrangements, while the latter are unincorporated, operating without a centralized budget, and without complex internal institutions or sub-units. APEC claims to be the only voluntary regional association in the world, while the Pacific Alliance may be the world's first informal regional institution. Now the Pacific Alliance will be introduced, including its background and structure, and then

Figure 1. Regional arrangement: formulization continuum
Source: (Author)

Less formalized				*More formalized*
Informal Association	**Voluntary Association**	**Binding Association**	**Union**	**Federating**
Unincorporated arrangement without a centralized budget and without complex internal institutions	Formal legal entity with a centralized budget, complex internal institutions and voluntary commitments	Formal legal entity with a centralized budget, complex internal institutions and binding commitments	Legal entity with complex internal institutions that integrates member action with binding commitments but not operating as a single nation	Process of federation: A regional arrangement evolves into a nation
Pacific Alliance	*Asia Pacific Economic Cooperation (APEC)*	*Andean Community*	*European Union*	*United States 1840–50s*

its operations are compared to the sources of resilience recently reviewed (see Table 1). First, though, the study's research methodology is introduced briefly.

PACIFIC ALLIANCE

Semi-structured interviews were conducted with government officials assigned to work with the Pacific Alliance (PA) and with members of the PA Business Council.[1] Interview questions sought a comprehensive understanding of the fundamental nature and operations of the PA given its unique structural characteristics. Questions about resilience were not asked and in fact, 'resilience' does not appear once in a word search of the 148 pages of typed interview notes derived from this field research project. Resilience, as a theoretical framework, only emerged after a review of the data and the extant literature. Thirty-nine (39) interviews were conducted primarily in PA capital cities – Santiago, Chile; Bogota, Colombia; Mexico City, Mexico; and Lima, Peru – during 2017. All respondents were assured confidentiality and assigned a number (e.g., 23PA), which is used when making reference to interview data. All interviews are documented, after the List of Reference, by number and the name of the respondent's organization, and the interview location and date (see Appendix 1).

The Pacific Alliance was established through the Declaration of Lima (2011) to seek deep integration through trade via the free movement of goods, services, capital and people. The PA emerged out of the Pacific Arc dialogue (2007–11), which included eleven Latin American countries with Pacific Ocean shoreline, but years of experience with regional institutions also contributed to PA formation. Member difficulties in the Andean Community help PA founding leaders understand that they needed another path (2PA, 10PA, 25PA). Mercosur also offered a point of reference, as it has a substantial agenda (like a mini-United Nations), is protectionist and restricts member sovereignty in establishing relations outside Mercosur (1PA, 2PA, 14PA, 18PA). PA founders appear to have reacted against the Andean Community (EU inspired) institutional model and the Mercosur customs union model: 'Currently, there is nothing new in Latin America regional integration except the Pacific Alliance' (31PA).

Peru President Alan Garcia Perez sensed that Pacific Arc talks were re-creating familiar problems and quietly proposed that a group of countries with similar economic and political systems, and similar levels of economic development, move beyond the Pacific Arc and establish a smaller dialogue in 2010. The Framework Agreement of the Pacific Alliance was adopted in 2012 (1PA, 3PA, 14PA, 15PA, 27PA) and establishes the PA structure and outlines the responsibilities of the Pro Tempore Presidency (Article 7) and the Council of Ministers (Articles 4–6), which includes External Affairs Ministers and Trade/Economy Ministers.[2] Engagement of Finance Ministers has emerged only recently, as the role of the Finance Ministry within the PA is still evolving, while other PA ministries (Health, Education, Labor, etc.) meet on an ad hoc basis (2PA, 9PA, 15PA, 20PA, 29PA, 31PA, 36PA, 37PA). Figure 2 is a summary overview of the PA organizational structure.

The Council of Ministers meets three times a year to frame and recommend many decisions taken at Presidential Summits. The High-Level Group of Vice Ministers is the PA Executive and meets four times a year. National Coordinators (both External Affairs and Trade/Economy) are in constant communication both vertically and horizontally, and work closely with the High-Level Group and the 24 Working Groups that operate along a diverse range of issues areas. The National Coordinators are the glue that make this informal system stick-together (2PA, 3PA, 7PA, 11PA, 29PA, 31PA, 34PA).

Private-sector processes such as the PA Business Council, with four national Chapters, include senior business leaders. Each National President and National Sherpa serves on the PA Business Council with access to Presidential Summits and the entire PA system by liaising with the PA 'Expert Group' (identified as a Working Group, although its only function is to link the Business Council/Chapters to each government). Business or private processes engage with PA governmental process, while respondents report that an effective system of business–government engagement has evolved, as the best ideas get to the right people within the system (13PA, 14PA, 15PA, 23PA, 26PA, 27PA, 34PA).

Most recently, six states (Australia, Canada, Ecuador, New Zealand, Singapore and South Korea) have been invited to engage in free trade negotiations with PA members. If agreement is achieved then each will become a PA Associated State, which is an interesting development with implications for PA resilience. The PA also has a diverse collection of 59 official observer states (as of July 2019) that sought such recognition and provide support to the PA (Pacific Alliance 2020). More on these observations shortly.

The fact that the PA is not incorporated and does not exist as a separate entity results in it not having a legal personality, which contradicts years of legal and managerial tradition and may appear unorthodox to some (Klabbers et al., 2011; Palacio, 2019). Such circumstance presents difficulties – for example, when the PA negotiate a free trade agreement, it is not signed by the PA, as no legal entity exists, but instead by each member. Nevertheless, the PA is a dynamic undertaking that remains a work in progress (VanGrasstek, 2019). The PA is highly innovative, and should continue to evolve, as it offers an opportunity to exam this uniquely informal regional institution.

The sections that follow utilize the resilience literature (Table 1) to examine this study's primary proposition that informal regional institutions contribute to member (national) resilience through an adaptation strategy and an adaptability (transformation) strategy.

Figure 2. Pacific alliance structure
Source: (Field Interviews; Alianza del Pacifico 2020)

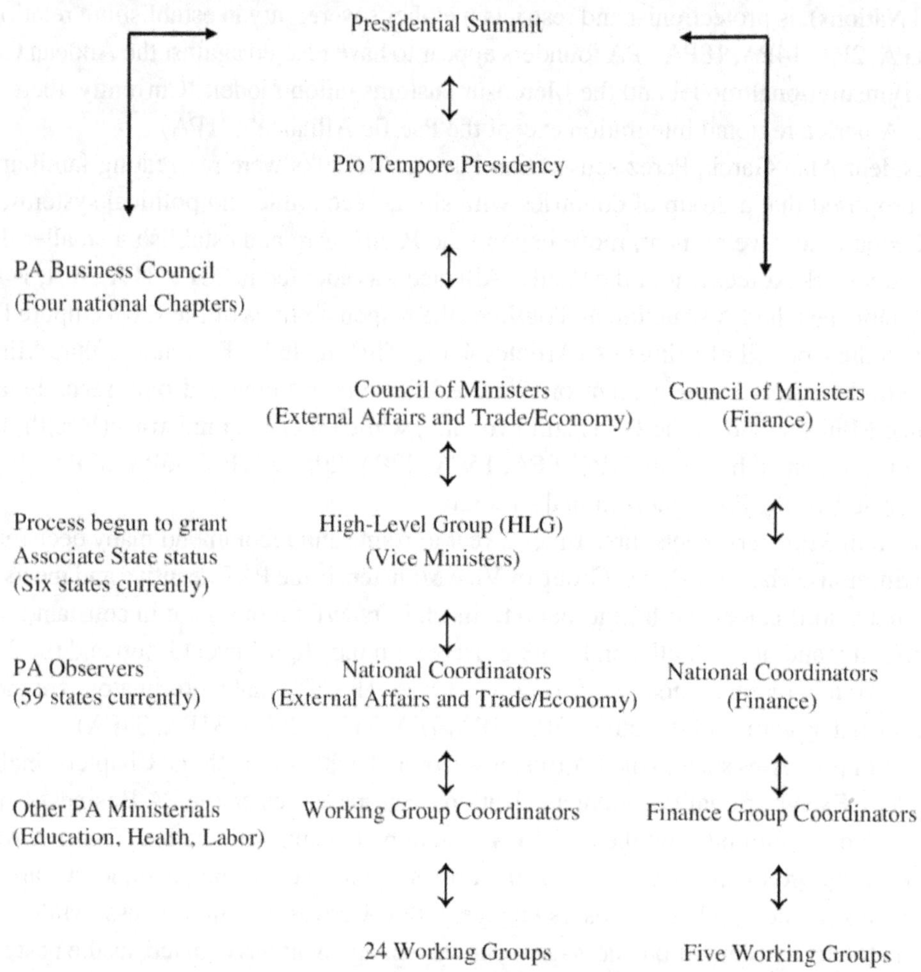

PA AND RESILIENCE: LEADERSHIP AND STRUCTURE

Leadership and structure are each fundamental to management and can be distinguished analytically, but this becomes difficult when engaged in case analysis, as structure is often created through leader decisions, and leadership is a critical part of the structure. Each are considered from a resilience perspective (each is defined in Table 1). The following discussion considers the PA and (1) control, creativity and hierarchical processes; (2) meaning, purpose and strategy that motivate and constrain actors; and (3) ongoing learning aimed at establishing behavioral routine.

Control and Creativity

Presidential mandates establish PA direction and the activities conducted. The adoption of mandates illustrates how PA structure includes elements of centralization, control, creativity and consensus. An idea for a mandate will be examined by the High-Level Group of Vice Ministers (HLG) before being reviewed by the Council of Ministers (Council), then considered for adoption via consensus at a PA Presidential annual summit. An idea for a mandate, however, can appear from anywhere within the PA system, thus supporting regional creativity. This annually managerial process drives a twelve-month PA planning and implementation cycle that is focused on practical short-term objectives (3PA, 7PA, 11PA, 13PA, 16PA, 22PA, 28PA, 29PA, 32PA). It is useful to examine the mandate adoption process conducted at a Presidential Summit more closely.

Presidential Summits are normally conducted at mid-year. Initially, National Coordinators meet together, followed by a meeting of the National Coordinators and the HLG, which is then followed by a meeting of the HLG on their own. The following day, the National Coordinators, the HLG and the Council meet together followed by a meeting of the Council on its own. This establishes the foundation for a full meeting that includes each level, plus the four Presidents, and then the Presidents meet on their own. The Business Council can be included anywhere in this process, although the Business Council and Presidents have a private meeting at each Summit (2PA, 6PA, 7PA, 11PA, 16PA, 22PA, 28PA, 29PA, 32PA, 34PA). 'These meetings establish mandates and the Summit Declaration that focus on short-term objectives. Adopted mandates are delegated to National Coordinators who pass them on to the relevant Working Group' (29PA).

This example illustrates how PA leadership established a hierarchical structure with defined roles and responsibilities at each level, supported by norms to collaborate within this hierarchy. The system appears to exert bottom-up and top-down control, while assuring that creativity is embedded into the process. This structure appears to serve collective ends, which provides a degree of legitimacy for the mandates and declarations that emerge. This process can be characterized as a 'collaborative-hierarchical structure'.

PA leadership also embeds control and creativity within the PA structure through initial critical decisions. Institutional design is innovative, as the overall approach is minimalist. Rather than build institutions and discuss political ideology, PA leaders initially focused on results and achieving an early harvest. In hindsight, the criteria used for regional member selection also demonstrate creativity – a small group with a common world-view, acceptance of free-market principles and democracy, similar levels of development and the completion of interlocking bilateral trade agreements among members. The institutional vision is long term and unending – integration through the free movement of goods, services, capital and people – but the focus is short-term: what are the easy things we can do right now, today, that will make a difference (1PA, 2PA, 3PA, 7PA, 8PA, 10PA, 12PA, 14PA, 25PA, 28PA, 33PA)? These structural decisions reflect creativity while concurrently imposing meaningful purpose and strategy throughout the entire system.

Meaning and Strategy

The PA's long-term vision has permeated beyond government and into commercial groups, communities and society. The PA project has even touched the hearts of officials who could just as easily feel 'jaded' by the additional work created by the PA. Examples are provided:

The Pacific Alliance has created a different kind of atmosphere among the commercial community. It could be called a 'philosophy of helping' where members concretely work together because the Pacific Alliance has created a kind of confidence in the commercial community to cooperate. Without Pacific Alliance assistance, Chilean and Peruvian farmers, as former competitors, are working together to gain access to foreign avocado markets since Peru's crop is harvested in the first half of the year and Chile's crop is harvested in the second half of the year (12PA). There was a time when Chile and Peru had a war and Peru lost, which has not been forgotten ... My father's generation says, 'Don't do business with Chile – they cannot be trusted.' Look how things have changed. Chile has had success exporting their retail system and now all of Peru buys from Chile (26PA).

Establishing real meaning is also a long-term political game, as a system has to endure the test of time. Although the PA is now ten years old it has survived several changes of government (at this writing) in Chile (twice), Colombia (once), Mexico (twice) and Peru (twice), while some presidential elections resulted in a change of political parties. In Chile, for example, a 'right-wing' government helped to establish the Pacific Alliance, which was replaced in 2014 with a 'left-wing' government. Initially, the new president appeared reluctant to embrace the PA – and even talked about joining Mercosur – but eventually this president recognized the PA's pragmatic approach and the direct benefit to trade and the economy. A national government (PA member) cannot ignore the bipartisan, broad-based support that currently exists for the PA (13PA, 22PA, 26PA, 31PA, 34PA).

Establishing real meaning is also a very human game, as one official stated: 'Working Group activities are secured by the government for free, as each engaged official essentially adds this work onto their normal duties. My Working Group colleagues believe in our project and are committed to the spirit of working-as-one' (33PA).

Observations of personal meaning are also revealing. A gruff Consular Services Director exclaimed, 'I'm in love with the Pacific Alliance.' An External Relations official with a 20-year government career described the Pacific Alliance as the most satisfying work conducted during her career. A Mexican official said, 'The Pacific Alliance provides a reason for members to care for each other. When I see a Peruvian on the street, I feel friendly to this stranger' (16PA, 29PA, 30PA, 32PA, 33PA, 34PA). Such comments are not unique but only expressed in settings where staff feel a personal alignment to regional goals and norms.

Learning and Routine

In the past, when some kind of international project commenced, the Presidents would jointly announce the purpose and then technical officials would be appointed to negotiate terms of reference, but this is not how the PA formed. The Presidents met four or five times before technical officials were included; they were then instructed to identify specific areas where they could work together, such as education or the movement of people. 'Clearly, there was political commitment, as the Presidents continued meeting, but no instructions came to produce terms of reference or even some kind of comprehensive framework. This approach to establishing a regional association was very strange and incremental' (10PA).

This incremental approach appears to be a PA hallmark. 'Establishing a uniform set of rules when each [PA] member operates with a different system requires a long-term vision and an incremental process' (23PA). 'All Working Groups and the entire system focus on achieving [PA] objectives through a step-by-step incremental approach' (29PA). Learning initially achieved through an evolving incremental approach – rather than comprehensive planning – stabilized and became routine throughout the PA.

Perhaps the most significant learning that has become routine has been the trial-and-error process of policy development and implementation at a systems level. All PA members have their own constitution, legal and regulatory environment, and implementation processes that must be considered when seeking to amalgamate, coordinate and/or integrate policy. After years of grappling and learning, the PA adopted a framework that provides direction. Congressional approval is required when policy development requires an international treaty. If policy development demands a change in national law for one or more members, then that/those member(s) must seek congressional approval. Policy development that does not require an international treaty and does not require a change in national law requires governmental approval. Regarding policy implementation, only governmental approval is required as each congress would previously have reviewed and approved the relevant policy (Second Protocol of Amendment, 2016).

This framework minimizes but does not remove the fact that each PA member has their own unique circumstances. For example, in seeking to adopt OECD standards on fiscal transparency, Peru is unable to move as quickly as other PA members because the Peruvian government must first work with its Congress to amend some laws. In Chile, the sale of government bonds to foreign entities (such as other PA members) requires an amendment to the Chilean Constitution (3PA, 23PA, 31PA, 34PA).

Finally, prior to the PA, these four states typically looked toward the US for ideas and learning. During formation, PA members agreed that more relevant learning could come from one another, especially when seeking best practice among them (1PA, 26PA, 30PA, 36PA, 37PA). Self-reliance and best practice found indigenously or borrowed from outside the region are other learning approaches that can establish behavioral routine.

PA AND RESILIENCE: COLLABORATION AND MEMBER CHARACTERISTICS

This section also utilizes a review of the resilience literature (see Table 1) and PA field data to examine this study's primary proposition: Informal regional institutions provide strategic benefits by contributing to member (national) resilience through an adaptation strategy and an adaptability (transformational) strategy. Pacific Alliance (PA) collaboration is considered first, followed by an examination of PA homogeneous and heterogeneous member characteristics (defined in Table 1).

PA Collaboration: Working Groups

Internally, each PA member engages with its counterparts horizontally, at each corresponding level, and engages vertically at a national and regional level (see Figure 2). National Coordinators and the Working Groups are especially active as '80 percent of the [PA] work is conducted by the National Coordinators and the Working Groups' (28PA). National Coordinators operate vertically by working closely with the High Level Group (HLG) and horizontally between all Working Groups[3] (3PA, 7PA, 11PA, 19PA, 29PA, 31PA, 34PA).

Externally, the PA collaborates horizontally. Initially, these four states saw each other as competitors but eventually moved beyond this view. Through internal collaboration, PA members created an external framework that allows members to cooperate and compete, as shared PA interests and private national interests are routinely separated (11PA, 14PA, 27PA). The PA Promotion Agencies Working Group, for example, is represented at an agreed-upon list of annual events (export or tourism fairs, investment meetings, technology conventions and so on). In addition, 'hundreds of requests are received by [PA] members annually, resulting in discussions on priorities and cooperation on many additional events annually … the focus is on a sharing benefits although this does not mean equal benefits at every event' (5PA). PA member collaboration achieves outcomes at a much lower cost, compared with working independently (5PA, 14PA, 16PA, 18PA, 38PA, 39PA).

Planning and implementation of innovation is the responsibility of each Working Group although the Innovation Working Group is directly involved in the commercialization of innovation including implementation of a public–private innovation agenda; an accelerator network to support commercial internationalization; and an investor network linking 'financial angels' to R&D opportunities. In one external collaborative project, 'the Innovation Working Group cooperated with the IDB [Inter-American Development Bank] in bringing together the Accelerator Network and the Investor Network' (16PA). Internal collaboration is vertical and horizontal, while external collaboration tends to be horizontal.

PA Collaboration: Business Council/Chapters

Business engagement with the PA began as a private initiative organized independently by business leaders in 2012, which evolved into the PA Business Council along with Chapters within each state – a collaborative system linking the internal work of each government to its business community. The Business Council includes the President and Sherpa of each national Chapter. Members of the Business Council/Chapter have access to the entire PA system including the Council, the HLG, National Coordinators and any Working Group. The Business Council is one of the keys to the success of the PA because of fluid communication between government and business (8PA, 27PA).

PA Collaboration: Observers

States may become PA Observers upon the unanimous approval of the Council. Nine Observers attended the 2013 PA Leaders' Summit with 59 PA Observers as of 2020 (7PA; Alianza del Pacifico). Having a large number of Observers provides the PA with opportunities, but it is also a burden, as such collaboration requires the attention of the National Coordinators who have roles that are already too demanding. Some Observers arrive with expertise or resources that they are willing to share, while others seek guidance on best practice. 'It is both a give-and-take arrangement between the observers and the PA' (7PA).

Australia and New Zealand assisted the PA on issues related to transport and logistics. Canada, Germany, Spain and the United Kingdom, for example, have separately offered the PA assistance in education related activities. Israel provided consultants to support the PA in studying droughts and Germany offered assistance in government procurement best practice (1PA, 2PA, 3PA, 7PA, 8PA, 10PA, 16PA, 19PA, 23PA, 26PA, 28PA, 30PA, 31PA, 38PA).

PA Collaboration: International Institutions

Reaching out to the Asia-Pacific has been a PA objective since inception. ASEAN and PA leaders began meeting in 2014, often on the sidelines of the UN General Assembly annual meeting, which produced a framework agreement in 2016 that supports cooperation in many areas. The PA and APEC have also held meetings, although a joint leaders' summit has not yet been achieved.

Without a secretariat, the PA is dependent on its members to conduct research, as there is no central budget, but the PA also depends on a number of international institutions for research support. The most engaged are the Inter-American Development Bank (IDB), the Andean Development Corporation (CAF) and the Organization for Economic Cooperation and Development (OECD). For example, The

IDB helped the PA to develop a migration software platform that supports the movement of people within the region while protecting state information and individual privacy. The IDB also conducted a study on PA member restrictions in services including taxes on services and supported the Innovation Working Group in linking relevant networks. This is only a sample of the work conducted by the IDB.

The OECD has provided support to the SME Working Group in studying SMEs and financing, and conducted research that established the foundation for the Gender Working Group. The CAF is cooperating with the Financial Integration Working Group to study tributary treatment, which examines each member's tax laws so that these laws can be amalgamated as a first step towards integration. The World Bank also provided support to the PA by conducting a comparative study on the tax structure of all four PA members. This is just a sample of the kind of external collaboration that is occurring between the PA and international institutions (1PA, 3PA, 4PA, 6PA, 7PA, 11PA, 17PA, 19PA, 21PA, 24PA, 27PA, 31PA, 35PA, 37PA).

The PA collaborates domestically to secure political and business support, and internationally through PA observers and international institutions. Such collaboration supplements the PA's limited resources. The norms supporting this process could be characterized as a 'collaborative-networked system'.

Homogeneous and Heterogeneous Member Characteristics

Internal collaboration is enhanced or diminished by the collection of characteristics that constitute the membership. Member inclusion and exclusion may be the single most significant factor that contributes to regional performance, which directly influences the resilience strategy that can be adopted. Achieving the right member mix – including and excluding members – in a political environment is especially challenging.

Initially, Costa Rica, Ecuador and Panama were each invited to join the PA, but declined or did not respond to invitations. Brazil expressed an interest in joining only after Mexico was invited. Others within this emerging body did not sense that Brazil would be a good fit when considering the shared vision that was evolving. Brazil was not excluded from the PA; it was just not included (1PA, 2PA, 3PA, 4PA, 14PA, 15PA, 27PA, 28PA, 31PA).

As mentioned initially, the PA established a new category of relationships in 2017: 'States Associated with the Pacific Alliance' and invited Australia, Canada, New Zealand and Singapore to begin negotiations to secure this status. It is premature to consider cooperation between PA-Associated States and PA members. It is unlikely that Associate Members will transition into full members given the high degree of PA integration to date. This new member category and the diversity it offers appears to contribute to greater degrees of heterogeneity, which could support an adaptability strategy though increased engagement between the PA and their Associated States will be necessary.

What is the right member mix? PA members repeatedly identify the following characteristics: 'No single member exerts more control or influence than any other member. There are no permanent coalitions although issue-based associations form' (3PA). 'Divergent views and disagreements exist between members but disagreements are managed through collaboration' (7PA). 'The PA is like a family, or a group of friends that have seen each other for a long time' (7PA, 8PA).

This study concludes that the PA is a small, highly cohesive regional institutional with member selection based on similarities not differences. Such conditions support a resilience adaptation strategy, but could inhibit an adaptability strategy (see Table 1). This question is examined further in the section that follows.

DISCUSSION

This study reasons that national resilience is supported by a small number of states engaged in a regional institution that contains a collaborative-hierarchical structure and a collaborative-networked system[4]. PA founders did not intentionally design a system to support member resilience; nevertheless, field data and empirical analysis indicates that PA founders created a system of continual national change that supports an 'adaptation' strategy. Implementation of an 'adaptability' strategy to achieve transformation is, on the other hand, elusive within the PA, as transformation appears to require heterogeneous actors if a significant external stress appears.

These four nations are not 'carbon copies' of each other. Chile is the smallest, with a population of almost 19 million. Reports indicate that culturally, Chile is so formal that its retail companies confront challenges when transplanting their retail systems in Central America (apparently, the least formal Latin American region). Mexico is the largest, with a population close to 130 million and a manufacturing base far more developed than those of other members. These are examples of meaningful differences within PA membership. Nevertheless, in a resilience context, PA membership does not contain sufficient heterogeneity to create friction, tension and productive disagreement to support the investigation of multiple frames, models and trajectories to support transformation.

Similarities not differences were the criteria used for PA member inclusion (a common world-view, acceptance of free-market principles and democracy, and similar levels of development). Such similarities provide strength in the day-to-day management of PA operations, but could serve as a barrier when seeking to implement a transformation strategy.

As a counterfactual, consider the heterogeneity that would exist if the PA and ASEAN were to establish much closer collaborative relations. The degree of heterogeneity apparent in a PA–ASEAN regional arrangement does not exist when compared to the PA as a stand-alone institution. The PA, however, is an evolving work-in-progress. The recently established status of 'associated states' could be a step toward developing an adaptability strategy if the PA further integrates associated states into the PA system. Such observations have strategic and managerial implications. Consider, for example, the inadequacy of an adaptation strategy and the necessity of an adaptability strategy when a national government is forced to manage a global pandemic such as COVID-19.

A regional arrangement can support national resilience if specific structures and processes are adopted. Empirically derived and grounded in a strategic and managerial perspective, this study identifies a 14-item framework that can guide states in building a regional institution able to achieve many goals including the goal of supporting member resilience.[5]

The following discussion examines and elaborates upon this policy framework to add clarity to the overview found in Table 2.

1. **Institutional Stability**: A collaborative-hierarchical structure infused with meaningful purpose contains top-down and bottom-up processes that exert control on each other. Meaningful purpose, perceived as legitimate, creates institutional norms that convert continual planning at the regional-level into the incremental implementation of innovation at the national-level, and provides system-level learning and routine that guide actor behavior.
2. **Institutional Agility**: Size and cohesion matter. Institutional flexibility can be achieved with a small group of states that have similar ideologies, world-views and levels of economic development. Transactions costs increase with diversity and with every additional member. If membership

Table 2. Framework for Building Regional Institutions that Support National Resilience

Institutional Stability: Collaborative-hierarchical structure infused with meaning and routine
Institutional Agility: Small cohesive membership with similar ideology, world views and development
Institutional Transformation: Ability to induct members to create friction and productive disagreement
Institutional Vision: Simple, long-term vision that inspires and motivates actors
Summit Leadership: Informal relations via regular meetings able to integrate new political leaders
Political Support: Broad and strong support able to withstand changes in national/member leadership
Resources: Collaborative-networked system that engages domestically and internationally
Strategy: Pragmatic and based on a realistic assessment of resources and the environment
Control and Creativity: Collaborative-hierarchical structure inspires and controls creative ideas
Structure: Less facilitates agility and member engagement through a joint-coordinative mechanism
Linking Policy and Operations: Responsibility of a single expert body that is adequately resourced
Policy Planning: Regional-level – Short-term incremental, monitored regularly and reviewed annually
Policy Approval: Policy development (congressional) and policy implementation (governmental)
Policy Action: National-level – Continual implementation of innovation to coordinate member policy

Source: Author

is too large, a formalized coordinative function, such as a secretariat and a centralized budget, is required thus increasing system complexity and reducing direct member contact and control.

3. **Institutional Transformation**: How often would a regional institution engaged in continual change and innovation, actually need to pursue an adaptability strategy? Transformation should not exist as a permanent ability, as it would be too disruptive to the entire system. If changes in the physical, political, economic and/or social environment are so dramatic that transformation is required, then the institutional ability to quickly induct heterogeneous members (or trusted advisors) could be essential, while the required expertise depends on the external challenge. It is possible that a collaborative-hierarchical structure combined with a collaborative-networked system could shift from an adaptation to an adaptability strategy. If drastic action is required (e.g., COVID-19) then continual implementation of innovation could produce greater system-level acceptance of structural change.
4. **Institutional Vision**: A simple long-term vision that inspires and motivates has utility. The vision must engage vertically and horizontally, and internally and externally, and contain meaningful purpose to establish norms that support strategy and action.
5. **Summit Leadership**: Formal relations between national political leaders are achieved easily, while informal relations are more difficult as transaction costs are incurred. Regular meetings are essential, as is the effective integration of recently elected leaders.
6. **Political Support**: Broad and strong support that is able to withstand changes in national/member leadership is essential. Support for or opposition against a recently established regional institution can become complicated by national party politics. Project survival requires that a broad spectrum of society become committed quickly.
7. **Resources**: Resilience is supported by resources, but resources can also serve as an alternative to resilience. Getting the balance right is essential. Note that a regional institution can secure international resources more effectively than a single nation.
8. **Strategy**: Pragmatic approaches that are based on a realistic assessment of resources and the environment. Build top-down and bottom-up structures that exert control on each other to achieve control and creativity.

9. **Control and Creativity**: A collaborative-hierarchical structure controls through a process of multiple reviews (e.g., National Coordinators ¬® HLG ¬® Council ¬® Presidential Summit), while securing creative ideas internally and externally through open cooperative processes and a collaborative-networked system.
10. **Structure**: Balance structure and agility. Less structure facilitates agility, as members collaborate directly and informally. Complex institutional structure contributes to stability but also inflexibility. Structure operates on four dimensions: internal-vertical, internal-horizontal, external-domestic and external-international.
11. **Linking Policy and Operations**: An effective regional arrangement has a unit responsible for linking policy and operations. Often, a secretariat performs this function, but a secretariat can be distracted with administrative, coordination, monitoring, and research duties. This function can be delegated to a committee that has authority, resources and regular meetings.
12. **Policy Planning**: Policy planning conducted at the regional-level with a focus on short-term incremental steps that is monitored regularly and reviewed annually. The first step is establishing how a problem/opportunity can be framed to coordinate member policy without resources and without legal modification in any member state. If the results lack meaning then the second step is to consider a solution that requires resources and/or changes in law in one or more member states.
13. **Policy Approval**: Separate policy development from policy implementation. Policy development, written as an international treaty, requires congressional approval. Policy implementation, written as an annex to a treaty, requires governmental approval as it previously received congressional approval. This framework reduces transaction costs for implementing innovation, while assuring member control and an orderly process of change.
14. **Policy Action**: Policy action is generally conducted at the national level via incremental action that effectively amalgamates, coordinates or integrates member policy. Each member confronts their own unique domestic circumstances in policy approval and implementation processes.

CONCLUSION

This 14-item framework for building an informal regional association that supports national resilience offers an alternative to the EU institutional model that dominated regionalization in the twentieth century. An institution-building model does offer substantial benefits – especially stability – but at substantial financial and political costs. This formal model may best fit the requirements or resources of developed countries, while the cost may be too great for developing countries. An informal regional institution, as described in this exploratory study, appears to balance costs and benefits from a developing country perspective.

The Pacific Alliance (PA) was conceived, built and managed by developing countries for developing countries based on their requirement to search for low-cost solutions to many problems and opportunities. The strategic and managerial dynamics of an informal regional institution deserve greater analytical and empirical attention and understanding – perhaps to the same degree as an institution-building model.

This exploratory study has sought to understand the strategic costs and benefits, and the management opportunities and challenges, of a regional institution that maintains an informal structure, while specifically examining the relationship between informal regional structure and member (national) resilience. This study began by seeking to understand regionalization and regional institutions in a Latin American context, which led directly to an examination of resilience, as resilience is recognized as an effective tool for understanding regional performance. The study examined the resilience literature generally and the national resilience literature specifically to develop a national resilience framework (see Table 1) that defined and operationalized critical concepts. A regional formalization continuum was also developed, based on a framework that distinguished federating, unions, formal associations (binding or voluntary) and informal associations (see Figure 1).

These two theoretical structures (a resilience framework and a regional formalization continuum) supported development of this study's primary proposition: that informal regional institutions contribute to member (national) resilience through an adaptation strategy and an adaptability or transformation strategy. This proposition was empirically tested utilizing PA field data.

The PA (Chile, Colombia, Mexico and Peru) may be the only informal regional institution on Earth, as this study cannot locate any other regional institution that operates without legal incorporation, without a central budget and without complex internal sub-units such as a secretariat (see Figure 2). Each member has established a government-based coordinative mechanism at the national level that combines with a joint coordinative mechanism at the regional level, aimed at continual planning and the incremental implementation of innovation.

PA norms and processes, and their relevance to national resilience, are examined by considering PA leadership and structure, including institutional control and creativity, meaning and strategy, and learning and routine. This study concluded that this arrangement is best characterized as a collaborative-hierarchical structure.

Internal and external collaboration between PA members and working groups, the PA business council/chapters, observer states and international organizations was also examined. The study concluded that this arrangement is best characterized as a collaborative-networked system.

In testing the primary proposition, this study reasons that a small and cohesive informal regional institution with a collaborative-hierarchical structure and a collaborative-networked system aimed at continual planning, and the implementation of incremental innovation supports member (national) resilience through an adaptation strategy but not through an adaptability strategy as the PA lacks sufficient heterogeneity to produce sufficient social friction to achieve transformation.

The study notes, however, that an ability to engage in transformation need not be a constant capability, as it could be too disruptive to the overall system. What is critical is an ability to adopt a transformational approach, when disruptive external forces require a shift to an adaptability strategy only after adaptation processes fail. A global pandemic such as COVID-19 was presented as an example of the kind of national challenge that requires the capacity to make an effective transition from an adaptation strategy to an adaptability strategy.

This exploratory study concludes by presenting a 14-part framework for building regional institutions that support national resilience (see Table 2). Although further research is required, this study concludes that an informal regional institution may be more cost-effective than an institution-building strategy for a collection of developing countries. Furthermore, solutions developed may have greater relevance to local conditions, as such solutions are often based on member 'best-practice' rather than importation from the 'global North'.

The model developed by the Pacific Alliance may have relevance to other regions, as the model provides guidance (see Table 2) and serves as a benchmark for states wishing to experiment with regional arrangements. Ultimately, a single state should develop a large network of cooperating states plus a much smaller collection of states that become long-term partners, which look after each other as the world is becoming more hostile and unpredictable, while the global framework – negotiated in the mid-twentieth century – gradually unravels.

ACKNOWLEDGMENT

The author is grateful to the Centre for Global Cooperation Research (Germany) for the invitation to serve as a Senior Fellow and for providing research funding [RAD #47767, 2016–2017] in support of this field research program. The author is also grateful to the Griffith Business School (Australia) for their continual support over many years. Special thanks to the Asia-Pacific Economic Cooperation (APEC) Policy Support Unit for providing valuable feedback during the conceptual stage of this research project. The author especially wishes to thank the many Pacific Alliance respondents who shared their time and observations during 37 interviews. In this regard, sincere appreciation must be expressed to Her Excellency Colombian Ambassador Clemencia Forero Ucros and the staff at the Colombian Embassy in Australia for their valuable support. The author is especially grateful to Ambassador Forero Ucros for her introduction to colleagues within the Pacific Alliance including Mr Carlos Moran of the Chile Embassy in Australia, Mr Alvaro Ayala Melendez of the Colombian Embassy in Australia, Ms Maria Luisa Gonzalez of the Mexico Embassy in Australia and Mr Gino Arciniega of the Peru Embassy. Each provided valuable support while conducting field research. The author is grateful to Professor Maria Alejandra Gonzalez Perez for first introducing the Pacific Alliance to the author and to Professor Enrique Ramirez for inviting the author to return to Latin America annually to teach for Universidad ICESI in Cali Colombia. Other colleagues were also helpful in conducting this research project including Jonathan Joseph, Ana Maria Palacio, Nicolas Chan, and Josie Nan Solorzano. Each provided support, guidance and/or insightful feedback. Blind reviews and panel sessions at the 25th World Congress of Political Science, the 18th International Conference on Group Decision and Negotiation, and blind reviews arranged by IGI Global also offered valuable insights, while any errors and omissions are the responsibility of the author.

REFERENCES

Abbott, K. W., & Snidal, D. (1998). Why states act through formal international organizations. *The Journal of Conflict Resolution*, *42*(1), 3–32. doi:10.1177/0022002798042001001

Alianza del Pacifico. El poder de la Integracion. (2020). [Pacific Alliance: The power of integration]. https://alianzapacifico.net/

Allen, C. R., Angeler, D. G., Garmestani, A. S., Gunderson, L. H., & Holling, C. S. (2014). Panarchy: Theory and application. *Ecosystems (New York, N.Y.)*, *17*(4), 578–589. doi:10.100710021-013-9744-2

Ancelovici, M. (2013). The origins of dynamic organizational resilience. In P. A. Hall & M. Lamont (Eds.), *Social resilience in the neoliberal era* (pp. 346–375). Cambridge University Press. doi:10.1017/CBO9781139542425.019

Asia Pacific Economic Cooperation. (2020). *About APEC*. https://www.apec.org/About-Us/About-APEC

Atkins, G. P. (2018). *Latin American and the Caribbean in the international system*. Routledge. doi:10.4324/9780429499395

Bourbeau, P. (2018). A genealogy of resilience. *International Political Sociology, 12*(1), 19–35. doi:10.1093/ips/olx026

Briceño-Ruiz, J., & Morales, I. (2017). *Post-hegemonic regionalism in the Americas: Toward a Pacific–Atlantic divide?* Routledge. doi:10.4324/9781315601663

Carranza, M. E. (2014). Resilient or declining? Latin American regional economic blocs in the postneo-liberal era. *Latin American Politics and Society, 56*(3), 163–172. doi:10.1111/j.1548-2456.2014.00244.x

Carranza, M. E. (2017). Resilient or declining? Mercosur and the future of post-neoliberal regionalism in Latin America. In J. Briceño-Ruiz & I. Morales (Eds.), *Post-hegemonic regionalism in the Americas* (pp. 125–140). Routledge. doi:10.4324/9781315601663-7

Comunidad Andina. (2020). http://www.comunidadandina.org

Crump, L. (2006). Global trade policy development in a two-track system. *Journal of International Economic Law, 9*(2), 487–510. doi:10.1093/jiel/jgl005

Crump, L. (2019). Trump on trade. *Negotiation Journal, 35*(1), 141–145. doi:10.1111/nejo.12250

Crump, L., & Downie, C. (2018). The G20 chair and the case of the global *economic* steering committee. *Global Society, 32*(1), 23–46. doi:10.1080/13600826.2017.1394818

Dabene, O. (2009). *The politics of regional integration in Latin America: Theoretical and comparative exploration*. Palgrave Macmillan. doi:10.1057/9780230100749

Dabene, O. (2012). Consistency and resilience through cycles of repoliticization. In P. Riggirozzi & D. Tussie (Eds.), *The rise of post-hegemonic regionalism: The case of Latin America* (pp. 41–64). Springer. doi:10.1007/978-94-007-2694-9_3

Declaration of Lima. (2011). [Declaracion de Lima: Alianza del Pacifico]. https://alianzapacifico.net/documentos-acuerdo-marco-de-la-alianza-del-pacifico/

Enderwick, P., & Buckley, P. (2020). Rising regionalization: Will the post-COVID-19 world see a retreat from globalization? *Transnational Corporations, 27*(2), 99–112. doi:10.18356/8008753a-en

Europa: Official Website of the European Union. (2020). https://europa.eu/european-union/index_en

Evans, P., & Stalling, B. (2016). Development studies: Enduring debates and possible trajectories. *Studies in Comparative International Development, 51*(1), 1–31. doi:10.100712116-016-9223-9

Folke, C. (2006). Resilience: The emergence of a perspective for social-ecological systems analysis. *Global Environmental Change, 16*(3), 253–267. doi:10.1016/j.gloenvcha.2006.04.002

Framework Agreement of the Pacific Alliance. (2012). [Acuerdo Marco de la Alianza del Pacifico]. https://alianzapacifico.net/documentos-acuerdo-marco-de-la-alianza-del-pacifico/

Gomez-Mera, L. (2013). *Power and regionalism in Latin America: The politics of MERCOSUR*. University of Notre Dame Press. doi:10.2307/j.ctvpj7g3t

Gray, J. (2018). Life, death, or zombie? The vitality of international organizations. *International Studies Quarterly*, *62*(1), 1–13. doi:10.1093/isqqx086

Grugel, J., & Riggirozzi, R. (2019). Facing the future: The legacies of post-neoliberalism in Latin America – Introduction to development and change virtual issue. *Development and Change*, *0*(0), 1–17. doi:10.1111/dech.12508

Hall, P. A., & Lamont, M. (2013). *Social resilience in the neoliberal era*. Cambridge University Press. doi:10.1017/CBO9781139542425

Joseph, J. (2013). Resilience as embedded neoliberalism: A governmentality approach, *Resilience: International Policy, Practices and Discourse*, *1*(1), 38–52. doi:10.1080/21693293.2013.765741

Joseph, J. (2018). *Varieties of resilience: Studies in governmentality*. Cambridge University Press. doi:10.1017/9781316551028

Keating, D., Siddiqi, A., & Nguyen, Q. (2013). National differences in population health and development. In P. A. Hall & M. Lamont (Eds.), *Social resilience in the neoliberal era* (pp. 239–263). Cambridge University Press. doi:10.1017/CBO9781139542425.014

Klabbers, J., Castren, E., & Wallendahl, A. (2011). *Research Handbook on the law of international organizations*. Edward Elgar. doi:10.4337/9780857931290

Koremenos, B., Lipson, C., & Snidal, D. (2001). The rational design of international institutions. *International Organization*, *55*(4), 761–799. doi:10.1162/002081801317193592

Martin, A., & Mercurio, B. (2017). Doha dead and buried in Nairobi: Lessons for the WTO. *Journal of International Trade Law & Policy*, *16*(1), 49–66. doi:10.1108/JITLP-01-2017-0001

Mattli, W. (1999). *The logic of regional integration: Europe and beyond*. Cambridge University Press. doi:10.1017/CBO9780511756238

Moller, J. O. (2021). Asia's transformation: From economic globalization to regionalization. ISEAS: Yusof Ishak Institute.

Montecinos, V. (1996). Ceremonial regionalism, institutions and integration in the Americas. *Studies in Comparative International Development*, *31*(2), 110–123. doi:10.1007/BF02719330

Odell, J. S. (2007). Growing power meets frustration in the Doha round's first four years. In L. Crump & J. Maswood (Eds.), *Developing countries and global trade negotiations* (pp. 7–40). Routledge.

Pacific Alliance. (2020). *What is the Pacific Alliance*. https://alianzapacifico.net/en/what-is-the-pacific-alliance/

Palacio, A. M. (2019). The Pacific Alliance: Building a pathway to the high-hanging fruit of deep integration. In P. Sauve, R. P. Lazo, & J. M. Alvarez Zarate (Eds.), *The Pacific Alliance in a world of preferential trade agreements* (pp. 3–27). Springer International. doi:10.1007/978-3-319-78464-9_1

Pendall, R., Foster, K. A., & Cowell, M. (2010). Resilience and regions: Building understanding of the metaphor. *Cambridge Journal of Regions, Economy and Society*, *3*(1), 71–84. doi:10.1093/cjres/rsp028

Phelan, W. (2015). Enforcement and escape in the Andean Community: Why the Andean Community of nations is not a replica of the European Union. *Journal of Common Market Studies*, *53*(4), 840–856. doi:10.1111/jcms.12222

Pike, A., Dawley, S., & Tomaney, J. (2010). Resilience, adaptation and adaptability. *Cambridge Journal of Regions, Economy and Society*, *3*(1), 59–70. doi:10.1093/cjres/rsq001

Riggirozzi, P., & Tussie, D. (2012). *The rise of post-hegemonic regionalism: The case of Latin America*. Springer. doi:10.1007/978-94-007-2694-9

Rivarola Puntigliano, A., & Briceño-Ruiz, J. (2013). *The resilience of regionalism in Latin America and the Caribbean: Development and autonomy*. Palgrave. doi:10.1057/9781137328373

Second protocol of amendment to the additional protocol of the framework agreement of the Pacific Alliance. (2016). [Alianza del Pacifico: Declaracion de Puerto Varas]. https://alianzapacifico.net/documentos-acuerdo-marco-de-la-alianza-del-pacifico/

Swidler, A. (2013). Cultural sources of institutional resilience. In P. A. Hall & M. Lamont (Eds.), *Social resilience in the neoliberal era* (pp. 319–345). Cambridge University Press. doi:10.1017/CBO9781139542425.018

US Government Services. (2020). *US history and historical documents*. https://www.usa.gov/history

VanGrasstek, C. (2019). Concluding remarks: The Pacific Alliance – stocktaking and the way forward. In P. Sauve, R. P. Lazo, & J. M. Alvarez Zarate (Eds.), *The Pacific Alliance in a world of preferential trade agreements* (pp. 251–262). Springer International. doi:10.1007/978-3-319-78464-9_14

Wang, Z., & Sun, Z. (2020). From globalization to regionalization: The United States, China and the Post-Covid-19 world economic order. *Journal of Chinese Political Science*, *28*(October). Advance online publication. doi:10.100711366-020-09706-3 PMID:33144822

Wolfe, D. A. (2010). The strategic management of core cities: Path dependency and economic adjustment in resilient regions. *Cambridge Journal of Regions, Economy and Society*, *3*(1), 139–152. doi:10.1093/cjres/rsp032

ENDNOTES

1 Griffith University Human Research Ethics Committee approved this research program (Policy Coordination in Regional Associations, application: 03/08/10326)

2 Framework Agreement of the Pacific Alliance, Article 7: The PA rotating Pro-Tempore Presidency serves from July to June and is responsible for establishing an annual program of activities with dates, venue and meeting agenda, including maintaining meeting records and documents. Articles 4–6: The PA Council of Ministers (Council) ensures compliance and implementation, evaluates the results of PA decisions, approves the PA program of activities, prepares Presidential Summit Declarations, convenes High-Level Group meetings, appoints working groups, grants observer status, and seeks support from international organizations in pursuing PA objectives (see: Framework Agreement of the Pacific Alliance 2012).

3 The Pacific Alliance Working Groups include the: Ad hoc Fishing Group, Committee of Experts–CEAP, Communication Strategy, Consumer Protection, Cooperation, Culture, Digital Agenda, Education, Environment, External Relations, Gender, Innovation, Institutional Affairs, Intellectual Property, Labor, Mining Development, Movement of People, Promotion Agencies, Public Purchasing, Services and Capital, Small and Medium-size Enterprises (SMEs), TBT-Regulatory Cooperation (technical barriers to trade), Tourism, and Trade Facilitation and Customs Cooperation (9PA; 31PA).

4 A regional association designed in this manner establishes norms and processes that balance control and creativity, and support a long-term vision at the institutional-level, continual planning at the regional-level and incremental implementation of innovation that converts learning into routine at the national-level. Structural and leadership qualities, as demonstrated by the PA, create meaningful purpose and legitimacy that motivate and constrain organizational actors to engage in guided performance – an approach central to resilience (please see Table 1).

5 It is important to note a limitation in the empirical development of Table 2, as this framework is the result of a single case. Researchers who wish to conduct similar work to critique, accept and/or reject this framework are most welcome by the author.

APPENDIX: FIELD INTERVIEWS

List of field interviews including the assigned number, the name of the respondent's organization, and the interview location and date:

1PA: Embassy of Colombia in Australia. Canberra (9/9/2016).
2PA: Colombia Ministry of Commerce, Industry and Tourism. Bogota (24/1/2017).
3PA: Colombia Ministry of Commerce, Industry and Tourism. Bogota (24/1/2017).
4PA: Colombia Ministry of National Education. Bogota (25/1/2017).
5PA: PROCOLOMBIA. Bogota (27/1/2017).
6PA: Colombia Ministry of Commerce, Industry and Tourism. Bogota (27/1/2017).
7PA: Colombia Ministry of External Relations. Bogota (27/1/2017).
8PA: Colombia Ministry of Commerce, Industry and Tourism. Skype (1/2/2017).
9PA: Colombia Ministry of Finance and Public Credit. Skype (7/2/2017).
10PA: Chile Ministry of Agriculture. Santiago (31/1/2017).
11PA: Chile Ministry of Foreign Affairs. Santiago (31/1/2917).
12PA: Chile Confederation of Production and Commerce. Santiago (31/1/2017).
13PA: Chilean Pacific Foundation. Santiago (1/2/2017).
14PA: Pacific Alliance, Chile Business Chapter. Santiago (2/2/2017).
15PA: Chile Ministry of Foreign Affairs. Santiago (3/2/2017).
16PA: Chile Ministry of Economy, Development and Tourism. Santiago (6/2/2017).
17PA: MILA (Integrated Latin American Market) Secretariat. Santiago (7/2/2017).
18PA: ProChile. Santiago (8/2/2017).
19PA: Chile Ministry of Woman and Gender Equality. Santiago (8/2/2017).
20PA: Chile Ministry of Foreign Affairs. Santiago (9/2/2017).
21PA: Chile Ministry of Foreign Affairs. Santiago (9/2/2017).
22PA: Peru Ministry of Foreign Affairs. Lima (13/2/2017).
23PA: Chamber of Commerce of Lima. Lima (14/2/2017).
24PA: Peru Ministry of Foreign Trade and Tourism. Lima (14/2/2017).
25PA: Peru Ministry of Foreign Trade and Tourism. Lima (15/2/2017).
26PA: COMEXPERU. Lima (15/2/2017).
27PA: PROMPERU. Lima (15/2/2017).
28PA: Peru Ministry of Foreign Trade and Tourism. Lima (16/2/2017).
29PA: Peru Ministry of Foreign Affairs. Lima (16/2/2017).
30PA: Mexico Secretary of Foreign Relations. Mexico City (22/2/2017).
31PA: Mexico Secretary of Foreign Relations. Mexico City (22/2/2017).
32PA: Mexico Secretary of Foreign Relations. Mexico City (22/2/2017).
33PA: Mexico Secretary of Tourism. Mexico City (22/2/2017).
34PA: Mexico Secretary of Economy. Mexico City (23/2/2017).
35PA: BBVA Bancomer. Mexico City (23/2/2017).
36PA: Mexico Secretary of Finance and Public Credit. Mexico City (24/2/2017).
37PA: Mexico Secretary of Labor and Social Welfare. Mexico City (24/2/2017).
38PA: ProMexico and ProChile. Casablanca, Morocco (24/4/2017).

39PA: Embassy of Colombia in Morocco. Rabat, Morocco (25/4/2017).

Chapter 3
Globalization, International Trade, and CO2 Convergence:
Evidence From G7 Countries

Furkan Yıldız
https://orcid.org/0000-0002-1822-1341
Kırklareli University, Turkey

ABSTRACT

The goal of this study is to investigate the potential effects of international trade on per-capita CO_2 emissions among trade partners. To achieve this purpose, the Group of Seven (G7) countries and each of their developing trade-partner countries with the highest trade volume have been selected as the sample. The stochastic convergence methodology has been employed using Augmented Dickey Fuller (ADF), Phillips-Perron (PP), and Enders-Lee Fourier unit root tests in order to test for convergence or divergence. Various results have been obtained from the unit root tests. These results suggest international trade to have no general or common effects on per capita CO_2 emissions.

INTRODUCTION

The economic borders between countries can be said to have weakened in the past few decades due to globalization. In the 1970s, in particular, the dominant policy in the international field was neo-liberalism, and this ideology also even became dominant in the field of economics. Foreign direct investments and the volume of international trade prominently increased as an obvious result of globalization. Multinational corporations became the important actors of the new economic order, and they engendered the homogenous expansion of production processes throughout the whole world. As such, some multinational corporations left only their strategic operations such as management and design in the central country, moving all their production operations in particular to less developed countries with abundant cheap labor. This implicit agreement between less developed and developed countries has provided the less developed countries with more employment and more production. However, multinational corporations (i.e., those in developed countries) achieved distinct advantages such as lower production costs and new

DOI: 10.4018/978-1-7998-7568-0.ch003

markets thanks to this agreement. However, in addition to the economic advantages that were created, this process has also increased energy consumption through the production increases in host countries. This increased energy consumption has also increased environmental degradation and the release of CO2 and other greenhouse gases into the atmosphere.

According to one part of the literature, developed countries have caused environmental pollution to be exported to the rest of the world through increased foreign trade volume and foreign direct investment as a result of globalization. Antweiler et al. (2001) investigated the effect a country's openness to international trade has on the environment using a theoretical model. In the study's theoretical section, they identified three different impacts free trade has had on the environment: the scale, technique, and composition effects. In their conclusion, they suggested that free trade has had a positive impact on environment. Cole and Elliott (2003) investigated whether compositional changes have occurred in inter-regional pollution due to trade liberalization. According to those authors, the suspected causes of these possible changes are dissimilarities in factor endowments (capital-labor composition) and/or inter-regional environmental regulations. They suggested trade liberalization as being able to reduce emissions based on biochemical oxygen demand while increasing NOx and CO2 emissions. The results from (Chakraborty & Mukherjee, 2013) indicate countries' environmental sustainability to be negatively related to their merchandise export and inward foreign direct investments while being positively related to service exports and outward foreign direct investments. Their results also indicate increased production in developing or less developed countries to lead to more energy consumption and more CO2 emissions. As a result, CO2 emissions per capita in the world are expected to converge over time.

These new circumstances have transformed environmental pollution into a transnational problem and increased concerns both politically and academically. In order to reduce the damage to the environment, climate summits such as Rio de Janeiro, Copenhagen, Paris, and Kyoto Protocols have been held. The Climate Change Framework Agreement and the Kyoto Protocol were signed, bringing measures on carbon trading and carbon tax to the agenda.

The main purpose of this study is to investigate whether the amount of CO2 emissions between G7 countries converge with each of their developing trade partner countries with the highest trade volume. For this purpose, ADF, PP and Enders-Lee Fourier unit root tests have been used to test for the convergence of CO2 emissions between the related countries. To the best of my knowledge, this study is relatively unique in literature in terms how it uses the unit root test and its sample. This feature makes up part of the study's contribution to the literature. The results reveal CO2 emissions to converge between Germany-China, Japan-Cuba, and the USA-Mexico. In contrast, no convergence was found between the United Kingdom-Turkey, Canada-Cambodia, France-Russia, or Italy-South Korea.

The remainder of the study is organized as follows. The next section is reserved to a review of the related literature. Following the literature review, the econometric model and method are introduced and the empirical results explained. Lastly, the study concludes with the discussion section.

LITERATURE REVIEW

In the literature, roughly three different approaches have been used regarding the investigation of CO_2 convergence across countries: the beta (β), sigma (σ), and stochastic convergence tests. In addition, these approaches are further divided into absolute and conditional convergence (Pettersson et al., 2014). β-convergence, which is derived from the neoclassical growth model (Solow, 1956), implies that countries with lower initial CO_2 levels will experience higher emission-growth levels. Hence, they will converge with countries that have higher-emissions. However, the β-convergence approach has been increasingly criticized because of the assumption that the growth rates of the individual countries is generated by an auto-regressive (1) process while controlling the persistent differences across countries (Friedman, 1992; Quah, 1997). To overcome these problems, sigma-convergence (σ), which was suggested by Quah (1993) regarding the dynamics over per capita growth, has been adapted and used to measure CO_2 convergence (see Aslan, 2009; Barassi et al., 2008; Bilgili & Ulucak, 2018; Churchill et al., 2020; Lee et al., 2008; Nourry, 2009; Romero-Ávila, 2008; Strazicich & List, 2003; Westerlund & Basher, 2008). The last approach, stochastic convergence, is another approach used for investigating CO_2 convergence across countries. This approach is an adaptation of Carlino and Mills's (1993) income convergence methodology and relies on scanning countries' CO_2 data over time using certain unit root tests. If the null hypothesis is accepted (no unit root test detected), then the result implies evidence of stochastic convergence to exist (Acar et al., 2017).

A brief summary of the related literature is provided in Table 1. While the studies from Apergis and Payne (2020), Boussemart et al. (2015), Jobert et al. (2010), Nguyen-Van (2005), Perkins and Neumayer (2008), Presno et al. (2018), Runar et. al. (2017), Strazicich and List (2003), Yang et. al. (2016), and Yavuz and Yilanci (2013) have used the β-convergence methodology, the studies from Aldy (2006) and Panopoulou and Pantelidis (2009) are comprised of the σ-convergence methodology. The stochastic convergence methodology, meanwhile, has been adopted in several studies (e.g., Ahmed et al., 2017; Apergis & Payne, 2020; Aslan, 2009; Barassi et al., 2008; Bilgili & Ulucak, 2018; Churchill et al., 2020; Lee et al., 2008; Nourry, 2009; Presno et al., 2018; Romero-Ávila, 2008; Strazicich & List, 2003; Sun et al., 2016; Westerlund & Basher, 2008; Yavuz & Yilanci, 2013).

According to Table 1's findings, mixed results are seen to have been obtained. Acar et al. (2017) composed a survey of the related literature and used the meta-analysis technique. They finally declared convergence of per capita CO_2 emissions. Payne (2020) also declared the same results following the same technique. Apergis and Payne (2020) investigated whether convergence exists among NAFTA countries. The results strongly indicated the presence of convergence for stochastic, club, and sigma convergence tests. Several studies used different unit root tests to investigate the convergence of CO_2 under the stochastic convergence approach. Bilgili and Uluocak (2018) found convergence in the ecological footprint among G20 countries. Lee et al. (2008) and Presno et al. (2015) investigated the convergence of CO_2 among OECD countries for different time periods using unit root tests. They both reported convergence within OECD countries. Romero-Ávila (2008) tested the convergence of 23 countries using panel stationarity and revealed the convergence of emissions. The CO_2 convergence among 10 South American economies was investigated by Robalino-López et al. (2016). According to their obtained test results, the CO_2 per capita among the sampled countries converges over 1980-2010 period. Another study, implemented by Strazicich and List (2003), analyzed the convergence of CO_2 emissions among 12 industrialized economies using the panel unit root test and found strong evidence for convergence. Westerlund and Basher (2008) also reached similar results in their study on 28 countries. Sun et al. (2016) determined a convergence among the largest 10 economies using the Enders-Lee Fourier unit root test. Boussemart et al. (2015) examined convergence throughout China's regions using the non-parametric approach. Brock and Taylor (2010) employed a cross-sectional method for 173 countries and reported a convergence of CO_2 emissions. Ezcurra (2007) uncovered convergence using the non-parametric approach. Meanwhile, Nguyen Van (2005) reported mixed results using the same approach. Perkins and Neumayer (2008) and

Table 1. Literature review

No.	Author(s) and Date	Period	Sample	Target Variable (s)	Methodology	Finding(s)
1.	Acar et al. (2017)			CO_2 emissions	meta-analysis	convergence
2.	Ahmed et al. (2017)	1960-2010	162 countries	CO_2 emissions	wavelet based unit root	mixed results
3.	Aldy (2006)	1960-2000	OECD and other 88 countries	CO_2 emissions	Markov transition matrix	mixed results
4.	Arslan (2009)	1950-2004	some country groups	CO_2 emissions	panel unit root	divergence
5.	Apergis and Payne (2020)	1970-2014	Canada, USA, Mexico	CO_2 intensity, energy intensity, carbonization index	stochastic, club, sigma convergence	convergence
6.	Barassi et al. (2008)	1950-2002	OECD countries	CO_2 emissions	panel unit root	no convergence
7.	Bilgili and Ulucak (2018)	1961-2014	G-20	ecological footprint indicator	panel KPSS club convergence	convergence
8.	Boussemart et al. (2015)	1997-2010	30 Chinese regions	CO_2 emissions	non-parametric	convergence
9.	Brock and Taylor (2010)	1960-1988	173 countries	CO_2 emissions	cross-sectional method	convergence
10.	Churchill et al. (2020)	1981-2014	17 emerging market economies	CO_2 emissions	panel unit root	mixed results
11.	Ezcurra (2007)	1960-1999	87 countries	CO_2 emissions	non-parametric	convergence
12.	Herrerias (2013)	1980-2009	162 countries	CO_2 emissions	pair-wise test club convergence test	mixed results
13.	Lanne and Liski (2004)	1870-2028	16 industrialized countries	CO_2 emissions	panel unit root	no convergence
14.	Lee et al. (2008)	1960-2000	OECD countries	CO_2 emissions	panel unit root	convergence
15.	Nourry (2009)	1950-2003	127 countries	CO_2 and SO_2 emissions	pair-wise test	mixed results
16.	Nguyen-Van (2005)	1966-1996	100 countries	CO_2 emissions	non-parametric	mixed results
17.	Panopoulou and Pantelidis (2009)	1960-2003	128 countries	CO_2 emissions	panel club convergence	convergence
18.	Payne (2020)			CO_2 emissions	meta-analysis	convergence
19.	Perkins and Neumayer (2008)	1980-2000	114 countries	CO_2 and SO_2 emissions	panel GMM	convergence
20.	Presno et al. (2018)	1901-2008	OECD countries	CO_2 emissions	stationarity	convergence
21.	Rios and Gianmoena (2018)	1970-2014	141 countries	CO_2 emissions	Green Solow growth model	weak convergence
22.	Romero-Ávila (2008)	1960-2002	23 countries	CO_2 emissions	Panel stationarity	convergence
23.	Jobert et al. (2010)	1971-2006	EU countries	CO_2 emissions	Bayesian shrinkage estimation method	convergence
24.	Robalino-López (2016)	1980-2010	10 south American countries	CO_2 emissions	panel unit root test	convergence
25.	Runar et al. (2017)	1985-2010	124 countries	CO_2 emissions	GMM	convergence
26.	Strazicich and List (2003)	1960-1997	12 industrialized countries	CO_2 emissions	panel unit root	convergence
27.	Sun et. al. (2016)	1971-2010	10 largest economies	CO_2 emissions	Enders-Lee Fourier unit root test	convergence
28.	Westerlund and Basher (2008)	1870-2002	16 developed 12 developing countries	CO_2 emissions	panel unit root	convergence
29.	Yang et al. (2016)	1998-2012	China provinces	CO_2 emissions	fixed and random effects	convergence
30.	Yavuz and Yilanci (2013)	1960-2005	G-7 countries	CO_2 emissions	threshold autoregressive panel unit root test	mixed results

Runar et al. (2017) investigated the convergence of CO_2 emissions by employing GMM methodology and both reported convergence.

Arslan (2009) is the only study in Table 1 to record divergence of CO_2 emissions. The author employed a panel unit root test in order to test the behavior of CO_2 emissions among a group of country and reported observing a divergence of carbon emissions among the countries. On the other hand, some studies such as Ahmed et al. (2017), Aldy (2006), Churchill et al. (2020), Herrerias (2013), Nourry (2009), and Yavuz and Yilanci (2013) have revealed mixed results.

As seen above, mixed results were obtained from the empirical studies. Several different motivations may cause these mixed results, such as the econometric technique being used, the sample, or the time period being tested. As understood from Table 1, the conventional unit root tests were generally used to test the stochastic convergence approach. Hence, these conventional unit root tests may have led to these mixed findings. Therefore, this study uses the Enders-Lee Fourier unit root test, which requires a small number of smooth breaks in the deterministic components of a time series, as a new unit root test.

METHODOLOGY

In order to measure the convergence of CO_2 emissions between each G7 country and its biggest developing trade partner country according to trade volume, the augmented Dickey-Fuller (Dickey & Fuller, 1981), Phillips-Perron (1988), and Enders-Lee Fourier (2012) unit root tests were employed under the stationarity approach. As such, this methodology creates an opportunity to measure the convergence of CO_2 emissions based on different unit root tests and to compare the obtained results. According to Perron (1989), if a structural break occurs in the series, the power to reject the unit root test decreases as long as the stationary alternative test holds true and the structural break is ruled out. Meanwhile, ignoring the presence of structural changes in the data makes the null hypothesis acceptable (Sun et al., 2016). Therefore, the Enders-Lee Fourier unit root test has been employed alongside the ADF and PP unit root tests in the current study. Enders and Lee developed their unit root test based on Gallant's Fourier flexible form (Enders & Lee, 2012; Gallant, 1981), which requires a small number of smooth breaks in the deterministic components of a time series. The function that provides the time-dependent deterministic term in Dickey and Fuller (1979) unit root test is as follows:

$$y_t = d(t) + \rho y_{t-1} + \gamma t + \varepsilon_t \tag{1}$$

In this equation, ε_t represents the stationary error term with σ_t^2 variance. If the deterministic component d(t) is known, the hypothesis of $p = 1$, which tests the presence of any unit root, can easily be tested. However, the testing process for this hypothesis has problems if d(t) is unspecified (Enders & Lee, 2012). Therefore, Enders and Lee developed the following unit root test so that the Fourier expansion of deterministic components occurs within the equation:

$$d(t) = \alpha_0 + \sum_{k=1}^{n} \alpha_k \sin(2\pi kt / T) + \sum_{k=1}^{n} \beta_k \cos(2\pi kt / T); \qquad n \leq T / 2 \tag{2}$$

In this equation, n represents the number of cumulative frequencies, k represents the particular frequency, and T stands for the number of observations. This equation transforms to the *DF* unit root test statistic when $\alpha k_= \beta k =_0$. In order to apply the test, the data generation process (DGP) starts with the following equation:

$$y_t = \alpha_0 + \gamma_t + \alpha_k \sin\left(2\pi kt / T\right) + \beta_k \cos\left(2\pi kt / T\right) + e_t; \qquad k \le T/2 \tag{3}$$

$$e_t = \rho e_{t-1} + \varepsilon_t \tag{4}$$

In Equation (4), e_t represents the error term. If the cointegration of p is equal to 1, then the series y_t has a unit root; if $p < 1$, then y_t is stationary.

As based on the methodologies from Schmidt and Philips (1992) and Amsler and Lee (1995), Enders and Lee developed their test procedure according to the Lagrange Multiplier (LM). The first variation of Equation (3) is based on the LM as follows:

$$\Delta y_t = \delta_0 + \delta_1 \Delta \sin\left(2\pi kt / T\right) + \delta_2 \cos\left(2\pi kt / T\right) + u_t \tag{5}$$

The detrend series using the coefficient estimates obtained by estimating Equation (5) is as follows:

$$\widetilde{S}_t = y_t - \widetilde{\psi}_0 - \widetilde{S}_0 t + \widetilde{\delta}_1 \sin\left(2\pi kt / T\right) - \widetilde{\delta}_2 \cos\left(2\pi kt / T\right), \qquad t = 2,\ldots,T \tag{6}$$

In the equation above, $\tilde{\psi} = y_1 - \tilde{\delta}_0 - \widetilde{\delta}_1 \sin\left(2\pi kt / T\right) - \widetilde{\delta}_2 \cos 2\pi kt / T$ and y_1 is the first observation of y_t. Equation (7) becomes the new created test equation after this step:

$$\Delta y_t = \phi \tilde{S}_{t-1} + d_0 + d_1 \sin\left(2\pi kt / T\right) + d_2 \cos\left(2\pi kt / T\right) + \varepsilon_t \tag{7}$$

This new equation is the final equation and is used to test whether the series has a unit root or not. The critical cointegration in this equation referencing whether it is a unit root or not is ϕ. If ϕ=0, then the series has a unit root; if ϕ<0, then this means the series is stationary. Assumptions in the application of this test are (1) E(ε0)=0 (2) $\sup_t E\left|\varepsilon_t\right|^{\delta+\omega} < \infty$ where (δ > 2; ω > 0), (3) $\delta^2 = \lim_{T\to\infty} T^{-1} E\left(S_T^2\right)\left(\delta^2 > 0; S_T = \sum_{t=1}^{T} \varepsilon_t\right)$, and (4) $\sum_{\infty}^{\infty} \alpha_m^{1-2/\delta} < \infty$. If εt $_i$n Equation (7) has an autocorrelation, then ΔS_{t-j} values must be added to the test equation for j = 1,…, p. The test statistics that must be examined in order to decide whether the series yt is stationary or not is $\tau_{LM} = \frac{\hat{\phi}}{s.d\left(\hat{\phi}\right)}$. If the τL$_M$ test statistic is more negative than the critical values Enders and Lee (2012) attained, then this result implies the series has no unit root and thus the null hypothesis is rejected.

DATA AND EMPIRICAL RESULTS

The Enders-Lee Fourier unit root test is performed using the per-capita CO_2 emissions for each G7 country and its respective developing trade-partner country with the largest trade volume. The time period of 1970-2016 has been selected due to the availability of data. All the data on per-capita CO_2 emissions have been taken from the World Bank's World Development Indicators (WDIs). The data have been transformed into logarithmic series.

Table 2. Descriptive statistics

	CAMB-CAN	CHN-GER	CUBA-JAP	MEX-USA	RUS-FRA	SKOREA-ITA	TR-UK
Mean	-0.985314	-0.666065	-0.319311	-0.285807	-0.267176	-0.255902	-0.402341
Median	-1.242964	-0.621073	-0.318814	-0.310734	-0.242716	-0.255352	-0.368454
Maximum	-0.357690	-0.301939	-0.222024	-0.122431	-0.184355	-0.034852	-0.210433
Minimum	-1.339956	-1.125868	-0.487087	-0.409707	-0.512364	-0.635120	-0.594084
Std. Dev.	0.378665	0.290190	0.048586	0.069546	0.084004	0.167921	0.135409
Skewness	0.627201	-0.139338	-1.211353	0.483053	-1.514402	-0.445221	-0.150521
Kurtosis	1.644981	1.463994	6.126625	2.607919	4.495714	2.397322	1.439249
T	47	47	47	47	27	47	47

The descriptive statistics of series are shown in Table 2. As understood from Table 2, the maximum and minimum values of the observations are -0.034852 and -1.339956, respectively. The mean values for the difference in CO_2 emissions between each G7 country and its developing trade-partner country vary between -0.985314 and -0.255902. The largest gap in CO_2 emissions is between Canada and Cambodia, while the smallest gap in CO_2 emissions is between Italy and South Korea.

LINEAR UNIT ROOT TEST RESULTS

Along with the Enders-Lee Fourier unit root test, the ADF and PP unit root tests have been applied to investigate and compare whether the difference in CO_2 emissions, if any, converges or diverges between the country pairs. Table 3 demonstrates the results from the ADF and PP unit root tests. Mixed results have been obtained when comparing the unit root test results for the constant with those for the constant and trend. According to the results, a specific divergence in CO_2 emissions has been found between Japan and Cuba and between Italy and South Korea for all cases. Along with these results, the per-capita CO_2 emissions in Cambodia, China, and Turkey have converged with those in Canada, Germany, and the United Kingdom, respectively, at varying degrees of significance when constant and trend are selected together. When the unit root tests are calculated with just the constant, results differing. The right side of Table 3 demonstrates the results with just the constant. China's CO_2 emissions still converge toward Germany's in respect to both the ADF and PP unit root tests at varying degrees of significance. A convergence in CO_2 emissions also occurs between Mexico and United States. Meanwhile, the convergence

Table 3. Linear unit root tests results

Country Groups	Constant & Trend		Constant	
	ADF	PP	ADF	PP
CAMB-CAN	-4.683*	-4.917*	-0.216	-0.295
CHN-GER	-3.357***	-3.210***	-2.943**	-2.941**
CUBA-JAP	-0.741	-0.684	-1.303	-1.414
MEX-USA	-1.840	-1.804	-2.776***	-3.181**
RUS-FRA	-2.588	-1.501	-0.607	-0.665**
KOREA-ITA	-2596	-1.911	-0.821	-1.079
TR-UK	-3520**	-3.320***	-2.112	-2.010

Note: *, **, and **** denote significances at the level of 1%, 5%, and 10%, respectively.

process between Cambodia and Canada and between Turkey and the United Kingdom transform into a divergence with just the constant.

ENDERS-LEE FOURIER UNIT ROOT TEST RESULTS

The results from the Enders-Lee Fourier unit root test are shown in Table 4. The calculated test statistics for the τL_M of each country pair is given in the second column. The third column represents the particular frequency (k), and the fourth column represents the number of cumulative frequencies (n). Finally the fifth column shows the critical values that were attained from the authors (Enders & Lee, 2012). The calculated test statistics are less negative than the critical values for Cambodia/Canada, South Korea/Italy, Russia/France, and Turkey/United Kingdom with the null hypothesis accepted at a critical value of 5%. This result implies the per-capita CO2 emissions to not converge across the country pairs. Meanwhile, when comparing the critical values from the Enders-Lee unit root test with the calculated test statistics for the 5% critical values, the per-capita CO2 emissions between China and Germany, between Cuba and Japan and between Mexico and United States converge over time.

Table 4. Enders-Lee Fourier nonlinear unit root test results

Country Groups	τ_{LM}	k	n	p	%5 C.V.	convergence
CAMB-CAN	-1.944	1	1	0	-4.10	-
CHN-GER	-4.647	1	1	0	-4.10	+
CUBA-JAP	-5.117	1	1	1	-4.10	+
MEX-USA	-4.273	1	1	0	-4.10	+
KOREA-ITA	-2.346	1	1	1	-4.10	-
RUS-FRA	-3.388	1	1	1	-4.10	-
TR-UK	-2.009	1	1	0	-4.10	-

CONCLUSION

The topic of this chapter has been the effects of international trade on the convergence of per-capita CO_2 emission levels between G7 countries and their respective developing trade-partner country with the largest trade volume. In order to investigate convergence process, stochastic convergence methodology was chosen, and the ADF, PP, and Enders-Lee Fourier unit root tests have been employed. The purpose of employing the nonlinear unit root test (i.e., Enders-Lee Fourier unit root test) is to test for a unit root without having to precisely model the breaks (Enders & Lee, 2012).

Mixed results have been derived from both the linear and nonlinear unit root tests. According to the linear unit root test results, a specific divergence of CO_2 emissions has occurred between Cuba and Japan and between South Korea and Italy in all circumstances. Meanwhile, a specific convergence occurred between China and Germany. However, the results for the other country pairs varied with respect to the type of unit root test.

The nonlinear unit root test results also demonstrate mixed results. While the per capita CO_2 emissions show converge between China and Germany, between Cuba and Japan, and between Mexico and the United States, diverging has been shown between Cambodia and Canada, between South Korea and Italy, between Russia and France, and between Turkey and the United Kingdom.

These mixed results imply a dissimilar effect of international trade on per capita convergence. These results may have been different as they tested the relationship between countries with different development levels. If convergence between countries at the same development level is tested, perhaps similar results can be obtained. Consequently, claiming a common argument as to whether or not international trade ensures the convergence or divergence of per-capita CO2 emissions between each G7 country and their biggest developing trade-partner country is difficult. This result does not allow a common policy to be recommended to countries in order to eliminate greenhouse gases originating from international trade. If this study is conducted by researchers for countries at the same level of development in the future, meaningful results may arise and the relevant literature can be enriched.

REFERENCES

Acar, S., Söderholm, P., & Brännlund, R. (2018). Convergence of per capita carbon dioxide emissions: Implications and meta-analysis. *Climate Policy*, *18*(4), 512–525. doi:10.1080/14693062.2017.1314244

Ahmed, M., Khan, A. M., Bibi, S., & Zakaria, M. (2017). Convergence of per capita CO_2 emissions across the globe: Insights via wavelet analysis. *Renewable & Sustainable Energy Reviews*, *75*, 86–97. doi:10.1016/j.rser.2016.10.053

Aldy, J. E. (2006). Per capita carbon dioxide emissions: Convergence or divergence? *Environmental and Resource Economics*, *4*(33), 533–555. doi:10.100710640-005-6160-x

Amsler, C., & Lee, J. (1995). An LM test for a unit root in the presence of a structural change. *Econometric Theory*, *11*(2), 359–368. doi:10.1017/S026646660000921X

Antweiler, W., Copeland, B. R., & Taylor, M. S. (2001). Is free trade good for the environment? *The American Economic Review*, *91*(4), 877–908. doi:10.1257/aer.91.4.877

Apergis, N., & Payne, J. E. (2020). NAFTA and the convergence of CO_2 emissions intensity and its determinants. *Inter Economics*, *161*, 1–9. doi:10.1016/j.inteco.2019.10.002

Aslan, A. (2009). Kişi başına karbon dioksit emisyon yakınsama analizi: 1950-2004. *Ege Akademik Bakış*, *9*(4), 1427–1427. doi:10.21121/eab.2009419683

Barassi, M. R., Cole, M. A., & Elliott, R. J. (2008). Stochastic divergence or convergence of per capita carbon dioxide emissions: Re-examining the evidence. *Environmental and Resource Economics*, *40*(1), 121–137. doi:10.100710640-007-9144-1

Bilgili, F., & Ulucak, R. (2018). Is there deterministic, stochastic, and/or club convergence in ecological footprint indicator among G20 countries? *Environmental Science and Pollution Research International*, *25*(35), 35404–35419. doi:10.100711356-018-3457-1 PMID:30350136

Boussemart, J. P., Leleu, H., & Shen, Z. (2015). Environmental growth convergence among Chinese regions. *China Economic Review*, *34*, 1–18. doi:10.1016/j.chieco.2015.03.003

Brock, W. A., & Taylor, M. S. (2010). The Green Solow model. *Journal of Economic Growth*, *15*(2), 127–153. doi:10.100710887-010-9051-0

Carlino, G. A., & Mills, L. O. (1993). Are U.S. regional incomes converging?: A time series analysis. *Journal of Monetary Economics*, *32*(2), 335–346. doi:10.1016/0304-3932(93)90009-5

Chakraborty, D., & Mukherjee, S. (2013). How do trade and investment flows affect environmental sustainability? Evidence from panel data. *Environmental Development*, *6*, 34–47. doi:10.1016/j.envdev.2013.02.005

Churchill, S. A., Inekwe, J., & Ivanovski, K. (2020). Stochastic convergence in per capita CO_2 emissions: Evidence from emerging economies, 1921-2014. *Energy Economics*, *86*, 104659. doi:10.1016/j.eneco.2019.104659

Cole, M. A., & Elliott, R. J. R. (2003). Determining the trade–environment composition effect: The role of capital, labor and environmental regulations. *Journal of Environmental Economics and Management*, *46*(3), 363–383. doi:10.1016/S0095-0696(03)00021-4

Dickey, D. A., & Fuller, W. A. (1979). Distribution of the estimators for autoregressive time series with a unit root. *Journal of the American Statistical Association*, *74*(366a), 427–431. doi:10.1080/01621459.1979.10482531

Dickey, D. A., & Fuller, W. A. (1981). Likelihood ratio statistics for autoregressive time series with a unit root. *Econometrica*, *49*(4), 1057–1072. doi:10.2307/1912517

Enders, W., & Lee, J. (2012). A unit root test using a fourier series to approximate smooth breaks. *Oxford Bulletin of Economics and Statistics*, *74*(4), 574–599. doi:10.1111/j.1468-0084.2011.00662.x

Ezcurra, R. (2007). Is there cross-country convergence in carbon dioxide emissions? *Energy Policy*, *35*(2), 1363–1372. doi:10.1016/j.enpol.2006.04.006

Friedman, M. (1992). Do old fallacies ever die? *Journal of Economic Literature*, *30*(4), 2129–2132.

Gallant, A. R. (1981). On the bias in flexible functional forms and an essentially unbiased form: The fourier flexible form. *Journal of Econometrics, 15*(2), 211–245. doi:10.1016/0304-4076(81)90115-9

Herrerias, M. J. (2013). The environmental convergence hypothesis: Carbon dioxide emissions according to the source of energy. *Energy Policy, 61*, 1140–1150. doi:10.1016/j.enpol.2013.06.120

Jobert, T., Karanfil, F., & Tykhonenko, A. (2010). Convergence of per capita carbon dioxide emissions in the EU: Legend or reality? *Energy Economics, 32*(6), 1364–1373. doi:10.1016/j.eneco.2010.03.005

Lee, C.-C., Chang, C.-P., & Chen, P.-F. (2008). Do CO_2 emission levels converge among 21 OECD countries? New evidence from unit root structural break tests. *Applied Economics Letters, 15*(7), 551–556. doi:10.1080/13504850500426236

Nguyen Van, P. (2005). Distribution dynamics of CO_2 emissions. *Environmental and Resource Economics, 32*(4), 495–508. doi:10.100710640-005-7687-6

Nourry, M. (2009). Re-examining the empirical evidence for stochastic convergence of two air pollutants with a pair-wise approach. *Environmental and Resource Economics, 44*(4), 555–570. doi:10.100710640-009-9301-9

Panopoulou, E., & Pantelidis, T. (2009). Club convergence in carbon dioxide emissions. *Environmental and Resource Economics, 44*(1), 47–70. doi:10.100710640-008-9260-6

Payne, J. E. (2020). The convergence of carbon dioxide emissions: A survey of the empirical literature. *Journal of Economic Studies* (ahead-of-print). doi:10.1108/JES-12-2019-0548

Perkins, R., & Neumayer, E. (2008). Fostering environment efficiency through transnational linkages? trajectories of CO_2 and SO_2, 1980–2000. *Environment and Planning A. Economy and Space, 40*(12), 2970–2989. doi:10.1068/a4089

Perron, P. (1989). The great crash, the oil price shock, and the unit root hypothesis. *Econometrica, 57*(6), 1361–1401. doi:10.2307/1913712

Pettersson, F., Maddison, D., Acar, S., & Soderholm, P. (2014). Convergence of carbon dioxide emissions: A review of the literature. *International Review of Environmental and Resource Economics, 7*(2), 141–178. doi:10.1561/101.00000059

Phillips, P. C. B., & Perron, P. (1988). Testing for a unit root in time series regression. *Biometrika, 75*(2), 335–346. doi:10.2307/2336182

Presno, M. J., Landajo, M., & Fernández González, P. (2018). Stochastic convergence in per capita CO_2 emissions. An approach from nonlinear stationarity analysis. *Energy Economics, 70*, 563–581. doi:10.1016/j.eneco.2015.10.001

Quah, D. T. (1997). Empirics for growth and distribution: Stratification, polarization, and convergence clubs. *Journal of Economic Growth, 2*(1), 27–59. doi:10.1023/A:1009781613339

Robalino-López, A., García-Ramos, J. E., Golpe, A. A., & Mena-Nieto, A. (2016). CO_2 emissions convergence among 10 South American countries. A study of Kaya components (1980–2010). *Carbon Management, 7*(1–2), 1–12. doi:10.1080/17583004.2016.1151502

Romero-Ávila, D. (2008). Convergence in carbon dioxide emissions among industrialised countries revisited. *Energy Economics*, *30*(5), 2265–2282. doi:10.1016/j.eneco.2007.06.003

Runar, B., Amin, K., & Patrik, S. (2017). Convergence in carbon dioxide emissions and the role of growth and institutions: A parametric and non-parametric analysis. *Environmental Economics and Policy Studies*, *19*(2), 359–390. doi:10.100710018-016-0162-5

Schmidt, P., & Phillips, P. (1992). LM tests for a unit root in the presence of deterministic trends. *Oxford Bulletin of Economics and Statistics*, *54*(3), 257–287. doi:10.1111/j.1468-0084.1992.tb00002.x

Solow, R. M. (1956). A contribution to the theory of economic growth. *The Quarterly Journal of Economics*, *70*(1), 65–94. doi:10.2307/1884513

Strazicich, M. C., & List, J. A. (2003). Are CO_2 emission levels converging among ındustrial countries? *Environmental and Resource Economics*, *24*(3), 263–271. doi:10.1023/A:1022910701857

Sun, J., Su, C.-W., & Shao, G. (2016). Is carbon dioxide emission convergence in the ten largest economies? *International Journal of Green Energy*, *13*(5), 454–461. doi:10.1080/15435075.2014.966373

Westerlund, J., & Basher, S. A. (2008). Testing for convergence in carbon dioxide emissions using a century of panel data. *Environmental and Resource Economics*, *40*(1), 109–120. doi:10.100710640-007-9143-2

Yang, J., Zhang, T., Sheng, P., & Shackman, J. D. (2016). Carbon dioxide emissions and interregional economic convergence in China. *Economic Modelling*, *52*, 672–680. doi:10.1016/j.econmod.2015.09.038

Yavuz, N. C., & Yilanci, V. (2013). Convergence in per capita carbon dioxide emissions among G7 countries: A TAR panel unit root approach. *Environmental and Resource Economics*, *54*(2), 283–291. doi:10.100710640-012-9595-x

KEY TERMS AND DEFINITIONS

CO_2 Emissions: The amount of CO_2 emissions stemming from the burning of fossil fuels.

Convergence: Is the concept that poorer economies' per capita incomes (in this study, CO_2 emissions) will tend to grow at faster rates than the richer economies. As a result, all economies should eventually converge in terms of per capita.

Enders-Lee Fourier Unit Root Test: A unit root test with a Fourier function which complements Fourier LM and DF-GLS unit root tests.

Globalization: A term that means the speed-up of movements and exchanges of capital, labor, goods and services etc. all over the earth.

Group of Seven (G7): An international economic organization consisting of seven advanced economies: Canada, France, Germany, Italy, Japan, the United Kingdom and the United States.

International Trade: The exchange of goods and services between countries.

Stochastic Convergence: A concept that essentially aims to formalize the idea that a random or unpredictable sequence of events is sometimes expected to fit into a pattern.

Chapter 4
Exchange Rate Regime Preferences and Budget Deficits in Open Economies: Evidence From FGLS and PCSE Estimation Methods

Mustafa Kiziltan
FEAS, Department of Public Finance, Hacettepe University, Turkey

ABSTRACT

This study investigates the impacts of exchange rate regime (ERR) choice, economic, institutional, and demographic factors on the budget deficit. The recent literature states that fiscal discipline is affected by the ERR preferences in open economies. In this study, the effect of de facto ERR preferences on fiscal discipline were analyzed between 1995 and 2016 for 76 countries classified into income groups. The estimates by Feasible Generalized Least Squares and Panel Corrected Standard Errors estimators show that flexible ERRs provide much more fiscal discipline. The findings highlight the importance of institutional quality, demographic factors, and inflation to ensure fiscal discipline. A country with a high level of trade openness is more vulnerable to exchange rate shocks, which leads to uncertainty in the fiscal policy. The results confirm that ERR preferences affect countries' fiscal disciplines differently, depending on the countries' characteristics.

INTRODUCTION

Fiscal policy is an essential tool in managing the economy. The effects of taxation, government spending, and borrowing on growth patterns are often reflected in the literature on developed and developing countries (Easterly & Rebelo, 1993). To successfully manage fiscal policy, governments strive to collect taxes at a level that can cover government spending and balance the budget. However, modern fiscal theories suggest that budget deficits can be tolerated to support economic growth, while a balanced

DOI: 10.4018/978-1-7998-7568-0.ch004

budget is rarely achieved. In this regard, there is extensive literature on the results and determinants of budget deficits. Determinants of the budget deficit differ depending on economic approaches. Various studies have been conducted within the framework of these approaches. A comprehensive and recent literature discussion on budget deficits' determinants can be found in Mawejje and Odhiambo (2020).

The literature on the budget deficit has been shaped according to economic views. For example, the classical approach to fiscal deficits emphasizes the inflationary effects that fiscal deficits can create by advocating the decline in the state's role in the economy. On the other hand, Keynesian economists reject the classics' arguments and advocate for governments to play a larger role in the economy. In their opinion, governments should intervene in the economy through tax, spending, and borrowing policies. These measures will inevitably lead to an increase in the budget deficit. It is emphasized that the implementation of policies stimulating the budget deficit to combat the deficit in demand in the economy will ensure economic growth through the multiplier effect (Bernheim, 1989). From a Keynesian perspective, budget deficits increase the current account deficit by increasing national income. This interconnection leads to a situation known in the literature as the twin deficit hypothesis. In the case of a flexible exchange rate in an open economy, an increase in the demand for money, resulting from increased income levels due to expanded government spending, will lead to higher interest rates. This situation provides capital inflow to the economy, leading to the national currency's appreciation and, indirectly, to a current account deficit. In other words, a current account deficit occurs along with a budget deficit, that is, a twin deficit (Kim & Roubini, 2008; Tobin, 1984). However, there are opposite results in the literature regarding this hypothesis. For example, Kim and Roubini (2008) analysed the relationship between the flexible exchange rate regime (ERR), the budget deficit, and the USA's current account deficit under the twin deficit hypothesis. Their findings indicate that the budget deficits arising from the expansionary public expenditures positively affect the current account balance and cause a loss in the value of the US exchange rate. On the other hand, Bahmani-Oskooee (1995) found evidence to support the twin deficit hypothesis, according to which budget and trade deficits are related.

According to the Ricardian equivalence hypothesis, taxes are deferred to the next generation by borrowing due to the budget deficit arising from tax cuts. In other words, taxes that are reduced today will be increased even more in the future. Individuals increase their savings because they know that their tax burden will increase in the future. For this reason, budget deficits caused by tax cuts do not have a real effect on variables such as the current account deficit, as stated in the twin deficit hypothesis (Barro, 1974, 1989). From a monetarism point of view, it is stated that the seigniorage used to finance budget deficits will cause inflation. Although, monetarists have seen inflation as a monetary situation since Friedman (1968, 1989). According to Sargent and Wallace (1981), the relationship between fiscal and monetary policies is explained with the inter-temporal budget constraint. This approach states that the financing of long-term chronic budget deficits through domestic borrowing will have a more inflationary effect than monetary financing in the long run. Tight monetary policy will reduce inflation in the current period and cause more inflation in the future. Therefore, chronic budget deficits cannot be sustained in the long run.

The fact that budget deficits are not sustainable in the long term has revealed the importance of ensuring fiscal discipline in the literature. In open economies, exchange rates have a crucial influence on fiscal discipline. Depending on the preferred ERR, fiscal policy in an open country has different effects on real variables. In this respect, the relationship between the budget deficit and the ERR has also been examined in the literature. For instance, Kim (2003), who investigated the relationship between capital flows and fiscal discipline, showed that the budget deficit would decrease under free capital flows. This discipline is more vital for countries applying a fixed ERR. In other words, it is stated that even if countries have high budget deficits, there will be no danger in liberalizing capital flows. In an analysis conducted for transition countries, Markiewicz (2006) found that the most important variables determining the ERR are the countries' economic sizes and the country group with which their trade is concentrated. It has been observed that flexible ERRs are applied more in countries with high budget deficits.

In a recent study, Chowdhury et al. (2016) examine fiscal discipline in developed and developing countries by considering the ERR and openness to trade. Their analysis is conducted by pooled panel and instrumental variables estimators. Various de facto regime classifications are used for the ERR in their analysis. This study's distinctive contribution to the literature is that they include the ERR and openness to trade as an interaction term in the analysis. Therefore, the ERR and the effect of the ERR on fiscal variables are investigated. The instrumental variables estimation approach was used to deal with the possible endogeneity problems in the ERR. A flexible ERR has been shown to provide more fiscal discipline.

In this respect this study's notable contributions are twofold. Political and institutional factors, economic variables such as inflation, and demographic factors affect the budget deficit differently. Therefore, in our study, these factors are taken into account in addition to per capita income, openness, and ERR variables. Besides economic factors, institutional and political factors are also crucial in explaining the budget deficit. For example, Roubini and Sachs (1989) examine the influence of political factors in industrialized countries, and Roubini (1991) in developing countries. In this regard, in our study, these effects are examined based on an up-to-date data set (Teorell et al., 2020). Additionally, it analyses the relationship between fiscal deficits and inflation for countries belonging to different groups according to income level classification. Fisher (2001) argues that countries' preferences for ERRs depend on their economic characteristics and inflationary background. Effective management under the chosen exchange rate system depends on the fiscal and financial systems' sustainability and soundness. Our findings demonstrate that the size of inflation impact on fiscal deficits yields different results for countries depending on their income groups. Moreover, in countries with aging populations, budget deficits can become a severe problem due to increased government spending on the one hand and lower tax revenues on the other. For this reason, the impact of demographic variables is also investigated in our study.

Second, as far as we know, there are no studies in the literature that examine the relationship between the ERR and the budget deficit by considering cross-dependence, serial autocorrelation, and heteroscedasticity between panel units. Taking these econometric issues into account, we conduct an analysis based on Feasible Generalized Least Squares (FGLS) and Panel Corrected Standard Errors (PCSE) estimators. In this study, the analysis is also carried out separately for countries with different income levels. Our analysis examines the situation for all countries and then repeat the analysis for high-income, high-middle-income, and low-middle-income countries, grouped according to the World Bank's income classification.

The rest of the study continues as follows: The second section presents empirical and theoretical literature on ERRs' effects on fiscal variables. The third section introduces the econometric model and data. The fourth section describes the econometric method and preliminary analysis results. The fifth section contains results and discussions. The last section concludes with the conclusion and policy implications.

THEORETICAL AND EMPIRICAL LITERATURE

The preference for a particular ERR has different political and economic dimensions. The macroeconomic preferred ERR is expected to support economic growth and meet governments' targets. From a microeconomic perspective, different ERRs affect income distribution in various ways (Li, 2019, p. 419). In this regard, the relationships between ERR preferences and various economic factors are frequently explored in the literature. It is argued that the exchange rate policy is subject to renewed discussion because of its macroeconomic role. It is emphasized that with the rise of inflation targeting, such policy choice issues, together with their numerous consequences, began to appear on the agenda. Montiel and Agenor (2008) can be explored for these conceptual debates and historical background on ERR preferences.

For example, Petreski (2012) examined the relationship between the ERR preference and economic growth and conducted an empirical and theoretical literature review. It is stated that the channel for the ERR's impact on growth is through foreign trade, investment, and productivity. A flexible ERR is considered vital as it reduces uncertainties. Moreover, it has been observed that the methods used in related studies differ. According to Petreski (2012), there are empirical research problems, such as the problem of endogeneity, sample bias, and different growth frames. Theoretically and econometrically based models that overcome these problems can provide compelling evidence between ERRs and growth.

The relationship between shocks arising from trade and foreign interest rates and macroeconomic variables is also revealed. Chia et al. (2012) analysed 33 Asian economies between 1980 and 2009 with Impulse-Response functions and a Panel VAR (PVAR) model. They found that the more flexible ERR causes smaller volatility for non-tradable goods. If the influence of external shocks is considerable, then, as a result, the volatility in the exchange rate will also be high. If a country moves from a fixed ERR to a flexible one, the exchange rate volatility will increase. Besides, the impact of foreign trade and interest rate shocks is longer in the flexible ERRs than in fixed ones.

Huang and Yang (2015) analysed 11 European countries that used the Euro between 1957 and 2013, using a method based on the unit root test with the relationship between purchasing power parity and ERR. They demonstrated that real exchange rates in the post-euro period were weaker than in the previous period. The results of the common correlated mean group estimators and the vector error correction model prove that the regime with the highest convergence rates for real exchange rates is the flexible floating ERR. After the euro, this relationship is reversing.

Jordaan (2015), in a study for 19 African countries, discussed the economic fundamentals, economic stability, and currency crises as the three main factors affecting the ERR. For example, it is stated that greater trade openness will result in a more flexible ERR. However, it is emphasized that there is no suitable model for every country regarding ERR preferences. Thus, the regime's preference should be determined according to the country's economic structure, institutional capacity, and political situation. Strong institutions will ensure fewer crises; thus, it is essential to have strong fiscal and monetary institutions.

The relationship between crises and ERRs is also examined in the literature. Chang and Velasco (2000) emphasized the importance of the ERR preference, the fiscal system structure, and central bank policies in preventing economic crises. They analysed each regime's effect in preventing financial vulnerabilities separately and found that ERRs are not the only cause of crises. The policies implemented as incentives for private-sector borrowing cause more crises. In a study (Combes et al., 2016) examining 90 countries between 1980 and 2009, it was observed that ERRs at the extremes did not cause crises more than the moderate regimes. This fact has been proven separately for crises such as debt, banking, and currency attacks. With this, it was stated that countries should focus on solid macro policies rather than on the ERR. Governments should take measures to prevent macroeconomic volatility within the country. It is argued that the perception that some ERRs are more open to crises is wrong.

According to Bohl et al. (2016), all ERRs increase economic growth. In principle, the determining factor of growth is not a country's ERR but its macroeconomic conditions. For this reason, studies conducted by countries and regions yield different results. Accordingly, while fixed ERRs perform well in developing countries, crawling regimes are appropriate for developed countries. It is also stated that fixed ERRs have more negative effects in economic crises. Bohl et al. (2016) findings point to transparency and accountability in developed countries, as expressed by Kimakova (2008).

Neaime and Gaysset (2017) used unit root and cointegration analysis for selected MENA countries. Egypt, Jordan, Tunisia, and Morocco were analysed separately using time series models. These countries struggled with severe external debt crises in the 1990s. Their findings demonstrated that the sustainability of ERR preferences and macroeconomic policies differ between countries. In these countries, it is recommended to increase the private sector's share in the economy, stimulate productive areas, and provide additional liquidity opportunities to the market. The effects of ERRs on foreign trade performance and crises were analysed in a sample of 191 countries (Santana-Gallego & Pérez-Rodríguez, 2019) for the period 1970–2016 in the framework of the gravity model by the Poisson pseudo maximum likelihood (PPML) estimator. It has been determined that the intermediate ERRs have an enhancing effect on foreign trade for both trading partners. For this reason, the crisis's impact varies depending on the situation in the country involved in foreign trade and on the type of currency used in foreign trade.

In a study for Mynamar, Hori and Wong (2013) showed the costs that can be caused by the simultaneous application of different ERR in a country. Myanmar is a very different example in terms of the ERR. In addition to a fixed ERR officially announced in this country, there are also separate ERRs emerging in unofficial markets. It is stated that this situation causes significant welfare losses in the country. It has been measured that the current ERR creates a wealth loss between 14% and 17% of a country's GDP.

The effects of ERRs on fiscal discipline for European countries are also examined. Jalles et al. (2018) attempted to analyse the economic situation that arises for countries in transition from the flexible ERR to the fixed ERR in the Euro regime with the synthetic control method. It has been shown that the move to a fixed ERR harms the fiscal discipline. A strong political stance can offset the negative fiscal implications of switching to a fixed ERR.

Turkey adopted the inflation targeting policy in 2001. The analysis of different ERRs and combinations of monetary and fiscal policies applied before and after inflation targeting between 1994 and 2010 was performed using the Markov-Switching Dynamic Stochastic General Equilibrium model and impulse-response. Results show that inflation targeting policy should be accompanied by central bank independence and fiscal discipline. Monetary and fiscal policy decisions should be made, considering such significant factors as the country's ERR (Çekin, 2018).

The relationship between fiscal rules, ERRs, and institutional quality was analysed for 153 countries between 1993 and 2015 with panel data analysis. In this analysis, the two-stage Least Squares (2SLS), an instrumental variable method, was used to address the endogeneity problem. Cyclical fiscal policies have been shown to be insufficient when strong financial institutions do not support fiscal rules. Accordingly, the impact of fiscal rules on fiscal discipline depends on the type of fiscal rules applied (Keita & Turcu, 2019).

Cavoli et al. (2019), on the other hand, analysing developing countries in Asia in the period 2001-2016 examined the impact of financial globalization. They argued that many countries are intervening in the foreign exchange market to eliminate exchange rate volatility despite flexible ERRs. This situation reveals that the financial independence of the monetary authority in countries is not credible in the face of global shocks. It makes these countries risky in terms of foreign capital fluctuations. Globalization reduces the effect of using exchange rates as a tool to achieve economic balance. However, it has been shown that the impossible trinity hypothesis, expressed as simultaneous free movement of capital, a fixed exchange rate, and independent monetary policies, is still valid for these countries.

Additionally, the relationship between country risk and ERR has also been examined in the literature. The period 1984-2013 was analysed using a panel logit model on a sample of 110 countries. The whole panel results show that the flexible ERR is more appropriate in case of low financial risk. European Union member countries have adopted a fixed ERR with low country risks. In general, it can be said that the flexible ERR is preferred in order to avoid financial shocks caused by increased risks. This situation reveals the ability of the flexible ERR to absorb shocks. The results point to the influence of political economy variables on the determination of exchange rate policy (Liu et al., 2020).

Research on the prevailing 1990s notion that fixed exchange rates provide more fiscal discipline than flexible exchange rates established a relationship between the chosen ERR and fiscal discipline and made recommendations on what countries should do for more fiscal discipline. It has been pointed out that expansionary fiscal policies in conjunction with a fixed ERR will deplete reserves and increase debt, and therefore a flexible ERR has been proposed (Tornell & Velasco, 1995; 1998; 2000). Inflation and fiscal policy practices influence the choice of ERR and its consistent implementation. While a fixed ERR protects countries from financial shocks that require increased government spending, it also carries fiscal and political risks. Therefore, fixed ERRs should be implemented with a good institutional infrastructure. In this regard, flexible ERRs provide greater fiscal discipline (Tornell & Velasco, 2000).

Especially for open economies with fixed ERRs, the possibility of financial turmoil due to government spending financed by the increase in money supply is critical. In such a shock situation, the question of the stability of the fixed ERR arises. Deciding when to abandon the fixed ERR is one of the most important policy decisions for countries open to trade. Rebelo and Veg (2008) stated that economics theory provides little information on this issue. It is emphasized that postponing the decision to leave because of severe fiscal turmoil will have huge costs. On the other hand, Agenor (2004, p. 98) pointed out that developing strong and reliable institutions for implementing monetary and fiscal policies is more important than the choice of ERR, but also emphasized that there are reasons to justify the examination of this issue. He stressed that the ERR choice was an essential topic of discussion, especially during the periods of reforms and institution building. In this regard, various studies are carried out on the fiscal aspect of the ERR preferences.

For example, Kimakova (2008) conducted a theoretical modeling study based on the relationship between monetary and fiscal policies, credibility, borrowing, and the ERR with financial markets for a small open economy. This study's findings indicate that a stable political structure based on accountability provides more fiscal discipline together with the flexible ERR. It is because the flexible exchange rate does not require excessive borrowing, as with a fixed exchange rate. Caporale et al. (2011) stated that Latin American countries are exposed to speculative exchange rates due to their volatility policies and ERRs. They emphasized that with proper fiscal policy, the economy would strengthen and become competitive. They demonstrated that monetary policy on real exchange rates is relatively small for these countries, with the main effect arising from fiscal shocks.

Ilzetzki et al. (2013) analysed the impact of ERR and fiscal shocks on output. They explained the macroeconomic effects of fiscal incentives through economic development, preference for ERRs, trade openness, and public debt. According to them, government spending will have a long-term impact on economic activity in countries closed to trade and have a fixed exchange rate. In contrast, in countries open to trade and with flexible exchange rates, the fiscal expansion will not lead to significant growth performance. Failure of countries to save during economic growth will lead to financial crises during a recession. Consequently, fiscal policy must be carried out considering periods of downturn in the economic cycle. When implementing these policies, of course, the chosen ERR's impact should be taken into account.

Model and Data

In this study, 22 years of data from 76 countries between 1995 and 2016 were used to analyse the relationship between budget deficits and ERR preferences. The frequency of the data used in the study is annual. Since it is desired to work with balanced panel data models under the study model, countries with missing data were excluded from the analysis. Since 1995 is the year when the analysis data can be fully obtained, the analysis period starts from that year. The data used in the study are drawn from the International Monetary Fund (IMF), IMF Direction of Trade Statistics (DOTS) (International Monetary Fund (IMF), 2020a), World Economic Outlook Database (International Monetary Fund (IMF), 2020b), and World Development Indicators (WDI) Database (The World Bank, 2020b). Besides, the Quality of Government Institute (QoG) (Teorell et al., 2020) and the classification of the ERR of Ilzetzki et al. (2019) were used.

To see the impact of differences in countries' income levels in the analysis, the World Bank's income classification was used (The World Bank, 2020a). This data set contains 38 high-income countries, 18 upper-middle-income countries, and 20 lower-middle-income countries. According to their income level, a list of countries included in the country groupings is presented in Appendix Table 4. Descriptive statistics of the variables used in the analysis are given in Table 1. This study analysed economic, institutional, and demographic variables following with the literature.

The model's basic specification at the empirical level in the study is shown in equation number 1. In the model, t denotes time, i is the country indicator, and ε is the error term. The ratio of the general government budget deficit to those countries' national income is used as the dependent variable in the models. In obtaining the budget deficit data (BD/Y = G/Y – T/Y), the ratio of general government total expenditures to national income (G/Y) and the ratio of general government revenues to national income (T/Y) data from the IMF (2020b) data set are employed.

$$\begin{aligned}\Delta \mathrm{BD}_{it} &= \alpha_0 + \alpha_1 open_{it} + \alpha_2 lngdppcap_{it} + \alpha_3 \mathrm{ERR}_{it} \\ &+ \alpha_4 \mathrm{qog}_{it} + \alpha_5 agedepold_{it} + \alpha_6 agedepyoung_{it} + +\alpha_7 lninf_{it} + \epsilon_{it}\end{aligned} \tag{1}$$

One of the model's explanatory variables is the trade openness variable (*open*), obtained by dividing the trade volumes, which are the sum of the exports and imports, by the respective countries' gross domestic products (current prices, US dollars). This variable is included in the analysis as a ratio. A country with a high level of trade openness is more vulnerable to external shocks. This leads to instability of the country's fiscal balances. Openness and budget deficit move together. When considered in conjunction with a flexible ERR, the external shocks that would arise from a larger external deficit would be absorbed by the flexible exchange rate. In the fixed ERR, the monetary policy that central banks

Table 1. Descriptive statistics and data sources

Variables	Data Sources	Number of observations	Mean	Standard Deviation	Min.	Max.
Budget Deficit (% of GDP) (*BD*)	IMF, WEO	1,672	0.01498	0.06263	-0.43303	0.32030
Trade openness (% of GDP) (*open*)	IMF, DOTS	1,672	0.68155	0.37879	0.09203	2.57707
GDP per capita (log) (*lngdppcap*)	IMF, WEO	1,672	8.92398	1.39711	5.47858	11.53837
Exchange rate regime (*ERR*)	Ilzetzki et al. (2019)	1,672	6.38636	4.19185	1	14
Quality of government (*qog*)	Teorell et al. (2020)	1,672	0.61753	0.20718	0.19444	1
Old age dependence (*agedepold*)	WB, WDI	1,672	0.12897	0.08235	0.00796	0.43958
Young age dependence (*agedepyoung*)	WB, WDI	1,672	0.43065	0.19048	0.14916	0.92071
Inflation (log) (*inf*)	IMF, WEO	1,672	4.41215	0.59423	0.98395	8.55336
*ERR*open*	Interaction Term	1,672	4.08667	3.94618	0.26333	28.34781

pursue to maintain the exchange rate at a certain level could lead to the depletion of foreign exchange reserves in that country. For this reason, it is recommended to apply flexible ERR in countries with high openness to foreign trade (Chihi & Normandin, 2013; Chowdhury et al., 2016; Combes & Saadi-Sedik, 2006). At the same time, this variable, defined by Summers (1988) as "current account targeting", also examines the existence of the impact of the current account on the budget deficit demonstrated by Baharumshah et al. (2006) and Helmy (2018, p. 330). This approach argues that an increase in the foreign trade deficit will negatively affect economic growth, while a shrinking economy will cause a budget deficit. Therefore, financing investments, especially in small countries with open economies, mainly requires external borrowing. External borrowing will increase the budget deficit, causing a worsening of the current account deficit.

Another explanatory variable used in the model is gross domestic product per capita (current prices, US dollars), reflecting the countries' income levels. Since it was desired to see the effect of the percentage change in the analysis, this variable was used by taking its natural logarithm (*lngdppcap*). This variable is used to determine the differences in income between countries.

Alesina and Perotti (1995; 1996), De Haan and Sturm (1994, 1997) and Leachman et al. (2007) showed that budget deficits are not only related to macroeconomic factors but that political and institutional factors are also crucial in determining budget deficits. For this reason, another vital variable in our analysis is the institutional quality (*qog*) selected to demonstrate the governance characteristics of countries. In this index, prepared by Teorell et al. (2020), countries are ranked in terms of bureaucratic quality, the rule of law, corruption, and transparency. The institutional quality variable is also related to the development levels of the countries. In this index, developed countries rank higher than developing countries. Improving institutional quality will provide more efficient public expenditures and more efficient tax collection, which can reduce the budget deficit. Therefore, in our analysis, we expect that as the level of development rises, the budget deficit decreases. However, while in developed countries, high social spending can increase budget deficits, in developing countries, an increase in budget deficits may result from spending on physical infrastructure. Considering this factor, it is clear that the expected sign of this variable in the analysis results is uncertain.

We used the average consumer price index (*lninf*) from the IMF World Economic Outlook Database (IMF, 2020b) to examine inflation's effect on budget deficits. Since high-income countries have not experienced inflationary problems in the recent period, it is expected that there is no relationship between inflation and budget deficits for these countries. In the middle-income group, the problem of inflation is still on the agenda of these countries. Consequently, a positive and significant relationship is expected between budget deficits and inflation in these countries. As a preliminary assessment, no difference is expected for high and low middle-income countries. In this regard, it is essential to note that the Fiscal Theory of Price Level (FTPL) (Leeper, 1991; Sims, 1994; Woodford, 1994) explains the relationship between inflation and fiscal policy. In this study, the literature on the relationship between budget deficits and inflation will not be given in detail to save space. For this purpose, McCallum and Nelson (2005) discussing monetarist and fiscal views of the price level, and Ssebulime and Edward (2019, pp. 4–5) comparing the monetarist view, Olivera-Tanzi effect, neoclassical, and new classical approaches could be examined.

Studies examining the population aging and the age dependence ratio analyse these two factors' effects on public fiscal variables, especially on budget deficits. These studies generally show that aging has a significant impact on the budget deficits in developed countries. In developed countries with an aging population structure, this elderly population is increasingly influencing budget deficits through social security, social protection, and pensions. For example, it is stated that the aging population causes fiscal stress (Auerbach, 2014). In these respects, various studies have examined the fiscal impacts of the population's demographic structure for countries or country groups with different income levels (Anderson et al., 2014; Chen & Chen, 2016; Kluge, 2013; Yoon et al., 2014; Zokalj, 2016). The aging population reduces total tax revenues (Felix & Watkins, 2013) and increases public spending (Hondroyiannis & Papapetrou, 2000) through social security and social protection spending. Therefore, determining the future level of social spending requires monitoring the age pyramid and demographic structure.

The young population dependence ratio (*youngagedep*) and the old population dependence ratio (*oldagedep*) variables coming from World Development Indicators (WDI) Database (The World Bank, 2020b) were used to examine the effect of countries' demographic structures on the budget deficits in our study. Here, while the young population dependence ratio is the ratio of the population aged 0-14 to the total working-age population, the old dependency ratio shows the population's ratio over 65 to the total working-age population. Our sign expectation is positive in terms of the old dependence ratio. In other words, when the old dependence ratio increases, budget deficits are expected to increase due to social expenditures. However, differences in the size of countries' effects are also expected depending on their income group. The magnitude of the impact is expected to be greater in high-income countries than in middle-income countries in terms of increasing fiscal deficits. Since young people in the young dependence ratio are at the age of education, it is expected that public expenditures will be increased through education expenditures. Therefore, budget deficits are expected to grow. However, it would not be surprising that the impact direction is different in middle-income countries since that there are young workers.

The literature on ERRs is often based on the IMF's de jure classification obtained from the governments. Since 1945, the IMF has also published the ERR preferences of countries. However, in these official classifications, changes in the market cannot be accurately and timely monitored. Besides, if de facto classifications are compared with de jure classification, it is shown that de facto regimes provide a broader category. For this reason, it is believed that (Levy-Yeyati & Sturzenegger, 2005) they catch the differences better. Although some studies showed that official classifications are used to classify ERRs, this de jure classification has also been misleading. Therefore, Chiu and Willett (2009, p. 1007) recommended using de facto classifications. This approach was found appropriate in this study. Ilzetzki et al. (2019, p. 631) have already stated that this classification is more suitable for studying fiscal issues. In this study, we used the ERR classification created by Reinhart and Rogoff (2004) and updated by Ilzetzki et al. (2019) and often preferred in the literature (Chowdhury et al., 2015; 2016), based on current data. This variable of preference for the ERR takes categorical values and consists of 14 separate classes. This variable ranges from 1 to 14, where 1 represents a fixed ERR preference, and 14 represents the flexible ERR preferences. Detailed information on this de facto ERR classification is described in Ilzetzki et al. (2019).

ECONOMETRIC METHODOLOGY AND PRELIMINARY ANALYSIS

This study decided to use the panel data method as an econometric approach because the analysis includes many countries and years. Ignoring cross-sectional dependence between series in panel data analysis can lead to biased results and, therefore, incorrect interpretations (Chudik et al., 2011; Pesaran, 2020). The cross-sectional dependence of the series in the panel may arise from various reasons such as spatial spillover effects, common unobservable shocks, social interaction, or a combination of all of these factors (Breitung & Pesaran, 2008). Cross-sectional dependence is a determining factor for selecting the panel unit root tests and co-integration tests to be used in the analysis. Also, in cases where co-integration is detected between variables, selecting the appropriate estimator to be used in estimating the magnitude of the long-term effect also depends on whether there is a cross-sectional dependence in the data. Therefore, obtaining reliable results requires starting the analysis by investigating the cross-sectional dependence.

Cross-section dependence is generally investigated by Lagrange Multiplier (LM) (Breusch & Pagan, 1980) and Cross-Section Dependence (CD) (Pesaran, 2020) tests. In the panel data analysis, cross-section dependence is evaluated depending on the model's structure within the framework of alternative approaches such as spatial dependence and factor structure (Moscone & Tosetti, 2009; Pesaran, 2020). Sarafidis and Wansbeek (2012) can be examined for detailed information about the tests applied in the investigation of cross-sectional dependency, and Hsiao et al. (2007) can be reviewed for the issue of testing cross-sectional dependence in nonlinear models.

LM test is used when the time dimension (T) of the panel is greater than the cross-section dimension (N), and the CD test is used when the time (T) and cross-section (N) dimensions are large. Since both time and cross-section dimensions are large in the models examined in our study, the cross-section dependence was tested by the CD test. The CD test statistic, which asymptotically normal distributed as N and T tending to infinity, is expressed as follows (Pesaran, 2020):

$$CD = \sqrt{\frac{2T}{N\left(N-1\right)}}\left(\sum_{i=1}^{N-1}\sum_{j=i+1}^{N}\hat{\rho}_{ij}\right) \sim N\left(0,1\right)$$

where T - time, N - unit, and $\hat{\rho}_{ij}$ – the estimated correlation coefficient. The CD test is based on the mean of pair-wise correlation coefficients of the residuals found from the regressions estimated by the Ordinary Least Squares (OLS) for each cross section unit in the panel.

Table 2. Preliminary tests: cross sectional dependence, heteroscedasticity and autocorrelation tests

Country Groups	Tests	Cross Sectional Dependence			Heteroscedasticity	Autocorrelation
		Pesaran's test	Frees' test	Friedman's test	Modified Wald test	Wooldridge test
Whole Panel	Fixed effect	32.208 0.0000	6.459 0.0000	231.035 0.0000	54439.49 0.0000	70.502 0.0000
	Random effect	34.558 0.0000	6.403 0.0000	249.050 0.0000		
High Income Countries	Fixed effect	28.360 0.0000	5.283 0.0000	193.040 0.0000	9321.42 0.0000	28.577 0.0000
	Random effect	29.346 0.0000	5.313 0.0000	199.782 0.0000		
Upper Middle Income Countries	Fixed effect	8.814 0.0000	1.293 0.0000	69.028 0.0000	4453.80 0.0000	24.342 0.0001
	Random effect	8.540 0.0000	1.179 0.0000	68.472 0.0000		
Lower Middle Income Countries	Fixed effect	3.181 0.0015	1.341 0.0000	41.447 0.0021	15830.87 0.0000	38.884 0.0000
	Random effect	5.169 0.0000	1.481 0.0000	48.785 0.0002		

Notes: The Friedman, Pesaran and Frees Tests test the null hypothesis of cross-sectional independence. The Modified Wald Test tests the null hypothesis of homoscedasticity. The Wooldridge Test tests the null hypothesis of no serial correlation.

According to the CD test results summarized in Table 2, the null hypothesis of no cross-section dependence between cross-sectional units is strongly rejected in all models. Thus, it was determined that there is a cross-sectional dependence in terms of the budget deficit, which should be considered. The CD test results indicate that a country's budget deficit's shock affects the budget deficits in the other country (s) in the group. Therefore, these findings show that countries affect each other, not only economically but also fiscal.

The modified Wald test developed by Greene (2003) was applied to detect variance between groups in fixed-effect models. For panel data, the modified Wald test as a group-wise heteroscedasticity test (Baum, 2001) is used to estimate the process of errors within cross-section units that may be homoscedastic. The null hypothesis of the modified Wald test for group-wise heteroscedasticity defined as follows:

$$H_0 : \sigma_i^2 = \sigma_i \text{ i= 1,......, Ng}$$

where Ng means the number of cross-sectional units. The Wald statistics' significance indicates that there is a heteroscedasticity problem that may affect the standard errors of the estimates. For this reason, regression estimation is not valid in the presence of heteroscedasticity. This test is called heteroskedastic according to the units since it is estimated with cross-sectional data. The heteroscedasticity problem can also occur in time series estimates.

According to the modified Wald test results in Table 2, the null hypothesis of "No problem of heteroscedasticity" was rejected. Accordingly, it has been concluded that there is a heteroscedasticity problem in our series. In other words, the heteroscedasticity test applied in our models has a statistically significant Chi-square statistic at a level of less than 1%. Hence, the null hypothesis of homoscedasticity at the panel level is rejected.

It is also assumed that the error terms in the established models are not related. If a relationship is detected between error terms, this indicates an autocorrelation problem. Autocorrelation occurs when the error terms in different observations are interrelated. Since this autocorrelation affects the standard error terms, the coefficients estimated in the autocorrelated model will not be valid. Results would also be biased. The null hypothesis of the Wooldridge (2009) autocorrelation test is no autocorrelation in the model:

H_0: $\mu t_{\mu} j$

where u*t* are residuals in a specific period t and u*j* are residues in a certain period j. The significance of the autocorrelation statistics of the Wooldridge test means autocorrelation in the model. For this reason, the estimated standard errors will not be valid when these estimation results are autocorrelated (Drukker, 2003).

The presence of autocorrelation in the panel data estimates of the fixed effects model for country groups with different income levels in our models was examined with the Wooldridge test developed for this. According to these results, the error terms in the models established for all country groups have an autocorrelation problem because the probability value is greater than the critical value. Thus, F-statistics are statistically significant at a level of less than 1% in models established for all income groups and indicating the presence of autocorrelation.

In the cross-sectional dependence between units, heteroscedasticity, and serial autocorrelation problems in analysis, the error terms' variance-covariance matrices will be in the form of a unit matrix. It causes estimates to be inefficient. For this reason, if there are one or more of these problems in the established models, then the appropriate estimation methods must be chosen for the analysis of the model. In our analysis, the models mentioned above were first estimated with panel data fixed effects and random effects estimators—these models determined through the relevant tests that there is a cross-sectional dependence problem between units.

The problem of heteroscedasticity has been identified through the Modified Wald Test. Also, the Wooldridge autocorrelation test was applied to detect the presence of correlation in the series. Therefore, cross-sectional dependence between units, heteroscedasticity, and serial autocorrelation problems was used to choose the estimation method that gives effective and consistent results. Following Reed and Ye (2011), estimates were made by using the Feasible Generalized Least Squares (FGLS) method and the Panel-Corrected Standard Errors (PCSE) methods, meeting the necessary criteria.

The feasible generalized least squares (FGLS) method is also known as Kmenta (Oberhofer & Kmenta, 1974) and Parks (Parks, 1967) method. It has been stated that FGLS can be an effective estimator when cross-sectional dependence and heteroscedasticity are strong and significant. However, these estimates' standard errors may not accurately reflect the sample variability (Beck & Katz, 1995). Therefore, the FGLS estimator tends to be extremely secure in small samples. For this reason, based on the selection criteria of Beck and Katz (1995), it was selected to use the FGLS method in the case of $T \geq N$ and the PCSE method in the case of $T < N$. It is stated that the PCSE estimator gives asymptotically better results than FGLS in the case of a finite sample. It allows the correlation of the error terms, the first-order autoregressive process over time, and heteroscedasticity (Marques and Fuinhas, 2012, p. 111). FGLS method is a suitable method if the time dimension T is greater than the cross-section dimension N. It has been shown that the FGLS method will be invalid when $N > T$ (Beck & Katz, 1995). In this case, it is impossible to obtain non-singular estimated coefficients of the cross-sectional covariance matrix. Also, acceptable standard errors cannot be produced (Kassi et al., 2019, p. 362).

RESULTS AND DISCUSSION

The estimation results are presented in Table 3. All results except for the group of high middle-income countries for ERR are statistically significant in estimates made without the interaction term. Besides, the direction of the impact was negative to all groups whose results were significant. The findings reveal that the choice of ERR has a significant (at 1% level) and adverse effect on budget deficits for relevant country groups. In other words, as the de facto ERR preference becomes flexible, the budget deficit decreases. These findings are consistent with the relevant literature stating that flexible ERRs provide fiscal discipline.

Flexible ERRs reduce uncertainties by absorbing currency shocks and provide an automatic mechanism to eliminate the vulnerabilities that result from greater openness. Thus, risks arising from external shocks do not cause significant damage to fiscal policies. Contrary, in our example, it was observed that the ERRs reduced budget deficits, albeit relatively low. In extended models, as in Chowdhury et al. (2016), the ERR preference variable and an interaction term, consisting of the ERR preference and openness variable, are used together; no significant results were found in any group, except for low-middle-income countries. For the low-middle-income countries, both the ERR preference and the interaction term are statistically significant at a 1% level. Notwithstanding, the ERR preference variable on its own has a positive effect. In other words, as the ERR has become more flexible, it is seen that budget deficits increase. On the other hand, when evaluated in terms of the interaction term, an adverse effect is observed in low-middle-income countries. That situation shows that flexible ERR preferences cannot be carried out effectively by autonomous central banks in low-middle-income countries and are supported by fiscal management increasing budget deficits. Nonetheless, in terms of the interaction term, ERR preferences lessen budget deficits through the foreign trade channel.

The ERR can absorb the impact of external deficit shocks on fiscal variables in low-middle-income countries. However, political goals such as central banks' inability to implement the ERR independently and macroeconomic problems of low middle-income countries cause increased public expenditures and budget deficits. As pointed out in Chang and Velasco (2000), this circumstance indicates that ERR is not the only problem leading to financial fragility. The vulnerability of ERR preferences in low-middle-income countries is forcing these countries to pursue fiscal policy. It increases budget deficits. Moreover, Chowdhury et al. (2016) show that long-term determination in ERRs in high-income countries and applying the same regime for many years may be the reason why the results do not fluctuate too much. In middle-income countries, the frequent changes in regime preferences due to political reasons enable these countries' estimation results to catch the changes better.

Table 3. Estimation results

	Whole Panel (T<N)		High Income Countries (T<N)		Upper Middle Income Countries (T>N)		Lower Middle Income Countries (T>N)	
	PCSE Corr (IND)		**PCSE Corr (IND)**		**FGLS (Correlated)**		**FGLS (Correlated)**	
ERR	-0.00077*** (0.00025)	-0.00043 (0.00044)	-0.00138*** (0.00033)	-0.00036 (0.00072)	0.00013 (0.00012)	0.00001 (0.00023)	-0.00028*** (0.00007)	0.00072*** (0.00019)
lngdppcap	-0.02543*** (0.00343)	-0.02561*** (0.00342)	-0.03962*** (0.00541)	-0.03956*** (0.00540)	0.00179*** (0.00057)	0.00188*** (0.00062)	-0.01371*** (0.00066)	-0.01420*** (0.00069)
open	-0.00538 (0.00389)	-0.00189 (0.00614)	0.001811 (0.00513)	0.01213 (0.01023)	-0.01517*** (0.00153)	-0.01654*** (0.00264)	-0.03511*** (0.00117)	-0.02542*** (0.00277)
qog	0.00777 (0.01207)	0.00820 (0.01199)	0.03934** (0.01999)	0.04048** (0.02017)	0.06117*** (0.00434)	0.06062*** (0.00460)	0.08880*** (0.00272)	0.09287*** (0.00289)
lninflation	0.00700** (0.00356)	0.00705** (0.00358)	0.01377 (0.00972)	0.01202 (0.01005)	0.01367*** (0.00092)	0.01355*** (0.00098)	0.00914*** (0.00066)	0.00975*** (0.00063)
agedepold	0.28478*** (0.05582)	0.28487*** (0.05596)	0.33623*** (0.05770)	0.33313*** (0.05768)	-0.01797 (0.01763)	-0.02056 (0.02001)	0.26489*** (0.02336)	0.28042*** (0.02368)
agedepyoung	-0.04769*** (0.01547)	-0.04886*** (0.01532)	-0.03814 (0.05543)	-0.04813 (0.06124)	-0.02870*** (0.00321)	-0.02904*** (0.00371)	-0.03705*** (0.00294)	-0.03808*** (0.00297)
Constant	0.19863*** (0.02294)	0.19771*** (0.02319)	0.27070*** (0.05745)	0.27299*** (0.05841)	-0.05015*** (0.00663)	-0.04872*** (0.00762)	0.07066*** (0.00541)	0.06271*** (0.00614)
ERR*open		-0.00051 (0.00059)		-0.00146 (0.00110)		0.00017 (0.00025)		-0.00161*** (0.00029)
Number of obs.	1,672	1,672	836	836	396	396	440	440
Number of groups	76	76	38	38	18	18	20	20
Time periods	22	22	22	22	22	22	22	22
Wald chi2	150.42***	151.24***	237.29***	233.10***	1954.43***	1963.04***	4619.49***	6315.47***

Note: The standard errors are in parentheses. *** significant at the 1% level, ** significant at the 5% level, * significant at the 10% level.

Although countries are categorized as high, upper-middle, and low middle-income countries according to the World Bank income classification, the per capita income variable is also used to indicate the economic development level in our models. The per capita income variable was appointed to control countries' development levels in the same group and statistically see the effects of their income levels. For the per capita income, all estimates produce statistically significant results at a 1% level. However, while the effect was negative for the whole panel, high-income countries, and low-middle-income countries groups, it was positive for high-middle-income countries. It can be said that the increase in per capita income in high-middle-income countries increases the budget deficits. In contrast, in the panel, high-income and low-middle-income countries, the increase in per capita income decreases the budget deficits.

Considering the results of the estimates related to the trade openness variable, the panel estimation covering all countries and the estimation for high-income countries group could not yield a statistically meaningful result. Nevertheless, upper and lower-middle-income countries' results reveal that the trade openness has a negative and significant (at 1% level) effect on budget deficits. It suggests that a one percent increase in trade openness will reduce budget deficits in high-middle-income countries by 0.01517 and

0.01654 percent, respectively. Concurrently, for low-middle-income countries, trade openness increases by one percent, decreasing their budget deficits by 0.03511 and 0.02542 percent, respectively. These findings indicate that trade openness in middle-income countries had a relatively low but positive effect on reducing budget deficits during the analysis period. However, Born et al. (2013, p. 452) emphasize that there is no consensus on the impact of trade deficits on fiscal shocks and the sign of this effect, and thus results differ from country to country.

In countries with a low level of trade openness, the magnitude of external shocks' impact on those countries' economies will not be very high. Though, in countries with a high level of trade openness, external shocks will significantly affect their fiscal system. Therefore, governments may allow external shocks to be automatically resolved through a flexible ERR and greater fiscal discipline. The next possible arguments explain variably related to the foreign trade yield statistically significant results in our analysis for both high-middle-income and low-middle-income countries. In countries in this income group, the choice of ERR has not been fully decided yet, and also fluctuations have occurred in their foreign trade over time. In these countries, governments continue to intervene in fiscal policy decisions to deal with external shocks (Chowdhury et al., 2016).

There are statistically significant and positive results when countries are classified according to income group. However, the institutional quality variable's estimation results do not give meaningful findings in the analysis covering all countries. This situation shows the importance of institutional factors on budget deficits, as stated by Alesina and Perotti (1995; 1996). One unit's increase in institutional quality for high-income countries leads to an increase in the budget deficit of 0.03934 and 0.04048 percent. On the other hand, this effect size is 0.06117 and 0.06062 percent in high middle-income countries and is 0.08880 and 0.09287 percent in low, middle-income countries. It is thought that different dynamics are underlying the positive relationship between institutional quality and budget deficits in all analysis results, including developed countries. While high social expenditures due to the aging population in developed countries may increase the budget deficits, it is presumed that in developing countries, the budget deficits increase due to the increase in public expenditures due to infrastructure expenditures. However, analysing this difference is, of course, the subject of other studies. In this study, the distinction, as mentioned earlier, is not discussed in detail. This research's primary purpose is to investigate the effect of ERR preferences and trade deficits on budget deficits.

The estimation results for the inflation variable support the literature findings and confirm a robust relationship between fiscal deficits and inflation in developing countries, but not in developed or high-income countries (Jalil et al., 2014, p. 121). When all countries are included in the analysis, or in other words, when there is no distinction according to income groups, a significant (at 5% level) relationship was found between inflation and budget deficit. In high-income countries, as expected, no significant relationship was found between inflation and budget deficit. On the other hand, a significant relationship was found in low and high middle-income countries in line with expectations. One possible reason for this situation in high-income countries is the independent implementation of monetary policy and high credibility. The findings obtained for developing countries can be explained by the fact that the monetary policies, applied for such reasons as the lack of wide tax bases and the inability to collect taxes effectively, create inflationary pressure. Budget deficits result in public borrowing, which leads to expansionary fiscal policies. These expansionist policies increase inflation by creating a demand-side pressure (Ghorbani Dastgerdi et al., 2018).

Estimates on the age dependence ratios also differ according to the countries' development levels. For estimation results covering all countries, the old dependence ratio increases the budget deficits, while the young dependence ratio decreases the budget deficits. On the other hand, in high-income countries, only the old dependence ratio has an increasing effect on budget deficits. However, in high-income countries, the young dependence ratio does not affect budget deficits. In upper-middle-income countries, the relationship between the old and young population dependence ratios and budget deficits is opposite to the high-income countries, as expected. In other words, while the increase of the young population decreases the budget deficits, the elderly population does not affect the budget deficits. In low-middle-income countries, while the old population dependence ratio increases the budget deficits, the young population dependence ratio decreases the budget deficits. All analysis results are highly consistent with the relevant literature.

CONCLUSION

Exchange rate shocks are significant economic risk sources that can disrupt countries' economic stability. These shocks affect different economic variables depending on the ERRs preferred by the countries. In open economies, indicators of these exchange rate shocks, which appear before the crises, differ according to ERRs. For example, pre-warning signals such as high-interest rates, increasing budget deficits, and central bank reserves' depletion should be considered in countries with a fixed ERR. On the other hand, countries with flexible ERRs experience deterioration in monetary factors such as inflation and credit growth before the exchange rate crises. These changes negatively affect the credibility of the country which highlights the importance of coordinating monetary and fiscal policies against exchange rate shocks in all countries (Zhao et al., 2014).

This study examined how the classification of countries, according to income groups, makes a difference in the effect of ERR preferences on budget deficits. It has been observed that the impact directions and sizes differ depending on the income groups of countries. The effect of flexible ERR's in reducing budget deficits and encouraging fiscal discipline has also been proven in this study. The results of the study provide important policy recommendations for different variables. With globalization, openness forces countries to apply flexible ERR and fiscal discipline policies. It is possible by increasing the institutional quality of the countries. A more transparent and accountable management style ensures countries to be prosperous in dealing with possible crises.

The study revealed that inflation is not only a monetary phenomenon but also has fiscal effects. Combating inflationary shocks and currency shocks depend on independent monetary authority, an influential fiscal authority, and treasury. Our findings demonstrate that the ERR has a significant negative impact on the budget deficit. Thus, it can be interpreted as more flexible ERRs significantly reducing the budget deficit. However, in most cases, the ERR's impact on reducing the budget deficit is found to be relatively low. This shows that the effectiveness of the budget deficit reduction policy based solely on the ERR is low. Thus, the importance of the practice of fiscal discipline in reducing the budget deficit becomes evident. On the other hand, in the long run, monitoring countries' demographic structures is also vital in determining policies for reducing budget deficits. Moreover, as Agenor (2004) stated, the effects of institutions and reforms are more important than these ERR preferences.

This study also has certain limitations. For example, in the literature, there are different *de facto* classifications in terms of ERR preferences. However, it was aimed to conduct a comprehensive analysis with the ERR preference classification covering many countries. For this purpose, the ERR classification of Ilzetzki et al. (2019) was used. Besides, this study attempted to demonstrate that there will not be a single appropriate ERR preference for all countries and that the ERR preferences change according to the country's economic, political, and demographic situation.

REFERENCES

Agenor, P. R. (2004). Orderly exits from adjustable pegs and exchange rate bands. *The Journal of Policy Reform*, *7*(2), 83–108. doi:10.1080/1384128002000242388

Alesina, A., & Perotti, R. (1995). The political economy of budget deficits. *IMF Staff Papers*, *42*(1), 1–31. doi:10.2307/3867338

Alesina, A., & Perotti, R. (1996). Income distribution, political instability, and investment. *European Economic Review*, *40*(6), 1203–1228. doi:10.1016/0014-2921(95)00030-5

Anderson, D., Dennis, B., & Hunt, B. (2014). *Is Japan's population aging deflationary?* IMF Working Paper Series No. WP/14/139. Retrieved from https://www.imf.org/en/Publications/WP/Issues/2016/12/31/Is-Japans-Population-Aging-Deflationary-41812

Auerbach, A. J. (2014). Budget rules and fiscal policy: Ten lessons from theory and evidence. *German Economic Review*, *15*(1), 84–99. doi:10.1111/geer.12023

Baharumshah, A. Z., Lau, E., & Khalid, A. M. (2006). Testing twin deficits hypothesis using VARs and variance decomposition. *Journal of the Asia Pacific Economy*, *11*(3), 331–354. doi:10.1080/13547860600764245

Bahmani-Oskooee, M. (1995). The long-run determinants of the U.S. trade balance revisited. *Journal of Post Keynesian Economics*, *17*(3), 457–465. doi:10.1080/01603477.1995.11490040

Barro, R. J. (1974). Are government bonds net wealth? *Journal of Political Economy*, *82*(6), 1095–1117. doi:10.1086/260266

Barro, R. J. (1989). The Ricardian approach to budget deficits. *The Journal of Economic Perspectives*, *3*(2), 37–54. doi:10.1257/jep.3.2.37

Baum, C. F. (2001). Residual diagnostics for cross-section time series regression models. *The Stata Journal*, *1*(1), 101–104. doi:10.1177/1536867X0100100108

Beck, N., & Katz, J. N. (1995). What to do (and not to do) with time-series cross-section data. *The American Political Science Review*, *89*(3), 634–647. doi:10.2307/2082979

Bernheim, B. D. (1989). A neoclassical perspective on budget deficits. *The Journal of Economic Perspectives*, *3*(2), 55–72. doi:10.1257/jep.3.2.55

Bohl, M. T., Michaelis, P., & Siklos, P. L. (2016). Austerity and recovery: Exchange rate regime choice, economic growth, and financial crises. *Economic Modelling*, *53*, 195–207. doi:10.1016/j.econmod.2015.11.017

Born, B., Juessen, F., & Müller, G. J. (2013). Exchange rate regimes and fiscal multipliers. *Journal of Economic Dynamics & Control*, *37*(2), 446–465. doi:10.1016/j.jedc.2012.09.014

Breitung, J., & Pesaran, M. H. (2008). Unit roots and cointegration in panels. In L. Matyas & P. Sevestre (Eds.), *The Econometrics of Panel Data Advanced Studies in Theoretical and Applied Econometrics* (pp. 279–322). Springer.

Breusch, T. S., & Pagan, A. R. (1980). The Lagrange Multiplier test and its applications to model specification in econometrics. *The Review of Economic Studies*, *47*(1), 239–253. doi:10.2307/2297111

Caporale, G. M., Ciferri, D., & Girardi, A. (2011). Fiscal shocks and real exchange rate dynamics: Some evidence for Latin America. *Journal of International Money and Finance*, *30*(5), 709–723. doi:10.1016/j.jimonfin.2011.04.001

Cavoli, T., Gopalan, S., & Rajan, R. S. (2019). Exchange rate policies in Asia in an era of financial globalisation: An empirical assessment. *World Economy*, *42*(6), 1774–1795. doi:10.1111/twec.12767

Çekin, S. E. (2018). Inflation targeting, fiscal policy, and the exchange rate regime. *Emerging Markets Finance & Trade*, *54*(9), 2093–2116. doi:10.1080/1540496X.2017.1358162

Chang, R., & Velasco, A. (2000). Financial fragility and the exchange rate regime. *Journal of Economic Theory*, *92*(1), 1–34. doi:10.1006/jeth.1999.2621

Chen, D. H. C., & Chen, D. H. C. (2016). Population age structure and the budget deficit. *Journal of Insurance and Financial Management*, *1*(4), 32–67.

Chia, W.-M., Cheng, T., & Li, M. (2012). Exogenous shocks and exchange rate regimes. *World Economy*, *35*(4), 444–460. doi:10.1111/j.1467-9701.2012.01445.x

Chihi, F., & Normandin, M. (2013). External and budget deficits in some developing countries. *Journal of International Money and Finance*, *32*(1), 77–98. doi:10.1016/j.jimonfin.2012.03.002

Chiu, E. M. P., & Willett, T. D. (2009). The interactions of strength of governments and alternative exchange rate regimes in avoiding currency crises. *International Studies Quarterly*, *53*(4), 1001–1025. doi:10.1111/j.1468-2478.2009.00566.x

Chowdhury, M. T. H., Bhattacharya, P. S., Mallick, D., & Ulubaşoğlu, M. A. (2015). Persistence, capital account openness, and financial sector health in exchange rate regime choice. *The Economic Record*, *91*(294), 279–299. doi:10.1111/1475-4932.12204

Chowdhury, M. T. H., Bhattacharya, P. S., Mallick, D., & Ulubaşoğlu, M. A. (2016). Exchange rate regimes and fiscal discipline: The role of trade openness. *International Review of Economics & Finance*, *45*, 106–128. doi:10.1016/j.iref.2016.04.013

Chudik, A., Pesaran, M. H., & Tosetti, E. (2011). Weak and strong cross-section dependence and estimation of large panels. *The Econometrics Journal*, *14*(1), C45–C90. doi:10.1111/j.1368-423X.2010.00330.x

Combes, J. L., Minea, A., & Sow, M. (2016). Crises and exchange rate regimes: Time to break down the bipolar view? *Applied Economics*, *48*(46), 4393–4409. doi:10.1080/00036846.2016.1158917

Combes, J. L., & Saadi-Sedik, T. (2006). How does trade openness influence budget deficits in developing countries? *The Journal of Development Studies*, *42*(8), 1401–1416. doi:10.1080/00220380600930762

De Haan, J., & Sturm, J. E. (1994). Political and institutional determinants of fiscal policy in the European Community. *Public Choice, 80*(1–2), 157–172. doi:10.1007/BF01047953

De Haan, J., & Sturm, J. E. (1997). Political and economic determinants of OECD budget deficits and government expenditures: A reinvestigation. *European Journal of Political Economy, 13*(4), 739–750. doi:10.1016/S0176-2680(97)00033-5

Drukker, D. M. (2003). Testing for serial correlation in linear panel-data models. *The Stata Journal, 3*(2), 168–177. doi:10.1177/1536867X0300300206

Easterly, W., & Rebelo, S. (1993). Fiscal policy and economic growth. *Journal of Monetary Economics, 32*(3), 417–458. doi:10.1016/0304-3932(93)90025-B

Felix, A., & Watkins, K. (2013). *The impact of an aging U.S. population on state tax revenues.* https://www.kansascityfed.org/publicat/econrev/pdf/13q4Felix-Watkins.pdf

Fischer, S. (2001). Exchange rate regimes: Is the bipolar view correct? *The Journal of Economic Perspectives, 15*(2), 3–24. doi:10.1257/jep.15.2.3

Friedman, M. (1968). The role of monetary policy. *The American Economic Review, 58*(1), 1–17. www.jstor.org/stable/1831652

Friedman, M. (1989). Quantity theory of money. In J. Eatwell, M. Milgate, & N. Peter (Eds.), *Money* (pp. 1–40). London: Palgrave Macmillan UK.

Ghorbani Dastgerdi, H., Yusof, Z. B., & Shahbaz, M. (2018). Nexus between economic sanctions and inflation: A case study in Iran. *Applied Economics, 50*(49), 5316–5334. doi:10.1080/00036846.2018.1486988

Greene, W. (2003). *Econometric analysis* (5th ed.). Prentice Hall.

Helmy, H. E. (2018). The twin deficit hypothesis in Egypt. *Journal of Policy Modeling, 40*(2), 328–349. doi:10.1016/j.jpolmod.2018.01.009

Hondroyiannis, G., & Papapetrou, E. (2000). Do demographic changes affect fiscal developments? *Public Finance Review, 28*(5), 468–488. doi:10.1177/109114210002800505

Hori, M., & Wong, Y. C. (2013). Costs of Myanmar's multiple exchange-rate regime. *The Journal of International Trade & Economic Development, 22*(2), 209–233. doi:10.1080/09638199.2011.555561

HsiaoC.PesaranM. H.PickA. (2007). *Diagnostic tests of cross section independence for nonlinear panel data models.* IZA Discussion Paper / CESifo Working Paper Series / IEPR Working Paper No. 2756 / No. 1984 / No. 07.17.

Huang, C. H., & Yang, C. Y. (2015). European exchange rate regimes and purchasing power parity: An empirical study on eleven eurozone countries. *International Review of Economics & Finance, 35*, 100–109. doi:10.1016/j.iref.2014.09.008

Ilzetzki, E., Mendoza, E. G., & Végh, C. A. (2013). How big (small?) are fiscal multipliers? *Journal of Monetary Economics, 60*(2), 239–254. doi:10.1016/j.jmoneco.2012.10.011

Ilzetzki, E., Reinhart, C. M., & Rogoff, K. S. (2019). Exchange arrangements entering the twenty-first century: Which anchor will hold? *The Quarterly Journal of Economics*, *134*(2), 599–646. doi:10.1093/qje/qjy033

International Monetary Fund (IMF). (2020a). *Direction of Trade Statistics (DOTS)*. Retrieved from https://data.imf.org/?sk=9D6028D4-F14A-464C-A2F2-59B2CD424B85

International Monetary Fund (IMF). (2020b). *World Economic Outlook Database (October 2019)*. https://www.imf.org/external/pubs/ft/weo/2019/02/weodata/index.aspx

Jalil, A., Tariq, R., & Bibi, N. (2014). Fiscal deficit and inflation: New evidences from Pakistan using a bounds testing approach. *Economic Modelling*, *37*, 120–126. doi:10.1016/j.econmod.2013.10.029

Jalles, J. T., Mulas-Granados, C., Tavares, J., & Correa Caro, C. (2018). Single currency and fiscal performance: The early Euro Area in perspective. *Applied Economics Letters*, *25*(6), 415–419. doi:10.1080/13504851.2017.1327119

Jordaan, A. C. (2015). Choice of exchange rate regime in a selection of african countries. *Journal of African Business*, *16*(3), 215–234. doi:10.1080/15228916.2015.1075645

Kassi, D. F., Sun, G., Ding, N., Rathnayake, D. N., & Assamoi, G. R. (2019). Asymmetry in exchange rate pass-through to consumer prices: Evidence from emerging and developing Asian countries. *Economic Analysis and Policy*, *62*, 357–372. doi:10.1016/j.eap.2018.09.013

Keita, K., & Turcu, C. (2019). *On promoting fiscal discipline: The role of exchange rate regimes, fiscal rules and institutions*. Policy Research Working Papers. doi:10.1596/1813-9450-8964

Kim, S., & Roubini, N. (2008). Twin deficit or twin divergence? Fiscal policy, current account, and real exchange rate in the U.S. *Journal of International Economics*, *74*(2), 362–383. doi:10.1016/j.jinteco.2007.05.012

Kim, W. (2003). Does capital account liberalization discipline budget deficit? *Review of International Economics*, *11*(5), 830–844. doi:10.1046/j.1467-9396.2003.00420.x

Kimakova, A. (2008). The political economy of exchange rate regime determination: Theory and evidence. *Economic Systems*, *32*(4), 354–371. doi:10.1016/j.ecosys.2008.04.001

Kluge, F. A. (2013). The fiscal impact of population aging in Germany. *Public Finance Review*, *41*(1), 37–63. doi:10.1177/1091142112439225

Leachman, L. L., Rosas, G., Lange, P., & Bester, A. (2007). The political economy of budget deficits. *Economics and Politics*, *19*(3), 369–420. doi:10.1111/j.1468-0343.2007.00320.x

Leeper, E. M. (1991). Equilibria under "active" and "passive" monetary and fiscal policies. *Journal of Monetary Economics*, *27*(1), 129–147. doi:10.1016/0304-3932(91)90007-B

Levy-Yeyati, E., & Sturzenegger, F. (2005). Classifying exchange rate regimes: Deeds vs. words. *European Economic Review*, *49*(6), 1603–1635. doi:10.1016/j.euroecorev.2004.01.001

Li, Y. (2019). RMB exchange rate reforms and exchange rate preferences of domestic interest groups in China. *Economic and Political Studies*, *7*(4), 413–432. doi:10.1080/20954816.2019.1667601

Liu, J., Wei, W., Shi, Y. B., & Chang, C. P. (2020). The nexus between country risk and exchange rate regimes: A global investigation. *The North American Journal of Economics and Finance*, *51*, 100842. doi:10.1016/j.najef.2018.08.025

Markiewicz, A. (2006). Choice of exchange rate regime in transition economies: An empirical analysis. *Journal of Comparative Economics*, *34*(3), 484–498. doi:10.1016/j.jce.2006.06.004

Marques, A. C., & Fuinhas, J. A. (2012). Are public policies towards renewables successful? Evidence from European countries. *Renewable Energy*, *44*, 109–118. doi:10.1016/j.renene.2012.01.007

Mawejje, J., & Odhiambo, N. M. (2020). The determinants of fiscal deficits: A survey of literature. *International Review of Economics*, *67*(3), 403–417. doi:10.100712232-020-00348-8

McCallum, B. T., & Nelson, E. (2005). Monetary and fiscal theories of the price level: The irreconcilable differences. *Oxford Review of Economic Policy*, *21*(4), 565–583. doi:10.1093/oxrep/gri032

Montiel, P., & Agenor, P. (2008). *Development macroeconomics* (3rd ed.). Princeton University Press.

Moscone, F., & Tosetti, E. (2009). A review and comparison of tests of cross-section independence in panels. *Journal of Economic Surveys*, *23*(3), 528–561. doi:10.1111/j.1467-6419.2008.00571.x

Neaime, S., & Gaysset, I. (2017). Sustainability of macroeconomic policies in selected MENA countries: Post financial and debt crises. *Research in International Business and Finance*, *40*, 129–140. doi:10.1016/j.ribaf.2017.01.001

Oberhofer, W., & Kmenta, J. (1974). A general procedure for obtaining maximum likelihood estimates in generalized regression models. *Econometrica*, *42*(3), 579–590. doi:10.2307/1911792

Parks, R. W. (1967). Efficient estimation of a system of regression equations when disturbances are both serially and contemporaneously correlated. *Journal of the American Statistical Association*, *62*(318), 500–509. doi:10.1080/01621459.1967.10482923

Pesaran, M. H. (2020). General diagnostic tests for cross-sectional dependence in panels. *Empirical Economics*, *60*(1), 1–38. doi:10.100700181-020-01875-7

Petreski, M. (2012). Exchange-rate regime and economic growth: A review of the theoretical and empirical literature. Kiel Institute for the World Economy (IfW) Economics Discussion Papers No. 2009–31. doi:10.2139srn.1726732

Rebelo, S., & Végh, C. A. (2008). When is it optimal to abandon a fixed exchange rate? *The Review of Economic Studies*, *75*(3), 929–955. doi:10.1111/j.1467-937X.2008.00479.x

Reed, W. R., & Ye, H. (2011). Which panel data estimator should I use? *Applied Economics*, *43*(8), 985–1000. doi:10.1080/00036840802600087

Reinhart, C. M., & Rogoff, K. S. (2004). The modern history of exchange rate arrangements: A reinterpretation. *The Quarterly Journal of Economics*, *119*(1), 1–48. doi:10.1162/003355304772839515

Roubini, N. (1991). Economic and political determinants of budget deficits in developing countries. *Journal of International Money and Finance*, *10*, S49–S72. doi:10.1016/0261-5606(91)90046-M

Roubini, N., & Sachs, J. D. (1989). Political and economic determinants of budget deficits in the industrial democracies. *European Economic Review*, *33*(5), 903–933. doi:10.1016/0014-2921(89)90002-0

Santana-Gallego, M., & Pérez-Rodríguez, J. V. (2019). International trade, exchange rate regimes, and financial crises. *The North American Journal of Economics and Finance*, *47*, 85–95. doi:10.1016/j.najef.2018.11.009

Sarafidis, V., & Wansbeek, T. (2012). Cross-Sectional Dependence in Panel Data Analysis. *Econometric Reviews*, *31*(5), 483–531. doi:10.1080/07474938.2011.611458

Sargent, T. J., & Wallace, N. (1981). Some unpleasant monetarist arithmetic. *Federal Reserve Bank of Minneapolis Quarterly Review*, *5*(3), 1–17. doi:10.21034/qr.531

Sims, C. A. (1994). A simple model for study of the determination of the price level and the interaction of monetary and fiscal policy. *Economic Theory*, *4*(3), 381–399. doi:10.1007/BF01215378

Ssebulime, K., & Edward, B. (2019). Budget deficit and inflation nexus in Uganda 1980–2016: A cointegration and error correction modeling approach. *Journal of Economic Structures*, *8*(1), 1–14. doi:10.118640008-019-0136-4

Summers, L. H. (1988). Tax policy and international competitiveness. In J. Frenkel (Ed.), *International Aspects of Fiscal Policies* (pp. 349–375). Chicago University Press.

Teorell, J., Dahlberg, S., Holmberg, S., Rothstein, B., Pachon, N. A., & Axelsson, S. (2020). *The Quality of Government Standard Dataset, version Jan20*. Retrieved from https://www.gu.se/en/quality-government/qog-data/data-downloads/standard-dataset

The World Bank. (2020a). *World Bank country and lending groups*. Retrieved from https://datahelpdesk.worldbank.org/knowledgebase/articles/906519-world-bank-country-and-lending-groups

The World Bank. (2020b). *World Development Indicators (WDI) Database*. The World Bank. Retrieved from https://data.worldbank.org/indicator

Tobin, J. (1984). A Keynesian view of the budget deficit. *California Management Review*, *26*(2), 7–14. doi:10.2307/41165063

Tornell, A., & Velasco, A. (1995). Fiscal discipline and the choice of exchange rate regime. *European Economic Review*, *39*(3–4), 759–770. doi:10.1016/0014-2921(94)00083-C

Tornell, A., & Velasco, A. (1998). Fiscal discipline and the choice of a nominal anchor in stabilization. *Journal of International Economics*, *46*(1), 1–30. doi:10.1016/S0022-1996(97)00039-1

Tornell, A., & Velasco, A. (2000). Fixed versus flexible exchange rates: Which provides more fiscal discipline. *Journal of Monetary Economics*, *45*(2), 399–436. doi:10.1016/S0304-3932(99)00057-4

Woodford, M. (1994). Monetary policy and price level determinacy in a cash-in-advance economy. *Economic Theory*, *4*(3), 345–380. doi:10.1007/BF01215377

Wooldridge, J. M. (2009). Introductory econometrics: A modern approach (4th ed.). Cengage Learning, George Mason University.

Yoon, J.-W., Kim, J., & Lee, J. (2014). *Impact of demographic changes on inflation and the macroeconomy.* Working Paper Series No. WP/14/210. Retrieved from https://www.imf.org/en/Publications/WP/Issues/2016/12/31/Impact-of-Demographic-Changes-on-Inflation-and-the-Macroeconomy-42463

Zhao, Y., de Haan, J., Scholtens, B., & Yang, H. (2014). Leading indicators of currency crises: Are they the same in different exchange rate regimes? *Open Economies Review*, *25*(5), 937–957. doi:10.100711079-014-9315-y

Zokalj, M. (2016). The impact of population aging on public finance in the European Union. *Financial Theory and Practice*, *40*(4), 383–412. doi:10.3326/fintp.40.4.2

ADDITIONAL READING

Alesina, A., & Tabellini, G. (1988). Voting on the budget deficit. *NBER Working Paper No. w2759.*

Ghosh, A. R., Gulde-Wolf, A. M., Wolf, H. C., & Wolf, H. C. (2002). *Exchange rate regimes: Choices and consequences* (Vol. 1). MIT press.

International Monetary Fund (IMF). (2018). Annual report on exchange arrangements and exchange restrictions. Washington (DC): International Monetary Fund (IMF).

James, J., Marsh, I., & Sarno, L. (Eds.). (2012). *Handbook of exchange rates* (Vol. 2). John Wiley & Sons. doi:10.1002/9781118445785

Klein, M. W., & Shambaugh, J. C. (2012). *Exchange rate regimes in the modern era*. MIT press.

Langdana, F. (1989). *Sustaining domestic budget deficits in open economies*. Routledge. doi:10.4324/9780203405864

Levy-Yeyati, E., & Sturzenegger, F. (2003). To float or to fix: Evidence on the impact of exchange rate regimes on growth. *The American Economic Review*, *93*(4), 1173–1193. doi:10.1257/000282803769206250

Masson, P. R. (2019). *Macroeconomic modelling and monetary and exchange rate regimes.* World Scientific Publishing Company Pte. Limited. doi:10.1142/11297

Rose, A. K. (2011). Exchange rate regimes in the modern era: Fixed, floating, and flaky. *Journal of Economic Literature*, *49*(3), 652–672. doi:10.1257/jel.49.3.652

KEY TERMS AND DEFINITIONS

Age Dependence: It shows the relationship between active population and passive population within the country.

Budget Deficit: It is the difference between government spending and tax revenues. There are various measurement methods.

Cross Section Dependence: It refers to the dependence between units, provinces, regions and countries subject to analysis.

De Facto: In practice, actual.

De Jure: Announced by official channels.

Exchange Rate Regime: An exchange rate system preferred by a country.

Trade Openness: It is calculated as the ratio of the sum of the exports and imports of the countries to the national income.

APPENDIX

Table 4. Country Groups by Income Levels

Income Groups	Countries
High Income Countries (38)	Australia, Austria, Bahrain, Brunei Darussalam, Canada, Chile, Cyprus, Czech Republic, Denmark, Finland, France, Germany, Greece, Hungary, Iceland, Ireland, Italy, Japan, Korea, Kuwait, Netherlands, New Zealand, Norway, Oman, Panama, Poland, Portugal, Qatar, Saudi Arabia, Singapore, Slovak Republic, Spain, Sweden, Switzerland, The Bahamas, Trinidad and Tobago, United Arab Emirates, United Kingdom
Upper-middle Income Countries (18)	China, Colombia, Costa Rica, Ecuador, Gabon, Guatemala, Iran, Jamaica, Jordan, Lebanon, Malaysia, Mexico, Namibia, Paraguay, Romania, Suriname, Thailand, Venezuela
Lower-middle Income Countries (20)	Algeria, Bangladesh, Bolivia, El Salvador, Ghana, Honduras, India, Indonesia, Kenya, Mongolia, Morocco, Nigeria, Pakistan, Papua New Guinea, Philippines, Republic of Congo, Senegal, Sri Lanka, Sudan, Tunisia

Source: (The World Bank, 2020a)

Chapter 5
Regional Centrality:
How Much Is Economics and How Much Is Geography?

M. Paula Fontoura
ISEG, University of Lisbon, Portugal

Nuno Crespo
https://orcid.org/0000-0002-6546-6325
ISCTE – Instituto Universitário de Lisboa, Portugal

Nadia Simoes
https://orcid.org/0000-0002-4334-4482
ISCTE – Instituto Universitário de Lisboa, Portugal

ABSTRACT

The theme of regional centrality, more commonly known as accessibility, has been increasingly invoked in recent years, mainly due to a clearer understanding that proximity to the markets is a key determinant of the location of firms. This chapter improves the most standard accessibility index using a decomposition method that allows considering the influence of (1) internal and external factors and (2) economic and geographical aspects. Each component identified has a specific interpretation and allows the identification of policy recommendations, such as the development of the transport and communication networks and active interventions to attract investment. The baseline decomposition method is adjusted in order to incorporate differences in spatial terms among the regional units considered. In order to illustrate the proposed methodology, the authors consider 171 countries. Results lead to the conclusion that the centrality level of the countries analyzed derives from different sources. Therefore, different countries may require different policy interventions to improve their centrality.

DOI: 10.4018/978-1-7998-7568-0.ch005

INTRODUCTION

Measures of regional centrality (commonly designated by accessibility) which aim to describe the centrality of the spaces assuming that the potential for economic activity of a location is a function of proximity to other economic centers and economic size or "mass" seems to have been rediscovered recently. Several reasons can be invoked to explain this renewed interest on accessibility and economic potential.

First, in spite of globalization being one of the most remarkable trends of the last decades (Head & Mayer, 2013), with trade growing faster than GDP since the 1980, the friction of distance on trade has remained consistently high since the middle of the last century, as shown by Disdier and Head (2008). The average result emerging from their meta-analysis points to the fact that a 10% increase in distance has a negative impact of 9% on bilateral trade.

Second, while proximity to the markets is one of the location determinants traditionally included in the empirical studies, in most cases only the demand that is specific to the region/country under analysis is considered, i.e., the importance of neighboring spaces is ignored (Head & Mayer, 2004). On the contrary, the concept of regional centrality explicitly incorporates and quantifies the external influence.

Third, since the beginning of the 1990s the new economic geography approach has put the importance of proximity to the markets into mainstream economics, discussing alternative mechanisms, based on the relative strength of centrifugal and centripetal forces, through which agglomeration of production may occur. In this group of models increasing returns and decreasing trade costs are key elements that generate an uneven spatial distribution of economic activity (Fujita et al., 1999). This perspective thus highlights that behind first nature aspects, second nature dimensions also matter for final location configurations. As stated by Krugman (1993, p. 131):

"\Firms that have an incentive to concentrate production at a limited number of locations prefer, other things equal, to choose locations with good access to markets; but access to markets will be good precisely where a large number of firms choose to locate.

Fourth, the centrality theme has extremely important implications for economic policy, namely in the areas of transports and economic and social cohesion (Ottaviano, 2008). In fact, as Spiekermann and Neubauer (2002, p. 7) affirm, "accessibility is the main 'product' of a transport system. It determines the locational advantage of an area (…)".

Fifth, different interventions can be requested in order to minimize the disadvantage associated with peripherality. Therefore, a clear understanding of the factors that constitute an obstacle to an easier access to the markets is valuable knowledge for policy actors.

Sixth, economic centrality has been the subject of an intense debate due not only to the negative impact of remoteness from the markets but also to the positive relationship between centrality and per capita income (Redding & Venables, 2004).[1]

A common approach to build an indicator of the family of accessibility indices is based on a gravity model to estimate "economic" or "market" potential. In its traditional formulation, this methodology assumes that the potential for economic activity of a location is a function of its proximity to other economic centres and economic size. This group of indicators has its origin in the pioneering contributions of Keeble et al. (1982) and Keeble et al. (1988) and includes the indexes suggested by Gutiérrez and Urbano (1996), Linneker (1996), and Schürmann and Talaat (2000), among others (see [Spiekermann & Neubauer, 2002] for a discussion of some of these measures).

While these centrality measures differ in some methodological options concerning, for instance, the measurement of "distance", a common shortcoming is the fact that they do not allow for identifying the relative contribution of geographical and economic components to the overall level of centrality. The present study addresses this specific issue by proposing an adaptation of the most commonly used centrality index and, based on that, a simple decomposition method that allows identifying the contribution of economics and geography at both internal and external levels of a country. An additional interest of this decomposition is to offer guidance on policy formulation aiming to improve the degree of centrality of a country. This index can be applied to any spatial unit; nonetheless, in what follows we will consider the country level, as this is the regional level adopted in the empirical example.

BACKGROUND

As mentioned in the Introduction, from the literature on economic centrality/peripherality several measures have emerged. The most commonly used index was proposed by Keeble et al. (1982) and Keeble et al. (1988). Using *i* for the country under analysis and *h* for other countries, the index can be expressed as:

$$P_i = \sum_h \frac{M_h}{\delta_{ih}} \tag{1}$$

where M_h is a mass variable for country *h* and δt_h the distance from i to h.

Taking this index as our inspiration we propose a new centrality measure:

$$C_i = \frac{l_i}{\delta_{ii}} + \sum_h \frac{l_h}{\delta_{ih}}, i \neq h \tag{2}$$

where l_i and l_h are the shares of countries *i* and *h* in the total value of the mass variable taken as reference, and δi_t is the internal distance of country i.

Equation (2) makes it clear that the level of centrality exhibited by country *i* depends on four dimensions, covering geographical and economic aspects at both internal and external levels. However, it does not allow us to identify how much each component contributes to the overall score of the country.

The main contribution of the study is to propose a simple method to decompose the global index into four parcels with specific interpretation.[2] This is obtained as follows:

$$C_i = \underbrace{\frac{\frac{1}{N}}{\delta_{ii}}}_{(C1)_i} + \underbrace{\underbrace{\frac{\left(l_i - \frac{1}{N}\right)}{\overline{\delta_{ii}}}}_{(C2.1)_i} \underbrace{\frac{\overline{\delta_{ii}}}{\delta_{ii}}}_{(C2.2)_i}}_{(C2)_i} + \underbrace{\sum_h \frac{\frac{1}{N}}{\delta_{ih}}}_{(C3)_i} + \underbrace{\sum_h \frac{\left(l_h - \frac{1}{N}\right)}{\delta_{ih}}}_{(C4)_i} \tag{3}$$

where $\overline{\delta_{ii}}$ is the average internal distance $\left(\frac{\sum_i \delta_{ii}}{N}\right)$ and N the total number of countries.

The *internal geographical component*, (C1), assumes an equal distribution of the economic activity (i.e., each country capturing a fraction $\frac{1}{N}$ of total economic activity). Thus, the values obtained by each country depend (negatively) only on its geographical dimension, evaluated through its area, as it is common in this type of measure. If the same portion of economic activity is located in a smaller country, we will then say that this country is more central than another one with a larger dimension, where the economic activity is more dispersed in space.

In turn, the *internal economic component* is measured through (C2), in which (C2.1) is a *pure internal economic component* and (C2.2) a *geographical adjustment factor*. (C2.1) assumes a positive value when an above-average share of economic activity is located in that country, indicating that its centrality level benefits from a favorable position in economic terms. A negative value occurs when the country captures a below-average fraction of economic activity. Given that we fixed the internal distance at its average, the differences between countries are fully attributable to this economic effect. (C2.2) has a value above 1 when the country is (geographically) smaller than the average and below 1 in the opposite case. The overall effect (C2) captures the internal economic component adjusted by the dimension of the country.

The centrality level of a given country depends not only on what happens at the internal level (the aspects analyzed so far) but also on external dimensions.

The *external geographical component*, (C3), is at the heart of the centrality concept. It assumes, once again, as in (C1), the equal distribution of economic activity in space and reveals how far country i is from the remaining countries. More remote countries suffer from a "tyranny of distance" (Battersby & Ewing, 2005), an expression, inspired by the title of the book by Geoffrey Blainey (1966) that became popular to summarize the idea that a negative position in this aspect is difficult to minimize and impossible to overcome in its full extension.

Finally, we should also consider the distribution of economic activity by the other countries. In this case, however, it is important to note that, unlike the preceding components, we cannot isolate a pure external economic component. The reason for that is straightforward. Obviously the share of economic activity located outside i is $(1-l_i)$ but this does not give us any new insight. What really matters is the spatial distribution of that part of the total economic activity and, more specifically, its proximity to i. Therefore, (C4) is a *residual component* influenced by both economic and geographical aspects, assuming a positive value when economic advantages are obtained by countries closer to i. Its minimum value is reached, for i, when all the economic activity is concentrated in the farthest country.

One of the most important insights gained in this decomposition methodology is that it offers guidance for policy interventions aimed at improving the centrality level of a country. In fact, distinct policy measures can be recommended depending on the main weaknesses detected. Let us consider each specific component. Improvement in the internal geographical component, (C1), can be obtained through better infrastructures, allowing a reduction in transport costs and times. In turn, if a country shows a low score on the internal economic component, (C2), interventions should be devoted to the attraction of more economic activity to the country, for instance through favorable conditions to FDI. For its part, rapid access to external countries is vital to improve centrality through component (C3). The creation and/or improvement of infrastructures that connect the country to foreign countries are adequate interventions to improve centrality. Component (C4) is the only one that is out of control of national authorities. It depends on the distribution of economic activity across the remaining countries, a factor that national policymakers do not influence in a direct way. Nevertheless, an indirect feature may help to improve this component, namely the formation of regional integration blocs, with the elimination (or, at least, reduction) of trade barriers between the members of the bloc. This may attract more economic activity for the whole bloc, which is commonly composed of adjacent countries.

At this point we have presented a simple procedure to identify the components that contribute to the level of economic centrality of each country. An obvious shortcoming of the method presented is the fact that to consider an equal distribution of economic activity across all countries is not a realistic assumption since the countries differ considerably in spatial terms. In fact, an equal distribution presupposes that a country as small as Luxembourg should locate the same share of economic activity than a much larger country like China. This can only be accepted as a first approximation. In order to overcome this problem, we suggest an adjustment to the baseline decomposition method in which, instead of using $\frac{1}{N}$ as reference, we consider the share of each country in spatial terms. This can be seen as a topographic adaptation, somewhat in line with the approach followed by Brülhart and Traeger (2005) to measure the level of specialization. This new version can therefore be expressed as:

$$C_i = \underset{(\dot{C5})_i}{\frac{\rho_i}{\delta_{ii}}} + \underset{(\dot{C6})_i}{\underset{(\dot{C6.1})_i}{\frac{(l_i - \rho_i)}{\overline{\delta_{ii}}}} \; \underset{(\dot{C6.2})_i}{\frac{\overline{\delta_{ii}}}{\delta_{ii}}}} + \underset{(\dot{C7})_i}{\sum_h \frac{\rho_h}{\delta_{ih}}} + \underset{(\dot{C8})_i}{\sum_h \frac{(l_h - \rho_h)}{\delta_{ih}}} \tag{4}$$

in which ρi and ρh $_a$re the shares of the internal distances of i *a*nd h *i*n the sum of all the internal distances, respectively.

Component (C5) is similar to (C1) in equation (3) but instead of $\frac{1}{N}$ we assume as reference the share of *i* in terms of its internal distance (p_i), which means that we are using internal distance as a proxy for area. Considering (C6), we can verify that, in (C6.1), the countries are ranked in accordance with the excess they exhibit vis-à-vis their share in spatial terms. A positive value is thus obtained when the country captures a greater proportion of economic activity than it has in terms of area. The interpretation of (C7) is also different from (C3) in equation (3). Now, the distances to the remaining countries are not equally weighted. Instead, each destination country is weighted by ρh Finally, (C8) evaluates the *geographical adjusted external economic effect* (*residual effect)*. This component assumes a positive value if the countries closer to i have a greater share of economic activity than they have in spatial terms.

AN EMPIRICAL EXAMPLE

In order to illustrate the method discussed in the previous section, we calculate the centrality level for a group of 171 countries.

Five methodological options have to be taken to calculate C_i. The first option regards the distance function considered. Despite the existence of other formulations and considerable study on this issue, the use of a linear function is the simplest and most common choice. The second one concerns inter-country distances as several options are available such as great circle distances, distances by road, time distances, transport costs; of course, the choice is strongly influenced by the availability of the data. The third option is related to the choice of location to consider as reference to measure the distance between countries. Two options are commonly used to capture that location: a dimensional criterion (population, economic activity) or an institutional criterion. However, usually the two possibilities do not imply significantly different results. The fourth option concerns the variable used to capture the economic dimension of the countries; GDP, population and employment are among the most common choices.

The final option is related to the measurement of the internal distance. This is the question that has been subjected to a more intense debate, namely in the context of the so-called "border effect" literature (Anderson & van Wincoop, 2003). Following Head and Mayer (2002), we can consider, on this topic, three types of measures (see also [Chen, 2004]). The first group of measures was suggested by Wolf (1997, 2000) and associates δi_i to a proportion (β) of the distance to neighbor countries. Wolf (2000) considers only the distance to the closest country and assumes β=0.25. In turn, Wolf (1997) considers β=0.5 and calculates the average distance from the countries with a common frontier. The second type of measures is based on the distribution of economic activity inside the national space. In general terms, these indicators require a demanding set of information for their construction. However, Wolf (1997) considered only the distance between the two largest cities of the country. Alternatively, Wolf (2000) proposed to multiply that distance by twice the weight of the second largest city on the sum of the two cities and Chen (2004) used the weighted average of the geographical distance between the major cities considering regional GDPs as weights. The indicators suggested by Head and Mayer (2000) and Helliwell and Verdier (2001) can also be classified in this second group of measures but are more complex. For example, in the measure proposed by Helliwell and Verdier (2001), the internal distance is expressed as the "weighted average of intra-city distances, intercity distances, the average distance between cities and rural areas, and the average distance from one rural area to another" (Helliwell & Verdier, 2001, 1026). The third group of indicators associates the internal distance with the area of the country, and is therefore easy to calculate. Representing the area of country i as ψi, Ni,sch (2000) and Melitz (2007) considered the radius of a hypothetical disk, i.e. $\sqrt{\frac{\psi_i}{\pi}}$. Other studies adopted alternative ways. For example, Keeble et al. (1982), Keeble et al. (1988) and Brülhart (2001, 2006) multiply the previous expression by $\frac{1}{3}$ while Head and Mayer (2000) and Redding and Venables (2004) multiply by $\frac{2}{3}$, aiming to obtain "the average distance between two points in a circular country" (Redding & Venables, 2004, 62).

In the case of this empirical example, the following methodological options were considered: (i) geodesic distances; (ii) inter-country (external) distances between the largest cities; (iii) internal distances calculated with $\frac{2}{3}\sqrt{\frac{\psi_i}{\pi}}$, as in Mayer and Zignago (2011); (iv) GDP data. For GDP we used data from World Bank for 2011. Internal and external distances were obtained from CEPII.

Table 1 shows the aggregate centrality index (C_i) for the 50 countries presenting highest scores in terms of this index. All the remaining evidence is available upon request.

Let us retain four main results from this evidence. First, there is an accentuated difference between the centrality levels of the most central countries and the remaining ones. In fact, only the first six countries

Table 1. The centrality index and its four components for the top 50 countries – 1st method

Rank	Country	C_i^{a}	$\frac{C_i}{max(C_i)}$	$(C1)_i^{b}$	$(C2)_i^{c}$	$(C2.1)_i^{d}$	$(C2.2)_i^{e}$	$(C3)_i^{f}$	$(C4)_i^{g}$
1	Belgium	0.00091	1.000	0.000085	0.000018	0.000006	3.096168	0.000413	0.000394
2	Netherlands	0.00089	0.978	0.000076	0.000070	0.000026	2.753691	0.000392	0.000353
3	Luxembourg	0.00080	0.878	0.000306	-0.000262	-0.000024	11.079399	0.000407	0.000348
4	Germany	0.00072	0.793	0.000026	0.000195	0.000206	0.942538	0.000409	0.000093
5	UK	0.00067	0.737	0.000031	0.000160	0.000140	1.140349	0.000330	0.000150
6	France	0.00064	0.702	0.000021	0.000116	0.000152	0.761774	0.000358	0.000145
7	Switzerland	0.00062	0.681	0.000077	0.000044	0.000016	2.772799	0.000367	0.000132
8	Macau	0.00059	0.650	0.003110	-0.002772	-0.000025	112.683509	0.000245	0.000008
9	Singapore	0.00057	0.627	0.000612	-0.000193	-0.000009	22.167367	0.000159	-0.000007
10	Canada	0.00054	0.588	0.000005	0.000017	0.000098	0.178381	0.000145	0.000368
11	Japan	0.00053	0.583	0.000025	0.000351	0.000383	0.916640	0.000121	0.000034
12	Slovakia	0.00052	0.567	0.000070	-0.000054	-0.000021	2.544327	0.000527	-0.000026
13	Hong Kong	0.00051	0.560	0.000470	-0.000162	-0.000009	17.049785	0.000244	-0.000043
14	Czech Rep	0.00049	0.538	0.000055	-0.000028	-0.000014	2.006277	0.000408	0.000055
15	Austria	0.00049	0.535	0.000054	0.000000	0.000000	1.945621	0.000521	-0.000088
16	Denmark	0.00048	0.525	0.000075	-0.000016	-0.000006	2.714076	0.000336	0.000084
17	Slovenia	0.00045	0.500	0.000109	-0.000097	-0.000024	3.958709	0.000452	-0.000009
18	Italy	0.00045	0.499	0.000028	0.000114	0.000111	1.026394	0.000354	-0.000042
19	Croatia	0.00043	0.476	0.000065	-0.000056	-0.000024	2.369519	0.000467	-0.000043
20	Korea	0.00043	0.471	0.000049	0.000090	0.000050	1.786298	0.000135	0.000155
21	Ireland	0.00042	0.466	0.000059	-0.000028	-0.000013	2.125196	0.000263	0.000131
22	Hungary	0.00042	0.458	0.000051	-0.000035	-0.000019	1.847201	0.000454	-0.000053
23	Poland	0.00039	0.432	0.000028	0.000006	0.000006	1.007574	0.000373	-0.000014
24	Bosnia & Herzeg	0.00038	0.414	0.000069	-0.000066	-0.000026	2.489175	0.000437	-0.000063
25	Norway	0.00038	0.413	0.000027	0.000007	0.000007	0.990203	0.000288	0.000054
26	Estonia	0.00037	0.404	0.000073	-0.000069	-0.000026	2.649302	0.000372	-0.000008
27	Sweden	0.00037	0.401	0.000023	0.000007	0.000009	0.839927	0.000319	0.000016
28	Serbia & Monten	0.00036	0.400	0.000049	-0.000044	-0.000025	1.762634	0.000439	-0.000079
29	Spain	0.00036	0.396	0.000022	0.000052	0.000065	0.792091	0.000266	0.000021
30	Lithuania	0.00036	0.393	0.000061	-0.000054	-0.000025	2.204823	0.000373	-0.000022
31	Latvia	0.00035	0.388	0.000061	-0.000057	-0.000026	2.216926	0.000354	-0.000005
32	Belarus	0.00034	0.378	0.000034	-0.000029	-0.000023	1.236579	0.000361	-0.000022
33	USA	0.00034	0.376	0.000005	0.000192	0.001052	0.182517	0.000152	-0.000007
34	Albania	0.00034	0.371	0.000092	-0.000089	-0.000027	3.322971	0.000410	-0.000076
35	Macedonia	0.00033	0.368	0.000097	-0.000095	-0.000027	3.513613	0.000433	-0.000101
36	Bulgaria	0.00033	0.365	0.000047	-0.000041	-0.000024	1.691144	0.000416	-0.000090
37	Finland	0.00033	0.365	0.000027	-0.000010	-0.000010	0.971131	0.000358	-0.000043
38	Romania	0.00033	0.360	0.000032	-0.000018	-0.000016	1.153946	0.000380	-0.000066
39	Ukraine	0.00032	0.347	0.000020	-0.000011	-0.000015	0.725150	0.000331	-0.000024
40	Rep Moldova	0.00031	0.343	0.000085	-0.000083	-0.000027	3.069131	0.000350	-0.000039
41	Tunisia	0.00031	0.340	0.000038	-0.000034	-0.000024	1.390625	0.000303	0.000002
42	Portugal	0.00031	0.338	0.000051	-0.000024	-0.000013	1.853618	0.000243	0.000037
43	Malta	0.00030	0.334	0.000875	-0.000856	-0.000027	31.694714	0.000305	-0.000020
44	Greece	0.00030	0.330	0.000043	-0.000016	-0.000010	1.552987	0.000332	-0.000058
45	Algeria	0.00030	0.328	0.000010	-0.000005	-0.000013	0.365076	0.000275	0.000018
46	Turkey	0.00029	0.322	0.000018	0.000017	0.000027	0.637709	0.000335	-0.000076
47	China	0.00026	0.283	0.000005	0.000098	0.000539	0.182104	0.000145	0.000010
48	Russian Fed	0.00025	0.279	0.000004	0.000015	0.000111	0.136347	0.000267	-0.000032
49	Morocco	0.00025	0.277	0.000018	-0.000014	-0.000021	0.668254	0.000239	0.000008
50	Lebanon	0.00025	0.271	0.000152	-0.000136	-0.000025	5.511003	0.000372	-0.000142

[a] C_i is the aggregate centrality index for country *i*

[b] $(C1)_i$ is the *internal geographical component* for country *i*

[c] $(C2)_i$ is the *internal economic component* for country *i*

[d] $(C2.1)_i$ is the *pure internal economic component* for country *i*

[e] $(C2.2)_i$ is the *geographical adjustment factor* for country *i*

[f] $(C3)_i$ is the *external geographical component* for country *i*

[g] $(C4)_i$ is the *residual component* for country *i*

show a centrality index above 70% of the maximum value (Belgium). Second, in aggregate terms, a very central position of the countries of the northern hemisphere is evident. Third, Europe clearly shows the most favorable situation regarding proximity to the markets, with seven countries in the best 10 (and 24 in the best 30) of the C_i index. Fourth, Africa and Oceania show the worst positions in terms of centrality, being penalized in their capacity to reach the markets.

The next step of our empirical example is to decompose the aggregate index with the aim of verifying the sources of centrality/peripherality in each specific case. The evidence is also shown in Table 1. Several interesting conclusions can be highlighted. The central idea to keep in mind is the fact that a high/low centrality level can be derived from very different sources. Regarding component (C1) we find, obviously, that the smallest countries have the highest values, meaning that the same amount of economic activity located in a more confined space corresponds to better access to that economic activity and therefore a higher level of centrality. A second and very important source of centrality is the internal economic component. Considering, more specifically, the component (C2.1) we see that the countries with the highest scores are, in this order: USA, China, Japan, Germany, France, UK, and Brazil. This group contains some of the most powerful economic countries, all of them members of the G20. As we emphasized above, component (C3) is critical to understand the concept of centrality, indicating the proximity to all the other countries. This proximity has an exclusive geographic dimension. The six countries that benefit the most from their location are from Africa (Republic of Congo and Democratic Republic of Congo) and Europe (Slovakia, Austria, Croatia, and Hungary). Finally, component (C4) corresponds to the *residual effect* representing the degree to which a large amount of economic activity locates close to the country under study. In this regard, Belgium, Canada, Netherlands, Luxembourg, and Korea comprise the group at the top of the classification.

The best way to make clear the crucial idea that the sources of centrality are very different is by providing a classification of the different countries according to the specific combination they show in the main components that contribute to their centrality score. Four criteria are used, leading to a total of 16 possible combinations:

- $(C1)_i$ above or below average, which we designate as $\left(\overline{C1}\right)_i$. The case of $(C1)_i > \left(\overline{C1}\right)_i$ occurs for the smallest countries, while $(C1)_i \leq \left(\overline{C1}\right)_i$ for the largest countries.
- $(C2.1)_i$ with a positive or negative value. $(C2.1)_i>0$ occurs when the country captures a proportion of total GDP above that associated with an equal distribution across all countries. In the opposite case, $(C2.1)_i$ takes a negative value.
- $(C3)_i$ above or below average, which we designate as $\left(\overline{C3}\right)_i$. $(C3)_i > \left(\overline{C3}\right)_i$ occurs in the case of the countries that benefit the most from their geographical position, i.e. that in a purely geographical sense are closer to the markets. Countries that locate far away from the markets have $(C3)_i \leq \left(\overline{C3}\right)_i$.
- $(C4)_i$ with a positive or negative value. $(C1)_i>0$ occurs if there is a concentration of economic activity in countries close to the country under consideration. $(C1)_i \leq 0$ corresponds to the case in which the largest part of economic activity is located far from the country considered.

Additionally, in order to establish the association between C_i and the four components mentioned, the names of the countries are presented:

- In bold and with an * if $\frac{C_i}{\text{Max}\, C_i} > 0.75$;
- In bold if $0.50 < \frac{C_i}{\text{Max}C_i} \leq 0.75$;
- With an * if $0.25 < \frac{C_i}{\text{Max}\, C_i} \leq 0.50$;
- Without any specific mention in the remaining cases.

The results from this exercise are presented in Table 2.

The empirical analysis conducted so far considers only the decomposition that assumes as reference an equal distribution across all countries. However, as we discussed in section 2, it is interesting to contrast the results from this case with those emerging from an analysis in which the spatial dimension of each country is taken as reference. This analysis was also undertaken in this study, following equation (4). The full range of results cannot be presented here due to space restraints but the classification of the countries according to criteria similar to those discussed above (with the necessary adaptation in terms of interpretation) is presented in Table 3.[3]

In this case, we consider only three components, namely (C6.1), (C7) and (C8). Component (C5) is not included because, by construction, it gives a constant value for all countries. Regarding the classification according to C_i, we follow the procedure already used in Table 2. Of course, the results show considerable differences when compared with the first decomposition method above reported. This derives directly from the concept inherent to each one of the decomposition methods proposed in this study (equations (3) and (4)), reinforcing the advantage of their joint consideration.

Considering the evidence in Table 3, we verify that only 27 countries have more economic activity than expected given their area (i.e. $(C6.1)_i>0$). This group of countries can be divided into 2 subgroups. A first one only includes European countries and corresponds to the case in which $(C7)_i > \left(\overline{C7}\right)_i$ while the second case refers to more peripheral countries in geographical terms, namely from Asia and (North, Central, and South) America.

FINAL REMARKS

Based on an adapted version of a standard index of regional centrality, this paper proposes a decomposition method which enables to simultaneously measure the degree of centrality and retain the influence of (i) factors that are internal or external to the region under study and (ii) economic and geographic aspects. This is an important issue because accessibility matters for business decisions about location and also because it provides guidelines on policy interventions aiming to overcome specific weaknesses detected with the proposed methodology. The baseline decomposition method is still adjusted in order to incorporate differences in spatial terms among the regional units considered.

Table 2. Countries' typology according to the four components – 1st method

		$(C1)_i \le \left(\overline{C1}\right)_i$ [a]		$(C1)_i > \left(\overline{C1}\right)_i$	
		$(C3)_i \le \left(\overline{C3}\right)_i$ [c]	$(C3)_i > \left(\overline{C3}\right)_i$	$(C3)_i \le \left(\overline{C3}\right)_i$	$(C3)_i > \left(\overline{C3}\right)_i$
$(C2.1)_i>0$ [b]	$(C4)_i>0$ [d]	**Canada**, China*, **Japan**, Korea*, Mexico	**Belgium***, **France**, **Germany***, **Netherlands***, Norway*, Spain*, Sweden*, **Switzerland**, **UK**		
	$(C4)_i \le 0$	Argentina, Australia, Brazil, India, Indonesia, USA*	Italy*, Poland*, Russian Fed*, Turkey*		
$(C2.1)_i \le 0$	$(C4)_i>0$	East Timor, Iceland*, Lao People Dem Rep, Mongolia*, Morocco*, Nepal, Papua New Guinea, Philippines, Portugal*, The Bahamas*, Vietnam	Algeria*, **Czech Rep**, **Denmark**, Ireland*, Tunisia*	Brunei Darussalam, F.S. Micronesia, **Macau**, Marshall Islands, Palau	**Luxembourg***
	$(C4)_i$£0	Angola, Bangladesh, Bhutan, Bolivia, Botswana, Burundi, Cambodia, Central Afric Rep, Chad, Chile, Colombia, Costa Rica, Côte d'Ivoire, Dominican Rep, Ecuador, El Salvador, Eritrea, Ethiopia, Fiji, Guatemala, Guyana, Haiti, Honduras, Jamaica, Kazakhstan, Kenya, Kyrgyzstan, Lesotho, Liberia, Madagascar, Malawi, Malaysia, Mali, Mauritania, Mozambique, Namibia, Nicaragua, Pakistan, Panama, Paraguay, Peru, Solomon Islands, South Africa, Sri Lanka, Sudan, Suriname, Swaziland, Tajikistan, Tanzania, Thailand, Turkmenistan, Uganda, Uruguay, Uzbekistan, Vanuatu, Venezuela, Yemen, Zambia, Zimbabwe	Albania*, Armenia, **Austria**, Azerbaijan, Belarus*, Benin, Bosnia & Herzeg*, Bulgaria*, Burkina Faso, Cameroon, Croatia*, Dem Rep Congo, Egypt, Equat Guinea, Estonia*, Finland*, Gabon, Georgia, Ghana, Greece*, Guinea, Guinea-Bissau, Hungary*, Iraq, Jordan, Latvia*, Lebanon*, Lithuania*, Macedonia*, Niger, Nigeria, Rep Congo, Rep Moldova*, Romania*, Rwanda, Senegal, Serbia & Monten*, Sierra Leone, **Slovakia**, Slovenia*, Syrian Arab Republic*, The Gambia, Togo, Ukraine*	Cape Verde, Comoros, **Hong Kong**, Kiribati, Maldives, Mauritius, Puerto Rico*, Samoa, Seychelles, **Singapore**, Tonga, Tuvalu	Antigua & Barbuda, Cyprus*, Dominica, Grenada, St. Kitts & Nevis, St. Lucia, Malta*, S. Tomé & Príncipe, St. Vincent & Grenad, Trinidad & Tobago

The names of the countries are presented: (i) in bold and with an * if $\frac{C_i}{\text{Max}\, C_i} > 0.75$; (ii) in bold if $0.50 < \frac{C_i}{\text{Max}\, C_i} \le 0.75$; (iii) with an * if $0.25 < \frac{C_i}{\text{Max}\, C_i} \le 0.50$; and (iv) without any specific mention in the remaining cases.

[a] $(C1)_i$ is the *internal geographical component* for country *i*; $\left(\overline{C1}\right)_i$ is the average value of this component
[b] $(C2.1)_i$ is the *pure internal economic component* for country *i*
[c] $(C3)_i$ is the *external geographical component* for country *i*; $\left(\overline{C3}\right)_i$ is the average value of this component
[d] $(C4)_i$ is the *residual component* for country *i*

Beyond the methodological contribution, we provide an empirical illustration considering data for 171 countries. This empirical analysis makes clear that the roots of the centrality level of each country

Table 3. Countries' typology according to the four components – 2nd method

		$(C7)_i \leq \left(\overline{C7}\right)_i$ [b]	$(C7)_i > \left(\overline{C7}\right)_i$
$(C6.1)_i>0$ [a]	$(C8)_i>0$ [c]	China*, **Hong Kong**, **Japan**, Korea*, **Macau**, Mexico, Puerto Rico*	**Austria**, **Belgium***, **Denmark**, **France**, **Germany***, Italy*, Ireland*, **Luxembourg***, **Netherlands***, Norway*, Poland*, Spain*, Sweden*, **Switzerland**, **UK**
	$(C8)_i\leq 0$	Brazil, India, **Singapore**, USA*	Turkey*
$(C6.1)_i\leq 0$	$(C8)_i>0$	Antigua & Barbuda, Brunei Darussalam, Cambodia, **Canada**, Dominica, Dominican Rep, East Timor, F.S. Micronesia, Fiji, Guatemala, Haiti, Iceland*, Indonesia, Jamaica, Kiribati, Lao People Dem Rep, Malaysia, Marshall Islands, Mongolia*, Morocco*, Palau, Papua New Guinea, Philippines, Russian Fed*, Samoa, Solomon Islands, St. Kitts & Nevis, Tonga, Tuvalu, Vanuatu, Venezuela, Vietnam, The Bahamas*	Albania*, Algeria*, Bosnia & Herzeg*, Croatia*, **Czech Rep**, Finland*, Hungary*, Latvia*, Malta*, Portugal*, Serbia & Monten*, **Slovakia**, Slovenia*, Tunisia*
	$(C8)_i\leq 0$	Angola, Argentina, Australia, Bangladesh, Bhutan, Bolivia, Botswana, Cape Verde, Chile, Colombia, Comoros, Costa Rica, Ecuador, El Salvador, Ethiopia, Grenada, Guinea, Guyana, Honduras, Kazakhstan, Kenya, Lesotho, Liberia, Madagascar, Malawi, Maldives, Mali, Mauritania, Mauritius, Mozambique, Namibia, Nepal, Nicaragua, Pakistan, Panama, Paraguay, Peru, St. Lucia, St. Vincent & Grenad, Seychelles, South Africa, Sri Lanka, Sudan, Suriname, Tanzania, Thailand, Trinidad & Tobago, Turkmenistan, Uruguay, Yemen, Zambia, Zimbabwe	Armenia, Azerbaijan, Belarus*, Benin, Bulgaria*, Burkina Faso, Burundi, Cameroon, Central Afric Rep, Chad, Côte d'Ivoire, Cyprus*, Dem Rep Congo, Egypt, Equat Guinea, Eritrea, Estonia*, Gabon, Georgia, Ghana, Greece*, Guinea-Bissau, Iraq, Jordan, Kyrgyzstan, Lebanon*, Lithuania*, Macedonia*, Niger, Nigeria, Romania*, Rwanda, S. Tomé & Príncipe, Senegal, Sierra Leone, Swaziland, Syrian Arab Rep*, Rep Congo, Rep Moldova*, Tajikistan, The Gambia, Togo, Uganda, Ukraine*, Uzbekistan

The names of the countries are presented: (i) in bold and with an * if $\frac{C_i}{\text{Max}\, C_i} > 0.75$; (ii) in bold if $0.50 < \frac{C_i}{\text{Max}\, C_i} \leq 0.75$; (iii) with an * if $0.25 < \frac{C_i}{\text{Max}\, C_i} \leq 0.50$; and (iv) without any specific mention in the remaining cases.

[a] $(C6.1)_i$ is the *pure internal economic component* for country *i;*

[b] $(C7)_i$ is the *external geographical component*; $\left(\overline{C7}\right)_i$ is the average value of this component

[c] $(C8)_i$ is the geo*graphical adjusted external economic effect* (*residual component*) of country *i*

can be very different, with positive and negative impacts of both economic and geographical factors. The final centrality score is therefore the net effect of a complex range of causes.

Based on the methodology discussed in this paper, several research avenues can be traced. First, the empirical exercise can be extended over a long-term period in order to capture historical trends about the level and the sources of regional centrality. Second, centrality level may be very different across sectors, pointing to the interest of obtaining the centrality level of a country in each sector and studying the corresponding determinants, as already explored for regions of a country by Crespo and Fontoura (2015). Third, the empirical analysis conducted here had essentially an illustrative purpose, but it could be easily expanded by using other methodological options to measure the variables that we have used to capture the centrality level, as in the case of distance. Finally, the robustness of the results obtained for the several components of regional centrality could be confirmed with additional methodologies.

REFERENCES

Anderson, J., & van Wincoop, E. (2003). Gravity with gravitas: A solution to the border puzzle. *The American Economic Review*, *93*(1), 170–192. doi:10.1257/000282803321455214

Battersby, B., & Ewing, R. (2005). *International trade performance: The gravity of Australia's remoteness.* Treasury Working Paper No. 2005-03.

Berthelon, M., & Freund, C. (2008). On the conservation of distance in international trade. *Journal of International Economics*, *75*(2), 310–320. doi:10.1016/j.jinteco.2007.12.005

Blainey, G. (1966). *The tyranny of distance: How distance shaped Australia's history.* Sun Books.

Brülhart, M. (2001). Evolving geographical concentration of European manufacturing industries. *Weltwirtschaftliches Archiv*, *137*(2), 215–243. doi:10.1007/BF02707264

Brülhart, M. (2006). The fading attraction of central regions: An empirical note on core-periphery gradients in Western Europe. *Spatial Economic Analysis*, *1*(2), 227–235. doi:10.1080/17421770601009866

Brülhart, M., & Traeger, R. (2005). An account of geographic concentration patterns in Europe. *Regional Science and Urban Economics*, *35*(6), 597–624. doi:10.1016/j.regsciurbeco.2004.09.002

Chen, N. (2004). Intra-national versus international trade in the European Union: Why do national borders matter? *Journal of International Economics*, *63*(1), 93–118. doi:10.1016/S0022-1996(03)00042-4

Crespo, N., & Fontoura, M. (2006). Economic centrality, per capita income and human capital – some results at regional and local level in 275 counties of Portugal. *Regional and Sectoral Economic Studies, 6.*

Crespo, N., Fontoura, M., & Simões, N. (2015). Spatial centrality: An approach with sectoral linkages. *Applied Econometrics and International Development, 15*(1), 45-56.

Disdier, A., & Head, K. (2008). The puzzling persistence of the distance effect on bilateral trade. *The Review of Economics and Statistics*, *90*(1), 37–48. doi:10.1162/rest.90.1.37

Fujita, M., Krugman, P., & Venables, A. (1999). *The spatial economy: Cities, regions and international trade.* MIT Press. doi:10.7551/mitpress/6389.001.0001

Gutiérrez, J., & Urbano, P. (1996). Accessibility in the European Union: The impact of the trans-European road network. *Journal of Transport Geography*, *4*(1), 15–25. doi:10.1016/0966-6923(95)00042-9

Head, K., & Mayer, T. (2000). Non-Europe: The magnitude and causes of market fragmentation in the EU. *Weltwirtschaftliches Archiv*, *136*(2), 284–314. doi:10.1007/BF02707689

Head, K., & Mayer, T. (2002). *Illusory border effects: Distance mismeasurement inflates estimates of home bias in trade.* CEPII Working Papers No. 2002-01.

Head, K., & Mayer, T. (2004). Market potential and the location of Japanese investment in the European Union. *The Review of Economics and Statistics*, *86*(4), 959–972. doi:10.1162/0034653043125257

Head, K., & Mayer, T. (2013). What separates us? Sources of resistance to globalization. *The Canadian Journal of Economics. Revue Canadienne d'Economique*, *46*(4), 1196–1231. doi:10.1111/caje.12055

Helliwell, J., & Verdier, G. (2001). Measuring internal trade distances: A new method applied to estimate provincial border effects in Canada. *The Canadian Journal of Economics. Revue Canadienne d'Economique*, *34*(4), 1024–1041. doi:10.1111/0008-4085.00111

Keeble, D., Offord, J., & Walker, S. (1988). Peripheral regions in a community of twelve Member States. Report for the European Commission, Brussels.

Keeble, D., Owens, P., & Thompson, C. (1982). Regional accessibility and economic potential in the European Community. *Regional Studies*, *16*(6), 419–432. doi:10.1080/09595238200185421

Krugman, P. (1993). First nature, second nature, and metropolitan location. *Journal of Regional Science*, *33*(2), 129–144. doi:10.1111/j.1467-9787.1993.tb00217.x

Linneker, B., & Spence, N. (1996). Road transport infrastructure and regional economic development: The regional development effects of the M25 London Orbital Motorway. *Journal of Transport Geography*, *4*(2), 77–92. doi:10.1016/0966-6923(96)00001-4

Mayer, T., & Zignago, S. (2011). *Notes on CEPII's distances measures: The Geodist Database.* CEPII Working Papers No. 2011-25.

Melitz, J. (2007). North, south and distance in the gravity model. *European Economic Review*, *51*(4), 971–991. doi:10.1016/j.euroecorev.2006.07.001

Melitz, M. (2003). The impact of trade on intra-industry reallocations and aggregate industry productivity. *Econometrica*, *71*(6), 1695–1725. doi:10.1111/1468-0262.00467

Nitsch, V. (2000). National borders and international trade: Evidence from the European Union. *The Canadian Journal of Economics. Revue Canadienne d'Economique*, *33*(4), 1091–1105. doi:10.1111/0008-4085.00055

Ottaviano, G. (2008). Infrastructure and economic geography: An overview of theory and evidence. *European Investment Bank Papers*, *13*, 8–35.

Redding, S., & Schott, P. (2003). Distance, skill deepening and development: Will peripheral countries ever get rich? *Journal of Development Economics*, *72*(2), 515–541. doi:10.1016/S0304-3878(03)00118-4

Redding, S., & Venables, A. (2004). Economic geography and international inequality. *Journal of International Economics*, *62*(1), 53–82. doi:10.1016/j.jinteco.2003.07.001

Schürmann, C., & Talaat, A. (2000). *Towards a European Peripherality Index*. Report for General Directorate XVI Regional Policy of the European Commission.

Spiekermann, K., & Neubauer, J. (2002). *European accessibility and peripherality: Concepts, models and indicators. Nordregio Working Paper No. 2002:9.*

Wolf, H. (1997). *Patterns of intra- and inter-state trade.* NBER Working Paper No. 5939.

Wolf, H. (2000). Intranational home bias in trade. *The Review of Economics and Statistics*, *82*(4), 555–556. doi:10.1162/003465300559046

ENDNOTES

1 Crespo and Fontoura (2006) confirm this causal link at the regional level using data from Portugal. Additionally, Redding and Schott (2003) establish a theoretical relationship between centrality and education attainment, reinforcing the advantage of a central position in terms of economic development.

2 For an alternative decomposition method, see Crespo et al. (2015). In this study, the method is applied to regions of a country and the main focus is to propose a method which includes sectoral linkages.

3 All the results are available upon request.

Chapter 6
Reshuffling the Negotiation Table:
The Agricultural G-20 During the Doha Round

Niels Søndergaard
INSPER, Brazil

ABSTRACT

This chapter analyses the participation of the agricultural G-20 coalition within the Doha Round of the World Trade Organization. The strategies, modes of operation, as well as the internal and external articulations of the group from its inception during the run-up to the Cancun Ministerial to its dissolution in 2008 are the object of scrutiny. Based on documental analysis of cables from the achieves of the Brazilian Ministry of Foreign Affairs and interviews conducted with stakeholders in the negotiation process, the chapter engages with the contextual circumstances and central factors which both permitted the rise of the G-20 within the negotiation process, but eventually also led to its disintegration.

INTRODUCTION

The outcome of trade negotiations can be very important in shaping the links that are formed between national economies and global markets. Concessions implying increased market access for developing countries to large developed markets can thereby wield a large impact on the economic development of the former group. This is not least the case within the field of agriculture, a sector within which certain developing states enjoy significant comparative advantages, and potential for significant export-driven growth. Conversely, far-reaching and drastic liberalizations of agriculture within other developing countries can also impact rural producers and ultimately threaten food security in these states. Moreover, developing states have often had a very limited leverage and faced a restricted room of *manoeuvre* within international trade negotiations, as rich countries often have enjoyed a disproportionate influence within these arenas. This has meant that both legitimate offensive and defensive interests of developing na-

DOI: 10.4018/978-1-7998-7568-0.ch006

tions frequently have faced very complicated prospects for advancing. This state of affairs has generally characterized the multilateral trading system throughout its development in the latter part of the 20th Century. However, the rise of a range of countries within the developing world from the early 2000s would eventually change this picture, as new power constellations within the global order spilled over into the global trading system. The formation of the G-20 within the field of agriculture during the Doha Round became emblematic of this change, as a range of developing countries rallied behind the goal of inclusive trade reform with special focus on agriculture. This chapter examines the surge, consolidation, and eventual disintegration of the agricultural G-20 within the Doha Round. More specifically, it analyses the strategies, the operational modalities, as well as the internal and external articulations of the group from its inception during the run-up to the Cancun Ministerial to its dissolution in 2008. Based on analysis of more than 1700 documents from the achieves of the Brazilian Ministry of Foreign Affairs and a range of interviews conducted with stakeholders in the negotiation process, this chapter seeks to present an empirically nuanced account of the contextual circumstances and structural key factors which both permitted the rise of this sweeping novel force within the negotiation process, but eventually also circumscribed its continuation.

THE DEVELOPMENT ROUND

Throughout the post-war period, a series of trade negotiations under the General Agreement of Trade and Tariffs (GATT) regime had led to growing liberalization of world trade. However, until the 1980s the agricultural sector had largely been left out of these negotiations and was therefore characterized by very elevated levels of subsidies, - especially within developed countries. The Uruguay Round (1986-1994) was meant to change this state of affairs. The agricultural sector, therefore, became a central part of these negotiations, and with the Agreement on Agriculture (AoA) entering into force in 1995, and market access, domestic support policies, and special safeguards of individual countries were inserted within a global framework for agricultural policy-making. Yet, developing countries who had hoped that the concessions they had to make as part of the AoA would lead to increased market access for agricultural products in the developed world, would be thoroughly disappointed. Even after the agreement, global agricultural trade remained highly distorted as especially the "Majors" (The European Union and the United States) would continue to significantly subsidize their agricultural producers while maintaining high tariffs which constituted a significant obstacle for developing country producers. As the reference period for reduction of agricultural support programmes had been a time with exceptionally high agricultural subsidies in the developed world, the reductions which the Majors had to make were very limited. All in all, the costs which farmers in many poor nations had to incur as a consequence of the AoA were thereby proportionately higher than those borne by agricultural producers in the developed world. This was often associated with significant impacts on vulnerable rural populations that had to face competition from heavily subsidized products from developed states (Clapp, 2006).

Consequently, many voices in developing states called out for a new round of multilateral trade negotiations that would be more attentive towards the interests of these countries. Agriculture would necessarily have to constitute a central issue within these talks. The preparations for the Doha Ministerial Conference at the World Trade Organization (WTO) were thereby characterized by a strong push to compensate for the lack of concessions to developing states, who mobilized in a range of groupings in order to prepare for what was termed as the "Development Round". This process would prove to be cumbersome from the very preparatory phase of the Doha Ministerial, which was set to take place in November 2001. From early 2001, contacts made between developed nations reflected an intent amongst these states to limit the scope of ambitions for reform within the field of agriculture. Approximations between the EU and the USA in the run-up to the Ministerial conference also hinted that although the Majors had accepted the need to signal that poverty and development-related themes were at the top of priorities, a consensus did exist about not making too substantial changes to the general *status quo* within the field of Agriculture. Experiences from previous rounds of negotiations had left developing states vary of any steps which might eventually sideline them. Hence, Brazil sought to create leverage in relation to the Majors through the Cairns Group of agricultural exporters, although the scattered positions of that group made it difficult to reach a common ground. China and India worked through the Like-Minded Group (LMG) of large states in the Global South aspiring to challenge the fundamental biases favoring agricultural producers in high-income countries. The phase leading up to the Doha Ministerial reflected an increasing degree of urgency amongst states demanding agricultural reform, as analyses of the outcome of the Uruguay Round corroborated the argument that developing states had not gained substantially from those negotiations. Both Brazil and India presented a high-profile engagement at Doha. India was especially active as part of the Like Minded-Group in opposing the Singapore Issues[1] which held a high priority amongst developed states. Developing countries countered this agenda by highlighting the need to emphasize implementation issues. Before the Ministerial Conference, Brazil had been very emphatic of the need to advance towards deep reforms of the three agricultural pillars of market access, internal support, and export subsidies, - an agenda which the country pursued intensely at Doha. These efforts made by the large developing states appear to have been somewhat successful in influencing the Doha Declaration, which was signed on November 14th 2001. The text in the working programme aiming at the conclusion of negotiations by January 2005 thus underscored the need for "a fair and market-oriented trading system through a programme of fundamental reform [within agriculture]" and that "the purpose is to correct and prevent restrictions and distortions in world agricultural markets".

Agricultural reform had thereby been established as a key objective for the Doha Round, along with the explicit intent of guaranteeing that the specific format chosen would be especially aimed at benefitting developing countries. Yet, despite the ostensive adherence to this agenda on behalf of the central players from both the global North and South, the events surrounding the Doha conference had also demonstrated that there were significant limits to how far the Majors would be willing to stretch themselves in order to concede to development-related agendas. Agricultural constituencies had proven to be a powerful force within domestic policies in both the United States and the European Union, which invariable would mean that even genuine attempts to accommodate parts of the demands for trade reform would face significant domestic opposition. Moreover, the complexities of trade negotiations and the technical resources needed in order to be able to present credible alternative proposals, - or often also just to be able to challenge pre-defined agendas by the Majors - meant that especially poor countries faced great obstacles within the WTO negotiations. In this situation, resource-endowed countries like India, Brazil, and China were in a special position, as their political leverage, as well as their human and knowledge-based capacities, made these states central to advancing the reform agenda. Different constellations of political opposition and alternative proposals for a new multilateral commercial order from Southern countries would therefore necessarily need to encompass these states.

THE CANCUN CONFERENCE AND THE G-20

Although the signature of the Doha Declaration constituted a significant expression of a will to reshape the global trading system, events the following year led to some concern regarding the level of ambition amongst major participants. The signature of the US Farm Bill in late 2002 provided a strong signal of the challenges to deep reform, as the contents of the law were seen as contradictory to the goal of diminishing distortive domestic subsidies. The EU was also hesitant to present a concrete proposal, which when finally laid forward in December 2002 contained a wide room for the Union to perpetuate existing tariff peaks within sensitive product categories. Amongst others, this also led Oxfam to criticize the draft for a lack of ambition. Proposals presented by President of the Special Session for Agriculture, Stuart Harbinson, by early 2003 did comprise of certain modalities that would lead the EU and the US to commit themselves more deeply to the core objectives of the Doha Declaration. Brazilian diplomatic correspondences nonetheless illustrate how the level of ambition displayed by the Harbinson text was viewed as falling short of the negotiations mandate in important fields within all three pillars[2].

Despite the high-level Ministerial Conference planned to take place in August 2003, progress in the negotiation process was slow throughout that year. Leading up to the Conference, an understanding around a common draft text was forming between the USA and the EU. The final proposal presented by the Majors comprised of a blended formula for tariff reductions, an extension of the Peace Clause from the Uruguay Round, and certain moderately trade distorting domestic support schemes. It also did not go further than suggesting a partial elimination of certain export subsidies and did not commit to specific levels of domestic support and tariff reductions. Especially the more competitive developing agro-exporters were likely to be negatively hit by the Majors' proposal, as they would be denied Special and Differential Treatment (SDT). The Brazilian WTO ambassador strongly attacked the draft text defended by the Majors and underlined how it would preserve privileges of developed countries while punishing developing states who had managed to become increasingly competitive agro-exporters.[3] Consensus between the Majors implied some potentially very serious implications for actors seeking significant multilateral trade reform, due to the combined leverage of these players and their capability in terms of imposing a continuation of the *status quo*. The fear that the United States and the EU would repeat the Blair House Accord from the Uruguay Round, through which they had dictated the terms of the agreement within the field of agriculture, led to preoccupations amongst many developing countries with otherwise highly diverging interests in this area (Hurrell & Narlikar, 2006).

The urgency brought about by the prospects of an imminent "Blair House 2.0" spurred a momentum for initiative amongst many developing countries. Since January 2003, Brazil and India had been approximating each other within the field of agriculture, a process that would bear fruit in the run-up to the Cancun Ministerial (Mariano & Ramanzini 2013, p. 1216). An initial text opposing this proposal was drafted by these two countries, and subsequently important support for an "alternative framework for agricultural negotiations" was ensured from China and other developing nations. Despite the fact that this group of states could not entirely agree concerning market access, it nonetheless managed to present a counter-proposal on August 20th, and was hereby initially referred to as "the Group of 17". This Group, - which with certain adherences and defections eventually would be known as the G-20, - comprised of countries from three different continents, and was formed on basis of a strong common ambition to see an agreement in line with that which was set out in the Doha mandate. The roles which especially India and Brazil played as the central vectors of organization and dynamism within the group imbued it with momentum and a certain degree of audacity in challenging the Majors. Despite the short time which Brazil had to prepare a counter-proposal, it did manage to bring a technically well-founded alternative text to the Conference, which became the core of the efforts to force the Majors to abandon their initial proposal.

At the Cancun Ministerial, the G-20 displayed an assertive stance and presented proposals for support and subsidy reductions targeting developed states. The group also defended the need for increased market access in these countries, especially about higher value-added products, as well as the elimination of export subsidies. The G-20 had entered the negotiations with the clear conviction that too little was offered by the USA and the EU within the field of agriculture, and too much was demanded by the Majors regarding Non-Agricultural Market Access (NAMA). The attempts to redefine the negotiation dynamics initially caught these heavyweights off guard, but soon hereafter spurred them to seek out different avenues to challenge the G-20. The Majors thereby sought bilateral engagements with individual G-20 members, one the one hand, offering both incentives for these states to reconsider their engagement within the G-20, and on the other, applying a large amount of pressure for them to split with the group. This divide-and-rule strategy did not prove effective at Cancun, as the G-20 maintained its cohesion throughout the entire bargaining process. Articulations with other developing country groups also proved to be vital in order to advance an alternative agenda to the one defended by the Majors, - a goal which was pursued through the presentation of demands with broad resonance within the developing world. The establishment of a tacit consensus with the G-90, the LDCs, and ACPs about making concessions within NAMA and the Singapore issues contingent upon results within agriculture was also an essential aspect of the G-20s agency. The central role, which this group assumed within the negotiations landscape at Cancun, meant that it eventually became evident that this Ministerial would not lead to any results.

What made the events at the Cancun Ministerial so distinctively unique in a historical perspective, was that it was the first time that developing states managed to significantly advance their agendas within the sphere of multilateral trade negotiations. Previously, such attempts had more often than not resulted in large developed players imposing their general agenda on these states. Although the result of these counter-efforts had been a deadlock in the negotiations at Cancun, the unity demonstrated by the G-20 when faced with pressures from the Majors was in itself a victory. This was obtained through a mixed strategy, which on the one hand had aimed at the technicalities of the negotiation process, in relation to which India and Brazil had spearheaded the G-20s efforts. On the other hand, an important discursive dispute had been fought in parallel within the public sphere, as developing states had attempted to win over sympathies for their cause (Doctor 2015, p.292). The Majors had sought to frame the G-20 as an obstructive force, attempting to sabotage vital efforts to advance with reform and liberalization of the global trading system. Countering such arguments thus became a fundamental part of the wider efforts to defend the G-20 agenda within agriculture. A central feature that defined this group was its highly developed capabilities for processing complex information and commercial data, and translating this into specific proposals. As such, thanks, especially to the Brazilian negotiation apparatus and close public-private cooperation between the foreign policy establishment and agribusiness sector, Brazil and the G-20, could engage within a privileged sphere of the negotiations where discussions reached a high level of technical sophistication (Carvalho 2010; Hopewell 2013; Søndergaard & Dias da Silva 2019). Contrary to the arguments initially advanced by the Majors in response to the sudden "Southern assertiveness" the specialized literature has tended to frame the G-20's agency at the Cancun Ministerial as a pro-active and constructive force (Mancini, 2010; Tussie & Narlikar 2004).

INTERNAL CONSOLIDATION AND OFFENSIVE ENGAGEMENT OF THE G-20

In the wake of the Cancun Ministerial, efforts by the Majors to fracture the G-20 intensified as the USA and the EU blamed this group for the collapse of the negotiations. A group of Latin American states eventually ceded and left the G-20, and members from the African group also experienced similar coercive tactics on behalf of the Majors. The G-20 nonetheless endured, and in December 2003, Brazil convoked a meeting in Rio de Janeiro in order to consolidate the group around a common negotiation strategy. The importance of removing trade distortions as part of a strategy for poverty reduction was highlighted at this occasion, and technical work was distributed on the key members of Brazil, India, China, South Africa, and Argentina. The G-20 opted for an open format, which permitted new memberships, and sought convergence with other negotiation groups within the Doha Round. As many G-20 members also were part of the Cairns Group, approximations were made with the goal of ensuring an outcome within the field of agriculture that would be in line with the Doha mandate. Although the Cairns was more offensively minded than the G-20, which also encompassed developing states with strong internal food security concerns, a common ground could be reached in relation to demands for larger agricultural market access in developed countries. Articulations were also sought in relation to the African Group with this agenda serving as a shared action-platform.

The offensive and defensive postures of the G-20 were clearly encapsulated by Brazil and India, respectively. As it gradually became evident that the G-20 invariably would continue as a central force within the negotiations process, the Majors eventually sought to include Brazil and India within a new core negotiations format that in time also would comprise of China. The negotiations dynamics had thereby changed, as the G-20 provided a platform for contestation of the agricultural *status quo*, with point of departure in which Brazil, India, and China had managed to launch themselves as central voices within the Doha Round (Hopewell, 2013). The G-20 should also be viewed in the light of changed geopolitical and geo-economic global power constellations, as the rise of large developing countries, such as the BRICS, constituted one of the most important trends of the 2000s. This hereby appears to have resulted in a generally permissive context for the G-20 as a specific initiative to challenge the *status quo* within the global trading system, and in relation to the sensitive field of agriculture. Hence, as highlighted by EU Commissioner in the early stages of the negotiation process, Pascal Lamy, the G-20 had a "geopolitical father", and "agriculture as its mother" (Hugueney, 2004).

The reshuffling of the negotiations scenario and acceptance of the new arrangement of power relations within this eventually led the EU to seek dialogue with the G-20 in order to resume the negotiations process. Similar messages were received from the US Trade Representative (USTR) the same month, which hinted at a possible momentum for the resumption of negotiations on basis of the new premises of increased G-20 influence. The technical work to define new negotiation proposals gained speed during 2004. Formulas for tariff reductions became a central object of analysis for both the Indian and Brazilian negotiations apparatus. Converging conclusions stressed how a blended formula would lead to large proportionate tariff reduction amongst developing countries compared to developed states. Together with the Cairns Group, the G-20 thereby questioned this modality for tariff reductions, and presented an alternative tiered formula. This proposal was marked by a strong emphasis on significant cuts in tariff peaks within developing countries, combined with a special attention to specific food security concerns of developing states. The tiered approach would eventually be adopted in the text presented by the President of the General Council, Shotaro Oshima, in July 2004. This draft, which came to be known as the July Package, was sensitive towards the Majors' demands regarding blue box payments and sensitive products, but importantly, also incorporated key demands of the G-20, such as a consequential elimination of export subsidies, substantial reductions in domestic support, and a tiered formula for tariff reductions. As the July package eventually was approved in the last days of that month, the G-20 could celebrate having fundamentally redefined the negotiation dynamics and reached a significant victory in terms of substantial changes to the negotiations agenda within the field of agriculture. According to Hurrell and Narlikar (2006), the passing of the July Package reflects how the G-20 reached beyond a temporary issue-coalition, and rather should be viewed as a block-type coalition which at least partly was held together by certain identity-based factors. In a similar vein, Efstathoupolos (2012) emphasizes the ideological elements related to North-South divisions within the negotiation process. This highlights the importance of deeper-lying political identities in shaping more durable actor-constellations bound together by factors that span beyond immediate rational benefit-oriented calculations. However, as Doctor (2015) underscores, the identity-based cohesion of the G-20 would eventually be faced with some clear limits posed by the strategic economic considerations of each of the G-20 members. Hence, while the strength of South-South politics should be kept in mind, by themselves, they would not be sufficient to guarantee the unity of the G-20 when tangible real challenges to its common posture would become more evident.

Upon the agreement on the July Package, the G-20 continued its work aiming towards the Hong Kong Ministerial conference planned for December 2005. With a significant overlap in membership between the two groups, a certain degree of coordination between the work taking place in the G-20 and within the Cairns Group also became evident. The conversion of Ad-Valorem Equivalents (AVEs) was a technical issue that at this point had gained much importance, and become a potential stumbling stone for the advance of the negotiations. At a G-20 meeting in New Delhi in March 2005, agreement on this issue was reached within the group. At this occasion, its members accentuated the utmost importance of ensuring the conversion of non-ad-valorem duties into AVEs. As the Hong Kong Ministerial approached and the Majors presented their negotiation proposals in the autumn of 2005, the G-20 very emphatically stressed the need to reach a higher level of ambition within agriculture. The time period for the phasing out of export subsidies also became a thorny issue within the negotiations, and developing countries argued in favor of a quick elimination. The increased leverage which developing countries had come to enjoy meant that they were able to more significantly influence the negotiations process, which eventually resulted in an agreement about the phasing out of agricultural export subsidies which was set at 2013. Generally, the Hong Kong Ministerial had led to moderately positive results for the G-20. Yet, certain internal divergences within the group had nevertheless become evident during the Ministerial. This was not least the case about Special Safeguard Measures (SSMs), defended by India and China, of which Brazil nonetheless was very critical. The country's very offensive profile as an agro-exporter meant that these mechanisms were seen as a potential threat to future Brazilian market access within other developing countries. These events should also be viewed on the backdrop of the rapid surge of especially China as an important destination for Brazilian agricultural exports during the early 2000s. Consequently, concessions which could lead to a certain degree of loss to this market increasingly became a Brazilian preoccupation, which eventually would provide a serious challenge to internal unity within the G-20.

FRICTIONS WITHIN THE G-20

A more cumbersome negotiations scenario arose in the wake of the Hong Kong Ministerial. The EU's signaling to the G-20 of its unwillingness to make further concessions within the field of agriculture led to suspicions that the Union sought an excuse for an eventual collapse of the Round. Consultations held between G-20 members and legal firms specialized in trade litigations also indicated that this group had begun to consider a more direct and assertive approach, especially in the case that the Majors proved reluctant towards further advances in the negotiations. After the Hong Kong meeting, the core format for the negotiations shifted towards the G6, comprising the EU, USA, Japan, Brazil, India, and Australia. However, discussions did not advance significantly within this forum, not least due to the United States' reluctance to make noticeable cuts in domestic support. In July 2006, 57 US Senators signed a letter in which they rejected the possibility of the United States making any further significant concessions within the field of agriculture, leading to an increased deterioration of the negotiation prospects. In addition to the Majors' lack of ambition, internal strife also became evident within the G-20. Compared to India and China, Brazil aimed for much more extensive liberalizations within the field of agriculture, while the former countries were more inclined to open markets for services and manufactures, respectively. The backing which Brazil had enjoyed within the global public sphere as a "champion of the developing world" also receded significantly, and especially NGOs and civil society organizations became more skeptical towards the possible implications of the country's hyper-offensive posture within the field of agriculture. With the main parties drifting apart throughout 2006, now WTO General-Secretary, Pascal Lamy, found it difficult to present proposals for formulas which would enjoy broad appeal. Repeated rejections of Lamy's negotiation drafts thereby eventually led him to temporarily suspend negotiations.

Despite the suspension of negotiations, the G-20 continued its activities, and at a meeting in Rio where the African Group, the LDCs, and ACPs alto took part, it sought to reenergize the discussions about how to advance with reform of the global trading system. Brazil and India also reaffirmed their understanding of the importance of developing country unity and of confronting the institutional asymmetries embedded within the WTO system. By 2007, a positive momentum had become apparent, and Lamy stressed the opportunity of resuming negotiations in order to conclude an agreement. As negotiations were reinitiated by February 2007, Brazil and India were positioned centrally within the G4 format adopted in the agricultural negotiations through which these leading states from the G-20 would seek an agreement with the USA and the EU. Although Brazil and India shared a mutual goal of concluding the negotiations in accordance with the Doha mandate, - an objective in which both parties had eventually invested significant amounts of resources and political capital - the fundamental divergences between their essential interests had not been attenuated. The preoccupation with Special Safeguards Measures (SSMs) which characterized Brazil and its agribusiness sector thus provided a substantial challenge, as SSMs were of absolute importance to India. Eventually, at the mini-ministerial conference in 2008, open disagreements between Brazil and India became evident. Brazil thus rejected a proposal presented by India, Indonesia, and China, and with the prospects of reaching a final agreement, chose to adhere to the package presented by Lamy during a G7 session. This package was nonetheless rejected by India who had assumed a clearly defensive position together with the G-33, which eventually forced Lamy to announce the breakdown of negotiations. Hence, after five years during which it had exercised significant influence in reshaping the dynamics of multilateral trade negotiations, the G-20 had eventually exhausted its potential. It might well be argued that the seed for disagreement between its central members had always been present within this coalition. Yet, faced with the mutual threat of being overruled by a new

Blair House Agreement, it had been possible to overcome the differences between developing countries. However, when a more specific common posture had to be defined, the wide-reaching differences between especially Brazil and India proved to be too deep to bridge.

CONCLUSION

At the point of its formation in the run-up to the Cancun Ministerial, the G-20 constituted a novel and sweeping force that profoundly reshuffled the dynamics of the negotiations within the WTO. In a very short time-span of only two years from Cancun to Hong Kong, issues and trade formulas which had been very difficult to imagine realistically would be part of the negotiations had not only been firmly inserted within the reform agenda but were eventually accepted by all participants. Emerging nations, such as Brazil and India, had thereby gained a space within the most central spheres of global agricultural policy-making (Hopewell 2013; Søndergaard 2020). This was part of a broader shift within the global order, as emerging economies came to account for an increasing part of global GDP and trade in the 2000s. This trend was possibly even more accentuated within the field of food production, trade, and consumption, as rapidly growing populations with increasing purchasing power demanded improved and more diversified diets. Yet, this circumstance also spurred a structural trend that would alter the dynamics of the negotiations and the underlying interests of the main players within the G-20. While India and China increased both their food production and exports, these countries also became very significant food importers, and especially India faced a complex situation in terms of guaranteeing both food supplies as well as the livelihoods of its substantial population of smallholder farmers. Brazil constitutes a very different case, as the country is characterized by more one-sidedly export-oriented offensive interests. The Brazilian Ministry of Foreign Affairs and agribusiness sector thus eventually reached the conclusion that the G-20 had become more of a liability than an effective tool for advancing the country's commercial interests in wide-ranging global agricultural market liberalization.

The current case of the agricultural G-20 within the Doha Rounds highlights how identity-based coalitions eventually face certain limits when divergence of economic interests and objectives characterize its core members. This does not mean that such identity-related factors are irrelevant, but rather that they constitute a superstructure that depends on a solid base of convergence of material interests. This also seems to be in line with scholarly observations that highlight the pragmatic nature of coalitions within the WTO, which most frequently revolve around issue-specific goals (Diego-Fernandes, 2008), and with contributions that stress how joint engagement on the technical level aimed at reaching shared interests has been adopted by coalitions within this sphere (Doctor, 2015, p.290). In a wider sense, the case examined calls attention to the implications of an increasingly multipolar world within the institutions of the global trading system. In the decade following the shipwrecking of the Doha Round, very few advances have been made in the multilateral sphere. While some developing countries have engaged in the "Spaghetti Bowl" of preferential trade agreements, these arrangements have not substituted multilateral solutions, and are themselves associated with a range of complex challenges (Bhagwati, 2008). This raises the question of whether substantial advances were only possible at historical moments of Western hegemony, or whether a redefinition of the global order will be able to accommodate the interests of emerging states.

REFERENCES

Calpp, J. (2006). WTO Agriculture negotiations: Implications for the Global South. *Third World Quarterly*, *27*(4), 563–577. doi:10.1080/01436590600720728

Bhagwati, J. (2008). *Termites in the trading system: How preferential agreements undermine free trade.* Oxford University Press. doi:10.1093/acprof:oso/9780195331653.001.0001

Carvalho, M. I. V. (2010). Condicionantes internacionais e domésticos: O Brasil e o G-20 nas negociações agrícolas da Rodada Doha. *DADOS Revista de Ciências Sociais*, *53*(2), 405–438. doi:10.1590/S0011-52582010000200005

Diego-Fernández, M. (2008). Trade negotiations make strange bedfellows. *World Trade Review*, *7*(2), 423–453. doi:10.1017/S1474745608003832

Doctor, M. (2015). Brazil's role in institutions of global economic governance: The WTO and G20. *Global Society*, *29*(3), 286–300. doi:10.1080/13600826.2015.1025041

Efstathopoulos, C. (2012). Leadership in the WTO: Brazil, India and the Doha development agenda. *Cambridge Review of International Affairs*, *25*(2), 269–293. doi:10.1080/09557571.2012.678294

Hopewell, K. (2013). New protagonists in global economic governance: Brazilian agribusiness at the WTO. *New Political Economy*, *18*(4), 603–623. doi:10.1080/13563467.2013.736957

Hugueney, C. (2004). *The G-20: Passing phenomenon or here to stay?* Dialogue on Globalization. Briefing Papers, Fes Berlin, March 2004.

Hurrell, A., & Narlikar, A. (2006). A new politics of confrontation? Brazil and India in multilateral trade negotiations. *Global Society*, *20*(4), 415–433. doi:10.1080/13600820600929762

Mancini, C. (2010). O esforço do setor agrícola para influenciar a agenda brasileira na Rodada Doha. *Revista Administração em Diálogo*, *14*(1), 135–161. doi:10.20946/rad.v12i1.2939

Mariano, M. P., & Ramanzini, H. R. J. (2013). Brazil and the G-20: Domestic pressures and the construction of the negotiating position in the Doha Round of the WTO. *Journal of World Trade*, *47*(6), 1203–1224.

Narlikar, A., & Tussie, D. (2004). The G-20 at the Cancun ministerial: Developing countries and their evolving coalitions in the WTO. *World Economy*, *27*(7), 947–966. doi:10.1111/j.1467-9701.2004.00636.x

Søndergaard, N., & Dias da Silva, R. (2020). Reshaping the policy arena: How the agro-export policy network propelled Brazil within global agricultural governance. *World Trade Review*, *19*(4), 550–566. doi:10.1017/S1474745619000375

Søndergaard, N. (2020). Food regime transformations and structural rebounding: Brazilian state–agribusiness relations. *Territory, Politics, Governance*, 1–20. doi:10.1080/21622671.2020.1786447

ENDNOTES

1 The Singapore Issues refer to government procurement, trade facilitation, competition, and investment.

2 Telegram from the Brazilian Mission at the WTO to the Brazilian Ministry of Foreign Affairs, nr.323 12/2, 2003.

3 Telegram from the Brazilian Mission at the WTO to the Brazilian Ministry of Foreign Affairs, 1845, 14/8, 2003.

Chapter 7
Economic Complexity and Trade Diversification in the Western Hemisphere Between 1962 and 2017

Jorge Mauricio Falcón Gómez
https://orcid.org/0000-0002-5187-2453
FLACSO, Ecuador

Fernando Martín Mayoral
FLACSO, Ecuador

ABSTRACT

Trade diversification patterns help explain the level of utilization of trade opportunities by countries, mainly the least developed. Empirical analyses show an inverse U relationship between trade diversification and level of development. Trade diversification measures used do not take into account differences in complexity of exports, and complexity indices only consider products with comparative advantages. This study seeks to cover both gaps by analyzing the differences in the determinants of trade diversification, considering the complexity of products exported by 19 Western Hemisphere countries from 1962 to 2017. The results show that after controlling for economic complexity, the inverted U relationship disappears. Development of financial markets positively affects the complexity of trade diversification in the long term, while the terms of trade that have a negative effect on trade diversification does not affect the complexity-corrected indices. In the short term, transaction costs and trade openness appear to have a significant effect.

DOI: 10.4018/978-1-7998-7568-0.ch007

INTRODUCTION

International trade offers countries important opportunities to expand markets and boost economies of scale, with the degree of trade diversification being one of the main determinants of this process (de Piñeres & Ferrantino, 1997; Haddad et al., 2013; Lederman & Maloney, 2003). However, most developing countries have not been able to insert themselves adequately into this dynamic. Taking advantage of these opportunities is for many the great task in public policy design (de Ferranti et al., 2002).

There exists consensus in the literature on the economic effects of diversification but not on its determinants (Jetter & Hassan 2015). They are usually associated with better use of the benefits of trade: on the one hand, diversification achieves greater macroeconomic stability by diversifying risk in an international price instability context (Haddad et al., 2013; Hamid, 2010); on the other hand, it generates positive externalities such as the learning process (*learning by exporting*) and *knowledge spillovers* (Hausmann & Klinger, 2007; Hausmann & Rodrik, 2002; Vettas, 2000). This in turn allows other exporters to access existing or potential markets (Vettas, 2000) with less uncertainty and therefore lower costs. This results in greater economic growth (Acemoglu & Zilibotti, 1997; de Ferranti et al., 2002; Hidalgo et al., 2007; Lederman & Maloney, 2003). In addition, the very dynamics of trade induce higher levels of productivity, by boosting both activities of the export sector and related sectors (Melitz, 2003). The extent and depth of these effects depend on diversification patterns, particularly if countries are specialized in certain products that use standardized inputs[1] that can serve many other products (*transversality*), since it reduces the costs of introducing new products (*information externalities*) (Hausmann & Rodrik, 2002). However, contributions in this area are still scarce.

The study of trade diversification patterns, has been addressed from different approaches at regional and global levels without a clear consensus. Two lines of analysis can be distinguished. The first one investigates the link between economic development (measured through GDP per capita) and diversification. De Benedictis et al. (2009) find a positive relationship between both variables. On the other hand, Imbs and Wacziarg (2003), Klinger and Lederman (2004) and Cadot et al. (2011) show the presence of an inverted "U", where countries as they develop increase their trade diversification towards a greater number of sectors, but after a certain (high) level of development, they start specializing again (Imbs & Wacziarg, 2003). This would confirm that trade specialization is a phenomenon of both less developed and more developed countries.

The second line has focused on analyzing different factors that influence trade diversification, emphasizing several aspects such as (1) the endowment of productive factors, particularly capital (human, physical or financial), elements of scale, which condition the absorption of knowledge and the use of both externalities and innovation (Acemoglu & Zilibotti, 1997; Aghion & Howitt, 2009); (2) trade costs (Dennis & Shepherd, 2011); (3) macroeconomic factors such as productivity, macroeconomic stability, competitiveness (Helpman & Krugman, 1989), volatility of terms of trade (Agosin et al., 2012), inflation or capacity to attract Foreign Direct Investment (FDI) (Fonchamnyo et al., 2017), among others; (4) political, cultural, and geographic factors, which reflect the influence of conflict and political governance (Makhlouf et al., 2015; Shepotylo, 2013); (5) the orientation of trade policy with respect to the degree of openness and market access, integration agreements, and export diversification programs (de Ferranti et al., 2002; Dennis & Shepherd, 2011; Estevadeordal & Martincus, 2006; Márquez-Ramos et al., 2015), or the role of the state as either facilitator or promoter (Lim & Saborowski, 2012).

The traditional diversification metrics (Herfindahl-Hirschman, Gini or Theil indices) have as their main limitation that they do not distinguish between the characteristics of exported products, that is, for these indices it is the same to increase exports of fruit or electronic devices. When the aim is to reflect the complexity of products, i.e. the amount of productive knowledge contained in each product exported by a country[2], the approach of Hausmann and Hidalgo (2011) and their index of economic complexity is capable of capturing these differences. However, this index is not completely satisfactory, since it discards those products in which the country does not have a competitive presence at the international level[3], so it does not take into account all the products exported by the country. Both limitations constitute an obstacle to the analysis of the complexity of trade diversification.

In order to achieve a better approach to the complexity of trade diversification, and taking into account the limitations in previous indicators, this research propose to merge Hausmann and Hidalgo's Economic Complexity Index (2011) with traditional diversification metrics, which will allow to evidence the differences in product complexity in the export baskets of each country, based on the knowledge they incorporate. This task will be done by giving greater weight to the more complex products, in order to capture the quality of commercial diversification.

With this background, this research aims to analyze the differences in the determinants of the patterns of trade diversification linked to the complexity of exports in Western Hemisphere countries during the period 1962-2017. In the following sections it will be analyzed the different theoretical approaches to trade diversification and its determinants, as well as to economic complexity and its determinants. Subsequently, different methodological considerations are reviewed based on empirical works that have addressed the analysis of trade diversification in order to justify the empirical strategy used. Then the empirical strategy is mentioned and results are exhibited. Finally, conclusions and recommendations are presented on the analysis carried out.

BACKGROUND

Trade Diversification and its Determinants

Throughout history, trade theories have sought to explain the patterns of trade specialization of countries and their different nuances. Classical economists as Adam Smith and David Ricardo, explained international trade as a technological change, where specialization and trade increase the possibilities of production (Krugman et al., 2006). Similarly, the neoclassical theory of international trade, based on the Ricardian perspective, assumes that countries specialize in products in which they have comparative advantages, and particularly in those products intensive in the most abundant productive factors (Heckscher 1919 - Ohlin 1933), giving rise to *inter-industrial trade*. Therefore, for classical and neoclassical models, the patterns of international trade are determined by productive specialization and differences in endowment of productive factors. In these models, trade diversification is not a positive factor because it limits the production possibilities associated with specialization and exchange (Krugman et al., 2006).

The New International Trade Theories introduced more complex trade determinants, considering economies of scale and product differentiation, giving rise to *intra-industry trade* (Krugman et al., 2006). Under this new approach, specialization transcends the product unit and allows for movement between attributes (*horizontal diversification*) and quality levels (*vertical diversification*) (Greenaway et al., 1995). Both patterns have also been typically associated with the level of development of countries. For example, among countries with exports concentrated in primary products, intra-industry trade is generally low (Martin-Mayoral et al., 2016) and with little room for differentiation.

Regarding the effects of trade diversification, there is consensus among authors that it is associated with greater use of the benefits of trade, because it allows diversification of risk arising from international price instability (Haddad et al., 2013; Hamid, 2010), in what Agosin (2009) calls the "portfolio effect". There are other channels through which diversification affects economic growth (Acemoglu & Zilibotti, 1997; de Ferranti et al., 2002; Hidalgo et al., 2007; Lederman & Maloney, 2003). The introduction of new products to the country's productive supply generates positive externalities through the learning process (*learning by exporting*) and *knowledge spillovers* (Hausmann & Klinger, 2007; Hausmann & Rodrik, 2002; Vettas, 2000). These externalities normally feedback. That is, the export of a new product reveals to current and potential exporters the presence of favorable domestic costs in their production (*information externalities*) (Hausmann & Rodrik, 2002), allowing them also to enter existing or potential markets (Vettas, 2000) with less uncertainty and costs.

In addition, increased commercial activity induces higher levels of productivity, generating economies of scale (Melitz, 2003) boosting sectors linked to commercial activities, which contributes to increased diversification[4].

The study of trade diversification patterns has been undertaken from different approaches at a regional and global scale. Two lines of analysis can be distinguished, the first one investigates the link between economic development (measured through GDP per capita) and diversification (Cadot et al., 2011; Imbs & Wacziarg, 2003; Klinger & Lederman, 2004). The second line has focused on analyzing the economic and institutional factors that influence trade diversification (Agosin et al., 2012; de Ferranti et al. 2002; Dennis & Shepherd, 2011; Fonchamnyo & Akame, 2017), including the effects of trade policy and particularly trade agreements (de Ferranti et al., 2002; Estevadeordal & Martincus, 2006; Márquez-Ramos et al., 2015; Martin-Mayoral et al., 2016).

With respect to the first approach, most researches that analyze the link between trade diversification and economic development assume a direct relationship between GDP per capita and diversification (De Benedictis et al., 2009). However, recent studies have identified that the dynamics of trade diversification are neither autonomous nor linear, i.e., that greater economic development does not necessarily imply greater diversification. Imbs and Wacziarg (2003) show how in an initial stage of development, productive diversification is accelerated, but above a certain level of per capita income, diversification is reduced. Klinger and Lederman (2004), Cadot et al. (2011), among others, show an inverted "U" against commercial diversification. Therefore, trade concentration is a phenomenon of both less developed and more developed countries, which implies that at the productive and commercial levels, diversification dynamics are complex. For these reasons, a very relevant aspect in the study of trade diversification patterns is to understand the relationship they have with the level of development of the countries, but also with the level of complexity of such diversification.

Regarding the economic and institutional factors that influence trade diversification (second line of analysis), the literature has focused mainly on five aspects.

1. *Factor endowment* between countries as the main determinant of *inter-industry trade* (Hecksher-Ohlin model). The literature validates these differences as determinants of diversification, and helps overcoming Leontief's paradox (1953) by controlling for labor qualification (Baldwin, 1971) or for technological differences (Davis & Weinstein, 2001). Thus, a broader concept of capital that includes human capital and technological progress are considered as determinants of diversification (Acemoglu & Zilibotti, 1997; Aghion & Howitt, 2009). This group includes elements of scale such as population size (Hummels & Klenow, 2005) or market size and capital accumulation (human,

physical, financial), which characterize the conditions of knowledge absorption and therefore the use of both externalities and innovation to explain trade diversification (Acemoglu & Zilibotti 1997; Aghion & Howitt 2009). This allows for greater development of export capacities, taking the domestic market as a starting point (Lim & Saborowski, 2012), and the efforts to discover new products associated with innovation capacity (Klinger & Lederman, 2006).

2. *Costs of trade*, which largely define the level of access and permanence in international markets (Dennis & Shepherd, 2011) and the possibilities for trade expansion (Shepotylo, 2013). The literature covers different ways of capturing these costs, such as distance to markets (Agosin et al., 2012), market entry, international transport and the costs of customs requirements and procedures (Dennis & Shepherd, 2011; Shepotylo, 2013).
3. *Macroeconomic factors* in terms of competitiveness, productivity, stability of the domestic market and its positioning in the international context (Helpman & Krugman, 1989), which determine trade and diversification patterns. Thus, greater macroeconomic instability (Jetter & Hassan, 2013), exchange rate instability (Fonchamnyo & Akame, 2017; Makhlouf et al., 2015), or terms of trade instability (Agosin et al., 2012) limit the possibilities of maintaining investment and trade flows over time and therefore the capacity to diversify into new products or markets. The improvement in the terms of trade could promote greater diversification by generating better profit conditions for exporters (Agosin et al., 2012), but at the same time they could also reaffirm the incentives to specialize, so the relationship depends on which effect dominates.

The country's productive characteristics also condition diversification patterns, since greater productive density allows for greater synergy between complementary sectors (Lim & Saborowski, 2012), while high comparative advantages in one sector could reinforce its subsequent expansion to other sectors (Hausmann et al., 2005; Lim & Saborowski, 2012).

Also, the capacity of countries to attract Foreign Direct Investment (FDI) (Fonchamnyo & Akame 2017; Mubeen & Ahmad, 2016) may facilitate technology transfer and trade externalities or limit them. On the other hand, higher *intra-industry trade intensity* (Martin-Mayoral et al., 2016) may influence sectoral diversification or limit the use of cross-sectoral complementarities.

4. *Political, cultural and geographical factors* on trade diversification, as political stability (Alemu, 2009), governance (Makhlouf et al., 2015; Shepotylo, 2013), conflict (Hammouda et al., 2006), cultural variables such as having been a colony or the country's dominant language (Jetter & Hassan, 2015), or geographical variables such as access to the sea (Makhlouf et al., 2015; Shepotylo, 2013).

The orientation of trade policy is, for many authors, the most important determinant of trade diversification (Edwards & Lawrence 2006; Estevadeordal & Martincus 2006; Lim & Saborowski 2012). It is reflected in the degree of openness and access to markets, making it possible to capture economies of scale (Dennis & Shepherd, 2011), the belonging to integration agreements (Estevadeordal & Martincus, 2006; Márquez-Ramos et al., 2015; Parteka and Tamberi 2013; Shepotylo 2013) or export diversification programs (Chakrabarti, 2018; Dennis & Shepherd, 2011) as well as the role of the state as facilitator or promoter of these processes.

However, in order to define a consistent trade policy, particularly in the context of Western Hemisphere countries, it is not only necessary to understand the diversification patterns, but also to consider the productive networks that the exportable portfolio uses and pushes (Hausmann & Hidalgo, 2011), as such differences determine the perspective of the very dynamics of trade diversification patterns.

Empirical Approach

Trade diversification has been analyzed from various methodological perspectives. These strategies include non-parametric, semi-parametric and parametric approaches. In the first group, descriptive analysis of concentration indicators are common. Koren and Tenreyro (2007) or Cadot et al. (2011) confirm the existence of a U-shaped relationship using the Theil Index (1972) with a beta=1 that gives equal weight along the income distribution. However, this first group of techniques does not allow multivariate analysis and therefore the effects of a particular variable cannot be isolated, nor can the effects of other recurrent biases in the literature be adequately controlled.

The use of semi-parametric techniques is also widespread (kernel smoothing regressions, local weight polynomial regressions and generalized additive models) since they allow to analyze the form and statistical significance of the relationship between specialization and income without making any a priori assumptions about the functional form of that relationship (De Benedictis et al., 2009). With these techniques this authors show a growing relationship between trade diversification and economic development after controlling for country heterogeneity.

Among the parametric approaches, the use of econometric models with panel data are also frequent (Amiti, 1999; Brasili et al., 2000; Estevadeordal & Martincus, 2006; Imbs & Wacziarg, 2003; Kalemli-Ozcan et al., 2003; Kim, 1995; Koren & Tenreyro, 2007; Proudman & Redding, 2000; Redding, 2002). This approach allows to directly evaluate the statistical significance of the relationship between both variables. Imbs and Wacziarg (2003), find the U-shaped relationship through fixed-effect estimates between the level of diversification and the quadratic function of GDP per capita. The parametric approach allows for the inclusion of a series of additional controls, and the evaluation of different functional forms and distributions, however, it also implies facing a series of empirical challenges. (1) *Short-term noise control* to avoid possible outliers in the data and reduce the effects of short-term cycles and shocks; (2) *Censored dependent variables*: the indices of trade diversification are usually normalized to values between [0.1]; (3) *Serial autocorrelation*: when the error terms are not independent of each other, the estimators obtained are not efficient; (4) *Cross-dependence between individuals* are usually found, reflecting knowledge spillovers or dependencies between them (Chudik & Pesaran, 2015). This is because countries commonly face common factors such as technological and institutional conditions, as well as macroeconomic factors. On an international scale, globalization also induces correlations between these factors. These aspects generate bias and inefficiency in estimators (De Hoyos & Sarafidis, 2006); (5) *Heterogeneity between units and common shocks in time*: which can generate heteroscedasticity and bias by omitted variable; (6) *Endogeneity and reverse causality* which generates bias and inefficiency. In particular, diversification and the same complexity drive knowledge accumulation and economic growth (Parteka & Tamberi, 2013). These biases are usually corrected by instrumental variables, where a common practice is to use the generalized moment estimator -GMM-, introduced by Hansen (1982).

An additional aspect that has been relegated in the literature with respect to both the determinants of diversification and economic complexity, has to do with the non-stationary nature of the series, and spurious regressions. To avoid this problem, cointegration analyses have been used (Engle and Granger 1987) after analyzing the order of integration of the series through unit-root tests.

As empirical alternative, here short and long-term relationships between variables is analyzed. In addition, assumptions about the order of integration of the variables must be taken into account. One possibility is to use traditional Error Correction Vectors models (VCEM), however they only allow the use of integrated variables of order one, I(1), while the Auto Regressive Distributed Lag models (ARDL) allow the joint use of variables I(0) and I(1) (Pesaran et al., 1999).

Following Pesaran et al. (1999), the generic ARDL model includes lags in levels of both dependent and independent variables[11], but it can also be rewritten as an Error Correction Vector, which allows verifying both the short term relationships (variables in differences), and the long term ones (variables in levels). When the long term parameter is significant, there is a long term relationship between the analyzed variables, and it is even possible to calculate the convergence speed to equilibrium (stationary state).

The starting point is an ARDL(1,1) model with homogeneous coefficients:

$$Diversity = D_{c,0} = \sum_{p} M_{cp} \tag{3}$$

where $\alpha 1$ expresses the dynamic relationship of the equation, so that if it is significant and less than 1, the model is stable, and converges towards a stationary state or long-term equilibrium, xi_t is a matrix of explanatory variables, ηi $_c$ollects the fixed effects, and vit $_i$s the error term considered iid(0, $Ubiquity = U_{p,0} = \sum_{c} M_{cp}$). As mentioned above, following Pesaran et al. (1999) this equation can be rewritten as an error-correction vector as follows:

$$y_{it} = \alpha_0 + \alpha_1 y_{it-1} + x_{it}\beta_{1k} + x_{it-1}\beta_{2k} + \eta_i + v_{it} \tag{4}$$

where σ_v^2 is the long term coefficient of x_{it} asumed homogeneous for all i, while ϕ=($\alpha 1-_1$) is the error correction coefficient, that verifies the long term relationship between $\Delta y_{it} = \alpha_0 + \phi\left(y_{it-1} - x_{it-1}\gamma_k\right) + \Delta x_{it}\beta_{1k} + \eta_i + v_{it}$ and $\gamma_k = \dfrac{\beta_{1k} + \beta_{2k}}{1-\phi}$. If this estimator is significant and negative, it implies that these variables have a stable long-term relationship, and therefore they are cointegrated (Shin et al., 1999). γk captures how the equilibrium changes and ϕ shows the speed of adjustment to their equilibrium values, after receiving an external shock; x_{it-1} are the short-term effects of xi_t in yi_t (Ditzen, 2019).

However, the existence of cross-dependency bias is frequent in international trade analyses, an aspect commonly neglected. The identification of cross-dependency is done through the cross-sectional dependence (CD) test of Pesaran (2004), Friedman (1937) and Frees (1995, 2004), which analyses the correlation matrix of errors between individuals (De Hoyos & Sarafidis, 2006). Among the possibilities to correct this problem here a CS – ARDL model is calculated, which allows to estimate the long term coefficient maintaining the autoregressive term. Chudik et al. (2013) and Pesaran et al. (1999) show, based on Monte Carlo simulations, that once cross-dependence is controlled, this methodological alternative is robust to endogeneity.

The definitive specification of the CS–ARDL model is the following:

$$y_{it-1} \quad (5)$$

where *i* refers to the country, t to the year. $y_{i,t}$ is the complexity adjusted concentration index, calculated from the normalized Herfindahl Hirschman Index (HHI) and Theil Index - generalized entropy (a=2). x_{it} and Δx_{it} is the matrix of explanatory variables as summarized in Table 1, expressed in levels (long term) and in differences (short term). ϕ is the error correction coefficient, which allows measuring the speed of convergence to the stationary state in presence of short-term shocks. β_{1k} is the cross-section means matrix introduced to control for spatial correlation. On the other hand, the long-term coefficients of the regressors φk cannot be directly interpreted and it is required to express them as - $\Delta y_{it} = \alpha_0 + \phi\left(y_{it-1} - x_{it-1}\varphi_k\right) + \Delta x_{it}\beta_{1k} + z_t\beta_{2k} + \eta_i + v_{it}$ (Pesaran et al., 1999). Finally $z_t = \left(\bar{y}_t, \bar{x}_t\right)'$ is a vector of time fixed effects (δt_j, country (ηi) and the error term ($\frac{\varphi_k}{\phi} = \gamma_k$).

DIVERSIFICATION AND ECONOMIC COMPLEXITY. DETERMINANTS AND MEASURES

Economic complexity expresses the amount of knowledge embedded into the productive structure (Hausmann & Hidalgo, 2011), considering that this structure is a reflection of the capacities and networks of factors and inputs that each country has available to produce (Utkovski et al., 2018) and which in turn translates into their respective export baskets.

The complexity of an economy is related to the multiplicity of useful knowledge embedded in it. Knowledge base can be only expanded through the interaction of individuals in complex networks around the economic activity. This is how economic complexity can be measured, taking the combination of products generated by countries (The Observatory of Economic Complexity - OEC, nd). This vision places capacities, in a broad sense, as the main determinant of competitiveness and economic development (Mariani et al., 2015).

Among the first attempts to measure a certain type of economic complexity, Hummels and Klenow (2005), nuance the analysis of trade diversification by breaking it down into *intensive* (products already exported) and *extensive* (new products). Additionally, there are approaches based on the sophistication of exports (Hausmann et al., 2005; Herédia et al., 2010), but they do not differentiate which product is growing or joining the export basket.

As Hausmann et al. (2005) point out, exporting bananas is not the same as exporting broccoli, even though both are agricultural products; the inputs, services, and actors that broccoli articulates are more standardized and can be more easily adapted than bananas to other products. This favors the development of new products nearby and therefore their presence in the export portfolio marks different types of diversification. Under this logic, each country must follow its own development pattern based on its particular productive structure which determines its capacity to process new knowledge (Utkovski et al., 2018) and therefore new products, so the way to increase its knowledge base is by facilitating the formation of more complex networks (Hausmann & Hidalgo, 2011).

The act of exporting shows international markets the availability of inputs needed to produce them competitively (Hausmann & Rodrik, 2002), that is, it generates *information externalities*, which reduce the costs of introducing new products; this effect is amplified if the exported products require inputs that can serve many other products and sectors (*transversality condition*).

Hidalgo et al. (2007) address the study of complexity with an "agnostic" approach[5]. This is based on the premise that the possibility of exporting a product depends on the export of other products (*conditional probability*), considering that similar inputs are required for their production and export. To this end, they estimate the structures of the observed relationships or networks between exported products, where the most complex products would be those exported competitively (with *revealed comparative advantages*) by the most commercially diversified countries. Under this perspective, the literature also refers to the role of centrality in international trade networks (Gala et al., 2018).

In this sense, a country's complexity is related to the amount of knowledge incorporated into their products, while a product is more complex the fewer complex countries that are capable of exporting it competitively. Therefore, an export basket would be more complex the more intermediate goods it contains and the fewer countries that are capable of exporting them with revealed comparative advantages (Hidalgo et al., 2007).

This vision involves the consideration of differences in learning between industries, intra-industrial externalities (Hausmann & Rodrik, 2002; Vettas, 2000), but also inter-industrial spillovers (Jaffe, 1984). According to Hausmann and Klinger (2006) it also implies that the assets (capacities and inputs) required for one product are not perfect substitutes for those required for another product and their adaptability would depend on their proximity. Thus, trade diversification would be more related to the *transversality* of accumulated assets than to productive linkages (Hirschman, 1958) or investment complementarities (Rosenstein-Rodan, 1943).

The analysis of inputs transversality therefore starts from the perspective of complexity, where the central concept is the space-product, which can be understood as the representation of the similarity or closeness between products. Two products are very similar or very close if the inputs they require are similar, so it is very likely that, being close, they will be exported by the same country. This network is characterized by being heterogeneous (O'Clery, 2015), where there are products that use very transversal inputs, and products that demand very specific inputs, which can only be used in the production of a few additional products.

This introduces the idea that diversification patterns are related to the specificities of the components of the productive basket, that is, its level of complexity. Thus, unlike the models of diversification by variety (Aghion & Howitt, 1990) and product quality (Grossman & Helpman, 1991), the costs of introducing a new product are higher the further away they are from the productive structure analyzed. In other words, there is persistence in the structure, but an adequate knowledge of it can be used to encourage a jump to nearby sectors and to promote greater quality (complexity) of diversification.

Although there is an important development in terms of the importance and effects of economic complexity, there is still little literature on its determinants. It is considered to be a factor with strong explanatory power of the countries' income level (Hausmann & Hidalgo, 2011) and therefore the level of development and economic growth (Stojkoski & Kocarev, 2017) and even the distribution of income and equity (Hartmann et al., 2017). One of the few contributions can be found in Daude et al. (2016) who find that, like diversification metrics, complexity can be understood as a stock over time, where there is significant persistence. Additionally, they find a negative relationship with the terms of trade where an increase in relative export prices reduces the incentives to increase complexity. The study also shows significant, but not conclusive results for the case of devaluation. Finally, they find positive relationships for the availability and consumption of energy, government spending and capital per worker, and negative relationships for the availability of arable land and capital flows, reflecting the tilt of complexity and the role of financial market stability. Javorcik et al. (2018) include variables such as integration and foreign investment as factors that positively influence complexity levels.

Traditional measures of trade diversification such as Herfindahl-Hirschman, Theil or Gini indices, describe the distribution of the amount or volume of exports among different products or groups of products. However, they do not consider differences between the products they analyze, that is, for these indices it is the same to export a fruit or an electronic device. This constitutes an important limitation, since they do not distinguish the amount of productive knowledge that each product incorporates, nor its contribution to the possible appearance of other products in a certain commercial basket.

Regarding the measurement of complexity, Mariani et al. (2015) point out that there are two approaches, the *linear economic complexity index* proposed by Hausmann and Hidalgo (2011), and a *non-linear index* proposed by Tacchella et al. (2012) Both indices try to measure the amount of productive knowledge that each product or country contains, through an iterative system that relates two dimensions of complexity, by product (*ubiquity*) and by country (*diversity*). Both approaches start from the country-product matrix (M_{cp}), that connects each country to the products that it makes. A country with *Revealed Comparative Advantages* is represented with 1, zero otherwise[6]. This avoids problems of scale and allows better comparison and analysis of the relevant information of each country:

$$v_{i,t} = \eta_i + \delta_t + u_{i,t} \tag{1}$$

$$u_{i,t} \bullet N\left(0,1\right) \tag{2}$$

In both linear and non-linear versions, *diversity* in a country is defined as the number of economic activities in which a country is specialized (sum of the rows of the M_{cp} matrix), while the *ubiquity* of a product is related to the number of countries that produce it (sum of the columns of the M_{cp} matrix).

However, exporting many products competitively does not make a country complex, it requires exporting complex products. Similarly, if we take again the case of bananas, few countries export them, but that does not make them a complex product. If we consider the linear version proposed by Hausmann and Hidalgo (2011), the system corrects a country's diversity by the average of the "ubiquity" of the products it exports competitively, while ubiquity is corrected by the average of the "diversity" of the countries that export it competitively. From here the country complexity index can be obtained.[7]

Beyond the similarities and differences between both approaches (*linear economic complexity index* and a *non-linear index*), none of them manages to completely characterize the complexity of a country's exportable basket, since products in which there are no revealed comparative advantages are discarded (Balassa, 1965). This constitutes an important limitation for the analysis of the complexity of trade diversification, mainly in the case of economies with primary exportable baskets and nascent development processes where products are incorporated into the exportable supply, but not necessarily with comparative advantages (in Balassa's sense). To overcome these limitations, this research proposes the combination of both metrics, including all exported products, but considering their differences. For this purpose, the Herfindahl Hirschman concentration (HHI)[8] and generalized entropy (GE) indices[9] are adjusted by the complexity of each product, based on the *linear perspective* proposed by Hausmann and Hidalgo (2011). The resulting index describes the complexity of export diversification.

Complexity is measured using the Product Complexity Index (PCI), published by the Economic Complexity Observatory (OEC - Data Sources n.d.). This is a standardized variable that gives different order of magnitude to each product making them comparable. To avoid negative values, the index is normalized between 1 and 2 using the min-max rescaling[10].

On this basis, Herfindahl Hirschman Index (HHI) and the Generalized Entropy Index are calculated using these new weighted values, where more complex products are assigned a greater weight, and therefore their inclusion and growth have a greater influence on the corrected indices.

Control Variables and Sources of Information

Based on the literature, the five groups of variables described above are considered. The first group includes the accumulation of human, physical and financial capital as they are the basis of production possibilities (Acemoglu & Zilibotti, 1997; Aghion & Howitt, 2009). The scale or market size effect has usually been measured using population or GDP per capita (Alemu, 2009; Hummels & Klenow, 2005; Jetter & Hassan, 2015; Parteka & Tamberi, 2013). Here GDP per capita and its quadratic term is also used as an approximation of the country's level of development.

For human capital, most studies take indicators of school enrollment, years of schooling and even interactions with other variables[12]. For this purpose, Caselli's (2005) methodology is applied, generating a human capital index, built on the basis of the decreasing returns of years of schooling in the population over 25 years old. For physical capital, the literature has used the formation or stock of capital, the provision of infrastructure or the attraction of foreign direct investment, in relation to GDP or in per capita terms (in many cases they are included in a quadratic form). Here capital stock per capita is used. Finally, financial development has usually been measured through indicators related to the deepening of financial services, credit to the private sector or reforms to the financial scheme. To capture this dimension, bank credit to the private sector is considered as a percentage of GDP.

Another aspect that literature controls is the weight of primary sectors in each country. For example, OPEC partners or shares of primary sectors in GDP or exports are considered. These controls are especially relevant in the analysis of the economies of the Americas. In this case, natural resource revenues are included as a percentage of GDP.

The second group of indicators refers to the *costs of trade*. Traditionally, studies use indicators that indirectly reflect transaction costs in international trade such as distance to markets, contiguity, if they have a common language, among others. In other cases, indicators are taken to directly quantify the costs of exporting per container. In this work, the average distance to the partner, weighted by the partner's weight in each country's exports, will be used as a transaction cost factor.

A third group of variables is the *characteristics of the mark*et, with respect to competitiveness, macroeconomic stability and trade composition. Competitiveness and productivity are measured through indicators such as revealed comparative advantages, the PRODY[13], introduced by Hausmann et al. (2005), or the capital-product ratio. To measure macroeconomic stability, inflation has usually been taken, as well as indicators on exchange policy and its volatility (standard deviation) or terms of trade (Agosin et al., 2012). Here inflation is calculated as the growth rate of the GDP deflator. Two additional factors of trade composition are also introduced, namely intra-industry trade using the Grubel Lloyd index[14] (Martin-Mayoral et al., 2016).

Institutional aspects are also considered as political, cultural and even geographical factors. In the political sphere, political conflict as well as governance are the main elements. With respect to the orientation of trade policy and the degree of state intervention in the dynamics of trade diversification, literature normally collects them through indicators of trade openness, where the weight of exports and imports in the GDP is evaluated. In other cases, the existence of deliberate trade diversification programs is considered. An indicator of trade openness, measured as the percentage of the sum of exports and imports over GDP, is included here. Finally, in the geographical field, variables such as distance, common border and access to the sea are taken into account. However, considering that fixed effects will be used in the proposed analysis, a good part of the influence of cultural and geographical factors is eliminated.

The analysis covers 55 years and 19 countries in the Western Hemisphere from 1962 to 2017[15]. The export data corresponds to the databases published by The Growth Lab at Harvard University (2019) and the MIT Observatory of Economic Complexity ("OEC - Data Sources" n.d.), which in turn is constructed and refined based on the work of (Feenstra et al., 2005). Both sources calculate the complexity index by product using the linear method. This information allows the calculation of several elements of the proposed model, such as concentration and its correction for complexity or intra-industrial trade.

For the national accounts indicators, "Penn World Tables version 9" database (Feenstra et al., 2015) is used, from which GDP and capital stock per capita are obtained, both adjusted by chained purchasing power parity to be comparable among countries and over time. This information also allows the calculation of inflation and terms of trade by using the deflators of consumption, exports and imports respectively. This database also incorporates a human capital index, calculated with the methodology proposed by Caselli (2005) including decreasing rates of return for education.

This information is complemented with the World Bank's WDI - World Development Indicators, from which bank credit to private sector and the percentage of primary income over GDP are taken. On the other hand, the political variables are taken from the "Center for Systemic Peace", particularly from the database "Polity version 4" (Marshal & Elzinga-Marshal, 2017). This allows for the inclusion of conflict and governance in the analysis. For the first case, the severity of the violence is taken, while for governance, the number of coups d'état and the durability of the political regime are considered, that is, years of democracy, anocracy or autocracy.

Geographic and transaction cost variables are collected from the Center for Prospective Studies and International Information (CEPII) by Head et al. (2010), complemented with the work of (Gurevich et al., 2018); this information has been specifically developed for dynamic gravitational models, and allows the inclusion of variables such as distance and access to the sea.

RESULTS

First, the main characteristics of the variables considered for the analysis are reviewed, starting from a discussion about the combination of the concentration and economic complexity indices. Second, the results of the econometric analysis and discusses their implications are presented.

The analysis of trends in both the complexity index and exports can be considered as a proxy for the characterization of export growth with respect to complexity; that is, in those cases where exports grow faster than complexity, it implies that this growth is mostly driven by products of similar complexity to those already in existence, while if the opposite is observed, it can be considered that there is a tendency to substitute less for more complex products within the export basket.

Table 1. Variables, abbreviations used and sources of information

Group of variables	Variable	Indicator	Transformation	Abbreviation	Source
Complexity of export diversification	Diversification	Concentration index: Helfindahl Hirschman (HHI) Generalized Entropy (GE - a = 2)	ln	hh ge	CID - Harvard
	Product complexity	Concentration index (HHI, GE-a=2) corrected for product complexity	ln	hhw gew	CID - Harvard OEC - MIT
Level of development	Level of development	GDP per capita	ln	y	PWT
		GDP per capita squared	ln	y2	PWT
Factor endowment	Human capital	Human capital index	diff ln	ch	PWT
	Physical capital	Capital stock per capita	diff ln	sk	PWT
	Financial development	Credit to the private sector by banks (% of GDP)	ln	fin	WDI
	Primary factor endowment	Natural resource income (% of GDP)	ln	prim	WDI
Costs	Trade costs	Average distance to markets considered	ln	dist	CEEPII - GEODIST - USITC
Market characteristics	Macroeconomic stability	GDP deflator growth rate	ln	inf	PWT
		Terms of trade	ln	ti	PWT
	Trade composition	Intra-industry trade	ln	gl	CID - HARVARD
Trade policy	Trade policy	Exports + Imports (% GDP)	ln	open	PWT
Others	Politics	Governance stability index	none	gov	Polity IV
		Severity of political violence events	none	viol	Polity IV

Source: (Authors elaboration)

As shown in Figure 1, in most countries there has been a growing trend over the last six decades in both exports and complexity, with parallel trajectories until the early 2000s, and a general slowdown in complexity indices from that point onwards. In this sense, the dynamics observed in the most advanced countries, United States and Canada, during the last decades have shown a consistent growth in exports, but a decrease in the complexity indices. One possible explanation can be found considering the vision of global value chains, where developed countries are focusing more on product innovation processes and geographic deconcentration of production than on the direct export of the complex final product (WTO et al., 2019).

When comparing the dynamics of the complexity index and the concentration indices (Figure 2 and 3), there are important differences between these indicators. If complexity index increases and the

Figure 1. Evolution of exports and product complexity (right axis)
Note: *Black line: Exports (ln). Blue dotted line: Product complexity index (normalized and weighted)*

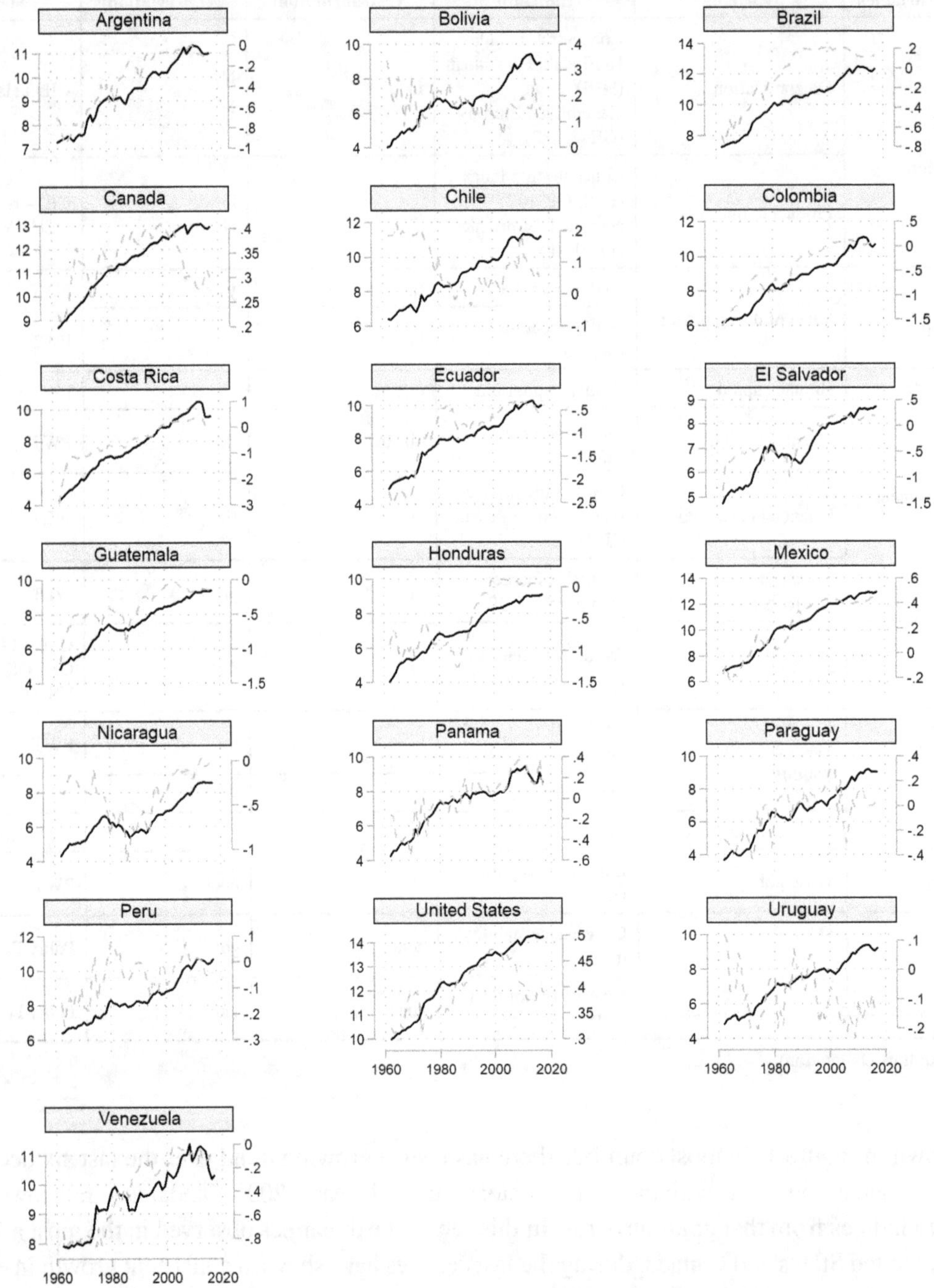

concentration index decreases, this implies that there have been gains in complexity, coupled with the introduction of new products (greater diversification), and that their dynamics are strengthening over time. If both indices grow, this implies that space is being gained in complexity in a few products (greater concentration).

Figure 2. Evolution of concentration (HHI index) and product complexity (right axis)
Note: *Higher HHI lower diversification Black line: Normalized HHI (ln). Blue dotted line: Product complexity index (normalized and weighted)*

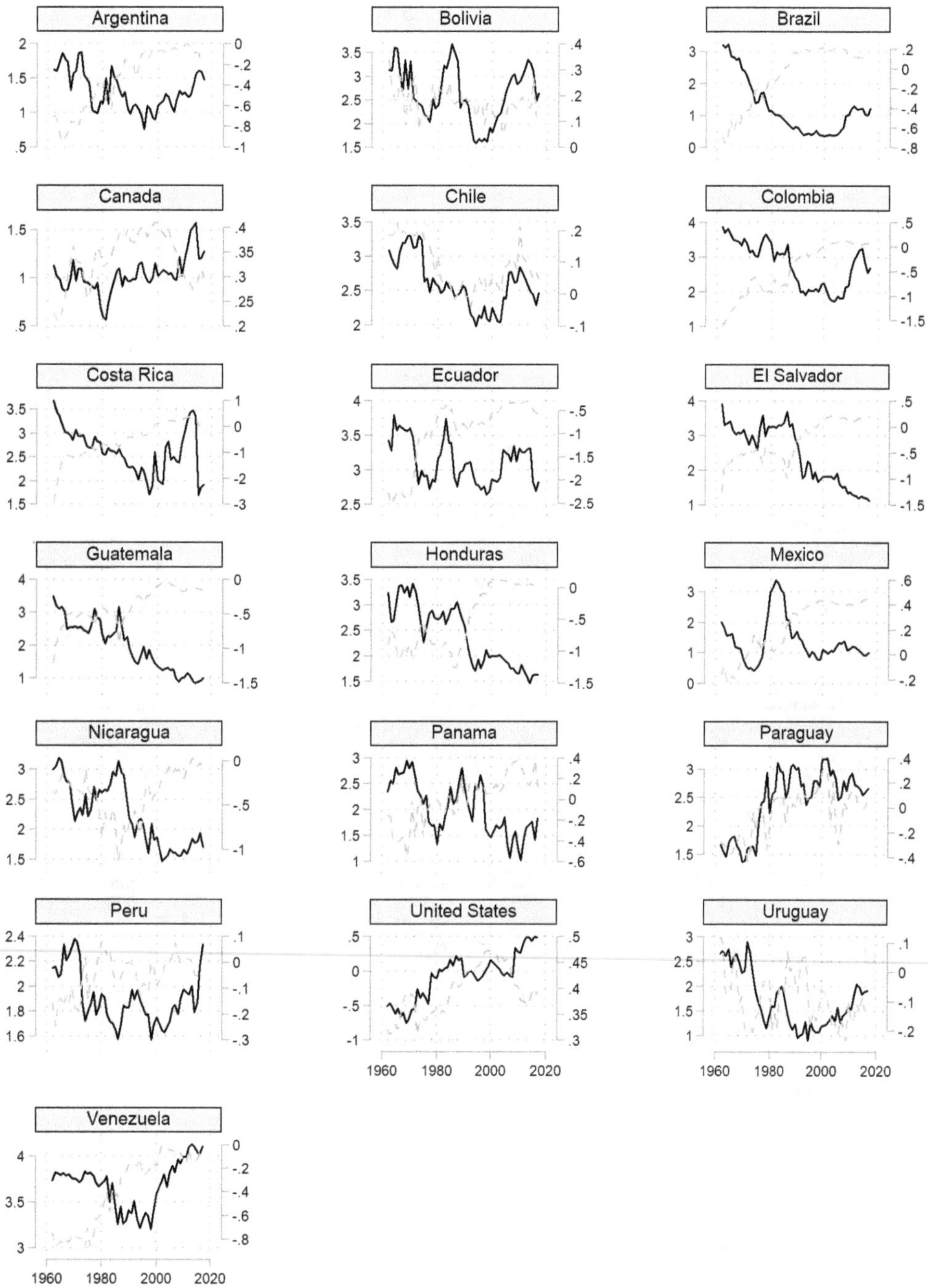

From the observation in Figure 1, 2 and 3, Brazil, El Salvador, Guatemala, Honduras, Panama and perhaps Costa Rica identify with the first case, gaining complexity and diversification at the same time. In the case of Brazil, the gap between complexity and export growth could be interpreted as reflect-

Figure 3. Evolution of the GE(a=2) index and the product complexity index (right axis)
Note: *Black line: GE(2) (ln). Blue dotted line: Product complexity index (normalized and weighted)*

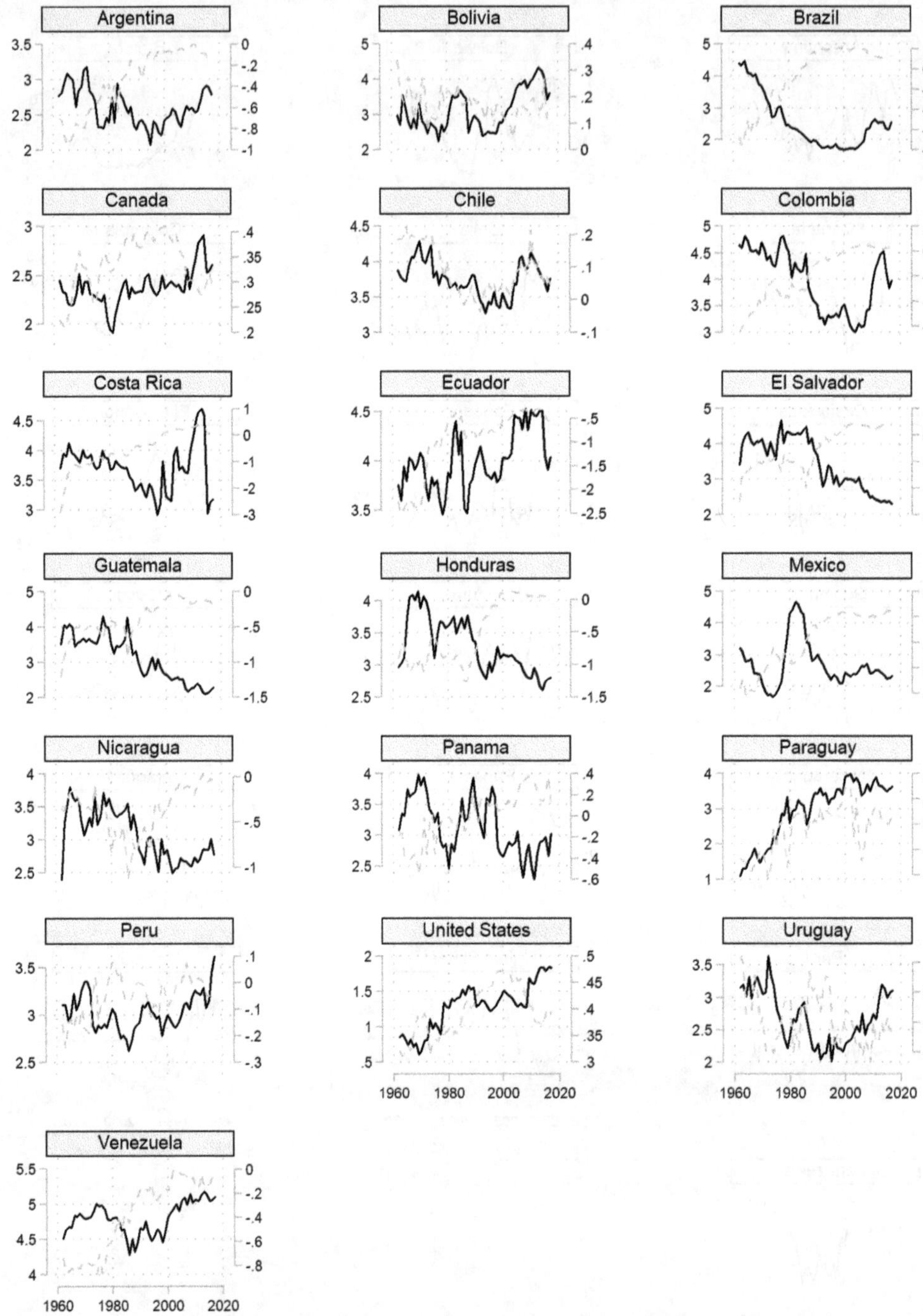

ing a substitution effect within the products in the export basket in favor of the more complex ones. In this sense, it can be inferred that the most complex products are concentrating and taking the lead in international trade. In the case of Argentina and Colombia, these characteristics were shared until the year 2000, while during the last decade they have increased the concentration of their export basket, but without gaining in trade complexity. Countries such as the United States, Paraguay and, to a lesser extent, Canada, have shown a trend towards concentration throughout the period analyzed, accompanied by greater complexity until 2000. Venezuela from 2000 onwards also seems to show this behavior. Finally, other countries such as Ecuador and Mexico seem to maintain their level of diversification although with ups and downs, but with an increase in complexity. Bolivia and Uruguay seem to have upward and downward peaks in the level of complexity.

Econometric Analysis

ARDL models have the advantage of being able to deal with different orders of integration between dependent and independent variables (Pesaran et al., 1999). However, it is important to first identify the order of integration of the different variables in order to avoid ending up exceeding the assumption made.

Table 2. Results of the unit roots tests (panel) - P-values for each test

Ha:	ADF-FISHER			P.Perron-Fisher			IPS			IPS with trend			Order of integration
	I(0)	I(1)	I(2)	I(0)	I(1)	I(2)	I(0)	I(1)	I(2)	I(0)	I(1)	I(2)	
Hh	0.03	-	-	-	-	-	0.03	-	-	0.39	-	-	I(0)
Hhw	-	-	-	-	-	-	-	-	-	0.05	-	-	I(0)
Ge	0.05	-	-	0.02	-	-	0.05	-	-	0.31	-	-	I(0)
Gew	0.00	-	-	-	-	-	0.00	-	-	0.09	-	-	I(0)
Y	1.00	-	-	1.00	-	-	1.00	-	-	0.80	-	-	I(1)
Lch	1.00	0.00	-	0.04	-	-	1.00	0.00	-	1.00	0.02	-	I(1)
Lsk	0.59	-	-	-	-	-	0.65	-	-	0.02	-	-	I(1)
Fin	0.09	-	-	0.21	-	-	0.09	-	-	0.09	-	-	I(1)
Prim	-	-	-	-	-	-	-	-	-	-	-	-	I(0)
Open	0.04	-	-	0.02	-	-	0.04	-	-	0.09	-	-	I(0)
Inf	-	-	-	-	-	-	-	-	-	-	-	-	I(0)
Ti	-	-	-	-	-	-	-	-	-	-	-	-	I(0)
Gl	-	-	-	-	-	-	-	-	-	0.05	-	-	I(0)
Viol	-	-	-	-	-	-							I(0)
Gov	-	-	-	-	-	-							I(0)

Note: P-values on the null hypothesis of unit root in all groups. In the case of Fisher-type tests, the p-value of the inverse of Z is taken as the most robust measure for the analysis (Choi, 2001)

Table 2 shows the p-values of the different tests that evaluate the unit-root null hypothesis for the variables in levels and first differences. Values greater than 0.05 imply that the unit-root null hypothesis cannot be rejected. In this way, all the variables included in the model are I(0) or I(1), which allows the original assumptions of the ARDL model to be maintained.

Another important element to review is the level of *collinearity* in the explanatory variables, since a high level of correlation between them could lead to premature rejection of the significance of the variables considered because they generate variance inflation (Das, 2019). One of the most widely used indices is the condition index proposed by Belsley et al. (1981), indicating that the problem is weak if an index of less than 10 is obtained, moderate if it is up to 30, and strong if it exceeds 30 points. By using auxiliary regressions between the regressors, the so-called Variance Inflation Factors (VIF) are constructed in order to measure the degree to which the variance of the different coefficients is over-estimated (inflated) due to the correlations with the other regressors. Values of VIF higher than 10 are defined as a serious problem (Das, 2019).

Table 3. Condition indices and variance inflation factor

Country	Condition index	Average IVF
Argentina	11.7	7.0
Bolivia	9.9	5.3
Brazil	9.5	4.9
Canada	17.0	11.2
Chile	13.0	8.2
Colombia	7.9	4.7
Costa Rica	6.1	3.0
Ecuador	8.1	4.5
El Salvador	7.2	4.0
United States	23.1	17.1
Guatemala	10.1	5.2
Honduras	7.5	4.5
Mexico	9.5	5.1
Nicaragua	5.3	2.5
Panama	5.6	3.0
Paraguay	7.3	3.4
Peru	9.8	4.7
Uruguay	7.1	3.9
Venezuela	8.9	4.4
All (Pooled)	2.8	1.4

Note: Estimated values without constant. It includes regressors for the dimensions of level of development (y), factor endowments (human, capital, financial, primary), macroeconomic factors and trade policy.

As can be seen in Table 3, the condition indices in the variables of each of the countries analyzed do not exceed a value of 30, while the value for the whole group reflects a condition indicator of 2.8; this shows that multicollinearity would not be a serious problem (Belsley et al., 1981). This is also reflected in the respective Variance Inflation Factors which on average do not exceed a value of 10, except for the case of the United States and Canada. However, the analysis of the group as a whole rule out the possibility of a serious problem, since the VIF reaches 1.4.

Another aspect to take into account is *cross sectional dependence* as it generates bias and inefficiency in the estimators, which can lead to erroneous conclusions about the level of significance of the variables, their magnitude, and even their sign (De Hoyos and Sarafidis, 2006). In this case, tests of Friedman (1937), Frees (1995) and Pesaran (2004) are considered.

These tests start from the ordinary least-squares version of the model, including fixed effects, and examine the structure of the cross-section correlation matrix. Thus, the null hypothesis is the absence of correlation or cross-dependence. Table 4 shows the p-values of each test against different specifications. In practically all cases the existence of cross independence is rejected, particularly in the simplest models where the incidence of spatial correlation is evident, while some specifications tested pass the Pesaran test, none pass the Friedman or Frees tests. De Hoyos and Sarafidis (2006) recommend considering only the Frees test in cases where the first two fail to reject the null hypothesis. This is because the latter also considers the possibility of alternate signs in the correlations within the model, so that they end up compensating each other and causing the first two tests to fail. In this sense, the tests indicate the existence of cross-dependence in all the specifications considered. To control these biases a transformation into deviations from the cross-sectional means for the variables of the model will be used.

Table 4. Cross-correlation tests (spatial correlation)

		HHI			HHI corrected			GE (α=2)			GE (α=2) corrected	
	a	b	c	a	B	c	a	b	c	a	b	c
Pesaran	0.00	0.00	0.30	0.00	0.00	0.14	0.00	0.00	0.65	0.02	0.27	0.21
Friedman	0.00	0.00	0.00	0.00	0.00	0.00	0.00	0.00	0.00	0.00	0.00	0.00
Frees	0.00	0.00	0.00	0.00	0.00	0.00	0.00	0.00	0.00	0.00	0.00	0.00

Note: p-values under the null hypothesis of absence of cross-dependence. a. Includes GDP and GDP squared as regressors; b. Includes factor endowment; c. Includes the other variables.

Finally, it is necessary to review the assumptions regarding homogeneity or heterogeneity both in the short- and long-term slopes, as well as in the adjustment coefficients. In this sense, following (Pesaran et al., 1999) it is required to test the consistency of these assumptions by evaluating if the model can adjust to the restrictions of homogeneity in the slopes (fixed-effect dynamic estimator - DFE), or to the version with heterogeneity in all the slopes (group mean estimator - MG), where the distribution of the slope vectors in each group is analyzed, or the intermediate version that allows weak homogeneity (group mean pool estimator - PMG), where homogeneity is assumed only in the long-term slopes.

To evaluate the different alternatives in the specification, an iterative process is considered that starts from a non-linear and linear relationship with respect to the GDP, and then the different variables considered in the analysis are included. For each group of regressors the three versions are estimated and compared using a Hausman test, so that the existence or not of homogeneity in the slopes can be identified in each specification (see Tables 5 and 6).

The results reflect that for most variables the null hypothesis of strict homogeneity cannot be rejected. On the other hand, when comparing the fixed-effects estimator with the PMG, the latter turns out to be less efficient in most cases, which reinforces the strict homogeneity hypothesis. On this basis, in this

Table 5. Homogeneity analysis of the coefficients, Hausman's test - quadratic specification for the GDP

Variable		Ho: Homogeneity		
		Strong	Weak	
Dependent	Independent+	MG vs DFE	MG vs PMG	DFE vs PMG
HHI	y	0.07	0.22	-
	ch	0.14	0.57	-
	sk	-	0.78	-
	fin	0.05	0.11	-
	prim	-	0.44	-
	open	0.40	0.39	-
	gl	0.05	0.52	-
	inf	0.41	0.59	-
	ti	0.06	0.59	-
HHI corrected	y	0.34	0.42	0.76
	ch	0.29	0.51	0.01
	sk	0.30	0.65	-
	fin	0.02	0.90	0.04
	prim	0.02	0.91	0.23
	open	0.04	0.07	0.53
	gl	0.11	0.39	-
	inf	-	0.53	0.02
	ti	0.09	0.07	-
GE (α=2)	y	0.34	0.48	-
	ch	-	0.74	-
	sk	1.00	0.49	-
	fin	0.15	0.28	0.18
	prim	0.91	0.39	-
	open	0.85	0.62	0.89
	gl	-	0.56	-
	inf	0.98	0.80	-
	ti	-	0.73	-
GE (α=2) corrected	y	0.26	0.48	0.01
	ch	0.41	0.75	-
	sk	0.07	0.72	-
	fin	0.32	0.79	0.02
	prim	-	0.60	0.03
	open	0.03	0.22	0.32
	gl	0.09	0.29	-
	inf	-	0.49	-
	ti	0.02	0.37	0.02

Note: p-values of the Hausman test under the different null hypotheses of homogeneity
MG: mean group, DFE: dynamic fixed effects, PMG: pooled mean group.
In all cases the regression includes a linear or non-linear relationship with respect to GDP, in this way the test is carried out considering this base specification and adding the respective variable. Additionally, in order to control for spatial correlation, all regressions include cross-section means for the dependent and independent variables.

Table 6. Coefficient homogeneity analysis, Hausman's test - linear specification for GDP

Variable		Ho: Homogeneity		
		Strong	Weak	
Dependent	Independent+	MG vs DFE	MG vs PMG	DFE vs PMG
HHI corrected - linear	y	0.29	0.47	0.70
	ch	0.02	0.10	0.58
	sk	0.88	0.63	0.04
	fin	-	0.99	0.16
	prim	-	0.64	0.43
	open	0.06	0.07	0.68
	gl	0.06	0.43	0.66
	inf	0.69	0.92	0.84
	ti	0.32	0.70	0.86
GE (α=2) corrected - linear	y	0.15	0.36	0.13
	ch	0.54	0.55	0.13
	sk	0.58	0.55	0.06
	fin	0.52	0.44	0.02
	prim	0.01	0.76	0.23
	open	0.08	0.24	0.43
	gl	0.07	0.34	0.07
	inf	0.55	0.61	0.77
	ti	0.01	0.46	0.08

Note: p-values of the Hausman test under the different null hypotheses of homogeneity
MG: mean group, DFE: dynamic fixed effects, PMG: pooled mean group.
In all cases the regression includes a linear or non-linear relationship with respect to GDP, in this way the test is carried out considering this base specification and adding the respective variable. Additionally, in order to control for spatial correlation, all regressions include cross-section means for the dependent and independent variables.

work the estimates will be made assuming strict homogeneity in the slopes and adjustment coefficients (i.e., the fixed-effects estimator - FED).

SOLUTIONS AND RECOMMENDATIONS

The results of the analysis for each of the specifications are summarized in Tables 7 and 8. Convergence is found in all equations, since their values ϕ are negative and significant at 1% of confidence and their absolute values are less than 1. The adjustment rate is between 10% and 20% higher in the models that include the correction for complexity, which means that there are more stable relationships.

The results for uncorrected concentration indices are consistent with the literature (Cadot et al., 2011; De Benedictis et al., 2009), since they present a non-linear relationship between GDP and each index, which implies that there is a maximum level of diversification from which countries tend to re-concentrate their export basket as they develop (Imbs & Wacziarg, 2003), presumably in more complex products. However, when the indices are corrected for product complexity, this non-linear relationship is no longer consistent (the quadratic term of GDP (*y2*) is no longer significant), since the knowledge factor is internalized. With these elements, the higher the income level, the higher the level of concentration in complex products.

In contrast to Agosin et al. (2012), the results suggest that the development of the financial market (*fin*) strengthens the dynamics of trade diversification (negative related to concentration index), mainly for more complex products, since the long-term elasticities of the model that consider the complexity correction are higher than the unweighted model.

On the other hand, intra-industry trade (*gl*) patterns do not influence the long-term dynamics of trade diversification, however, in the short term they do allow for a reduction in concentration indices, possibly because they contribute to stimulate trade between countries with a similar set of inputs, which in turn allows for the influence of learning patterns within the same basket of products (Hausmann & Rodrik, 2002; Vettas, 2000). However, there is no evidence that they are significant in the models weighted by complexity.

Considering the dynamics of the terms of trade (*ti*), significant parameters are found in the long term, where it is shown that an increase in the relative prices of exports versus imports favors specialization patterns by reducing incentives to diversify the export basket (Agosin et al., 2012; Daude et al., 2016). However, no significant evidence is found on the complexity corrected indices, which could imply that this relationship does not affect the more complex products.

Regarding transaction costs (*distw*), it is found that in all cases it generates difficulties for diversification (Parteka & Tamberi, 2013), both in the short and long term.

With respect to the discussion on trade policy orientation (*open*), it is found that trade liberalization puts pressure on specialization in the short term, but, although the evidence is not conclusive, it would seem to encourage a long-term diversification trajectory. On the other hand, in complexity-corrected models, openness seems to positively influence concentration on complex products in the long term. However, to confirm these results, a bilateral version would be required to identify the heterogeneities existing in the different processes of trade opening.

Finally, no significant results are found in the inclusion of political and governance variables in the long term, only the events of violence present short-term effects in the diversification patterns, since political instability introduces more uncertainty in markets and even adds transaction costs that complicate the permanence of trade flows.

FUTURE RESEARCH DIRECTIONS

There are important aspects to deepen the analysis in order to advance in the understanding of the trade dynamics expressed by the indicators analyzed, and which constitute important areas of future work:

- Based on the tests applied, specification alternatives should be examined with respect to the homogeneity of the short and long term slopes, however, it is important to extend the analysis to include two sources of heterogeneity:
    - A bilateral version of the model: This would allow the identification of differentiated impacts between different variables, trade integration agreements, type of bilateral trade, etc.

Table 7. CS-ARDL estimation: HHI and GE (a=2) uncorrected indices

	HHI				GE (a=2)			
	Fixed effect		EE corrected		Fixed effect		EE corrected	
	Quadratic	Linear	Quadratic	Linear	Quadratic	Linear	Quadratic	Linear
Coef. adjust (Φ)	-0.15***	-0.15***	-0.12***	-0.13***	-0.13***	-0.13***	-0.12***	-0.13***
Long term coefficients								
y	-0.57***	-0.63***	-0.70***	-0.61***	-0.46***	-0.51***	-0.59***	-0.47**
y2	0.03***	0.04***	0.04***	0.03***	0.03***	0.03***	0.03***	0.03**
fin	-0.03***	-0.03***	-0.02	-0.02	-0.03**	-0.03**	-0.01	-0.01
open	-0.01	0.01	-0.06*	-0.03	0.00	0.02	-0.03	0.00
ti	0.15***	0.13***	0.16***	0.16***	0.15***	0.14**	0.20***	0.20***
distw		0.04*		0.13**		0.04*		0.10**
Sort term coefficients								
D.fin	-0.03	-0.03	-0.05*	-0.04**	-0.03	-0.02	-0.04**	-0.04**
D.open	0.06	0.08	0.09*	0.08	0.12*	0.14*	0.14***	0.14***
D.gl	-0.29***	-0.25***	-0.30***	-0.26***	-0.22***	-0.18***	-0.24***	-0.20***
D.distw		0.67***		0.65***		0.60***		0.58***
Cross-dependency								
Averages CS	Yes	Yes	No	No	Yes	Yes	No	No
Average in i	Yes	Yes	No	No	Yes	Yes	No	No
r2_w	0.20	0.27	0.16	0.23	0.17	0.22	0.14	0.20
r2_b	0.28	0.40			0.07	0.22		
r2_o	0.20	0.27			0.17	0.22		
rho	0.00	0.00			0.00	0.00		
N	966	966	966	966	966	966	966	966

$^{*} p < 0.10$, $^{**} p < 0.05$, $^{***} p < 0.01$

Note: Fixed effects: dynamic estimator of fixed effects, with spatial correlation controls incorporating averages between individuals at each t, and averages over time for each individual.

EE-Corrected: fixed-effects dynamic estimator, which controls for cross-dependence by correcting for variables based on (Driscoll & Kraay, 1998) deviations from cross-sectional means and adjusted variance matrix.

    ◦ Relaxing the assumption of homogeneous slopes and examining the case by case of the countries.
- It is important to examine the different combined effects between the explicative variables, for example Agosin et al. (2012) show how the terms of trade impact differently between countries with greater human capital.
- In some cases, the evidence presented does not allow for conclusive results; further analysis is needed in the case of distance, terms of trade, complexity and trade diversification.
- Finally, there are other areas of analysis that could be incorporated, including as determinants of diversification, for example, the role of centrality in international trade networks.

Table 8. CS ARDL estimation: HHI and GE (a=2) corrected for complexity

	HHI corrected				GE (a=2) corrected			
	Quadratic		Linear		Quadratic		Linear	
	EF	EE corr	EF	EE corr	EF	EE corr	EF	EE corr
Coef. adjust (Φ)	-0.15***	-0.16***	-0.15***	-0.16***	-0.14***	-0.15***	-0.14***	-0.14***
Long term coefficients								
y	-0.06	0.53*	0.03***	0.10***	0.03	0.71**	0.03***	0.10***
y2	0.01	-0.02			-0.00	-0.03**		
fin	-0.04***	-0.05*	-0.04***	-0.05*	-0.04***	-0.04*	-0.04***	-0.04
open	0.03*	0.01	0.03*	0.01	0.04***	0.05	0.04***	0.05
distw	0.05**	0.11*	0.05**	0.09*	0.05**	0.08	0.05**	0.06
Sort term coefficients								
D.distw	0.96**	0.93***	0.96**	0.93***	0.85**	0.83***	0.85**	0.84***
D.viol	0.03	0.03**	0.03	0.03**	0.03	0.03**	0.03	0.03**
Cross-dependency								
Averages CS	Yes	No	Yes	No	Yes	No	Yes	No
Average in i	Yes	No	Yes	No	Yes	No	Yes	No
r2_w	0.20	0.18	0.20	0.18	0.17	0.16	0.17	0.16
r2_b	0.47		0.42		0.34		0.34	
r2_o	0.20		0.20		0.17		0.17	
rho	0.00		0.00		0.00		0.00	
N	970	970	970	970	970	970	970	970

* $p < 0.10$, ** $p < 0.05$, *** $p < 0.01$

Note: Fixed effects: dynamic estimator of fixed effects, with spatial correlation controls incorporating averages between individuals at each t, and averages over time for each individual.

EE-Corrected: fixed-effects dynamic estimator, which controls for cross-dependence by correcting for variables based on (Driscoll & Kraay, 1998) deviations from cross-sectional means and adjusted variance matrix.

CONCLUSION

This study has focused on analyzing differences in the determinants of trade diversification patterns when considering the complexity of exports. To this end, the complexity index per product proposed by Hausmann and Hidalgo (2011) was merged with the traditional measures of diversification (generalized entropy and HHI). From the methodological point of view, a CS-ARDL parametric model was used to control, among other biases, the cross-section dependence and at the same time to distinguish the short and long-term dynamics.

The approach used allows visualizing the importance of including complexity in the analysis of trade diversification. The results show differences in the main determinants of trade diversification patterns after considering the complexity of exports. One of the main ones is that under these adjustments a U-shaped relationship is no longer maintained between diversification and the level of development reported in the literature (Cadot et al., 2011; Imbs & Wacziarg, 2003). In other words, after considering complexity it is observed that the higher the income level, the greater the concentration in complex products.

The proposed adjustments reflect more stable relationships, since the models that consider complexity adjust between 10% and 20% faster to their long-term trend than with traditional indicators. In general, there is a correspondence between the determinants of traditional trade diversification and the complexity-corrected indicators, however, there are significant differences in both short-term and long-term perspectives.

With respect to the long-term relationships, the results underline the importance of the development of financial markets as it drives the dynamics of diversification, especially for the more complex products. Important policy challenges for further financial deepening emerge from these results.

Terms of trade affect the less complex products to a greater extent, as their negative effect is not significant in the complexity adjusted indices. In this sense, it can be considered that when confronting an increment in the relative prices of exports, the incentives to maintain a certain structure end up dominating, as opposed to the possibility of capturing better commercial conditions, thus favoring specialization patterns (Agosin et al., 2012; Daude et al., 2016).

The introduction and maintenance of more complex products implies a series of different incentives that are not significantly affected by transaction costs, trade openness and intra-industry trade, which have a greater influence on less complex products, especially in the long term. Thus, in the case of intra-industrial trade it is found that in the short term, if they allow for a reduction in concentration rates, these dynamic feeds the learning patterns within the same basket of products (Hausmann & Rodrik, 2002; Vettas, 2000), however this dynamic does not generate significant impacts on the more complex products.

In sum, policy implications include the importance of financial deepening, especially for the incorporation of more complex products into the export basket, as well as the role of political and economic stability within trade patterns. On the other hand, considering that the costs of introducing a new product are higher the further away they are from the productive structure analyzed which means that there is persistence in the structure, an adequate knowledge of it can be used to encourage a jump to nearby sectors and to promote greater quality (complexity) of diversification.

REFERENCES

Acemoglu, D., & Zilibotti, F. (1997). Was Prometheus unbound by chance? Risk, diversification, and growth. *Journal of Political Economy*, *105*(4), 709–751. doi:10.1086/262091

Aghion, P., & Howitt, P. (1990). A model of growth through creative destruction. *Econometrica*, *60*(2), 323–351. doi:10.2307/2951599

Aghion, P., & Howitt, P. (2009). *The economics of growth*. The MIT Press. http://eprints.ucl.ac.uk/17829/

Agosin, M. R. (2009). Crecimiento y diversificación de exportaciones en economías emergentes. *Revista CEPAL*, *97*(97), 117–134. doi:10.18356/0e25c429-es

Agosin, M. R., Alvarez, R., & Bravo-Ortega, C. (2012). Determinants of export diversification around the world: 1962-2000. *World Economy*, *35*(3), 295–315. doi:10.1111/j.1467-9701.2011.01395.x

Alemu, A. M. (2009). Determinants of vertical and horizontal export diversification: Evidences from Sub-Saharan Africa and East Asia. *Ethiopian Journal of Economics*, *17*(2), 1–56. doi:10.4314/eje.v17i2.47311

Amiti, M. (1999). Specialization patterns in Europe. *Weltwirtschaftliches Archiv*, *135*(4), 573–593. doi:10.1007/BF02707385

Balassa, B. (1965). Trade liberalisation and "revealed" comparative advantage 1. *Manchester School*, *33*(2), 99–123. doi:10.1111/j.1467-9957.1965.tb00050.x

Baldwin, R. E. (1971). Determinants of the commodity structure of U.S. Trade. *The American Economic Review*, *61*(1), 126–146.

Belsley, D., Kuh, E., & Welsch, R. (1981). Regression diagnostics - identifying influential data and sources of collinearity. *The Journal of the Operational Research Society*, *32*(2), 157–158. doi:10.1057/jors.1981.33

Brasili, A., Epifani, P., & Helg, R. (2000). On the dynamics of trade patterns. *De Economist*, *148*(2), 233–258. doi:10.1023/A:1004065229330

Cadot, O., Carrere, C., & Strauss-Kahn, V. (2011). Export diversification: What's behind the hump? *The Review of Economics and Statistics*, *93*(2), 590–605. doi:10.1162/REST_a_00078

Caselli, F. (2005). Accounting for cross-country income differences. In P. Aghion & S. Durlauf (Eds.), *Handbook of Economic Growth* (pp. 679–741). North-Holland.

Chakrabarti, A. S. (2018). Dispersion in macroeconomic volatility between the core and periphery of the international trade network. *Journal of Economic Dynamics & Control*, *88*, 31–50. doi:10.1016/j.jedc.2018.01.019

Chudik, A., Mohaddes, K., Pesaran, M. H., & Raissi, M. (2013). *Debt, inflation and growth: Robust estimation of long-run effects in dynamic panel data models. Center for Applied Financial Economics*. CAFE.

Chudik, A., & Pesaran, M. H. (2015). Common correlated effects estimation of heterogeneous dynamic panel data models with weakly exogenous regressors. *Journal of Econometrics*, *188*(2), 393–420. doi:10.1016/j.jeconom.2015.03.007

Das, P. (2019). *Econometrics in Theory and Practice*. Springer. doi:10.1007/978-981-32-9019-8

Daude, C., Nagengast, A., & Perea, J. R. (2016). Productive capabilities: An empirical analysis of their drivers. *The Journal of International Trade & Economic Development*, *25*(4), 504–535. doi:10.1080/09638199.2015.1073342

Davis, D. R., & Weinstein, D. E. (2001). An account of global factor trade. *The American Economic Review*, *91*(5), 1423–1453. doi:10.1257/aer.91.5.1423

De Benedictis, L., Gallegati, M., & Tamberi, M. (2009). Overall trade specialization and economic development: Countries diversify. *Review of World Economics*, *145*(1), 37–55. doi:10.100710290-009-0007-4

De Ferranti, D., Lederman, D., Maloney, W. E., & Perry, G. E. (2002). *From natural resources to the knowledge economy: Trade and job quality*. Wold Bank. *Latin American and Caribbean Ethnic Studies*. Advance online publication. doi:10.1596/0-8213-5009-9

De Hoyos, R. E., & Sarafidis, V. (2006). Testing for cross-sectional dependence in panel-data models. *The Stata Journal*, *6*(4), 482–496. doi:10.1177/1536867X0600600403

De Piñeres, S. A. G., & Ferrantino, M. (1997). Export diversification and structural dynamics in the growth process: The case of Chile. *Journal of Development Economics*, *52*(2), 375–391. doi:10.1016/S0304-3878(96)00446-4

Dennis, A., & Shepherd, B. (2011). Trade facilitation and export diversification. *World Economy*, *34*(1), 101–122. doi:10.1111/j.1467-9701.2010.01303.x

Ditzen, J. (2019). *Estimating long-run effects in models with cross-sectional dependence using xtdcce2*. CEERP Working Paper Series 007, Centre for Energy Economics Research and Policy, Heriot-Watt University.

Driscoll, J. C., & Kraay, A. C. (1998). Consistent covariance matrix estimation with spatially dependent panel data. *The Review of Economics and Statistics*, *80*(4), 549–559. doi:10.1162/003465398557825

Edwards, L., & Lawrence, R. (2006). *South African trade policy matters: Trade performance and trade policy*. NBER Working Paper Series 12760. doi:10.1111/j.1468-0351.2008.00338.x

Engle, R. F., & Granger, C. W. J. (1987). Co-integration and error correction: Representation, estimation, and testing. *Econometrica*, *55*(2), 251–256. doi:10.2307/1913236

Estevadeordal, A., & Volpe Martincus, C. (2006). *Specialization and diverging manufacturing structures: The aftermath of trade policy reforms in developing countries*. Development Studies Working Papers 220.

Feenstra, R. C., Inklaar, R., & Timmer, M. P. (2015). The next generation of the Penn World Table. *The American Economic Review*, *105*(10), 3150–3182. doi:10.1257/aer.20130954

Feenstra, R. C., Lipsey, R. E., Deng, H., Ma, A. C., & Mo, H. (2005). *World Trade Flows: 1962-2000*. NBER Working Paper 11040. doi:10.3386/w11040

Fonchamnyo, D. C., & Akame, A. (2017). Determinants of export diversification in Sub-Sahara African region: A fractionalized logit estimation model. *Journal of Economics and Finance*, *41*(2), 330–342. doi:10.100712197-016-9352-z

Frees, E. W. (1995). Assessing cross-sectional correlation in panel data. *Journal of Econometrics*, *69*(2), 393–414. doi:10.1016/0304-4076(94)01658-M

Friedman, M. (1937). The use of ranks to avoid the assumption of normality implicit in the analysis of variance. *Journal of the American Statistical Association*, *32*(200), 675–701. doi:10.1080/01621459.1937.10503522

Gala, P., Camargo, J., & Freitas, E. (2018). The Economic Commission for Latin America and the Caribbean (ECLAC) was right: Scale-free complex networks and core-periphery patterns in world trade. *Cambridge Journal of Economics*, *42*(3), 633–651. doi:10.1093/cje/bex057

Ghani, E., Grover Goswami, A., & Kharas, H. (2012). *Service with a smile*. openknowledge.worldbank.org

Greenaway, D., Hine, R., & Milner, C. (1995). Vertical and horizontal intra-industry trade: A cross industry analysis for the United Kingdom. *Economic Journal (London)*, *105*(433), 1505–1518. doi:10.2307/2235113

Grossman, G. M., & Helpman, E. (1991). Quality ladders in the theory of growth. *The Review of Economic Studies*, *58*(1), 43. doi:10.2307/2298044

Gurevich, T., Herman, P., Abbyad, N., Demirkaya, M., Drenski, A., Horowitz, J., & Kenneally, K. (2018). *The Dynamic Gravity Dataset: 1948-2016.* Economics Working Paper 2018-02-A. U.S. International Trade Commission.

Haddad, M., Jerome Lim, J., Pancaro, C., & Saborowski, C. (2013). Trade openness reduces growth volatility when countries are well diversified. *The Canadian Journal of Economics. Revue Canadienne d'Economique*, *46*(2), 765–790. doi:10.1111/caje.12031

Hamid, Z. (2010). Concentration of exports and patterns of trade: A time-series evidence of Malaysia. *Journal of Developing Areas*, *43*(2), 255–270. doi:10.1353/jda.0.0065

Hammouda, H. B., Karingi, S., Njuguna, A., & Sadni Jallab, M. (2006). Diversification: Towards a new paradigm for Africa's development. Munich Personal RePEc Archive, 35.

Hansen, L. P. (1982). Large sample properties of generalized method of moments estimators. *Econometrica*, *50*(4), 1029. doi:10.2307/1912775

Hartmann, D., Guevara, M. R., Jara-Figueroa, C., Aristarán, M., & Hidalgo, C. A. (2017). Linking economic complexity, institutions, and income inequality. *World Development*, *93*, 75–93. doi:10.1016/j.worlddev.2016.12.020

Hausmann, R., & Hidalgo, C. A. (2011). *The Atlas of Economic Complexity - mapping paths to prosperity*. Massachusetts Institute of Technology. https://atlas.cid.harvard.edu/media/atlas/pdf/HarvardMIT_AtlasOfEconomicComplexity.pdf

Hausmann, R., Hwang, J., & Rodrik, D. (2005). *What you export matters.* NBER Working Paper 11905. doi:10.3386/w11905

Hausmann, R., & Klinger, B. (2006). *Structural transformation and patterns of comparative advantage in the product space*. Center for International Development. doi:10.2139srn.939646

Hausmann, R., & Klinger, B. (2007). *The structure of the product space and the evolution of comparative advantage.* CID Working Paper 146.

Hausmann, R., & Rodrik, D. (2002). *Economic development as self-discovery.* NBER Working Papers 8952. doi:10.3386/w8952

Head, K., Mayer, T., & Ries, J. (2010). The erosion of colonial trade linkages after independence. *Journal of International Economics*, *81*(1), 1–14. doi:10.1016/j.jinteco.2010.01.002

Helpman, E., & Krugman, P. R. (1989). *Trade policy and market structure*. The MIT Press.

Herédia, M., Cabral, C., & Veiga, P. (2010). *Determinants of export diversification and sophistication in Sub-saharan Africa.* FEUNL Working Paper Series wp550.

Hidalgo, C. A., Klinger, B., Barabasi, A. L., & Hausmann, R. (2007). The product space conditions the development of nations. *Science*, *317*(5837), 482–487. doi:10.1126cience.1144581 PMID:17656717

Hirschman, I. I. (1958). On multiplier transformations. United States Air Force, Office of Scientific Research.

Hummels, D., & Klenow, P. J. (2005). The variety and quality of a nation' s exports. *The American Economic Review*, *95*(3), 704–723. doi:10.1257/0002828054201396

Imbs, J., & Wacziarg, R. (2003). Stages of diversification. *The American Economic Review*, *93*(1), 63–86. doi:10.1257/000282803321455160

Jaffe, A. B. (1984). *The effects of market demand, technological opportunity and research spillovers on R&D intensity and productivity growth. NBER Working Paper 1432*. doi:10.3386/w1432

Javorcik, B. S., Lo Turco, A., & Maggioni, D. (2018). New and improved: Does FDI Boost production complexity in host countries? *Economic Journal (London)*, *128*(614), 2507–2537. doi:10.1111/ecoj.12530

JetterM.HassanA. (2013). *The roots of export diversification.* Documentos de Trabajo 13–02. Medellín. doi:10.2139srn.2193650

Jetter, M., & Hassan, A. (2015). Want export diversification? Educate the kids first. *Economic Inquiry*, *53*(4), 1765–1782. doi:10.1111/ecin.12213

Kalemli-Ozcan, S., Sørensen, B. E., & Yosha, O. (2003). Risk sharing and industrial specialization: Regional and international evidence. *The American Economic Review*, *93*(3), 903–918. doi:10.1257/000282803322157151

Kim, S. (1995). Expansion of markets and the geographic distribution of economic activities: The trends in US regional manufacturing structure, 1860–1987. *The Quarterly Journal of Economics*, *110*(4), 881–908. doi:10.2307/2946643

Klinger, B., & Lederman, D. (2004). *Discovery and development: An empirical exploration of new products.* World Bank Policy Research Working Papers 2004-11. doi:10.1596/1813-9450-3450

Klinger, B., & Lederman, D. (2006). *Diversification, innovation, and imitation inside the global technological frontier.* Policy Research Working Papers 3872.

Koren, M., & Tenreyro, S. (2007). Volatility and development. *The Quarterly Journal of Economics*, *122*(1), 243–287. doi:10.1162/qjec.122.1.243

Krugman, P. R., Obstfeld, M., & Melitz, M. J. (2006). *Economía internacional: Teoría y Política*. Pearson.

Lederman, D., & Maloney, W. F. (2003). *Trade structure and growth.* Policy Research Working Papers 3025. Washington, DC: The World Bank. doi:10.1596/1813-9450-3025

Leontief, W. (1953). Factor proportions and the structure of American trade: Further theoretical and empirical analysis. *The Review of Economics and Statistics*, *38*(4), 386–407. doi:10.2307/1926500

Lim, J. J., & Saborowski, C. (2012). Export diversification in a transitioning economy: The case of syrialim and saborowski export diversification in Syria. *Economics of Transition*, *20*(2), 339–367. doi:10.1111/j.1468-0351.2011.00430.x

Makhlouf, Y., Kellard, N. M., & Vinogradov, D. (2015). Trade openness, export diversification, and political regimes. *Economics Letters*, *136*, 25–27. doi:10.1016/j.econlet.2015.08.031

Mariani, M. S., Vidmer, A., Medo, M., & Zhang, Y. C. (2015). Measuring economic complexity of countries and products: Which metric to use? *The European Physical Journal B*, *88*(11), 1–9. doi:10.1140/epjb/e2015-60298-7

Márquez-Ramos, L., Florensa, L., & Recalde, M. (2015). Economic integration effects on trade margins: Sectoral evidence from Latin America. *Journal of Economic Integration*, *30*(2), 269–299. doi:10.11130/jei.2015.30.2.269

Marshal, M. G., & Elzinga-Marshal, G. (2017). *Global Report 2017: Conflict, Governance, and State Fragility*. http://www.systemicpeace.org/globalreport.html

Martin-Mayoral, F., Morán Carofilis, G., & Cajas Guijarro, J. (2016). The effects of integration agreements in Western Hemisphere trade, 1970–2014. *The Journal of International Trade & Economic Development*, *25*(5), 724–756. doi:10.1080/09638199.2015.1125519

Melitz, M. J. (2003). The impact of trade on intra-industry reallocations and aggregate industry productivity. *Econometric Society*, *71*(6), 1695–1725. doi:10.1111/1468-0262.00467

Mubeen, N., & Ahmad, N. (2016). Towards measurement and determinants of export diversification: An empirical analysis of Pakistan. *Pakistan Journal of Commerce and Social Sciences*, *10*(3), 588–605.

O'Clery, N. (2015). A tale of two clusters: The evolution of Ireland's economic complexity since 1995. *Journal of the Statistical and Social Inquiry Society of Ireland, 45*(2009), 16–66.

OEC - Data Sources. (n.d.). Author.

Parteka, A., & Tamberi, M. (2011). Export diversification and development: An empirical assessment. *Quaderni Di Ricerca*, *359*, 1–38. doi:10.2139srn.1890767

Parteka, A., & Tamberi, M. (2013). What determines export diversification in the development process? Empirical assessment. *World Economy*, *36*(6), 807–826. doi:10.1111/twec.12064

Pesaran, M. H. (2004). General diagnostic tests for cross-sectional dependence in panels. *Empirical Economics*, 1–38. http://www.dspace.cam.ac.uk/handle/1810/446

Pesaran, M. H., Pesaran, M. H., Shin, Y., & Smith, R. P. (1999). Pooled mean group estimation of dynamic heterogeneous panels. *Journal of the American Statistical Association*, *94*(446), 621–634. doi:10.1080/01621459.1999.10474156

Proudman, J., & Redding, S. (2000). Evolving patterns of international trade. *Review of International Economics*, *8*(3), 373–396. doi:10.1111/1467-9396.00229

Redding, S. (2002). Specialization dynamics. *Journal of International Economics*, *58*(2), 299–334. doi:10.1016/S0022-1996(01)00169-6

Rosenstein-Rodan, P. N. (1943). Problems of Industrialisation of Eastern and South-Eastern Europe. *Economic Journal (London)*, *53*(210/211), 202–211. doi:10.2307/2226317

Shepotylo, O. (2013). Export diversification across countries and products: Do Eastern European (EE) and Commonwealth of Independent States (CIS) countries diversify enough? *The Journal of International Trade & Economic Development*, *22*(4), 605–638. doi:10.1080/09638199.2011.577797

Stojkoski, V., & Kocarev, L. (2017). *The relationship between growth and economic complexity: Evidence from Southeastern and Central Europe*. Munich Personal RePEc Archive, no. 77837. https://mpra.ub.uni-muenchen.de/77837/3/MPRA_paper_77837.pdf

Tacchella, A., Cristelli, M., Caldarelli, G., Gabrielli, A., & Pietronero, L. (2012). A new metrics for countries' fitness and products' complexity. *Scientific Reports*, *2*(1), 723. Advance online publication. doi:10.1038rep00723 PMID:23056915

The Growth Lab at Harvard University. (2019). International Trade Data (SITC, Rev. 2). Harvard Dataverse, 3166. doi:10.7910/DVN/H8SFD2

Utkovski, Z., Pradier, M. F., Stojkoski, V., Perez-Cruz, F., & Kocarev, L. (2018). Economic complexity unfolded: Interpretable model for the productive structure of economies. *PLoS One*, *13*(8), 1–24. doi:10.1371/journal.pone.0200822 PMID:30086166

Vettas, N. (2000). Investment dynamics in markets with endogenous demand. *The Journal of Industrial Economics*, *48*(2), 189–203. doi:10.1111/1467-6451.00118

WTO, IDE-JETRO, OECD, VIBE, & World Bank. (2019). *Technological Innovation, Supply Chain Trade, and Workers in a Globalized World*. Authors.

ADDITIONAL READING

Allen, J. (1985). Comments on complexity and trade: A view from Melanesia. *Archaeology in Oceania*, *20*(2), 49–57. doi:10.1002/j.1834-4453.1985.tb00102.x

Altomonte, C., & Békés, G. (2009). *Trade complexity and productivity. Nota di Lavoro 62.2009*. Fondazione Eni Enrico Mattei.

Cristelli, M., Gabrielli, A., Tacchella, A., Caldarelli, G., & Pietronero, L. (2013). Measuring the intangibles: A metrics for the economic complexity of countries and products. *PLoS One*, *8*(8), e70726. doi:10.1371/journal.pone.0070726 PMID:23940633

Hartmann, D. (2014). *Economic complexity and human development: How economic diversification and social networks affect human agency and welfare*. Taylor & Francis.

Hidalgo, C. A., & Hausmann, R. (2009). The building blocks of economic complexity. *Proceedings of the National Academy of Sciences of the United States of America*, *106*(26), 10570–10575. doi:10.1073/pnas.0900943106 PMID:19549871

Imbs, J., & Wacziarg, R. (2003). Stages of diversification. *The American Economic Review*, *93*(1), 63–86. doi:10.1257/000282803321455160

Tacchella, A., Cristelli, M., Caldarelli, G., Gabrielli, A., & Pietronero, L. (2013). Economic complexity: Conceptual grounding of a new metrics for global competitiveness. *Journal of Economic Dynamics & Control, 37*(8), 1683–1691. doi:10.1016/j.jedc.2013.04.006

ENDNOTES

1 Inputs are considered in a broad sense: knowledge, capital, labor, technology, intermediate goods and institutions involved in the productive process.

2 More complex products require more knowledge and therefore fewer countries can export them in a competitive way, while a country is more complex if it exports competitively products with more knowledge incorporated.

3 We refer to competitive presence in the sense of Balassa (1965), where a product has *Revealed Comparative Advantages* if it has a higher share in the country's total exports than the world average, and is more competitive the higher this ratio is.

4 The scope and depth of these effects also depends on the complexity of diversification, an aspect that will be explained in the next section.

5 Hidalgo et al. (2007) refer to this term to indicate that they do not start from assumptions about factor endowments or technological differences to build their index, but from the observed export structures.

6 Diversity indicates the number of economic activities in which a country specializes. Revealed Comparative Advantages (RCA) are calculated as: $RCA = \frac{X_{cp}}{\sum_c X_{cp}} / \frac{\sum_p X_{cp}}{\sum_{c,p} X_{cp}}$ where Xcp is the quantity (in USD) of a product p that a country c exports; C = number of considered countries P = number of considered products (Observatory of Economic Complexity).

7 See Tacchella et al. (2012) for an extensive explanation of this index.

8 The normalized HHI index is calculated considering the minimum and maximum possible in its construction (min-max scaling), as follows: $HHI = \frac{\sum_i s^2 - 1/N}{1 - 1/N}$ where s is the participation of each element of study, in this case the exports of each product. The higher this index is, the more concentration there is.

9 The generalized entropy index is a family of inequality indices that, depending on the parameter a, gives more or less weight to each tail of the distribution. In particular, the higher a is, the more weight is given to the upper part of the distribution of the variable. In this research, to give more weight to the more complex products, it is calculated as follows:

$$Ge(a=2) = \frac{1}{a(a-1)}\left[\frac{1}{N}\sum_i^N \left(\frac{x_i}{\bar{x}}\right)^a\right] - 1$$

10 $X = \frac{X_i - min(X)}{max(X) - min(X)} + 1$

11 The lag order of the variables can be determined by the different information criteria as Akaike, Hannan-Quinn and Schwarz (Baltagi, 2014).

12 Agosin et al. (2012) by including a term of interaction between human capital and terms of trade found that countries with more human capital are more robust to terms of trade shocks.

13 PRODY is defined as a weighted average of the per capita incomes of all countries exporting a particular product, with the weights given by the revealed comparative advantage (RCA) of the exporting country (Ghani et al., 2012).

14 The Grubel - Lloyd Index measures the degree to which similar products are exported and imported. For sector i the index would be $Gl_i = 1 - \frac{|X_i - M_i|}{X_i + M_i}$, where 1 would imply that only intra-sector trade exists and 0 that only inter-sector trade exists.

15 The countries considered in the analysis are Argentina, Bolivia, Brazil, Canada, Chile, Colombia, Costa Rica, Ecuador, El Salvador, Guatemala, Honduras, Mexico, Nicaragua, Panama, Paraguay, Peru, United States, Uruguay and Venezuela.

Chapter 8
China's Geostrategic Approach to Trade in Pursuit of Global Centrality

Guy-Maurille Massamba
https://orcid.org/0000-0003-3350-8401
Model Praxis, USA

ABSTRACT

The geostrategic approach refers to China's method to rise as global power through worldwide trade expansion and the development of its military and naval capabilities. It creates clusters of countries interlinked as China's trade partners, thus being assets to its global ascent. China's importance in global trade is a function of its partners' behavior embracing its trade mechanism. The edges connecting nodes are multidirectional, implying that countries are as much interested in their China-induced interlinkages as they are in their partnership with China. This results in China's centrality, a quality gained from being dominant in trade partnerships in terms of numbers and significance. This chapter examines the approach, process, and historical, geographic, and behavioral components that China uses in its ascent as central node in the international trade network. It explores how underlying dimensions making China's national character conjointly devise its behavior in global trade.

INTRODUCTION

In the study of China's emergence as global power, trade is a relevant analytical tool for development analysis, and the examination of the degree of integration in the international trade network (ITN). Interest in China as central node in trade networks justifies the scrutiny of the role of its leadership in masterfully engineering the process leading to such outcomes. Trade policy encompasses the geographic and historical factors influencing China's past, present, and future. Another determinant element worth examining is institutional functionality, the systemic conditions to implement trade policy. How are institutions, such as the Belt and Road Initiative (BRI), used for trade promotion? What norms are used to induce participation? This study highlights the underlying factors of China's behavior in trade partnerships.

DOI: 10.4018/978-1-7998-7568-0.ch008

Geostrategy is a complex approach to politics compelling decision makers to tackle the interlacing domestic and international issues with political realism. It consolidates, asserts, and perpetuates a nation's existence among self-interested nations. It envisions national development through the use of international factors, such as trade. Geostrategy entails ensuring the preservation of national interest through institutions translating policies. Such policies as China's trade reforms have a geostrategic meaning for national development through trade expansion within institutional networks. China has resorted to a geostrategic approach not only to widen its trade partnerships, but also to gain centrality in trade networks. This study aims to elucidate the constructs of a center-periphery framework stemming from China's actions. It explores the nature of trade networks and the underlying factors - historical and geographic, of China's strategy.

The central argument is stated as follows: China's geostrategic approach addresses historical, geographic, and economic necessity impelling the aggregate development of security capabilities, economic objectives, and trade. This resulted in its ascent as global power able to exert influence through expanded horizontally configured trade networks, thereby becoming a central node in the ITN.

This study adopts an analytical approach inspired by network analysis. Network configuration outlines the edges connecting to China's central node. The role of peripheral states is defined as contribution of BRI participating economies. Analyzing the geostrategic approach implies deciphering the realist intentionality of Chinese leadership to give meaning to China's history and geography in modern circumstances. Three key concepts are the focus of this analysis: geostrategic approach; trade; and centrality. They are presented through deductive reasoning to highlight their interrelationship: Geostrategic behavior has induced trade expansion, which produced China's centrality.

Six steps make the structure of this analysis, beginning with the literature review focused on the significance of geography in politics in order to elucidate the concepts of geostrategy and geopolitics. The second step presents the conceptual framework, explaining the concepts of nodes and edges, and China's as a central node in trade networks. The third section is about China's geostrategic objectives, with emphasis on China's ascent as global power based on its continental strategy. The fourth section offers an insight into the BRI, the multiform global trade structure devised by China. Emphasis is on the significance of the BRI to global trade, and the significance of South Asia to China's geostrategic interests. In the fifth section the impact of the COVID-19 pandemic on global trade is examined. Finally, the reflection on the BRI instigates policy recommendations, which are attempted in this study.

LITERATURE REVIEW

This literature review deals first with the importance of geography. Afterwards, scholarship on geostrategy and geopolitics is presented, particularly in their application in policy making.

The Significance of Geography

Geography is regarded as the inexorable framework within which politics evolves, and defined in accordance with interests and security necessity. Politics, whether domestically or internationally, takes place as geographically contextualized. Gray (1999, p. 164) states that "geography cannot be an optional extra for consideration by the strategic theorist or planner, because it drives the character and the potential contemporary reach of tactical, hence operational prowess." The strategic skills of the political planner as operational prowess delineate one's interest within spatial features. This is not limited to national politics. The political planner views the international scene as a stage in the pursuit of national interest. The description of geography as inescapable is one of the strongest assertions about the setting in which politics evolves. It implies a fundamental character, stressed in Dibb's (2018) correlation of geography and strategic defense planning perspectives. Dibb argues that the hopes pinned on economic interdependence and globalization to moderate realist views of national interest have not obliterated the strategic inclinations to control national boundaries and territory.

The challenge to a nation's geography can arise from ambitious states seeking to assert influence beyond their borders. Dibb reflects on Vladmir Putin's geopolitical intent toward Europe, which comprises a challenge to the liberal political and economic order and nostalgia of a lost world once under Soviet influence. Included in Dibb's consideration are China's ambitions in the South China Sea, and the relevance of Australia's location to US policy as regards Asia. This highlights security issues, which Sloan (2017) conceptualizes as underpinned in the coalescence of geography, history and strategy. This "trinitarian perspective," as Sloan calls it, inspires state security actions, which are the assertive geopolitical expression of their national interest. The triad guides the interactions between states.

Inescapable geography encloses state activities in primordial facts, encasing politics in time and space as sine qua non conditions. Human development in all its forms, including politics, unfolds primarily and exclusively as spatially and temporally determined history. Kaplan's (2012, p. 42) notion of "backdrop" expresses the primordial character of geography as the first order of things that the state has to manage in its self-definition and relations to others. Kaplan unambiguously asserts that "a state's position on the map is the first thing that defines it, more than its governing philosophy even." The use of cartographic observations helps to depict a government's perspectives and objectives, thus taking geography as necessary reference in the elaboration of strategic plans. Kaplan cautions on the use of geography for policy making, instructing that "geography informs, rather than determines. Geography, therefore, is not synonymous with fatalism" (p. 43). Insights from geographic position serve in strategic foreign policy and state objectives based on geographic reality.

Gray's (1999) presents a similar view considering geography as an inescapable fact for political actions, military ambitions, and mythical embrace of its characteristics. Geography is not only a country's identity. It also serves as an "ally" favorably propelling a country's political, economic and cultural ambitions beyond the territorial space. As physical boundaries, a country's geographic dimensions delineate the constraints on state capabilities for the allocation of resources of the national community. However, this very organizational necessity requires the deployment of geographic elements, such as sea, borders, resources, and population, springing open as forces and capabilities supporting a country's actions, presence, and effects beyond its borders. Geography is a strategic factor whose relation to politics cannot be severed without detrimental consequences. It is a consideration stemming from geostrategic thinking.

Geostrategy and Geopolitics

An analysis by Rogers (2011) introduces a relationship between geography, politics and strategy, and evokes a complex and conflict-laden prospect with an assertive pursuit of national interest. Interactions between countries are not always amiable cooperation. With this viewpoint, Rogers alludes to a country's use of pressure and coercion for influence and leverage. This rejects a Hegelian reading of history as gradual perfected evolution of human and social interaction. International relations are not frictionless human activities. The paradigm that idealized international relations as globalized cooperation overlooks particular characteristics established by geography. It ignores tensions exploding into open or tacit conflicts, such as World Wars and the Cold War, in which -- States engage in the region with similar ambitions.

THE CONCEPTUAL FRAMEWORK OF CENTRALITY

Centrality is used in network analysis to qualify a node within a network. In sociology, centrality is appropriately identified in circumstances of leadership, popularity and reputation enjoyed by social actors in a network (Zhang & Luo, 2017). Higher centrality denotes a social actor's close proximity to the center. It indicates the actor's power, position of influence, and access to available resources in the system. The location and driving factors constitute the circumstances of nodal motions. Bloch et al. (2017) emphasize the relation of centrality to the context, accounting for the interactions that determine a country's economic capabilities, including trade.

It is important beforehand to provide brief explanations of some important concepts. Most prevalent in the analysis are nodes or vertices, and edges or links. Networks have two primary aspects: a multitude of separate entities and the connections that link them. These numerous entities are called nodes or vertices, whereas their connections are the edges or links. A central node is so called because of its size resulting from the number of other nodes connected to it through edges.

Hojman and Szeidl (2008) propose a network formation resulting from decisions by participating actors to connect with one another. For instance, the BRI, as network, reflects the commitment by participating economies to enter trade partnership with China, the central node in the network, and with one another. Network formation is not random, and is dependent upon the actions, behavior and strategic options available to, and used by, interconnected nodes. It is multidirectional and purposeful in that "direct and indirect access to other agents in the network generates benefits, which can depend on the network distance between players" (p. 297). BRI participating economies embrace the norms of the partnership with expectations of gains in economic growth, and the system is so established as to allow economies to connect with as many members as possible. In network analysis, optimal presence and effectiveness depend on each member's expansive and cross-directional activities. Each operates "as a unit or node of a social network as well as a social actor" (Bandyopadhyay et al., 2011, p. 1). BRI trade and investments incentivize potential partners to expand their development capabilities through mutually beneficial agreements.

Cingolani et al. (2017) measure centrality and economic performance in terms of the countries' capacity to add value to trade networks via production and the extent of involvement in economic transactions. A World Bank (2019b, p. 19) analysis of all BRI corridor economies has determined that "all regions experienced a gradual rise in the share of Chinese value added in their imports, and a rise in the share of China in their domestic value added embodied in other economies' exports." China's share in these economies has reinforced their integration with the world and with each other, although with variations between participating economies. Network analysis explain the variations through the years, and in trade volume, as well as commodities. Variations indicate "the role of the extensive and intensive margins" (De Benedictis & Tajoli, 2011, p. 1419), and the density of interconnections between numerous trade partners, as well as the correlations of various economic phenomena (Guha et al., 2016). Consequently, nodes are indicative of the country's qualitative and quantitative presence. Such presence reflects the country's capacity to add value to other countries through production and exports (Amador & Cabral, 2016). It shows the position of countries in the international production. As a measure, it considers the production chain as an essential variable in the study of trade by including the volumes of production and the goods produced as ways of adding value to trade partnerships.

Centrality is a shifting quality assessed on the basis of the positions of countries in the production chain. For instance, Mexico and Brazil are "more central in the intermediate positions of the international production network of electronic goods than their trade volumes would lead to expect, while many advanced European countries are much less central." (Cingolani et al., 2017, p. 16). China's centrality has also been viewed in similar terms due its "supply of goods inputs to the exports of goods of other countries" (Amador & Cabral, 2016, p. 3). China's centrality in global trade is not only reflected in the total number of edges linking to it (Figure 1). Its advancement in the global value chain, effected by its "domestic capacity to produce industrial goods," also contributes to its central position (Meng & Wang, 2019, p. 43). With 59% in 2010, China is among the top 10 developing economies with the highest GVC participation rate, as shown in Figure 2. Over the period from 2000 to 2017, China had increased its production of intermediates.

A study by McKinsey Global Institute (2019) highlights gains by Chinese technology producers in market share in key sub segments. China exposure to the world has increased as an important "market, supplier, and provider of capital." Citing the World Bank, the study notes that "in many categories in-

Figure 1. China's centrality due to export growth 2016
Source: (World Bank Integrated Trade Solution, WITS)
https://wits.worldbank.org/Networkchart/countrychart/en/country/CHN/nomenclature/H0/year/2016/tradeflow/Export/product/Total/threshold/0.01/viewpoint/Supplier
China: *Weighted Outdegree: 21.897; Weighted Indegree: 0.869*
United States: *Weighted Outdegree: 15.595; Weighted Indegree: 0.864*
Node size depends on the Weighted OUT-degree; it is proportional to relevance of each country as a supplier in the selected sub-network.

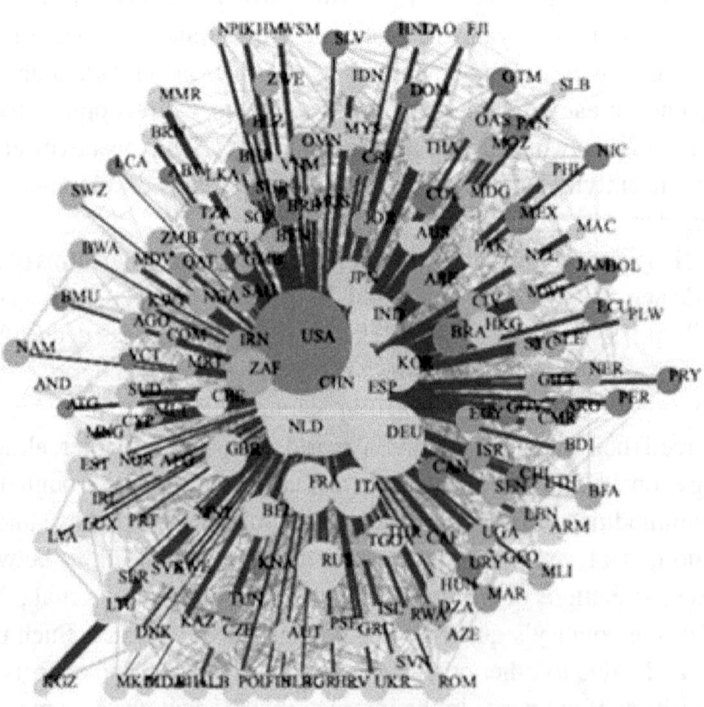

cluding automobiles, spirits, luxury goods, and mobile phones, China is the largest market in the world, accounting for about 30 percent (or more) of global consumption" (p. 5). Moreover, China's market share in terms of multinational corporation penetration for a number of brands has surpassed that of the United States. This evolution results from a well-thought strategic objectives of policy of "reform and openness" (*gaige kaifang*), adopted by Chinese leadership with incrementalism, gradually transforming China's economic basis, thereby creating the conditions for a more assertive multiform engagement with the world.

Figure 2. Twenty-five developing economies with highest GVC participation rate, 2010 (per cent)
Source: (UNCTAD (2013); UNCTAD–Eora GVC database)

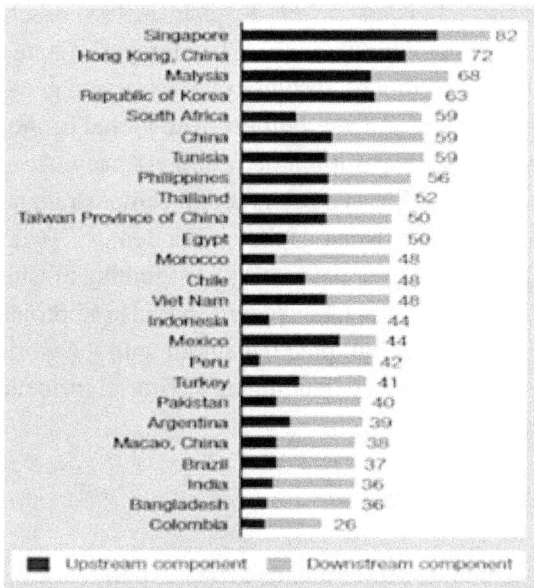

CHINA'S GEOSTRATEGIC OBJECTIVES

China's geostrategic approach involves expanding and consolidating its economic and military position both regionally and globally. Zicheng et al. (2011) identify three pillars of China's geostrategy. These are territorial integrity and national sovereignty; regional stability aligned with geopolitical security along its borders; and global influence based on its position as regional power and global trading partner. This last pillar has the significance of countering the hegemonic influence of the United States. Therefore, "China's strategy of multipolarization involves developing its strategic partnership with Russia, encouraging Europe to become a pole, and helping Japan escape from U.S. control and become an independent pole" (p. 205-206). Joining the World Trade Organization (WTO) in 2001 was a geostrategic move to advance economic interests through trade partnerships. The security front involves securing trade routes with regional maritime power. China's investments on the Makran seacoast of southwest Pakistan, amount to U.S. $1 billion for the construction of a deep-water port at Gwadar, "in order to establish a trade and transport hub for Central Asian nations and simultaneously expand China's geostrategic influence" (Qi et al., 2006, p. 58). Chinese leadership recognizes the importance of maritime strategy for security in the

Asia-Pacific region (Bitzinger, 2011). Hartnett and Vellucci (2011, p. 81) state that "China's continued economic growth is dependent on maritime access and security." The buildup of maritime infrastructure has economic underpinnings. It includes "the capacity to maintain and support foreign trade, transportation, and strategic resources" (Zicheng et al., 2011, p. 22). This is but one dimension of a long-term vision.

As China emerges as a continental power, it assumes a history of territorial losses and imperial demise reflected in the decline of an imperial rule over a territorially unified and single empire. The united China, heralded as an achievement by Qin Shi Huangdi, stretched back as far as 221 BCE. It made China a great power culturally dominating the East Asia region. For over 2000 years China was and remained an imperial power until the nineteenth century when the Qing dynasty weakened, also marked by important territorial losses, due to land grab by Western powers (Kaplan, 2012). From most of the second half of the twentieth century to the present, China's rulers have signaled a determination to overcome the unease of territorial dispossession. Kaplan (p. 198) describes Mao Zedong as "an irredentist who had internalized the wounds of a once vast and imperial state surviving the centuries only to be humiliated in the recent past." Although disputes over lands and geographic reconstitution are far from settled, China has consolidated its current borders. The global economic ambitions aim at reviving China, and counterbalancing and dispelling a demeaning legacy. According to Kaplan, "the very economic and diplomatic strategies of China's rulers today demonstrate an idea of China that reaches beyond the territorial extent of even the China of the eighth-century Tang and the eighteenth-century High Qing." History and geography coalesce in the strategic thinking of China's leadership to determine trade policies, not only as efforts to surpass China's past, but also to project power within and beyond its geographic boundaries. "China, a demographic behemoth with the world's most energetic economy for the past three decades, is, unlike Russia, extending its territorial influence much more through commerce than coercion" (p. 198).

China's Ascent as a Global Power

China's emergence as global economic power and its growing political clout reflect developments conceptualized by the power transition theory. The global transformation signaling a power shift toward China has been interpreted by scholars who envision China replacing the United States (Danner & Martín, 2019; Lemke & Tammen, 2003). It causes structural change within the international regime (Lai, 2011), resulting in a constant push-and-pull process in which national policies and institutional mechanisms, such as defense and trade, are set to foster change or maintain the status quo. Power transition theory, as originally formulated by Organski, ascribes a bellicose attitude to rising powers. China's rise is interpreted as a challenge to the United States. Its behavior is seen to offset the U.S. global influence (Yang, 2013). Tensions resulting from China's trade policy have given credence to the bellicose suggestion of power transition theory.

China's rise is generally associated to its economic growth, trade expansion, although other components, such as military buildup should not be neglected in the analysis. China has military ambitions included in its national strategy, as it seeks to implement "the great rejuvenation" of the Chinese nation. A U.S. Department of Defense report discusses the objective of the People's Liberation Army (PLA) to achieve levels of a "world-class" military by the end of 2049. "Within the content of the PRC's national strategy it is likely that Beijing will seek to develop a military by mid-century that is equal to—or in some cases superior to—the U.S. military, or that of any other great power that the PRC views as a threat" (Department of Defense, 2020, p. i). Figure 3 shows an increase in 2010-2019 China's defense budget, nearly doubled during the past 10 years. The increase represents an average annual growth of about 8 percent, in inflation-adjusted terms. Ikenberry (2014, p. 43) assesses in no uncertain terms China's long-term vision and the transformative aim inherent in its military-supported multi-faceted development goals. "The rise of China is perhaps the defining drama of East Asia and the global order. The extraordinary growth of the Chinese economy—and its active diplomacy and military buildup—is already transforming East Asia." The transformation involves shifting, reconstructing, and reinforcing alliances within global political and economic networks, as well as the reconfiguring centers of power.

Figure 3. China's defense budget 2010—2019
Source: (U.S. Department of Defense, Annual Report to Congress, 2020. Military and Security Developments Involving the People's Republic of China)

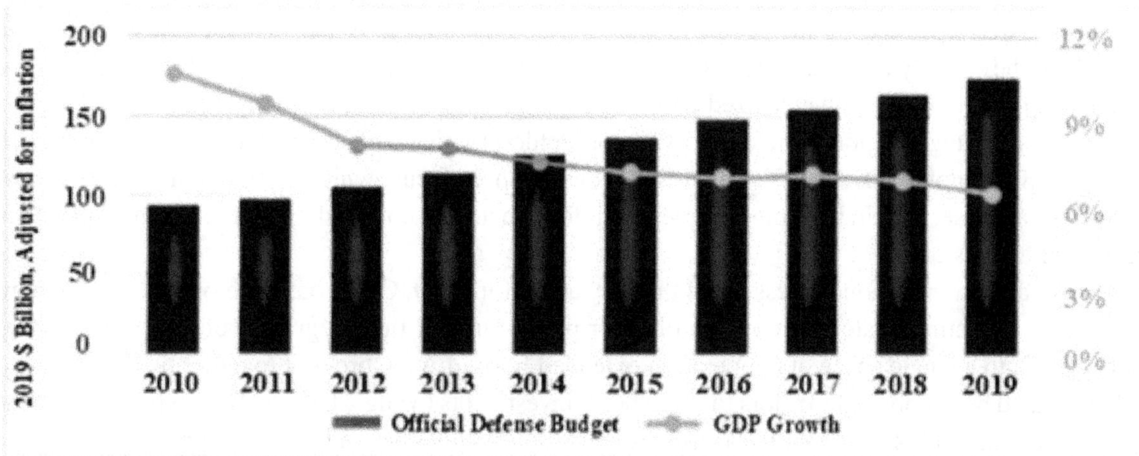

The decline in U.S. global dominance as hegemonic power, observed though the lens of its diminished appeal (Regilme, 2019), is consequential for global governance (Chase-Dunn et al., 2011). It creates room for the growing influence of other states. Signs of relative dispersion of global power signal political and economic unsteadiness in the global political economy. Discernible facets of instability include "the growing political salience of various forces and activities that appear to transcend and impinge not only upon existing political boundaries and forms of economic production and distribution, but also on the values that underpin social institutions and existing modes of social and cultural differentiation" (McBride et al., 2002, p. 1). Trade engagement and performance by the United States in the Asia-Pacific region, for instance, established a geopolitical order transforming the region. This led countries into open liberalized economic systems, coupled with security ties with such countries as Japan and South Korea. This order is being transformed into a multipolar configuration (Ikenberry, 2014), as yet undefined, with China's rise as a dominant fact sustained by its global effort to bolster and diversify its trade through the BRI.

China's trade bold initiatives are grounded in its approach to international politics and views about the moral tenets and liberal economic value systems uniting world democracies. Through what is identified as China's revisionist behavior, a collusion of interests between China and Russia signals aggressive determination "to shape a world consistent with their authoritarian model—gaining veto authority over other nations' economic, diplomatic, and security decisions" (Mattis, 2018, p. 2). Scholars have even argued for containment to restrain China's military potential before it becomes overwhelming (Huiyun, 2009). The idea is advanced from the perspective of power transition theory highlighting challenges from a rising power displeased with the existing international political system (Kastner & Saunders, 2012). Trade policy, coupled with great power aspirations, is symptomatic of a comprehensive approach to international politics, instilling gradual strategic pursuits that span continents through initiatives of cooperation and aid, including financial policy.

Continental Approach to Global Expansion

China's trade strategy begins close to home. Its relations with its neighbors are defined by policy of security concerns for a region in which it wants to assert leadership. At the Fourth Summit of the Conference on Interaction and Confidence Building Measures in Asia (CICA), in May 2014, President Xi Jinping declared that "it is for the people of Asia to run the affairs of Asia, solve the problems of Asia and uphold the security of Asia. The people of Asia have the capability and wisdom to achieve peace and stability in the region through enhanced cooperation."[1] This declaration is among the actions designed to establish a strategic regional enclosing of a geographic area that China cannot disregard without risk to its pursuit of global influence. It demonstrates geographic focus, which in terms of China's global aspirations and rise, first and foremost suggests reinforcement and consolidation of its regional presence for greater expansion.

The Asian continent nonetheless is not the only area of interest. China has developed a view of continentalism reflecting strategic extension of a periphery through the integration of BRI participating economies into a single space of cooperation extended beyond Asia, brought together by connectivity, and facilitated by economic corridors through hefty investments (Yang, 2018, p. 2). In other words, "the geographic space of BRI starts with peripheral diplomacy, but goes beyond this to encompass most of the world" (Callahan, 2016, p. 237). The BRI platform cannot be viewed merely in terms of its geoeconomic considerations. Zheng (2020) suggests to view it as China's strategic effort to cast its continentalism in expansionist terms, in contrast with its early isolationist behavior. Continentalism is an expansionist impetus contrasting with the heavily Sino-centric antiquated significance of the concept. The old approach restrained seaward extensions, and limited China's naval operations by insisting on land power (Qi et al., 2006; Zheng, 2020). Interestingly this old brand of continentalism was opposed to maritime perspective, which is fashionable today in China. It constructed an identity that China is shedding off, albeit not entirely, in its current embrace of maritime development. Nohara (2017, p. 211) describes this process as "hybridization of the two" identities—old-fashioned and maritime. Current foreign policy synchronizes continentalism with the development of naval identity, two formerly antithetical perspectives. The result is continentalism that is at once new, in the sense of being different from the old continentalism, and revisited.

The new continentalism, configured and materialized through the BRI, expands its territory by including Eurasia or the entire landmass forming Africa and Eurasia and their seas (Zheng, 2020). According to Cáceres (2014, p. 107) "Chinese strategists have examined the dynamic geopolitical links that are reconfiguring Eurasian spaces from the western edge of Europe (and shaky model of a Union) through to the eastern edge of Asia, including the Korean peninsula and Japan." Chinese geostrategic logic efficiently defined Eurasian socioeconomic and political developments with its expansionist perspective challenging deep-rooted cooperation arrangements. The BRI geoeconomic structure in the Afro-Eurasian space, as Petranek (2019, p. 11) points out, "is destabilizing and derailing the old triad

(USA, Europe, and Japan) with a concrete proposal to Asia, Eurasia, Arabia, and the northern African Continent." Eurasia is the scene of geopolitical competition for influence between China, Russia, United States, and the European Union (Umbach, 2019).

Under President Xi, the continentalist doctrine has engineered an "expansionist foreign policy" (Zheng, 2020, p. 3). Xi's approach includes, among others, trading strategies to strengthen regional cooperation, which could not be sustained without structured regional interactions. As a course of action, China has institutionally embedded the approach in institutions, such as the New Development Bank (NDB) under BRICS, the Asian Infrastructure Investment Bank (AIIB), and the new Silk Road Fund (SRF) under BRI (Baruah & Panda, 2019). Continentalism consists of strategically and institutionally "bringing in" the outer geographic expanse. It is implemented through initiatives that Xi has launched at regional seminars and conferences. These gatherings, such as the May 2014 CICA and the November 2014 Asia-Pacific Economic Cooperation (APEC) summit create a functional context operating, according to President Xi's words, as "multi-dimensional infrastructure of networks" in which trade links of multiple countries intersect with China's interests and geostrategic goals.

Continentalism comprises structured arrangements supporting interdependence and making means of production accessible worldwide to meet the needs of member countries. Calder (2012, p. 48) states that "when economic interdependence is substantial, and technological change rapid, as has recently been the case within Eurasia, there tends to be demand from national leaders for new, stabilizing institutions, although that demand often remains unarticulated." The new continentalism is embodied in the BRI geographically and institutionally. Its expansionist strategy is embodied in investments that span a wide expanse for the purpose of facilitating trade and access to strategic commodities such as oil and gas. Calder's focused analysis emphasizes the structural conditions as they determine the context, geography, and policy underlying the formulation and implementation of China's continental approach. The context is China's growing need for resources to sustain its production capabilities. The new continentalism is the geostrategic solution through unimpeded and expanded trade defined in BRI statements, and access to diversified sources of energy. Scholars, including Calder, have established the link between China's needs for energy and its trade configuration (Ratner, 2018; Ziegler, 2006). Zweig et al. (2005, p. 25) state that "now that China is the workshop of the world, its hunger for electricity and industrial resources has soared." Chauhan (2019, p. 120) considers that China's energy consumption places the country at the top of the world's largest energy consumers, accounting for "24 percent of global energy consumption and 34 percent of global energy consumption growth in 2018." China's demand for energy rose by "4.3 per cent in 2018, the highest since 2012." Such growing demands generate incentives to pave the way for an energy geography. This is not without consequences, as it affects the competitiveness of business in other economies, pushing for enhanced control of these markets.

In addition to the context, there are geographic and policy aspects considered as structural conditions shaping continentalism, and operating therein as agencies. Geography and policy concomitantly frame geopolitical developments in China's Eurasian vision. China's policy contrives a new Eurasian reality based on geographic contiguity and inherent economic interactions. It grasps the convenience and convergence of the Eurasian geographic contiguity, energy and infrastructural capabilities. The BRI connectivity investments materialize policy that projects and entails regional trends that Calder (2012, p. 3) sees as potentially reducing impediments. "Propinquity provides, once political obstacles are removed, a dynamic basis for deepening—and synergistic—economic and strategic interaction among the nations of Eurasia, especially through physical channeling mechanisms such as pipelines, which simultaneously create a distinctive geopolitical intimacy".

THE SIGNIFICANCE OF THE BRI AS TRADE AGENCY

The BRI exists since 2013, and includes economic corridors and trade agreements. It spans a wide geographic space comprising countries in Asia, Europe, and Africa, and the Middle East. The BRI includes investments in connectivity infrastructures, which incentivize countries in need of infrastructure development. As a "crucial dimension" (Schneider, 2021, p. 14) of the BRI, trade is what makes the BRI a living organism, an expanding and dynamic geostrategic reality. Trade functions as the modus operandi directing all BRI participating economies to China one way or the other, either through infrastructure investments, import and export, or financial enticement, while making China the central node of this trading network. This is made possible as the BRI's role is "to create land and maritime trade routes linking China with Europe, through Asia (including the Middle East) and Africa" (Liangxiang & Janardhan, 2020, p. 35). The BRI has evolved to "become an umbrella term under which a variety of Chinese developmental projects focused on regional connectivity and infrastructure have been placed" (Links, 2021, p. 119). Observers have noted with skepticism the process, conditions, and narrative about China's initiative Schortgen (2018). The ambition of the program testifies to China's search for "international status," (*Guoji Diwei*), an objective pursued since the mid-1990s (Deng, 2008). In addition to skepticism, major powers, such as India and the United States, have "expressed developmental and geopolitical concerns" with the BRI (Gong, 2020, p. 88). India's concern has evolved into geopolitical contest with China in a regional competition, which has intensified to involve an extensive part of the Indian Ocean (Baruah, 2018; Ghiasy, 2018).

This does not imply that BRI participating economies do not benefit from the program. African countries welcome cooperation through the BRI, given their difficulties in funding infrastructure projects (Links 2021). Middle East countries seize investment opportunities. Research by Liangxiang and Janardhan (2020) shows participation by Chinese companies in infrastructure connectivity, for instance, in the construction of the Ain Sokhna Port of Egypt and the New Hamad Port of Qatar. Infrastructure connectivity is perceived as an engine of economic growth. Gong (2020, p. 78) points to World Bank projections that "the BRI will increase trade for countries along the route by 4.1 percent." Another World Bank study (2019b, p. 67) estimates that "policies to promote trade facilitation in Belt and Road corridor economies would boost their exports, thus complementing infrastructure projects." The European Union has also reinforced cooperation with China through the BRI, with prospects of joint investment and co-financing, some of which target infrastructure in Southeast Europe (Casarini, 2015).

The existence of economic corridors is the implement of the connectivity objective. As geographic connectivity they "reterritorialize" the global trade order. Forough (2019, p. 275) considers this reordering as "gradual but palpable tectonic shifts unfolding in global geo-economics." This process has generated a re-centering whereby particular geographic points in the network have gained relative importance as connecting zones, and for bringing China the central node closer to faraway territories. For instance, Central Asia, "has become an increasingly important in-between regional space for transport logistics and relaying hubs" (Chen & Fazilov 2018, p. 9; Hans-Peter, 2013). The region, and in particular Kazakhstan, is "bringing China and Europe closer together and more linked via long-distance overland trade." The re-centering creates opportunities based on the location of participating economies, in terms of trade volume and costs. Connections through transport networks between China, Central Asian, and European countries are effective. "The Eurasian transport network provides people and firms in China with better access to foreign markets than to people and firms in Central Asian and European countries" (Chen & Fazilov, 2018, p. 9). The World Bank (2019b, p. 48) also evaluates the effectiveness in quantitative terms by looking at the reduction in shipment time, a crucial factor in trade costs likely to improve trade growth. The study estimates that "corridor economies can on average experience a 3.2 percent reduction in shipment times with the rest of the world and 4 percent with other corridor economies. Along individual economic corridors shipment times come down on average by 8.5 percent and by as much as 12 percent." This Chinese advantage does not negate the gains for corridor economies, shown in Figure 4.

Figure 4. The belt and road's six economic corridors
Source: (Global Infrastructure Connectivity Alliance)

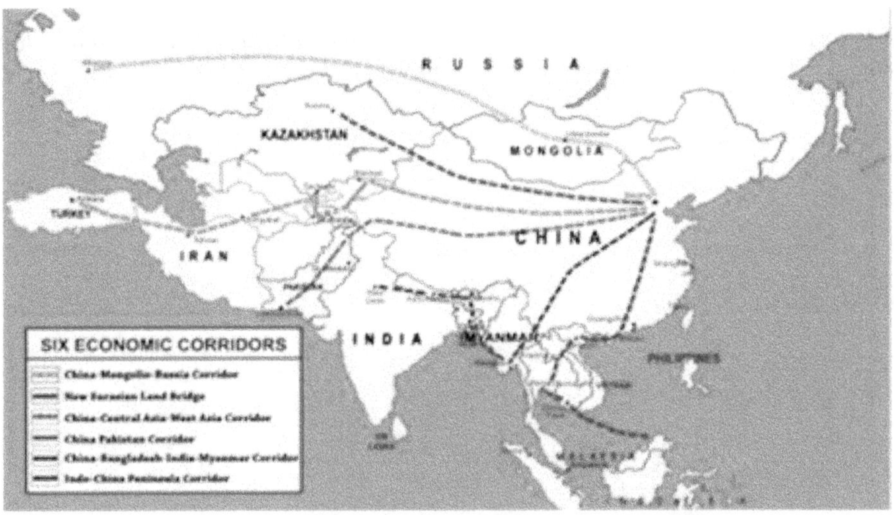

BCIM Bangladesh-China-India-Myanmar Economic Corridor
CAWA China-Central Asia-West Asia Economic Corridor
ICP China-Indochina Peninsula Economic Corridor
CMR China-Mongolia-Russian Federation Economic Corridor
NELB New Eurasia Land Bridge Economic Corridor
CPEC China-Pakistan (CP) Economic Corridor

Trade Growth in Economic Corridors

The overall outlook of trade growth in economic corridors is marked by variations resulting partly from trade facilitation procedures in each region and between trade partners. In this analysis, the total value of trade is evaluated as an indication of BRI-induced change. In the case of Africa, although the years following the launching of the BRI, from 2013 to 2019, have witnessed fluctuations, as Figure 5 shows, there was a steady increase in the volume of exports and imports, kept substantially above pre-BRI levels. China's exports to Africa reached their highest level in 2015 at $155.70 billion, while imports from the continent were at $47.56 billion. There was gradual resurgence of trade, although minimal after a slowdown in 2016. In 2018 and 2019, two-way trade between China and Africa amounted to $185.29 billion and $191.73 billion respectively, the latter being the highest in the decade. The fact that most post-BRI trade volumes are higher than those of the pre-BRI, despite fluctuations, can be interpreted as

BRI momentum. Furthermore, in the same figure, the comparison between China and the United States in terms of their respective trade with Africa shows a higher China-Africa trade volume than US-Africa. Another indicator of China-Africa trade steadiness is the flow of Chinese foreign direct investment (FDI) to Africa, as shown in Figure 6. Chinese FDI has surged from US$ 75 million in 2003 to US$2.7 billion in 2019, exceeding U.S. FDI to the continent. The momentum is expected to continue as China's investments continue to make inroads into the continent. The 2018 Forum for China–Africa Cooperation in Beijing provided China-Africa development partnership with an opportunity to consolidate trade, as China committed US$60 billion for development financing until 2021 (ORF, 2020).

Figure 5. Trade levels in Africa before and after the BRI in partnership with China and the USA
Source: (Compiled by Author, based on Data from Johns Hopkins University SAIS-CARI)

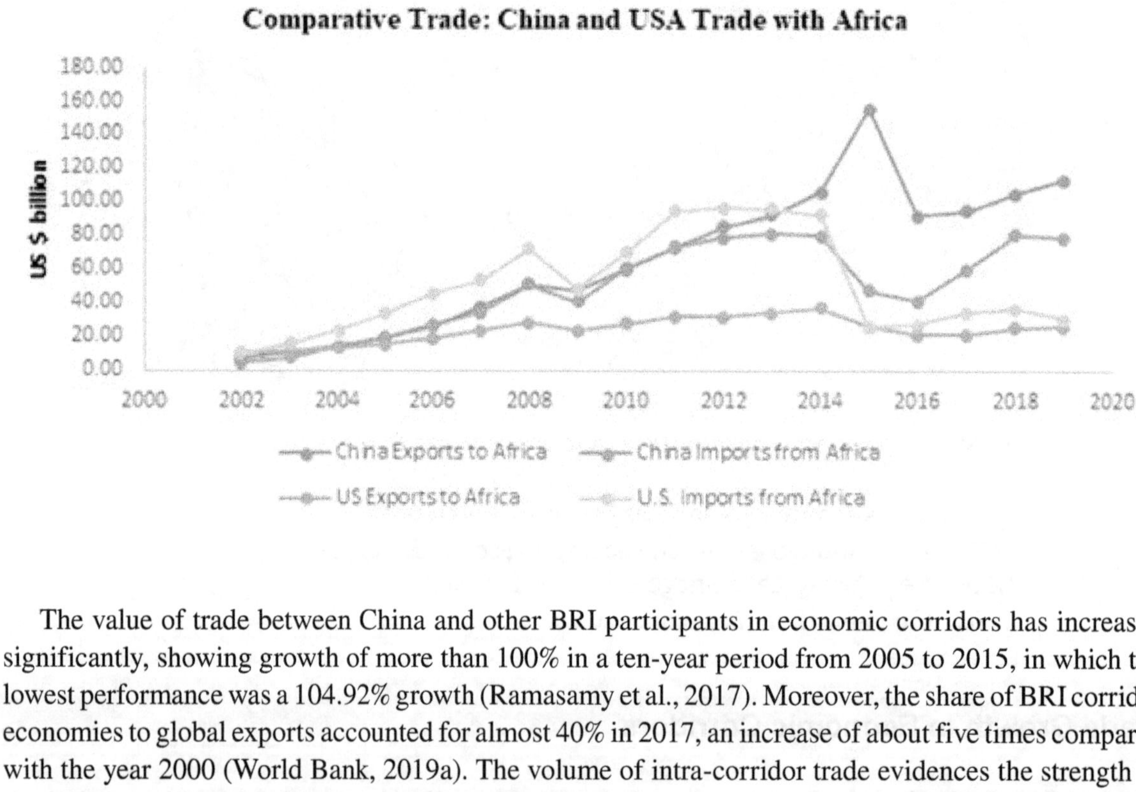

The value of trade between China and other BRI participants in economic corridors has increased significantly, showing growth of more than 100% in a ten-year period from 2005 to 2015, in which the lowest performance was a 104.92% growth (Ramasamy et al., 2017). Moreover, the share of BRI corridor economies to global exports accounted for almost 40% in 2017, an increase of about five times compared with the year 2000 (World Bank, 2019a). The volume of intra-corridor trade evidences the strength of the corridor and its contribution to global trade. The lowest level of total trade, US$ 4,030 billion, is in the CPEC (China-Pakistan Economic Corridor). Nonetheless, the total growth in this corridor is still high, amounting to 352.92% in 2015 compared to 2005 (Ramasamy et al., 2017). The trends are similar in all economic corridors. In every corridor the highest trade flows have consistently involved China, as indicated in Figure 7.

The BRI has also contributed to increasing trade volume through the integration of corridor economies. Integration reinforces trade among corridor economies, despite differences in the levels of integration. According to World Bank findings, the corridor economies comprising countries of East Asia and Pacific and those of Europe and Central Asia have deeper integration. High levels of intra-corridor integration reflect on high values of intraregional exports and imports. BRI economies have increased their share

Figure 6. Chinese FDI vs U.S. FDI to Africa
Source: (Compiled by Author, based on Data from Johns Hopkins University SAIS-CARI)

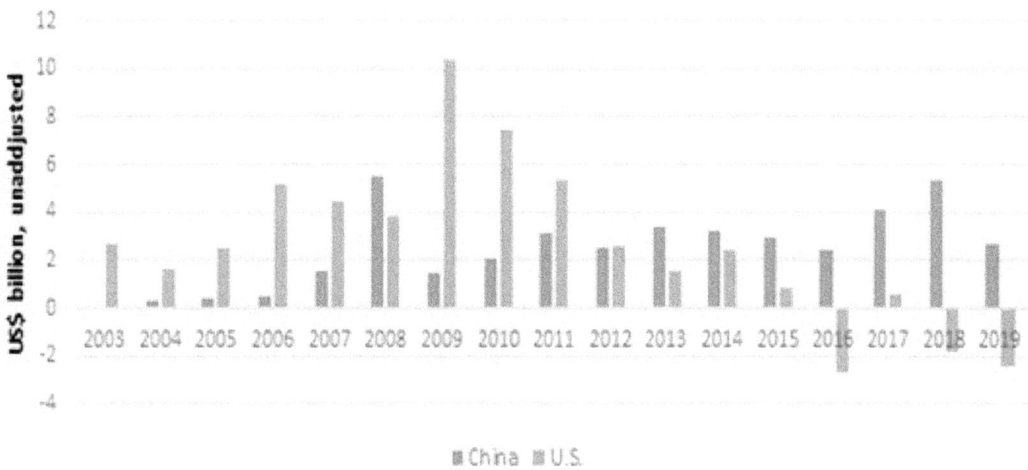

in the global production chain, combining intraregional trade with extra-regional trade, including FDI. The share of most BRI economies in global exports has nearly doubled since the mid-1990s, as shown in Figure 8. In 1995, East Asia and Pacific contributed to global exports with 14%, and reached 21% in 2015. Europe and Central Asia stood at 4%, and in 2015 they were at 8%. The Middle East and North Africa contributed to global exports with 2% in 1995. In 2015, this share reached 4%. Finally, South Asia's share in global exports was 1%, and gradually rose over two decades to reach 3% in 2015.

Figure 7. Largest trade flows in economic corridors, in $billion
Source: (Data compiled by Author, on basis of information extracted from Ramasamy et al. (2017). Trade and Trade Facilitation along the BRI Corridors)

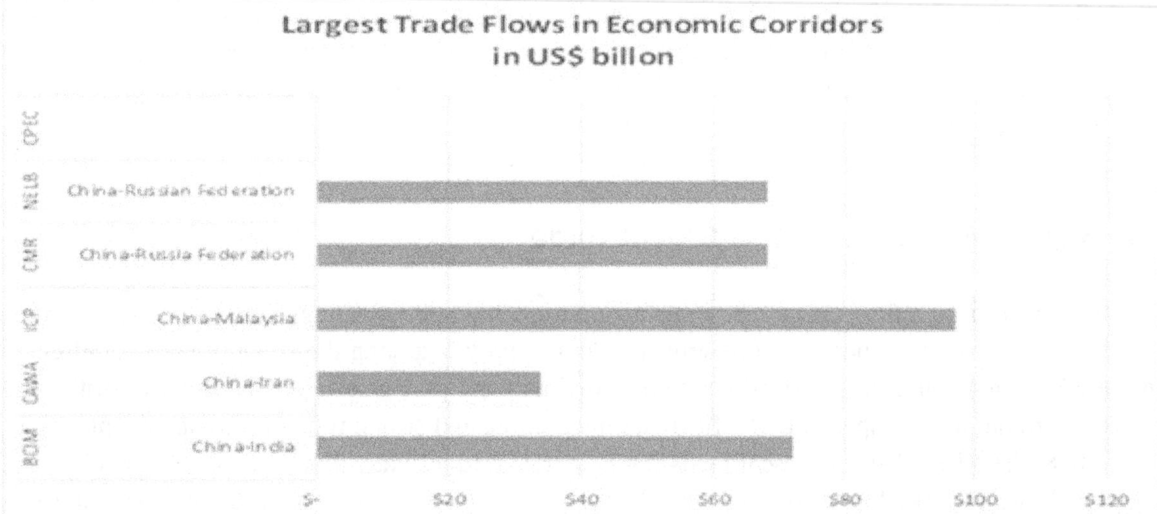

Figure 8. Share of BRI economies in global exports
Source: (Compiled by Author from 2019 World Bank data. Three Opportunities and Three Risks of the Belt and Road Initiative (worldbank.org))

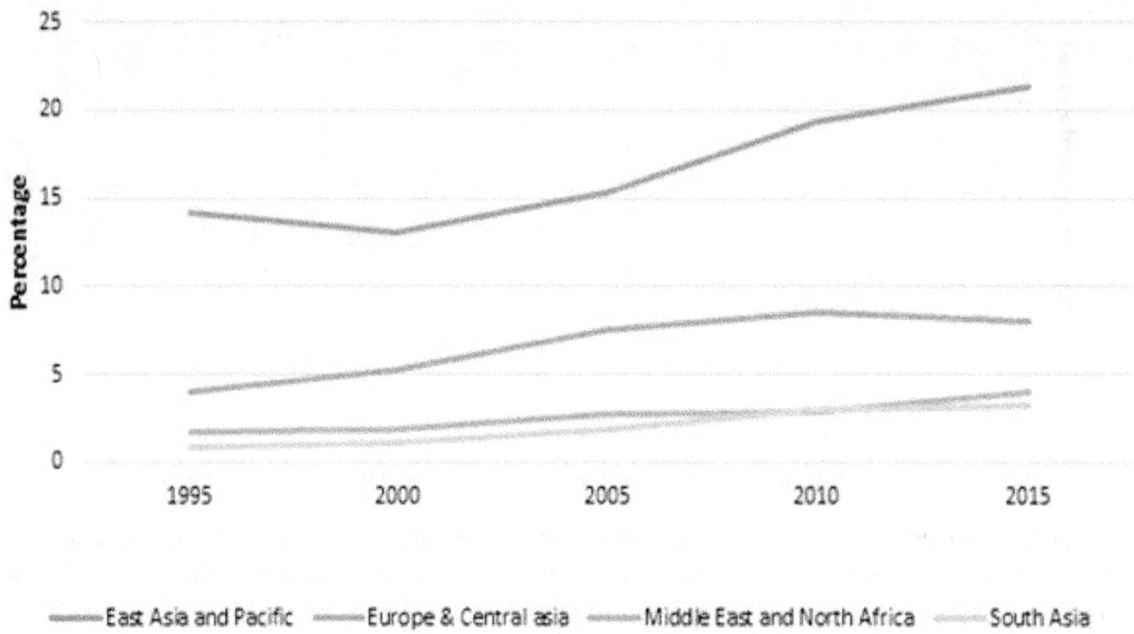

A growing number of BRI countries have ranked China among the three most important sources of foreign value added included in their exports. As China's economic activities span the world, its growing presence creates a significant shift in the global economy, displacing the center of gravity and transforming global patterns of accumulation and production networks (Jenkins, 2019). The growing number of countries that consider China as major trade partner constitutes an indicator of gravitational pull (World Bank, 2019a). Furthermore, not only does the gravitational shift derive from increased numbers of countries pulled towards China, but it also transforms the global economy in ways that affect U.S. dominance. For Lairson (2018, p. 2) China's centrality is mostly about structural change of the global order. "The BRI will increase the gravitational pull on states and firms to participate as success breeds additional opportunities, even for many states and firms clearly involved in the US global order. Such is the nature and power of a liberal and open world that China can operate such an effort to build structural power and attract a very broad set of states to this effort."

The Significance of the BRI to Global Trade

The BRI makes a significant structural contribution to global trade as China strives to close the infrastructure gap through connectivity investments. Connectivity is among the five priorities highlighted in the BRI, interconnecting overland economic corridors and port gateways. The other priorities are policy coordination, unimpeded trade, financial integration, and strong relations among people (Konings, 2018). The BRI does not discard existing bilateral and multilateral trade blocs. These blocs get integrated into the BRI framework as expanded cooperation and inter-regional trade. The result is a wider integration including countries situated outside dominant trade groups structured as bilateral or multilateral agreements or exclusive trade partnerships. Alon et al. (2018, p. 2) present the BRI as intended "to consolidate and upgrade a dense network of bilateral Free Trade Agreements (FTA) into a multilateral arrangement, anchored by China's gravitational pull and vast open market." Unimpeded trade is multilateral trade involving various partners located at distant geographic corners, facilitated by connectivity, enabled by coordinated policy, and supported by financial integration. The BRI is distinctive by the number of participants—65 countries, 62% of the global population. The wide cast is "fostering broader and deeper connectivity with the expanding middle class" making the BRI a global interaction "bound to (re-)shape the global economic order in consequential ways" Schortgen (2018, p. 25). The BRI is spreading trading dots in regional geographies, and by so doing it "territorializes" in the form of "spatial fixes". This essentially contextualizes the plan in participating economies, integrating the BRI with local development goals. The contextualization is necessary because "the grand project nature of the BRI, represented in a series of maps of linkages is comprised of the ideas and practices of strategic coupling, and hence requires a variety of local spatial arrangements compiled by the agency of many geopolitical actors (Flint & Zhu, 2018, p. 98)."

The *Vision and Actions* published by the Chinese government states, among other objectives, the need "to connect Asian, European and African countries more closely." The document, however, does not rule out cooperating with other regions. The *Vision and Actions* presents the initiative as "open to all countries, and international and regional organizations for engagement." A reminiscence of the ancient Silk Road, the BRI expands the boundaries of the ancient Road by establishing "new transport corridors, comprising physical and virtual communications infrastructures and nodal cities, coastal and inland ports, trade and industrial zones and industrial clusters" (Liu & Dunford, 2019, p. 152). Connectivity is the underlying function of this global establishment, not only of territories, but also of production processes thus interlinked, whereby local economic activities are integrated in an extended spatial outreach (Flint & Zhu, 2019). Not only does the BRI achieve economic and infrastructural realizations, but it also represents a matrix of a worldview for a trade environment envisioned to embody values. Liu and Dunford (2016, p. 336) conceptualize its scope with an intimation of the potency of its intended impact. "The BRI should therefore be understood as an organizational notion that employs the cultural meaning of the Silk Road to lay cultural foundations for international cooperation and create a global platform for further globalizing China".

Along the BRI distinctive trade blocs operate, and China has established trade with individual countries and blocs, becoming in many cases, the largest trade partner for many of them. Song et al. (2018) identified 30 countries for which China is the largest trade partner. How does the BRI as global trade project interact with each pocket of countries organized as regional trade blocs operating within its institutional parameters? Song et al. (2018, p. 1252) describe this situation as "spatial interaction between globalization and regionalization," meaning that preexisting regional multilateral or bilateral trade institutions connect to a global framework that incorporates activities of diverse communities distinct with their cooperation and development models. The situation makes China "the core node in terms of both trade volume and trade relationships" (Song et al., 2018, p. 1253) of the global multidirectional network of various regional trade partnerships clustered together. In addition, the emergence of the BRI has produced a complex topology of trade relationships featuring extra and intra BRI core nodes, given that pre-BRI trade groups continue to operate with their specific centers, such as the United States and Europe, linked to some BRI countries. Furthermore, intra-BRI trade functions as an integrated network, while containing various centers. Song et al. (2018) identified three BRI regions as centers to which

BRI economies are attached. China, Russia, and India-United Arab Emirates are core nodes of those BRI centers. This configuration is characterized as segmentation of a trade network that is at the same time integrated.

Regionalization is not antithetical to the BRI logic. Rather, it reinforces the capacities of individual nations to transcend their economic limits, such as market size. Regionalization is spatial extension for national economies readied for the integration into the BRI global framework through connected regional economic corridors. The alignment of regionalization and globalization is significant of "the degree of overall spatial continuity" (Song et al., 2018, p. 1255), reinforcing national economies through regionalization, which in turn brings regional trade into a global structure.

The Significance of South Asia to China's Geostrategic Interests

On the first line of China's pathway to global centrality stands its backyard, its South Asian neighbors. In some of these countries critical economic and financial conditions, such as deficits in infrastructure financing, offered China an opportunity to weigh in (Anwar, 2020). The region is also marked by differences, and perceptions about cooperation with China also differ. While Pakistan, Bangladesh, Sri Lanka, Maldives, Nepal, and Afghanistan support China's initiative, India and Bhutan, on the other hand, have been aloof with it. Anwar (2020, p. 163) explains that "Indian opposition is due to its confrontational relationship with China, which has been marked by competition rather than cooperation." Grossman (2020, p. 2) also points out persistent suspicions over China's economic engagement with its neighbors, "as it could support Beijing's broader geopolitical goals—namely the potential geostrategic encirclement of India."

The longstanding antagonism between China and India is no doubt recognized by China's leadership as likely to impede the pursuit of strategic goals in the region, given existing policy differences between the two countries. Moreover, India occupies a dominant position in the regional geography, with such imposing factors as large population, military power, and economic capabilities. Efforts to resolve disagreements over a number of issues, particularly territorial and border disputes, include diplomatic formal and informal initiatives most notably resorted to by Chinese leadership (Grossman, 2020). Border issues between the two countries have dominated their relations, with significant changes over five decades, alternating from the 1950s to the end of the 1980s between warmth, hostility, rapprochement and readjustment. The post-cold war era has brought opportunities for easing tensions. Jain (2004, p. 253) notes that "both countries have realized the imperative need for cooperation in diverse areas, especially in the trade and economic domains, in the long-term interest of peace and stability in Asia as well as of faster economic development and prosperity at home." However, viewing itself in competition with China, India has grown reluctant to some of China's actions, such as "attempts to secure port access agreements along the Indian Ocean," (Grossman, 2020, p. 4) through small states interested in China's BRI. Furthermore, India is also concerned with the relationship between China and Pakistan.

By its contiguity with China, South Asia is within the immediate continental perimeter of China's geostrategic thrust, and its geographic situation presents factors capable of affecting the BRI in the region. Three conditions underlie the rationale for China's interest in South Asia in the context of the BRI. They facilitate to incorporate the BRI in the social, political, and economic fabric of countries of the region. Their interconnectedness creates a useful geopolitical framework for China's objectives. First, in spite of variations among countries and the challenges for their domestic economies, the region has demonstrated rapid growth in the 1990s. Since the 2000s, the region's GDP has climbed to 5.3 percent even though its rising economic growth has been lagging behind China's. These trends cannot be ignored in the context of trade with China. Economic policies implemented in the region have contributed to overcoming constraints such as corruption, civil conflicts, and macroeconomic instability (International Growth Center, 2010). At the same time economic fragility may serve China's interests as ground to entice countries into aid that they are likely to welcome.

The second aspect has a clear strategic connotation involving the security of uninterrupted supply chains in the Indian Ocean for energy imports and other products from Africa and the Middle East needed for manufacturing (Ghiasy, 2021). The region extends China's access to sea lines by being a terrestrial gateway to the Indian Ocean. The China-Pakistan Economic Corridor (CPEC) is strategically important as a network comprising roads, highways, railways and power generation plants (Forough, 2019; Grossman, 2020). Its embedded transportation infrastructure is to "connect the north-western Chinese province of Xinjiang with the Pakistan port of Gwadar" (Indian Council of World Affairs (ICWA, 2015, p. 1). Security matters particularly intertwine with the commercial dimension in the CPEC. They constitute the reason behind China's interest in promoting dialogue with the Taliban in Pakistan and Afghanistan, "as this is seen as necessary for CPEC's security" (Forough, 2019, p. 278). From a commercial standpoint, China's commitment to the region gives CPEC particular significance in that it "reduces China's dependence on the strategic chokepoint of the Strait of Malacca." CPEC is significant as a key passage strategically redirecting China's commercial routes for imports and exports.

The third aspect is revealed by India's interpretation of China's intents as a mixed effort of "spinning a web of win-win economic ties built from trade strength, which could make China the nucleus of regional integration" (ICWA, 2015, p. 3). Critics of the BRI have often pointed to this mixture of assertiveness and narratives of shared interests as "a strategic ploy to gain access and build influence through diplomatic and economic coercion" (Mobley, 2019, p. 53). A complex set of circumstances determine the geopolitical setting of the region. The most determinant of these is the persistence of tense relationships between Pakistan and India, in which China is not a silent observer. China's activities in Pakistan have contributed to fanning an already tense situation, increasing India's disgruntlement and concern with being encircled by China's ports or naval bases throughout the Indian Ocean once naval facilities at Gwadar are established by China (Grossman, 2020). Moreover, as Ghiasy (2021, p. 267) notes, "these tensions and divisions have extended and continue to extend extra-regionally. China still sides with Pakistan, while the US has shifted away from Pakistan and towards India to counter China in the Indo-Pacific." Long-standing border disputes occasionally break out between India and Pakistan, while China and India have faced each other over the issue of Tibet that has remained central in a conflict that has contributed to increasing tensions between them (Anwar, 2020). Border disputes between China and India continue to plague their relationships, in particular over the Line of Actual Control (LAC) that separates territories they respectively control. This, in addition to India's rejection of China's BRI, and the competition for regional dominance, does not bode well for China's geostrategic plan, as it seeks "to gain economically from India's involvement in BRI" (Grossman, 2020, p. 4).

The United States withdrawal from the Trans-Pacific Partnership agreement in January 2017 boosted China's chances to be the regional dominant player. As Baruah and Panda (2019, p. 164) state, "whether it is in South Asia, Southeast Asia or East Asia, China's key foreign policy goal as stated by the government is to ensure regional stability, fostering the principles of good state-to-state relations in international relations through mutual respect, win-win cooperation and promoting fairness and justice." In his speech at the 19th Party Congress, President Xi highlighted the vision of shared community, emphasizing BRI-supported neighborly relations. The BRI makes Xi's rule consequential in the development of regional relations and beyond. His potential life-term presidency implies that "Asian countries worried about China's increasing assertiveness can no longer pin their hopes on a more benign and mild leader arising in the future. Strategically, they would have to meet a more robust China as a geopolitical fact for decades to come" (Dylan, 2018).

South Asia, not unlike all trade regions, has been hit by the outbreak of the novel coronavirus, COVID-19, which has followed the global value chain. China's productions had been temporarily suspended by many multinational companies when the pandemic was at its highest in the country. Baldwin and Tomiura (2020) see the magnitude of the effects from its impact on other world's major economies - the United States, Japan, Germany, Britain, France, and Italy. Along with China, these countries account for 60% of world supply and demand (GDP), 65% of the world manufacturing, 41% of world manufacturing exports. The next section examines some effects of the pandemic.

THE COVID-19 PANDEMIC AND GLOBAL TRADE

Affected by the pandemic, China's central role in global production networks could not but affect the transmission channels. As Arezki and Nguyen, (2020, p. 56) state, "when China's production is disrupted, countries with strong value chain connections with China will likely also be affected." Supply disruptions affect production, since the heartland of manufacturing (East Asia) is where the pandemic originated as it rushed to other industrial hubs, such as the United States and Germany. Additionally, supply chain "will amplify the direct supply shocks as manufacturing sector in less-affected nations find it harder and/or more expensive to acquire the necessary imported inputs from the hard-hit nations, and subsequently from each other" (Baldwin & di Mauro, p. 4). According to Friedt and Zhang (2020), China experienced a 45% reduction in exports during the first half of 2020. About 75% of the reduction occurred as a reflection of GVC effect. A World Bank (2021, p. 115) assessment determined that "concerns about the viability of global value chains and the course of the pandemic have weighed on international trade and tourism." Global networks contributing to trade, such as production chains and commodity exports, have been hampered by reduced productivity. Supporting facts include concurrent increase in the number of Chinese and global coronavirus infections during the first quarter of 2020 and the decline of new export orders by as much as 50% of both goods and services (World Bank, 2021).

Trade interconnections are generally explained through causality. For instance, Sforza and Steininger (2020, p. 3) state that "a higher degree of integration in the global production network implies that a shock in one country directly diffuses through the trade linkages to other countries." However, the correlation is not one-directional. Disruptions in two interconnected factors—supply and demand—have reverberations throughout the economic system and their waves return to affect the source of disruptions. Friedt (2021, p. 2) argues that "the real danger of the pandemic-induced disruption of global production networks lies in the feedback effects that amplify the original shock and spread it through the entire chain of production."

POLICY RECOMMENDATIONS

Transparency

A World Bank report (2018) found that procurement methods in the BRI favor Chinese firms, disproportionately awarding infrastructure contracts. This finding also reveals lack of transparency, as well as scarcity of information related to BRI procurement procedures. Three aspects should be addressed: the availability of data on procurement procedures implemented in the BRI; transparency in the decision making regarding contracts awarded in project host countries; and the consideration of local investors and contractors in countries where projects are conducted. Addressing these issues in an inclusive manner will increase confidence in the BRI and Chinese leadership. Although Chinese funding justifies the lion share of contracts for Chinese companies, it would be appropriate to consolidate the BRI's integration through policies and trade agreements of joint investments with host country.

Global Oversight

International development institutions, such as the World Bank, UNDP, UNCTAD should establish a joint platform to continually assess China's BRI implementation and serve as leverage for less developed nations. This can be done in conjunction with the U.S. government and the European Union, and like-minded countries, such as Canada, India, Japan, and South Korea, which are concerned with China's growing influence on global trade and its impact on global security. For less powerful BRI participating economies the platform would provide global institutional support, should they encounter difficulties in their cooperation with China.

Forced Technology Transfer

The United States, Canada, the European Union, along with like-minded countries, such as India, Japan, South Korea and Australia, should work on increasing levers through a consortium for technology transfer surveillance. The goal is to enforce the protection of technology and curtail forced technology transfer, a practice used by the Chinese government to access the know-how from Western companies.

Project Preparation

The plan should also include transparent project preparation processes, which should take into account financial, environmental, social, workforce, health concerns, and legal considerations. In addition, the plan would have added value if it contained key performance indicators (KPI) to be predetermined in the preparation process of trade agreements by policy makers. The idea of specific KPI would facilitate evaluation at the global level by independent observers. Introducing KPI would ensure project high quality and sustainability.

Anticorruption Units

Procurement practices and project implementation should be monitored with mechanisms designed to enforce compliance to best practices and anticorruption principles. The *Thematic Forum on Clean Silk*

Road of the second Belt and Road Forum for International Cooperation adopted measures calling to work in the spirit of the United Nations Convention Against Corruption. This should be reinforced through national units tasked with oversight for accountability where projects are implemented to curtail wasteful spending. The BRI legal framework should contain guidance for prosecution of corruption behaviors in accordance with international standards.

CONCLUSION

The various networks of China's trade partnerships are built upon institutional determinants, and carry meanings whereby China as the central node sets the norms. The incorporation of norms into national entities seeking to partake in the networks is the work of a strategy deployed by China on a global scale. The strategy contributes to the creation of trade regime, bolstered by regulative, normative, and cognitive elements. The BRI is no doubt a different trade structure, but it has not deviated from the framework of the WTO's liberal trade regime (Weinhardt & Brink, 2020). This is significant in that inconsistency with established principles of global trade would lessen the persuasive influence of China's initiative. It is more rewarding for an aspiring power to challenge the system from within than without. This explains the strategy of more assertive international involvement already activated under Hu Jintao. China has been seen "taking greater interest in international affairs to the point of becoming more of a "rule shaper" in many cases, instead of a mere follower" (Mishra, 2019, p. 282). Therefore, the outcomes of China's political and economic actions reflect heeding domestic and international historical and geopolitical factors.

China's actions in the global economy are translated into network edges whose multitude expands China's place as central node. The BRI, as trade network, produces multiple links spanning the world and reflecting China's geostrategic approach. The number of geographically situated nodes linked to China will increase as investments in economic corridors and beyond yield satisfactory outcomes. Trade dominance through widespread partnerships and the taming of geographic conditions has strategically resulted in China's centrality in the ITN. China is not a hegemon yet, but its rise is a significant fact in the contemporary global political economy in which the United States continues to act as the dominant power. Any concern with China's growing influence is faced with apprehension from the standpoint of the United States, not only in the context of trade disputes, but also from the perspective of unipolarity. This is the reaction of a dominant systemic rule setter to the challenge by the increased global centrality of a country whose geostrategic emergence has sometimes been viewed as rule breaking or perhaps institutional revisionism.

In sum, China's geostrategic approach includes safeguarding global institutions deemed necessary, as well as expanding its trade networks as institutional frameworks embodying its geopolitical and geoeconomic objectives. When existing institutions might not facilitate its ambitious plans, China has resorted to initiating enticing structural conditions with horizontal patterns of interactions. With a persuasive approach embedded in peripheral diplomacy, China has induced participants to embrace its trade mechanisms, such as the BRI, thus successfully establishing communities of "shared beliefs" through financial institutions, security protocols, and trade commitments.

REFERENCES

Alon, I., Zhang, W., & Lattermann, C. (2018). Introduction. In I. Alon, W. Zhang, & C. Lattermann (Eds.), *China's Belt and Road initiative: Changing the rules of globalization* (pp. 1–13). Palgrave. doi:10.1007/978-3-319-75435-2_1

Amador, J., & Cabral, S. (2016). *Networks of value added trade.* ECB Working Paper No. 1931.

Anwar, A. (2020). Report, South Asia and China's Belt and Road Initiative: Security implications and ways forward. In A. L. Vuving (Ed.), *Hindsight, insight, foresight: Thinking about security in the Indo-Pacific* (pp. 161–178). Daniel K. Inouye Asia-Pacific Center for Security Studies.

Arezki, R., & Nguyen, H. (2020). Novel coronavirus hurts the Middle East and North Africa through many channels. In R. Baldwin & B. W. di Mauro (Eds.), *Economics in the Time of COVID-19* (pp. 53–58). Centre for Economic Policy Research.

Baldwin, R., & Tomiura, E. (2020). Thinking ahead about the trade impact of COVID-19. In R. Baldwin & B. W. di Mauro (Eds.), *Economics in the Time of COVID-19* (pp. 59–71). Centre for Economic Policy Research.

Bandyopadhyay, S., Rao, A., & Sinha, B. (2011). *Models for social networks with statistical applications.* Sage. doi:10.4135/9781452226538

Baruah, A. G., & Panda, J. P. (2019). Xi Jinping's authoritarianism, Chinese foreign policy and India. *Megatrend Review, 16*(1), 151–172. doi:10.5937/MegRev1901151G

Baruah, D. M. (2018). *India's answer to the Belt and Road: A road map for South Asia* (Report). Carnegie Endowment for International Peace Working Paper.

Bhattacharya, K., Mukherjee, G., Saramäki, J., Kashi, K., & Manna, S. (2008). The international trade network: Weighted network analysis and modelling. *Journal of Statistical Mechanics, 2008*(02), 1–10. doi:10.1088/1742-5468/2008/02/P02002

Bitzinger, R. (2011). Recent developments in naval and maritime modernization in the asia-pacific: implications for regional security. In P. C. Saunders, C. D. Yung, M. Swaine, & A. Yang (Eds.), *The Chinese navy: Expanding capabilities, evolving roles* (pp. 23–40). National Defense University Press for the Center for the Study of Chinese Military Affairs.

Bloch, F., Jackson, M., & Tebaldi, P. (2017). *Centrality measures in networks.* arXiv:1608.05845v3. https://arxiv.org/pdf/1608.05845v3.pdf

Brill, H. (1985). Political geography, geopolitics, and geostrategy: An attempt at systematization. *Strategic Studies, 8*(2), 86–98.

Cáceres, S. B. (2014). *China's strategic interests in the South China Sea: Power and resources.* Routledge.

Calder, K. E. (2012). *The new continentalism: Energy and twenty-first-century Eurasian geopolitics.* Yale University Press.

Callahan, W. A. (2016). China's "Asia Dream": The Belt Road Initiative and the new regional order. *Asian Journal of Comparative Politics*, *1*(3), 226–243. doi:10.1177/2057891116647806

Casarini, N. (2015). *Is Europe to benefit from China's Belt and Road Initiative?* Istituto Affari Internazionali (IAI).

Chase-Dunn, C., Kwon, R., Lawrence, K., & Inoue, H. (2011). Last of hegemons: U.S. decline and global governance. *International Review of Modern Sociology*, *37*(1), 1–29.

Chauhan, P. (2019). Energy dimension of the Belt and Road Initiative. *Indian Journal of Asian Affairs*, *32*(1/2), 119–115.

Chen, X., & Fazilov, F. (2018). Re-centering Central Asia: China's "New Great Game" in the old Eurasian Heartland. *Palgrave Communications*, *4*(71), 1–12. doi:10.105741599-018-0125-5

Chinese Government. (2015). *Vision and actions on jointly building Silk Road Economic Belt and 21st Century Maritime Silk Road.* Academic Press.

Cingolani, I., Panzarasa, P., & Tajoli, L. (2017). Countries' positions in the international global value networks: Centrality and economic performance. *Applied Network Science*, *2*(1), 2–21. doi:10.100741109-017-0041-4 PMID:30443576

Danner, L. K., & Martín, F. E. (2019). China's hegemonic intentions and trajectory: Will it opt for benevolent, coercive, or dutch-style hegemony? *Asia & the Pacific Policy Studies*, *6*(2), 186–207. doi:10.1002/app5.273

De Benedictis, L., & Tajoli, L. (2011). The world trade network. *World Economy*, *34*(8), 1417–1454. doi:10.1111/j.1467-9701.2011.01360.x

Deng, Y. (2008). *China's struggle for status: The realignment of international relations*. Cambridge University Press. doi:10.1017/CBO9780511790768

Department of Defense. (2020). *Military and security developments involving the People's Republic of China.* Annual Report to Congress.

Dibb, P. (2018). The return of geography. In R. Glenn (Ed.), *New Directions in Strategic Thinking 2.0: ANU Strategic & Defence Studies Centre's Golden Anniversary Conference Proceedings* (pp. 91-104). Acton, Australia: ANU Press. 10.22459/NDST.07.2018.08

Dylan, L. (2018). How Xi Jinping's 'Lifetime Presidency' could change China – for better or worse? *The Conversation, 2*.

Economy, E. (2010). The game changer: Coping with China's foreign policy revolution. *Foreign Affairs*, 1–10.

Flint, C., & Zhu, C. (2019). The geopolitics of connectivity, cooperation, and hegemonic competition: The Belt and Road Initiative. *Geoforum*, *99*, 95–101. doi:10.1016/j.geoforum.2018.12.008

Forough, M. (2019). Intervention with Chinese characteristics: The Belt and Road Initiative reconfiguring (Afro-) Eurasian geo-economics. *Conflict Security and Development*, *19*(3), 275–281. doi:10.1080/14678802.2019.1608023

Friedt, F. (2021). The triple effect of COVID-19 on Chinese exports: GVC contagion effects dominate export supply and import demand shocks. *VOX, CEPR Policy Portal*.

Friedt, F., & Zhang, K. (2020). The triple effect of Covid-19 on Chinese exports: First evidence of the export supply, import demand & Gvc contagion effects. *Covid Economics*, *53*, 72–109.

Ghiasy, R. (2018). *China's Belt and Road Initiative: Security implications and ways forward for the European Union*. Stockholm International Peace Research Institute.

Ghiasy, R. (2021). The Belt and Road Initiative in South Asia: Regional impact and the evolution of perceptions and policy responses. In F. Schneider (Ed.), *Global perspectives on China's Belt and Road Initiative: Asserting agency through regional connectivity* (pp. 265–290). Amsterdam University Press.

Gompert, D. (2013). *Sea power and American interests in the Western Pacific*. The Rand Corporation.

Gong, X. (2020). China's Belt and Road Initiative financing in Southeast Asia. *Southeast Asian Affairs*, 77-95.

Grant, R. (1994). The geography of international trade. *Progress in Human Geography*, *18*(3), 298–312. doi:10.1177/030913259401800302

Gray, C. S. (1999). Inescapable geography. In C. S. Gray & G. Sloan (Eds.), *Geopolitics, geography and strategy* (pp. 161–177). Frank Cass Publishers.

Grossman, D. (2020). What China wants in South Asia. *ORF Issue Brief*, *368*, 1–16.

Guha, N., Han, A., & Lin, A. (2016). Network analysis of global trade. *CS224W*, 1-8.

Hans-Peter, B. (2013). *What is economic corridor development and what can it achieve in asia's sub-regions?* ADB Working Paper Series on Regional Economic Integration, No. 117, Asian Development Bank (ADB). http://hdl.handle.net/11540/2308

Hartnett, D. M., & Vellucci, F. (2011). Toward a maritime security strategy: An analysis of Chinese views since the early 1990s. In P. Saunders, C. Yung, M. Swaine, & A. Yang (Eds.), *The Chinese Navy: Expanding Capabilities, Evolving Roles* (pp. 81–108). National Defense University Press for the Center for the Study of Chinese Military Affairs.

Hojman, D. A., & Szeidl, A. (2008). Core and periphery in networks. *Journal of Economic Theory*, *139*(1), 295–309. doi:10.1016/j.jet.2007.07.007

Huiyun, F. (2009). Is China a revisionist power? *The Chinese Journal of International Politics*, *2*(3), 313–334. doi:10.1093/cjip/pop003

Ikenberry, G. J. (2014). From hegemony to the balance of power: The rise of China and American grand strategy. *International Journal of Korean Unification Studies*, *23*(2), 41–63.

Indian Council of World Affairs (ICWA). (2015). China Pakistan Economic Corridor (CPEC). *Issue Brief*, 1–15.

International Growth Center. (2010). *Economic growth and structural change in South Asia: Miracle or Mirage?* Working Papers 10/0859.

Jain, B. M. (2004). India–China relations: Issues and emerging trends. *The Round Table*, *93*(374), 374. doi:10.1080/0035853041000167960[2]

Jenkins, R. (2019). *How China is reshaping the global economy: Development impacts in Africa and Latin America*. Oxford University Press.

Kano, L., & Oh, C. H. (2020). Global value chains in the post-COVID world: Governance for reliability. *Journal of Management Studies*, *57*(8), 1773–1777. doi:10.1111/joms.12626

Kaplan, R. (2012). *The revenge of geography: What the map tells us about coming conflicts and the battle against fate*. Random House Publishing Group.

Kastner, S. L., & Saunders, P. C. (2012). Is China a status quo or revisionist state? Leadership travel as an empirical indicator of foreign policy priorities. *Studia Quaternaria*, *56*, 163–177.

Kimura, F., Thangavalu, S., Narzioko, D., & Findlay, C. (2020). Pandemic (COVID-19) policy, regional cooperation and the emerging global production network. *Asian Economic Journal*, *34*(1), 3–27. doi:10.1111/asej.12198

Konings, J. (2018). Trade impacts of the Belt and Road Initiative. *ING, Economic & Financial Analysis*, 1-12.

Lai, D. (2011). The Power Transition Theory. In The United States and China in Power Transition. Strategic Studies Institute, US Army War College.

Lairson, T. D. (2018). *The global strategic environment of the BRI: Deep interdependence and structural power.* Academic Press.

Lemke, D., & Tammen, R. L. (2003). Power transition theory and the rise of China. *International Interactions*, *29*(4), 269–271. doi:10.1080/714950651

Li, X., Meng, B., & Wang, Z. (2019). Recent patterns of global production and Gvc participation. In *Technological Innovation, Supply Chain Trade, and Workers in a Globalized World*. Geneva: Centre William Rappard.

Liangxiang, J., & Janardhan, N. (2020). Belt and Road Initiative: Opportunities and obstacles for the Gulf. In N. Janardhan (Ed.), *The Arab Gulf's Pivot to Asia: From Transactional to Strategic Partnerships* (pp. 35–48). Gerlach Press. doi:10.2307/j.ctv15r56r3.5

Links, S. (2021). Ascertaining agency Africa and the Belt and Road Initiative. In F. Schneider (Ed.), *Global perspectives on China's Belt and Road Initiative: Asserting agency through regional connectivity* (pp. 113–139). Amsterdam University Press.

Liu, W., & Dunford, M. (2019). Chinese perspectives on the Belt and Road Initiative. *Cambridge Journal of Regions, Economy and Society*, *12*(1), 145–167. doi:10.1093/cjres/rsy032

Matsumura, M. A. (2019). A realist approach to Japan's free and open Indo-Pacific Strategy vs. China's Belt and Road Initiative: A propaganda rivalry. *International Journal of China Studies*, *10*(2), 131–154.

Mattis, J. (2018). *Summary of the 2018 national defense strategy of the United States of America*. US Department of Defense.

McBride, S., Cohen, M., Dobuzinskis, L., & Busumtwi-Sam, J. (2002). Global instability: Uncertainty and new visions in political economy. In S. McBride, L. Dobuzinskis, M. Cohen, & J. Busumtwi-Sam (Eds.), *Global instability* (pp. 1–6). Social Indicators Research Series. Springer. doi:10.1007/978-94-010-0251-6_1

McKinsey Global Institute. (2019). *China and the world: Inside the dynamics of a changing relationship*. Author.

Mishra, R. (2019). China's global maritime engagement and the Indian Ocean Region. In J. Wang & H. Boon (Eds.), *China's omnidirectional peripheral diplomacy* (pp. 281–316). World Scientific Publishing Co. doi:10.1142/9789813141797_0012

Mobley, T. (2019). The Belt and Road Initiative: Insights from China's backyard. *Strategic Studies Quarterly*, *13*(3), 52–72.

National Development and Reform Commission. (2015). *Vision and Actions on Jointly Building Silk Road Economic Belt and 21st Century Maritime Silk Road*. reconasia-production.s3.amazonaws.com

Nohara, J. J. (2017). Sea power as a dominant paradigm: The rise of China's new strategic identity. *Journal of Contemporary East Asia Studies*, *6*(2), 210–232. doi:10.1080/24761028.2017.1391623

O'Loughlin, J. (1994). *Dictionary of geopolitics*. Greenwood Press.

ORF (2020) Issue Brief, No. 395.

Qi, X., Erickson, A., & Goldstein, L. (2006). Maritime geostrategy and the development of the Chinese navy in the early twenty-first century. *Naval War College Review*, *59*(4), 46.

Ramasamy, B., Yeung, M., Utoktham, C., & Duval, Y. (2017). *Trade and trade facilitation along the Belt and Road Initiative Corridors*. ARTNetT Working Paper Series No. 172.

Ratner, E. (2018). *Geostrategic and military drivers and implications of the Belt and Road Initiative*. Council on Foreign Relations.

Regilme, S. Jr. (2019). The decline of American power and Donald Trump: Reflections on human rights, neoliberalism, and the world order. *Geoforum*, *102*, 157–166. doi:10.1016/j.geoforum.2019.04.010

Rogers, J. (2011). A new geography of European power? (Rep.). Egmont Institute.

Schneider, F. (2021). Actors and agency in China's Belt and Road Initiative: An Introduction. In F. Schneider (Ed.), *Global perspectives on China's Belt and Road Initiative: Asserting agency through regional connectivity* (pp. 11–32). Amsterdam University Press.

Schortgen, F. (2018). China and the twenty-first-century Silk Roads: A new era of global economic leadership? In China's Belt and Road Initiative: Changing the rules of globalization (pp. 17-33). Cham, Switzerland: Palgrave.

Sforza, A., & Steininger, M. (2020). *Globalization in the time of COVID-19*. CESifo Working Paper, No. 8184, Center for Economic Studies and ifo Institute (CESifo), Munich.

Sloan, G. (2017). *Geopolitics, geography and strategic history*. Routledge. doi:10.4324/9780203489482

Song, Z., Che, S., & Yang, Y. (2018). The trade network of the Belt and Road Initiative and its topological relationship to the global trade network. *Journal of Geographical Sciences, 28*(9), 1249–1262. doi:10.100711442-018-1523-8

Swartz, P. M. (2011). Rising powers and naval power. In P. Saunders, C. Yung, M. Swaine, & A. Yang (Eds.), *The Chinese navy: Expanding capabilities, evolving roles* (pp. 1–21). National Defense University Press for the Center for the Study of Chinese Military Affairs.

Umbach, F. (2019). *China's Belt and Road Initiative and its energy-security dimensions.* S. Rajaratnam School of International Studies, RSIS Working Paper, 320.

UNCTAD. (2015). *Tracing the value added in global value chains: Product-level case studies in China.* United Nations.

Wang, Y. (2016). Offensive for defensive: The Belt and Road Initiative and China's new grand strategy. *The Pacific Review, 29*(3), 455–463. doi:10.1080/09512748.2016.1154690

Weinhardt, C., & Brink, T. (2020). Varieties of contestation: China's rise and the liberal trade order. *Review of International Political Economy, 27*(2), 258–280. doi:10.1080/09692290.2019.1699145

World Bank. (2018). *Public procurement in the Belt and Road Initiative.* Author.

World Bank (2019a). *Three opportunities and three risks of the Belt and Road Initiative.* worldbank.org

World Bank. (2019b). Belt and road economics: Opportunities and risks of transport corridors. Washington, DC: Author.

World Bank. (2020). East Asia and the Pacific economic update: From containment to recovery. Washington, DC: Author.

World Bank. (2021). Global Economic prospects, A World Bank Group Flagship Report. Washington, DC: Author.

Xi, J. (2017). *Secure a Decisive Victory in Building a Moderately Prosperous Society in all Respects and Strive for the Great Success of Socialism with Chinese Characteristics for a New Era.* Delivered at the 19th National Congress of the Communist Party of China.

Yang, S. (2013). Power transition, balance of power, and the rise of China: A theoretical reflection about rising great powers. *China Review, 13*(2), 35–66.

Zhang, B. (2014). Xi Jinping, 'Pragmatic' offensive realism and China's Rise. *Global Asia, 9*(2), 71–79.

Zhang, J., & Luo, Y. (2017). Degree centrality, betweenness centrality, and closeness centrality in social network. *2nd International Conference on Modelling, Simulation and Applied Mathematics (MSAM)*, 300-303.

Zhang, Z. (2018). The Belt and Road Initiative: China's new geopolitical strategy? *China Quarterly of International Strategic Studies, 4*(3), 327–343. doi:10.1142/S2377740018500240

Zheng, Y. (2020). Rediscovering continentalism: The new geographic foundations of Chinese Power. *International Politics*, 1–35. doi:10.105741311-019-00206-7

Zhu, Z., Cesina, F., Chessa, A., Caldarelli, G., & Riccaboni, M. (2014). The rise of China in the international trade network: A community core detection approach. *PLoS One*, *9*(8), 1–8. doi:10.1371/journal.pone.0105496 PMID:25136895

Zicheng, Y. (2011). *Inside China's grand strategy: The perspective from the People's Republic*. University Press of Kentucky.

Ziegler, C. E. (2006). The energy factor in China's foreign policy. *Journal of Chinese Political Science*, *11*(1), 1–23. doi:10.1007/BF02877031

Zweig, D., & Jianhai, B. (2005). China's global hunt for energy. *Foreign Affairs*, *84*(5), 25–38. doi:10.2307/20031703

KEY TERMS AND DEFINITIONS

Belt and Road Initiative: Economic and trade development initiative launched by China in 2013 involving several countries in trade partnerships connected through infrastructure transports.

Connectivity: Method for establishing lifeline linkages between economic corridors and to the outside world in order to achieve transport network completeness.

Continentalism: An expansionist approach used by China to include countries of Eurasian landmass in its sphere of trade.

Economic Corridors: Partnerships of countries connected through dynamic interactions aimed at creating patterns of regional economic development.

Edge: An edge is a line drawn to connect two vertices and they constitute a set of two elements characterized by the connecting points.

Eurasia: Continental landmass comprising Asia and Europe, which China, through its geostrategic approach to trade, has expanded to include Africa for the purpose of its trade expansion.

Geoeconomic: Characteristics of economic activities as they relate to the spatial, temporal, and political aspects.

Geography: Physical location of a country as it determines its political, economic, and trade development through its dealing with other countries in the world.

Geopolitics: Geopolitics is mostly used in international relations as the study of the influence of geographic factors on politics, both domestic and international.

Node: In network analysis, a point at which lines or pathways intersect or branch in a network or diagram.

ENDNOTE

1 New Asian Security Concept For New Progress in Security Cooperation (fmprc.gov.cn).

Chapter 9
The Era of the Dragon: How China Is Preparing to Be the World's Top Economy in 21st Century

Maria João Tomás
https://orcid.org/0000-0003-4922-6724
Universidade Autónoma de Lisboa, Portugal

ABSTRACT

The upcoming decades are expected to be marked by the rise and consolidation of the People's Republic of China, PRC, as the world's first economy, dethroning the U.S. and altering global economic geopolitics. The Dragon Age will mark the 21st century, with all the consequences that can come from it. This chapter analyzes the changes that are already underway and that prepare China to be the world's great economy. The departure point will be the examination of China's economic situation. Following, the authors move on to analyzing the Belt and Road Investment, the Chinese mega investment that aims to connect China to Europe inspired by the ancient Silk Road, making a geoeconomic analysis of the main world markets and how China has long prepared this economic rise and implicates a political and military ascension statement.

INTRODUCTION

China is looking to be the top world's economy in the 21st century. To understand this path, it is essential to understand how China is dealing with the different markets and how it has managed to address the challenges that each one offers. The globalization of the Chinese economy, as will be seen in the next chapters, has a local focus, to be accepted without major objections, and not rejected either by the populations nor by their governments. The way China is operating in African countries is not the same as in in the Middle East. The strategy, agreements and partnerships are substantially different in each one of the markets, adapted to the existing reality, whether political, social, economic, and even military in nature.

On the other hand, it is also important to understand what China is looking for in each region. It is certain that one of the main objectives is the search for hydrocarbons to boost the high energy consump-

DOI: 10.4018/978-1-7998-7568-0.ch009

tion of its industry. China is not only the world's largest energy consumer; it is the second largest consumer of oil and the third largest consumer of natural gas. The need to diversify hydrocarbon suppliers, not to be held hostage by any, has taken China to several continents, although its main partner remains Russia. This precaution has consolidated large agreements, such as the one with Saudi Arabia, or major interventions, such as the ones in Sudan or Nigeria.

However, China is not only looking for hydrocarbons. The geographical isolation that led to the creation of the Ancient Silk Road is the same reason for the creation of the Belt and Road Initiative. The need to sell its production, and have good access, without being dependent on third parties, was one the main reasons for the creation of this mega investment that connects China to the world, with various land and sea routes, construction of ports, hubs, and hinterlands. The choice of the country partners is also strategic, to consolidate its position, not only economically but also politically, by becoming an agent of power in the region. As we shall see, China installed military bases in strategic locations. On the other hand, the way China has been dealing with other Asian countries is essential to understand how has achieved the leadership in this competitive part of the world.

This article aims to address all these issues to explain the rise of China and how will lead the world's economy in the 21st century.

PEOPLE'S REPUBLIC OF CHINA, PRC

The preliminary numbers of the Council of the People's Republic of China for the pandemic year of 2020 points towards a gross domestic product (GDP) of China 72,278.6 billion yuan in the first three quarters. This corresponds to a growth of 0.7 percent at comparable prices, mostly based on the growth of 3.2 percent for the second quarter, and up to 4.9 percent for the third quarter. The projections of the International Monetary Fund for 2020 were 6% lower.

China remains on the back of the world's largest economies affected by the consequences of the pandemic. The country, where the first case of COVID-19 disclosed in 2019 seems unscathed to the increasingly severe and widespread economic crisis. To realize this rise of China, which aims to be the world's largest economy even before 2023, one must understand a little of its history and figures.

The first aspect to retain is the fact that according to the world Economic Forum (2019) "China home to almost a fifth of the world's population"[1], being the most populous country of the planet, with 1,38 billions of people (Figure 1), making the Chinese domestic market an important protection bubble of the Chinese economy (Ho et al., 2019). China's GDP has consistently grown 10%, although it has slowed in the last 10 years, and now walks by 6.3% (Statistica, 2020). Figure 2 shows this evidence. The world average in 2020 is 3.3%. China's poverty rate fell from 53% in 1981 to 8% in 2001 (Chen & Ravallion, 2008). It also has the largest number of unicorns, companies worth more than $1 billion, an estimated number of almost 10 million market entities, and new companies and industries already are 15,7% of GDP of China in 2019 (Statistica 2020). China is buying important companies all over the world, like Volvo, is making investments in a variety of others, like the technological Lenovo from IBM, purchasing mineral and hydrocarbons reserves, and seeks to be self-enough in value of chain, ranging from as "commoditized manufacturing and lower-skilled assembly to design, logistics, financial and business services, high-tech industries and life sciences" (Coleman et al., 2014).

China leads in technologies, registering more than half of the world's intellectual property patents in 2020, surpassing the United States. Inflation despite having risen in recent years has stopped during

Figure 1. Total population of China from 1980 to 2019 with forecasts until 2025
Source: (IMF; CEIC; National Bureau of Statistics of China)

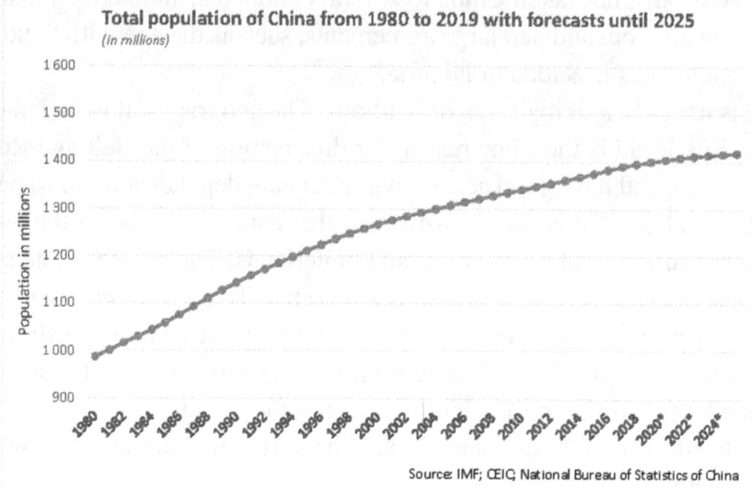

the pandemic, and projections point to a decrease in the coming years. It is in 2020 the largest exporter and the third largest carrier of goods on the planet. As shown in Figure 3, the main Chinese importers are the United States and the European Union while the import of goods in China remains on the rise (Statistica 2020).

Figure 2. Gross domestic product (GDP) at current prices in China from 1985 to 2019 with forecasts until 2025 (in billion U.S. dollars)
Source: (IMF)

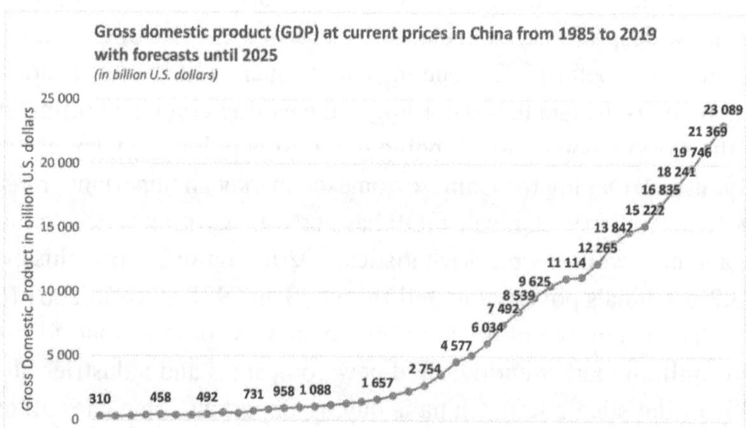

Figure 3. China's leading import partners, by import value
Source: (National Bureau of Statistics of China)

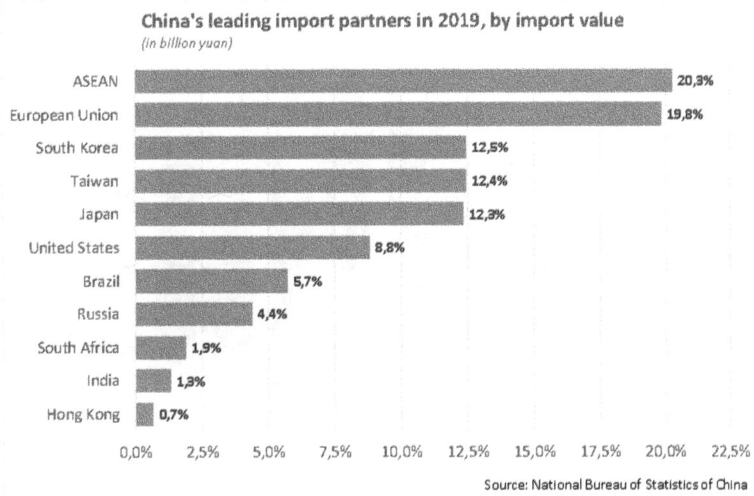

Figures 4 and 5, below, complement this evidence, providing additional detail.

Figure 4. Inflation rate in China from 2008 to 2018 with forecasts until 2025
Source: (IMF)

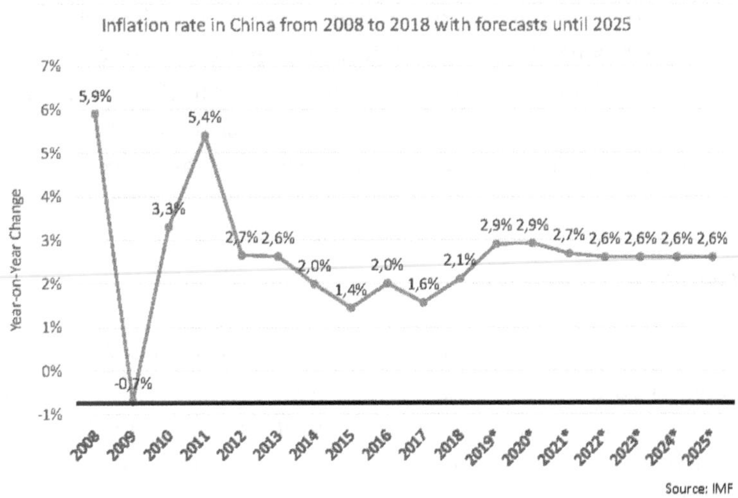

The fact that the economy has grown by an average of 10% a year, make People's Republic of China, the world's second largest economy by 2020, getting closer and closer to the leader, the United States. The emerging superpower is preparing to be the world's largest economy, an explicit strategy of current President Xi Jingiping, which began with Deng Xiaoping's economic reforms in 1978, with the introduction of market socialism and economic openness. In November 2017, president Xi Jinping in

Figure 5.Value of imports of goods in China from 2009 to 2019 (in billion U.S. dollars)
Source: (WTO)

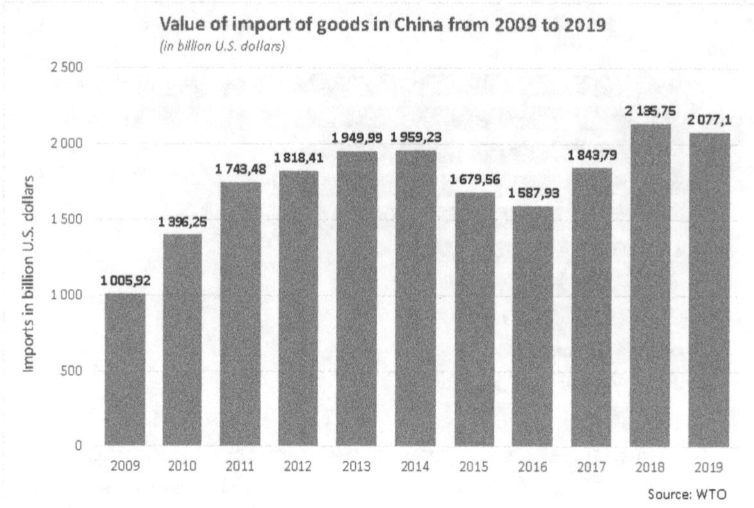

his opening address to the 19th Congress of the Chinese Communist Party (PCC) declared that China "comes day after day, approaching the center of the world stage".

China's role as the global economic leader will create a new order of global movement of goods and energy supplies, but also a new geopolitical reality, with a China leading the diplomatic, military, and political order (Dahlman & Aubert, 2001). This new era, "The Dragon Era" will end the American hegemony, consolidated in the 20th century, after the dissolution of the Soviet Union on December 26th, 1991, when the bipolar order came to an end, and the axel America/USSR disappeared, leading to Russia opusculum as a world leader. For China it was the opportunity to start asserting itself independently.

To be the world's largest economy, Xi Jinping began the construction of the Belt and Road Initiative, BRI, the most important tool for China geopolitical and economic ambition.

BELT AND ROAD INITIATIVE, BRI

The Belt and Road Initiative (Figure 6), BRI, is undoubtedly one of the biggest economic and foreign policy projects of China. In May of 2017, president Xi Jinping declared at the opening of Belt and Road forum: "China will actively promote international co-operation through the Belt and Road Initiative. In doing so, we hope to achieve policy, infrastructure, trade, financial, and people-to-people connectivity and thus build a new platform for international co-operation to create new drivers of shared development" (Xi, 2017, p. 61). The ambitions of China are very clear, and the Belt Road Initiative is a central part of this plan.

The name Belt and Road Initiative was coined in 2013 by China's President Xi Jinping, who drew inspiration from the concept of the Silk Road established during the Han Dynasty 2,000 years ago – an ancient network of trade routes that connected China to the Mediterranean via Eurasia for centuries (Ohashi, 2018).

Figure 6. The Belt and Road Initiative
Source: (Merics)

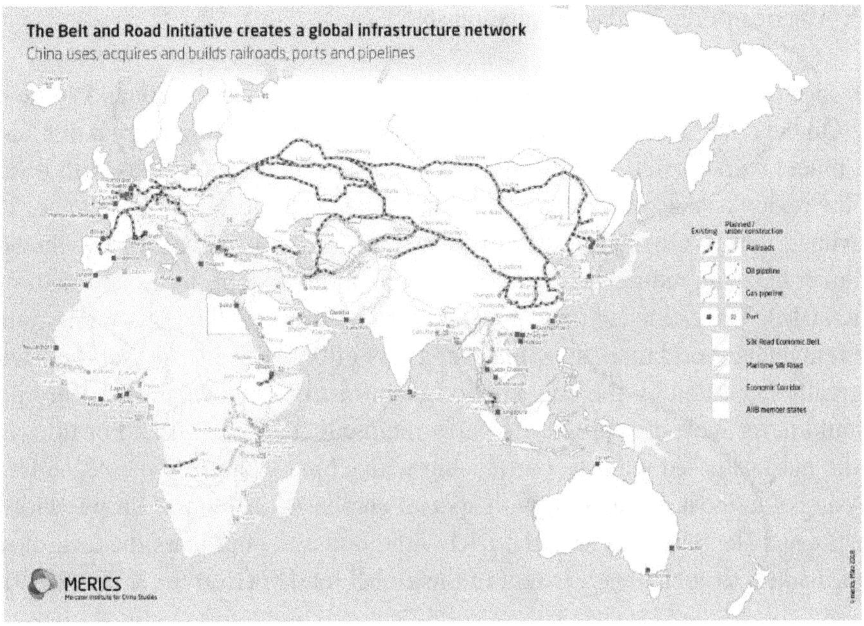

This huge investment of 50 billion dollars is already nicknamed as the great economic project of the 21st century. This mega project includes the construction of sea, rail and road routes. This will facilitate the transportation of people, goods and energy, covering an area that involves bilateral agreements with 66 countries, more than 4.4 billion people and almost 40% of the world's economy, with an economic impact of 21 trillion of dollars, and a direct investment of 1 trillion dollars. 90% of the investment is financed by the Silk Road Fund, founded in December 2014, with the following composition: 65% of the investment provided by the State Administration of Foreign Policy, 15% by the Investment Corporation of China, 5% by the Development Bank of China and 15% by the Export and Import Bank of China. The remaining 10% are from European banks (OECD, 2018; People's Republic of China, 2015). Showing well the strategic economic and political importance of this project, China's State Councillor Yang Jiechi and EU High Representative for Foreign And Security Policy and Vice-President of the European Commission Federica Mogherini chaired in Brussels the celebrations of the 40th anniversary of Sino-European diplomatic relations, where negotiations for "Sino-European Strategic Cooperation Planning 2020" were strengthened, which included several investment and cooperation treaties in the financial sector. The new Silk Road is equivalent to 13 times the value of the Marshall Plan and is often compared with it, despite the fact that China vehemently rejects the analogy (Herrero & Xu, 2016).

According to the report, "China's Belt and Road Initiative in the global trade, investment and finance landscape" from *OECD Business and Finance Outlook* 2018 (OECD, 2018), the first links of the Chinese Economic Belt routes will be ready to operate in 2023. The Chinese government has made cooperation agreements and direct investments with more than 60 countries belonging to six trading associations:

- the Association of Southeast Asian Nations (ASEAN) and China Free Trade Area (ASEAN+1)[2];
- the Bangkok Agreement (BA)[3]; the Economic Co-operation Organisation (ECO)[4];

- the South Asian Association of Regional Co-operation (SAARC)[5];
- the European Union (EU)[6]; and
- the North American Free Trade Association (NAFTA)[7].

Despite the success of the initiative, not all projects have been successful, and some have even had to be changed. On the other hand, the high amount required is increasing the risk of Chinese debt, and the influx of Chinese workers into the various countries has generated tensions with residents. China's dominance in the region has also been criticized and challenged (Hurley & Portelance, 2018).

On the other hand, there is also the question of the real sustainability of the project, whether investments and loans will ever have the return. It is certain that China thinks long-term, and with much planning (Herrero & Xu, 2016). The estimated trade generated from Europe will be 6%, while from Asia will be only half. The remaining world markets will suffer a loss of 0.004. It is true that the African countries involved are greatly benefited by the construction of infrastructure, which if it were not for China's investment, would never have the capacity to carry them out (Breuer, 2017). For this reason, African countries are the most satisfied with the partnership with China, alongside the Asian East and Center, while South Asia is the most displeased, with special emphasis on India. Europe, with the exception of Poland, Bosnia and Herzegovina, sees the BRI with good eyes, but fears the lack of regulation and coordination of markets to such a wide extent of the global market (Herrero & Xu, 2019).

USA RESPONSE

This "Silk Road Economic Belt" rehabilitates the economy of all the countries geographically involved, leaving the U.S. on the sideline. Although China and the U.S. are both members of APEC, The Asia-Pacific Economic Cooperation, established in 1983, and which is considered the world's largest economic block, the U.S. obviously fears Chinese leadership. The Chinese economic dominance in the medium term will translate into more American unemployment because the price of Asian labor is substantially lower than that of the U.S.A. and many American companies fear to leave the country in search of a lower production price. Patents and intellectual and industrial property rights are also being debated, especially regarding pharmaceutical companies, which makes negotiations slower and more time-consuming (Geeraerts, 2019).

Obama's response to China rise was to find ways to isolate China through treaties and economic platforms, excluding China from them, while Trump opted for sanctions and embargoes.

Obama negotiated with the European Union the Transatlantic Trade and Investment Partnership Agreement, TTIP, allowing the United States to strengthen its influence in Europe, especially at commercial level. In the Pacific, Obama proposed a Trans-Pacific Partnership with 12 Asian countries covering 800 million people, representing 40 percent of world GDP. The aim was to bind Pacific nations closer through lower tariffs, liberalize markets, services, and investments, facilitate reciprocal access to public goods and contracts, eliminate and reduce customs duties, as well as barriers to trade between the two sides of the Atlantic, barring China's growing regional influence (Garrett, 2018).

The isolationism of Trump, a strategy quite different from Obama's neoliberalism, withdrew USA from the Trans-Pacific Partnership Agreement (TPP) arguing that it facilitated the entry of foreign workers. Trump chose instead a trade war, imposing tens of billions of dollars of tariffs on Chinese goods, and a set of import taxes, embargoes to telecommunications, and high customs duties, trying to weaken China economy. These measures have led to a lose-lose situation, with heavy consequences on the global value of chains, impacting industries structures, investment, innovation, and consumer welfare across the world, heightened in 2020 with the economic crisis of the pandemic (Chen & Zhang, 2020; Paterson, 2018).

China does not like sanctions, does not enter political alliances, meddle internal affairs or support regimes change (Chen, 2016).

CHINA AND ASIA

Central Asia

Central Asia is a crucial intersection point between the "Silk Road Economic Belt" and the "21st Century Maritime Silk Road". However, this "priority zone" points out problems of balancing India with Pakistan, two nuclear countries. Although India is more politically stable and economically strong, its ties with the USA and Japan are not well seen by China. On the other side, although Pakistan is more instable, has internal societal problems, a weaker economic development and its ties with US are not so strong (Mehmood et al., 2019).

The bet fell on Pakistan, not only at the Deepwater Port of Gwadar in Pakistan, then connected to a 3,000-kilometer-long corridor of roads and railways, coming close to the Arabian Sea. On the other hand, it also focuses on coal mining in the Thar Desert, a project that includes the construction of power plants to expand electricity capacity.

India does not like the approach China-Pakistan, especially because it empowers Pakistan at a political and economic level.

Other important BRI project in Asia is the Kyaukpyu pipeline in Myanmar, a project of $1.5 billion designed to carry 22 million tons of crude oil per year from the Middle East and Africa to reach China, representing 5% of China's annual oil imports. This pipeline makes the transfer of oil supplies faster because shipments no longer need to be transported through the Strait of Malacca and the South China Sea (Li, 2018).

Easter and South Eastern Asia

China's main territorial problem, apart from Hong Kong, Taiwan, and Tibet, is the dominance in the China Sea. The neighboring countries do not like to have China as the dominant power with ambitions to be the world leader.

Several associations isolate China to the East, such as the ASEAN - Association of Southeast Asian Nations, The Shanghai Cooperation Organization, or The Southeast Asia Treaty Organization.

It is said that until the 19th century, the Chinese Empire had a sinocentric perspective of East and South Asia, being the dominant political, economic, and cultural force. The Middle Empire granted a special status to the countries of Southeast Asia or "Nanyang" in exchange for vassalage and payment of taxes. In return, they received military recognition and support and assistance in crises. Alternating periods of stability with others of greater intervention, relations were mostly peaceful and balanced. China played a stabilizing role, never seeking to impose its direct political presence, if its neighbors did not pose a threat to the balance of the area, with trade intense exchanges. Perhaps because of this millennial heritage, China still claims its sinocentric role in the region (Shouyi, 1982).

After the end of the Cold War in the 1990s, the region began to experience a dynamic of its own, trying to eliminate any trace of the occupation of the Western powers. Also began the dispute the islands called Paracels, Silvers, Macclesfiels Bank and Spratly, also claimed Vietnam, Malaysia, Philippines, Taiwan and Brune.

The so-called "Kuala Lumpur Declaration", 1971, led to the creation of a Zone of Peace, Freedom and Neutrality in Southeast Asia, ZOPFAN, which attempted to limit the increased presence of the two blocs led by the US and the USSR (Shouyi, 1982).

China's economic opening in 1978 leads to aspirations to have a greater influence in this region, proposing a free trade area with ASEAN, in 2001, the "Agreement on Trade in Goods", and in 2004 the proposal for a Framework Agreement on Comprehensive Economic Cooperation between ASEAN and China emerged. It was the beginning of China's further intervention in the region. It follows the "Strategic Partnership" which includes broad cooperation in the security and political sectors, the "Treaty of Friendship and Cooperation", the Declaration on the Conduct of the Parties to the South China Sea", the Protocol to the Treaty of the Southeast Asia Nuclear Weapon-Free Zone, SEANFZ, and agreements with the Shanghai Cooperation Organization and the Boao Forum (Chakraborty & Kumar, 2012).

In 2020 the hypothesis of developing a "Community of East Asia" is on the table, among the countries of 10 ASEAN plus China, Japan, and South Korea. If concretized, it will be a historic transformation towards the creation of an unprecedented regionalism in East Asia, which will greatly affect the world's American hegemony (Kian, 2013).

China is also constructing several high-speed railway lines, connecting Southeast Asian countries with the Chinese Yunnan region: the central route linking Laos, Thailand, and Malaysia to Singapore; the westbound route that follows Myanmar; the route east that goes through Vietnam and Cambodia.

CHINA AND RUSSIA

During the decades of the Cold War, 1947-1991, the world was divided into two blocs, led by the United States and the USSR. China remained in the shadow of the soviets. In 1956, Mao Zedong started to defend a different Marxism doctrine and more interventionist and belligerent measures, instead of the international peaceful coexistence of the Eastern Bloc with the Western world. Moscow rejected the idea. This Sino-Soviet split lasted until 1966, when China decided to leave the agreement. The monolithic Communism block fractured, and China and Russia starting to compete for the control of the worldwide Communist movement. China supported revolutions against European colonialism in Africa, and gained influence and international recognition (Schlesinger, 1967).

With the dissolution of the Soviet Union on December 26th, 1991, and the Yalta Paradigm, the bipolar world, disappeared, as well as one of the traditional sources of threat, and the United States emerged as the only world power. Foreign military interventions such as Operation Desert Storm in 1990 had already advocated the U.S. as the dominant military power (Korolev, 2015).

The decades that followed confirmed American hegemony in all fields, not only because of the United States' determination to act unilaterally but also because of the use of military force after the attacks of 11 September 2001. Russia, one of ultimate symbols of communism, lost the importance of Cold War times, in what is considered by the Russians one of the worst times in Russia history. During this period of American hegemony, which lasted from 1991 to 2014, USA through NATO actively extended its sphere of influence, with special focus on the former Soviet Republics, integrating several countries of the former Warsaw Pact, such as Hungary, Poland, Bulgaria, for a total of 28 members. Besides establishing itself as the military force of the European Union through the agreement "Berlin Plus", USA even tried to accomplish Russia with the NATO, the so-called Russia Council (Tsygankov, 2015).

In December 1998, Russia and China signed the first post-Cold War treat, with the aim of weakening American hegemony. In 2001, with Vladimir Putin as prime minister, they signed the Treaty of Good-Neighbour and Friendly Cooperation, with the same objective of diminishing American power, especially in central Asia. Despite having the same common purpose, China wants to lead the world economy, dethroning USA, while Russia wants to recover the position as world leader, lost after the Cold War, to maintain the sphere of influence in former USSR states, preventing the U.S.A. and NATO from getting closer, being closer to Europe and less isolated (Karaganov, 2018).

The Russo-Chinese strategic cooperation is made in different fronts, and Russia has benefited with China industrialization, economic ambitions, and energy needs.

Since 2010, China is the largest trading partner of Russia. China exports to Russia, machinery and equipment, clothing, chemical products, fur products, footwear, and furniture, while Russia mineral fuels and petroleum products, and wood and wood products, non-ferrous metals, fish and seafood, as well as chemical products. Both China and Russia decided to de-dollarize, having a currency swap in to reduce the role of dollar in international trade and make the rubble and the yuan more stable (Sakwa, 2008).

Russia is the world leader energy potency, has 1,688 trillion cubic feet of natural gas reserves and has 80 billion barrels of oil reserves. In 2020, it is the biggest gas supplier of Europe and Eastern Europe. To secure his pole position, Putin started the construction of diverse pipelines, made multilateral alliances, firming Russia political international influence. The most important Russia trade partnership is with China. 15.3 percent of Chinese oil imports are from Russia and China is the second Russia gas customer. 70% of gas projects of Belt and Road Initiative are Russian. By 2024, the Siberia Gas Pipeline Project will be finished, by Gazprom, a $55 billion project, 3,000 kilometers, suppling Russian gas to the north east of China. It is an estimated bilateral trade of $200 billion (38 billion cubic meters annually for 30 years). As a response, USA started to impose sanctions on Russia (Hillman, 2020).

To mitigate the impact of U.S. coercive economic, Moscow and Beijing decided, in early 2019, to convert the mutual trade into national currencies up to 50 percent, expecting to have surpass $100 billion by the end of 2019, believing to achieve the goal of doubling the volume of trade to $200 billion by 2024 (Shin, 2020).

The Sino-Russia partnership is beneficial to both countries since they do not collide with each other interests. The economic closeness does not mean a political alliance, because they do not share the same political ambitions. The "strategic partnership" works as far as both interests do not collide and share a common target, weakening USA hegemony (Götz & Merlen, 2019).

Twenty years after the fall of the Soviet Union, Russia is rising again, but now on the shadow of China (Blank, 2018; Karaganov, 2018).

CHINA IN AFRICA

The Chinese presence on the African continent is not recent, and dates to Cold War, when China supported coups and revolutions against European colonialism. The most significant case was in South Africa. With the implementation of economic reforms of Deng Xiaoping, in 1978, China began to search Africa for raw materials and hydrocarbons for its economic and industrial growth. In exchange for cheaper materials, China built infrastructure that improved quality of life but also facilitated transportation of the raw materials and hydrocarbons.

The China-Africa Cooperation Forum (FOCAC), which took place in Beijing in October 2000, marked the beginning of peaceful development of a non-interventionist African-China relations and a pronouncer of what would become the following decades. In comparison, U.S. had "very little traditional strategic interests in Africa", mainly after the Cold War. However, American interests have proved to be primarily of a military and interventionist nature with the creation in 2007 of AFRICOM, a formation of a new combatant command for a rapid intervention in Africa (Walker, 2008).

The creation of FOCAC was the first step in political institutionalization of the relationship between China and African countries. The objective of the strategy was to search for foreign markets for excess installed capacity in China in industrial and construction sectors, combined with the demand for raw material and energy sources - one third of the oil supply to China comes from Africa, mainly from Angola and Niger. The 'Go Out Strategy', the economic strategy of internationalization of the economy, related to the demand for strategic assets, was complemented, regarding Africa, with the publication by the China State Council of the *China's Africa Policy documents,* or *China's strategy for Africa* in 2006, and *China's Foreign Aid* in 2011, specifying the modalities of aid and priorities of China's cooperation policy (Brautigam, 2010).

There are more than 800 Chinese private companies operating in Africa, mainly in infrastructure, energy, and banking. Despite bringing with them the workers from China, they can create indirect employment. The operation of these Chinese multinationals in Africa is steppingstone to start operating in more developed and complex markets. On the other hand, it is an attempt to better control global value chains, in particular distribution. The trade cooperation with China could be increased, and investments in infrastructure could help develop local areas, add new economic opportunities and socioeconomic development, especial in zones under the BRI (Breuer, 2017).

Of course, huge investment may trigger problems, like pollution, and state debt. Measures to improving the environment are necessary as well as encouraging local labour participation (Calabrese & Can, 2016).

CHINA AND THE "MIDDLE EAST"

Middle East was the name given by Europeans to this part of the planet because it is halfway to the far East, where China is located. Being the crossroads between Africa, Asia, and Europe, is a key point in terms of world trade circulation. Connects East to West, Asia to Europe and Africa, and access to the Mediterranean Sea. "Marching West" or "marching East" must be made passing the "Middle East". No wonder that through Bab El Mandab and the Suez Canal passes 13% of the volume of world trade. If for the Ancient Silk Road, this was the most important checkpoint, it is a key hub for the Belt and Road Initiative (Tomás, 2013).

However, the Middle East has two thirds of hydrocarbon reserves on the planet. Saudi Arabia, Iran, Emirates or Kuwait are the world's largest exporters of gas and oil. China is very deficient in energy and its growing economy make it the world's largest energy consumer and importer (Tomás, 2013). According to China's General Administration of Customs, in 2018, almost 30% of its total imports came from this region, 462m tons of oil, or 2.9m barrels per day, as presented in Figures 7 and 8. Its main supplier in 2019 was Saudi Arabia (GACPRC, 2020).

Figure 7. Dependence of Middle Eastern countries on the Chinese energy market
Source: (China Med)

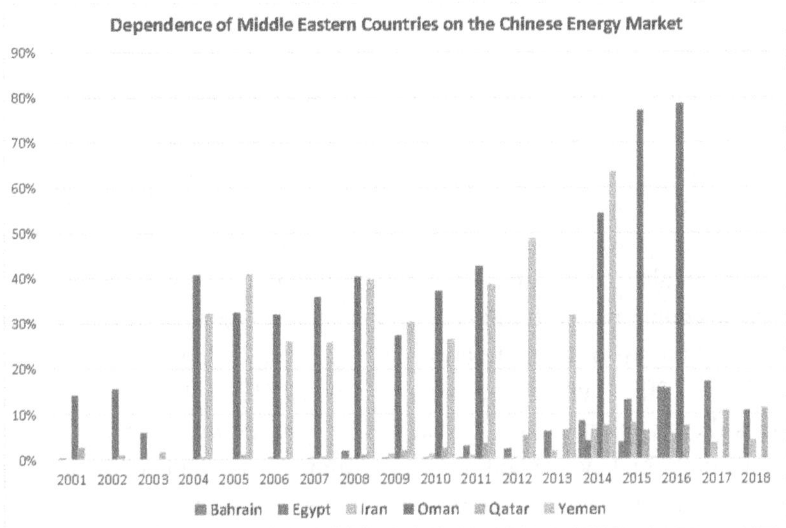

China's cooperation with this region is therefore not only an energy issue but also a geostrategic issue. It represents a strategic approach to affirm its influence and power in this crucial region of the planet. Nevertheless, China is also aware of the American presence in the Middle East. Since the Operation Desert Storm in 1990, the USA reinforced its position in Iraq, more recently involved in war in Syria,

Figure 8. Chinese dependence on energy imports from the Middle East
Source: (China Med)

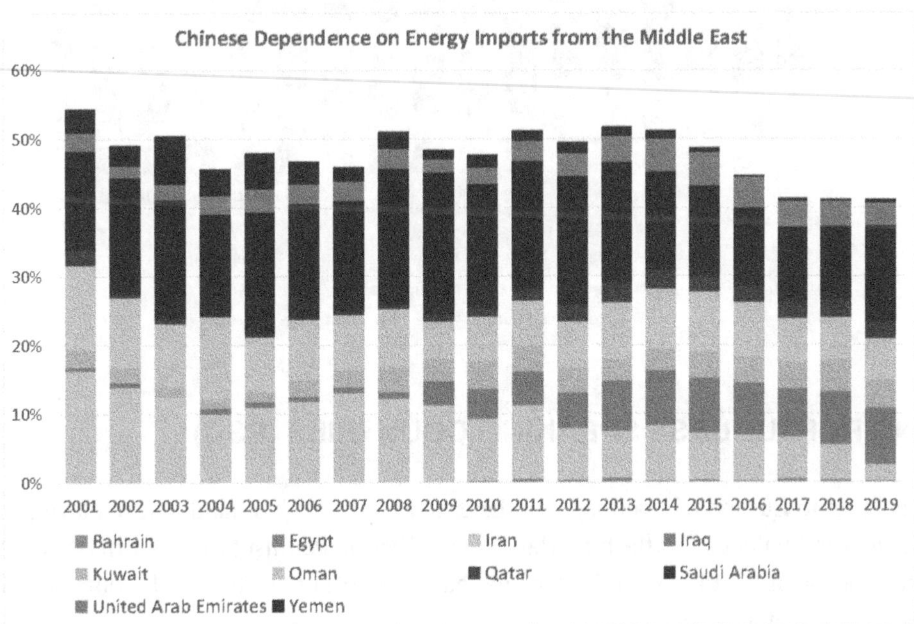

is partner of Saudi Arabia, Kuwait, Emirates, Iraqi Kurdistan, Bahrain, Jordan and is the great allied of Israel (Chaziza, 2019).

Aware of this chess game, and to assure the needed energy supply, China has built its presence in the Middle East by increasing in its economic engagement, becoming a major trading partner with energy exporters, establishing multilateral relations with 11 of these countries, from Iran to the Gulf Countries, steadfastly alienating no one, and avoiding policies that would challenge American interests in the region. China opted for a policy of non-interference in the internal affairs of each country, which is very pleased in this region, marked by the American bellicose intervention. China is being recognized as of central importance for trade, investments, diplomatic consultations, and even security cooperation, and become more and more an alternative for USA (Calabrese, 2017).

China has marked an economic position in the region and became the largest extra-regional source of FDI in the Middle East. In terms of trade, relationship in Dubai, China has more than 4,200 businesses worth almost \$7 billion in 2018 but also investment, almost \$123 billion, especially in infrastructure construction. Besides the reconstruction of Syria and Iraq in the post-war period, and the ambitious Saudi plan, Saudi Vision 2030, key projects were also signed with the Emirates, Oman, Saudi Arabia, Djibouti, and Egypt, an investment of \$23 billion. Evidence on this topic is shown in Figures 9 and 10.

Figure 9. Number of Chinese contract workers in the Middle East
Source: (China Med)

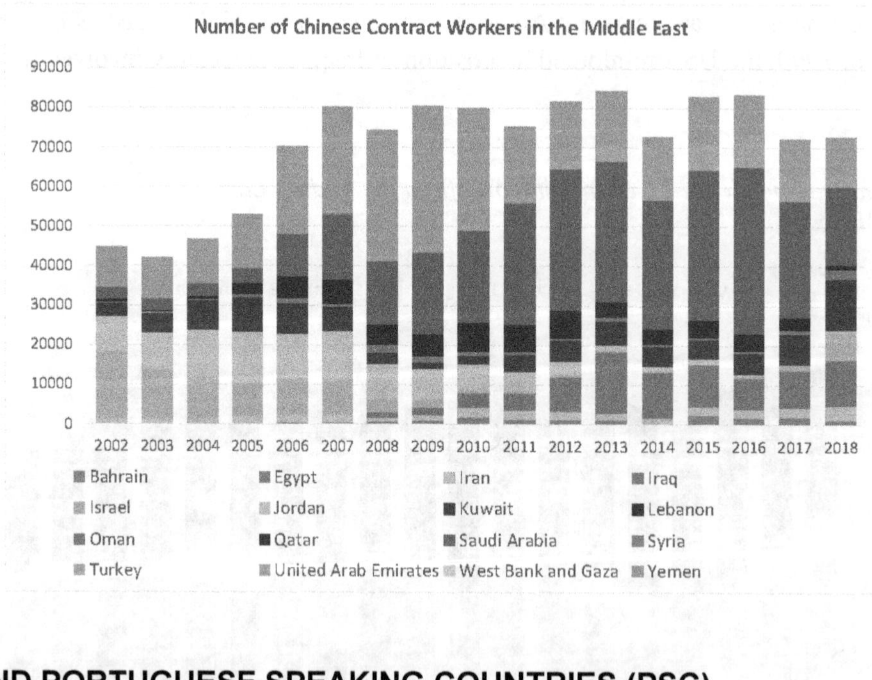

CHINA AND PORTUGUESE SPEAKING COUNTRIES (PSC)

China's connection to Europe will be made on the eastern side, both at land and sea level. The Spanish ports of Algeciras and Valencia are the hinterland for the Iberian Peninsula and North Africa, and Madrid is the terminal station of the railway link. Portugal has been left out of this trade route, at least for now, but has a very important asset: Lusophony.

Figure 10. Chinese contribution of troops and other personnel to UN peacekeeping operations in the Middle East
Source: (China Med)

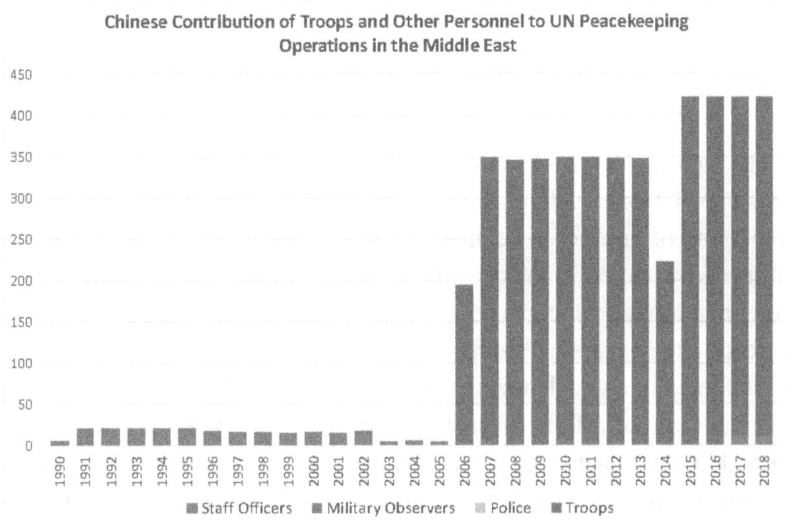

Sharing the same language is definitely an important factor of economic success. Language facilitates communication and avoids second interpretations, which can be very harmful to business. On the other side, they all share a common historical context that provides an understanding of attitudes and habits, difficult for outsiders. This perspective helps the flow of business (Esperança et al., 2017).

The Portuguese Speaking Countries, (PSC) - Angola, Brazil, Cape Verde, Guinea Bissau, Mozambique, Sao Tome and Principe, Timor-Leste, and Equatorial Guinea - belong to CPLP, Community of Portuguese-Speaking Countries. All the countries are coastal or island, belong to different continents and keep good political and economic relations (Mendes, 2014). Besides the common history context, there is business and economic development, cooperation, proximity, and mutual interests. These countries are the first choice for PSCs companies and China is very close, because of former Portuguese autonomic region of Macau. In addition to increase commercial relations, China created in Macau the Forum for Trade and Economic Cooperation between China and Portuguese-speaking Countries, the Macau Forum (Alves, 2008).

The PSC market, in addition to facilitating trade between the countries that are part of it, is also a gateway to regional markets, such as the European Union or Africa. Trade cooperation between China and Portuguese-speaking countries has become an indispensable part of global economic cooperation.

GLOBAL AND GLOCALLY CHINA

Chinese economic growth began with the opening of the economy in 1978. This economic liberalization has never been accompanied by political reforms, which has not prevented the PRC from having its own process of economic growth. China, in 2021, is preparing to dethrone the U.S.A. as the world's largest economy, and as the major global player. In the past decades, Chinese economic growth contributed to accelerate the global integration of markets and convergence of consumer preferences, showing that globalization is not a homogenous process.

While acting on a global scale, Chinese firms have been able to adapt, adopting internationalization strategies to get into local markets, competing with existing brands. This glocation has been fundamental to the success of the Chinese global market (Gianinazzi, 2018).

The glocation of Chinese firms consists of integrating local cultural characteristics into their brands' strategies, adapting to culture, society, and the local market. This knowledge turns out to be decisive because culture marks patterns of consumption and behavior. Cross Culture has long been studied, with proven results (Hofstede, 1994; Hofstede, 2001). The adaptation to moral standards, habits and local traditions allows the brand or product to be accepted in the target market of internationalization, allowing greater competitive advantage. On the other hand, it facilitates final communication to the customer, with effective marketing campaigns, capable of appealing to the consumption of the brand or product. These Cross-Culture skills are responsible for the successful globalization of Chinese companies because they adapt to the local market. (Hofstede, 2010; Tomás, 2017). This is reinforced by the principle of non-meddling in the internal affairs of each country, or to provoke regime changes. The Chinese Principles of Peaceful Coexistence remain valid: mutual respect for territorial integrity and sovereignty, non-interference in internal affairs, equality and mutual benefit, and peaceful coexistence. This policy is complemented with multilateralism, which guarantees bilateral relations with countries all over the world (Chen, 2016; Grauer, 1989).

However, the safety of Chinese citizens abroad in areas of political instability, such as the Middle East and certain African countries, led to install military capability to protect their own interest. The Chinese base in Djibouti, the port of Gwadar, Pakistan, or some of the ports in the Middle East, are some of these examples. This strategy also makes the political position of China in these geographies stronger. China has developed a program of modernization of the military and its armed forces, increasing its capacity for intervention. It is not expected to be used, unless it is to assert itself before its East Asian neighbors, in control of the China Sea, or to show strength in Hong Kong, Taiwan or Tibet. China's long tradition shows that it will only go to war when provoked or when its interests and sovereignty are threatened (Erickson et al., 2019).

CONCLUSION

China developed, very early on a sinocentric view of the world. The Chinese nation has preserved its identity and isolation, always playing through its own interests, not yielding to external pressures. The ambition to be the economic potency of the world, which is very close to concretizing, also entails a change in the paradigm of forces worldwide. Whoever has control of the world economy will also have political control and forcibly, power at the military level. China, aware of all this, has been preparing at all these levels for the coming times.

Trump's protectionism eased the task for Xi Jinping, isolating U.S.A., weakening American foreign intervention. It is certain that pressure from economic sanctions has had its consequences, but nothing stopped the rise of Beijing, even in times of pandemic, by riding against the cycle with the rest of the world. The victory of Joe Biden and the return of Obama's neoliberal policies will help to make America stronger again, at least in terms of foreign affairs, but the country is divided, and the new president will face many challenges.

The decline of the American hegemony, the de-dollarization and the concretization in 2020 of the "Community of East Asia", corresponding to 30% of World GDP, will greatly help China to be leading the world's economy, with all political, geopolitical and military consequences. Europe must be prepared for this new scenario.

REFERENCES

Alves, A. (2008). China lusophone connection. *China in Africa Report, 2*.

Blank, S. (2018). Paradoxes abounding Russia and the South China Sea issue. In C. Anders (Ed.), Great powers, grand strategies: The new game in the South China Sea. Naval Institute Press.

Brautigam, D. (2010). *The dragon's gift: The real story of China in Africa*. Oxford University Press.

Breuer, J. (2017). *Two belts, one road? The role of Africa in China's Belt and Road Initiative*. BlickWechse.

Calabrese, J. (2017). *China's role in post-hegemonic Middle East*. Middle East Institute.

Calabrese, L., & Can, C. (2016). *China-Africa: A maturing relationship? Growth, change and resilience*. DFID-ESRC Growth Research Programme.

Chaziza, M. (2019). China's economic diplomacy approach in the Middle East conflicts. *China Report (New Delhi, India), 55*(1), 24–39. doi:10.1177/0009445518818210

Chen, S., & Ravallion, M. (2008). *The developing world is poorer than we thought, but no less successful in the fight against poverty*. The World Bank Policy Research Working Paper 4703.

Chen, Z. (2016). China debates the non-interference principle. *The Chinese Journal of International Politics, 9*(9), 349–374.

Chen, Z. (2016). China, the European Union and the fragile world order. *Journal of Common Market Studies, 54*(4), 775–792. doi:10.1111/jcms.12383

Chen, Z., & Zhang, X. (2020). Chinese conception of the world order in a turbulent Trump era. *The Pacific Review, 33*(3-4), 1–31. doi:10.1080/09512748.2020.1728574

Coleman, G., Kalish, I., Konigsburg, D., & Sitao, X. (2014). *Competitiveness: Catching the next wave China*. Deloitte.

Dahlman, C. J., & Aubert, J. E. (2001). *China and the knowledge economy: Seizing the 21st century*. World Bank Publications. doi:10.1596/0-8213-5005-6

Erickson, A. S., Goldstein, L. J., & Li, N. (2010). *China, the United States, and 21st-Century Sea power: Defining a maritime security partnership*. Naval Institute Press.

Esperança, J. P., Reto, L. A., & Machado, F. L. (2017). Países de destino das multinacionais portuguesas: A importância da lusofonia. In N. Crespo & M. J. Tomás (Eds.), *A internacionalização da economia portuguesa, casos de sucesso empresarial* (pp. 71–89). Temas e Debates, Círculo de Leitores.

GACPC - General Administration of Customs of People's Republic of China. (n.d.). http://english.customs.gov.cn/

Garrett, C. (2018). Constructing narratives of global order: The Obama presidency, TPP, TTIP, and the contested politics of geoeconomics. *Atlantic Studies*, *16*(2), 261–281. doi:10.1080/14788810.2018.1434107

Gianinazzi, W. (2018). Penser global, agir local: Histoire d'une idée. *EcoRev*, *46*(1), 19–30. doi:10.3917/ecorev.046.0019

Götz, E., & Merlen, C. R. (2019). Russia and the question of world order. *European Political Science*, *20*(2), 133–153.

Grauer, S. (1989). *Think globally, act locally: A Delphi Study of educational leadership through the development of international resources in the local community*. University of San Diego.

Herrero, A. G., & Xu, J. (2016). *China's Belt and Road Initiative: Can Europe expect trade gains?* Bruegel Working Paper Issue 5.

Hillman, J.E. (2020). *China and Russia: Economic Unequals*. CSIS.

Ho, J., Poh, F., Zhou, J., & Zipser, D. (2019). *China consumer report 2020: The many faces of the Chinese consumer*. McKinsey & Company.

Hofstede, G. (1991). *Cultures and organizations: Software of the Mind*. McGraw-Hill.

Hofstede, G. (1994). The business of international business is culture. *International Business Review*, *3*(1), 1–14. doi:10.1016/0969-5931(94)90011-6

Hofstede, G. (2001). *Culture's consequences: Comparing values, behaviors, institutions and organizations across nations*. Sage Publications.

Hurley, J., S., & Portelance, G. (2018). *Examining the debt implications of the Belt and Road Initiative from a Policy Perspective*. Center for Global Development Policy Paper 121.

Korolev, A. (2015). Russia's reorientation to Asia: Causes and strategic implications. *Pacific Affairs*, *89*(1), 53–73. doi:10.5509/201689153

Li, Y. (2018). The greater Euroasian partnership and the Belt and Road Initiative: Can the two be linked? *Journal of Euroasian Studies*, *9*(2), 94–99. doi:10.1016/j.euras.2018.07.004

Mehmood, F., Fatima, N., & Ullah, K. (2019). Impact of China-Pakistan economic corridor on Pakistan's future energy consumption and energy saving potential: Evidence from sectoral time series analysis. *Energy Strategy Reviews*, *25*, 34–46. doi:10.1016/j.esr.2019.04.015

OECD. (2018). *China's Belt and Road Initiative in the global trade, investment and finance landscape*. OECD Business and Finance Outlook.

Ohashi, H. (2018). The Belt and Road Initiative (BRI) in the context of China's opening-up policy. *Journal of Contemporary East Asia Studies*, *7*(2), 85–103. doi:10.1080/24761028.2018.1564615

Paterson, S. (2018). *China, Trade and Power: Why the West's economic engagement has failed*. London Publishing Partnership.

Sakwa, R. (2008). New Cold War or twenty years crisis? Russia and international politics. *International Affairs*, *84*(2), 241–267. doi:10.1111/j.1468-2346.2008.00702.x

Schlesinger, A. (1967). Origins of the Cold War. *Foreign Affairs*, *46*(1), 22–52. doi:10.2307/20039280

Shin, F. (2020). A financial alliance won't help China and Russia Dethrone the US Dollar. *The Diplomat, 26*.

Shouyi, B. (1982). An outline history of China. Pequim: China Knowledge Series, Foreign Languages Press.

Statista. (2020). *The Statistics Portal for Market Data, Market research and market data modelling*. Author.

Tomás, M. J. (2013). *Da Primavera ao Inverno Árabe*. Temas e Debates, Círculo de Leitores.

Tomás, M. J. (2017). Os desafios culturais na internacionalização. In N. Crespo & M. J. Tomás (Eds.), *A Internacionalização da economia portuguesa, Casos de sucesso empresarial* (pp. 179–195). Temas e Debates, Círculo de Leitores.

Tsygankov, A. (2015). The Sino-Russian challenge to the World order: National identities, bilateral relations, and East versus West in the 2010s. *The Journal of Asian Studies*, *74*(3), 731–732. doi:10.1017/S0021911815000698

Walker, J. (2008). *China, U.S. and Africa: Competition or cooperation?* (Master Thesis). U.S. Army War College.

Xi, J. (2017). *Work together to build the Silk Road economic Belt and the 21st Century Maritime Silk Road*. Full text of President Xi's speech at opening of Belt and Road forum.

ADDITIONAL READING

Almond, R. G. (2016). China and the Iran Nuclear Deal. *The Diplomat*, 8 March.

Calabrese, L. (2017). *Chinese investment and knowledge transfer in Africa*. DFID-ESRC Growth Research Programme.

Calabrese, L., & Weng, X. (2018). *Chinese investment and small-scale commodity producers in Africa*. DFID-ESRC Growth Research Programme.

Chakraborty, D., & Kumar, A. (2012). ASEAN and China: New dimensions in economic engagement. *China Report (New Delhi, India)*, *48*(3), 327–349. doi:10.1177/0009445512462300

Chan, A. (2020). Rethinking the rise of China and its implications on international order. *Chinese Journal of International Review*.

Checchinato, F., Hu, L., Perri, A., & Vescovi, T. (2013). Internationalization of a chinese "born glocal" brand in a foreign sector: the case study of goodbaby. China Goes Global 2013- September 25-27, Bremen, Germany.

Collinson, S., & Rugman, A. M. (2007). The regional character of Asian multinational enterprises. *Asia Pacific Journal of Management*, *24*(4), 429–446. doi:10.100710490-006-9035-y

Gaspar, C. (2013). A China e a transformação da Ásia. *Relaciones Internacionales*, 38.

Geeraerts, G. (2019). The EU-China partnership: Balancing between divergence and convergence. *Asia Europe Journal*, *17*(3), 281–294. doi:10.100710308-019-00554-2

Johnson, C. K. (2016). *President Xi Jinping's 'Belt and Road' Initiative: A Practical Assessment of the Chinese Communist Party's Roadmap for China's Global Resurgence.* Center for Strategic and International Studies, March.

Kian, H. K. (2013). Chinese economic dominance in Southeast Asia: A Longue Duree Perspective. *Comparative Studies in Society and History*, *55*(1), 5–34. doi:10.1017/S0010417512000564

Kim, J.Y. (2017). *Remarks of World Bank Group President Jim Yong Kim at the Belt and Road Forum for International Co-operation – Opening Plenary Session*, May.

Kuik, C. C. (2008). China's evolving multilateralism in Asia: The aussen politik and innen politik explanations. In K. Calder & F. Fukuyama (Eds.), *East Asian Multilateralism: Prospects for Regional Stability* (pp. 109–140). The Johns Hopkins University Press.

Kuik, C. C., Idris, N. A., Nor, M., & Rahim, A. (2012). The China factor in the US "reengagement" with Southeast Asia: Drivers and limits of converged hedging. *Asian Politics & Policy*, *4*(3), 315–344. doi:10.1111/j.1943-0787.2012.01361.x

Lewis, R. (2006). *When cultures collide: Leading across cultures*. Nicholas Brealey International.

Luthans, F., & Jonathan, P. (2015). *International Management, Culture, Strategy and Behavior* (9th ed.). McGraw-Hill.

Mathews, J. A. (2002). *Dragon multinational: A new model for global growth*. Oxford University Press.

Minkov, M. (2011). *Cultural differences in the globalizing world*. Emerald.

Muekalia, D. J. (2004). Africa and China's strategic partnership. *African Security Review*, *13*(1), 5–11. doi:10.1080/10246029.2004.9627264

Nicole, E. (2011). *Is your business glocal? How to think globally and act locally*. YFS Magazine - Startups, Small Business News and Entrepreneurial Culture.

Paal, D. (2013). Contradictions in China's Foreign Policy. *Carnegie Endowment for International Peace*, 13 December 2013.

Taylor, I. (1998). China's foreign policy towards Africa in the 1990s. *The Journal of Modern African Studies*, *36*(3), 443–460. doi:10.1017/S0022278X98002857

Taylor, I. (2009). *China's New Role in Africa*. Zed Books.

Zhaou, S. (2010). The China Model: Can it replace the western model of modernisation. *Journal of Contemporary China*, *19*(65), 419–436. doi:10.1080/10670561003666061

ENDNOTES

1 https://www.weforum.org/agenda/2019/06/china-by-numbers-10-facts-to-help-you-understand-the-superpower-today/

2 Brunei-Darussalam, Cambodia, Indonesia, Lao People's Democratic Republic, Malaysia, Myanmar, Philippines, Singapore, Thailand, Vietnam, and China.

3 Bangladesh, China, Lao People's Democratic Republic, India, Korea, and Sri Lanka.

4 Afghanistan, Azerbaijan, Iran, Kazakhstan, Kyrgyz Republic, Pakistan, Tajikistan, Turkey, Turkmenistan, and Uzbekistan.

5 Bangladesh, India, Pakistan, Maldives, Nepal, and Sri Lanka.

6 28 members of the union.

7 United States, Canada, and Mexico.

Chapter 10
Cultural Impact on Global Trade

Anusha Thakur
https://orcid.org/0000-0001-8761-2250
University of Petroleum and Energy Studies, India

ABSTRACT

As in any international business relation, factors such as political, economic, social, technological, and legal dimensions are expected to significantly impact trade activities. Social factors include the cultural aspects of exports and imports along with the differences among foreign markets. Culture poses to be complementary to FDI and exports. Cultural components include food, language, clothing, values, traditions, and beliefs, which differ from region to region across the world. When the countries are culturally different, investing and trading becomes a risk. Hence, in today's scenario, it is very important for the organizations to understand cultural differences in order to compete with their competitors. Understanding these cultural differences owes the opportunity to make or break the success of a foreign trade opportunity. The global businesses need to adhere to the demands and perceptions of different cultures in the countries when they purchase different products.

INTRODUCTION

Barter of goods and services among people is one of the oldest practices in the history. Over the years, internationalization and globalization have significantly gained traction in the market. More companies are nowadays emphasizing towards the expansion of their businesses across the different regions in the world.

One of the prominent features in the world economy is the boom in financial globalization and trade over the past few years. Global Trade, or International Trade, is the import and export of goods and services across the international boundaries. International trade, an inclusion of all transactions performed between the countries, stimulates the long-term growth via multiple channels (Calderóna, 2010). The trade process allows the countries to specialize, thereby enabling the businesses to exploit the economies of scale.

Companies emphasize on the execution of international practical structures in the target market in order to perform transactions. Along with the implementation of international strategies of manage-

DOI: 10.4018/978-1-7998-7568-0.ch010

ment knowledge, it becomes increasingly important to analyze and focus on the financial scenario for these strategies as well. Few of the most significant differences between international commerce and local commerce activities include the economic activities, financial and managerial decisions, cultural differences and legal structures of different countries, and the goals of the organizations. Hence, it is essential for the organizations to understand the importance of culture as part of international transactions and marketing strategies.

Strategically investigating the cultural aspects of the nation enables the brands to develop effective cross-cultural strategies in order to sustain the businesses. The process of cultural trade offers several avenues to the developing countries, thereby posing advantageous for the increasing interest in cultural goods and services across the globe. International competitiveness plays an important role in the potential development of firms and overall prosperity. More companies are nowadays emphasizing the expansion of their businesses across the different regions in the world. Most of the cultural layers, such as language, religion, ethnic background, artistic interests, and ideological orientation, tumble over the national boundaries. Hence, variation in the culture of countries plays an important role in the process of export and import of the materials/products across the world.

LITERATURE REVIEW

Transnational flows of financial resources, people, culture, information, and goods across the nations have been witnessing significant rise over the years, thereby drastically transforming the world (Ritzer, 2001). Globalization is a multidimensional phenomenon which encompasses not only the economic components but also the political, ideological, and cultural, along with other similar facets (Prasad & Prasad, 2006). For years, globalization has been equated with the economic growth across the nations in the world. In addition to this, the process has also been addressed from the perspective of social sciences, international relations, politics, and economics. Hence, the term globalization comprises a system or a policy which promotes global interconnection and interdependence among the nations via advanced technologies. With the help of advancements in the information technologies, people in the Western regions are able to get familiar with the styles in the Eastern regions, and vice-versa.

The period of globalization, with its unparalleled intensification and acceleration of the flows of information, labor, and capital, across different regions is significantly impacting the culture across the globe. In any international business relation, the uncontrollable factors, such as economics, politics, legal, technological, and culture, are expected to impact the trade processes and relations within the nations. Globalization enables the individuals across the globe to understand the beliefs, ideas, and cultures. One of the advantages posed by globalization is the fact that the process brings the worldwide identity together. Any country owes the independence to share and represent culture in the businesses. With the proper understanding of the cultures of the different countries, any foreign trade opportunity can be made successful or unsuccessful.

Cross-border trade impacts the culture, habits, and lifestyle of the individuals. Culture of a country is expected to directly influence negotiations. One of the ways that leads to the success of companies across the nations, in the field of commercial activities, is the cultural recognition in the markets, across the globe. The companies in marketing sector consider cultural factors from different dimensions in the segments such as packaging, advertising, marketing & distribution and also distinguishes the traditions, conduct, religion, language, communication and other factors related to such segments. When the individuals from two different countries live together or share a common land, blending and mix of cultures always takes place.

Definition of Culture

Every nation is professed differently for its culture, whether it is in terms of the standard of living or the quality of people in the world. Few countries are significantly known for the good things, while some are known in terms of bad things. Culture is a strong element in individual's lives. One of the basic definitions of culture emphasizes "the way we do things around here" (Deal & Kennedy, 2000). Culture is expected to control the values, hopes, and views of the individuals. So, building partnering relationships among the countries significantly caters to the understanding of their cultural differences as well (Hattangadi, 2019).

According to Hofstede, culture refers to "carrying within herself or himself patterns of potential acting, and thinking learned throughout their lifetime" (Schmitz, 2012). The word culture offers diversified ways for the interpretation of environment and the world, along with relating the same to the other people. Culture particularly refers to a diversified and large set of intangible aspects of life. Cultures are not identical among the countries. They refer to the totality of a particular cluster or a group of individual's patterns of behaviour and experiences, along with the various assumptions and values related to life and how do these evolve with different cultures. Few definitions of culture have witnessed widespread acceptance, including:

- Culture is a set of beliefs, orientations to life, policies, values and assumptions, behavioral and procedural conventions which are shared by a group of individuals, and further impacts the member's behavior along with their respective interpretations with respect to other people's behavior as well (Spencer-Oatey, 2008).

Culture refers to the joint programming of the mind, which differentiates between the members of one group and the other (Hofstede, 1994). The impact of culture on international market and the necessity of businesses to understand the cross-cultural management before expanding their market into different territories is briefly described below.

Role of Culture in International Market

Cross-cultural management plays a vital role and has a significant impact on the businesses operation in the different regions of the world. Businesses are closely devoted to patterned cultural behaviors owing to the fact that culture embodies values, norms, symbols, and beliefs which guides and impacts the lives of individuals. The businesses need to abide and follow a particular country's culture in order to expand or witness significant rise in their market. With the implementation of proper strategies, possible impacts and risks of cross-cultural discrepancies can be minimized, thereby delivering effective outcomes for their businesses (Siriphattrasophon, 2012).

International business marketing is significantly different from local market owing to the difference in promotional strategy, product pricing, and place, which differs from that of the local customers (Johansson, 2000). With significant growth in information technology, cross border marketing has not been merely difficult. However, one of the challenges faced by the multinational firms nowadays is in terms of culture, which varies according to countries. Culture is a set of beliefs, knowledge, language, literature, and traditional values, which are practiced by the natives of a country at any particular time. The process of international marketing engages the firm in establishing the manufacturing facilities overseas as well as coordinating the strategies across the different regions in the world (Keegan, 2002).

International commerce includes transactions performed between different countries. In order to perform these transactions, the companies need different structures to execute them in the target market. One of such structures, which often leads to the success of global transactions, is the proper understanding and knowledge of culture.

The term "Culture" functions on a multitude of levels, thereby making cross-country, cross-cultural business as well as trade more complicated. Hence, with increasing globalization, it becomes essential to understand the different expressions of culture across the globe.

Culture can be broadly classified into:

Table 1. Levels of culture

National Culture	Industry Culture
This is the broadest level of cultural influence. When businesses are done in foreign countries, negotiations are often impacted by the national cultures, along with the laws and regulations in the country.	This level is impacted by the behavioral practices and norms within the industries. The industrial products are less impacted by the culture of a particular country, and more impacted by the industry standards and norms.
Company Culture	**Individual Behavior**
Every company has their own set of opinions, beliefs, values, communication standards, as well as norms and expectations.	An individual's behavior is usually influenced by all the other levels of culture, and it is the personal expression of other cultural beliefs. The individuals are impacted by the national as well as subcultures of social groups.

National culture can be defined as the values held by the majority of individuals within a country. These values are invariably unconscious and are developed in individual's childhood. Within the national cultures, values are stable over time, however slight changes can occur from one generation to the other. National and organizational cutures vary in aspects wherein, the organizational culture referes to sociology and national culture belongs to anthropology. Organizational culture can be changed, but the national culture can never be changed. Organizational culture refers to the culture that is only relevant to a particular organization, thereby differentiating the firm from the competitors. These organizational cultures are at times called as the "corporate cultures" which focuses on the values, assumptions, and the beliefs of an organization. For instance, the culture of a school in a town is expected to differ from that of another school in the same town. The individual differences in culture refers to the preferences of an individual via his/her own personal experiences, which includes the impact of peers, family, media, and school on them. An individual working in an organization might have the same team or organizational culture, however, might vary in their individual cultures, owing to the fact that it varies on an individual's upbringing.

The above mentioned levels of culture are vital to recognize and think about the businesses in order to cater to the changing scenario and competitiveness.

Cultural Factors Affecting International Markets

Cultural factors play a key role in international commerce, in terms of values, lifestyle, and language. Culture is divided into foreign culture or local culture. In today's scenario, it is very important for the companies to understand the difference in cultures in the context of internal businesses. The cultural differences affect the businesses in three main areas:

- Communication
- Organizational hierarchy
- Etiquette

Proper knowledge, and understanding of the same, helps to avoid differences with foreign colleagues and clients.

Communication

Effective communication plays a crucial role in determining the success of a business, whether it is a big company or a start-up. In the international business arena, language is one of the most important factors in bridging the cultural differences. Hence, it is very important for the businesses to properly understand the language of the target market and then convey the appropriate message accordingly.

In certain cultures, there are people who speak directly, are loud, or at times even blunt during any conversation. At the same time, in other cultures, there are people who are soft-spoken, wait patiently when in conversation, and also use flowery languages. For instance, in India, the business professionals communicate in an indirect and nuanced way. This might prove opposite to the countries wherein people tend to be briefer and more direct in their communication styles. During any business meeting, such differences are probable to come to the forefront. Hence, it becomes essential for the partners and clients to communicate properly in the business meetings and put more emphasis on the verbal as well as non-verbal communication styles.

Hierarchies also play a pivotal role on communication styles in the businesses and firms. At times, lack of respect and acknowledgement with the seniors, within the company, often leads to a negative situation.

Organizational Hierarchy

Cultural norms direct how attitude towards the organizational and management hierarchy are perceived. In some cultures, individuals and staff in middle management are at times not allowed to speak during the conversations or meetings. In some countries, it is at times difficult to query or express the opinions made by the senior officers which are indeed different from the rest. In terms of attitude, these are dependent on the social values of any particular country. In countries such as South Korea and Japan, respect for senior people or the people in positions of authority and elders are deep-rooted in society as well as workplaces.

Etiquette in the Workplace

In the case of multinational firms, with multiple differences, proper learning of business etiquettes often proves to be significantly important. Hence, paying importance on the way an individual is addressed while dealing with clients and partners is significantly important.

The Americans and Canadians often use first names, while dealing with new acquaintances. However, in several Asian countries, such as South Korea, China, and Singapore, as a basic etiquette, it becomes necessary to add Mr. or Ms. while addressing before anybody's surname.

Punctuality is also one of the important factors to be considered in businesses. For instance, in Germany, it is always expected to arrive prior to the scheduled time given. In addition to this, countries such as Japan, United States, Russia and South Korea expect their clients and partners to be on time, rather than being late or early.

Hence, working in a diversified environment becomes an essential factor in solving the problems owing to inter-cultural conflicts. The cultural norms have positive impact on the interpersonal relationships at the workplace. There are few frameworks for conducting the businesses across different cultures in different nations across the world.

Models such as Hofstede's six dimensions of culture are widely being used in the cross-cultural fields such as international management, cross-cultural psychology, and cross-cultural communication.

RESEARCH METHODOLOGY

This study includes information collected through different secondary sources such as journals, research papers, articles, trade reports and company annual reports. Various cultural differences across different countries, in different regions, were particularly considered. Additionally, the study was based on the Hofstede's Cultural Dimensions, for in-depth analysis of cross-cultural communications in different countries in the North American, Asia-Pacific, European and Middle-Eastern regions. The Hofstede framework offers a distinct comparative approach to the study of cultures by identifying as well as measuring the different aspects of cultures in the world.

Research Questions

- What is the impact of culture in global trade across the different countries in the world?
- What are the strategies that organizations need to implement in order to understand the cultural differences and compete accordingly in the international market?
- In addition to this, the chapter also discusses the cultural challenges of globalization (challenges related to culture of one particular country, relative to the other cultures in the world).

Significance of the Study

This study aims to provide in-depth analysis of the different cultures and strategies adopted by the countries to keep in pace in the trade processes despite the culural differences. Further, this study emphasizes several topics, such as:

- To understand the different factors that favorably impacts the operation of international trade processes.
- To understand how the cultural dimensions differ among different countries.

Scope of the Study

- This study provides emphasis on various cultural dimensional trends in the regions of North America (USA), Europe, (UK), and Asia-Pacific (Japan).
- In addition, this study also emphasizes the case of Coca-Cola across India and China.

Hofstede's Six Dimensions Of Culture

Power Distance Index (PDI): This is the first dimension of Hofstede's Cultural Dimension theory. This dimension refers to the inequality that exists between the individuals with and without power. A lower index implies that people are enquiring the authority and making efforts to allocate the power. In addition to this, a low power distance index implies that the power is shared, dispersed and is not distributed unevenly. Higher index implies that the society also includes an established hierarchy, and there is an acceptance of the unequal distribution of power. Important traits of the high-power index include:

- Centralized organizations
- Complex hierarchies
- Large compensation gaps

Individualism Versus Collectivism (IDV): IDV is the next dimension of Hofstede's Cultural Dimension theory. This factor discovers the extent to which the individuals in a society are integrated in a specific group, along with the type of individual relations within the community.

Individualistic societies relate to the relation of an individual with his/her family and indicates that the concerned person is not dependent on anyone, and is focused upon attaining his/her personal goals. However, collectivism refers to the integrated relationships existing in a society which extends to the others and families. The higher IDV score inspires the achievement of an individual.

Masculinity versus Femininity (MAS): The next dimension of Hofstede's Cultural Dimension theory refers to what values are considered more important in the society. A masculine society is more competitive, being characterized by a strong drive for achievement, success, and material rewards. In turn, a feminine society is more consensus-oriented, with a strong preference for cooperarion, caring, and quality of life.

Uncertainty Avoidance Index (UAI): This index refers to the ways an individual caters to anxiety and stress in a society. The term is described as the tolerance level of society for vagueness and uncertainty. Societies with high Uncertainty Avoidance Index score determine rigid guidelines, different code of behaviour, and laws.

Long-term versus Short-term orientation (LTO): The long-term orientation versus short-term orientation refers to the connection of the current with the past as well as future challenges. The businesses with high long-term orientation specify that traditions and persistence is valued in the organizations.

Indulgence Versus Restraint (IVR): The factor indulgence versus restraint considers the tendency of the society to fulfil the desires. Countries with higher IVR scores boosts the free fulfilment of an individual's drives and emotions. The businesses foster debate and dialogues in the company meetings, pays emphasis to the work-life balance of the individuals, and prioritizes mentoring in the company.

This study provides an analysis on various cultural trends in the regions of North America (US), Europe, (UK), and Asia-Pacific (Japan). It also describes the relationship between the behavior and values, with the help of a structure on the basis of factor analysis. In other words, the Hofstede theory studies the significant aspects of culture and offers a rating on the comparison scale. Hence, appropriate knowledge of the varied features in a business, observed in different cultures, enables the manager to understand the international business market.

EMPIRICAL EVIDENCE AT THE COUNTRY LEVEL

North American Region – The Case of the United States

The analysis of the United States is illustrated in the figure below:

Figure 1. Analysis of the Hofstede cultural dimensions in United States of America

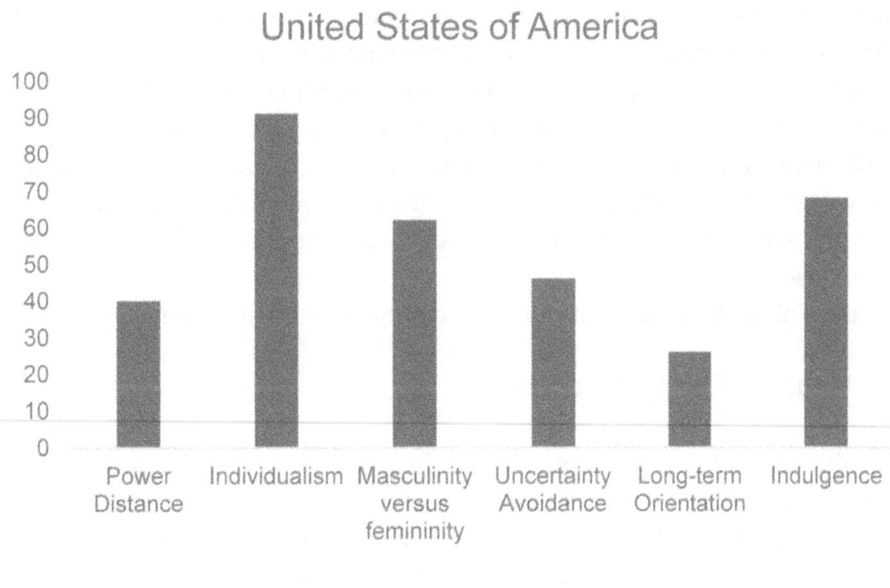

Power Distance: in terms of power distance, the score in America is 40. The power distance dimension deals with the fact that all the individuals in the societies are not equal, and also it expresses the cultural attitude towards power inequalities amongst us. The inequality of a society is endorsed by the leaders and followers.

Individualism: when it comes to understanding culture, the American culture is more than Disney World and Hollywood. One of the main cores in the American culture is Individualism, which accounts for a score of 91. Individualism has been critically influencing the different fields of economics, society, culture and politics. Individualism is characterized by the engagement in competitive tasks, along with an emphasis on how an individual becomes distinct. The Americans follow the principles of "justice and liberty for all". Key emphasis is on equal rights in all the aspects of American government and society.

Individualistic cultures in the American region are basically self-centered, the key emphasis lies mostly on their individual goals. One of the major views is that every person has a moral significance along with certain rights which are either of inherent or divine origin in nature. There are different ways in which every individual perceives, exists, experiences, acts, and thinks (Younkins, 1998). In the United States, most of the people are considered to be individualists, who are particularly motivated by what is good for them personally, and are usually self-reliant and independent. The society at such places is loosely-knit in which the expectation is that people are engaged in looking after their immediate families and themselves and do not rely on authorities for support.

Masculinity versus femininity: the score of the Masculinity is 62 in the American region. The number can be explained by combining the high masculinity drive with the individualist drive across the world. Rising inequality is endangering democracy, owing to a broadening gap among the classes which are thereby expected to slowly push the Individualism factor down and Power Distance up.

Uncertainty Avoidance (UAI): in terms of the Uncertainty Avoidance dimension, the region scores 46. Hence, the perceived context in which the Americans usually find themselves are expected to impact their behavior more than the culture would have scored lower or higher.

The degree of acceptance among the Americans is fairly well for innovative products, new ideas, along with the willingness to try something different or new, whether it is in terms of businesses, or technology. The Americans are considered to be more tolerant in terms of ideas or opinions from any individual from any country with freedom of expression. In addition to this, the Americans do not need a lot of rules and are also less expressive emotionally in comparison to the higher-scoring cultures.

Long-term Orientation: in terms of long-term orientation, the Americans account for the fifth dimension with a score of 26. The businesses in America measure their performance on a short-term basis, with their quarterly profit and loss statements, thereby enabling the individuals to strive for quicker results at the workplace.

Indulgence: the United States accounts for a score of 68 in the sixth dimension.

Asia-Pacific Region: The Case of Japan

The analysis for the case of Japan is illustrated in the figure below.

Power Distance: Japan does not score as high as other Asian countries, and accounts for a score of 54 in the power distance dimension. The Japanese are very much conscious about their hierarchical position in a social setting and hence, act accordingly. However, some of the individuals from other countries experience the slow decision-making process, thereby proving it more hierarchical.

Individualism: in terms of Individualism, Japan accounts for 46. Japanese society is basically a collectivistic society, where the harmony of a group is prioritized over the expression of the individual opinions. The Japanese society are mainly experienced as collectivistic by Asian standards and Western standards.

Masculinity: the Masculinity score in Japan is 95, owing to the fact that Japan is one of the most Masculine societies in the world. The businesses in the country are majorly driven by factors such as achievement, competition as well as success.

The expression of Masculinity in Japan is majorly driven for perfection and excellence in material sciences, and production in every industry and businesses among the different countries.

Figure 2. Analysis of the Hofstede Cultural Dimensions in Japan

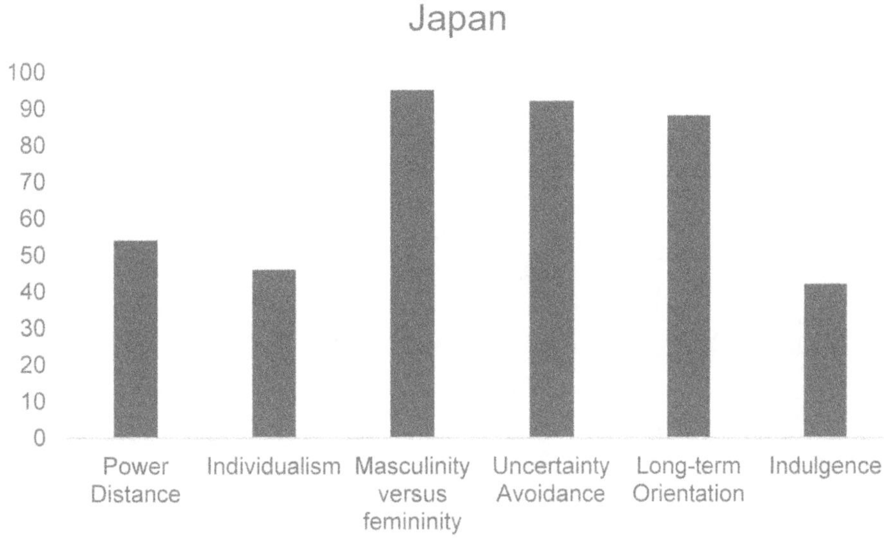

Uncertainty Avoidance: the uncertainty avoidance dimension score for Japan is 92, and is one of the most uncertainty avoiding countries in the world. This can mainly be attributed to the fact that Japan is regularly threatened by the natural disasters, such as tsunamis, earthquakes, volcano eruptions, and typhoons, which are expected to prepare the individuals for uncertain situations. This high need for Uncertainty Avoidance is one of the factors explaining why changes seem to be difficult to be realized in a country like Japan.

Long-Term Orientation: the long-term orientation score in Japan is 88, which seems to be high. In the history of mankind, the Japanese people see their lives as very short. The corporate segments in Japan offer constant higher rate of investment in the Research & Development segments economically, with the higher capital rate, along with the priority to a stable market share growth.

Indulgence: Japan accounts for a relatively lower score of 42 in terms of indulgence cultural dimension. The Japanese society with such low score of indulgence offer the tendency to pessimism and cynicism. Individuals with this type of orientation have the perception that their actions might be restrained by the social norms.

European Region: The Case of the United Kingdom

The analysis of the case of United Kingdom is illustrated in the figure below.

Power Distance: in terms of power distance dimension, UK accounts for a score of 35, which reflects that the British society believes in the fact that inequalities amongst the individuals should be minimized. According to the reports, the power distance index is usually lower amongst the higher class in Britain in comparison to that of the working classes.

Individualism: the individualism cultural dimension accounts for a score of 89 in the UK, which is one the highest Individualist scores. British individuals are a group of private and individualist people. The people in Britain emphasize on developing their unique purpose in life and how uniquely they can contribute to the businesses and societies.

Figure 3. Analysis of the Hofstede Cultural Dimensions in the United Kingdom

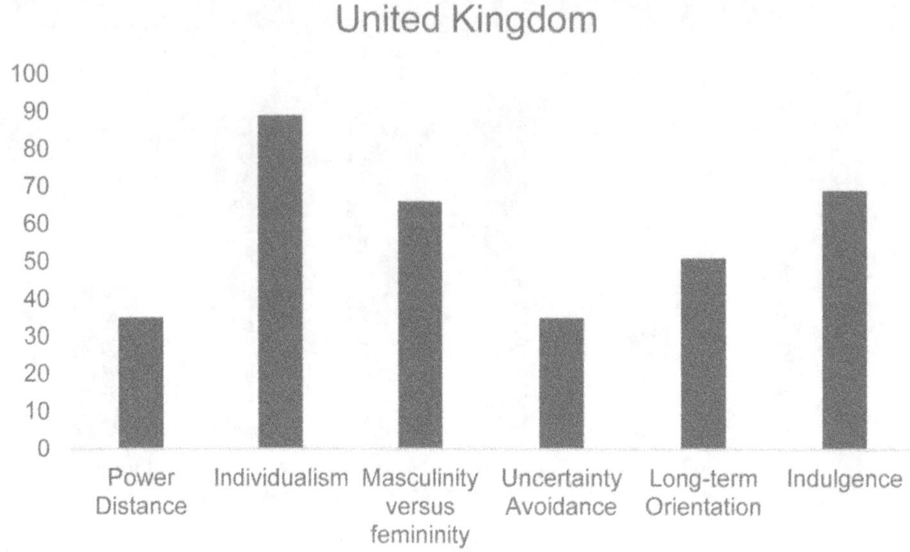

Masculinity versus femininity: with a score of 66 in terms of masculinity versus femininity, UK is a masculine society, which emphasizes on being highly success driven and oriented. The individuals in the UK, in comparison to the other countries, live in order to work, with a clear understanding of their goals and ambitions.

Uncertainty Avoidance (UAI): the UK has a score of 35 in terms of Uncertainty Avoidance, which emphasizes the fact that the nation goes along with the new information and plans that comes with each day. The British people are merely comfortable in their ambiguous situations, owing to the fact that Britain is a low UAI country. The country differs with the work culture of the other countries in terms of the fact that there is heavy consumerism for the innovative and new products in the industries such as financial engineering, marketing, and advertising.

Long Term Orientation: the long-term orientation dimension accounts for a score of 51 in the UK. Thus, a dominant preference in the British culture is difficult to be determined. The country prefers to maintain time-honored norms and traditions in their businesses.

Indulgence: cultural dimension indulgence accounts for a score of 69, which indicates that the British culture is an indulgent culture. The individuals with higher indulgence scores exhibit the willingness to realize their desires in regards to their lives with an optimistic attitude. In addition to this, the individuals in the region emphasize on spending their money according to their time, needs and wishes.

EMPIRICAL EVIDENCE: THE CASE OF "COCA-COLA"

The Coca-Cola is the largest beverage company in the world, which offers its consumers nearly 500 sparkling brands. The Coca-Cola Company is engaged in the manufacturing and selling of beverage bases. The authorized bottlers combine concentrate or beverage bases as the case may be with water or carbonated water, sweetener (as per the product), in order to produce canned or bottled beverages. These beverages are packaged in approved containers with trademarks - such as refillable or non-refillable glass or PET bottles, tetra packs, and cans to the retailers.

The brand has one of the largest beverage distribution networks in the world, which is consumed in more than 200 countries across the different nations. The globalization factor for competitiveness in the industry impacted the brand in the market.

Coca-Cola has a strong fan base ranging from Bahrain to Budapest and Boston, with its drinking brands such as Frescolita, Vegitabeta, as well as Ambasa. Coca-Cola has its availability in the remotest corners across the globe. The brand is committed to local markets, wherein it emphasizes on the cultural and background differences among the countries. With its bottling partners, the company ranges from the local communities to the foreign communities that it serves, thereby making the brand refresh and benefit every individual. Being one of the largest companies in the world, Coca-Cola owes the capability to adapt to different cultures and markets.

Cultural Impact

Every brand operating in foreign markets need to understand the culture of that particular nation. One of the key objectives of the customers in marketing processes is to gain knowledge about the cultural and social influences of the customers. In addition to this, emphasis on the determinants of purchase behavior also contributes to the success of marketing in the cultural aspects. One of the major factors to be focused upon also includes the proper knowledge, understanding and respect for the other's culture and also set one's own cultural values according to the same. Such important considerations are expected to differentiate the brand from its lesser known counterparts. The global marketers focus upon addressing the particulars of cross-cultural consumer behaviors via various models and theories, which explains the consumer needs, and cultural influences, and then develop various methods to contrast and compare the behavior of the buyers and consumers across different cultures.

Over the past few years, various socio-cultural effects are recognized as critical elements of marketing behavior. The cultural components include aspects such as religion, language, attitudes, and values. Technology and aesthetics are also expected to impact the consumer perception for a brand.

Cultural Impact in India

Untill 1977, Coca-Cola was one of the leading brands in the world and in India as well. However, due to FERA (Foreign Exchange Regulation Act), the brand had to leave India and didn't return till the year 1993. Owing to the quality, price quality trade-offs, market exploitation, and resource exploitation, the brand had to face a lot of problems in the country. Coca-Cola was criticized for affecting the quantity and quality of the ground water. Due to such issues, the brand faced a lot of criticism in India.

However, due to its strong brand reputation, the brand could make it back in the country. With the in-depth analysis and market analysis in India for the cultural aspects, and needs of the customers, the brand could regain its market share in India.

Coca-Cola gave more importance to the country's culture, owing to the fact that it is one of the major elements in India for deciding the consumer purchase decisions and behavior. Hence, the uncertainty avoidance in India is low and it is difficult for individuals in the country to adopt to sudden changes. The uncertainty avoidance score in India is 50, which implies that the people are emotional and sensitive towards the invasions and exploitation from other cultures. Hence, before entering the Indian market, proper understanding of the culture is vital.

Cultural Impact in China

One of the key strategies for entry in China is the effective implementation of cross-cultural communication. Proper knowledge and understanding of the formality of language in China, with proper business practices and etiquettes are expected to minimize the chances of miscommunications among the individuals in the country (Watkins, 2013). China is engaged in reforming its state-owned enterprises in order to widen its businesses. This is further anticipated to impact the inability of the international businesses to operate freely within the country. There are few countries easier to navigate in comparison to China. Hence, in order to ensure success in the businesses, the firms are engaged in hiring intelligent employees to train, manage and educate the staffs, thereby improving its profitability. One of the major reasons for Coca-Cola to hold a successful market in China is its cross-cultural strategies and leadership.

Coca-Cola has established a popular and strong brand in China. The brand is engaged in connecting the employees to the cross-cultural training, developing cultural competence, and cross-cultural communication education (Gomez, 2013). Hence, Coca- Cola has developed the necessary expertise in order to navigate through the various aspects of the Chinese market.

STRATEGIES TO ADDRESS THE CULTURAL DIFFERENCES

Cross-cultural communication is one of the key strategies in addressing cultural differences. Communications are non-verbal as well as verbal. Hence, it becomes very much important for the individuals and the firms/businesses to be well-aware of the expressions, gestures, and the body language of the same. Display of inappropriate non-verbal communication methods are expected to pose offensive at times. If the employees are sensitive to the culture of any nation, then it helps in eliminating the cultural barriers in the process of trade. In addition to all of the above factors, intercultural communications needs to be effective to advance cross-cultural communications (Watkins, 2013). In order to enhance the intercultural communications, it becomes essential for the businesses/firm to properly understand and navigate through the cultural practices of the nation.

In the future, trade tensions among the countries are expected to pose problems for the businesses that are operating in the foreign markets. For instance, factors such as rising product prices, and increase in the labor costs for international businesses are expected to increase the market barriers for the businesses operating in that particular country. In addition to all of the above factors, cultural aspects within the businesses in a country, such as conflicting working styles, coupled with the employment laws, navigating the visa requirements, and lack of professional etiquettes also poses to be a matter of concern at the firm level in different countries with different culture, impacting on the business profitability as well.

CONCLUSION

The process of globalization enables the movement of cultural norms and practices along with the cross-border exchange of goods and products. It becomes an essential factor for the brands/companies to understand the cultural differences in different nations, and hence formulate their strategies to enter the market. Proper understanding of the culture leads to better interactions with other cultures along with the efficient management of firms/businesses.

Hence, in today's scenario, the companies are investing heavily on establishing cross-cultural communication training and techniques, with a focus on reduction of misunderstandings. The businesses are putting a lot of efforts on gaining knowledge and investigating about the country's culture before entering that particular market. However, country's legislative policies and frameworks, which support the cultural factors, should be specific. This paper focused on encouraging the different new market players to adapt to the relevant cultural differences and gain profits by understanding the different cultural dimensions country-wise.

REFERENCES

Calderóna, C. (2010). *Trade and economic growth: Evidence on the role of complementarities for CAFTA-DR countries.* The World Bank: Latin America and the Caribbean Region.

Deal, T., & Kennedy, A. (2000). *Corporate cultures: The rites and rituals of corporate life.* Perseus Book Publishing.

Gomez, M. B. (2013). *Coca Cola: International business strategy for globalization.* International Trade & Academic Research Conference.

Hattangadi, V. (2019). *Six dimensions to understand cultural differences in the world.* Financial Express.

Hofstede, G. (1994). The business of international business is culture. *International Business Review, 3*(1), 1–14. doi:10.1016/0969-5931(94)90011-6

Javetski, B. F. (1996). Old world, new investment. *Business Week*, 50-51.

Johansson, J. (2000). *Global marketing - Foreign entry, local marketing, and global management.* McGraw-Hill.

Keegan, W. (2002). *Global Marketing Management.* Pearson Education.

Livermore, D. (2015). *Leading with cultural intelligence: The real secret to success.* Amacom.

Prasad, P., & Prasad, A. (2006). Global transitions: The emerging new world order and its implications for business and management. *Business Renaissance Quarterly, 1*, 91–113.

Ritzer, E. M. (2001). *Globalization theory: Lessons from the exportation of McDonaldization and the new means of consumption.* Sage Publications.

Siriphattrasophon, S. (2012). Cross-cultural management of a multinational enterprise: A case of Thailand and Vietnam. *International Journal of Business and Management Studies, 1*(3), 379–390.

Spencer-Oatey, H. (2008). *Culturally speaking: Culture, communication and politeness theory* (2nd ed.). Bloomsbury.

Watkins, M. (2013). *Culture and society.* Harvard Business Review, Fontana Press.

Younkins, E. (1998). *Individualism and freedom: Vital pillars of true communities*. Retrieved from https://fee.org/articles/individualism-and-freedom-vital-pillars-of-true-communities/

KEY TERMS AND DEFINITIONS

Business: A person's regular trade, occupation, or profession.

Culture: The customs, ideas, and social behaviour of a particular society or an imdividual.

Economic: Related to the economy or economics.

Globalization: The process by which organizations or businesses develop international impact or start operating on an global scale.

International Trade: International trade is defined as a set of actions which aims to exchange the goods, capital and services between the countries across their international borders.

Market: A regular gathering of people for the purchase and sale of provisions, as well as other commodities.

Strategy: A plan of action designed to achieve a long-term aim.

Chapter 11
Evaluation of India's Proposed Regional Trade Agreements With Major Economies Using General Equilibrium Analysis

Somesh Mathur
Indian Institute of Technology, Kanpur, India

Naman Agarwal
Indian Institute of Technology, Kanpur, India

ABSTRACT

This chapter attempts to analyze trade effects of India's liberalization with the Association of Southeast Asian Nations and five Asia-Pacific countries (ASEAN Plus Five), Bay of Bengal Initiative for Multi-Sectoral Technical and Economic Cooperation (BIMSTEC), European Union (EU), India-Japan-Australia trilateral framework, and Southern African Customs Union (SACU). It also tries to look at how they can create new opportunities for trade among the member countries. The authors sort out which of the above-recorded arrangements will be the most welfare upgrading for India. The chapter attempts to comprehend whether India ought to pull out for the occasions to be essential for value-chains in the areas. Maximum gains occur when India liberalizes with all, that is, liberalizes multilaterally followed by ASEAN 10, RCEP, Indo Pacific, CPTPP, MENA, EU 27, 54 nations African FTA, GCC, among others. Services and investment liberalization would bring further dividends to India.

INTRODUCTION

Trade always have unequal impact on returns to factors of production. We need to undertake a holistic view and understand economic wide impact of external liberalization. Besides economic concerns, safeguarding security interests are primary factors if we need to look east and act east. India gains the most in terms of welfare when we align with the east. We need to go beyond our discussion of get-

DOI: 10.4018/978-1-7998-7568-0.ch011

ting constrained by trade deficits with the countries and study economy wide impact of liberalization measures. Maybe trade deficits have to be reflected in changes in our exchange rates. The best strategy remains Liberalize Multilaterally.

After doing more than 500 simulations in GTAP10, it seems very clear that India has comparative advantage in unskilled and skilled labor and capital-intensive goods in form of textiles and light manufacturing. We have heavy disadvantage in terms of natural capital as a group including forestry, fishing, coal, oil extraction and construction. Returns to land sometimes comes positive sometimes negative when we align with ROW because of heavy subsidies provided by developed and developing countries alike. We also gain in terms of meat and meat products, dairy products, rice and motor vehicle production. We also have advantages in transport and communication and other services. In South Asia, we gain in terms of utilities also. Next set of reforms need to take care of regulatory burdens and promote competition as far as trade in services and investments are concerned.

We have negative trade balance of merchandise where we export 323 billion US dollars in 2019 but import 478 billion US dollars of merchandise from the world. This shortfall is met by positive trade balance in terms of exports of services of the level of 321 billion US dollars and imports of 188 billion dollars, but not enough to cover up for having net current account deficit. This current account deficit is more than matched by capital account surplus, leading to a BOP surplus. The latter has led to appreciation of Indian rupee. What is surprising to note is that we have Capital account surplus at the time of pandemic. Second, all GTAP simulations of trade Liberalization show that India's trade balance falls negative with external Liberalization, meaning that our exchange rate may be overvalued and may see depreciation in coming months. What is disturbing is however to note that exports are not increasing while tariff increase has led to constrains on imports and especially intermediate imports where such protectionism in the economy may force other countries to adopt tit for tat strategy of imposing duties on our products. We need to focus on three E's, Electronics, Engineering and Electrical products and boost trade in services and investments. For latter regulatory burdens and competition need to go up with fall in non-tariff barriers. Our manufacturing, trade and MSMEs trade all are intertwined with each other. Our overvalued exchange rate and lower growth in pandemic may be the reason that we saw our PCY fell below that of Bangladesh.

Non-tariff measures in India product wise distinguished by technical and non-technical or price measures. Footwear, fuels and wood faces price measures in India like licensing, quotas, paratariffs, anti-competitive export measures. Animals, chemical, hides, vegetables and skin imports face TBTs and SPS non-tariff measures. AMS command is used in GTAP to account for NTMs in the general equilibrium model. The NTMs data comes from UNESCAP, WTO designed TINA and WITS platforms. Textile and clothing face both price and non-price measures to safeguard our economic interest. NTMs and NTBs have very thin line separating them, meaning when NTMs are used as protectionist device they become barriers and therefore are subject to discussion. Stones, plastics and rubber imports faces more price measures. Anti-Competitive measures include state trading enterprises for importing and measures affecting competition. SPS includes registration requirements for importers, tolerance limits for residue and restricted use of substance, prohibitions and temporary geographic prohibitions. TBT includes licensing, marking and packaging requirements, and other prohibitions.

Many economists suggest that free trade improves welfare, yet we systematically measure it and see if India will profit by these FTA's. These agreements are strategically significant to India as they grant free access to these markets for Indian products.

At the point when a nation takes an interest in a free-trade region, it might encounter gains because of trade creation and either an increase or a decrease because of trade diversion. The previous has a constructive effect on welfare since the evacuation of taxes inside the area permits the nation to dispense its assets all the more efficiently underway. The nation is now ready to import the merchandise that is in the past created inefficiently behind its levy divider from member regions that are more efficient producers. Trade diversion, in the context of a free trading region, may change the source of imports from a more efficient producer to the free trading area that is not as productive. Nonetheless, this loss might be counterbalanced by the increase in welfare that results from tariff removal. Both of these impacts go into the consequences of the liberalization experiments.

The five trade agreements analyzed in this paper are:

1. **RCEP:** The Regional Comprehensive Economic Partnership (RCEP) is a proposed free trade agreement between the ten member states of ASEAN, namely Brunei, Cambodia, Indonesia, Laos, Malaysia, Myanmar, the Philippines, Singapore, Thailand, and Vietnam, and their free trade partners - Australia, China, Japan, New Zealand, and South Korea.
2. **BFTAFA:** The BIMSTEC Free Trade Area Framework Agreement (BFTAFA) is under negotiation, also referred to as mini-SAARC. The member states are - Bangladesh, Bhutan, India, Myanmar, Nepal, Sri Lanka, and Thailand.
3. **India-EUAgreement:** It is a proposed FTA which is not negotiated further since 2013. It comprises of India and 27 member states of European Union - Austria, Belgium, Bulgaria, Croatia, Republic of Cyprus, Czech Republic, Denmark, Estonia, Finland, France, Germany, Greece, Hungary, Ireland, Italy, Latvia, Lithuania, Luxembourg, Malta, Netherlands, Poland, Portugal, Romania, Slovakia, Slovenia, Spain, and Sweden.
4. **India-Japan-Australia:** India, Japan and Australia are likely to set up a trilateral framework to address trade and investment barriers along with trade and investment promotion.
5. **India-SACUAgreement:** The Southern African Customs Union (SACU) is a customs union among five countries of Southern Africa - Botswana, Eswatini, Lesotho, Namibia and South Africa. Negotiation of a free trade agreement with SACU is planned to be held in the coming future.

LITERATURE REVIEW

Numerous papers have been published examining the effect of different economic accords on various nations; however, there is an insignificant exploration on RCEP, BIMSTEC, India-EU, India-Japan-Australia and India-SACU countries. Consequently, this paper itself contributes to our knowledge in the case of India as this will reveal to us potential effects on India's welfare because of these FTA's. To more readily comprehend the current situation of these nations, we will be taking a gander at various exchange proportions like import/export imbalance, export and import shares, as examined in the Handbook of Trade Statistics policymaking.

Gaur (2020) recommended that both India and different member states of RCEP ought to perceive complementarities between them. India's getting together with RCEP is fundamental for India concerning different states from the association. The comprehensive image of Asian reconciliation will not rise without India in RCEP. Complete segregation would not work for any nation in this financially reliant world.

In any case, if India depends on an elective methodology of respective bilateral economic accord course, it might be tedious and would likewise not ensure a superior economic accord than RCEP. The eventual fate of RCEP seems to be like that of CPTPP (Comprehensive and Progressive Agreement for Trans-Pacific Partnership) after the US pulled out from the understanding except if RCEP part nations locate a center way to determine the particular issues.

As an issue of compromise, RCEP countries can return to their choice of not permitting auto-trigger and snap-back choices for imports for India. Interestingly, India can investigate different modes in trade in services like 'consumption abroad' for foreigners and medical services and 'business presence'.

METHODOLOGY

Economy wide impact of tariff liberalization means that businesses in source country goes up due to decline in tariffs or taxes along with businesses from other countries getting transferred to the source country whose sourced products to host country now faces lower tariffs. Lower tariffs means lower outputs due to supply impacts. Further, a decline in prices of a commodity decreases the real returns of the factors used intensively. The same happens when, due to tariff decline, some factors move out of the production of this good to the production of other goods. In addition, now that imports are cheaper, domestic production gets impacted. In the partner country, trade grows up, leading to changes in investment and savings with commensurate impacts on the GDPs of the partner countries. The terms of trade improve for the partner country, raising their welfare levels. However, it is also important to know whether tariffs are imposed on final or intermediate products. If they are applied to intermediate products, then the cost of production comes down to raise profits to increase production and prices. The adjustment matters whether they are entirely happening in prices or production or both. GTAP model allows all the Tariff liberalization and escalations to be analyzed due to one integrated model of production, consumption, equilibrium markets and traded sector. Elasticities play an important role to gauge the economy wide changes due to shocks in the economy. GTAP model are identified by model equations, data in input - output format and parameters, like the elasticities. The latter can also be changed. Nonlinear simultaneous deterministic equations are solved to know the economy wide impact of exogenous variable changes on all endogenous variables. Closure allows you to fix or change the endogenous and exogenous variables. A huge effort has to be done in order to model general equilibrium impacts of variable change in real sector on economy wide variables comprising of 141 regions and 65 sectors and 5 factors of production, namely land, unskilled and skilled labor, capital and natural resources. Seminal work done in GTAP modelling in Monash University in Australia and Purdue University are very useful in this regard.

The paper will utilize the GTAP (Global Trade Analysis Project) model and apply linear and nonlinear techniques for the purpose and to calculate the correlations of the models of various FTAs. Gragg's technique with extrapolation will be favored over Johansen's strategy. We will utilize this for all the various situations consistently.

The agglomerations will be made for economic partnership among the five proposed arrangements, RCEP, BFTAFA, and with EU, Japan-Australia and SACU that incorporates just their full-time part states. It would investigate which of the accompanying agreements gives India the best open door for economic development and collaboration. It will research different *ad valorem* import tariff conditions with India:

- *Experiment 1*: India removing the import tariffs when source country is from the proposed aggregation but not vice-versa.
- *Experiment 2:* liberalizing the trade altogether between India and aggregation but maintained with the rest of the world.

Even though it is far-fetched that an arrangement would bring about the total removal of all import tariffs, these experiments give an upper bound to the advantages of the individual nations that can be caught by the model.

It will likewise search for the effect of every one of these collaborations changing with India as far as trade creation, trade diversion, terms of trade, trade balance, import and export quantities, level of employment and increase in market share and other trade indicators.

EXPERIMENTAL DESIGN

All analyses/simulations are designed with a multi-nation, general equilibrium closure. The general equilibrium closure is fitting for catching the substation in production and consumption that happens among goods and the subsequent changes in trade flows and values. Output levels, prices and income are endogenous for all regions. Finally, the worldwide bank's distribution of investment is fixed (*ROR-DELTA*= 0).

The database going with the GTAP model is appropriate to analyze the results of a free trade area since, except for Bhutan, all the nations concerned have detailed data. The commodities are isolated into three gatherings: food and agriculture (*FoodAgri*), resources and manufacturing (*ResoManuf*), and services (*Services*).

RunGTAP offers a wide range of arrangement strategies. The **SINGLE-STEP SOLUTION**, or Johansen strategy, regards the model as a straight framework, linearized around the underlying arrangement. This methodology is the easiest and speediest computationally. Notwithstanding, since GTAP is a non-direct framework, Johansen results are not exactly precise, aside from little shocks. The errors are super-relative to the size of the shock: twofold the size of the shock, and the size of the errors will dramatically increase.

MULTI-STEP SOLUTION methodology is utilized to diminish linearization blunders which emerge from the default one-step or Johansen arrangement technique. Briefly, the Euler multi-step system naturally isolates the exogenous shock into various equivalent segments. The outcomes from the two stages might be consolidated to create an answer that is more accurate than that got by a single step: the more steps, the more exactness. The **Gragg and Midpoint** techniques are minor variations of the Euler strategy - they can sometimes create more precise outcomes for a given number of steps. We decide to run Gragg solutions with respectively 2, 4 and 6 steps. GEMPACK consequently utilizes these outcomes to extrapolate to an answer that is more precise than any of the three individual arrangements.

GENERAL EQUILIBRIUM IMPACT OF TARIFF REDUCTION

Think about a decrease of the tariff on imports of *i* from *r* into *s*, *tms*(*i,r,s*). This brings down *pms*(*i,r,s*) via price linkage equation:

$$pms(i,r,s) = tm(i,s) + tms(i,r,s) + pcif(i,r,s). \quad (1)$$

Domestic users immediately substitute away from competing imports as per the condition:

$$qxs(i,r,s) = qim(i,s) - \sigma_M(i) * [pms(i,r,s) - pim(i,s)]. \quad (2)$$

Likewise, the composite cost of imports confronting sector *j* falls through conditions:

$$pim(i,s) = \sum_{k \in REG} MSHRS(i,k,s) * pms(k,s); \quad (3)$$

$$pfm(i,j,s) = tfm(i,j,s) + pim(i,s). \quad (4)$$

This builds the aggregate demand for imports through equation:

$$qfm(i,j,s) = qf(i,j,s) - \sigma_D(i) * [pfm(i,j,s) - pf(i,j,s)] \quad (5)$$

Less expensive imports serve to bring down the composite cost of intermediates through condition beneath:

$$pf(i,j,s) = FMSHR(i,j,s) * pfm(i,j,s) + [1 - FMSHR(i,j,s)] * pfd(i,j,s)]. \quad (6)$$

This causes excess profits at current prices, via condition:

$$VOA(j,s) * ps(j,s) = \sum_{i \in ENDW} VFA(i,j,s) * pfe(i,j,s) + \sum_{i \in TRAD} VFA(i,j,s) * pf(i,j,s) + VOA(j,s) * profitslack(j,s). \quad (7)$$

This thus incites output to expand, which in turn generates an expansion effect through conditions

$$qva(j,s) + ava(j,s) = qo(j,s) - ao(j,s); \quad (8)$$

$$qf(i,j,s) + af(i,j,s) = qo(j,s) - ao(j,s) \quad (9)$$

The expansion effect induces increased demands for primary factors of production via equation:

$$qfe(i,j,s)+afe(i,j,s)=qva(j,s)-\sigma_{VA}(j)*[pfe(i,j,s)-afe(i,j,s)-pva(j,s). \tag{10}$$

In the general equilibrium model, this expansion generates an excess of demand via the mobile endowment market-clearing condition equation:

$$VOM(i,s)*qo(i,s)=\sum_{j\in PROD} VFM(i,j,s)*qfe(i,j,s)+VOM(i,s)*endwslack(i,s). \tag{11}$$

This shoots up the prices of these factors and transmits the shock to other sectors in the liberalizing region.

Now turn to region *r*, which produces the goods for which *tms(i,r,s)* is reduced. Equation (2) may be used to determine the implications for total sales of *i* from *r* to *s*, given the responses of agents in region *s* to the tariff shock.

$$\begin{aligned} VOM(i,r)*qo(i,r)&=VDM(i,r)*qds(i,r)+VST(i,r)*qst(i,r)\\ &+\sum_{s\in REG} VXMD(i,r,s)*qxs(i,r,s)+VOM(i,r)*tradslack(i,r) \end{aligned} \tag{12}$$

Above equation dictates the resulting implications for total output: *qo(i,r)*. Now, the equations (8) and (9) again transmit the expansion effect back to intermediate demands and region *r*'s factor markets.

RESULTS

The consequences of the Experiment 1 (only India removing the trade barriers with the agglomerates) are examined first. These results are then compared to reform on India entering bilateral free trade policies with the groups.

The economy-wide impacts and macroeconomic effects of the trade policies are measured by variables:

- *DTBAL*= change in trade balance X–M, \$US million
- *DTBALi*= change in trade balance by i and by r, \$US million
- *EV*= equivalent variation, \$US million
- *pm*= market price of commodity i in region r
- *pr*= ratio of domestic to imported prices in r
- *qo*= industry output of commodity i in region r
- *qxw*= aggregate exports of i from region r, FOB weights
- *tot*= terms of trade for region r: tot(r)=psw(r)–pdw(r)
- *vgdp*= change in value of GDP

General Simulations

GTAP10 simulation helps us to answer several questions. Who, among ASEAN 10 partners, gains the most by having free trade both ways with India? Calibration based on country parameters, VGDP and welfare as defined by the GTAP model, shows that Indonesia, followed by South East Asia comprising of Malaysia and Singapore, then D2 ASEAN 10 countries comprising of Vietnam and Thailand, followed by developing ASEAN 10 comprising of Laos, Cambodia, Philippines and Myanmar have welfare gains in that order. Brunei has marginal negative welfare when it has free trade with India both ways. India gains more than 5800 million US dollars welfare gain while Indonesia has more than 1400 million US dollars welfare gain, 1162 million US dollars welfare gain for Malaysia and Singapore, 875 million US dollars gain for Vietnam and Thailand, nearly 100 million US dollars gain for developing ASEAN 10. Indonesia sees 0.82 percent growth rate, Singapore and Malaysia together 0.34 per cent growth while India has nearly 0.08 percent growth due to free trade with ASEAN 10 nations. However, India's trade balance becomes negative basically due to negative fall on trade in grains and vegetables, processed food and extraction industry. All factors in India however gain, except natural resource comprising of shipping, forestry, coal and oil extraction, basic metals. Light manufacturing, textiles, meat and meat products, utilities, transport and communication and other services in India gets a boost due to the free trade deal of India with ASEAN 10 nations. Surprisingly, China, which has historical and cultural ties with ASEAN 10 nations, gains by having free trade with ASEAN 10 of the level of nearly 4500 million US dollars but ASEAN 10 as a group has negative welfare losses due to their free trade with China. China alternatively has massive investments and trade in services with ASEAN 10 nations. China may be imposing lower tariffs on ASEAN 10 exports leading to relatively lower welfare for ASEAN 10 nations. Agriculture, Processed food, Light and Heavy Manufacturing gain the most in ASEAN 10 nations due to free trade deal with India. Domestic investments in India gets a fillip due to its free trade deal both ways with ASEAN 10 nations. What happens if ASEAN 10 also has free trade among themselves along with having free trade with India? In that case, India's welfare gain are still higher while now Vietnam and Thailand's welfare gains are relatively maximum, followed by that of Singapore and Malaysia. Indonesia is third but still grows at the highest rate. Processed food trade from Singapore and Malaysia, like vegetable oils and fats, sugar, dairy products, food products, among others bring gains to their economies.

Let us evaluate now the 15 nations RCEP trade deal with ASEAN 10, China, Japan, Korea and Oceania comprising of Australia and New Zealand. Surprisingly, Japan followed by Korea, then China followed by Oceania gain the most in terms of welfare gains. ASEAN 10 have negative 4000 million US dollars as welfare loss. Japan gains more than 22000 million US dollars followed by South Korea gain of more than 11000 million US dollars as welfare changes. China gains around 10000 million US dollars with more than 3300 million US dollars gain for Oceania countries. Japan and Korea are gaining in terms of GDP growth and welfare despite massive losses to factors like land and natural resources. Korea gains because of higher trade and output of textile, light manufacturing, heavy manufacturing and public utilities. Japan sees growth in light manufacturing and utilities like electricity generation, gas, water and construction. China gains more than any other RCEP partner if RCEP think of aligning with Latin America, MENA or CPTPP in future. If India joins RCEP, gains for India nearing 6000 million US dollars, with RCEP partners gaining more than China. It is one such unique deal and that may be the reason that RCEP 14 including ASEAN 10 and Japan were keen to have trade deal with India. India however witnesses negligible changes in growth of GDP as trade balances of India become negative due to losses in extraction and grains and vegetable sector due to being part of RCEP. ASEAN 10 free trade deal both ways with India seems to be mutually beneficial. Massive gains occur for Japan and Korea due to RCEP in its present form due to increase in domestic investments.

Specific Simulations

In the first case, when India liberalizes itself for RCEP but there is no reciprocity, India's GDP depreciates by 1.67% and also loses in terms of trade by 1.32% (Table 1 and Table 2). Also, India's trade balance decreases by more than 6000 million USD, which is caused primarily due to a decrease in the trade balance in the primary sector, which ranges about 14000 million USD. This strong decrease in the primary sector trade balance is due to a decrease of about 36% in import prices due to which India imports an enormous amount of cheap agricultural commodities than it exports. However, India's trade balance increases in secondary and tertiary sectors. Between India and RCEP, RCEP countries gain slightly with their GDP increasing by 0.25%.

In Table 3 and Table 4, for trade between India and RCEP but with the case that RCEP also liberalizing the trade with India completely, India still loses by 0.87% GDP, and there is little effect on RCEP. India's trade balance slightly improves in the agricultural sector but deteriorates enormously in manufacturing and services so that India's total trade balance is worse than in the first case. India's price ratio of domestic and imported agricultural products still increases more than 36%, but in the latter case, India's exports for food has increased by more than 37%, which was only 19% increase in the first case. By looking at EV, consumer welfare increases strongly for RCEP in both cases, but it increases enough for India only in the second case.

Now, between India and BIMSTEC group of countries, for the first case when only India gets rid of tariffs and the second case when BIMSTEC follows India and removes its tariffs, Tables 5, 6, 7 and

Table 1. Economy-wide impacts when India liberalizes trade with the RCEP, but RCEP does not reciprocate (percentage change)

pm	RCEP	ROW	IND
Land	1.64	-0.30	-9.73
UnSkLab	0.27	-0.06	-1.06
SkLab	0.22	-0.05	-0.24
Capital	0.23	-0.05	-0.53
NatRes	0.14	-0.04	0.31
FoodAgri	0.34	-0.07	-3.70
ResoManuf	0.19	-0.04	-1.13
Services	0.22	-0.05	-0.78
CGDS	0.18	-0.04	-1.19

qo	RCEP	ROW	IND
FoodAgri	0.75	-0.15	-3.97
ResoManuf	-0.12	0.02	1.08
Services	-0.03	0.00	0.28
CGDS	0.07	-0.06	0.99

qxw	RCEP	ROW	IND
FoodAgri	8.42	-0.57	19.05
ResoManuf	-0.16	0.02	9.07
Services	-0.59	0.16	2.78

pr	RCEP	ROW	IND
FoodAgri	0.40	0.05	35.81
ResoManuf	0.13	-0.04	0.91
Services	0.25	-0.01	-0.77

Table 2. Macroeconomic effects when India liberalizes trade with the RCEP, but RCEP does not reciprocate (percentage change)

DTBAL	(Sim)
RCEP	-242.32
ROW	6493.88
IND	-6251.54

DTBALi	RCEP	ROW	IND
FoodAgri	19281.22	-6632.13	-13963.47
ResoManuf	-13508.18	7884.80	4373.37
Services	-6015.35	5241.21	3338.56

tot	(Sim)
RCEP	0.16
ROW	-0.03
IND	-1.32

EV	(Sim)
RCEP	11205.73
ROW	-3205.08
IND	920.33

vgdp	(Sim)
RCEP	0.25
ROW	-0.05
IND	-1.67

8 summarize the results. Consumer welfare measured by EV increases for BIMSTEC countries but decreases for India in the former case. There is very little change in every variable, including GDP, which decreases by 0.10%. One thing to note here is that the trade balance of both India and BIMSTEC countries decreases overall and the rest of the world benefits from this.

In the latter case, there is an increase in consumer welfare for both India and BIMSTEC countries. India's GDP also rises slightly by 0.5%, and food exports rise by 4%. However, there are very high loses in the overall trade balances for both India and BIMSTEC.

Running the same set of simulations for India and EU trade, we find that there is no significant economy-wide impact when EU does not decrease their trade barriers in response to India (Table 9 and

Table 3. Economy wide-impacts when India liberalizes trade with the RCEP and RCEP reciprocates (percentage change)

Pm	RCEP	ROW	IND
Land	1.30	-0.39	-5.78
UnSkLab	0.23	-0.08	-0.17
SkLab	0.20	-0.07	0.32
Capital	0.20	-0.08	0.14
NatRes	0.13	-0.06	0.78
FoodAgri	0.24	-0.09	-2.34
ResoManuf	0.15	-0.06	-0.63
Services	0.18	-0.07	-0.14
CGDS	0.14	-0.06	-0.74

qo	RCEP	ROW	IND
FoodAgri	0.58	-0.18	-2.51
ResoManuf	-0.09	0.02	0.79
Services	-0.02	0.01	0.12
CGDS	0.08	-0.09	1.30

qxw	RCEP	ROW	IND
FoodAgri	8.48	-0.78	37.04
ResoManuf	-0.04	0.03	8.72
Services	-0.49	0.21	0.45

Pr	RCEP	ROW	IND
FoodAgri	0.91	0.02	37.86
ResoManuf	0.15	-0.04	1.45
Services	0.21	-0.04	-0.11

Table 4. Macroeconomic effects when India liberalizes trade with the RCEP and RCEP reciprocates (percentage change)

DTBAL	(Sim)		DTBALi	RCEP	ROW	IND	
RCEP	-1683.18		FoodAgri	14718.53	-8609.22	-7566.87	
ROW	9167.26		ResoManuf	-11367.50	10273.71	-345.25	
IND	-7484.08		Services	-5034.22	7502.77	428.04	
tot	(Sim)		EV	(Sim)		vgdp	(Sim)
RCEP	0.14		RCEP	10154.12		RCEP	0.20
ROW	-0.04		ROW	-5609.55		ROW	-0.08
IND	-0.69		IND	4258.02		IND	-0.87

Table 10). Overall, trade balances shoot up for the rest of the world primarily due to the effect in the services sector of about 5000 million USD. India's market prices decrease by 0.3% in the secondary sector due to liberalizing, which alongside increases the manufacturing outputs and exports of India but not in a significant amount. EU gains significantly in consumer welfare, terms of trade and GDP.

When EU also retaliates by decreasing the trade barriers for Indian goods and services, there are similar macroeconomic effects on EU, but India starts gaining in terms of trade, GDP and consumer welfare slightly (Table 11 and Table 12). Net exports still decline for both India and EU as compared to no tariff relief. One significant change is seen in the costs of factors of production. Endowment costs, which decreased in the former case, increases in the latter case almost for all factors.

Table 5. Economy-wide impacts when India liberalizes trade with the BIMSTEC, but BIMSTEC does not reciprocate (percentage change)

pm	ROW	BIMSTEC	IND		qo	ROW	BIMSTEC	IND
Land	0.00	1.04	-0.31		FoodAgri	0.00	0.29	-0.12
UnSkLab	0.00	0.41	-0.04		ResoManuf	0.00	-0.07	0.05
SkLab	0.00	0.35	-0.02		Services	0.00	-0.04	0.00
Capital	0.00	0.36	-0.03		CGDS	-0.01	0.28	0.06
NatRes	0.00	0.30	0.01					
FoodAgri	0.00	0.43	-0.13		qxw	ROW	BIMSTEC	IND
ResoManuf	0.00	0.21	-0.06		FoodAgri	-0.01	1.81	0.71
Services	0.00	0.32	-0.04		ResoManuf	0.00	0.14	0.51
CGDS	0.00	0.19	-0.07		Services	0.01	-1.14	0.15
pr	ROW	BIMSTEC	IND					
FoodAgri	-0.01	0.43	1.08					
ResoManuf	0.00	0.21	0.07					
Services	0.00	0.32	-0.04					

Table 6. Macroeconomic effects when India liberalizes trade with the BIMSTEC, but BIMSTEC does not reciprocate (percentage change)

DTBAL	(Sim)		DTBALi	ROW	BIMSTEC	IND	
ROW	745.88		FoodAgri	6.24	612.23	-662.89	
BIMSTEC	-357.54		ResoManuf	113.84	-288.41	85.94	
IND	-388.35		Services	625.80	-681.35	188.61	
tot	(Sim)		EV	(Sim)		vgdp	(Sim)
ROW	0.00		ROW	-685.41		ROW	0.00
BIMSTEC	0.25		BIMSTEC	1049.20		BIMSTEC	0.40
IND	-0.07		IND	-451.09		IND	-0.10

In Table 13 and Table 14, effects of India liberalizing trade with Japan and Australia (not vice-versa) are shown. Aggregate exports of India rise in all sectors and market prices decrease for all commodities, and factors of production in India. India loses in macroeconomic variables slightly as expected, whereas Japan and Australia benefit mostly in terms of consumer welfare.

When Japan and Australia also liberalize trade with India, the three countries form a trilateral chain of aggregates. The prices of commodities and endowment costs do not decrease as it was in the former case (Table 15 and Table 16). This is the only significant difference observed between both the cases. The trade policies of Japan and Australia as a group have very similar macroeconomic effects on both India and themselves.

Table 7. Economy-wide impacts when India liberalizes trade with the BIMSTEC and BIMSTEC reciprocates (percentage change)

pm	ROW	BIMSTEC	IND		qo	ROW	BIMSTEC	IND
Land	-0.03	0.21	0.98		FoodAgri	-0.01	-0.13	0.17
UnSkLab	-0.02	0.48	0.62		ResoManuf	-0.01	0.17	0.13
SkLab	-0.02	0.48	0.51		Services	0.00	-0.06	-0.12
Capital	-0.02	0.51	0.54		CGDS	-0.02	0.88	0.34
NatRes	-0.03	0.66	0.69					
FoodAgri	-0.02	0.12	0.56		qxw	ROW	BIMSTEC	IND
ResoManuf	-0.02	0.03	0.35		FoodAgri	-0.06	3.08	4.32
Services	-0.02	0.33	0.49		ResoManuf	-0.01	1.28	2.04
CGDS	-0.02	-0.02	0.31		Services	0.07	-1.19	-1.73
pr	ROW	BIMSTEC	IND					
FoodAgri	-0.02	2.33	1.82					
ResoManuf	-0.01	0.56	0.50					
Services	-0.02	0.33	0.51					

Table 8. Macroeconomic effects when India liberalizes trade with the BIMSTEC and BIMSTEC reciprocates (percentage change)

DTBAL	(Sim)		DTBALi	ROW	BIMSTEC	IND
ROW	3328.04		FoodAgri	-512.80	-356.73	720.42
BIMSTEC	-1568.68		ResoManuf	489.02	-546.40	-266.25
IND	-1759.36		Services	3351.82	-665.55	-2213.52

tot	(Sim)		EV	(Sim)		vgdp	(Sim)
ROW	-0.01		ROW	-3042.14		ROW	-0.02
BIMSTEC	0.07		BIMSTEC	500.66		BIMSTEC	0.14
IND	0.43		IND	2017.24		IND	0.50

Economy-wide effects of India decreasing the levy on SACU products and services presents an interesting case (Table 17 and Table 18). There is no significant change for India. The demand rises in Southern Africa, following which prices and quantity produced rises there. At the macroeconomic front, the rest of the world benefits as a whole in trade balances in every sector while India loses in manufacturing. Overall, there is a slight drop in consumer welfare and GDP of India but those rise more for SACU in absolute terms.

When SACU union also reciprocates with Indian trade policy of removing tariffs, prices in India also increases along with SACU for every good and service (Table 19 and Table 20). There is a slight drop in demand for agricultural activities and services, but manufacturing activities cover up for those.

Table 9. Economy-wide impacts when India liberalizes trade with the EU, but EU does not reciprocate (percentage change)

pm	ROW	IND	EU_27
Land	-0.01	-0.35	0.12
UnSkLab	-0.03	-0.06	0.16
SkLab	-0.03	-0.05	0.14
Capital	-0.03	-0.05	0.15
NatRes	-0.04	0.01	0.21
FoodAgri	-0.02	-0.23	0.12
ResoManuf	-0.02	-0.36	0.11
Services	-0.03	-0.13	0.13
CGDS	-0.02	-0.42	0.10

qo	ROW	IND	EU_27
FoodAgri	0.01	-0.13	-0.02
ResoManuf	-0.02	0.07	0.07
Services	0.01	-0.01	-0.02
CGDS	-0.04	0.53	0.10

qxw	ROW	IND	EU_27
FoodAgri	0.04	1.05	-0.01
ResoManuf	-0.05	2.80	0.20
Services	0.18	0.54	-0.33

pr	ROW	IND	EU_27
FoodAgri	-0.02	1.09	0.05
ResoManuf	-0.02	0.76	0.06
Services	-0.05	-0.16	0.10

Table 10. Macroeconomic effects when India liberalizes trade with the EU, but EU does not reciprocate (percentage change)

DTBAL	(Sim)		DTBALi	ROW	IND	EU_27	
ROW	5066.98		FoodAgri	634.80	-487.78	-220.96	
IND	-2837.35		ResoManuf	-1073.75	-3058.85	3703.83	
EU_27	-2229.63		Services	5505.93	709.28	-5712.45	
tot	**(Sim)**		**EV**	**(Sim)**		**vgdp**	**(Sim)**
ROW	-0.02		ROW	-3044.06		ROW	-0.03
IND	-0.27		IND	-1281.12		IND	-0.35
EU_27	0.07		EU_27	5262.16		EU_27	0.15

In the macroeconomic view, trade balances for both India and SACU drop. The trade balance of the rest of the world benefits the most in the services sector since both India and SACU start importing more. The coming together of India and SACU benefits both by increasing terms of trade, equivalent variation and real GDP for both of the groups.

Where should 15 nations RCEP, an Asian and Pacific alliance look for maximum gains? It seems that in any free trade deal both ways with EU28, or North American region or Latin American countries or Middle East and North African region, it is China that gains the most, the exception being when RCEP 14 and China aligns with India. Maybe that is the reason why RCEP countries were keen on having a trade deal with India. RCEP14 gains the most when it aligns with Latin American region, followed by

Table 11. Economy wide-impacts when India liberalizes trade with the EU and EU reciprocates (percentage change)

pm	ROW	IND	EU_27		qo	ROW	IND	EU_27
Land	-0.01	0.02	0.07		FoodAgri	0.02	-0.15	-0.04
UnSkLab	-0.04	0.38	0.14		ResoManuf	-0.02	0.20	0.06
SkLab	-0.04	0.35	0.13		Services	0.01	-0.08	-0.02
Capital	-0.04	0.36	0.13		CGDS	-0.05	0.74	0.11
NatRes	-0.06	0.56	0.18					
FoodAgri	-0.03	0.14	0.09		**qxw**	**ROW**	**IND**	**EU_27**
ResoManuf	-0.03	-0.07	0.08		FoodAgri	0.06	1.05	-0.02
Services	-0.04	0.26	0.11		ResoManuf	-0.06	4.40	0.22
CGDS	-0.03	-0.15	0.07		Services	0.21	-0.82	-0.28
pr	**ROW**	**IND**	**EU_27**					
FoodAgri	-0.03	1.47	0.07					
ResoManuf	-0.02	1.06	0.08					
Services	-0.06	0.24	0.08					

Table 12. Macroeconomic effects when India liberalizes trade with the EU and EU reciprocates (percentage change)

DTBAL	(Sim)	DTBALi	ROW	IND	EU_27
ROW	6640.85	FoodAgri	948.55	-535.66	-484.23
IND	-3861.53	ResoManuf	-732.98	-2300.92	2448.02
EU_27	-2779.32	Services	6425.28	-1024.95	-4743.03

tot	(Sim)	EV	(Sim)	vgdp	(Sim)
ROW	-0.03	ROW	-4462.51	ROW	-0.04
IND	0.07	IND	712.79	IND	0.07
EU_27	0.06	EU_27	4599.32	EU_27	0.12

MENA and followed by North American region. The welfare gain for RCEP14 is minimum when it aligns with EU28 along with maximum gain for China of more than 26000 million US dollars. India gains more when it aligns with RCEP14 without China. With China, it brings lower dividends to India. Grains and meat products are adversely affected by its trade with North American countries.

When ASEAN 10 has free trade both ways with China, the entire ASEAN group as one entity has negative welfare and negative GDP growth while when India has free trade both ways with ASEAN 10, there are mutual welfare gains for both ASEAN 10 and India, ASEAN 10 gaining more than 3400 million US dollars while India has more than 5800 million US dollars gain with 0.10 change in Indian GDP. Indian trade is 100 billion US dollars with ASEAN 10 but skewed towards the East Asian partners,

Table 13. Economy-wide impacts when India liberalizes trade with the Japan-Australia, but Japan-Australia does not reciprocate (percentage change)

pm	JapAus	ROW	IND
Land	0.29	-0.01	-0.18
UnSkLab	0.16	-0.01	-0.04
SkLab	0.16	-0.01	-0.03
Capital	0.16	-0.01	-0.04
NatRes	0.15	-0.01	0.00
FoodAgri	0.13	-0.01	-0.10
ResoManuf	0.12	-0.01	-0.12
Services	0.15	-0.01	-0.06
CGDS	0.11	-0.01	-0.14

qo	JapAus	ROW	IND
FoodAgri	0.08	0.00	-0.06
ResoManuf	-0.01	0.00	0.04
Services	0.00	0.00	-0.01
CGDS	0.12	-0.01	0.15

qxw	JapAus	ROW	IND
FoodAgri	1.16	-0.01	0.44
ResoManuf	0.14	-0.01	0.91
Services	-0.43	0.03	0.19

Pr	JapAus	ROW	IND
FoodAgri	0.14	0.00	0.52
ResoManuf	0.12	-0.01	0.21
Services	0.16	0.00	-0.05

Table 14. Macroeconomic effects when India liberalizes trade with the Japan-Australia, but Japan-Australia does not reciprocate (percentage change)

DTBAL	(Sim)	DTBALi	JapAus	ROW	IND
JapAus	-1379.97	FoodAgri	289.60	-23.33	-286.26
ROW	2198.77	ResoManuf	-642.36	1075.19	-763.26
IND	-818.80	Services	-1027.21	1146.91	230.72
Tot	**(Sim)**	**EV**	**(Sim)**	**vgdp**	**(Sim)**
JapAus	0.13	JapAus	1804.83	JapAus	0.16
ROW	-0.01	ROW	-1262.37	ROW	-0.01
IND	-0.10	IND	-649.00	IND	-0.14

where we have trade deficit with many of the ASEAN trading partners. What gets impacted negatively with ASEAN 10 are trade in grains and vegetables, trade in processed food and extraction industry. With China, textile, heavy and light manufacturing gets impacted negatively in the ASEAN nations and hence returns to skilled and unskilled labor and capital loses. For India, when it has free trade with ASEAN 10, all factors gain except returns to natural capital. China welfare gains are 4500 million US dollars, 1000 million US dollars lower than India, when it has free trade both ways with ASEAN 10. In India, meat and meat products, light manufacturing, textiles, transport and communications, domestic investments and other services gain by having free trade with ASEAN 10. Strategically, it is advisable to align with

Table 15. Economy wide-impacts when India liberalizes trade with the Japan-Australia and Japan-Australia reciprocates (percentage change)

pm	JapAus	ROW	IND	qo	JapAus	ROW	IND
Land	0.27	-0.02	-0.12	FoodAgri	0.07	0.00	-0.07
UnSkLab	0.16	-0.01	0.03	ResoManuf	-0.01	0.00	0.05
SkLab	0.16	-0.01	0.03	Services	0.00	0.00	-0.02
Capital	0.16	-0.01	0.03	CGDS	0.14	-0.02	0.18
NatRes	0.15	-0.02	0.08				
FoodAgri	0.13	-0.01	-0.05	**qxw**	**JapAus**	**ROW**	**IND**
ResoManuf	0.12	-0.01	-0.08	FoodAgri	1.18	0.00	0.42
Services	0.14	-0.01	0.00	ResoManuf	0.17	-0.01	1.16
CGDS	0.10	-0.01	-0.10	Services	-0.43	0.03	-0.03
pr	**JapAus**	**ROW**	**IND**				
FoodAgri	0.16	0.00	0.58				
ResoManuf	0.14	-0.01	0.26				
Services	0.16	-0.01	0.01				

Table 16. Macroeconomic effects when India liberalizes trade with the Japan-Australia and Japan-Australia reciprocates (percentage change)

DTBAL	(Sim)		DTBALi	JapAus	ROW	IND	
JapAus	-1565.63		**FoodAgri**	252.60	30.10	-302.48	
ROW	2530.47		**ResoManuf**	-810.06	1074.11	-619.69	
IND	-964.84		**Services**	-1008.16	1426.26	-42.68	
tot	**(Sim)**		**EV**	**(Sim)**		**vgdp**	**(Sim)**
JapAus	0.13		**JapAus**	1763.17		**JapAus**	0.15
ROW	-0.01		**ROW**	-1565.81		**ROW**	-0.01
IND	-0.04		**IND**	-245.17		**IND**	-0.07

ASEAN 10. Culture and democratic traditions therefore should become the pillar of the economic and strategic partnership. Any discredit on democratic values lowers the value of the partnerships

It seems that developed ASEAN, comprising of Brunei, Vietnam, Singapore, Indonesia, Malaysia and Thailand, gains the most in terms of the level of welfare by having free trade among ASEAN 10, figuring 414 million US dollars while Laos, Cambodia and South East Asia loose in terms of welfare. Philippines also gains in terms of welfare - 162 million US dollars. All developing ASEAN however loose in terms of GDP by ASEAN FTA. The developed ASEAN gains in terms of trade in grains and vegetables while the developing part gains in terms of unskilled labor, skilled labor and capital by trading in textiles, light manufacturing with their richer counterpart. India's FTA with ASEAN 10 brings in

Table 17. Economy-wide impacts when India liberalizes trade with the SACU, but SACU does not reciprocate (percentage change)

pm	ROW	IND	SACU		qo	ROW	IND	SACU
Land	0.00	-0.01	-0.02		**FoodAgri**	0.00	0.00	-0.43
UnSkLab	0.00	-0.01	0.67		**ResoManuf**	0.00	0.01	0.14
SkLab	0.00	-0.01	0.66		**Services**	0.00	-0.01	-0.03
Capital	0.00	-0.01	0.67		**CGDS**	-0.01	0.06	0.73
NatRes	0.00	0.00	0.80					
FoodAgri	0.00	-0.02	0.54		**qxw**	**ROW**	**IND**	**SACU**
ResoManuf	0.00	-0.04	0.49		**FoodAgri**	0.01	0.09	-1.79
Services	0.00	-0.02	0.58		**ResoManuf**	0.00	0.36	0.97
CGDS	0.00	-0.05	0.37		**Services**	0.01	0.05	-2.17
pr	**ROW**	**IND**	**SACU**					
FoodAgri	0.00	0.01	0.38					
ResoManuf	0.00	0.09	0.44					
Services	0.00	-0.01	0.59					

Table 18. Macroeconomic effects when India liberalizes trade with the SACU, but SACU does not reciprocate (percentage change)

DTBAL	(Sim)		DTBALi	ROW	IND	SACU	
ROW	845.01		FoodAgri	237.47	18.44	-244.90	
IND	-345.62		ResoManuf	205.59	-426.50	116.15	
SACU	-499.39		Services	401.95	62.44	-370.64	
tot	(Sim)		EV	(Sim)		vgdp	(Sim)
ROW	0.00		ROW	-473.38		ROW	0.00
IND	-0.04		IND	-249.34		IND	-0.04
SACU	0.45		SACU	647.39		SACU	0.65

around 5900 million US dollars welfare gain for India while more than 3500 million US dollars welfare gain for ASEAN 10. ASEAN 10 grows at vGDP of the level of 0. 24 percent while India grows at 0.11 percent. If India joins RCEP, India's welfare may be more or matching the gains when India liberalizes and have free trade with ASEAN 10. However, vGDP changes are negligible when India liberalizes with 15 nations RCEP having China as one of the members. In net, liberalizing with ASEAN 10 may be the best way to move forward economically and strategically.

Let us now evaluate India ASEAN FTA, signed since 2009, India Japan FTA and India Korea FTA using GTAP 10 simulations. ASEAN India total trade touching 100 billion US dollars but we have trade deficit with the group as such. Maximum welfare gains of India of the level of more than 5800 million

Table 19. Economy wide-impacts when India liberalizes trade with the SACU and SACU reciprocates (percentage change)

pm	ROW	IND	SACU		qo	ROW	IND	SACU
Land	0.00	0.04	-0.03		FoodAgri	0.01	-0.04	-0.43
UnSkLab	-0.01	0.14	0.66		ResoManuf	0.00	0.06	0.18
SkLab	-0.01	0.13	0.64		Services	0.00	-0.03	-0.05
Capital	-0.01	0.14	0.66		CGDS	-0.01	0.14	1.19
NatRes	-0.01	0.20	0.83					
FoodAgri	-0.01	0.09	0.47		qxw	ROW	IND	SACU
ResoManuf	-0.01	0.06	0.37		FoodAgri	0.02	-0.32	-1.60
Services	-0.01	0.12	0.53		ResoManuf	-0.01	0.99	1.59
CGDS	-0.01	0.04	0.18		Services	0.02	-0.42	-1.97
pr	ROW	IND	SACU					
FoodAgri	-0.01	0.12	0.44					
ResoManuf	0.00	0.20	0.74					
Services	-0.01	0.12	0.53					

Table 20. Macroeconomic effects when India liberalizes trade with the SACU and SACU also reciprocates (percentage change)

DTBAL	(Sim)
ROW	1553.33
IND	-695.70
SACU	-857.63

DTBALi	ROW	IND	SACU
FoodAgri	412.63	-164.01	-236.65
ResoManuf	134.75	2.32	-287.71
Services	1005.96	-534.00	-333.27

tot	(Sim)
ROW	0.00
IND	0.08
SACU	0.35

EV	(Sim)
ROW	-1075.37
IND	571.20
SACU	481.50

vgdp	(Sim)
ROW	-0.01
IND	0.10
SACU	0.50

US dollars while ASEAN gains more than 3800 million US dollars. Grain trade, processed food, heavy manufacturing and extraction industry gets impacted while all factors gain except natural resource. Transport and Communication and other services gain relatively more by India ASEAN FTA. Physical and IT connectivity, services and investment Liberalization, maritime security, and education and cultural ties would further strengthen India ASEAN FTA. We may also need ASEAN for China containment policies. India Japan and India Korea brings nearly 1000 million and more than 1700 million US dollars gain for Japan and Korea, respectively. India's welfare and GDP though goes down because heavy manufacturing gets impacted by the free trade deal.

What happens when we consider a two way free trade between India and China? We lose in terms of trade balance, welfare and GDP. We lose in terms of trade in grains, trade in meat products and heavy manufacturing. We have negative trade balance due to mainly negative trade balances in extraction and heavy manufacturing. Returns to unskilled labor, skilled labor, capital and much more than the former three, returns to natural capital would go up, namely those who are involved in forestry, fishing, coal and oil extraction and metals. Chinese would have positive 0.17 growth in vGDP and more than 4200 million US dollars welfare gain if it aligns with India. Gains would double for China and maybe some gains for India if services and investment liberalization are included. As of today free trade with China brings negative welfare for India. The basic idea is to shift comparative advantage in its own favor in India by investing in Electrical, Electronics, Engineering goods and 4IR technologies, promote village development, ports, telecommunications, among others, to match the Chinese superiority. Pharma and medical products and GVCs can be further developed in India.

It is said that, if one wishes to look east, it is inevitable that one would need to align with China. However, all GTAP simulations show that India China, Pak China, ASEAN China or RCEP deal has negative welfare for India, Pakistan and ASEAN 10, respectively. China gains in all the alignments. This is happening despite all South Asian and East Asian countries, including Oceania major imports from China. Of course, South Asia exports reach more to the west. East Asian countries are more linked in their exports and imports and investments with China. GVCs in South Asia can be linked to textile production where inputs are provided by China. Maybe if one looks at tariff structure we may have some answers. The highest tariff rates are 165 percent in Bangladesh, 44 percent in India, 65 percent in Pakistan, 29 percent in SL, 7 percent in China, 5 percent in Japan, 36 percent in Indonesia, while the other ASEAN nations have an average of 25 percent. With the reduction in tariffs, consumers gain, producers loose, government lose revenue, the returns to factors intensive in production of the goods whose tariffs came down decrease, loss regarding terms of trade and possibly a trade balance. On the other hand, tariff reduction in home country provides trade to partners and substantial improvement in GDP via trade and higher investments and savings. India needs to invest outside in terms of telecommunications, ports, build roads and have physical connectivity and village development with investment in 4IR technology to shift comparative advantage in our favor. Strategic industrial policy may be the answer keeping that protectionism needs to be kept at check

CONCLUSION

It seems that our welfare goes down when China is part of RCEP, from 5400 million US dollars when it is not part of it to 4735 million US dollars when China is in RCEP. At present, China is part of RCEP. We have larger gains when China is not part of RCEP and we have free trade with 15 nations RCEP both ways. The paper also tries to evaluate and simulate India's free trade gain both ways with 54 nations African Free Trade area, 5 nations South African Customs Union, with BIMSTEC countries, having free trade with South Asian countries, having alliance with Ganga Mekong nations and having free trade with 6 nations Latin American MERCOSUR countries. The welfare gains are of 4200 million US dollars if we have two way free trade with African FTA nations. The highest gain remains when India aligns with ASEAN 10 followed by RCEP and Indo Pacific alliance. BIMSTEC, South Asian alliance brings around 2000 million US dollars welfare gain for India. Half the amount is obtained if we align with Ganga Mekong nations. SACU alliance gives more relative welfare gain to India than aligning with MERCOSUR, but gains are not exceeding 1000 million US dollars. East Asia gains more if we look east.

The results of the experiment highlight the importance of experimental design and the usefulness of GTAP in analyzing regional integration. Two different scenarios for five different regional trade aggregations were examined further and compared. The macroeconomic effects on India of all the 10 experiments above are summarized in Table 21.

Comparing real GDP, consumer welfare and terms of trade changes, we analyze that India gains with BIMSTEC in both type of policies and with EU and SACU only when the trade has been liberalized both ways. Among these four policies, India gains the most in the free trade liberalization policy with BIMSTEC, followed by only India getting rid of tariffs to BIMSTEC, and free trade policies with EU and SACU. In the above results, we see that India loses by removing tariffs on RCEP countries in any manner, though the consumer welfare peaked for free trade with RCEP. The change in trade balances of India is negative for all the cases, worst with RCEP. India also loses with the trilateral free trade with Japan and Australia in any tariff policy.

From the above results, it can be explained why withdrawing from RCEP group of countries is in India's benefit. It protects the Indian domestic industries from cheap foreign goods from industrialized nations and saves the nation from dumping of goods by China. Moreover, from a macroeconomic point of view, India would not have performed well by joining with RCEP nations.

BIMSTEC and ASEAN comes out to be most beneficial for India, but talks for BIMSTEC FTA was started in 2004 but is yet to be concluded. Since the BIMSTEC region is notable for its diversity, the member states need to build on the regional synergies and work towards utilizing the available resources most optimally. It also allows India to pursue its three core policies: Neighborhood First, Act East and Economic development of India's north-eastern states.

Table 21. Summary of the macroeconomic effects on India for all the experiments

Experiment	*DTBAL*	*tot*	*EV*	*vgdp*
RCEP-1	-6251.54	-1.32	920.33	-1.67
RCEP-2	-7484.08	-0.69	4258.02	-0.87
BIMSTEC-1	-388.35	0.25	1049.20	0.40
BIMSTEC-2	-1759.36	0.43	2017.24	0.50
EU-1	-2837.35	-0.27	-1281.12	-0.35
EU-2	-3861.53	0.07	712.79	0.07
JAPAUS-1	-818.80	-0.10	-649.00	-0.14
JAPAUS-2	-964.84	-0.04	-245.17	-0.07
SACU-1	-345.62	-0.04	-249.34	-0.04
SACU-2	-695.70	0.08	571.20	0.10

The benefits from the trilateral supply chain resilience initiative proposed between India, Japan and Australia is also under scrutiny. Overall, we found that India would lose with the free trade with Japan and Australia, but the proposed initiative is more specific to particular sectors and to reduce the dependence on China at times of emergencies. Hence, commenting on this initiative requires further research directed deep into the policy's roots.

Finally, note that the benefits of a preferential trading agreement cannot be fully captured by a perfectly competitive, static model. The benefits of increased competition, potential economies of scale, and the incentives for investment brought by a preferential agreement will be fully realized only in the long run. These forces will likely increase incomes and, with them, imports from the rest of the world (outside trading region). While the GTAP model cannot capture all these dynamic effects from trade liberalization, it is useful for generating comparative static results for different trade scenarios, which can provide direction in the path toward further trade reform:

- Trade always have unequal impact on returns to factors of production. We need to undertake a holistic view and understand economic wide impact of external liberalization.
- Besides economic concerns, safeguarding security interests are primary factors if we need to look east and act east.
- India gains the most in terms of welfare when we align with the east. We need to go beyond our discussion of getting constrained by trade deficits with the countries and study the impact of liberalization measures. Maybe trade deficits have to be reflected in changes in our exchange rates.
- The best strategy remains liberalize multilaterally.

REFERENCES

Gaur, P. (2020). India's withdrawal from RCEP: Neutralising national trade concerns. *Journal of the Asia Pacific Economy*, 1–19. doi:10.1080/13547860.2020.1809772

Hertel, T., Powell, A., Frisvold, G., Gehlhar, M., Gray, D., Hanslow, K., Huff, K., Ianchovichina, E., Kuhn, B., Lanclos, D., MacLaren, D., Martin, W., McDonald, B., McDougall, R., Pearson, K., Perroni, C., Swaminathan, P., Tsigas, M., Tyers, R., . . . Young, L. (1997). *Global Trade Analysis: Modeling and Applications* (University of Cambridge). Purdue University, West Lafayette, IN: Global Trade Analysis Project (GTAP). Retrieved from https://www.gtap.agecon.purdue.edu/resources/res_display.asp?RecordID=4840

Pearson, K., Horridge, M., & Corong, E. (2018). *Hands-on Computing with RunGTAP and WinGEM To Introduce GTAP and GEMPACK* (Center of Policies Studies). Purdue University, West Lafayette, IN: Global Trade Analysis Project (GTAP). Retrieved from https://www.gtap.agecon.purdue.edu/resources/res_display.asp?RecordID=1638

APPENDIX

Sets

CGDS_COMM = capital goods commodities
DEMD_COMM = demanded commodities
ENDW_COMM = endowment commodities
ENDWC_COMM = capital endowment commodity
ENDWM_COMM = mobile endowment commodities
ENDWS_COMM = sluggish endowment commodities
MARG_COMM = margin commodities
NMRG_COMM = non-margin commodities
NSAV_COMM = non-savings commodities
PROD_COMM = produced commodities
REG = regions in the model
TRAD_COMM = traded commodities

Variables

af composite intermed. input i augmenting tech change by j of r
Afe primary factor i augmenting tech change by j of r
ao output augmenting technical change in sector j of r
ava value added augmenting tech change in sector i of r
endwslack slack variable in endowment market clearing condition
pcif CIF world price of commodity i supplied from r to s
pf firms price for commodity i for use by j in r
pfd price index for domestic purchases of i by j in region s
pfe firms price for endowment commodity i in ind. j, region r
pfm price index for imports of i by j in region s
pim market price of composite import i in region r
pm market price of commodity i in region r
pms domestic price for good i supplied from r to region s
profitslack slack variable in the zero profit equation
ps supply price of commodity i in region r
pva firms price of value added in industry j of region r
qds domestic sales of commodity i in r
qf demand for commodity i for use by j in region r
qfe demand for endowment i for use in ind. j in region r
qfm demand for i by industry j in region s
qim aggregate imports of i in region s, market price weights

qo industry output of commodity i in region r
qst sales of m from r to international transport
qva value added in industry j of region r
qxs export sales of commodity i from r to region s
qxw aggregate exports of i from region r, FOB weights
Tfm power of the tax on imported tradable commodity I demanded by firms in sector j of region r
tm source-gen. change in tax on imports of i into s
tms source-spec. change in tax on imports of i from r into s
tradslack slack variable in tradeable market clearing condition

Coefficients

RORDELTA binary coefficient to switch mechanism of allocating investment funds
FMSHR share of firms imports in dom. composite, agents prices
MSHRS share of imports from r in import bill of s at mkt prices
VDM domestic sales of i in r at mkt prices (tradeable only)
VFA producer expenditure on i by j in r valued at agents prices
VFM producer expenditure on i by j in r valued at mkt prices
VOA value of commodity i output in region r at agents prices
VOM value of commodity i output in region r at market prices
VST exports of m from r for intl transport valued at mkt p (tradeable only)

Chapter 12
Renegotiation of USCM and Its Impact on the Agricultural Exports of Sinaloa

José G. Vargas-Hernández
https://orcid.org/0000-0003-0938-4197
University Center for Economic and Managerial Sciences, University of Guadalajara, Mexico

ABSTRACT

Mexico, like other countries, invested in measures to attract foreign direct investment. It therefore signed the USCM Agreement in 1994, a treaty that imposed Mexico as the largest direct exporter to the United States, a country that is likely to leave the treaty by renegotiating USMC. Therefore, this research is carried out to determine the advantages and disadvantages of renegotiation based on Sinaloa's agricultural exports, with the question of whether it would negatively affect Sinaloa's agricultural exports.

INTRODUCTION

In Eduardo Galeano's book "The Open Veins of Latin America" he stipulates the phrase: "The people who buy rule, the people who sell served; trade must be balanced to ensure freedom; the people who want to die sell to only one people, and the people who want to save sell to more than one" (Galeano, 1970).

The regional agreement called the Mexico, North American Free Trade Agreement (NAFTA) was signed between the governments of Mexico, Canada and the United States in 1992 and entered into force in 1994, aiming to create a free trade area, at a reduced cost for the exchange of goods between the three countries. Since 1994, it is one of the largest free trade zones in the world, establishing the basis for strong economic growth and greater prosperity for Canada, the United States, and Mexico.

For 15 years, the NAFTA has demonstrated how free trade contributes to increased wealth and competitiveness by providing true benefits to families, farmers, workers, manufacturers and consumers (NAFTA de hoy, 2017).

The NAFTA or United States, Canada and Mexico Agreement (TMEC) is the set of rules that Mexico, the United States and Canada agree to sell and buy products and services (Castro, 2008). It was an in-

DOI: 10.4018/978-1-7998-7568-0.ch012

novative treaty aimed at opening and expanding the North American market. Since then, the NAFTA has systematically removed most of the tariff and non-tariff barriers to trade and investment between Canada, the United States and Mexico, leading to the establishment of a stable framework for long-term investments.

The TMEC was preceded by the Canada-United States Free Trade Agreement (Expansion, 2017). President Donald Trump was in a renegotiation crisis due to the entry into power of the government of the United States, who proposed to rearrange the rules established in the treaty with faithful benefits in his favor and if not, he announced the departure of his country from the agreement. The renegotiation has already been finalized, but there is in Mexico a wave of uncertainty about what would happen to its exports, since it is the main supplier of raw materials and a variety of merchandise to the United States.

Currently, a series of changes have emerged in the decisions of the governments involved in the TMEC, mainly the United States. Therefore, it is of utmost importance to conduct a viable investigation about the impact of the renegotiation on Sinaloa exports, since the state Sinaloa has earned the nickname of being the breadbasket of Mexico for the large amount of raw materials that the state produces. It is the number one state in supplying its agricultural products to the neighboring country (United States). That is why the present project is delimited in a spatial way to firmly base ourselves on determining the advantages and disadvantages that, by the renegotiation of the TMEC, were implemented in Sinaloans agricultural exports.

Therefore, it is of utmost importance to investigate and determine the impact of the renegotiation of the TMEC on Sinaloan agricultural exports, a state called "the granary of Mexico" for its wealth in agricultural crops and which has earned the first place of exploitation of these raw materials to be exported to the neighboring country, the United States.

That is why this research work is aimed at determining the advantages and disadvantages in production, trade and distribution network that will prevail after the renegotiation. Taking as indicators Mexico's exports and trade, the gross domestic product (GDP), GDP per capita, and transportation logistics for export shipments, this chapter intends to:

1. Analyze the renegotiation of the TMEC;
2. Determine the advantages of Sinaloan exports;
3. Determine the disadvantages of Sinaloan exports;
4. Analyze the production of agriculture in Sinaloa;
5. Analyze Sinaloa's trade in relation to the USA.

Some of the questions that this study tries to answer are:

1. Will the renegotiation of the TMEC negatively impact Sinaloa agricultural exports?
2. What would be the production in Sinaloa's agricultural exports based on the renegotiation of the TMEC?
3. How would trade in agricultural exports in Sinaloa be based on the renegotiation advantages of the TMEC?
4. What would the distribution network in Sinaloa's agricultural exports look like depending on the disadvantages of renegotiating the TMEC?

Mexico, like other countries, invested in measures to attract foreign direct investment to its territories. Consequently, in 1994, it signed the NAFTA with the United States of America and Canada, a treaty that imposed Mexico as the largest direct exporter to the United States, a country that will possibly exit the treaty by renegotiating the TMEC. Therefore, it is important to carry out this research to determine the advantages and disadvantages that for the above mentioned were implemented in Sinaloenses agricultural exports, which is one of the main export productions and source of employment for many Sinaloenses.

The main objective of the study is to determine the advantages and disadvantages of renegotiating the TMEC based on Sinaloa's agricultural exports. The specific objectives are to determine production in Sinaloa's agricultural exports based on the renegotiation of the TMEC, determine trade in agricultural exports from Sinaloa based on the renegotiation advantages of the TMEC and to determine the distribution network in Sinaloa's agricultural exports based on the disadvantages of renegotiation of the TMEC.

THE IMPACT OF THE AGROECONOMY SECTOR OF SINALOA IN MEXICO

This paper reviews the impact of the renegotiation of TMEC on agricultural exports from the State of Sinaloa, which is expected to benefit from the change in the country's orientation abroad, given its traditional specialization in vegetables for export to the U.S.A. In order to have reference parameters, Sinaloa is approached in the broader context of Mexico, while reflecting on basic aspects of its economic structure and the dynamics of agriculture, showing that it is still very important in the economic dynamics of the state of Sinaloa, but which, at the same time, is in other sectors of activity where the key is to attack the problem of low growth (CEDRSSA, 2020).

During several six-year terms of government, the objective was to promote structural reforms that benefit the inefficient economy through exports. For example, a crusade against hunger is generated when, incongruously, the majority of the population that produces food is in a situation of extreme poverty. The lack of importance given to the agricultural sector is serious without highlighting the role that this sector plays in the Mexican economy.

Mexico has had a productive increase of 82.4 percent in 25 years. In 2019, the sector closed with a production of 282.5 million metric tons, a result 1.4 percent better than the previous year, although a decrease of 25 percent by 2020, this derived from some drought problems suffered, mainly in beans and sugar cane. In the case of the state of Sinaloa there was a lack of water for the dams. Likewise, in Sinaloa, a production of 5.5 million tons of white corn was achieved in the recent season (CODESIN, 2021).

Sinaloa is the most important agricultural state in the production of grains in Mexico, which has earned it the nickname of "the granary of Mexico", since grains such as corn, beans and chickpea are produced and occupy the first national places regarding the value of production. Likewise, the state stands out as the main producer and exporter of vegetables, such as red tomato, chili peppers and cucumber. One out of every two tomatoes that Mexico exports are from Sinaloa (Reyes Rodríguez & Quintero Reyes, 2020).

In the first semester of 2019, Sinaloa managed to export 2,414.03 million dollars in products from the agri-food, agriculture, agribusiness, manufacturing, and fishing and mining sectors, against 2 thousand 139.86 million dollars in the same period of 2018, registering a growth of 12.8% in exports. The main export destinations were: The United States, Canada, Japan, Spain, South Korea, Venezuela and the Netherlands. Likewise, the main exportable products are: tomatoes, meat and beef cuts with and without bone, mango, bell pepper, beef viscera, fruit juices, frozen tuna and fillets, chickpeas, peppers, grapefruit oils, tapas and aluminum cans, plastics, corn, wheat, fish meal and sound equipment (Toledo, 2020).

The dynamics of the agricultural GDP of Sinaloa and Mexico tend to be very similar throughout the period, highlighting only that in the case of the agricultural GDP of Sinaloa the variations are more abrupt, but in general the dynamics are similar. Although both the agricultural GDP of the Sinaloa river and the national GDP have had periods of stagnation, the rate of growth continues to rise. Regarding this, despite the weakening of the policy aimed at the primary sector, the growth of agricultural productivity has been notable thanks to the strengthening of production chains and contract farming (Fiscal et al., 2017).

REVIEW OF THE LITERATURE

According to the classic trade theory developed by David Ricardo, all countries win when they participate in a free trade zone. Theoretically, the idea that each country should specialize according to its comparative advantages is logic (Dillon, 1991). The TMEC drives economic growth and dynamic trade, stimulates investment and, at the same time, creates productive alliances, adapts to small and medium-sized companies in a framework of fairness and certainty. TMEC partners promote environmental protection and offer greater job opportunities in North America (Audley et al., 2003).

The Secretary of Commerce of the United States, Wilbur Ross, seems to have given the TMEC a breather, after having said in an interview with the NBC network that a "sensible" renegotiation of the treaty would strengthen the weight, and experts agreed (El Financiero, 2017). "(This statement) indicates that not only (Trump) is taking a negotiating stance, it indicates that this stance, this softness, reflects the broad consensus that exists in the US, at least among companies, that there are great benefits for both countries (with the TMEC)", said David Shirk of the University of San Diego. On the Mexican side of the border, the analysis is similar. For Jessica de Alba, a researcher at the Anahuac University, this first warning from Ross is a positive and encouraging reaction in terms of investments and free trade in North America (El Financiero, 2017).

For Ernesto O'Farrill, president of Bursamétrica, Ross's comments indicate that in the US they are willing to modernize the trade agreement and not abandon it. "The statements are far from the initial position that Mexico was going to bend in the TMEC negotiation, and threatened to leave unilaterally. The statements are showing that the TMEC is alive and can undergo a modernization process", he assured. The decision to strengthen the Mexican peso may have the objective of preventing Mexico from having an unfair advantage, in order to reduce its currency appreciation, which, in turn, means that the United States wants to continue trading with the country, added O'Farril. He explained that the third line of actions focuses on discovering ways to raise wages and improve the living conditions of Mexican workers (El Financiero, 2017).

With this it is understood that it can be a measure to discourage migration to the northern country. For ranchers, the situation shows an opening gesture. "(Washington) has made it clear that they are clear today of negotiating the treaty and that this is convenient for us. In this situation that we have a sensible dialogue on foreign trade, we applaud and congratulate it because it is what our countries require", said Rogelio Pérez, director of Mexican Beef, the exporting branch of the Mexican Association of Livestock Fattening (AMEG) (El Financiero, 2017).

However, Shrik warned that while it may be perceived that the balance is now tilting more on the side that the TMEC will be maintained, it should not be thought that what a cabinet member says is precisely the same as Trump thinks, because a constant of the period that Trump had been in office is the uncertainty in his relationship with Mexico. "We don't know who we're going to wake up with tomorrow," Shrik said, referring to Trump's fickleness. In contrast, Arturo Pérez Behr, president of the National Association of Importers and Exporters of the Mexican Republic, expressed caution before Trump's comments (El Financiero, 2017).

"The fact that there is talk of renegotiation, and no longer a cancellation of the TMEC, is a positive issue, the threat issues are decreasing, it is a good way, but that does not mean that we no longer have to be on the lookout for statements that President Donald Trump makes, hopefully that is already the speech of the government in general", he said. He explained that Asian countries such as China have taken advantage of what the TMEC establishes legally, so it cannot be considered as abuse. "We have to advocate for our country, whatever suits Mexicans", he added (El Financiero, 2017).

In a bilateral FTA it is not feasible to negotiate internal aid because it is impossible in practice to identify which products enter a country with aid and which do not. Therefore, domestic aid has not been negotiated in this treaty with the United States (Mypimes, 2017). Today there is a general consensus regarding the benefits of the economic integration of nations. Free trade is good because it allows access to a greater number of goods and at lower prices, which should increase social welfare. It allows access to cheaper inputs and capital goods, which should increase the competitiveness of the productive sectors that add value.

Free trade promotes the efficient allocation of resources because price signals are not distorted: when there is a shortage of a good, its price rises and producers receive the signal to increase supply (and consumers to reduce demand); when there is abundance of a good, its price falls and producers receive the signal to reduce supply (and consumers to increase demand) (Mypimes, 2017).

AGRICULTURAL FREE TRADE: THEORY AND REALITY

From a macroeconomic point of view, opening the current account of the economy is equivalent to opening the economy to the savings of the rest of the world. However, the reality of international trade, in the specific case of the agricultural sector, is far from that first best theoretician called free trade. Why? To resolve this question, it is necessary to understand that the agricultural sector is special and different from the other sectors of the economy and that the conservation of agricultural activities translates into a benefit for all of society. When a product is purchased from a peasant, not only the product itself is received, but also the lawful and peaceful occupation of the national rural territory (Mypimes, 2017).

In other words, in addition to a product, peace and tranquility is also received from the peasant in the countryside and, therefore, peace and tranquility in the cities. Of course, this positive externality for society would never be reflected in the free market price of agricultural products. But since societies value this positive externality, we then accept distortions in the price of some products in the agricultural sector in order to make them economically viable and profitable for farmers (Mypimes, 2017).

In practice, international trade in the agricultural sector suffers from three types of distortions or barriers.

First, there are the tariff barriers. These include ad-valorem tariffs (percentage of the price of the good), specific tariffs (a certain value on the price of the good), and quotas (import quotas). Second, there are non-tariff barriers, whose restrictive effects on trade are in many cases greater than the tariff barriers. Among these types of distortions, the sanitary technical and phyto/zoo standards that are imposed for the importation of products stand out. Third, we have export subsidies. Given their fiscal capacity, developed countries prefer to protect the rural sector with domestic aid and export subsidies.

An export is to send national or nationalized goods for use or consumption abroad (Minister of Foreign Affairs and Cooperation, 2017). Exports are sent abroad to obtain plant products through knowledge developed by man, destined to cultivate the land. Production sent abroad from the primary sector that uses cultivation as its main activity obtains raw materials. Developing countries have to resort to tariff barriers to protect rural producers. It is very important to keep in mind that what is negotiated in an FTA is border support (tariffs).

CONTEXTUAL FRAMEWORK OF EXPORTS IN SINALOA

According to data from the SEDECO COFOCE information system, in Sinaloa, at the end of 2015, the agro-food and agriculture sectors represent 62 percent of total exports of the State. According to this source, the main exporting company in Sinaloa is Sukarne SA de CV Grupo VIZ, with a participation of almost 28 percent of total exports. This company is followed by the auto parts company located in the city of Los Mochis, Deplhi de México SA de CV, and Envases Universales de México which is in Mazatlán and the agro-industrial sector Citrofrut and Conservas La Costeña, with operations in Rosario and Guasave. The existing companies at the end of 2015 registered in this system was 607 exporting companies (CODESIN, 2017). See Table 1 below.

Table 1. Companies at the end of 2015 registered in the Sinaloan export system

NUM	COMPANY NAME	EXP ENE - NOV 2015 (USD)		SHARE
1	SU KARNE SA DE CV GRUPO VIZ	$	706,613,325.39	27.64
2	DELPHI DE MEXICO SA DE CV	$	190,609,983.35	7.46
3	ENVASES UNIVERSALES DE MEXICO SA DE CV	$	121,929,090.41	4.77
4	CITROFRUT	$	91,670,524.68	3.59
5	CONSERVAS LA COSTEÑA	$	90,508,024.29	3.54
6	TERRA WEALTH TRADER SA DE CV	$	81,213,869.37	3.18
7	COMPAÑIA MINERA PANGEA SA DE CV	$	69,077,770.88	2.70
8	BIOPARQUES DE OCCIDENTE	$	54,389,001.85	2.13
9	CEUTA PRODUCE SA DE CV	$	46,667,563.19	1.83
10	GRANOS LA MACARENA	$	43,010,555.81	1.68
11	GENERAL BRANDS MANUFACTURAS DE MEXICO, S.	$	36,893,112.75	1.44
12	GRANEROS UNIDOS	$	34,534,093.89	1.35
13	PRODUCTORES DEL MAR DE MEXICO	$	32,790,797.17	1.28
14	AGROIDNUSTRIAS DEANDAR DE DELICIAS SA DE CV	$	28,883,344.55	1.13
15	EXPORTALIZAS MEXICANAS SA DE CV / RENE PRODUCE	$	25,718,963.07	1.01
16	AGROEXPORTADORA DEL NOROESTE SA DE CV	$	24,127,318.57	0.94
17	VALORES HORTICOLAS DEL PACIFICO SA DE CV	$	22,847,270.70	0.89
18	CONDUCTORES TECNOLOGICOS DE JUAREZSA DE CV	$	22,696,553.50	0.89
19	INDUSTRIAS MARINO SA DE CV	$	21,622,249.26	0.85
20	EXPORTADORA AGRICOLA SACRAMENTO SA DE CV	$	21,562,663.95	0.84

Source: CODESIN Sinaloa Council for Economic Development (2015).

In 2016, 14 countries opened their markets to receive, some of them for the first time, others after certain limitations, animal products from Mexico. As a result of the negotiations of sanitary protocols carried out by SAGARPA with the authorities of 14 countries and the European Union, the opening of markets was achieved in 2016 for 18 Mexican products, nine of animal origin and nine vegetables, explained the federal agency. Due to the negotiations that were carried out through the National Service of Health, Safety and Agro-Food Quality (Senasica), the prohibition to export pathogen-free eggs and egg products to the European Union was lifted and the market for Mexican honey reopened in Saudi Arabia (Torres, 2017).

Agro will have a privileged place in any negotiation. Regarding products of plant origin, since last year, Mexico has exported blueberry to China; table grape from Sonora to Australia; tomato seedlings to the United States and sugar cane (in vitro or hardened) to Peru, in addition to sorghum brushes to Chile; stevia plants to Guatemala; corn seed to Ecuador; Chili seed to Portugal and amaranth grain for consumption in the neighboring northern country, Turkey and the European Union (Torres, 2017). According to information from SAGARPA, this year it is expected to expand the offer of Mexican products abroad, for which talks have already started with health services from more than 15 nations. About 13 Mexican products of Mexican origin are expected to "step on" the land of countries such as Russia, China, Indonesia, Iran, Singapore, Vietnam, Taiwan and Japan for the first time (Torres, 2017).

MATERIALS AND METHODS

Type of Research

It is an exploratory investigation, aiming to facilitate a greater penetration and understanding of the problem that is faced. It is analytical because it is descriptive and is more linked to statistical and control data, in order to generate a hypothesis about what happened, or to occur, predict failures or events. It is also of an empirical type since it is based on experimentation or observation (evidence).

Research Design

Research Construct

Research Instrument

The instrument used in this research project is bibliographic analysis and hemerographic analysis because it focuses on the renegotiation of the NAFTA for which this research is based mainly on agricultural exports of the state of Sinaloa.

Data Analysis

Quarterly GDP Growth Annual Rate

The Mexican economy grew 2.9 percent at an annual rate in the first quarter of 2016, according to preliminary figures from the National Institute of Statistics and Geography (INEGI).

This advance represents the best first quarter for Mexico since 2013, and the highest quarterly growth since the second quarter of 2014.

Table 2. Research design

Variable	Description	Dimensions	Indicators	Research instruments	Operacionalization of variables	Statistical analysis
X0 TMEC	"The North American Free Trade Agreement or NAFTA is a trade agreement between the three countries in North America: Canada, the United States of America and Mexico." (TMEC, 2016: s.p.). (NAFTA, 2016: s.p.).	Renegotiation Advantage Disadvantages	US exit from the treaty. Exports Commerce	Bibliographic analysis Hemerographic Analysis	Review of practical case Bibliographic analysis	Analytical Study Exploratory study Empirical study
Y0 Agricultural Exports	Product of the primary sector that you dare from cultivation as a production activity obtains raw materials	Production Commerce Red de distribution	GDP distribution network GDP per capita in Sinaloa Opening to new markets Logistics	Bibliographic analysis Hemerographic analysis	Review of practical case Hemerographic Analysis	Analytical Study Exploratory study Empirical study

Source: self-made

Growth of the Primary Sector

In turn, the primary activities, that is, those related to agriculture, advanced 3 percent at the annual rate, surpassing the 2.9 percent advance that occurred last year.

Figure 1. Research construct

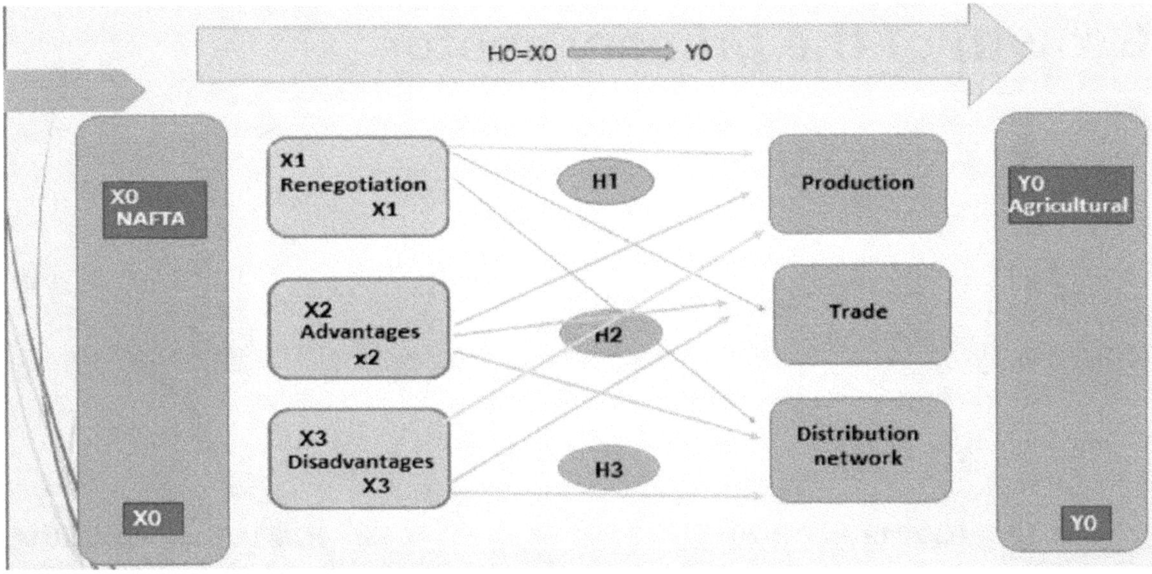

Depreciation Impact on Wealth of Mexicans

GDP per inhabitant represents the economic value of the goods and services generated by a nation that would correspond to each inhabitant if wealth were distributed equitably (BANXICO, 2017) (CONAPO, 2017). The Gross Domestic Product (GDP) is the value of the final goods and services produced by a country during an established period. GDP per capita is this same measure but divided by the population of a country. In 2014, the GDP per capita for Mexico reached its highest level in history, but, only two years later, this measure registered a drop of more than 20 percent.

Figure 2. Quarterly GDP growth annual rate

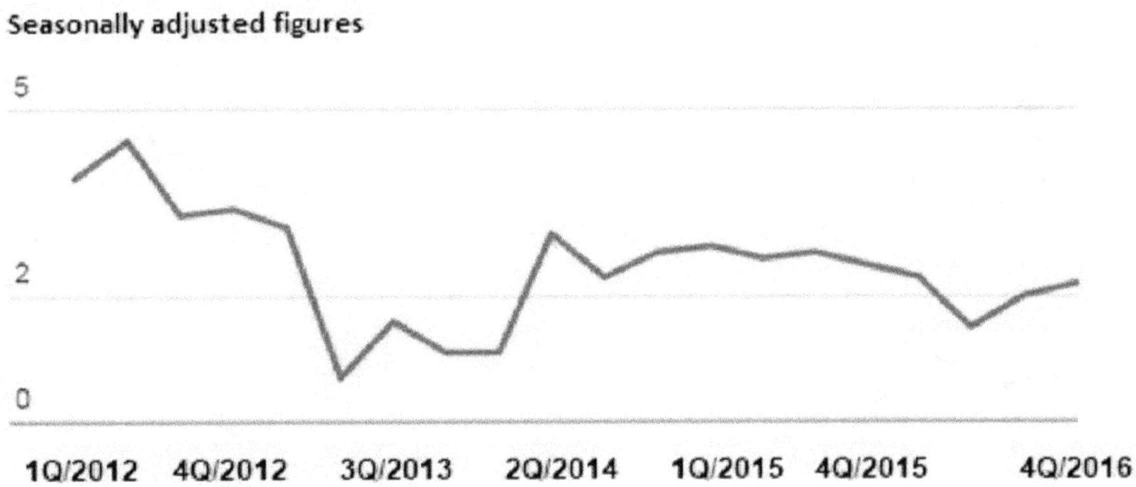

Figure 3. Growth of the primary sector

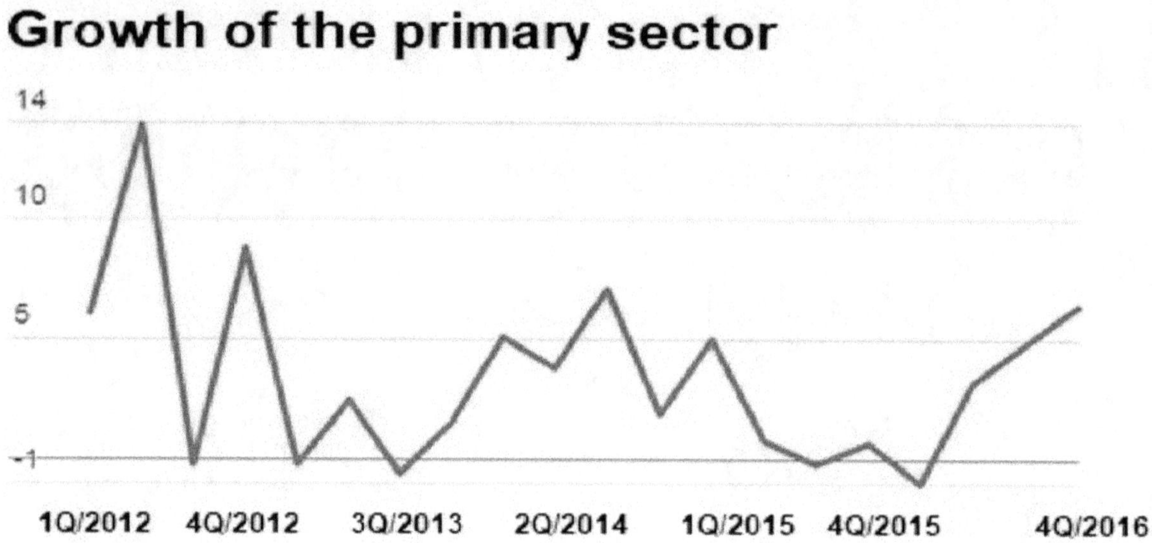

Export Logistics

In Mexico, the port of Veracruz is an example of the country's commercial and industrial development since the 16th century. Today, its importance is indisputable and its challenges are increasingly complex, as the evolution of industrial processes and the type of goods test any logistics system. The logistics chain begins with the production of the raw materials and ends at consumption centers. In this sense, seaports are nodes in the physical network of maritime transport and their competitiveness depends on the fact that those they offer are fast, flexible and safe for international trade and shipping lines.

Figure 4. Depreciation Impact on the Wealth of Mexicans

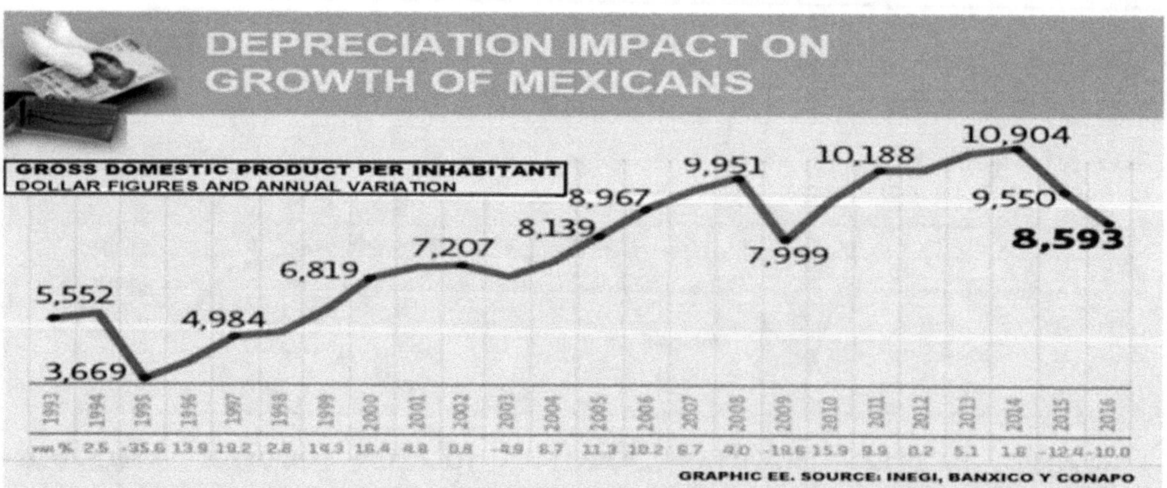

According to a study by the Inter-American Development Bank (IDB, 2017) on cargo logistics in Latin America and the Caribbean, there are at least three perspectives to consider to understand the importance of the logistics process in an economy: the generator cargo (industry), cargo operator (services) and the public policy environment. It is the orderly interaction of these three elements that allows logistics operation costs to be consistently reduced over time.

In the first stage of the expansion, 16,000 million pesos will be invested by the Federal Government. By the end of the project, in 2030, they will have invested 70,000 million pesos (42,000 would be private and 28,000 from public sources). The World Bank (Banco Mundial, 2010) (WB) ranked Mexico, in 2010, in 50th place out of 155 countries with a performance of 3,051. Some consultancies have estimated that logistics costs in Mexico represent 15.3% of the Gross Domestic Product (GDP). The logistics costs of Mexican companies are 10.3% of sales, of which 40% correspond to transportation costs and 60% to inventories, order processing, storage and planning of transportation operations management (Real Estate Market, 2017).

Recently, the federal government and the IDB carried out a study on the National System of Logistics Platforms (SNPL) (National System of Logistics Platforms, 2017), which defined that the system would be made up of 85 logistics platforms, highlighting the investment in infrastructure and services to increase the efficiency of supply chains. In this context, it can be observed the performance of Mexican ports in recent years. For example, in 2010, commercial imports by sea were 75.2 million tons and 122.2 million tons were exported to all regions of the world. In 2013, 81.1 million tons were imported and 129.1 million were exported (Real Estate Market, 2017). This increase was possible because Mexico traded this way, both on the Gulf and Caribbean coast (15 ports) and in the Pacific Ocean (20 ports), the port of Veracruz being the most representative for the manufacturing industry.

According to the Economic Commission for Latin America and the Caribbean (CEPAL, 2014), in the ranking of containerized port movements in the 2010 region, the port of Veracruz ranked 18th while for the first semester of 2013 it was ranked 16. On the other hand, in 2014, according to the study of port technical efficiency, prepared by the IDB, the port of Veracruz occupies the 22nd position in terms of efficiency in a total of 63 ports in Latin America and the Caribbean (Real Estate Market, 2017).

Trade has as a priority to carry out the expansion of the port because this will promote employment and will boost the economy of the region and the state. The entities where most of these vehicles come from are: Puebla, Estado de México, Aguascalientes, Coahuila, Tamaulipas, Nuevo León and Veracruz. This port is the most representative for the export and import of motor vehicles. According to the following table, the port of Veracruz moves 66% of total vehicle exports by sea (Real Estate Market, 2017).

In addition, the port of Veracruz, with respect to the movement of vehicles in roll-on / roll-off, has a performance of 128.8 UHBO (unit of hour ship in operation). Currently, the port of Veracruz has 48 companies that offer related services. For the Mexican State, the development of the maritime-port subsector is vital to the economic growth of the country. Therefore, the interaction between the private sector and the government is important. The latter has the task of carrying out public policies in order to strengthen and make it more efficient and modern.

In the coming decades, the port of Veracruz will be one of the most important logistical-maritime enclaves in the country and on the Atlantic coast to communicate the central region of Mexico with the markets of the United States and Europe. Likewise, it will connect the national industry with global supply chains, which will allow it to be more competitive and face the challenges of global trade and manufacturing (Real Estate Market, 2017).

Export Movements by System, Mexico 2013

Figure 5. Exports by transport model

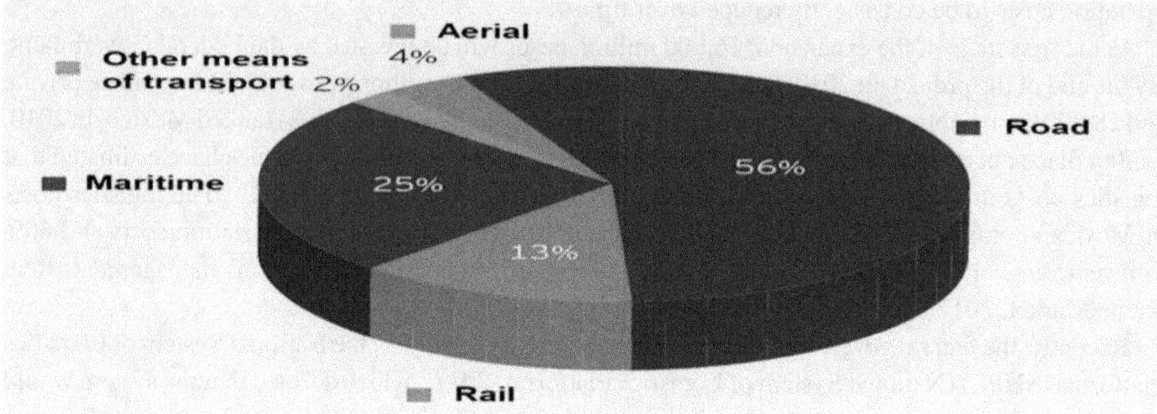

In this pie chart it is made clear that the most used transportation in Mexico for 2013 is by land, followed by sea.

The three products with the highest export of Sinaloa are tomato, corn and wheat. 82.5 percent of Sinaloan exports correspond to sales to the United States market. In terms of income, this represents 8.9 percent of the State Gross Domestic Product. During 2014, Sinaloa exported products for about 770 million dollars, which represented 0.2 percent of the national total. The main shipments were tomato, chickpea, beef, fish oil and flour, shrimp, squid and tuna. The TMEC has represented a 339 percent growth in the value of Mexican exports to the United States since its implementation.

Nationally, more than 80 percent of exports go to the United States. This represents a high dependency of the country's productive sectors with the neighbor to the north. And the larger a state's trade with the United States, the greater its vulnerability. Vegetables were the main product in the period from January to June 2010. In the same period, the 10 main imports from the North American market to Mexico were corn, soy, soy residues, wheat, pork ham, other foods, boneless meat, powdered milk and cream, fructose and starch waste.

Twenty-two states in Mexico export vegetables to the United States, Guanajuato being the leading state. In 2014, Sinaloa exported vegetables to the northern neighbor. In turn, it imported American vegetables for $84,628. Thus, the value of the exports of vegetables from 22 states to the United States exceeds their imports.

The bilateral relationship is key. If the United States market is important to Mexico, the same thing happens in reverse. According to the United States Department of Commerce, Mexico is the second destination for exports from that country, with 15.7 percent of the total, preceded by Canada with 18.6 percent and is the third largest provider, with 13.1 percent of imports, after China, which accounts for 21.5 percent, and Canada, which accounts for 13.2 percent. For example, Mexico is the second commercial partner of the state of Michigan (Mexico receives 31.03 percent of the total exports of that North American state). In the case of California, the Mexican market imports 12.53 percent of the products that that state sends abroad. For Nebraska this value is 14.53 percent.

Vegetable Exports and Imports, Mexico-EU

It is noteworthy that the US content of Mexican exports to the American market is almost 40 percent of the components of these products, according to the National Bureau of Economic Research. The revision of the Free Trade Agreement draws the attention of the economic sectors of Mexico. Achieving maintenance and expansion of the agreements is an urgent need for many states highly dependent on the United States market for their exports.

In the case of Sinaloa, this commercial relationship represents 8.9 percent of the state GDP and this is mainly for food. There are other more vulnerable entities. Examples of this are Chihuahua, Baja California, Coahuila and Tamaulipas. For all these states, exports to the United States represent more than 50 percent of its Gross Domestic Product and, for the most part, are from the manufacturing sector (El Debate, 2017).

RESULTS

Mexico has quarterly GDP growth at an annual rate of 2% in the last three years. GDP per capita has been increasing until 2014 and since then it has been decreasing, following the behavior of the primary sector that has been in constant change for 2015, down to minus 1, but for 2016 it has increased up to 6%. According to the financier, Mexico's exports to the US have grown by 339% in real terms since the implementation of the NAFTA.

Mexico-US trade has been in constant change. In 2014 the Mexican states exported to the United States a total value of 583 million 794 thousand 468 dollars. Mexico imported a smaller quantity of US vegetables for a total value of 23 million 139 thousand 098 dollars.

Considering the Sinaloan exporting companies, in first place is Graneros United with 34, 893, 112.75 (USD) with participation of 1.35 and in the general ranking of exporting companies is in 12th place. In second place, Agroindustrias de Andar de Delicias SA de CV with 28, 883, 344.53 with participation of 1.13 in the general position 14, and in third place Agroexportadora del Noroeste SA de CV with 24, 127, 318.57 participation 0.94 according to CODESIN.

In 2010, the World Bank places Mexico in 55th place out of 155 countries with transportation performance while the economic commission for Latin America puts Mexico in the 15th position regarding port technical efficiency. According to Yuridia Torres, the financier Mexico can expand and open its market to new countries, such as China, Australia, Peru, Chile, Guatemala, Portugal, Turkey, Russia, Indonesia, Iran, Singapore, Vietnam, Taiwan, Japan, and the European Union. It would be a greater advantage if the renegotiation of the TMEC were not to be satisfactory for Mexico.

It was questioned in this study that the renegotiation of the TMEC has a negative effect on Sinaloan agricultural exports. With the in-depth investigation that was carried out, we can conclude that an American exit would greatly affect Sinaloa.

Renegotiation has a direct impact on agricultural production in Sinaloa, with a serious negative effect, since overproduction would be created if the new destination for exporting from Sinaloa was not quickly available.

The renegotiation has also a direct effect on the agricultural distribution network in Sinaloa, affecting the sea and land ports since they are the most popular transportation routes in Mexico, the most used being the one in Veracruz.

DISCUSSION

Mexico is a very capable country, with sufficient resources to stand out before other countries in Latin America and the world, it is only a matter of having an efficient president who knows how to take advantage of and exploit the riches of this country, who focuses on being persevering and growing every day more to become a developed country, increasing the quality of life of its inhabitants. Mexico should not be so dependent on the United States since it can maintain its economy even without its support. It must eliminate prejudices and uncertainties and export its productions to new markets, risking out of their comfort zone to obtain even more favorable results for the Mexican economy.

In Sinaloa, while the activities belonging to the industrial and services sectors registered a decrease of 6.5% and 6% respectively, the activities corresponding to the primary sector had a growth of 8.1% in 2020 (CODESIN, 2021). In this sense, Sinaloa producers continue to take advantage of the business opportunities offered by the national and international agri-food markets, maximizing the efficiency of production processes, the responsible use of natural resources, social responsibility, modernization and expansion of capacity.

The main component analysis establishes that in the state of Sinaloa the most relevant crops in terms of planted area are cereals, fruit trees, industrial plants, legumes and tubers. The harvested area is similar to that sown, except that industrial crops disappear from the first component. Regarding the volume of production, cereals, fruit trees, forages, tubers and oilseeds are the most important in Sinaloa (Bruno Fiscal, Restrepo and Holmes Rodríguez, 2017).

Thanks to the fact that Sinaloa has an important strength in the agri-food, agriculture, agroindustry and mining sectors, it managed to cushion the fall in the export indicator of its different products for the month of April. Despite the fact that at the national level the drop in total exports was - 40.9%, Sinaloa registered - 14.4% in April thanks to the agri-food, agriculture, agribusiness and mining sectors, so we will continue to promote Mexican exports and manage in favor of the Sinaloan producers (Redacción, 2020).

The analysis of the evolution of the agricultural production structure of Sinaloa since NAFTA and later TEMEC (USMEC) shows a growth in the production of fruit trees and oilseeds, that is, crops with an export vocation, to the detriment of peasant economy crops. The growth of the basic products of the state food basket, although it has been constant, is not enough to cover all the needs of the internal market, which generates a crisis to satisfy a part of the national demand, which was covered with surplus production (Fiscal et al., 2017).

The year 2020 was full of challenges, but also many opportunities. The approval of the United States of North America with the Free Trade Agreement, gives certainty to Mexico and with it great positive repercussions to the various sectors. But, on the other hand, the pandemic also had negative effects on product exports (Toledo, 2020).

This research can be of great help to the main agricultural exporting companies in Sinaloa, to different secretaries such as, secretary of economy, SAGARPA, SEDECO, SENASICA, PROMEXICO, Chambers of Commerce, students of the Autonomous University of Sinaloa (UAS) to the degrees of Economy and International Commerce.

In this context, the expansion of the Veracruz port complex, which is expected to be completed in 2025, is an indicator of public policy aimed at strengthening the port network. With a total investment of 60,000 million pesos, and 23,933 million pesos between 2013 and 2018, the port will achieve the highest number of maritime entries and freight mobility in accordance with the National Infrastructure

Program 2014-2018. With this, an expansion of the port in the north is expected in breakwater, navigation channel, piers and specialized terminals, specialized equipment, new yards and storage area.

CONCLUSION

As a general conclusion of this research project, it is contended that the renegotiation of the TMEC does not have to put the agricultural commodities and products from the State of Sinaloa in a wave of uncertainty regarding its exports, since it was accepted that the renegotiation and a fair agreement was reached for the three countries. Included in this agreement, there are different clauses that protect agricultural exports from any unfair act that is intended to be done. Besides, this made us investigate new possibilities for agricultural export growth for Mexico since countries like China, Australia, Singapore and others have opened their markets to receive imports of agricultural goods from Mexico. Finally, the results are satisfactory regarding the growth of agricultural products from Sinaloa to Canada and United States, the TMEC partners.

REFERENCES

Audley, J. J., Papademetriou, D., Polaski, S., & Vaughan, S. (2003). *La promesa y la realidad del TLCAN.* Lecciones de México para el Hemisferio.

Banco Mundial. (2010). *PIB y PIB per capita de México.* Banco Mundial.

BANXICO. (2017). *Desarrollo económico mexicano.* Banco de México.

Castro A. (2008, June 15). Que es el tratado de libre comercio. *El Universal.*

CEDRSSA (2020). *Reporte del sector agropecuario en México.* Centro de Estudios para el Desarrollo Rural Sustentable la Soberanía Alimentaria. Poder legislativo de San Lázaro, Cd. De México.

CEPAL. (2014). *Tratados de libre comercio, América Latina y el Caribe.* Comisión Económica para América Latina y el Caribe.

CODESIN. (2017). *Las exportaciones en Sinaloa.* Consejo para el Desarrollo Económico de Sinaloa.

CODESIN. (2021). *Reporte 07 del 2021. Indicador trimestral de la actividad económica estatal (ITAEE) en Sinaloa.* Consejo para el Desarrollo Económico de Sinaloa.

CONAPO. (2017). *Estadísticas de exportación.* Consejo Nacional de Población.

Dillon, J. (1991). *Bases teóricas y prácticas de los tratados de libre comercio.* Institution Ecumencial Coalition for Economic Toronto.

El Debate. (2017). *Exportaciones de Sinaloa (05.03.2017).* El Debate.

El Financiero. (2017). El PIB de México en cinco gráficas. El financiero.

Expansion. (2017). Economía internacional. *Expansión.*

Fiscal, C., Restrepo, B. L., & Rodríguez, H. (2017). Estructura productiva agrícola del estado de Sinaloa, México, y el tratado de libre comercio de América del Norte (TLCAN). *Chilean Journal of Agricultural & Animal Science*, *33*(1), 0. doi:10.4067/S0719-38902017005000102

Galeano, E. (1970). Las venas abiertas de América latina (Vol. 2). Montevideo, Uruguay: Siglo XXI Editores.

Ministro de Asuntos Exteriores y de Cooperación. (2017). *Exteriores de gobierno.*

Mypimes. (Ed.). (2017). *Libre comercio agrícola, teoría y realidade*. México: Mypimes.

NAFTA de hoy. (2014). Tratado de libre comercio de américa del norte. *TMEC de hoy*. https://www.sec-TMEC-mex.org/Inicio/Bienvenida

Real Estate Market. (2017). Artículos, Infraestructura y construcción, puerta para la industria-mexicana. Market, Real estate, México.

Redacción. (2020). *Gobierno de Sinaloa fortalece sectores primários (09.06.2020)*. El Economista.

Reyes Rodríguez, E., & Quintero Reyes, G. (2020). *Agronegocios oportunidades de inversión en el sector agroalimentario en Sinaloa (02.04.2020)*. El Economista.

Secretariado del TLCAN. (2017). NAFTA, Secretariado del TMEC.

Toledo, M. (2020). Sinaloa, en el primer lugar en exportación de productos cárnicos. *El Sol De Mazatlán.*

Torres Y. (2017). 14-paises-abrieron-su-mercado-a-productos-mexicanos-en-2016. *El financiero.*

KEY TERMS AND DEFINITIONS

Agricultural: Belong or relating to agriculture or farmer.
Exports: To send goods to another country for sale.
NAFTA: North America Free Trade Agreement.
Renegotiation: Negotiation whose purpose is to introduce modifications to something already agreed.
Sinaloa: One of the 32 federal states of Mexico, located in the Northwest.
TMEC: México, United States, and Canada treaty.
USCM: United States, Canada, and Mexico.

Chapter 13
Determinants of Specialization and Main Trends in International Trade

Iulia Monica Dumitrescu
Babeş-Bolyai University, Romania

ABSTRACT

This chapter presents a review of the determinants of specialization and the main trends in international trade. Globalization, trade agreements, new economic poles, and regional integration represent the most influential trends in international trade. Research in this field shows that the main determinants of specialization are demographic change; advances in technology, investment, and energy; and natural resources. Each of the mentioned determinants of specialization and trends will be discussed and constitute a separate section with relevant research and key findings.

INTRODUCTION

Trade competition is one of the most important topics related to international economics in the last decades. Firstly, the major trends in international trade will be detailed: globalization, international agreements, regionalization, and emerging markets. Secondly, a more detailed view will be offered regarding four groups of specialization determinants: demographic change, technological advance, energy and natural resources, and investment.

There are four main trends that appear in the literature on the topic and are believed to be critical. These main trends in international trade are international agreements, globalization (openness of markets), regionalization, and the emergence of new markets that have become new economic poles.

The aim of this chapter is to present a summary of the major trends in international trade and the main determinants of specialization.

DOI: 10.4018/978-1-7998-7568-0.ch013

TRENDS IN INTERNATIONAL TRADE

Globalization

In the last 50 years, we have been witnessing an openness of markets at a scale unmatched until this moment, which means that the external dimension is of critical importance. This fact can be noticed at macroeconomic level regarding the relations between countries and, at the microeconomic level, taking into consideration the companies. Globalization is undoubtedly one the most researched topics by the academic community and economists worldwide as it is a main trend in international trade (Arribas et al., 2009). Globalization is a phenomenon that debuted after the World War II but it has been able to rapidly grow due to the rounds of negotiations of the GATT/WTO, namely since the mid-1980s.

The definition of globalization according to IMF (2002) is "the process through which an increasingly free flow of ideas, people, goods, services, and capital leads to the integration of economies and societies" and it represents "a political choice in favor of international economic integration, which for the most part has gone hand-in-hand with the consolidation of democracy". The World Trade Organization (WTO) general director explained in a speech that globalization can be defined as "a historical stage of accelerated expansion of market capitalism, like the one experienced in the 19th century with the industrial revolution. It is a fundamental transformation in societies because of the recent technological revolution which has led to a recombining of the economic and social forces on a new territorial dimension" (Lamy, 2006). The former general director also identifies international trade as one of the most visible dimensions of globalization.

The first person that used the term globalization was Levitt (1983) aiming to explain the changes in the international economy between 1950 and 1985. He was also the first to stress the importance of technology: "a powerful force drives the world towards a converging commonality, and that force is technology. It has proletarianized communication, transport and travel. (…) Almost everyone everywhere wants all the things they have heard about, seen, or experienced via the new technologies" (Giddens, 1990, p. 64). Almost 30 years later, his revolutionary statements continue to be true as the average consumer has more and more diverse requests and little to none regard to the market boundaries consequently influencing international trade. In his book, Anthony Giddens shares a perspective on the matter of geographic distances and globalization and explains it as an "intensification of worldwide social relations which link distant localities in such a way that local happenings are shaped by events occurring many miles away and vice versa" (Giddens, 1990, p. 60). The term globalization can be found in research papers as associated with the term integration, in the context of societies and economies becoming more integrated due to the reduced cost of transportation, lower trade barriers and faster communication (World Bank, 2002). The same report explains that the phase of globalization studied in this paper, that started around 1980 and continues today as being "spurred by technological advance in transport and communications technologies and by the choice of large developing countries to improve their investment climates and to open up to foreign trade and investment". Therefore, we can deduce the important effect of globalization on international trade, mainly in the last 50 years.

A more recent definition by Kopp (2020) explains globalization as a spread of products, technology, jobs and information across borders and cultures and from the economic stand point as an interdependence of nations stimulated by free trade.

Several researchers link the fast development of technology and science as factors that contribute to the reduction of costs with transportation and communication and that facilitate international trade. In the time frame 1930-2000, the cost of ocean shipping was reduces by half, the airfreight was reduced by a 6th of its cost, the cost for telecommunication was reduced significantly and the price of computers became accessible (Gao, 2000), therefore bringing advantages to the organization and coordination of global production.

However, in all of the above definitions, the common understanding is that globalization is a process of integration between economies with an existing fast flow of trade, people, ideas, and money that has diverse effects in each national economy. This integration at an international level can be seen in the market for labor, technology, products and services. Nowadays, the internet technologies are facilitating the circulation of these elements regardless of the geographic boundaries of the countries. Therefore, it is clearer that the countries have become more interdependent than ever and we are witnessing an unseen movement of international trade. Globalization is so much known for these elements that it is habitually used to express the fast spread of connectivity, production, technology, and communication around the world.

Some of the main elements of the economic globalization are human migration, movement of capital and international trade (Mukherjee, 2008). The IMF defines the economic globalization as "a historical process, the result of human innovation and technological progress (IMF, 2008). It refers to the increasing integration of economies around the world, particularly through the movement of goods, services, and capital across borders. The term sometimes also refers to the movement of people (labor) and knowledge (technology) across international borders. There are also broader cultural, political, and environmental dimensions of globalization". Upon measuring globalization in any given country, the main indicators are exports and imports, namely the country's international trade ratio to GDP or GNP. Consequently, a clear interconnection exists between globalization and international trade.

It has been researched and commonly agreed upon among scientists that distance is the most important proxy regarding costs in the case of international trade (Anderson & Wincoop, 2004; Head & Mayer, 2014). It has also been established that the effect of distance has fallen over time along the last 50 years. This difference can be explained by the new technologies, evolution of transportation, production fragmentation, etc., that are frequently associated with globalization. However, these effects have not been equally effective in all the countries. In their empirical study, Borchert and Yotov (2017), considering 69 countries from various continents, reach the conclusion that the main beneficiaries of globalization in international trade have been the countries in the middle of per-capita income distribution. On the other hand, concerning the low-income countries, distance friction is still heavily reflected on trade.

The above figure presents the data obtained after testing a panel of 69 countries and presents the effects of globalization on the per capita income of the countries.

Arribas et al. (2009) evaluates the degree of trade integration and the degree of openness for 59 countries. The conclusions of this empirical study show that globalization is mainly driven by technological advance and the decline in transportation costs but its magnitude is however fueled by the gradual removal of political barriers to trade and investment, human and capital flows. Therefore these indirect drivers are paramount in the speeding up of the globalization process that has been facilitated by the reduction in the transportation costs, the lower transaction fees and a greater reliance on international markets as a mechanism of resource allocation (Grossman & Helpman, 2005).

Figure 1. Globalization effect on GDP
Source: (Borchert & Yotov, 2017)

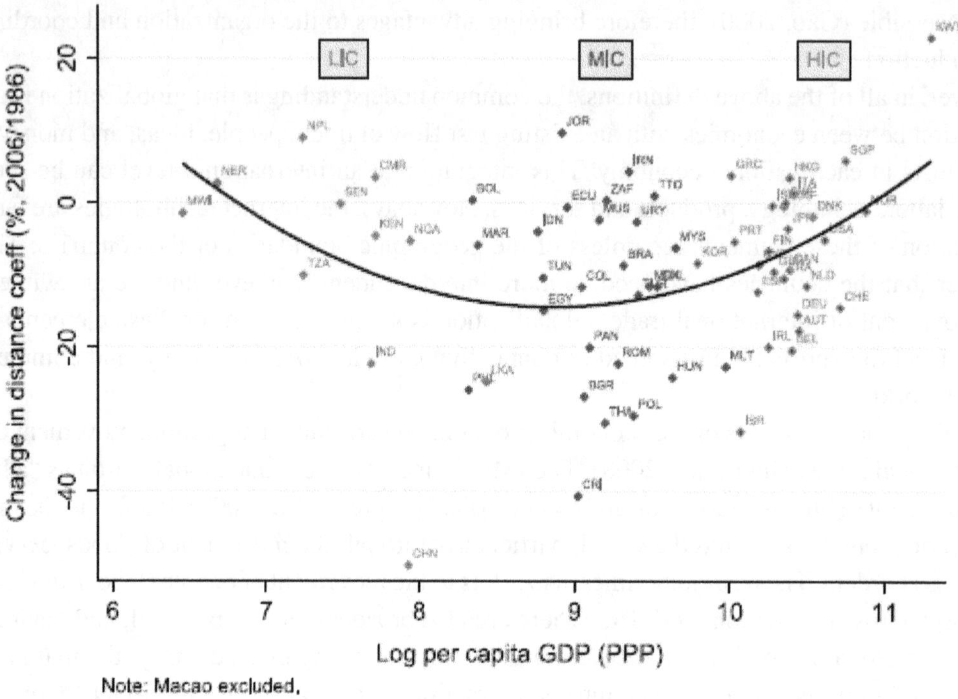

Regionalization

Regional integration is explained as a process through which national states willingly decide to merge with their neighboring countries in order to gain new techniques for resolving disputes among themselves (Haas, 1970). van Langenhove and de Lombaerde (2007) define it as a global phenomenon where territorial structures interact among each other and construct new forms of organization alongside with the existence of traditional state led organization forms at the national level. Scientific articles generally view regional integration as occurring among countries with the purpose of increasing their level of interaction in economy, politics, security, social and cultural fields. The study by Claar and Nölke (2013) concludes that regional integration is the union of individual states within a region into a larger ensemble, with a level of integration depending on the willingness towards sharing sovereignty. They define the most important functions of regional integration as being the strengthening of trade integration in the region, the creation of an appropriate enabling environment for private sector development, the development of infrastructure programs in support of economic growth and regional integration, the development of strong public sector institutions and good governance; the reduction of social exclusion and the development of an inclusive civil society, contribution to peace and security in the region, the building of environment programs at the regional level and the strengthening of the region's interaction with other regions of the world.

It is very important to mark a contrast between regionalism and regionalization, although they also have many common aspects. Regionalization is viewed by many theoreticians as the process of regional interaction creating a regional space and on the other hand regionalism is explained as a collection of ideas, identities and ideologies related to a regional project (Warleigh-Lack, 2006). These distinctions do not however exclude the fact that regional projects are tied to political plans. Regionalization is hardly a new concept as for the last twenty years the concept of regional blocs has appeared in the literature regarding international economy (Gittelman, 1992). Regional integration can be perceived as a modality of protecting groups of countries from outsiders through the creation of large internal markets. On the positive side, regionalism may facilitate a more open international environment through the implementation at a regional level of free cross-border movement of goods, services and people. Governments and transnational corporations are responsible through their actions by the regulatory frameworks adopted. Regional economic integration can be beneficial to developing countries by grouping together in regional blocks with bigger economies.

From the etymology of the word, regionalism refers to an activity or phenomenon taking place cross border, or in between world regions. The majority of the studies in the field consider such regions at the level of nations, therefore becoming connected to the globalization trend. When discussing the topic of regionalization it would be more accurate to talk about the different waves of regionalism. Nowadays regionalism can be witnessed in all parts of the world. If the old waves of regionalization were mainly centered in Europe and had a similar focus on trade arrangements and security alliances, regionalization nowadays is versatile and has a global reach (Schulz et al., 2001).

Regionalization is a term that can often be found in the literature as linked to globalization. Globalization is a cumulus of ideas, frameworks, international markets collaboration and needs of the society. This means that it is driven by a changing division of labor and power that is manifested in a new wave of regionalism. Mittelman (2000) also outlines that " the most important features of the new regionalism are its worldwide reach, extending to more regions, with greater external linkages". Globalization and regionalization occur simultaneously as they are both processes of social transformation that produce countries that benefit from them and others who do not. A large number of countries and communities has gained from these processes but, of course, the effects of these processes have been highly uneven. The biggest question that stands is if sophisticated systems of communication and the development of integrated commodity and financial markets have not demolished cultural, ethnic, economic or political diversity. It is important to apprehend that if globalization and regionalization have global reach, upon trying to analyse their effects one must consider not only the activity of the official institutions (states, firms, civil societies) but also the intersection between these actors within processes of so called informal regionalization.

The effects of regionalization and globalization include an increase in production and commodity chains, therefore creating regionalized regimes of wealth accumulation. If the world dynamic before the first wave of regionalization (Cold War) was transparent and clear, it has now become "a set of intricate networks of strategic alliances and highly flexible markets" (Bøås et al., 2003). This new dynamic, which has implications in the economic and political sphere, have made it more complicated to keep under control drugs, gangs, guns, migration, networked terrorism and other associated branches. Principles of regionalization can be found in many contexts, for example the regional security complex can be defined as "a set of units whose major processes of securitization, desecuritization, or both, are so interlinked that their security problems cannot reasonably be analyzed or resolved apart from one another" (Buzan, 2003, p. 41).

New regionalism is defined by Söderbaum (2003) as "a range of formal/informal mid-level triangular relations among not only states but also non-state actors, notably civil societies and private companies" and puts it as one of the most important facets of transnational relations. The study also creates a link between diverse forms of regionalization that can be witnessed and the biggest unions of countries created through international cooperation, such as the European Union, the North American Free Trade Agreement, and Mercosur.

The new regionalism approach explores new forms of transnational cooperation and cross-border flows through comparative and multilevel perspectives (Mittelman, 2000). During a process of regionalization, the said regions are being assembled to consequently obtain a series of objectives. Regionalization is expressed by intensive cooperation, integration and convergence regarding a set of elements concerning politics, culture, security, economics and diplomacy leading us to the concept of multidimensional regionalization (Schulz et al., 2001). None of the above dimensions is easily manageable. Therefore, upon the integration of several regions, it may lead to a series of contradictions. Regionalization strategies are frequently created in an alignment with globalization, in order to reinforce and take advantage of its benefits. The new regionalism is state assisted and majorly market driven with the purpose of increasing productivity, efficiency, external and internal/regional trade. The process in the East Asian network is viewed as rather dynamic and successful, and can be witnessed through the regionalization of trade, investment, technology and business practices.

The regional integration theory aims to explain the initiation and the evolution of regional international organizations (Schimmelfennig, 2018). The primary focus of the regional integration theory was regarding the European integration and namely the European Union. Through regional integration, governments can obtain their objectives by maximizing their economic interests and national security. However, governments pass on their authority to regional organizations in order to secure their bargaining outcomes but continue to supervise the integration process and the respective organizations. The regional international organizations usually have the following common features: the fact that they are state members, they have an organizational capacity, multilateralism, and the fact that they are geographically close to each other. Two or more states that become members initiate the regional international organizations with headquarters, own staff and functioning procedures. The activity of the regional international organizations is centred on the development and dynamics of regional integration based on three dimensions: their scope, the level of centralization and the territorial extension. The scope of the organization is part of the functional dimension, namely the distribution of policymaking competences between the members. The dimension related to level refers to the distribution of decision-making competences inside the organizations between governments and non-governmental bodies. Territorial extension dimension refers to the number of countries that are integrated or the reach of the organization and its integrated policies over the region. All of these dimensions are consolidated in the European Union multidimensional process of integration.

Finally, in a modern age, where trade blocks exist hand in hand with free trade areas and regional trading agreements, we have witnessed the creation of significant groups: the European Union, the North American Free Trade Agreement, Mercosur and the Association of Southeast Asian Nations (ASEAN). All these blocks of countries develop their activity and coexist with the World Trade Organization in the pursuit of global free trade.

International Agreements

One of the main tools that facilitate international trade is through international agreements that fasten the process of goods and services trade to different countries. Trade agreements regulate international trade between two or more nations. One agreement may comprise all imports and exports, certain categories of goods, or just a single category. A trade agreement is a wide-ranging taxes, tariff and trade settlement that might include investment guarantees. It habitually takes place between two or more countries upon an agreement on terms that help them to trade among each other (Corporate Finance Institute). There are numerous types of agreements that are split in three main categories: unilateral, bilateral and multilateral. Unilateral trade agreements are the least commonly used as they only benefit the one country in matter. A unilateral trade agreement occurs when a country wants to put in place certain restrictions while no other countries want them to be instituted. Unilateral trade agreements fundamentally leave no space for negotiation since they are imposed without a commerce treaty between countries (Amadeo, 2020a). The bilateral trade agreements clearly take place between two sides, with the mention that these sides may be countries, an informal group of countries, or existing trade blocks. Bilateral trade agreements manage to lower taxes and most often rotate around subsidized domestic industries, such as automotive, oil, or food industries. Such an agreement offers a preferential status for the two nations by giving them access to their respective markets, managing to increase trade and economic growth. This type of agreement would aim to: eliminate tariffs, agreement not to dump products al low costs, withhold unfair subsidies, agreement not to steal each other's innovative products and to standardize regulations, labor standards, environmental protection in order to create a competitive advantage (Amadeo, 2020b). The third category is the multilateral agreements and they are being signed by more than two sides. Multilateral agreements commonly take place between neighbor countries and tend to be more problematic until reaching a consensus in negotiation and implementation. However, such an agreement becomes highly relevant after a proper implementation. North American Free Trade Agreement is the largest multilateral agreement including The United States, Mexico and Canada (Amadeo, 2020c). Nevertheless the most significant free trade zones at the moment are the European Union (EU), the North American Free Trade Agreement (NAFTA), and the Association of Southeast Asian Nations (ASEAN).

Trade agreements can have different effects on the level of economic integration depending on the policies and trade pacts adopted by the block. The most common trade agreements are the preferential and free trade types, which are concluded in order to reduce (or eliminate) tariffs, quotas and other trade restrictions on items traded between the signatories.

One of the most commonly used is the Free Trade Agreement establishing a Free Trade Area (FTA) with the purpose of an extensive reduction or elimination of tariffs on a great extent of trade, therefore permitting the free movement of goods. In some of these agreements, a reduction of restrictions on investment and establishment can exist allowing the free movement of capital and free movement of services. In case a common market is also established, the benefits include a reduction of restrictions on the freedom of movement for all factors of production, freedom of movement of labor and of enterprise and coordination in economic policy.

Preferential Trade Agreements (PTAs) are also often encountered and they have limited scope and depth of tariff reduction between the customs territories. Preferential Trade Agreements nowadays cover a larger number of issues, alongside lowering tariffs, and involve more structured institutional arrangements (World Trade Report, 2011).

Regardless of the category of trade agreement there must be a number of countries or at least one country willing to undertake it. Among the European countries the impulse to enter a trade agreement mainly comes from the reinforcement of strategic alliances and the possibility to form part of security arrangements. Such a position seems favorable for smaller countries who gain more security for their access to larger country markets by partnering with larger countries. European arrangements usually cover sectoral arrangements in agriculture, steel, transfer of resources through social and regional funds and free labor mobility. On the other hand, trade agreements in North America include special dispute settlement procedures for anti-dumping, environment and labor standards and complex sectoral arrangements in autos and textiles (Whalley, 1998). Regional trade agreements may incorporate discriminatory trade barrier reductions, factors and goods mobility, harmonized arrangements for financial services, transportation and other categories of services. However, each country enters trade agreements for diverse objectives and clearly, trade agreements are very diverse in structure. Trade agreements differ by the coverage of the agreements, the balance of concessions between the parties of the agreement and if the mentioned agreement is part of an on-going process of wider economic integration.

Above, the reasons for a country to joining a trade agreement have been presented. However, it is equally important to outline the motivation of governments to negotiate such agreements (Grossman, 2016). Trade treaties are a formal statement of intergovernmental cooperation. Governments decide to renounce their sovereign rights to choose their own trade policies in order to receive the same privileges from the others. A government does so for the purpose of interdependence. Each country is interested in achieving several objectives from their trade treaties and they are concerned by the decisions of their trade partners. Since the decision-making is multilateral in the case of a trade agreement, this is a mean to internalize such international externalities.

There are a number of agreements that have outlined the trade policy at a wide-raging level. The most important general trade agreement is called the General Agreement on Tariffs and Trade (GATT). The Uruguay Round negotiations were the birth place of the World Trade Organization and by the year 2016 they had 164 member countries that stand for more than 96% of the world trade (WTO, 2020). A main tendency of trade agreements in recent years has been the creation and growth of free trade zones among nations with the purpose of forming regional trade blocs. The agreements that create free trade zones all have the same objectives: liberalize trade, promote economic growth, and provide equal access to markets among the member nations.

Thus, the main institutions that are in charge of international agreements are the World Trade Organization (WTO) and the International Monetary Fund (IMF). The main objective of the WTO is "to facilitate, embody, and arbitrate over trade and trade-related agreements among its sovereign members" while the role of the IMF is to "finance short-term disequilibria in a world of fixed exchange rates and commitments to achieve convertibility on current account" (Wolf, 2004). During the second wave of globalization, commonly assumed as covering the years 1950-1980, the series of multilateral trade liberalization facilitated by the General Agreement on Tariffs and Trade (GATT) gave the opportunity to Japan, Northern America and European countries to restore trade relations (World Bank, 2002). Fast transportation, rapid communication and trade agreements created a possibility for countries such as Brazil, China, Hungary, India, and Mexico to participate in global trade heavily, especially with manufactured goods and services.

Goldstein et al. (2007) analyze the effects of the GATT/WTO on world trade and empirically show that they influenced patterns of international trade. Trade among the members of the GATT/WTO was considerably higher than what one would predict, based purely on proximity, national income, and other non-political variables.

The international system is comprised by a multitude of commercial agreements, some more generous than others. If two countries strike an agreement that replace the GATT/WTO, by giving more generous benefits than what the GATT/WTO provides, the effect of the GATT/WTO may be minimal. According to Subramanian and Wei (2007), free trade agreements "represent the culmination of trade integration, whereas the WTO represents some intermediate way station". Therefore, two countries that belong to

GATT/WTO and also belong to a FTA are predicted to trade between each other as much as they would have traded by being simply members of a common FTA but not members of the WTO.

Emergence of New Economic Poles

Firstly, the features of an economic power should be emphasized, mainly the capacity of an international participant to impact the behavior of other players in order to influence them in undertaking particular movements with the purpose of obtaining their objectives. A powerful country has to possess key elements such as technological progress, education, natural resources, population, economic and military strength (Tellis et al., 2000).

Nowadays, when technology has carved the world economies structure, it has facilitated the creation of a multipolar world system (World Bank, 2011). After the Second World War end and up until the fall of the Berlin wall the world was existing under a bi-polar international system. These poles were controlled by a small number of developed countries that were controlled by the American regime. The openness of markets towards the global economy, privatization and deregulation happened through the "Washington Consensus". These events led us to the present international landscape where numerous countries with remarkable influence exist together with other powerful players such as NGO's and international organizations (Kobrin, 2015).

Therefore, we are living in a multipolar world order where the United States and the traditional European countries no longer have the sole influence and they co-exist with multiple emerging poles of power. Regardless of the categorization of the current situation, either it is multipolarity or nonpolarity (Haass, 2008), the international system is characterized by multiple centers with significant power. The six most powerful international poles are USA, Japan, Russia, China, India, and the European Union. Side by side, we have countries such as Brazil, Indonesia, Turkey and South Korea who are gaining more power year after year. When grasping a panoramic view over the last decades, a shift from a period of international multipolar organization in the early twentieth century towards an intricate networked system can be witnessed. Recent years have shown the collaboration of very diverse countries that reveal that a clear center of power does not exist but more so a tendency towards shifting alliances.

During the second part of the twentieth century, the United Stated of America was the core of the developed world. In the same period, other countries marked their position as poles of economic power in different regions of the world, such as Germany, United Kingdom and France in Europe, Brazil in Latin America, Japan and China in Asia and Russia at the convergence of Europe and Asia. New associations and groups were created leading us to today's landscape: the European Union with its center in Germany, NAFTA with its nucleus in USA, Asia with its core in China, the three mentioned countries becoming universe-economies (Poladian & Oehler-Şincai, 2014). These authors have evaluated the great economic powers in the world by considering their shares in global GDP, global trade and investment flows. The change in the landscape of economic powers is explained through the advance of technology, integration mechanisms and the ability to acquire strategic resources. The conclusion was that, based on worldwide exports, by the year of 2012 the power was transferred from the western countries (USA, Germany, France, United Kingdom, Canada, Italy, Spain, Switzerland, Belgium) to the eastern countries (China, Japan, South Korea, Hong Kong, Singapore, Taiwan, India, Thailand, Malaysia, Indonesia). In a period of twenty years, the exports of the western countries from the total global exports dropped from 53% to 36% and the eastern countries exports grew to 30% of the total, raising from 21%.

In their study, Inkpen and Ramaswamy (2007) explain the importance of multinational companies in certain countries and their link to the same countries being seen as emerging economic powers. Due to the benefits of globalization, entire industries have searched for the optimal location to perform value chain activities. Manufacturers and suppliers were mainly based in China, South Korea, India, Hungary, Israel, and Mexico, whereas the process of assembly took place in countries with higher knowledge and cost benefits. The majority of the sales of the multinational companies are in the area of the European Union, the rich Asian countries and the countries who are NAFTA members (Rugman & Verbeke, 2004). However, the global economic environment evolved, turning China and India into two emerging markets who manage to keep low costs for manufacturing but also have service capabilities.

At a global level, China has registered remarkable GDP increases, with even higher rates of growth than the most powerful developed countries, therefore becoming an engine of economic growth in the last thirty years. This information results from the study of the compound annual growth rate in the time frame of 1980-2013 (Poladian & Oehler-Şincai, 2014).

Based on the World Bank Report (World Bank, 2011), by the year of 2025, the world economy will be dominated by emerging economies. This report places China, India at the top of the list alongside with Brazil, Indonesia, Russian Federation and the Republic of Korea.

DETERMINANTS OF SPECIALIZATION

This section is going to detail the main classical and modern theories related to trade specialization.

David Ricardo elaborated the law of comparative advantage. The theory refers that a country possessing a comparative advantage over a certain good will produce more (Dixit & Norman, 1980). Comparative advantage for a country over a type of good means that the country manages to produce the good at a lower relative marginal cost or at a lower opportunity cost than its trading partners. A comparative advantage would give a country the potential to sell goods and services at a lower price than its competition, therefore obtaining higher sales. Comparative advantage can be used to explain the economic reality from historical stand point for individuals, firms, or nations and the differences between them that originate from the different levels of technological development or the level of endowment.

In his theory, Ricardo illustrates that when taking two countries into comparison, even though one of the countries has more efficient labor at producing every type of product than the other country, it would still be beneficial to engage in trade for both parties. The theory demonstrates that if two countries are able to produce two types of goods and engage in free trade, each of the countries will expand their overall consumption through the export of the good in which it has a comparative advantage while importing the other good (Baumol & Blinder, 2015). Before David Ricardo's theory of comparative advantage, from 1817, the literature that suggested this concept belonged to Adam Smith and Robert Torrens. In his theory, Ricardo takes as an example two countries who engage in trade, each producing two products of identical quality but with different costs of production. The example makes one of the countries more efficient in producing both goods, therefore having an absolute advantage. The applied example demonstrates that it is more advantageous for both countries to specialize in producing only one of the goods if possibilities for trading the goods exist. Ricardo's theory implies that comparative advantage stimulates international trade even more so than absolute advantage.

Another key mathematical model related to international trade is the Heckscher-Ohlin model. It was created at the Stockholm School of Economics by Eli Heckscher and Bertil Ohlin. An important link exists between the theory of David Ricardo earlier presented and the Heckscher-Ohlin model. The theory is based on comparative advantage and uses the factor endowment of a trading region in order to predict patterns of commerce and production.

Blaug (1992) explains that the model is based on the fact that countries will export the products that can be produced within the country with available and cheap resources whereas the products that require sparse resources for production would be imported. Also Leamer (1995) explains the hypotheses that the traded commodities have at base a number of factors such as labor, land and capital. He further explains that "the exchange of commodities internationally is therefore indirect factor arbitrage, transferring the services of otherwise immobile factors of production from locations where these factors are abundant to locations where they are scarce. Under some circumstances, this indirect arbitrage can completely eliminate factor-price differences".

The initial Heckscher–Ohlin theoretical model assumption was that the only difference between two countries would be the wealth in capital and labor and did not consider variations in production technology between countries. The model also assumed that the two countries could only be producing two types of goods. Nevertheless, the main addition of the H-O model compared to the Ricardian model is the introduction of variable factor proportions, namely variable capital endowments. This refers to the developing countries and the highly developed ones, specifically to the fact that developing countries would have an abundance of labor force whereas developed countries have abundant capital.

Between the modern theories that have shaped the view on international trade, the ones that cannot be excluded are the ones that Paul Krugman contributed to, consequently making him the winner of the Nobel prize in economic sciences. Krugman (1980) presents a framework for analyzing trade based on product differentiation and economies of scale. The study included the reasons for the existence of trade between countries that have factor endowments that are alike and how a big domestic market could stimulate exports. Earlier studies only include the concept of increasing returns influencing the pattern of comparative advantage whereas the new theory includes the idea of specialization influencing comparative advantage.

The basic model from 1980 by Krugman was actually a derived version of the work by Dixit and Stiglitz (1977). Among the new additions to the model, the perception of Krugman when elaborating this study was different than the one of his predecessors. The new perspective of the study was related to countries who trade abundantly and share a multitude of common characteristics whereas the studies produced before concentrated on trade among countries with well-defined comparative advantage and highly different characteristics. The justification presented in the study regarding trade among similar countries was based on the consumers' preference for a diverse choice of brands and that production is more efficient with economies of scale. In other words, as stated by Panagariya (2008): "consumers like variety in what they consume. For the same expenditure, their satisfaction is greater if they have a larger variety of products available. This creates the incentive for firms to produce a large variety of products. But the production of a new variety has setup costs. This leads to declining per-unit costs as a larger quantity of the variety is produced and places a limit on the number of varieties the market can profitably supply. A firm produces a new variety only if it can capture a large enough market to allow profitable sales". The conclusion of the theory is that each country can specialize in producing a few brands of any specific category of product in order to be efficient but they would be less efficient if they were to specialize on different categories of products. This model is a key contribution in the context of the new trade theory.

The factor that was considered new in the new trade theory was the use of mathematics in the economic model in order to measure the increasing returns to scale and the use of the network effect. The network effect was applied to explain the importance that industrial planning and tariffs have in the development of industries. In the models that were developed what resulted as a prognosis was a specialization by industry at national level and some of the most visible examples was the watch industry in Switzerland or the movie industry in Hollywood. Another result of these models was that industries that depend on the above mentioned elements may lead to situations of monopolistic competition or oligopoly.

What has been considered as the new wave of New Trade Theory or better known as the "New" New Trade Theory in international trade was developed by Marc Melitz and Pol Antràs. The work by the authors (Antràs & Helpman, 2004; Melitz, 2003) concentrates on intermediate goods and their growing importance in recent years. Their theory highlights the existence of differences in the framework of a company in the same industry of the same country. The models explained with the new trade theory were centered around countries and industrial sectors while the "new" new trade theory focuses on companies and their relevance in international trade.

Another highly important academic contribution by Paul Krugman came through the articles written during 1991-1999, where he presented the New Economic Geography theory. The new economic geographic theory is an evolution of the new trade theory. A more clear view regarding the geographic theory was firstly presented in his article from 1991 (Krugman, 1991). This article is the first place where Krugman draws attention over the fact that the very limited existing literature of the time on economic geography portrayed countries without putting them in dimension. In this sense transportation costs between countries were always calculated as zero. The purpose of the paper was to present and further encourage the use of theoretical industrial organization techniques with an addition of economic geography. More importantly, the paper presented a model of geographical concentration of manufacturing based on the interaction of economies of scale with the inclusion of transportation costs.

His article from 1998, Krugman (1998) has a clear view on the theory and explains that one of the most relevant implications was the validation of the issue of location and the inclusion of economic geography in economic theory. More than that, the new economic geography showed the versatility of the economic studies and opened the door for other ideas that might not have had a natural link to the topic.

The heterogeneity of firms is clearly impacted by trade and trade liberalization and therefore has an effect on specialization and export patterns. Characteristics of firms interact with the industry they fall under and industries further interact with the countries they belong to subsequently reacting to trade. The study by Oi (1983) is one of the base studies regarding heterogeneity of companies. His study explains the systematic differences between companies operating in the same industry regarding employment and the organization of production. The study underlines that entrepreneurial ability has a great effect on the dimension of a firm and it has to extend to monitoring the workers activity and production coordination. Finally, the study concludes that dissimilarities may arise between heterogeneous firms due to differences in monitoring costs that lead to further differences in worker productivity, design of products and the organization of production.

Firstly, one must understand the nature of heterogeneous firms, the starting point being that not all the firms in a given country become exporters. In fact, more companies do not export than the ones that do. The exporting companies tend to be much larger than the non-exporting ones, however only a part of the total output is exported. Questions arise regarding the difference in productivity between the exporting companies and non-exporters. Bernard and Jensen (1999) address this topic in their article regarding export performance. They determine that companies that are competitive become exporters and register growth rates and success while exporting firms have a higher survival rate and employment growth. Their study clearly shows a higher level of productivity within exporting companies, a higher output, higher wages paid to all categories of workers, higher capital-labor ratio and more skilled labor.

Trade liberalization combined with heterogeneous firms in a model of comparative advantage is studied by Bernard et al. (2007) in a more modern approach. Their study finds that reallocations of economic activity within industries create jobs among all sectors. They also prove that a relative growth in the case of high production firms can have a positive effect on all industries as it increases aggregate productivity, although with a higher impact on comparative advantage sectors. Ultimately, they demonstrate that the behavior of heterogeneous firms enhances the comparative advantage of the country they operate in, thus producing gains from trade.

Even more recent research by Redding (2010) concludes that trade liberalization can affect income distribution through the reallocation across firms within industries. The study underlines that heterogeneity in productivity and size of firms exists between industries. Few companies in a specific industry participate in international trade, usually the highly productive ones. Resources are reallocated within industries, therefore raising the average industry productivity through trade liberalization. This creates a filter effect within industries as firms with lower productivity exit the industry and make room for expansion towards international markets for the high productivity suppliers.

In this section, various important theories were presented regarding the factors that shape world trade and the patterns of trade. In the following sections, the elements that will be presented are nowadays perceived as having great importance in the dynamic of international trade. More importantly, these elements are not new influence factors in this field but their evolution in the last decades requires a closer approach.

Demographic Variations

Demography is an ever changing dimension that has witnessed great transformations in the last twenty years. Globalization is a key factor in the appearance of the following events: migration, development of education, higher participation in the labor force by women and an ageing population (WTO, 2013). All of these factors have critical effects on the way countries develop and choose to specialize, therefore shaping their comparative advantages. Ultimately, these changes affect the export possibilities and the demand for imports, thus influencing global trade.

According to the data offered by the Population Reference Bureau (Kaneda et al., 2020) the population of the world by mid-July 2020 has reached 7.8 billion inhabitants. The prediction from this report is that by the year 2050 the world population would be of 9.9 billion inhabitants. The growth rate however is not considered to be equally distributed globally; therefore the prognosis is that certain African countries (Angola, Benin, Niger) will most probably double their population alongside with some Asian countries, the American population will also increase but in a slower rhythm while the Chinese population will decrease by 2050 (Li et al., 2012).

We are now experiencing the highest life expectancy rates at birth that have ever existed. In the study by Lee (2003), all the four phases of a demographic transition are explained, and believed to have started around 1800 with a debut in the European countries. A demographic transition implies an initial decline in mortality, followed by a decline in fertility; therefore boosting a rise in population growth rates only to be followed by a decrease that leaves countries with an ageing population and long life expectancy. The phenomenon has reached all the parts of the globe and is believed to be completed by the year 2100.

The economic effects of a global population that has a higher life expectancy imply more citizens with a legal working age, therefore increasing the labor force.

According to Yakita (2012) changes in the demography of a country, in a sense of a longer life expectancy, imply a longer period of retirement. The article argues that countries with an aging population will bring effects on international capital flows and will naturally have differences in domestic savings but they need not necessarily become net exporters of capital intensive goods. The author concludes that a country with an aging population will export labor intensive goods and import capital intensive goods as long as the relative price is lower than the free trade relative price. In a later article, Yakita (2014) also studies the great difference between countries with a constant fertility and countries with endogenous fertility and their diverse reactions regarding capital taxation, reactions that further impact international trade in the long run.

However, all countries find themselves at different phases of transition (Eberstadt, 2012). The most visible difference in timing can be observed between developed countries and developing countries. The inception of the process for developed countries is linked to the 19th century while for the developing countries around the 20th century. In recent times, the developing countries have had higher fertility and growth rates, generating a more dynamic evolution of the process despite the significant difference in years for the debut. All these phases of demographic transition bring diverse effects as they produce changes regarding comparative advantage and the structure of demand, therefore potentially shaping the trade patterns of countries. Precisely these variations of the demography of countries are components that aid the movement of people towards developing economies.

For countries such as the ones in Africa, Middle East, East Asia, India, which are witnessing high fertility rates, an enhancement in the public sector and education could positively affect their economies in the years to come (The Economist, 2012). Putting aside the benefits of the early stages of demographic transition, the later stages bring a whole different set of characteristics. As detailed by Li et al. (2012), if countries with high numbers of young employees had cheap labor manufacturing as a result, a shift in the age distribution towards an elderly population will cause in increase in the cost of labor.

Naito and Zhao (2009) and Sayan (2005) argue that the Heckscher–Ohlin model is applicable and that capital abundant countries are going to be the ones with low population growth while the countries that are labor abundant will be the ones with high population growth. This would mean that each country has a different comparative advantage and it will react differently when engaging in international trade.

Changes in the demography of a country may affect their comparative advantage but they also affect the composition of the consumption and the general level of consumption. When considering households, the number of family members can understandably influence the level of consumption. Several authors (Bonke & Browning, 2011; Browning & Ejræs, 2009) confirm through their studies that a family with more children will have a higher rate of consumption. Developed countries that find themselves in later stages of the demographic transition will have an aggregate consumption highly influenced by the elderly population who are responsible for the greatest share of consumption. Lührmann (2005) and Martins et al. (2005) show that the categories of consumption with a higher share will be health, transport, communication, entertainment and community services. In a more elaborated research, focused on Chinese consumers from 60 cities (Atsmon & Magni, 2016), conclusions also reveal a growing desire of the citizens towards spending more money for travel, leisure and healthcare products. The study further underlines the importance of the growing age group of consumers over 50, who aspire to improve their quality of life and are willing to pay more for high quality goods.

Developing countries, on the other hand, face themselves in a different demographic transition phase with most commonly high fertility rates. Countries such as these face a period in which their middle class is growing and therefore could positively influence economic growth. Based on the study by Lim and Saner (2011), another phenomenon occurring in developing economies is the rise in the education level. Countries such as Korea, Germany, India, United States and the Latin American and Middle Eastern market were the ones with a high increase in education services during 2002-2007. For the period of time between 1960 and 2010, countries from North Africa, Sub Saharan Africa, Middle East and South Asia have had the highest rates of growth regarding education according to the study. Studies such as Schofer and Meyer (2005) and Chou and Ravinet (2015) also depict a rise in higher education. That increase in demand for education can presently be perceived in the changes regarding the composition of the labor force.

Figure 2. Educational attainment of the total population over age 15, 1950-2010
Source: (Barro & Lee, 2013)

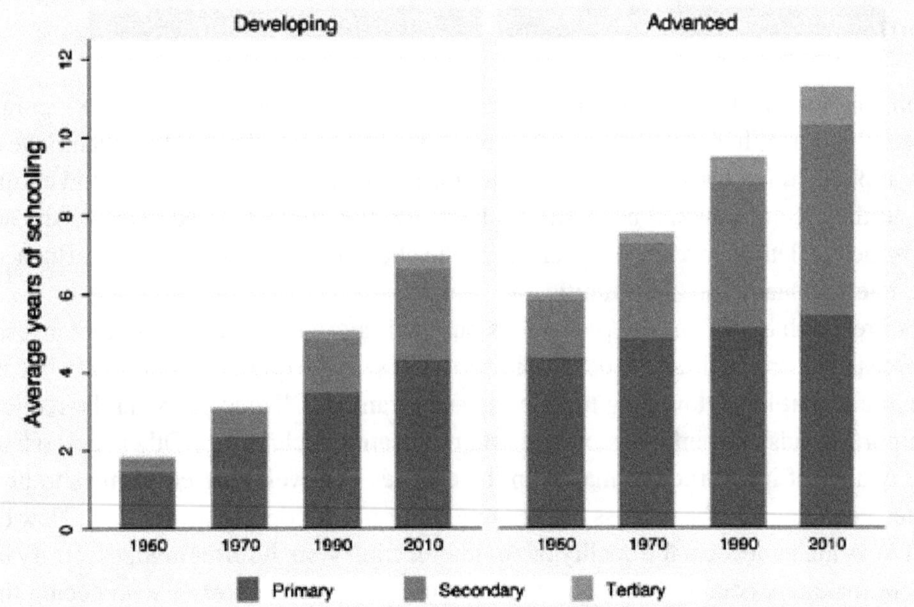

Note: Advanced countries = Australia, Austria, Belgium, Canada, Denmark, Finland, France, Germany, Greece, Iceland, Ireland, Italy, Japan, Luxembourg, Netherlands, New Zealand, Norway, Portugal, Spain, Sweden, Switzerland, Turkey, USA, United Kingdom.

The increase of female participation in the workforce is one of the most notable changes regarding the demographic transition. Galor and Weil (1993) relate it to technological progress and physical capital. These factors have shaped labor in becoming more productive and, at the same time, have increased the opportunity cost of raising children. Also Soares and Falcao (2008) agree that such elements have decreased fertility but have influenced women to return to education and participate in the workforce.

Based on Mammen and Paxson (2000), female labor force participation rates depend on the level of development of the country. Economies with a higher level of development present educational gains for women and also ensure a high opportunity cost for raising children while increasing high female labor market participation.

According to the report by the International Labor Market (ILO, 2010) the main determinants for women to participate in the workforce are: culture, social norms, possibilities of education and religion. A study that takes into consideration a panel of women from numerous countries that have mainly similar determinants from the ones specified above however discovers a difference in levels of employment. These differences in low rates of employment by women in certain regions are justified by Tsani et al. (2013) through specific social norms. An interesting article by Humlum et al. (2019) explains some of the determinants for young ladies in their education choices. The empirical results reveal that sons will reflect the fathers' behavior while daughters will take after both parents but will be more influenced by their mothers regarding education and further career choices.

The global demographic transition has presented important ramifications that have brought changes to the global economic landscape. These demographic changes have restructured populations and we are witnessing a highly populated planet, an aging population, less children born, lower fertility rates and a lengthy life expectation.

Investment

By definition, an investment is a distribution of money with the expectation of future income or appreciation (Chen, 2020b). When studying investment at national level, the most relevant investments are investments in public infrastructure, human capital infrastructure, and information and communication technology. In the case of national economies, classically the domestic resources are the sources that finance investment. Clearly, investment in either of the above mentioned fields can influence in a positive way the international trade opportunities of a country.

Even older research by Jimenez (1994) points out the importance of infrastructure investment from public resources, with an emphasis on developing countries. In the quest of a country in becoming more competitive at a global level, lowering trade costs are paramount. Trade costs can be reduced through investing in ports, roads, and information and communication technology. Other research also proves that a better quality of infrastructure may help the chances of developing economies to be associated with advanced economies in the process of production of final goods (Baldwin, 2012; Hew et al., 2009; Kimura, 2013). A higher level in the quality of communication systems offer higher security in transmission, therefore making a country more eligible for those advanced countries who decide to outsource certain parts of the production process (Grossman & Helpman, 2005).

Several studies conclude that a country with high saving rates will export mostly capital intensive goods (Chen, 2020b; Stiglitz, 1970). There are numerous examples of countries that through the attraction of foreign resources have managed to invest in physical capital and therefore gain a comparative advantage. Costa Rica is one of the countries that over the years has managed to be highly develop in the fields of technology and has become a knowledge-driven economy (Rodríguez-Clare, 2001). Several companies from the electronic sector have started manufacturing plants in the country and have helped Costa Rica to become specialized in technology.

An increase in international factor mobility, through foreign direct investment can finance investment and increase trade. A foreign direct investment is "an investment made by a firm or individual in one country into business interests located in another country" (Chen, 2020a). Foreign direct investment occurs when an investor establishes foreign business operations or gains foreign business assets in a foreign company. If capital is invested in production capacity, according to Grossman et al. (2006), the receiving country will further export to countries in proximity. Overall, greater foreign direct investment will positively affect trade.

Figure 3. FDI stocks, GDP 2019
Source: (OECD, 2020)

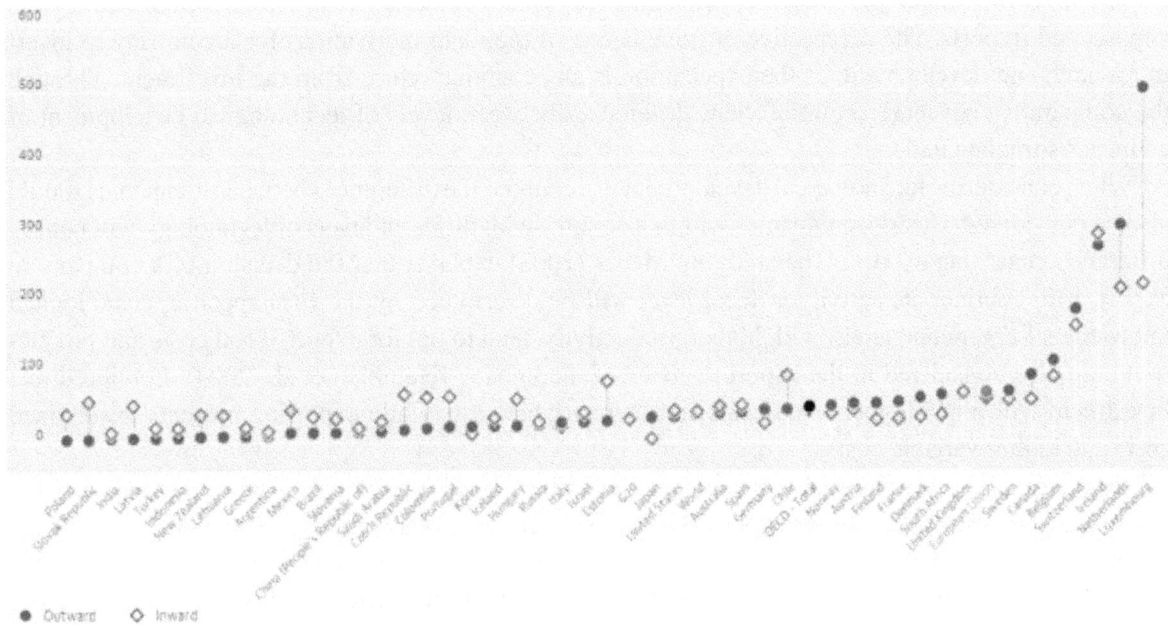

Overall, foreign direct investment is viewed as a positive factor in increasing world trade and for the development of countries. The study by Crespo and Fontoura (2007) evaluates the foreign direct investment spillovers to domestic firms. A multinational company brings its technology and processes to the country where it opens a new subsidiary but these elements are not necessarily transferred to the domestic firms. The indirect benefits of foreign direct investment are represented by the capacity of absorption of domestic firms. The results of the study show that the available information about FDI spillovers reflects a greater absorptive capacity of local firms in developed regions.

Advance in Technology

The level of advance in technology differs from country to country and influences trade and income levels as well. In the previous sections, it has been outlined that accumulations of human capital and physical capital influence trade patterns and specialization. However, development in technology is also an important factor that shapes trade and produces differences in income levels between countries (Easterly & Levine, 2001; Prescott, 1998). The level of technological development explains differences within countries but is also a driver of economic growth. Even more so, technology has been responsible for the fast growth of the last two centuries through electricity, telephones, combustion engine, speed internet, etc.

In order to analyse the level of technological advance in a country, one must measure technological progress by including research and development, total factor productivity and patent applications (Keller, 2010). Technological transfers can be measured through analysing technology spillovers and the purchase of technology, such as royalty payments, R&D services trade, trade in technology-intensive goods, the share of foreign-owned employment in total employment, and foreign direct investment.

The level of technological development influences the countries' trade participation and also its exports and imports. The perspective of trade is one of the main motivations for a company to invest in research and development, as the expectation is an economic return from the investment. Through the comparative advantage point of view, differences between levels of technological development of countries stimulate trade.

When considering technological development in a country, the differences between companies should also be considered. Clearly, companies within a country with different levels of technology will behave differently regarding exports. The study by Melitz (2003) explains that the decision of a company to export or to continue its activity at local level will be determined by the firm-specific technological knowledge. Larger companies, with higher productivity, tend to opt for export. Total costs and productivity are also considered in the export decision of a company (Helpman et al., 2004). Foreign direct investment will imply higher fixed costs and low variable costs while exporting presents lower fixed costs and higher variable costs.

Nowadays, the functioning of companies has overall changed. Production is now represented as the assembling process of intermediate goods. The decision of using locally produced intermediate goods in the process of production and then exporting or moving the whole process to a different country depends on the level of technology. In the case of multinationals, the headquarter company will often transfer technology to the affiliate company. Keller and Yeaple (2013) present a positive relationship between the complexity of exports and geographical distance to the destination markets regarding American exports. Usually, goods that demand technologically complex processes will be produced in home countries and exported while the inputs that require a more standardized process of production will be produced abroad when the transfer of technology has higher costs.

As discussed in earlier sections, the new economic geography theory (Krugman, 1998) alongside the reality of inequality between countries in technology diffusion influence trade patterns. Technology is transferred more easily between companies that are geographical closer to each other. This phenomenon benefits the companies as they lower production costs and become more competitive upon engaging in international trade. This will further produce change to the regional concentration of companies, as they will want to benefit from technology spillover and further reduce trade and transportation costs, therefore producing concentration of firms from the same industry. Ultimately, countries that have a broader home market advantage for a certain product will choose to export.

Technological advance has brought great changes to trade costs, as costs regarding transportation and communication have been reduced. In any given field or industry, one main concern is keeping the trade costs as low as possible. As mentioned in earlier sections, great technological breakthroughs have brought changes to air, sea and land transportation. These technological changes have made transportation costs cheaper and, therefore, have a positive impact on trade. Advance in technology has facilitated the reduction of communication costs and, as shown by (Fink et al., 2011) it has majorly benefited trade in the industries that produce differentiated goods, such as technologically advanced manufacturing goods.

Communication costs reduction has also benefited the agriculture and standardized manufacturing goods industries but not in such a high measure.

Cheaper transport costs have had a great influence on online sales as shown by Lendle et al. (2016) and subsequently small business have had to benefit from lower cross-border trade costs through the internet. Figure 4 shows the average distance travelled by goods by product category. The results of the study on the Ebay website show that through online sales almost all categories of products travel more kilometres than in the case of classical shopping. Overall, the data provided proves that online shopping (data regarding the ebay website) has a smaller distance effect on trade flows by 65%. The high difference in distance effects is attributed to the advance in online technology.

Figure 4. Average distance of exports by product category
Source: (Lendle et al., 2016)

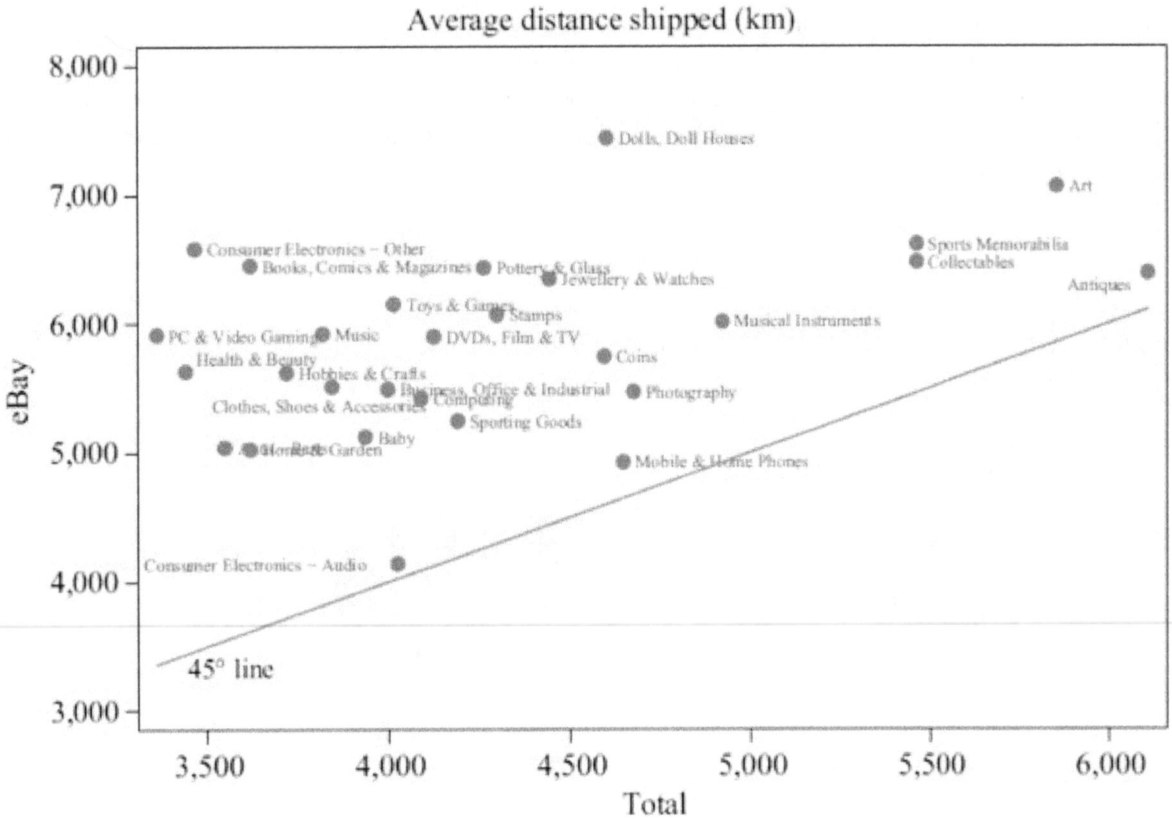

The evolution of technology has also facilitated the appearance of new economic poles. Countries that were the initiators of technological innovation have managed to develop further and to attract funds for research and development. The book by Fu and Soete (2010) channels the rise of new economies like the BRICS countries (Brazil, Russia, India, China, South Africa) but also the rise of the Asian Tigers. The authors underline that advance in technology has been one of the main drivers of national competitiveness and that investment in research and development has also been growing in these emerging countries. The book by Lundvall et al. (2009) also researched the link between innovation systems and their effect on economic development. In an ever changing geographic landscape of innovation, countries that were formerly executing the production phases for advanced economies have now managed to grow economically through their own innovation and contribution to technology (Mahmood & Singh, 2003).

Finally, advance in technology and innovation has influenced trade patterns through the emergence of new economic poles. The transfer of technology has been regionalized, trade costs have been reduced and information and communication technology has increased the share of services in world trade.

Energy and Natural Resources

In the previous sections, several factor endowments have been presented and, as pointed out in the theoretical section, the natural resources of a country are also considered. The amount of natural resources that a country possesses and that can be exploited is an important element in their economic development. Economic research is typically considering the amount of land, water and natural resources that can be utilized in diverse production functions within a country.

According to Ruta and Venables (2012), natural trade accounts for one-fifth of worldwide merchandise trade, out of which fuels have the highest share. The next figure will represent the countries of the world that hold 80% of the world crude oil reserves and are members of the Organization of the Petroleum Exporting countries.

Figure 5. OPEC share of world crude oil reserves, 2018
Source: (OPEC, 2019)

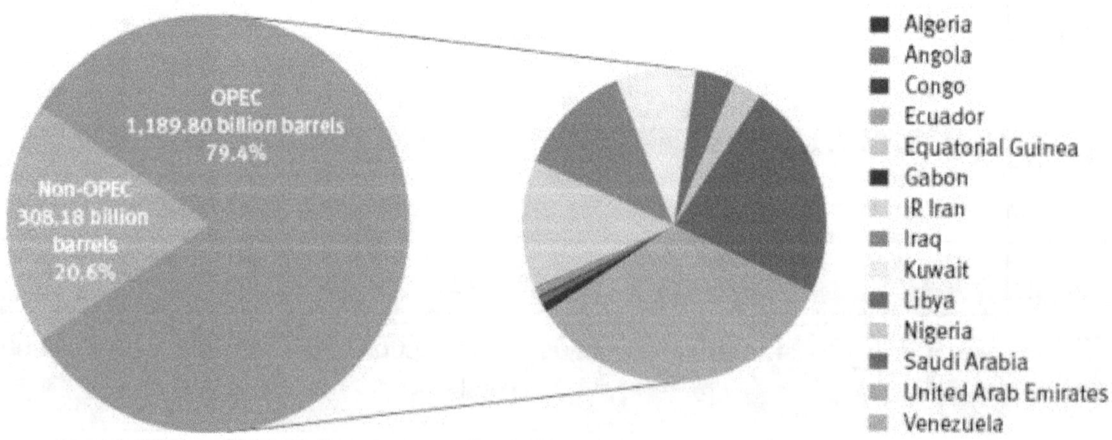

OPEC proven crude oil reserves, at end 2018 (billion barrels, OPEC share)

Venezuela	302.81	25.5%	Kuwait	101.50	8.5%	Algeria	12.20	1.0%	Gabon	2.00	0.2%
Saudi Arabia	267.03	22.4%	UAE	97.80	8.2%	Ecuador	8.27	0.7%	Equatorial Guinea	1.10	0.1%
IR Iran	155.60	13.1%	Libya	48.36	4.1%	Angola	8.16	0.7%			
Iraq	145.02	12.2%	Nigeria	36.97	3.1%	Congo	2.98	0.3%			

Natural resources are undoubtedly an important factor in trade but, for 21 countries, they represent the vast majority of their exports and have a high contribution to their GDP. Natural resources are defined in the World Trade Report (WTO, 2010) as the totality of forestry products, fish, fuels and mining products.

The study by Romalis (2004) starts from the economic theory that forecasts that countries which are relatively abundant in a factor of production will most likely export the commodity which uses that factor intensively. Two conclusions emerge from this research: countries that have a fast accumulation of a factor will switch their export structures and production in the direction of industries that use that factor abundantly and countries that use their abundant factors will seize a greater share of world production and trade of commodities.

As discussed before, oil is the most traded natural resource. Therefore, the few countries that possess it influence prices through their availability to export to the rest of the countries. Since oil is a commodity that involves all the world economies, importers or exporters, changes in its price affect positively the exporters (Backus & Crucini, 2000) while cause challenges to importing countries. Countries that are large oil importers tend to base their industrial activity on this resource in order to obtain energy. A rise in prices of oil will generate a decrease of the industrial sector and therefore impact the economic result at country level. Upon an increase in the cost of energy, the import and export patterns of a country may change (Sadorsky, 2012).

The exhaustibility of natural resources has diverse effects on international trade as countries with higher shares of resources are in advantage. Based on an extensive study by Álvarez and Fuentes (2012), a comparative advantage in manufactured goods is more persistent than a comparative advantage in resource-intensive goods. The study also finds that the specialization of a country is not necessarily held back by possessing an abundance of natural resources. In conclusion, countries that possess exhaustible natural resources presently have a competitive advantage but must be more preoccupied of alternatives for the future, such as clean energies, if they wish to maintain their economic position.

CONCLUSION

The previous sections have provided extensive research on the topic of international trade and specialization patterns. Globalization has proven to have a general positive impact on global trade, however the different effects on countries has positioned certain economies more in advantage than others. Regional integration has created specific advantages for collaborating groups of countries, advantages that further facilitated an easier trade between them. International trade agreements have also eased the flow of products, information and technology among countries and helped loosen trade barriers. Globalization also created a unique context for countries that might not have presented the most economic potential or competitive advantages to become new economic powers. Changes regarding the global demography such as migration, female participation in the workforce, fertility, and aging have completely changed the workforce spectrum for countries, creating different advantages for countries that are in different phases of demographic transition. Technological advance and great innovations have facilitated trade and reduced trade costs, especially regarding transportation costs. The uneven geographical distribution of natural resources at global level has produced countries with an abundance of resources and with great comparative advantages. On the other hand, countries with scarce natural resources became importers and their economies are influenced greatly upon increases in prices. Investment in infrastructure has proven to be a great modality of economic development that has made countries more competitive regarding international trade.

REFERENCES

Álvarez, R., & Fuentes, J. R. (2012). Specialization dynamics and natural resources abundance. *Review of World Economics*, *148*(4), 733–750. doi:10.100710290-012-0130-5

Amadeo, K. (2020a). See why Afghan rugs cost you more today than a year ago. *Unilateral Trade Agreements, Their Pros and Cons, with Examples.* Retrieved from https://www.thebalance.com/unilateral-trade-agreements-definition-examples-3305904

Amadeo, K. (2020b). *Bilateral trade agreements with their pros and cons*. Retrieved from https://www.thebalance.com/what-are-bilateral-trade-agreements-pros-cons-and-list-3305911

Amadeo, K. (2020c). *5 pros and 4 cons to the world's largest trade agreements*. Retrieved from https://www.thebalance.com/multilateral-trade-agreements-pros-cons-and-examples-3305949

Anderson, J. E., & Wincoop, E. (2004). Trade costs. *Journal of Economic Literature*, *42*(3), 691–751. doi:10.1257/0022051042177649

Antràs, P., & Helpman, E. (2004). Global sourcing. *Journal of Political Economy*, *112*(3), 552–580. doi:10.1086/383099

Arribas, I., Pérez, F., & Tortosa-Ausina, E. (2009). Measuring globalization of international trade: Theory and evidence. *World Development*, *37*(1), 127–145. doi:10.1016/j.worlddev.2008.03.009

Atsmon, Y., & Magni, M. (2016). Chinese consumers: Revisiting our predictions. *The McKinsey Quarterly*, *4*, 71–81.

Backus, D. K., & Crucini, M. J. (2000). Oil prices and the terms of trade. *Journal of International Economics*, *50*(1), 185–213. doi:10.1016/S0022-1996(98)00064-6

Baldwin, R. (2012). *Global supply chains: Why they emerged, why they matter, and where they are going*. CEPR Discussion Papers No. 9103.

Barro, R. J., & Lee, J. W. (2013). A new data set of educational attainment in the world, 1950–2010. *Journal of Development Economics*, *104*, 184–198. doi:10.1016/j.jdeveco.2012.10.001

Baumol, W. J., & Blinder, A. S. (1988). *Economics: Principles and policy* (13th ed.). Cenfage Learning.

Bernard, A. B., & Jensen, J. B. (1999). Exceptional exporter performance: Cause, effect, or both? *Journal of International Economics*, *47*(1), 1–25. doi:10.1016/S0022-1996(98)00027-0

Bernard, A. B., Redding, S. J., & Schott, P. K. (2007). Comparative advantage and heterogeneous firms. *The Review of Economic Studies*, *74*(1), 31–66. doi:10.1111/j.1467-937X.2007.00413.x

Blaug, M. (1992). *The methodology of economics, or how economists explain* (2nd ed.). Cambridge University Press. doi:10.1017/CBO9780511528224

Bøås, M., Marchand, M., & Shaw, T. (2003). The Weave-World: The regional interweaving of economies, ideas and identities. In F. Söderbaum & T. Shaw (Eds.), *Theories of New Regionalism. International Political Economy Series* (pp. 197–210). Palgrave Macmillan. doi:10.1057/9781403938794_11

Bonke, J., & Browning, M. (2011). Spending on children: Direct survey evidence. *Economic Journal (London)*, *121*(554), F123–F143. doi:10.1111/j.1468-0297.2011.02444.x

Borchert, I., & Yotov, Y. V. (2017). Distance, globalization, and international trade. *Economics Letters*, *153*, 32–38. doi:10.1016/j.econlet.2017.01.023

Browning, M., & Ejræs, M. (2009). Consumption and children. *The Review of Economics and Statistics*, *91*(1), 93–111. doi:10.1162/rest.91.1.93

Buzan, B. (2003). Regional security complex theory in the Post-Cold War world. In F. Söderbaum & T. Shaw (Eds.), *Theories of New Regionalism* (pp. 140–159). Palgrave Macmillan. doi:10.1057/9781403938794_8

CarolK. (2020). *Globalization.* Retrieved from https://www.investopedia.com/terms/g/globalization.asp

Chen, J. (2020a). Foreign direct investment (FDI). *International Markets.* Retrieved from https://www.investopedia.com/terms/f/fdi.asp

Chen, J. (2020b). Investment. *Investing essentials.* Retrieved from https://www.investopedia.com/terms/i/investment.asp#:~:text=An%20investment%20is%20an%20asset,the%20future%20to%20create%20wealth

Chou, M.-H., & Ravinet, P. (2015). The rise of 'Higher Education Regionalism': An agenda for higher education research. In J. Huisman, H. de Boer, D. D. Dill, & M. Souto-Otero (Eds.), *The Palgrave International Handbook of Higher Education Policy and Governance* (pp. 361–378). Springer. doi:10.1007/978-1-137-45617-5_20

Claar, S., & Nölke, A. (2013). Deep integration in North–South relations: Compatibility issues between the EU and South Africa. *Review of African Political Economy*, *40*(136), 274–289. doi:10.1080/03056244.2013.794726

Corporate Finance Institute. (n.d.). *Regional trading agreements.* Retrieved from https://corporatefinanceinstitute.com/resources/knowledge/economics/regional-trading-agreements/

Crespo, N., & Fontoura, M. P. (2007). Determinant factors of FDI spillovers – What do we really know? *World Development*, *35*(3), 410–425. doi:10.1016/j.worlddev.2006.04.001

Dixit, A., & Norman, V. (1980). *Theory of international trade: A dual, general equilibrium approach.* Cambridge University Press. doi:10.1017/CBO9780511628627

Dixit, A. K., & Stiglitz, J. E. (1977). Monopolistic competition and optimum product diversity. *The American Economic Review*, *67*(3), 297–308.

Easterly, W., & Levine, R. (2001). What have we learned from a decade of empirical research on growth? It's not factor accumulation: Stylized facts and growth models. *The World Bank Economic Review*, *15*(2), 177–219. doi:10.1093/wber/15.2.177

Eberstadt, N. N. (2012). Looking towards 2030: A new world coming into focus. *Economic Affairs, 32*(1), 17–25. doi:10.1111/j.1468-0270.2011.02123.x

Fink, C., Mattoo, A., & Neagu, I. C. (2011). Assessing the impact of communication costs on international trade. In J.-C. Maur. & J. S. Wilson (Eds.), Trade costs and facilitation: Open trade and economic development (vol. 2, pp. 24-41). Elgar.

Fu, X., & Soete, L. (2010). *The rise of technological power in the South*. Palgrave Macmillan. doi:10.1057/9780230276123

Galor, O., & Weil, D. N. (1993). *The gender gap, fertility, and growth.* National Bureau of Economic Research No. w4550.

Gao, S. (2000). *Economic globalization: Trends, risks and risk prevention. Economic and Social Affairs, No. 1*. CDP Background Paper.

Giddens, A. (1990). *The consequence of modernity*. Polity Press.

Gittelman, M. (1992). Foreign direct investment in the Triad: A framework for understanding regionalization in the 1990s. *International Executive, 34*(6), 469–483. doi:10.1002/tie.5060340602

Goldstein, J. L., Rivers, D., & Tomz, M. (2007). Institutions in international relations: Understanding the effects of the GATT and the WTO on world trade. *International Organization, 61*(1), 37–67. doi:10.1017/S0020818307070014

Grossman, G. M. (2016). *The purpose of trade agreements.* National Bureau of Economic Research 22070.

Grossman, G. M., & Helpman, E. (2005). Outsourcing in a global economy. *The Review of Economic Studies, 72*(1), 135–159. doi:10.1111/0034-6527.00327

Grossman, G. M., Helpman, E., & Szeidl, A. (2006). Optimal integration strategies for the multinational firm. *Journal of International Economics, 70*(1), 216–238. doi:10.1016/j.jinteco.2005.07.011

Haas, E. B. (1970). The study of regional integration: Reflections on the joy and anguish of pretheorizing. *International Organization, 24*(4), 607. doi:10.1017/S0020818300017495

Haass, R. N. (2008). The age of nonpolarity: What will follow U.S. dominance. *Foreign Affairs, 87*(3), 44–56.

Head, K., & Mayer, T. (2014). Gravity equations: Workhorse, toolkit, and cookbook. In G. Gopinath, E. Helpman, & K. Rogoff (Eds.), *Handbook of International Economics* (Vol. 4, pp. 131–195). Elsevier.

Helpman, E., Melitz, M. J., & Yeaple, S. R. (2004). Export versus FDI with heterogenous firms. *The American Economic Review, 94*(1), 300–316. doi:10.1257/000282804322970814

Hew, D., Das, S. B., & Sen, R. (2009). *ASEAN economic integration and implication for CLMV countries. In Plugging into Production Networks: Industrialisation Strategy in Less Developed Southeast Asian Countries*. Institute of Southeast Asian Studies.

Humlum, M. K., Nandrup, A. B., & Smith, N. (2019). Closing or reproducing the gender gap? Parental transmission, social norms and education choice. *Journal of Population Economics, 32*(2), 455–500. doi:10.100700148-018-0692-1

ILO. (2010). *Women in labor markets: Measuring progress and identifying challenges.* ILO.

IMF. (2002). *Globalization: A framework for IMF involvement.* IMF.

IMF. (2008). *Globalization: A brief overview.* IMF.

Inkpen, A., & Ramaswamy, K. (2007). End of the multinational: Emerging markets redraw the picture. *The Journal of Business Strategy, 28*(5), 4–12. doi:10.1108/02756660710820776

Jimenez, E. (1994). *Human and physical infrastructure: Public investment and pricing policies in developing countries.* The World Bank Policy Research Working Paper Series No. 1281.

Kaneda, T., Greenbaum, C., & Kline, K. (2020). *2020 World population data sheet shows older populations growing, total fertility rates declining.* Population Reference Bureau.

Keller, W. (2010). International trade, foreign direct investment, and technology spillovers. In B. H. Hall & N. Rosenberg (Eds.), *Handbook of the Economics of Innovation* (Vol. 2, pp. 793–829). North-Holland. doi:10.1016/S0169-7218(10)02003-4

Keller, W., & Yeaple, S. R. (2013). The gravity of knowledge. *The American Economic Review, 103*(4), 1414–1444. doi:10.1257/aer.103.4.1414

Kimura, F. (2013). The development of logistics infrastructure in ASEAN: The comprehensive Asia Development Plan and the Post-AEC initiative. In S. Basu Das (Ed.), *Enhancing ASEAN's Connectivity* (pp. 37–58). Institute of Southeast Asian Studies.

Kobrin, S. J. (2015). Is a global nonmarket strategy possible? Economic integration in a multipolar world order. *Journal of World Business, 50*(2), 262–272. doi:10.1016/j.jwb.2014.10.003

Krugman, P. (1980). Scale economies, product differentiation, and the pattern of trade. *The American Economic Review, 70*(5), 950–959.

Krugman, P. (1991). Increasing returns and economic geography. *Journal of Political Economy, 99*(3), 483–499. doi:10.1086/261763

Krugman, P. (1998). What's new about the New Economic Geography? *Oxford Review of Economic Policy, 14*(2), 7–17. doi:10.1093/oxrep/14.2.7

Lamy, P. (2006). *Humanising Globalization.* World Trade Organization.

Leamer, E. E. (1995). Princeton Studies in International Finance: Vol. 77. *The Heckscher-Ohlin model in theory and practice.* Princeton University.

Lee, R. (2003). The demographic transition: Three centuries of fundamental change. *The Journal of Economic Perspectives, 17*(4), 167–190. doi:10.1257/089533003772034943

Lendle, A., Olarreaga, M., Schropp, S., & Vézina, P. L. (2016). There goes gravity: eBay and the Death of Distance. *Economic Journal (London), 126*(591), 406–441. doi:10.1111/ecoj.12286

Levitt, T. (1993). The globalization of markets. *Readings in international business: A decision approach, 249*, 249-252.

Li, H., Li, L., Wu, B., & Xiong, Y. (2012). The end of cheap Chinese labor. *The Journal of Economic Perspectives, 26*(4), 57–74. doi:10.1257/jep.26.4.57

Lim, A. H., & Saner, R. (2011). Rethinking trade in education services: A wake-up call for trade negotiators. *Journal of World Trade, 45*(5), 993–1034.

Lührmann, M. (2005). *Population aging and the demand for goods & services.* Munich Center for the Economics of Aging (MEA) Discussion Paper Series 05095.

Lundvall, B.-A., Joseph, K. J., Chaminade, C., & Vang, J. e. (2009). *Handbook of innovation systems and developing countries: Building domestic capabilities in a global setting.* Elgar. doi:10.4337/9781849803427

Mahmood, I. P., & Singh, J. (2003). Technological dynamism in Asia. *Research Policy, 32*(6), 1031–1054. doi:10.1016/S0048-7333(02)00109-9

Mammen, K., & Paxson, C. (2000). Women's work and economic development. *The Journal of Economic Perspectives, 14*(4), 141–164. doi:10.1257/jep.14.4.141

Martins, J. O., Gonand, F., Antolin, P., de la Maisonneuve, C., & Yoo, K.-Y. (2005). *The impact of ageing on demand, factor markets and growth.* OECD Economics Department Working Papers 420.

Melitz, M. J. (2003). The impact of trade on intra-industry reallocations and aggregate industry productivity. *Econometrica, 71*(6), 1695–1725. doi:10.1111/1468-0262.00467

Mittelman, J. H. (2000). *The globalization syndrome: Transformation and resistance.* Princeton University Press. doi:10.1515/9781400823697

Mukherjee, I. (2008). Impact of globalization on international trade. *ICFAI Journal of International Business, 3*(1), 28–45.

Naito, T., & Zhao, L. (2009). Aging, transitional dynamics, and gains from trade. *Journal of Economic Dynamics & Control, 33*(8), 1531–1542. doi:10.1016/j.jedc.2009.02.006

OECD. (2020). *FDI Stocks.* https://data.oecd.org/fdi/fdi-stocks.htm

Oi, W. Y. (1983). Heterogeneous firms and the organization of production. *Economic Inquiry, 21*(2), 147–171. doi:10.1111/j.1465-7295.1983.tb00623.x

OPEC. (2019). *OPEC share of world crude oil reserves, 2018.* Retrieved from: https://www.opec.org/opec_web/en/data_graphs/330.htm

Panagariya, A. (2008). Paul Krugman, Nobel. *Forbes.*

Poladian, S. M., & Oehler-Şincai, I. M. (2014). Emerging of new poles of economic power in the world. *Procedia Economics and Finance, 8*, 474–483. doi:10.1016/S2212-5671(14)00116-6

Prescott, E. C. (1998). Needed: A theory of total factor productivity. *International Economic Review, 39*(3), 525–551. doi:10.2307/2527389

Redding, S. (2010). Theories of heterogeneous firms and trade. *C.E.P.R. Discussion Papers, 3.*

World Trade Report. (2011). *The WTO and preferential trade agreements: From co-existence to coherence.* Author.

Rodríguez-Clare, A. (2001). Costa Rica's development strategy based on human capital and technology: How it got there, the impact of Intel, and lessons for other countries. *Journal of Human Development, 2*(2), 311–324. doi:10.1080/14649880120067301

Romalis, J. (2004). Factor proportions and the structure of commodity trade. *The American Economic Review, 94*(1), 67–97. doi:10.1257/000282804322970715

Rugman, A. M., & Verbeke, A. (2004). A perspective on regional and global strategies of multinational enterprises. *Journal of International Business Studies, 35*(1), 3–18. doi:10.1057/palgrave.jibs.8400073

Ruta, M., & Venables, A. J. (2012). International trade in natural resources: Practice and policy. *Annual Review of Resource Economics, 4*(1), 331–352. doi:10.1146/annurev-resource-110811-114526

Sadorsky, P. (2012). Energy consumption, output and trade in South America. *Energy Economics, 34*(2), 476–488. doi:10.1016/j.eneco.2011.12.008

Sayan, S. (2005). Heckscher-Ohlin revisited: Implications of differential population dynamics for trade within an overlapping generations framework. *Journal of Economic Dynamics & Control, 29*(9), 1471–1493. doi:10.1016/j.jedc.2004.08.008

Schimmelfennig, F. (2018). Regional integration theory. In Oxford Research Encyclopedia of Politics. doi:10.1093/acrefore/9780190228637.013.599

Schofer, E., & Meyer, J. W. (2005). The worldwide expansion of higher education in the twentieth century. *American Sociological Review, 70*(6), 898–920. doi:10.1177/000312240507000602

Schulz, M., Soderbaum, F., & Ojendal, J. (2001). Key issues in the new regionalism: Comparisons from Asia, Africa and the Middle East. In B. Hettne, A. Inotai, & O. Sunkel (Eds.), *Comparing regionalisms: Implications for global development* (pp. 234–276). Palgrave.

Soares, R. R., & Falcao, B. L. (2008). The demographic transition and the sexual division of labor. *Journal of Political Economy, 116*(6), 1058–1104. doi:10.1086/596102

Stiglitz, J. E. (1970). Factor price equalization in a dynamic economy. *Journal of Political Economy, 78*(3), 456–488. doi:10.1086/259644

Subramanian, A., & Wei, S. J. (2007). The WTO promotes trade, strongly but unevenly. *Journal of International Economics, 72*(1), 151–175. doi:10.1016/j.jinteco.2006.07.007

Tellis, A. J., Bially, J., Layne, C., & McPherson, M. (2000). *Measuring National Power in the Postindustrial Age.* RAND Corporation.

The Economist. (2012). A tale of three islands. *The Economist, 401*(8756), 28-30.

Tsani, S., Paroussos, L., Fragiadakis, C., Charalambidis, I., & Capros, P. (2013). Female labor force participation and economic growth in the South Mediterranean countries. *Economics Letters*, *120*(2), 323–328. doi:10.1016/j.econlet.2013.04.043

van Langenhove, L., & de Lombaerde, P. (2007). Regional integration, poverty and social policy. *Global Social Policy*, *7*(3), 379–385. doi:10.1177/1468018107082240

Warleigh-Lack, A. (2006). Towards a conceptual framework for regionalisation: Bridging 'new regionalism' and 'integration theory'. *Review of International Political Economy*, *13*(5), 750–771. doi:10.1080/09692290600950639

Whalley, J. (1998). Why do countries seek regional trade agreements? In J. A. Frankel (Ed.), The regionalization of the world economy (pp. 63-83). NBER Project Report series. University of Chicago Press.

Wolf, M. (2004). Globalization and global economic governance. *Oxford Review of Economic Policy*, *20*(1), 72–84. doi:10.1093/oxrep/grh005

World Bank. (2002). *Globalization, Growth and Poverty*. The World Bank.

World Bank. (2011). *Global development horizons 2011: Multipolarity - The new global economy*. The World Bank.

World Trade Organization. (2020). *Members and Observers*. Retrieved from https://www.wto.org/english/thewto_e/whatis_e/tif_e/org6_e.htm

WTO. (2010). *World trade report 2010: Trade in natural resources*. Retrieved from https://www.wto.org/english/res_e/booksp_e/anrep_e/world_trade_report10_e.pdf

WTO. (2013). *Factors shaping the future of world trade*. Retrieved from https://www.wto.org/english/res_e/booksp_e/world_trade_report13_e.pdf

Yakita, A. (2012). Different demographic changes and patterns of trade in a Heckscher-Ohlin setting. *Journal of Population Economics*, *25*(3), 853–870. doi:10.100700148-011-0363-y

Yakita, A. (2014). Effects of capital taxation on economies with different demographic changes: Short term versus long term. *Journal of Population Economics*, *27*(1), 257–273. doi:10.100700148-013-0480-x

Chapter 14
Greenfield FDI Determinants in the MENA Region: An Empirical Analysis Using Dynamic Panel Data Model

Youssra Ben Romdhane Loukil
LED, University of Sfax, Tunisia

Souhaila Kammoun
IHEC, CODECI, University of Sfax, Tunisia

Imen Ouerghi
ESC, QuARG, University of Manouba, Tunisia

ABSTRACT

The purpose of the chapter is twofold. Firstly, the authors intend to identify the main determinants of Greenfield FDI in a context of political and economic changes by choosing inflation, trade freedom, and investment freedom as macroeconomic variables and political instability as an institutional variable. Secondly, they determine which environmental sector may affect this mode of foreign investment in MENA region. Using dynamic panel models on a sample of 13 countries over the period 2010-2018, they perform econometric modeling to measure the relationship between Greenfield FDI, macroeconomic aggregates, and the relationship between FDI and the environmental sector. They find that trade openness stimulates foreign investment in MENA region and that the lack of inflation control may disrupt the inflow of Greenfield FDI since it reflects the economic stability of the host countries. Furthermore, there is a positive relationship between Greenfield FDI and environmental sectors. The chapter suggests some relevant practical implications to improve the attractiveness of Greenfield FDI in the MENA region.

DOI: 10.4018/978-1-7998-7568-0.ch014

INTRODUCTION

The literature on business investment is largely dominated by studies on how the cost of production, the size of the domestic market, and the growth of host countries affect the amount of Foreign Direct Investment (FDI). Perhaps not surprisingly, the empirical literature has identified a positive relationship between the level of macroeconomic and political stability and the corresponding level of inward FDI (Adeseyoju, 2001; Anyanwu, 1998; Aremu, 1997; Aremu, 2005; Blonigen & Piger, 2014; Chete, 1998; Ekpo, 1995; Froot & Stein, 1991; Harms & Méon, 2018; Hood & Young, 1979; Jaiblai & Kammoun et al., 2020; Jenkins & Thomas, 2002; Kojima, 1973; Kojima, 1982; Kojima & Ozawa, 1984; Kottaridi et al., 2019; Li & Rajan, 2020; Masayuki & Ivohasina, 2005; Obadan, 1982; Odozi, 1995; Oke et al., 2012; Osinubi, 2010; Palangkaraya & Waldkirch, 2008; Pfeffermann & Madarassy, 1992; Prakash & Assaf, 2001; Root, 1990; Shenai, 2019; Uremadu, 2010; Vernon, 1966; World Bank, 2010; WTO, 1996).

Several researchers suggest that macroeconomic and political instability in host countries may be due to rising inflation, exchange rate deterioration and domestic and international market disruption (Ali et al., 2017; Alobari et al., 2016). In this context, it should be noted that the literature has generally focused on an unattractive axis that aims at "the relocation of production to other economically stable host countries" (Emmanuel et al., 2018; Jacob & Kattookaran, 2019). In the same vein, some countries have moved towards the green economy in recent years by focusing on a new type of investment called "greenfield investments" to stimulate value addition in their economies (Akhtaruzzaman et al., 2017; Asiedu, 2006; Caccia et al., 2018; Kolstad & Wiig, 2012; Stevens et al., 2016; Yeung et al., 2012). A 'Greenfield' Investment is "a form of foreign direct investment where a parent company starts a new venture in a foreign country by constructing new operational facilities from the ground up". Despite vast empirical enquiry, the empirical studies have largely ignored the possibility of certain macroeconomic aggregates but also sectors of activity that may affect the mode of engagement in foreign markets, such as freedom of investment, industry, agriculture and services in relation to local production by Greenfield FDI.

The motivation for this research stems from the results of a growing number of empirical studies examining the relationship between Greenfield FDI, macroeconomic aggregates and environmental sectors. To our knowledge, our study is the first to propose a theoretical and empirical explanation which chooses in a first part the Greenfield FDI as endogenous variable to know the nature of the relationship between this type of investment and inflation, commercial freedom, freedom to invest and political instability as an institutional variable. The second part studies the influence of the Greenfield FDI on three environmental sectors: agriculture, industry and services in the MENA region. Concerning the added value, our research is the first carried out to assess together these two relationships in the MENA region using dynamic panel modeling via the method DPM because this method has a higher power than the traditional method. Our choice is mainly justified by two reasons: on the one hand, the MENA zone has undergone political changes like the countries of the Arab Spring, Syria and Yemen and, on the other hand, this region is characterized by the variation of wealth between countries like oil and non-oil countries.

The overarching purpose of this study is to test whether the improvement of high value-added production, the creation of high-skilled jobs for local people and technological spin-offs, as well as the geographical location and the agricultural and industrial modes of operation could affect the results associated with Greenfield FDI. However, few attempts have been made to identify on the one hand the complexity of the relationship between the Greenfields and macroeconomic aggregates through inflation and, on the other hand, the Greenfields and the environment across the industrial and agricultural sectors in political uncertainty. To our knowledge, several researchers have used unit-root tests based on time series to explain the relationships of FDI such as Burger et al. (2014), Han and Phillips (2010), and Harms and Meon (2018). This paper goal is to explain the effect of Greenfield FDI on macroeconomic aggregates and environmental sectors in the MENA zone. We collected a dataset describing key variables over the period 2010-2018. The choice of the period is justified by the constraint of the political uncertainty prevailing in MENA region. Based on data from 13 countries, we perform econometric modeling to measure this relationship using a new dynamic panel modeling (DPM) method.

Our central finding is that trade openness stimulates foreign investment in MENA region and helps some countries to improve their positions on the world market. However, a negative relationship with the inflation rate was marked. This explains why the lack of inflation control may disrupt the inflow of Greenfield FDI since it reflects the economic stability of the host countries. The second model reveals a positive relationship between Greenfield FDI and the industrial and agricultural sectors. On the channels of manifestation, we find that the transmission effect of FDI is significant only for the agriculture and services sectors and generally negative for the manufacturing sector, although insignificant. Our results can be seen as an important contribution to the empirical evidence on the link between FDI and growth. Research is needed to suggest relevant practical implications to help firms adopt financial technologies to satisfy consumers and meet their needs, in line with local culture and attract more potential customers.

The rest of the paper is organized as follows. The following section presents a review of the literature on the relationship between Greenfield FDI, macroeconomic aggregates in the first part and the relationship between FDI and the environment in the second part. The next section describes the data set and research methodology. After that, we interpret the results of the two estimation models. Lastly, we conclude and present the significance of the study and the practical implications.

THEORETICAL BACKGROUND

In recent years, multinational companies have been making foreign direct investments mainly in the FDI Greenfield mode. In the extensive empirical literature that examines the determinants of these investments, very few studies have examined the relationship between Greenfield FDI and macroeconomic aggregates and sectors of environments in the MENA region. A thorough review of empirical literature on the topic reveals that in the pre-revolutionary period, Greenfield FDIs increased significantly in the MENA region in the interest of financial stability, taking into account the trade openness that facilitates the entry of Greenfield FDIs. In the post-revolutionary period, which was marked by a severe economic recession, Greenfield FDI fell, particularly for the Arab Spring countries, Syria, and Yemen, as a result of rising inflation. In a situation of political instability, the results reveal a positive relationship between Greenfield FDI and industry, agriculture and services, which could lead to positive externalities.

Economic Determinants of Greenfield FDI

The issue of Greenfield foreign direct investment is attracting the interest of researchers and practitioners alike. Despite growing academic research on Greenfield FDI to develop a theoretical framework, there is still no common definition for this type of investment, and the question of its determinants is still on-going (Caccia et al., 2018; Ibrahim, 2019; Levasseur, 2014; Moghadam et al.; Neto et al., 2014). Within this framework, various research papers have attempted to understand the main determinants of Greenfield investments and to explain their relationship with the financial market and the economic environment of countries around the world (Chayawisan, 2015; De Beule et al., 2012). In this line of research, Chakrabarti (2001) and Jordaan (2004) have analyzed the relationship between Greenfield FDI and economic growth and found that Greenfield FDI is directed towards countries with the largest markets so that companies can earn a higher return on their capital. This result is confirmed by several studies such as Ang (2008), Asiedu (2002), Pärletun (2008), and Tsai (1994) but it is refuted by Edwards (1990) and Jaspersen et al. (2000). Other studies have explained the relationship between Greenfield investment and social openness (Edwards, 1990; Ghodsi, 2020; Gorodnichenko et al., 2020) confirming that exporting firms seek more openness but this is not the case for firms seeking closed markets. In this framework, Kosekahyaoglu (2020) studied the main economic and political determinants of Greenfield FDI for Turkey, countries in the European Union and Central and Eastern European countries during the period 1980-2004. Based on the Granger causality methodology, the empirical results show a two-way relationship between Greenfield FDI and foreign trade on the one hand and a one-way relationship between Greenfield FDI and exports on the other.

Similarly, Ghodsi (2020) has analyzed this relationship in 17 CESEE countries over the period 1996-2016. The empirical results of a stochastic frontier specification of the Knowledge Capital (KK) model indicate that technical barriers to trade have negative market influences, such as certification and compliance costs at the frontier, which encourage female entrepreneurs to make Greenfield investments in the host market instead of exporting to that market. Furthermore, Moghadam et al. (2019) have investigated the causal direction between the determinants of Greenfield FDI on macroeconomic aggregates Greenfield FDI and found a strong relationship between market opening and foreign firms preferring mergers with Greenfield investment. The authors concluded that the degree of openness of a country to international trade is a relevant factor in the investment decision. In the same vein, Culem (1988), Edwards (1990) and Kravis and Lipsey (1982) have highlighted the positive effect of openness on Greenfield FDI, while Schmitz and Bieri (1972) found a weak positive relationship between these two approaches. In addition, Xaypanya at al. (2015) studied the determinants of Greenfield FDI in the Association of Southeast Asian Nations using differentiation techniques to estimate parameters on panel data over the period 2000-2011. They found that, although there are significantly positive effects of infrastructure and openness level on Greenfield FDI inflows in this region, the inflation rate has a negative impact. Based on this finding, many studies have examined the effect of Greenfield investment on inflation. Similarly, Mina (2020) confirmed that the inflation rate argument discourages Greenfield FDI flows and that an increase in the money supply could signal inflationary pressures and depreciation in the value of money, which discourages Greenfield FDI flows. Moreover, Faroh and Shen (2015) analyzed this relationship for Sierra Leone over a period between 1985- 2012. The empirical results showed that the inflation rate is weakly related to Greenfield FDI inflows. These results are contradicted by the studies of Obiamaka (2011) and Omankhanlen (2011).

Effect of Political Stability on Greenfield FDI in the MENA Region

It's noteworthy to mention that political uncertainty is a factor that imposes more constraints on the economies of global countries (MIGA, 2014). Shocks to political stability affect expected rates of return for firms in all sectors. Similarly, political instability in the MENA region and particularly in the Arab Spring countries is intense since 2011 (Campante & Chor, 2012). However, political instability has negatively affected the economic environment of these countries (Tunisia, Libya, Egypt, Syria and

Yemen) which has led to a disruption of FDI inflows into the MENA area (Burger et al., 2014). Caccia et al. (2018) are among the researchers who have analyzed the relationship between Greenfield FDI and political stability in the MENA region. They noted that such investments are much more sensitive to cultural ties between the investing country and the host country than in other regions. They mentioned that religious and linguistic ties favor investment in these countries more than in other regions. In addition, they confirmed that the absence of corruption, business freedom and political stability would favor Greenfield FDI in the region. That being said, and from an investor perspective, the MENA region remains a rich region in natural resources, which encourages Greenfield FDI and the growth of the service sector and industry. The main contribution of this study is to identify the main economic determinants of Greenfield and which sector attracts Greenfield FDI in MENA region.

DATA AND RESEARCH METHODOLOGY

Scope and Aim of the Study

This section explains the data sources. We then describe the measures of key variables used in this study and the methodological approach. In order to identify relevant explanatory variables for Greenfield FDI in the MENA region in a context of macroeconomic and political instability, we use control variables such as macroeconomic variables like inflation rate, trade freedom and investment freedom. We collect information from databases on political uncertainty, such as political stability for 13 countries from 2010 to 2018. We collect all the data in our sample from the World Bank database and The United Nations Conference on Trade and Development (UNCTAD).

Specification of the Model

In this study, we use a dynamic specification to evaluate the impact of economic determinants on the evolution of Greenfield Foreign Direct Investment in MENA countries. The dynamic panel equation structure is presented as follows:

$$FDI_{i,t} = \beta_0 + \beta_1 FDI_{i,t-1} + \beta_2 INF_{i,t} + \beta_3 STAB_{i,t} + \beta_4 TRFR_{i,t} + \beta_5 INFR + \varepsilon_{i,t} \quad (1)$$

where FDI is Foreign Direct Investment; STAB is Stability; INF is Inflation; TRFR is Trade Freedom; and INFR is Investment Freedom.

Unit Root Tests on Panel Data

Recent literature suggests that panel-based unit root tests have a higher power than unit root tests based on individual time series. Although these tests are commonly referred to as "panel-based unit root" tests, they are theoretically only multi-series unit root tests that have been applied to panel data structures (where the presence of country cuts generates "multiple series" from a single series). Therefore, this alternative approach to panel unit root tests uses the results of Fisher (1932) to derive tests that combine p-values from individual unit root tests. This idea has been proposed by Choi (2001) and Maddala and

Wu (1999). The results of the stationarity tests conducted in our study on all variables are shown in the following tables:

Table 1. Stationarity test results

Variables	Method	Statistics	P-values
STABILITY	ADF - Fisher Chi-square	21.6261	0.7090
	ADF - Choi Z-stat	0.86741	0.8071
INFLATION	ADF - Fisher Chi-square	29.5272	0.2877
	ADF - Choi Z-stat	0.93773	0.8258
TRADE_FREEDOM	ADF - Fisher Chi-square	33.3675	0.1517
	ADF - Choi Z-stat	-0.92661	0.1771
INVESTMENT_FREEDOM	ADF - Fisher Chi-square	34.9557	0.1126
	ADF - Choi Z-stat	0.47304	0.6819
FDI	ADF - Fisher Chi-square	45.8692	0.0046
	ADF - Choi Z-stat	-2.73013	0.0032

Source: (Authors' own calculations)

We note that the variables are stationary in first differences, so we can conclude that the variables are first-order integrated. On this ground, we need to perform a co-integration test of these variables in order to choose the appropriate model for our analysis.

Table 2. Stationarity tests of variables on first difference -Augmented Dickey Fuller (ADF) test

Variables	Method	Statistics	P-values
DSTABILITY	ADF - Fisher Chi-square	61.7412	0.0001
	ADF - Choi Z-stat	-3.86579	0.0001
DINFLATION	ADF - Fisher Chi-square	41.7994	0.0257
	ADF - Choi Z-stat	-2.32492	0.0100
DTRADE_FREEDOM	ADF - Fisher Chi-square	71.0905	0.0000
	ADF - Choi Z-stat	-5.08392	0.0000
DINVESTMENT_FREEDOM	ADF - Fisher Chi-square	71.4256	0.0000
	ADF - Choi Z-stat	-4.56502	0.0000
DFDI	ADF - Fisher Chi-square	54.8242	0.0003
	ADF - Choi Z-stat	-3.46472	0.0003

Source: (Authors' own calculations)

Co-Integration Test

Co-integration tests on panel data have been proposed by Bai and Ng (2001), Kao (1999), and Pedroni (1999, 2004). These authors have deduced that the tests for the absence of co-integration in panel data are residual tests similar to the tests proposed by Engle and Granger (1987) in the context of time series. Pedroni (1995, 1997) proposed various tests to address the null hypothesis of the absence of intra-individual co-integration for homogeneous and heterogeneous panels, and proposes an extension to the case where co-integrating relationships include more than two variables. Thus, like the unit root tests, Pedroni's tests take into account heterogeneity through parameters that may differ between individuals and make it possible to compensate for the low power of small-sample time series tests (Hurlin & Mignon, 2006). The tests presented here all have the null hypothesis that there is no co-integration between several variables. The test results are presented in the following table:

Table 3. Co-integration test results

Panel tests	Statistics	P-values
v-Statistic	0.991021	0.1608
rho-Statistic	0.613463	0.7302
PP-Statistic	-6.398740	0.0000***
ADF-Statistic	-5.737187	0.0000***
Group Mean Tests	**Statistics**	**P-values**
rho-Statistic	2.324848	0.9900
PP-Statistic	-13.55858	0.0000***
ADF-Statistic	-7.852682	0.0000***

Source: (Authors' own calculations)

When Pedroni's co-integration test is carried out for all the variables, we notice that out of the seven statistics, there are four that are in favor of the existence of a long term relationship between the different variables. All of these tests require the existence of a co-integrating relationship. Thus, it is necessary to apply an efficient estimation method in order to test the model presented above.

Estimation Method

In order to estimate the selected model, we follow the approach used by Arellano and Bond (1991). We apply the generalized method of moments (GMM) in first differences, which makes it possible to estimate a model with dynamic panel data. This method is given by several econometricians such as: Arellano and Bond (1991), Arellano and Bover (1995), and Hanssen (1982). It controls, for unobserved individual effects, the endogeneity of explanatory variables and the use of a lagged dependent variable. The basic principle of the GMM first-difference estimator is to first rewrite the equation to be estimated in first differences in order to eliminate individual and temporal specific effects and then instrument the explanatory variables of the first difference equation by their level values lagged by one period or more.

The first-difference equation is as follows:

$$\text{Ä}FDI_{i,t} = \beta_1 \text{Ä}FDI_{i,t-1} + \beta_2 \text{Ä}INF_{i,t} + \beta_3 \text{Ä}STAB_{i,t} + \beta_4 \text{Ä}TRFR_{i,t} + \beta_5 \text{Ä}INFR + v_{i,t} \,. \quad (2)$$

The estimation of this equation by the first-difference method of Arellano and Bond (1991) yields the results presented in Table 4.

Table 4. Results of the estimation by the method of Arellano and Bond (1991) in first differences (model 1)

	Coef.	T-Stat	Significance
FDI(-1)	0.520797	13.91796	0.0000***
INF	-2.051158	-2.890735	0.0047***
STAB	-0.038046	-2.803555	0.0061***
TRFR	-0.001577	-0.049811	0.9604
INFR	0.007950	0.447730	0.6553

(*) denotes statistical significance at the 10 percent level and, (**) denotes statistical significance at the 5 percent level and (***) denotes statistical significance at the 1 percent level.

Source: (Authors' own calculations)

The second model tests the impacts of sectorial variables on FDI:

$$FDI_{i,t} = \beta_0 + \beta_1 FDI_{i,t-1} + \beta_2 AGR_{i,t} + \beta_3 IND_{i,t} + \beta_4 DEP_{i,t} + \varepsilon_{i,t} \,. \quad (3)$$

The estimation of the equation by the method of Arellano and Bond (1991) in first difference produces the results shown in Table 5.

Table 5. Results of the estimation by the method of Arellano and Bond (1991) in first differences (model 2)

	Coef.	T-Stat	Significance
FDI(-1)	0.480839	30.36925	0.0000***
AGR	0.025010	2.959066	0.0039***
IND	0.046024	2.326371	0.0220**
DEP	0.461055	1.925825	0.0570*

(*) denotes statistical significance at the 10 percent level and, (**) denotes statistical significance at the 5 percent level and (***) denotes statistical significance at the 1 percent level.

Source: (Authors' own calculations)

RESULTS AND DISCUSSION

For the first model, the results of the estimates show a negative and significant effect of Inflation on FDI. Thus, an increase in inflation by 1 point generates a decrease in FDI by 2.05 points. This is in line with the expected result. Similarly, the stability variable has a significant and positive effect on FDI (an increase in instability of 1 point leads to a decrease in FDI of 0.038 point). This can be explained by the political instability experienced by most of the countries of the panel considered in our work. However, the variables TRFR and INFR are not significant. Furthermore, empirical results suggest a positive relationship between Greenfield FDI and trade openness in the MENA region. In fact, the political transition in this region has led to an increase in trade openness, especially in Morocco, as a large number of investors closed their businesses in Libya and Tunisia following the revolution and preferred to move to Morocco. Consequently, trade openness can promote technical innovation and accelerate enterprise restructuring (Candau, 2020; Ghali & Rezgui; 2011; Kosekahyaoglu, 2020). On the other hand, the Gulf countries are the richest in the region as a result of their oil production. These results are confirmed with the study by Kammoun et al. (2020). This requires the development of the eco-systemic services sector and the adoption of a new law on green investments supported by tax breaks and subsidies and the creation of new jobs. Furthermore, there is a negative relationship between Greenfield FDI and inflation, which requires more macroeconomic stabilization in the markets. Our results are confirmed by the studies of Jaiblai and Shenai (2019). On the other hand, Faroh and Shen (2015) and Xaypanya et al. (2015), found that a decrease in inflation leads to an increase in FDI inflows. In contrast, Obiamaka et al. (2011) and Omankhanlen (2011) found no effect of inflation on Greenfield FDI inflows.

In the second model, there is a positive relationship between Greenfield FDI and the sectors of industry and agriculture. These results are confirmed by Ewing & Yang (2014), Ghali & Rezgui (2014) and Kinda (2014). Overall, the results show that the industrial sector can have a greater impact on the economy than other sectors of the economy.

Regarding the growth of FDI via the agricultural sector, we find systematically positive and significant coefficients of the interaction terms. This finding is strong relative to the model specifications, suggesting that the creation of an added value in the agricultural sector could amplify the impact of FDI on countries' growth. The agricultural sector thus appears as a promising channel through which FDI can have an impact on economic growth in the MENA region. Consequently, it can be argued that MENA countries benefit from Greenfield FDI in the food, chemicals and machinery and electronics sectors. This result highlights the existence of a minimum condition to ensure investment prosperity and thus attract FDI. A large number of economic activities (especially industrial ones) requires a minimum communication infrastructure that facilitates access to raw and intermediate materials but also access to markets, reducing production costs.

CONCLUSION

There is no doubt that FDI, as an important inflow of foreign capital, provides financial resources to countries to improve their economies, but the existing literature on the impact of FDI on macroeconomic aggregates and the environment has not been instructive. With political uncertainty, countries' economies and environments are influenced positively or negatively. This study first explores the effect of Greenfield investment on the inflation rate, trade freedom and investment freedom as macroeconomic variables by adding an institutional variable such as political stability. In the second part, it analyses the relationship between this type of investment and environmental sectors such as industry and agriculture. We provide empirical evidence using a new technique Dynamic panel modeling via the method DPM, over the period 2010-2018. in the MENA region.

Based on the empirical results of our first model, we find a positive relationship between Greenfield FDI and trade openness in the MENA region. Therefore, it can be concluded that trade openness is an important factor in stimulating foreign investment in the region and helps countries to improve their positions in the global market. On the other hand, there is a negative relationship with the inflation rate. This is because inflation control can disrupt the inflow of Greenfield FDI because it reflects macroeconomic stability.

In the second model, we find a positive relationship between Greenfield FDI and the industry, agriculture and services sectors. Thus, FDI inflows open an important channel for export trade in both goods and services, mainly in the garment and tourism industries. This development strategy could create employment opportunities and generate more output for the economy in the long term. However, an outsourcing of services provided abroad in a service sector such as tourism and hospitality (travel, hotels, and restaurants) is insignificant despite the fact that the economy lacks skilled labor.

However, the implications of the green investment approach could be founded in the formation of new consumer markets, the stability of small and medium-sized enterprises, the development of new carbon reduction policies to maximize the value of investments and greater social responsibility.

On the basis of the above conclusions, we provide key policy implications for policy makers. First, policies and regulations aimed at creating a favorable investment environment are recommended for the sustainable absorption of foreign direct investment, which can be accompanied by the promotion of environmentally sound technologies. Second, the tilting of FDI towards processing exports further improves the environmental performance of processing exporters by facilitating the adoption of cleaner technologies. Thirdly, greening of industries, based on the use of clean energy, is necessary. Fourthly, there is an urgent need to preserve the environment with ICT-based emission control technologies, including the use of renewable energy mixes, power grid optimization, sustainable agricultural mechanization, intelligent energy distribution and management, green logistics activities and eco-design, which could be achieved by ICT applications in a region.

From the above, we note that political stability, macroeconomic stability and protection of property rights and the rule of law are becoming imperatives for the attractiveness of FDI in the MENA region.

REFERENCES

Adeseyoju, A. (2001). *Attracting foreign investors to Nigeria.* Dailynews Paper n°31.

Akhtaruzzaman, M., Berg, N., & Christopher, H. (2017). *Expropriation risk and FDI in developing countries: Does return of capital dominate return on capital? Bank of Canada Staff Working, 9.* Bank of Canada.

Ali, A., Ibrahim, M., & Omar, Z. (2017). Impact of changes in the exchange rate on foreign direct investment: Evidence from Somalia. *African Journal of Economic and Sustainable Development, 8*(8), 27–54.

Alobari, C., Paago, J., Igbare, F. N., & Emmah, D. (2016). Exchange rate and foreign direct investment. Implication for economic growth in Nigeria. *Equatorial Journal of Finance and Management Science, 1*(1), 10–23.

Ang, B. J. (2008). Determinants of foreign direct investment in Malaysia. *Journal of Policy Modeling, 30*(1), 185–189. doi:10.1016/j.jpolmod.2007.06.014

Anyanwu, J. C. (1998). An econometric investigation of the determinants of foreign direct investment in Nigeria. *Nigerian Economic Society Annual Conference Publication.*

Arellano, M., & Bond, S. (1991). Some test of specification for panel data: Monte Carlo evidence and application to employment equations. *The Review of Economic Studies, 58*(2), 277–297. doi:10.2307/2297968

Aremu, J.A. (1997). Foreign private investment: Determinants, performance and promotion. C*BN Bulletin*, 108–112.

Aremu, J. A. (2005). *Attracting and negotiating foreign direct investment with transnational corporations in Nigeria.* Market Link Communications.

Asiedu, E. (2002). On the determinants of foreign direct investment to developing countries: Is Africa different? *World Development, 30*(1), 107–119. doi:10.1016/S0305-750X(01)00100-0

Asiedu, E. (2006). Foreign direct investment in Africa: The role of natural resources, market size, government policy, institutions and political instability. *World Economy, 29*(1), 63–77. doi:10.1111/j.1467-9701.2006.00758.x

Beule, D., Van, D., & Bulcke, D. (2012). Locational determinants of outward foreign direct investment: An analysis of Chinese and Indian Greenfield investments. *Transnational Corporations, 21*(1), 1–34. doi:10.18356/66d08267-en

Blonigen, B., & Piger, J. (2014). Determinants of foreign direct investment. *The Canadian Journal of Economics. Revue Canadienne d'Economique, 47*(3), 775–812. doi:10.1111/caje.12091

Burger, M., Ianchovichina, E., & Rijkers, B. (2014). Risky business political instability and Greenfield foreign direct investment in the Arab world. *The World Bank Economic Review, 30*(2), 306–331. doi:10.1093/wber/lhv030

Caccia, F. C., Baleix, J. M., & Paniagua, J. (2018). Foreign direct investment in oil abundant countries: The role of institutions. *PLoS One, 14*(4), e0215650. doi:10.1371/journal.pone.0215650 PMID:31013300

Campante, F. R., & Chor, D. (2012). Why was the Arab world poised for revolution? Schooling, economic opportunities, and the Arab Spring. *The Journal of Economic Perspectives, 26*(2), 167–187. doi:10.1257/jep.26.2.167

Candau, F. (2020). Trade, FDI and migration. *International Economic Journal, 27*(3), 441–461. doi:10.1080/10168737.2012.676058

Chakrabarti, A. (2001). The determinants of foreign direct investments: Sensitivity analyses of cross-country regressions. *International Review of Social Sciences, 54*(1), 89–114. doi:10.1111/1467-6435.00142

Chayawisan, N. (2015). The interaction between domestic and foreign direct investment in Thailand. *British Journal of Economics*, *9*(2), 1–6. doi:10.9734/BJEMT/2015/19274

Chete, L. N. (1998). Determinants of foreign direct investment in Nigeria. Niser Monograph Series 7.

Choi, I. (2001). Unit root tests for panel data. *Journal of International Money and Finance*, *20*(2), 249–272. doi:10.1016/S0261-5606(00)00048-6

Culem, G. C. (1988). The locational determinants of direct investments among industrialized countries. *European Economic Review*, *32*(4), 885–904. doi:10.1016/0014-2921(88)90051-7

Edwards, S. (1990). *Capital flows, foreign direct investment, and dept - equity swaps in developing countries.* NBER Working Paper No. 3497.

Ekpo, A. H. (1995). Foreign direct investment in Nigeria: Evidence from time series data. *CBN Economic and Financial Review*, *35*(1), 59–78.

Eluwole, K. K., & Akadiri, A. A. (2019). Does the interaction between growth determinants a drive for global environmental sustainability? Evidence from world top 10 pollutant emissions countries. *The Science of the Total Environment*, 705.

Emmanuel, B., Criscent, I. E., & Alhasan, Y. (2018). Effect of exchange and interest rates on foreign direct investment in Nigeria 2006-2018. *International Journal of Contemporary Research and Review*, *10*(7), 21572–21585. doi:10.15520/ijcrr.v10i07.717

Faroh, A., & Shen, H. (2015). Impact of interest rates on foreign direct investment: Case study Sierra Leone economy. *International Journal of Business Management and Economic*, *6*(1), 124–132.

Froot, K. A., & Stein, J. C. (1991). Exchange rates and foreign direct investment: An imperfect capital markets approach. *The Quarterly Journal of Economics*, *106*(4), 1191–1217. doi:10.2307/2937961

Ghali, S., & Rezgui, S. (2011). FDI contribution to technical efficiency in the Tunisian manufacturing Sector: Evidence from Micro-Panel Data. *International Economic Journal*, *25*(2), 319–339. doi:10.1080/10168737.2010.504215

Ghodsi, M. (2020). How do technical barriers to trade affect foreign direct investment? Tariff jumping versus regulation haven hypotheses. *Structural Change and Economic Dynamics*, *52*, 269–278. doi:10.1016/j.strueco.2019.11.008

Gorodnichenko, Y., Svejnar, J., & Terrell, K. (2020). Do foreign investment and trade spur innovation? *European Economic Review*, *121*, 103343. doi:10.1016/j.euroecorev.2019.103343

Harms, G., & Méon, P. (2018). Good and useless FDI: The growth effects of Greenfield investment and mergers and acquisitions. *Review of International Economics*, *26*(1), 37–59. doi:10.1111/roie.12302

Hood, N., & Young, S. (1979). *The economics of multinational enterprise*. Longman.

Hurlin, C., & Mignon, V. (2006). *Une synthèse des tests de cointégration sur données de panel.* halshs-00070887.

Jacob, T., Kattookaran, T., & Paul, S. (2019). Impact of exchange rate volatility on Foreign Direct Investment in India: An Empirical Analysis. *Journal of Management, 8*(1), 13–22.

Jaiblai, P., & Shenai, P. (2019). The determinants of FDI in Sub-Saharan economies: A study of data from 1990–2017. *International Journal of Financial Studies, 7*(43), 1–32. doi:10.3390/ijfs7030043

Jaspersen, F., Aylward, A.H., & Knox, A.D. (2000). The effects of risks on private investment: Africa compared with other developing countries. *Investment and Risk in Africa*, 71–95.

Jenkins, C., & Thomas, L. (2002). *Foreign direct investment in Southern Africa: Determinants, characteristics and implications for economic growth and poverty alleviation*. https://www.csae.ox.ac.uk/reports

Jordaan, J. C. (2004). *Foreign direct investment and neighbouring influences* (Unpublished doctoral thesis). University of Pretoria.

Kammoun, S., Romdhane, Y., & Fakhfakh, M. (2020). Effects of economic and political risks on Foreign Direct Investment: A panel data analysis in MENA region. In A. Prabhakar, T. Dutta, G. Kaur, V. Sarin, & V. Erokhin (Eds.), *Regional Trade and Development Strategies in the Era of Globalization*. doi:10.4018/978-1-7998-1730-7.ch012

Kojima, K. (1973). A macroeconomic approach to foreign investment. *Hitotsubashi Journal of Economics, 16*, 1–12.

Kojima, K. (1982). Macroeconomics versus international business approach to foreign direct investment. *Hitotsubashi Journal of Economics, 23*, 1–19.

Kojima, K., & Ozawa, T. (1984). Micro and macro economic models of direct foreign investment: Toward a synthesis. *Hitotsubashi Journal of Economics, 25*, 1–20.

Kolstad, I., & Wiig, A. (2012). What determines Chinese outward FDI? *Journal of World Business, 47*(1), 26–34. doi:10.1016/j.jwb.2010.10.017

Kolstad, I., & Wiig, A. (2012). What determines Chinese outward FDI? *Journal of World Business, 47*(1), 26–34.

Kosekahyaoglu, L. (2006). A comparative analysis of FDI in Turkey and the CEECs: Is there any link between FDI and trade? *Journal of Business Economics and Management, 7*(4), 183–200. doi:10.3846/16111699.2006.9636140

Kottaridia, C., Giakoulas, C., & Manolopoulos, D. (2019). Escapism FDI from developed economies: The role of regulatory context and corporate taxation. *International Business Review, 28*(1), 36–47.

Kravis, L. B., & Lipsey, R. E. (1982). The location of overseas production and production for export by US multinational firms. *Journal of International Economics, 12*(3/4), 201–223.

Li, J., & Rajan, R. (2009). Foreign direct investment and technology transfer under uncertainty in a liberalizing host economy. *International Economic Journal, 23*(1), 23–41. doi:10.1080/10168730802696483

Lien, D., Selmier, W. T., & Oh, C. (2012). Confucius Institute effects on China's trade and FDI: Isn't it delightful when folks Afar Study Hanyu? *International Review of Economics & Finance, 2*, 147–155.

Maddala, G. S., & Wu, S. (1999). A comparative study of unit root tests with panel data and a new simple test. *Oxford Bulletin of Economics and Statistics*, *61*, 631–652.

Mahbuba, T., & Jongwanich, J. (2019). Determinants of foreign direct investment (FDI) in the power sector: A case study of Bangladesh. *Energy Strategy Reviews*, *24*(1), 178–192.

Mina, W. (2020). Do GCC market-oriented labor policies encourage inward FDI flows? *Research in International Business and Finance*, *5*, 101092.

Moghadam, A. T., Mazlan, N. S., Chin, L., & Ibrahim, S. (2019). Mergers and acquisitions and Greenfield foreign direct investment in selected ASEAN countries. *Journal of Economic Integration*, *34*(4), 746–765.

Neto, P., Brandão, A., & Cerqueira, A. (2008). The impact of FDI, cross-border mergers and acquisitions, and Greenfield investments on economic growth. *The IUP Journal of Business Strategy,* 24–44.

Obadan, M. I. (1982). Direct investment in Nigeria: An empirical analysis. *African Studies Review*, *25*(1).

Obiamaka, P. E., Onwumere, J. U., & Okpara, G. C. (2011). Foreign direct investment and economic growth in Nigeria: A Granger causality analysis. *International Journal of Current Research*, *3*(11), 225–232.

Odozi, V. A. (1995). *An overview of foreign investment in Nigeria 1960–1995.* Central Bank of Nigeria Occasional Paper No. 11.

Oke, O. B., Ezike, E. J., & Ojogbo, E. S. (2012). Locational determinants of foreign direct investment in Nigeria. *International Business Research*, *5*(4), 103.

Omankhanlen, A. E. (2011). The effect of exchange rate and inflation on foreign direct investment and its relationship with economic growth in Nigeria. *Economics and Applied Informatics*, *1*, 5–16.

Osinubi, T., & Amaghionyeodiwe, L. A. (2010). Foreign private investment and economic growth in Nigeria. *Review of Economic Business Studies*, *10*(2), 105–127.

Palangkaraya, A., & Waldkirch, A. (2008). Factor abundance and FDI factor intensity in developed countries. *International Economic Journal*, *22*(4), 489–508.

Pärletun, J. (2008). *The determinants of foreign direct investment: A regional analysis with focus on Belarus*. http://biblioteket.ehl.lu.se/olle/papers/0002948.pdf

Pedroni, P. (1995). *Panel cointegration, asymptotic and Önite sample properties of pooled time series tests with an application to the PPP hypothesis.* Indiana University Working Paper in Economics 92–013.

Pedroni, P. (1996). *Fully modified OLS for heterogeneous cointegrated panels and the case of purchasing power parity.* Indiana University Working Paper in Economics.

Pedroni, P. (1999). Critical values for cointegration tests in heterogenous panels with multiple regressor. *Oxford Bulletin of Economics and Statistics*, *61*, 653–670.

Pedroni, P. (2004). Panel cointegration: Asymptotic and finite sample properties of pooled time series tests with an application to the PPP hypothesis. *Econometric Theory*, *20*(3), 597–625.

Pfeffermann, G.P., & Madarassy, A. (1992). *Trends in private and investment in developing countries.* World Bank Paper 16.

Prakash, L., & Assaf, R. (2001). How beneficial is foreign direct investment for developing countries. *Finance & Development, 38*(2), 7–9.

Root, F. R. (1990). *International trade and investment.* South Western Publishing Co.

Schmitz, A., & Jurg, B. (1972). EEC tariffs and U.S. direct investment. *European Economic Review, 3*(3), 259–270.

Stevens, C. E., Xie, E., & Peng, M. W. (2016). Toward a legitimacy-based view of political risk: The case of Google and Yahoo in China. *Strategic Management Journal, 37*(5), 945–963.

Tsai, P. (1994). Determinants of FDI and its impact on economic growth. *Journal of Economic Development, 19*, 137–162.

Uremadu, S. O. (2010). The impact of foreign private investment on capital formation in Nigeria, 1980 - 2004: An Empirical Analysis. *Lex et Scientia, XV*(2), 166–182.

Vernon, R. (1966). International investment and international trade in the product life cycle. *The Quarterly Journal of Economics, 80*, 190–207.

World Bank. (2010). *World Development Indicators.* The World Bank.

WTO. (1996). *International Trade.* Trends and Statistics.

Xaypanya, P., Rangkakulnuwat, P., & Paweenawat, P. S. (2015). The determinants of foreign direct investment in ASEAN: The first differencing panel data analysis. *International Journal of Social Economics, 42*(3), 239–250.

Yuriy, G., Jan, S., & Katherine, T. (2020). Do foreign investment and trade spur innovation? *European Economic Review*, 121.

Chapter 15
A Roadmap to India Liberalizing With Major Economic Groups

Somesh Mathur
Indian Institute of Technology, Kanpur, India

Sachin Kumar Angural
Indian Institute of Technology, Kanpur, India

ABSTRACT

This chapter aims to look at various existing international economic cooperation groups and analyze the impact of India liberalizing with each of them using the GTAP model. This chapter aims to discuss each of these economic groups composition and identify the key sectors they are specialized in. Further, they analyze the product aggregations in which India and these groups would benefit if we liberalize with them. This chapter looks at different linear and nonlinear methods while performing the simulations and compares them. The chapter looks at the different scenarios with (1) India reducing tariff by 10%, (2) both Indian and the economic group reducing tariff by 10%, (3) both reducing the tariffs to 0%. The chapter then further looks at the impact of each cooperation liberalizing with India in terms of terms of trade (ToT), trade balance, and import and export quantities. Thus, this chapter attempts to get some insights into what product aggregates would be beneficial for India and the economic groups and therefore build a roadmap for the same.

INTRODUCTION

We have seen a significant liberalization in India, with the economy opening up in the early 1990s. This has helped India's growth, and with increasing connectedness, it becomes essential to look at the roadmap of the liberalization and evaluate the way forward. Furthermore, from 2010 onwards, India had become a significant player in the world market. In this period, Indian exports almost reached $54 billion, starting at $13 billion if we consider just the US. Also, India's imports from the US increased to $32 billion from $6 billion in the same period. This shows how vital India has become in the international market.

DOI: 10.4018/978-1-7998-7568-0.ch015

Currently, GTAP is being used to analyze these agreements in a research and policy setup. GTAP is essentially a powerful Computable General Equilibrium (CGE) model. It is a very transparent, powerful tool that can solve very particular issues of impact on ToT, the balance of trade, and other related factors. Therefore, along with a brief methodology, we will focus mainly on its application in the context of the problem defined by us and use the results for the trade analysis, conclusion, and results.

This work can help to form a policy framework for India to negotiate with these economic groups and make the necessary setup for differentiated products to derive the most out of India liberalizing with them.

LITERATURE REVIEW

The paper "Economic Potential of an India-US Free Trade Agreement" by Emiko Fukase and Will Martin, published in the Journal of Economic Integration studies the impact of integration, as we look forward in this paper (Fukase & Martin, 2016). However, we take a step forward and look at the potential at each product level rather than aggregate. The paper by Fukase and Martin explores the economic implication of a potential free trade agreement between India and the United States and we extend this over integration with different economic groups.

The seminal paper "Global Trade Analysis: Modeling and Applications" by Hertel gives us a thorough understanding of the GTAP model and the criticalities needed to be kept in mind while performing the analysis and interpretation of results.

Cirera et al. (2013) have analyzed the effect of tariff reduction in developing countries. They argue that the impact is country and policy specific. They observed that employment is likely to suffer in the short-run post-liberalization and is consistent with the existent theory that winners and losers post the trade policy reform.

Also, Hoque (2005) analyzed the impact of tariff reduction in Bangladesh using a CGE model. He found out that reduction in all tariffs expands the gross domestic product and employment, that is, they have a short-run positive effect on growth.

This paper adopts the CGE approach given by Hertel (1996) and uses the GTAP model to simulate scenarios.

DATA AND METHODOLOGY

This paper refers to the GTAP 10 database for the data and performing the simulation scenarios. It considers the following scenarios for setting up the liberalization conditions between India and the various economic groups:

1. CASE1: 10% reduction in tariff by India, nothing by groups in consideration
2. CASE 2:10% reduction in tariffs by both India and the group countries
3. CASE 3: Both India and group countries reducing tariffs to 0%

For each of the scenarios above, the paper discusses the impact on:

1. Prices

2. Balance of Trade
3. Welfare related terms like TOT, EV, etc.
4. Goods with maximum benefits for both India and group countries

The paper covers the following economic groups for which the aforementioned cases have been considered:

1. MERCOSUR: Argentina, Brazil, Paraguay, and Uruguay
2. BIMSTEC: Bangladesh, Bhutan (NA), India, Myanmar, Nepal, Sri Lanka, Thailand
3. GCC: Bahrain, Kuwait, Oman, Qatar, Saudi Arabia, and the United Arab Emirates
4. Mekong-Ganga: India, Thailand, Myanmar, Cambodia, Laos, and Vietnam
5. RCEP: Brunei, Cambodia, Indonesia, Laos, Malaysia, Myanmar, Philippines, Singapore, Thailand, Vietnam, China, Japan, South Korea, Australia, and New Zealand

For each of these groups, the paper considers only the member states and ignores the observer or non-member states. The paper also looks at the product aggregates to provide a meaningful picture: Grains and Crops, Livestock and Meat Products, Mining and Extraction, Processed Food, Textiles and Clothing, Light Manufacturing, Heavy Manufacturing, Utilities and Construction, Transport and Communication and Other Services.

For solving the CGE model, this paper relies on the Gragg's method with extrapolation and does not follow Johansen's method. By default, we use Gragg's method while solving the GTAP model, with extrapolation. It solves the model several times, with every next iteration having thinner grid. We extrapolate using Gragg 2, 4, 6 steps results in 3 solutions at 2-4-6 steps. This paper uses this method consistently for all the scenarios.

The GTAP model is a multiregional, multisector, CGE (Computable General Equilibrium) model, which assumes perfect competition & constant returns to scale. It uses a standard structure as given in Hertel (1996) and inherently solves non-linear model by performing simulations using GEMPACK. The basic policy shock of tariff reduction using this model is solved from the standard equations in the model.

Considering reduction of bilateral tariff on imports of good *i* from country *r* into *s*. This is similar to the policy shock variable given in the RunGTAP software as *tms(i,r,s)*. This reduction in tariffs lowers the market price of the tradable commodity *i* sourced from country *r* to *s* via the price linkage equation given as:

$$pms(i,r,s) = tm(i,s) + tms(i,r,s) + pcif(i,r,s) \quad (1)$$

where, *pms(I,r,s)* is the market price by source of the tradeable commodity *i* imported from source *r* to destination *s, tm(i,s)* is the power of the variable import tax on imports of the tradeable commodity *i* in the region *s, tms(i,r,s)* is the power of the tax on imports of the tradeable commodity *i* from source *r* to destination *s* and *pcif(i,r,s)*is the world *(cif)* price of the tradable commodity *i* imported from source *r* to destination *s* after including the transport margin.

Now, post this tariff reduction, the domestic users can immediately substitute away from the competing imports according to the equation:

$$qxs(i,r,s) = qim(i,s) - \sigma_M(i)*[pms(i,r,s) - pim(i,s)] \tag{2}$$

where *qxs(i,r,s)* is the quantity of exports of tradeable commodity *i* from source *r* to destination *s*, *qim(i,s)* is the quantity of aggregate imports of tradeable commodity *i* demanded by region *r* using the market prices as the weights, σ_M is the coefficient of substitution and *pim(i,s)* is the market price of the aggregated imports of tradeable commodity *i* in the region *s*.

Also, the composite prices of the imports facing sector *j* fall according to the equation:

$$pim(i,s) = \sum_{k \in REG} MSHRS(i,k,s)*pms(i,k,s) \tag{3}$$

where *MSHRS(i,k,s)* is the market share of source *k* in the aggregate imports of the tradeable commodity *i* in the region *s* computed at market prices; and

$$pfm(i,j,r) = tfm(i,j,r) + pim(i,r) \tag{4}$$

where *pfm(i,j,r)* is the demand price of imported tradeable commodity *i* for firms in sector *j* of region *r*, *tfm(i,j,r)* is the power of the tax on imported tradeable commodity *i* demanded by firms in sector *j* of region *r*.

This fall in composite price then increases the aggregate demand of the imports via the equation:

$$qfm(i,j,s) = qf(i,j,s) - \sigma_D(i)*[pfm(i,j,s) - pf(i,j,s)] \tag{5}$$

where *qfm(i,j,s)* is the quantity of the imported tradeable commodity *i* demanded by firms in sector *j* of region *s*, *qf(i,j,s)* is the quantity of composite tradeable commodity *i* demanded by firms in sector *j* of region *s*, and *pf(i,j,s)* is the demand price of composite tradeable commodity *i* for firms in sector *j* of region *s*.

These cheaper imports bring down the composite price of the intermediaries through equation:

$$pf(i,j,r) = FMSHR(i,j,r)*pfm(i,j,r) + [1 - FMSHR(i,j,r)]*pfd(i,j,r) \tag{6}$$

where, *FMSHR(i,j,r)* is the share of the imports in the composite for tradeable commodity *i* used by firms in sector *j* of region at agents' prices, and *pfd(i,j,r)* is the demand price of the domestic tradeable commodity *i* for firms in sector *j* of region *r*.

The lowering of composite price causes excess profit at current prices via the accounting relationship:

$$\begin{aligned} VOA(j,r)*ps(j,r) &= \sum_{i \in ENDW} VFA(i,j,r)*pfe(i,j,r) \\ &+ \sum_{i \in TRAD} VFA(i,j,r)*pf(i,j,r) + VOA(j,r)*profitslack(j,r) \end{aligned} \tag{7}$$

where *VOA(j,r)* is the value of nonsavings commodity *i* output or supplied in region *r* evaluated at the agents' prices, *ps(j,r)* is the supply price of the nonsavings commodity *i* in region *r*, *VFA(i,j,r)* is the value of purchases of demanded commodity *i* by firms in sector *j* of region *r* evaluated at agents' prices, *pfe(i,j,r)* is the demand price of endowment commodity *i* for firms in sector *j* of region *r*, and *profitslack(j,r)* is the exogenous slack variable in the zero-profits equation.

This, in turn, leads to an expansion in outputs which further generates an expansion effect via equation:

$$qva(j,r)+ava(j,r)=qo(j,r)-ao(j,r) \tag{8}$$

where *qva(j,r)* is the quantity index of value added (land-labor composite) in firms of sector *j* in region *r*, *ava(j,r)* is the value added augmenting technical change in sector *j* of region *r*, *qo(j,r)* is the quantity of non-saving commodity *i* output or supplied in region *r*, and *ao(j,r)* is the output augmenting the technical change in the sector *j* of region *r*.

$$qf(i,j,r)+af(i,f,r)=qo(j,r)-ao(j,r) \tag{9}$$

where *qf(i,j,r)* is the quantity of the composite tradeable commodity *i* demanded by firms in sector *j* in region *r*, and *af(I,j,r)* is the composite intermediate input *i* augmenting technical change in sector *j* of region *r*.

Here, it must be noted that in case of partial equilibrium model where the non-food sector aggregates' activity levels are exogenous to the model, the expansionary effect by the above two equations will be presented only when *j* refers to the food sector.

The expansion effect mentioned above induces an increase in the demand of the primary factors of production through equation:

$$qfe(i,j,r)+afe(i,j,r)=qva(j,r)-\sigma_{VA}(j)*\left[pfe(i,j,r)-afe(i,j,r)-pva(j,r)\right] \tag{10}$$

where *qfe(i,j,r)* is the quantity of endowment commodity *i* demanded by firms in sector *j* of region *r*, and *afe(i,j,r)* is the primary factor *i* augmenting the technical change in sector *j* of region *r*.

In the partial equilibrium model, the labor and capital might be assumed forthcoming perfectly elastic supply from the non-food sectors. Therefore, *pfe(i,j,r)* remains unchanged for *i* = labor, capital. On the other hand, in the general equilibrium model this expansion would generate an excess demand via the mobile endowment market clearing equation which would as a result bid up the prices of these factors and transmitting the shock to other sectors also which employ these factors in the liberalizing region.

Now, for region *r*, which produces the goods for which the tariff *(tms(i,r,s))* has been reduced, the following equation determines the total sales from *r* to *s* because of the response of the agents in region *s* to the tariff shock, as mentioned above also:

$$qxs(i,r,s)=qim(i,s)-\sigma_M(i)*\left[pms(i,r,s)-pim(i,s)\right] \tag{11}$$

The following equation

$$VOM(i,r)*qo(i,r) = VDM(i,r)*qds(i,r) + VST(i,r)*qst(i,r) + \sum_{r \in REG} VXMD(i,r,s)*qxs(i,r,s) + VOM(i,r)*tradslack(i,r) \quad (12)$$

determines the implications for the total output $qo(i,r)$, given that the market clearing equation has been eliminated and $pm(i,r)$ is fixed, as under the partial equilibrium model. Then the expansionary equations as stated in previous page come into play which transmit the expansion effect back into the intermediate demands and also to the region r's factor markets.

Simulation Scenarios

This paper uses the GTAPAgg2 database based on GTAP 10 version. The aggregation data has been chosen from the year 2014. For each of the economic group in consideration, aggregations scheme has been modified. The regions have been mapped from 141 old regions to 3 new regions, namely the economic group in consideration, India, and rest of the world. The sectoral and factor aggregation has been utilized as in the default setup. A total of 5 data base have been created for 5 economic groups post which RunGTAP software has been used to perform simulations.

Figure 1. This shows the version of the database used for the study

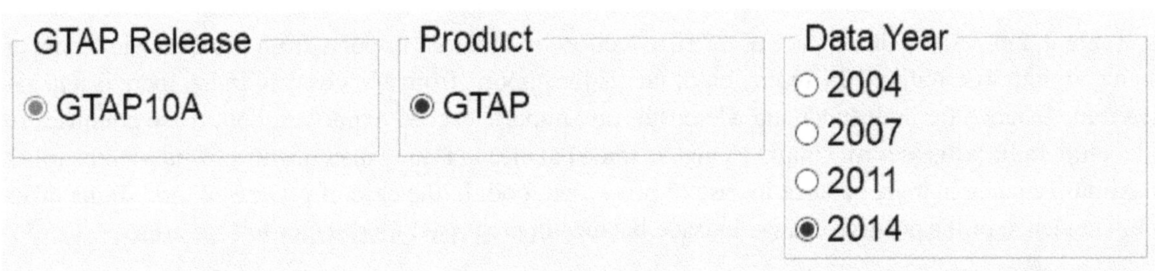

The RunGTAP software takes input as the aggregated zip file, the shocks and closures to solve the non-linear equations using the method specified. The next section discusses some of the findings from this exercise.

RESULTS

Case 1: 10% Reduction of Tariff by India

India and Mercosur

Table 1, below, represents the initial tariff rate imposed by India and nations in Mercosur on the imports from Mercosur and India respectively. India imposes maximum tariff on imports of *grains and crops* from Mercosur and Mercosur, on the other hand, imposes maximum tariffs on imports of *textile and clothing* coming from India. Utilities and Construction, Transport and Communication and other Services are a few sectors that face zero tariff; either being freely allowed to trade or no trade taking place in these sectors.

Table 1. Tariffs imposed by India and Mercosur

Sector	Initial Tariff Rate by India (%)	Initial Tariff Rate by Mercosur (%)
Grains and Crops	33.18	6.70
Livestock and Meat Products	5.95	11.08
Mining and Extraction	0.61	3.88
Processed Food	15.96	10.69
Textiles and Clothing	10.54	24.05
Light Manufacturing	7.55	14.76
Heavy Manufacturing	7.64	4.43
Utilities and Construction	0.00	0.00
Transport and Communication	0.00	0.00
Other Services	0.00	0.00

Table 2 and 3 show the impact of tariff reduction by India on imports from Mercosur in terms of change in imports. With a 10% reduction of tariffs for imports from Mercosur in India, there is a negative trade balance for both India and Mercosur, i.e., imports exceed exports in both these countries in this setup. India witnesses maximum change in trade balance in Heavy manufacturing and Mercosur has maximum change in trade balance in case of processed food. In the case of processed food, India takes 67% incidence of the positive change in trade balance in processed food sector in Mercosur.

Table 2. Change in trade balance (in $ US Mn)

DTBAL	(Sim)
India	-2.78
Mercosur	-58.55
RoW	61.33

Overall, India has negative change trade balance in case of processed food but a positive one in case of Heavy Manufacturing. Table 4 below provides a summary of changes in market prices of factors and commodities. India sees a lowering of prices for almost all the items given except for natural resources. Mercosur, on the other hand, sees a rise in prices of all commodities except natural resources.

The equivalent variation represents the additional income that needs to be given to reach the given level of utility that an individual could have reached if the prices would have changed. The EV for India

Table 3. Change in trade balance by commodity and region (in $ US Mn)

DTBALi	RoW	India	Mercosur
Grains and Crops	13.46	7.33	-20.33
Livestock and Meat Products	14.76	3.83	-17.85
Mining and Extraction	13.52	-4.44	-8
Processed Food	-39.98	-81.8	119.96
Textiles and Clothing	-6.04	11.11	-5.21
Light Manufacturing	19.54	13.89	-32.98
Heavy Manufacturing	16.95	24.91	-42.08
Utilities and Construction	1.95	0.39	-2.34
Transport and Communication	11.61	8.2	-20.35
Other Services	15.56	13.81	-29.37

Table 4. Market price of factors and commodities by regions (% change)

Pm	RoW	India	Mercosur
Land	0.002	-0.0202	0.0111
Unskilled Labor	-0.0005	-0.006	0.0169
Skilled Labor	-0.0005	-0.005	0.0164
Capital	-0.0005	-0.0051	0.0165
Natural Resources	0.0011	0.0126	-0.0429
Grains and Crops	0	-0.0102	0.0141
Livestock and Meat Products	-0.0002	-0.0106	0.014
Mining and Extraction	-0.0001	-0.0017	0.004
Processed Food	-0.0003	-0.0135	0.0142
Textiles and Clothing	-0.0004	-0.0053	0.0135
Light Manufacturing	-0.0004	-0.0046	0.0124
Heavy Manufacturing	-0.0004	-0.0038	0.0105
Utilities and Construction	-0.0004	-0.0046	0.0136
Transport and Communication	-0.0005	-0.0055	0.015
Other Services	-0.0005	-0.005	0.0157

Table 5. Equivalent variation by regions ($ US Mn)

EV	(Sim)
RoW	-32.74
India	-34.42
Mercosur	64.51

is negative, which means that consumers in India are worse off. Mercosur however has a positive EV (Table 5).

Table 6 presents the industry output in the various regions. The metric here is not straightforward with a few sectors experiencing expansion and a few experiencing contraction.

Table 6. Industry output by commodity and regions (% change)

Qo	RoW	India	Mercosur
Grains and Crops	0.0007	-0.0053	0.0014
Livestock and Meat Products	0.0008	0.0023	-0.0088
Mining and Extraction	0.0002	0.0027	-0.0079
Processed Food	-0.0009	-0.037	0.0454
Textiles and Clothing	-0.0005	0.0106	-0.009
Light Manufacturing	0.0001	0.0055	-0.0075
Heavy Manufacturing	0	0.0049	-0.0054
Utilities and Construction	-0.0002	-0.0006	0.0058
Transport and Communication	0	-0.0002	0.0001
Other Services	0	0.0009	-0.0011

The terms of trade in this case, however, show that India has become worse off, with a negative change. Mercosur has on the other hand observed improved terms of trade.

Table 7. Terms of trade by region

tot	(Sim)	Pre	Post	Ch/%Ch
RoW	-0.0001	1.0000	1.0000	0.0000
India	-0.0051	1.0000	0.9999	-0.0001
Mercosur	0.0111	1.0000	1.0001	0.0001

The GDP has also decreased for India and, on the contrary, has made Mercosur better off.

Table 8. Change in value of GDP (% change)

vgdp	(Sim)
RoW	-0.0005
India	-0.0088
Mercosur	0.0157

We can conclude that India reducing tariffs by 10% makes India worse off in terms of terms of trade, GDP and EV. Thus, this definitely isn't a policy decision that India should look forward too.

Table 9. Tariffs imposed by India and BIMSTEC

Sector	Initial Tariff Rate by India (%)	Initial Tariff Rate by BIMSTEC (%)
Grains and Crops	10.94	7.87
Livestock and Meat Products	11.47	41.72
Mining and Extraction	14.03	10.52
Processed Food	28.36	14.81
Textiles and Clothing	4.95	9.46
Light Manufacturing	7.12	6.50
Heavy Manufacturing	5.83	7.18
Utilities and Construction	0.00	0.00
Transport and Communication	0.00	0.00
Other Services	0.00	0.00

Table 10. Change in trade balance (in $ US Mn)

DTBAL	(Sim)
RoW	61.87
BIMSTEC	-37.54
India	-24.33

Table 11. Change in trade balance by commodity and region (in $ US Mn)

DTBALi	RoW	BIMSTEC	India
Grains and Crops	1.09	4.83	-6.44
Livestock and Meat Products	3.08	-5.32	2.31
Mining and Extraction	-7.33	0.71	5.46
Processed Food	-3.07	18.3	-16.84
Textiles and Clothing	25.51	-27.9	2.28
Light Manufacturing	-2.83	12.35	-10.4
Heavy Manufacturing	-5.38	12.73	-12.8
Utilities and Construction	1.52	-1.76	0.24
Transport and Communication	34.09	-29.74	5.31
Other Services	15.17	-21.73	6.56

Table 12. Market price of factors and commodities by regions (% change)

Pm	RoW	BIMSTEC	India
Land	0.0005	0.0432	-0.015
Unskilled Labor	-0.0002	0.0273	-0.0022
Skilled Labor	-0.0002	0.0266	-0.0016
Capital	-0.0002	0.0289	-0.002
Natural Resources	-0.0017	0.141	0.0006
Grains and Crops	-0.0001	0.0293	-0.007
Livestock and Meat Products	-0.0001	0.0249	-0.0062
Mining and Extraction	-0.0005	0.0457	-0.0022
Processed Food	-0.0001	0.022	-0.0071
Textiles and Clothing	-0.0001	0.018	-0.0047
Light Manufacturing	-0.0002	0.0143	-0.0052
Heavy Manufacturing	-0.0002	0.0141	-0.0044
Utilities and Construction	-0.0002	0.0196	-0.0032
Transport and Communication	-0.0002	0.024	-0.0032
Other Services	-0.0002	0.0249	-0.0022

Table 13. Equivalent variation by regions ($ US Mn)

EV	(Sim)
RoW	-51.18
BIMSTEC	74.95
India	-15.43

Table 14. Industry output by commodity and regions (% change)

Qo	RoW	BIMSTEC	India
Grains and Crops	0.0002	0.0061	-0.0046
Livestock and Meat Products	0.0002	-0.0185	0.0019
Mining and Extraction	-0.0002	0.0157	0.0004
Processed Food	0	0.0265	-0.0087
Textiles and Clothing	0.0018	-0.0673	0.0039
Light Manufacturing	-0.0001	0.0151	-0.0001
Heavy Manufacturing	-0.0001	0.0092	0.0001
Utilities and Construction	-0.0002	0.0127	0.0021
Transport and Communication	0.0001	-0.0027	0.0004
Other Services	0	-0.0022	-0.0001

India and BIMSTEC

In the case of India and BIMSTEC, India levies most tariffs on processed food from BIMSTEC nations and experiences most tariffs on livestock and meat products going to these nations. Table 9 provides a peek into the base tariffs in the two regions under consideration. The impact of tariff reduction by India is that both India and BIMSTEC nations incur a negative change in trade balance (see Table 10).

The most negative change on trade balance has been observed in case of processed food in the case of India and transportation and communication in case of BIMSTEC nations. Table 11 summarizes the change in prices in case of tariff reduction.

Table 15. Terms of trade by region

tot	(Sim)	Pre	Post	Ch/%Ch
RoW	-0.0002	1.0000	1.0000	0.0000
BIMSTEC	0.0182	1.0000	1.0002	0.0002
India	-0.0042	1.0000	1.0000	0.0000

Table 16. Change in value of GDP (% change)

Vgdp	(Sim)
RoW	-0.0002
BIMSTEC	0.03
India	-0.0056

Table 17. Tariffs imposed by India and GCC

Sector	Initial Tariff Rate by India (%)	Initial Tariff Rate by GCC (%)
Grains and Crops	29.72	0.61
Livestock and Meat Products	2.04	3.26
Mining and Extraction	1.42	1.89
Processed Food	9.72	18.16
Textiles and Clothing	11.95	5.00
Light Manufacturing	10.00	4.85
Heavy Manufacturing	6.15	3.37
Utilities and Construction	0.00	0.00
Transport and Communication	0.00	0.00
Other Services	0.00	0.00

Table 13 shows that EV is negative in the case of India, showing an overall reduction in consumer welfare. BIMSTEC nations, on other hand, seem to reap the benefits of these lowered prices because of tariff reduction.

The terms of trade, again, have worsened here for India. Also, there is a decline in the GDP. Thus, this scenario will also hurt the Indian Economy (Table 15 & 16).

India and GCC

Table 17 shows the initial AV tax/tariff. In India, the most significant tariff is levied on Grains and Crops and processed food in case of Gulf countries (GCC).

Table 18. Change in trade balance (in $ US Mn)

DTBAL	(Sim)
RoW	151.6793
India	-155.5003
GCC	3.8211

The *grains and crops* from GCC countries face the maximum tariff from India and *processed food* from India faces maximum tariff in GCC countries.

This scenario also leads to a negative change in the trade balance in India and positive in case of the GCC countries.

Table 19 shows that the positive change in trade balance for the GCC countries is concentrated in the *Heavy Manufacturing* countries. On the other hand, India observes a negative change in trade balance in the case of *mining and extraction* and also in *heavy manufacturing* sectors.

Table 19. Change in trade balance by commodities and regions ($ US Mn)

DTBALi	RoW	India	GCC
Grains and Crops	2.69	-0.96	-2.07
Livestock and Meat Products	6.33	-0.51	-5.89
Mining and Extraction	129.07	-64.84	-64.45
Processed Food	11.84	-4.15	-8.08
Textiles and Clothing	8.11	4.46	-12.84
Light Manufacturing	3.93	-0.14	-5.24
Heavy Manufacturing	-148.38	-71.68	210.26
Utilities and Construction	4.77	0.12	-4.89
Transport and Communication	61.98	-2.34	-47.08
Other Services	71.34	-15.45	-55.89

Table 20. Market price of factors and commodities by regions (% change)

Pm	RoW	India	GCC
Land	-0.0009	-0.0055	-0.0485
Unskilled Labor	-0.0015	0.0095	0.0496
Skilled Labor	-0.0014	0.0069	0.0404
Capital	-0.0014	0.0063	0.0484
Natural Resources	0.0199	-0.1024	-0.0417
Grains and Crops	-0.001	-0.0007	0.0345
Livestock and Meat Products	-0.0011	0.0013	0.0303
Mining and Extraction	0.0032	-0.0184	0.0197
Processed Food	-0.0009	-0.0006	0.03
Textiles and Clothing	-0.001	-0.0031	0.0408
Light Manufacturing	-0.0007	-0.0122	0.037
Heavy Manufacturing	0.0002	-0.0175	0.0342
Utilities and Construction	-0.0006	-0.0045	0.0312
Transport and Communication	-0.0011	0.0011	0.0378
Other Services	-0.0012	0.0046	0.0441

Table 21. Equivalent variation by regions ($ US Mn)

EV	(Sim)
RoW	-66.35
India	-43.94
GCC	142.96

Table 22. Industry output by commodity and regions (% change)

Qo	RoW	India	GCC
Grains and Crops	0.0001	-0.003	-0.0267
Livestock and Meat Products	0.0002	-0.003	-0.0454
Mining and Extraction	0.0029	-0.0165	-0.0123
Processed Food	0.0002	-0.0043	-0.0236
Textiles and Clothing	0.0002	0.0038	-0.0947
Light Manufacturing	-0.0005	0.0147	0.0278
Heavy Manufacturing	-0.0012	0.0047	0.0439
Utilities and Construction	-0.0007	0.016	0.0216
Transport and Communication	0.0001	0.0005	-0.0122
Other Services	0.0001	-0.0074	-0.0161

Table 23. Terms of trade by region

tot	(Sim)	Pre	Post	Ch/%Ch
RoW	-0.0007	1.0000	1.0000	0.0000
India	-0.0116	1.0000	0.9999	-0.0001
GCC	0.0234	1.0000	1.0002	0.0002

Table 24. Change in value of GDP (% change)

vgdp	(Sim)
RoW	-0.001
India	-0.0071
GCC	0.0371

The market prices of factors of production increase in India, except for land. However, the average market prices of commodities decline in India. GCC countries, on the other hand, see an increase in the prices of commodities in all the sectors.

Table 21 shows that EV is negative in the case of India, showing an overall reduction in consumer welfare, which has been observed in the previous two cases as well.

Table 25. Tariffs imposed by India and Mekong-Ganga

Sector	Initial Tariff Rate by India (%)	Initial Tariff Rate by Mekong-Ganga (%)
Grains and Crops	24.05	6.50
Livestock and Meat Products	13.36	17.31
Mining and Extraction	9.27	5.53
Processed Food	50.23	11.15
Textiles and Clothing	11.31	5.21
Light Manufacturing	8.51	6.70
Heavy Manufacturing	5.84	2.67
Utilities and Construction	0.00	0.00
Transport and Communication	0.00	0.00
Other Services	0.00	0.00

Table 26. Change in trade balance (in $ US Mn)

DTBAL	(Sim)
RoW	77.1703
Mekong	-32.2791
India	-44.8912

Table 27. Change in trade balance by commodities and regions ($ US Mn)

DTBALi	RoW	Mekong	India
Grains and Crops	-4.75	37.12	-34.62
Livestock and Meat Products	4.42	-11.94	7.31
Mining and Extraction	-12.94	5.89	1.70
Processed Food	1.27	3.86	-5.76
Textiles and Clothing	6.97	-13.12	5.85
Light Manufacturing	12.85	3.41	-16.65
Heavy Manufacturing	1.81	7.15	-14.18
Utilities and Construction	1.74	-2.01	0.27
Transport and Communication	41.50	-33.52	6.38
Other Services	24.32	-29.12	4.81

Table 28. Market price of factors and commodities by regions (% change)

Pm	RoW	Mekong	India
Land	0.0006	0.1145	-0.0555
Unskilled Labor	-0.0002	0.0341	-0.0026
Skilled Labor	-0.0002	0.0291	-0.0003
Capital	-0.0002	0.0293	-0.0011
Natural Resources	-0.0021	0.0781	-0.007
Grains and Crops	-0.0001	0.0593	-0.0208
Livestock and Meat Products	-0.0001	0.035	-0.0167
Mining and Extraction	-0.0006	0.0355	-0.0039
Processed Food	0	0.0275	-0.0152
Textiles and Clothing	-0.0001	0.0139	-0.0072
Light Manufacturing	-0.0002	0.0148	-0.007
Heavy Manufacturing	-0.0002	0.0141	-0.0063
Utilities and Construction	-0.0002	0.0189	-0.004
Transport and Communication	-0.0002	0.0245	-0.0039
Other Services	-0.0002	0.0264	-0.0016

Table 29. Equivalent variation by regions ($ US Mn)

EV	(Sim)
RoW	-69.92
Mekong	106.56
India	6.55

Table 30. Industry output by commodity and regions (% change)

Qo	RoW	Mekong	India
Grains and Crops	0.0002	0.025	-0.0197
Livestock and Meat Products	0.0003	-0.034	0.0091
Mining and Extraction	-0.0003	0.0067	-0.0008
Processed Food	0.0001	-0.003	-0.0023
Textiles and Clothing	0.0005	-0.046	0.0077
Light Manufacturing	0.0001	0.0007	-0.0001
Heavy Manufacturing	0	0.004	0.0019
Utilities and Construction	-0.0003	0.0174	0.0039
Transport and Communication	0.0001	-0.0078	0.0021
Other Services	0	-0.0031	-0.0001

Overall, this scenario also reflects that unilateral deviation from protection hurts India in terms of ToT, EV and trade balance.

India and Mekong-Ganga

Table 25 shows the initial tariffs faced by imports sourced at India and Mekong-Ganga, destined to Mekong-Ganga and India respectively. *Processed food* faces the most tariffs in India and *livestock and meat products* face maximum tariffs in the case of Mekong-Ganga nations.

Post the unilateral reduction of tariffs by India, both Mekong-Ganga and India face a negative change in the trade balance. This shows that none of the partners in this liberalization process is benefitting from it in terms of trade balance.

Table 27 shows that the most of the negative change in trade balance is concentrated in grains and crops in the case of India and transportation & communication in the case of Mekong-Ganga nations.

Table 31. Terms of trade by region

tot	(Sim)	Pre	Post	Ch/%Ch
RoW	-0.0003	1.0000	1.0000	0.0000
Mekong	0.0184	1.0000	1.0002	0.0002
India	-0.0065	1.0000	0.9999	-0.0001

Table 32. Change in value of GDP (% change)

vgdp	(Sim)
RoW	-0.0002
Mekong	0.0358
India	-0.0073

Table 28 finds very striking observation that all the factors and commodities in India see a decline in their market prices. On the other hand, an increase in market prices has been observed in the case of Mekong-Ganga nations.

Table 33. Tariff imposed by India and RCEP

Sector	Initial Tariff Rate by India (%)	Initial Tariff Rate by RCEP (%)
Grains and Crops	26.50	15.04
Livestock and Meat Products	15.50	14.29
Mining and Extraction	3.25	0.58
Processed Food	72.63	9.36
Textiles and Clothing	12.92	4.02
Light Manufacturing	9.14	5.30
Heavy Manufacturing	5.60	1.62
Utilities and Construction	0.00	0.00
Transport and Communication	0.00	0.00
Other Services	0.00	0.00

Table 34. Change in trade balance (in $ US Mn)

DTBAL	(Sim)
RCEP	-104.3178
RoW	476.2012
India	-371.8835

Table 35. Change in trade balance by commodities and regions ($ US Mn)

DTBALi	RCEP	RoW	India
Grains and Crops	24.25	-59.79	23.43
Livestock and Meat Products	-46.12	15.17	30.54
Mining and Extraction	57.13	-104.08	-2.33
Processed Food	690.66	-349.43	-365.80
Textiles and Clothing	-87.33	61.42	17.99
Light Manufacturing	-272.19	242.88	20.53
Heavy Manufacturing	11.26	234.47	-296.14
Utilities and Construction	-35.42	30.88	4.55
Transport and Communication	-196.77	257.53	92.73
Other Services	-249.78	147.16	102.61

In terms of equivalent variation, both India and Mekong-Ganga have been benefitted by this scenario, with Mekong-Ganga gaining significantly. The industry output in India see a significant impact only in the case of grains and crops, with a 0.02% decrease.

Table 31 and 32 show that India loses in terms of terms of trade and also observes a decrease in GDP. Mekong-Ganga, on the other hand, observes a gain in terms of both ToT and GDP. This, as in the previous three cases, doesn't show a very promising policy decision for India.

India and RCEP

India and RCEP see tariffs being imposed in lot of sectors. Exports from RCEP from *processed food* sector faces the maximum tariffs in India (72.6%). On the other hand, exports from India face relatively low tariffs in RCEP countries.

Post 10% reduction in tariffs by India, both RCEP and India see a negative change in the trade balance, which means that countries other than RCEP are able to benefit from this scenario because of diversion of trade.

Table 36. Market price of factors and commodities by regions (% change)

Pm	RCEP	RoW	India
Land	0.0525	-0.024	-0.3298
Unskilled Labor	0.0176	-0.0045	-0.046
Skilled Labor	0.0167	-0.0042	-0.0227
Capital	0.017	-0.0044	-0.0363
Natural Resources	0.0216	-0.0126	0.0107
Grains and Crops	0.0241	-0.0072	-0.145
Livestock and Meat Products	0.0186	-0.0054	-0.1429
Mining and Extraction	0.0162	-0.006	-0.0412
Processed Food	0.0155	-0.0048	-0.1786
Textiles and Clothing	0.0142	-0.0036	-0.0874
Light Manufacturing	0.0135	-0.0035	-0.0898
Heavy Manufacturing	0.0123	-0.0038	-0.0806
Utilities and Construction	0.014	-0.004	-0.0579
Transport and Communication	0.0152	-0.0041	-0.06
Other Services	0.0157	-0.0042	-0.038

Table 37. Equivalent variation by regions ($ US Mn)

EV	(Sim)
RCEP	845.07
RoW	-310.34
India	225.17

As expected, the negative change in trade balance is concentrated in *processed food* and *heavy manufacturing* in India whereas in the case of RCEP it is in the *light manufacturing* and *transportation* sector that most of the negative change is concentrated.

Table 38. Industry output by commodity and regions (% change)

Qo	RCEP	RoW	India
Grains and Crops	0.0148	-0.0082	-0.0963
Livestock and Meat Products	-0.0046	-0.0007	0.0243
Mining and Extraction	0.0006	-0.0011	0.0076
Processed Food	0.0459	-0118	-0.4542
Textiles and Clothing	-0.0182	0.0086	0.0405
Light Manufacturing	-0.009	0.0035	0.0588
Heavy Manufacturing	-0.0031	0.0026	0.0039
Utilities and Construction	0.0035	-0.0021	0.0367
Transport and Communication	-0.0019	0.0009	0.0117
Other Services	-0.0008	0.0001	0.0113

Table 39. Terms of trade by region

tot	(Sim)	Pre	Post	Ch/%Ch
RCEP	0.0113	1.0000	1.0001	0.0001
RoW	-0.0023	1.0000	1.0000	0.0000
India	-0.0794	1.0000	0.9992	-0.0008

Table 40. Change in value of GDP (% change)

vgdp	(Sim)
RCEP	0.0177
RoW	-0.0046
India	-0.0902

Table 41. Change in trade balance (in $ US Mn)

DTBAL	(Sim)
RoW	131.2205
India	-61.5622
Mercosur	-69.6583

Table 42. Change in trade balance by commodities and regions ($ US Mn)

DTBALi	RoW	India	Mercosur
Grains and Crops	17.57	-3.94	-13.16
Livestock and Meat Products	12.77	-1.20	-11.07
Mining and Extraction	38.48	-40.99	2.15
Processed Food	-40.68	-90.76	129.24
Textiles and Clothing	-25.66	69.23	-45.01
Light Manufacturing	28.41	10.07	-39.05
Heavy Manufacturing	3.51	59.06	-65.13
Utilities and Construction	2.50	-1.16	-1.33
Transport and Communication	36.85	-20.00	-10.66
Other Services	57.49	-41.86	-15.64

Table 43. Market price of factors and commodities by regions (% change)

Pm	RoW	India	Mercosur
Land	0.0017	-0.0195	0.0265
Unskilled Labor	-0.0009	0.0163	0.0099
Skilled Labor	-0.0009	0.0142	0.0082
Capital	-0.0009	0.0153	0.0096
Natural Resources	0.0031	-0.0318	-0.0167
Grains and Crops	-0.0004	0.0029	0.0095
Livestock and Meat Products	-0.0005	0.0033	0.0085
Mining and Extraction	0	0.0046	0.0027
Processed Food	-0.0006	0.0015	0.0076
Textiles and Clothing	-0.0007	0.0105	-0.005
Light Manufacturing	-0.0007	0.0082	0.0042
Heavy Manufacturing	-0.0006	0.0061	0.0036
Utilities and Construction	-0.0007	0.0106	0.0066
Transport and Communication	-0.0008	0.0122	0.0077
Other Services	-0.0008	0.0139	0.0083

Table 44. Equivalent variation by regions ($ US Mn)

EV	(Sim)
RoW	-95.95
India	66.64
Mercosur	45.81

In terms of EV, India & RCEP both are benefitted from this liberalization. However, here also non-deviant countries benefit the most.

Table 39 and 40 show more welfare impacts of this liberalization. Here, India loses significantly in terms of trade and also observes a significant decline in the GDP. These tables also show that India loses in this type of policy decision.

CASE 2: 10% Reduction of Tariff by India and Economic Group

India and MERCOSUR

Tables 41 to 47 reflect the impact of 10% tariff reduction by both India and Mercosur nations.

Both India and Mercosur observe the maximum change in trade balance of *processed food* in opposite way. India also observes a positive change in the case of *textiles and clothing.*

Table 45. Industry output by commodity and regions (% change)

Qo	RoW	India	Mercosur
Grains and Crops	0.0008	-0.0103	0.0086
Livestock and Meat Products	0.0005	-0.001	-0.0025
Mining and Extraction	0.0005	-0.0071	-0.0035
Processed Food	-0.001	-0.0417	0.0504
Textiles and Clothing	-0.0015	0.0588	-0.0834
Light Manufacturing	0	0.0073	-0.0086
Heavy Manufacturing	-0.0002	0.0135	-0.0073
Utilities and Construction	-0.0005	0.0074	0.0073
Transport and Communication	0	0.0008	0.0007
Other Services	0.0001	-0.0058	-0.0008

Table 46. Terms of trade by region

tot	(Sim)	Pre	Post	Ch/%Ch
RoW	-0.0003	1.0000	1.0000	0.0000
India	0.0091	1.0000	1.0001	0.0001
Mercosur	0.0058	1.0000	1.0001	0.0001

Table 47. Change in value of GDP (% change)

vgdp	(Sim)
RoW	-0.0008
India	0.0108
Mercosur	0.0073

Table 48. Change in trade balance (in $ US Mn)

DTBAL	(Sim)
RoW	321.1311
BIMSTEC	-156.066
India	-165.0651

Table 49. Change in trade balance by commodities and regions ($ US Mn)

DTBALi	RoW	India	BIMSTEC
Grains and Crops	11.91	-23.72	9.01
Livestock and Meat Products	-32.66	-7.07	41.84
Mining and Extraction	66.15	-2.53	-70.62
Processed Food	-17.20	8.67	5.25
Textiles and Clothing	-17.59	-16.49	32.74
Light Manufacturing	-45.22	3.69	41.73
Heavy Manufacturing	30.78	-42.09	-4.39
Utilities and Construction	6.58	-2.48	-4.10
Transport and Communication	143.93	-42.17	-73.92
Other Services	174.46	-31.86	-142.59

Table 50. Market price of factors and commodities by regions (% change)

Pm	RoW	India	BIMSTEC
Land	-0.0021	-0.0758	0.1168
Unskilled Labor	-0.0024	0.047	0.062
Skilled Labor	-0.0022	0.0485	0.0486
Capital	-0.0023	0.0537	0.0524
Natural Resources	0.0038	0.101	-0.0973
Grains and Crops	-0.002	0.0039	0.0658
Livestock and Meat Products	-0.0021	-0.0112	0.0753
Mining and Extraction	-0.0008	0.0477	0.0201
Processed Food	-0.0018	0.0036	0.0474
Textiles and Clothing	-0.0018	-0.006	0.0409
Light Manufacturing	-0.0019	-0.008	0.0305
Heavy Manufacturing	-0.0017	0.0073	0.0232
Utilities and Construction	-0.002	0.0222	0.039
Transport and Communication	-0.0021	0.0334	0.0465
Other Services	-0.0021	0.0383	0.0486

Table 43 shows that the prices of almost all factors and commodities increase in this scenario, with land and natural resources becoming cheaper.

Combining results from Tables 44, 46 and 47, we see that bilateral liberalization, with tariffs being reduced by both the partners, benefit both in terms of EV, ToT and change in GDP. This shows that, if both partners open up, there are more chances of liberalization being mutually beneficial.

India and BIMSTEC

Tables 41 to 47 reflect the impact of 10% tariff reduction by both India and BIMSTEC nations.

The most important change in trade balance is concentrated in *mining* in the case of BIMSTEC nations and *heavy industries* and *transport* in the case of India.

Table 51. Equivalent Variation by regions ($ US Mn)

EV	(Sim)
RoW	-274.70
BIMSTEC	90.99
India	220.12

Table 52. Terms of trade by region

tot	(Sim)	Pre	Post	Ch/%Ch
RoW	-0.0009	1.0000	1.0000	0.0000
BIMSTEC	0.0064	1.0000	1.0001	0.0001
India	0.0386	1.0000	1.0004	0.0004

Table 53. Change in value of GDP (% change)

vgdp	(Sim)
RoW	-0.0022
BIMSTEC	0.0225
India	0.0502

Table 54. Change in trade balance (in $ US Mn)

DTBAL	(Sim)
RoW	345.7947
India	-288.1233
GCC	-57.6713

Table 55. Change in trade balance by commodities and regions ($ US Mn)

DTBALi	RoW	India	GCC
Grains and Crops	28.39	-28.49	0.68
Livestock and Meat Products	9.37	-1.65	-7.72
Mining and Extraction	185.60	-149.96	-38.81
Processed Food	-14.14	41.93	-28.82
Textiles and Clothing	43.00	-17.93	-24.62
Light Manufacturing	-69.26	118.25	-49.02
Heavy Manufacturing	-154.82	-35.92	175.44
Utilities and Construction	7.09	-3.52	-3.57
Transport and Communication	122.63	-68.32	-35.80
Other Services	187.93	-142.50	-45.43

Table 56. Market price of factors and commodities by regions (% change)

Pm	RoW	India	GCC
Land	0.0008	0.0266	-0.0555
Unskilled Labor	-0.003	0.0617	0.0404
Skilled Labor	-0.0028	0.0501	0.0335
Capital	-0.0028	0.0529	0.042
Natural Resources	0.0237	-0.1831	-0.0213
Grains and Crops	-0.0017	0.0381	0.0236
Livestock and Meat Products	-0.0021	0.0436	0.0146
Mining and Extraction	0.003	0.0005	0.0192
Processed Food	-0.002	0.0373	0.0132
Textiles and Clothing	-0.002	0.0338	0.0296
Light Manufacturing	-0.0018	0.0174	0.0263
Heavy Manufacturing	-0.0008	0.0054	0.0279
Utilities and Construction	-0.0018	0.0307	0.0208
Transport and Communication	-0.0024	0.042	0.0277
Other Services	-0.0025	0.0478	0.0364

Table 57. Equivalent Variation by regions ($ US Mn)

EV	(Sim)
RoW	-287.84
India	165.49
GCC	158.10

Table 51 to 53 reflect the welfare impact of the tariff reduction. Overall, both BIMSTEC nations and India benefit from this setup. Moreover, the impact is higher than that of India & Mercosur aligning together.

India and GCC

Tables 54 to 60 reflect the impact of 10% tariff reduction by both India and GCC countries. The most important change in trade balance is concentrated in *mining* in case of India and *heavy industries* in case of GCC nations.

Table 57 represents the EV as a result of liberalization. Both India and GCC countries see a positive EV, that is, consumer becoming better off with new prices.

Combining observations in Tables 57, 59 and 60, we find that both India and GCC countries benefit from the trade being liberalized in terms of EV, ToT and also the change in GDP.

Table 58. Industry output by commodity and regions (% change)

Qo	RoW	India	GCC
Grains and Crops	0.0014	-0.0097	-0.0184
Livestock and Meat Products	0.0002	0.0002	-0.0663
Mining and Extraction	0.0037	-0.0359	-0.0086
Processed Food	-0.0005	0.0273	-0.0854
Textiles and Clothing	0.003	-0.0213	-0.1657
Light Manufacturing	-0.0016	0.0677	0.0006
Heavy Manufacturing	-0.0016	0.023	0.0417
Utilities and Construction	-0.0015	0.0331	0.0269
Transport and Communication	0.0001	0.0014	-0.0058
Other Services	0.0003	-0.0235	-0.0161

Table 59. Terms of trade by region

tot	(Sim)	Pre	Post	Ch/%Ch
RoW	-0.0013	1.0000	1.0000	0.0000
India	0.0224	1.0000	1.0002	0.0002
GCC	0.0201	1.0000	1.0002	0.0002

Table 60. Change in value of GDP (% change)

vgdp	(Sim)
RoW	-0.0024
India	0.0379
GCC	0.0253

Table 61. Change in trade balance (in $ US Mn)

DTBAL	(Sim)
RoW	147.8334
Mekong	-74.7149
India	-73.1186

Table 62. Change in trade balance by commodities and regions ($ US Mn)

DTBALi	RoW	Mekong	India
Grains and Crops	7.59	59.11	-67.93
Livestock and Meat Products	-75.46	-87.75	172.47
Mining and Extraction	-16.28	-0.75	11.34
Processed Food	-44.57	5.90	37.78
Textiles and Clothing	30.98	-6.96	-24.24
Light Manufacturing	-11.32	28.55	-18.52
Heavy Manufacturing	107.88	-11.86	-101.88
Utilities and Construction	3.75	-2.24	-1.50
Transport and Communication	63.97	-29.90	-28.16
Other Services	81.29	-28.81	-52.48

Table 63. Market price of factors and commodities by regions (% change)

Pm	RoW	Mekong	India
Land	-0.0042	-0.0044	0.1437
Unskilled Labor	-0.0012	0.0335	0.0265
Skilled Labor	-0.0011	0.0341	0.0183
Capital	-0.0011	0.0354	0.0196
Natural Resources	-0.0016	0.0754	-0.0639
Grains and Crops	-0.0013	0.0292	0.0422
Livestock and Meat Products	-0.0014	-0.0465	0.082
Mining and Extraction	-0.0012	0.0352	0.0023
Processed Food	-0.0009	0.0014	0.0196
Textiles and Clothing	-0.0009	0.0078	0.0136
Light Manufacturing	-0.0009	0.0044	0.0082
Heavy Manufacturing	-0.0009	0.0119	0.005
Utilities and Construction	-0.001	0.0179	0.0134
Transport and Communication	-0.001	0.021	0.0177
Other Services	-0.001	0.0265	0.0181

Table 64. Equivalent variation by regions ($ US Mn)

EV	(Sim)
RoW	-141.90
Mekong	101.74
India	111.48

Table 65. Industry output by commodity and regions (% change)

Qo	RoW	Mekong	India
Grains and Crops	0.0005	0.0471	-0.0303
Livestock and Meat Products	-0.0042	-0.2756	0.1649
Mining and Extraction	-0.0001	0.0057	-0.0129
Processed Food	-0.0014	-0.012	0.0214
Textiles and Clothing	0.0024	-0.0156	-0.0226
Light Manufacturing	-0.0003	0.0305	-0.0022
Heavy Manufacturing	0.0005	0.0122	-0.0139
Utilities and Construction	-0.0005	0.0312	0.0068
Transport and Communication	0.0001	-0.003	0.0002
Other Services	0.0001	-0.0074	-0.0075

India and Mekong-Ganga

Tables 61 to 67 reflect the impact of a 10% tariff reduction by both India and countries in Mekong-Ganga. The most important change in trade balance is concentrated in *livestock and meat products* in the case of India and *grains and crops* in the case of Mekong-Ganga nations.

Table 66. Terms of trade by region

tot	(Sim)	Pre	Post	Ch/%Ch
RoW	-0.0006	1.0000	1.0000	0.0000
Mekong	0.0112	1.0000	1.0001	0.0001
India	0.0143	1.0000	1.0001	0.0001

Table 67. Change in value of GDP (% change)

vgdp	(Sim)
RoW	-0.0011
Mekong	0.0216
India	0.0203

Table 65 reflects the impact of tariffs in terms of equivalent variation. Both India and Mekong-Ganga nations benefit from the trade liberalization in terms of EV.

Tables 64, 66 and 67 summarizes the overall impact of trade liberalization on India and Mekong-Ganga. Both the partners benefit from liberalization in terms of all the welfare parameters.

India and RCEP

Tables 68 to74 reflect the impact of a 10% tariff reduction by both India and countries in RCEP. The most change in trade balance is concentrated in *processed food* in the case of RCEP and *livestock and Meat products* in the case of India.

Table 68. Change in trade balance (in $ US Mn)

DTBAL	(Sim)
RCEP	-225.0982
RoW	713.1676
India	-488.0703

Table 69. Change in trade balance by commodities and regions ($ US Mn)

DTBALi	RCEP	RoW	India
Grains and Crops	-74.12	-82.85	144.57
Livestock and Meat Products	-185.68	-67.59	253.66
Mining and Extraction	56.48	-92.69	-14.67
Processed Food	643.85	-373.84	-296.99
Textiles and Clothing	-88.87	89.81	-9.78
Light Manufacturing	-314.20	259.44	43.97
Heavy Manufacturing	125.80	321.70	-501.07
Utilities and Construction	-32.57	33.78	-1.21
Transport and Communication	-151.41	331.96	-17.49
Other Services	-204.38	293.45	-89.06

Table 71 shows the impact of tariff reduction by both partners in terms of equivalent variation. Both RCEP and India benefit from this liberalization.

Overall, using data from Tables 71, 73 and 74, it can be concluded that the impact of a 10% tariff reduction by both India and countries in RCEP is positive for RCEP but not India.

Table 70. Market price of factors and commodities by regions (% change)

Pm	RCEP	RoW	India
Land	-0.0136	-0.0325	0.1876
Unskilled Labor	0.0137	-0.0071	0.0468
Skilled Labor	0.0138	-0.0065	0.0412
Capital	0.0142	-0.0068	0.0328
Natural Resources	0.029	-0.0116	-0.1765
Grains and Crops	0.007	-0.0101	0.046
Livestock and Meat Products	0.0042	-0.008	0.0853
Mining and Extraction	0.0145	-0.0075	-0.0213
Processed Food	0.0059	-0.0067	-0.0729
Textiles and Clothing	0.0084	-0.0056	-0.0208
Light Manufacturing	0.0094	-0.0056	-0.0409
Heavy Manufacturing	0.0088	-0.0058	-0.0439
Utilities and Construction	0.0105	-0.0062	-0.0012
Transport and Communication	0.0113	-0.0063	0.0096
Other Services	0.0123	-0.0064	0.028

Table 71. Equivalent variation by regions ($ US Mn)

EV	(Sim)
RCEP	786.45
RoW	-520.35
India	573.69

Table 72. Industry output by commodity and regions (% change)

Qo	RCEP	RoW	India
Grains and Crops	0.0001	-0.0081	-0.0486
Livestock and Meat Products	-0.0251	-0.0071	0.23
Mining and Extraction	0.0021	-0.0007	-0.0322
Processed Food	0.0429	-0.0131	-0.4244
Textiles and Clothing	-0.0154	0.0119	0.0027
Light Manufacturing	-0.0089	0.0031	0.0664
Heavy Manufacturing	-0.0006	0.0028	-0.0271
Utilities and Construction	0.0045	-0.0033	0.0544
Transport and Communication	-0.0008	0.0011	0.0049
Other Services	-0.0005	0.0004	-0.0131

Table 73. Terms of trade by region

tot	(Sim)	Pre	Post	Ch/%Ch
RCEP	0.0089	1.0000	1.0001	0.0001
RoW	-0.0032	1.0000	1.0000	0.0000
India	-0.0139	1.0000	0.9999	-0.0001

Table 74. Change in value of GDP (% change)

vgdp	(Sim)
RCEP	0.0128
RoW	-0.007
India	-0.0039

CASE 3: Reduction of Tariffs to 0% by Both

India and MERCOSUR

Overall, using data from *Tables 78, 80 and 81,* it can be concluded that the impact of tariff reduction by

Table 75. Change in trade balance (in $ US Mn)

DTBAL	(Sim)
RoW	1797.7344
India	-994.4606
Mercosur	-803.2732

Table 76. Change in trade balance by commodities and regions ($ US Mn)

DTBALi	RoW	India	Mercosur
Grains and Crops	217.93	-124.47	-90.59
Livestock and Meat Products	145.72	-27.35	-113.16
Mining and Extraction	442.71	-443.81	-2.54
Processed Food	-524.84	-1345.86	1833.86
Textiles and Clothing	-591.78	1695.52	-1146.83
Light Manufacturing	347.79	172.81	-533.99
Heavy Manufacturing	378.85	117.05	-529.01
Utilities and Construction	30.98	-19.07	-11.90
Transport and Communication	537.56	-332.58	-82.99
Other Services	812.83	-686.70	-126.13

Table 77. Market price of factors and commodities by regions (% change)

Pm	RoW	India	Mercosur
Land	0.0176	-0.2762	0.4977
Unskilled Labor	-0.012	0.2801	0.086
Skilled Labor	-0.0113	0.2337	0.0591
Capital	-0.0114	0.251	0.0858
Natural Resources	0.0388	-0.5847	-0.0771
Grains and Crops	-0.0053	0.0673	0.1128
Livestock and Meat Products	-0.0072	0.0743	0.0858
Mining and Extraction	0.0002	0.0686	0.0306
Processed Food	-0.0077	0.0568	0.0698
Textiles and Clothing	-0.0086	0.1794	-0.1908
Light Manufacturing	-0.009	0.141	0.0193
Heavy Manufacturing	-0.0076	0.1063	0.0221
Utilities and Construction	-0.0093	0.1791	0.0519
Transport and Communication	-0.0101	0.2055	0.0615
Other Services	-0.0105	0.2307	0.0671

Table 78. Equivalent variation by regions ($ US Mn)

EV	(Sim)
RoW	-1344.91
India	819.47
Mercosur	158.27

Table 79. Industry output by commodity and regions (% change)

Qo	RoW	India	Mercosur
Grains and Crops	0.0097	-0.1537	0.1871
Livestock and Meat Products	0.0055	-0.0265	-0.0067
Mining and Extraction	0.0069	-0.1271	-0.0212
Processed Food	-0.0126	-0.5686	0.7178
Textiles and Clothing	-0.0352	1.4379	-1.6603
Light Manufacturing	0.0003	0.1124	-0.1025
Heavy Manufacturing	-0.0008	0.0959	-0.0358
Utilities and Construction	-0.007	0.1123	0.0818
Transport and Communication	0.0006	0.0135	0.0083
Other Services	0.0013	-0.101	-0.0163

Table 80. Terms of trade by region

tot	(Sim)	Pre	Post	Ch/%Ch
RoW	-0.0042	1.0000	1.0000	0.0000
India	0.1545	1.0000	1.0015	0.0015
Mercosur	0.0516	1.0000	1.0005	0.0005

Table 81. Change in value of GDP (% change)

vgdp	(Sim)
RoW	-0.0107
India	0.1762
Mercosur	0.0421

Table 82. Change in trade balance (in $ US Mn)

DTBAL	(Sim)
RoW	3131.1243
BIMSTEC	-1520.944
India	-1610.179

Table 83. Change in trade balance by commodities and regions ($ US Mn)

DTBALi	RoW	India	BIMSTEC
Grains and Crops	107.47	-236.00	101.09
Livestock and Meat Products	-301.54	-53.62	375.60
Mining and Extraction	659.96	-32.64	-693.35
Processed Food	-165.82	76.21	58.57
Textiles and Clothing	-170.03	-158.13	315.44
Light Manufacturing	-450.01	27.83	424.66
Heavy Manufacturing	281.21	-392.24	-41.67
Utilities and Construction	64.17	-24.21	-39.96
Transport and Communication	1401.51	-414.30	-720.23
Other Services	1704.19	-313.85	-1390.34

Table 84. Market price of factors and commodities by regions (% change)

Pm	RoW	India	BIMSTEC
Land	-0.0205	-0.7302	1.1151
Unskilled Labor	-0.0237	0.4606	0.6033
Skilled Labor	-0.0218	0.4763	0.4735
Capital	-0.0222	0.5257	0.5105
Natural Resources	0.0384	0.8857	-0.9538
Grains and Crops	-0.0195	0.0398	0.6362
Livestock and Meat Products	-0.0204	-0.0932	0.7221
Mining and Extraction	-0.0078	0.4484	0.1947
Processed Food	-0.0178	0.0346	0.4606
Textiles and Clothing	-0.0177	-0.0561	0.3981
Light Manufacturing	-0.0184	-0.0754	0.2969
Heavy Manufacturing	-0.0166	0.071	0.2261
Utilities and Construction	-0.019	0.2166	0.3795
Transport and Communication	-0.02	0.3271	0.453
Other Services	-0.0207	0.3756	0.4733

Table 85. Equivalent variation by regions ($ US Mn)

EV	(Sim)
RoW	-2681.78
BIMSTEC	930.83
India	2154.77

Table 86. Industry output by commodity and regions (% change)

Qo	RoW	India	BIMSTEC
Grains and Crops	0.0084	-0.1554	0.0178
Livestock and Meat Products	-0.0168	-0.8654	0.3631
Mining and Extraction	0.0084	0.0529	-0.225
Processed Food	-0.0053	0.1845	0.0351
Textiles and Clothing	-0.0062	-0.1654	0.2173
Light Manufacturing	-0.0104	0.4346	0.3193
Heavy Manufacturing	-0.0036	0.0311	0.1232
Utilities and Construction	-0.0119	0.4706	0.2035
Transport and Communication	0.0031	0.0421	-0.0053
Other Services	0.0027	-0.114	-0.1906

Table 87. Terms of trade by region

tot	(Sim)	Pre	Post	Ch/%Ch
RoW	-0.0089	1.0000	0.9999	-0.0001
BIMSTEC	0.0639	1.0000	1.0006	0.0006
India	0.3752	1.0000	1.0038	0.0038

Table 88. Change in value of GDP (% change)

vgdp	(Sim)
RoW	-0.0217
BIMSTEC	0.2265
India	0.4886

both India and countries in Mercosur to target rate of 0% is positive for both in terms of EV, ToT and change in GDP. India benefits more than Mercosur in this setup.

Table 89. Change in trade balance (in $ US Mn)

DTBAL	(Sim)
RoW	3457.9463
India	-2881.233
GCC	-576.7127

Table 90. Change in trade balance by commodities and regions ($ US Mn)

DTBALi	RoW	India	GCC
Grains and Crops	283.90	-284.94	6.76
Livestock and Meat Products	93.73	-16.49	-77.17
Mining and Extraction	1855.98	-1499.59	-388.14
Processed Food	-141.41	419.28	-288.17
Textiles and Clothing	430.00	-179.32	-246.19
Light Manufacturing	-692.57	1182.45	-490.20
Heavy Manufacturing	-1548.19	-359.25	1754.43
Utilities and Construction	70.88	-35.16	-35.72
Transport and Communication	1226.33	-683.24	-357.99
Other Services	1879.29	-1424.97	-454.31

Table 91. Market price of factors and commodities by regions (% change)

Pm	RoW	India	GCC
Land	0.0084	0.2661	-0.5553
Unskilled Labor	-0.0301	0.6173	0.4037
Skilled Labor	-0.0283	0.5012	0.335
Capital	-0.028	0.5287	0.4198
Natural Resources	0.2372	-1.8313	-0.2125
Grains and Crops	-0.0174	0.3815	0.236
Livestock and Meat Products	-0.0207	0.4356	0.1463
Mining and Extraction	0.0297	0.0048	0.192
Processed Food	-0.0195	0.3731	0.132
Textiles and Clothing	-0.0198	0.338	0.2961
Light Manufacturing	-0.0182	0.1737	0.2631
Heavy Manufacturing	-0.0083	0.0541	0.2785
Utilities and Construction	-0.0179	0.3068	0.2081
Transport and Communication	-0.0235	0.4204	0.2774
Other Services	-0.0252	0.4781	0.3642

Table 92. Equivalent variation by regions ($ US Mn)

EV	(Sim)
RoW	-2878.43
India	1654.92
GCC	1581.01

Table 93. Industry output by commodity and regions (% change)

Qo	RoW	India	GCC
Grains and Crops	0.0145	-0.0974	-0.1844
Livestock and Meat Products	0.0022	0.0022	-0.6628
Mining and Extraction	0.0367	-0.3587	-0.0859
Processed Food	-0.0046	0.2732	-0.8544
Textiles and Clothing	0.0296	-0.2125	-1.6567
Light Manufacturing	-0.016	0.6766	0.0061
Heavy Manufacturing	-0.016	0.2302	0.4169
Utilities and Construction	-0.0151	0.3308	0.2688
Transport and Communication	0.0012	0.0135	-0.0582
Other Services	0.0032	-0.2345	-0.1613

Table 94. Terms of trade by region

tot	(Sim)	Pre	Post	Ch/%Ch
RoW	-0.0135	1.0000	0.9999	-0.0001
India	0.2238	1.0000	1.0022	0.0022
GCC	0.2010	1.0000	1.0020	0.0020

Table 95. Change in value of GDP (% change)

vgdp	(Sim)
RoW	-0.0243
India	0.3792
GCC	0.2529

India and BIMSTEC

Overall, using data from Tables 86, 87 and 88, it can be concluded that the impact of tariff reduction by both India and countries in BIMSTEC to target rate of 0% is positive for both in terms of EV, ToT and change in GDP. India benefits more than BIMSTEC in this setup.

Table 96. Change in trade balance (in $ US Mn)

DTBAL	(Sim)
RoW	1890.0155
Mekong	-935.5219
India	-954.4932

Table 97. Change in trade balance by commodities and regions ($ US Mn)

DTBALi	RoW	Mekong	India
Grains and Crops	206.81	878.70	-1117.97
Livestock and Meat Products	-783.42	-1397.61	2264.45
Mining and Extraction	-221.15	114.34	3.78
Processed Food	-708.10	550.11	117.96
Textiles and Clothing	324.58	-91.56	-238.64
Light Manufacturing	-152.30	275.31	-139.30
Heavy Manufacturing	1409.23	-438.55	-1035.14
Utilities and Construction	45.22	-30.22	-15.00
Transport and Communication	861.74	-408.56	-274.62
Other Services	907.40	-387.37	-520.03

Table 98. Market price of factors and commodities by regions (% change)

Pm	RoW	Mekong	India
Land	-0.0295	0.6251	1.6193
Unskilled Labor	-0.0136	0.4757	0.2809
Skilled Labor	-0.0128	0.4413	0.1774
Capital	-0.0131	0.4659	0.1991
Natural Resources	-0.0214	1.6187	-0.7005
Grains and Crops	-0.0126	0.6499	0.4309
Livestock and Meat Products	-0.0146	-0.4924	0.9501
Mining and Extraction	-0.014	0.6001	0.0122
Processed Food	-0.0096	0.1034	0.151
Textiles and Clothing	-0.0101	0.1196	0.1232
Light Manufacturing	-0.0112	0.0785	0.07
Heavy Manufacturing	-0.0111	0.1767	0.0328
Utilities and Construction	-0.0118	0.2553	0.128
Transport and Communication	-0.0119	0.2932	0.1754
Other Services	-0.0122	0.363	0.1796

Table 99. Equivalent Variation by regions ($ US Mn)

EV	(Sim)
RoW	-1775.08
Mekong	1199.48
India	664.60

Table 100. Industry output by commodity and regions (% change)

Qo	RoW	Mekong	India
Grains and Crops	0.0127	0.7772	-0.454
Livestock and Meat Products	-0.0452	-3.7331	2.1355
Mining and Extraction	-0.0011	0.1607	-0.1402
Processed Food	-0.02	0.4847	0.1655
Textiles and Clothing	0.0249	-0.2379	-0.2113
Light Manufacturing	-0.0042	0.3225	0.0236
Heavy Manufacturing	0.006	-0.0045	-0.117
Utilities and Construction	-0.0068	0.3781	0.0732
Transport and Communication	0.002	-0.0714	-0.0018
Other Services	0.0011	-0.1149	-0.0958

Table 101. Terms of trade by region

tot	(Sim)	Pre	Post	Ch/%Ch
RoW	-0.0073	1.0000	0.9999	-0.0001
Mekong	0.1825	1.0000	1.0018	0.0018
India	0.1329	1.0000	1.0013	0.0013

Table 102. Change in value of GDP (% change)

vgdp	(Sim)
RoW	-0.0133
Mekong	0.3026
India	0.1654

India and GCC

Overall, using data from Tables 92, 94 and 95, it can be concluded that the impact of tariff reduction by both India and countries in GCC to target rate of 0% is positive for both in terms of EV, ToT and change

Table 103. Change in trade balance (in $ US Mn)

DTBAL	(Sim)
RCEP	-2904.62
RoW	8306.00
India	-5401.39

Table 104. Change in trade balance by commodities and regions ($ US Mn)

DTBALi	RCEP	RoW	India
Grains and Crops	-1245.36	-1209.85	2202.55
Livestock and Meat Products	-3218.02	-1062.62	4272.89
Mining and Extraction	891.11	-702.82	-792.35
Processed Food	13658.70	-3845.50	-10561.87
Textiles and Clothing	-1457.32	823.00	506.67
Light Manufacturing	-4527.50	2764.35	1624.52
Heavy Manufacturing	-2020.17	4760.72	-3351.70
Utilities and Construction	-407.74	389.72	18.03
Transport and Communication	-1843.10	3861.88	471.76
Other Services	-2735.22	2527.11	208.10

Table 105. Market price of factors and commodities by regions (% change)

Pm	RCEP	RoW	India
Land	0.0993	-0.4249	2.1644
Unskilled Labor	0.1837	-0.0766	0.0993
Skilled Labor	0.1799	-0.0697	0.0032
Capital	0.1868	-0.0725	-0.0487
Natural Resources	0.3448	-0.0522	-0.8207
Grains and Crops	0.1612	-0.1192	0.1596
Livestock and Meat Products	0.08	-0.091	0.7708
Mining and Extraction	0.1877	-0.0636	-0.3201
Processed Food	0.0912	-0.0736	-1.7248
Textiles and Clothing	0.1154	-0.0605	-0.601
Light Manufacturing	0.1288	-0.0589	-0.7315
Heavy Manufacturing	0.1221	-0.0583	-0.7001
Utilities and Construction	0.1426	-0.0646	-0.3348
Transport and Communication	0.1515	-0.067	-0.2969
Other Services	0.1632	-0.0686	-0.1024

Table 106. Equivalent Variation by regions ($ US Mn)

EV	(Sim)
RCEP	9257.73
RoW	-4808.15
India	1322.30

Table 107. Industry output by commodity and regions (% change)

Qo	RCEP	RoW	India
Grains and Crops	0.1219	-0.1108	-0.8815
Livestock and Meat Products	-0.3784	-0.0983	3.7294
Mining and Extraction	0.0227	0.0028	-0.1258
Processed Food	0.91	-0.1379	-7.678
Textiles and Clothing	-0.248	0.1084	0.7122
Light Manufacturing	-0.1312	0.0325	1.2154
Heavy Manufacturing	-0.0576	0.0414	0.1879
Utilities and Construction	0.0518	-0.0378	0.4826
Transport and Communication	-0.01	0.0134	-0.022
Other Services	-0.0125	0.003	-0.137

Table 108. Terms of trade by region

tot	(Sim)	Pre	Post	Ch/%Ch
RCEP	0.1158	1.0000	1.0012	0.0012
RoW	-0.0316	1.0000	0.9997	-0.0003
India	-0.5077	1.0000	0.9949	-0.0051

Table 109. Change in value of GDP (% change)

vgdp	(Sim)
RCEP	0.1681
RoW	-0.0737
India	-0.7885

Table 110. Impact of tariff reduction by India (-10%)

Indian aligning with	Overall Impact	Recommended Policy Decision	Most Beneficial Product Agg.	
			India	Partner
Mercosur	Negative	No	-	-
BIMSTEC	Negative	No	-	-
GCC	Negative	No	-	-
Mekong-Ganga	Negative	No	-	-
RCEP	Negative	No	-	-

in GDP. India benefits more than GCC in this setup. The product aggregates *light manufacturing* in case India and *heavy manufacturing* in GCC are the most beneficial for each.

Table 111. Impact of tariff reduction by both India and Economic Groups (-10%)

Indian aligning with	Overall Impact	Recommended Policy Decision	Most Beneficial Product Agg.	
			India	Partner
Mercosur	Positive	Yes	Textile & Clothing	Processed Food
BIMSTEC	Positive	Yes	Utilities & Const.	Light Industries
GCC	Positive	Yes	Light Industries	Heavy Industries
Mekong-Ganga	Positive	Yes	Livestock & Meat	Grains & Crops
RCEP	Negative	No	-	-

Table 112: Impact of tariff reduction by both India and Economic Groups (Target 0%)

Indian aligning with	Overall Impact	Recommended Policy Decision	Most Beneficial Product Agg	
			India	Partner
Mercosur	Positive	Yes	Textile & Clothing	Processed Food
BIMSTEC	Positive	Yes	Utilities & Const.	Light Industries
GCC	Positive	Yes	Light Industries	Heavy Industries
Mekong-Ganga	Positive	Yes	Livestock & Meat	Processed Food
RCEP	Negative	No	-	-

India and Mekong-Ganga

Overall, using data from Tables 99, 101 and 102, it can be concluded that the impact of tariff reduction by both India and countries in Mekong-Ganga to target rate of 0% is positive for both in terms of EV, ToT and change in GDP. However, Mekong-Ganga countries benefit more than India in this setup.

India and RCEP

Overall, using data from Tables 106, 108 and 109, it can be concluded that the impact of tariff reduction by both India and countries in RCEP to target rate of 0% is negative for India but positive for RCEP in terms of EV, ToT and change in GDP. This also validates the India's walkout from RCEP as India is not benefitting in any sense from this liberalization.

Tables 110 -112 summarise the three simulation scenarios considered in this paper.

CONCLUSION

The overall finding of this paper states that the unilateral deviation or one-way liberalization policies by India do not benefit India in any way. The bilateral tariff reduction helps both the partner countries and India, except in the case of India liberalizing with RCEP. Moreover, a similar conclusion can be drawn up in case of reducing tariffs to 0% by both the partners as well. The paper also discusses the product aggregates where the countries and groups can focus for maximum benefits. This can be essential for policy formation as in trade there are winners and losers and every country try to adopt that policy that increases its overall welfare.

Highest gain remain when India aligns with ASEAN 10 followed by RCEP and Indo Pacific alliance. BIMSTEC, South Asian alliance brings around 2000 million US dollars welfare gain for India. Half the amount if we align with Ganga Mekong nations. SACU alliance gives more relative welfare gain to India than aligning with MERCOSUR, but gains are not exceeding 1000 million us dollars. East Asia gains more if we look east.

REFERENCES

Cirera, X., Willenbockel, D., & Lakshman, R. W. (2014). Evidence on the impact of tariff reductions on employment in developing countries: A systematic review. *Journal of Economic Surveys*, *28*(3), 449–471. doi:10.1111/joes.12029

Fukase, E., & Martin, W. (2016). The Economic Potential of an India-US Free Trade Agreement. *Journal of Economic Integration*, *31*(4), 774–816. doi:10.11130/jei.2016.31.4.774

Hertel, T., Ivanic, M., Preckel, P., & Cranfield, J. (2003). *Trade liberalization and the structure of poverty in developing countries.* GTAP Working Paper 25.

Hertel, T. W. (1996). *Global trade analysis: Modeling and applications*. Cambridge University Press. doi:10.1017/CBO9781139174688

Hoque, S. (2005). *The impact of tariff reduction on Bangladesh economy: a computable general equilibrium assessment. MPRA Paper 16246*. University Library of Munich.

Chapter 16
Gastronomic Entrepreneurial Profile and Factors Influencing the Potential of Business Internationalization:
The Case of Metropizza

José G. Vargas-Hernández
https://orcid.org/0000-0003-0938-4197
University Center for Economic and Managerial Sciences, University of Guadalajara, Mexico

Mario Guadalupe Zazueta-Félix
Universidad Autónoma Indígena de México, Mexico

ABSTRACT

The current challenge for the survival and growth of international businesses is the appropriation of innovation in all its senses. This chapter attempts to analyze the contextual framework of international entrepreneurship and the importance of the entrepreneur's profile that influences the potential to generate innovative environments in relation to success in doing business abroad. This analysis aims to answer the questions of strategic thinking that can be a critical factor in business competitiveness and contribute to its success.

INTRODUCTION

The purpose of a scientific paper is, according to Hernández et al. (2014), to present an argument, backed by evidence, to detect or identify keywords, approaches, concepts, variables and potential definitions, to find examples, and from then interpret the conclusions.

Entrepreneurship in external markets for a company that employs 100 or up to 250 people in the case of the industrial sector (SME) in Latin America is extremely arduous. There is research that illustrates

DOI: 10.4018/978-1-7998-7568-0.ch016

that 10.8% of entrepreneurs have the possibility to internationalize, but these efforts are not competitive enough (Amorós et al., 2012). That is why the presence of SMEs is little in the international arena.

We found answers in several cases of proven success and failure, where they indicate causes or different reasons to achieve or not achieve internationalization. In some cases, we found internal details of the organization, for example: inconsistencies on organization, production, or financial aspects (see, among others, Pavón (2010)). Likewise, we aim to identify and analyze the factors and characteristics of the entrepreneurs that influence the potential for business internationalization.

The objective of this chapter is to identify and analyze the personality factors or elements that influence the potential for internationalization of a business, from a theoretical perspective. The present study focuses on the personal and environmental aspects that foster innovative subjects and leaders, as well as attitude and aspects of the personality (Rodríguez & Prieto, 2009).

BACKGROUND

The organizations arise through actions that are intended to create value and meaning. Thanks to the contributions of Oviatt and McDougal (2005), entrepreneurship is known as a progressive action of man to break down borders: international entrepreneurship comes to mark the combination of behaviors of man with the outside world where we can point out innovation, proactivity with the firm purpose of not only trying but creating value in the company.

The human condition does not escape trial and error, so dealing with entrepreneurship issues is trying to build a career based on mistakes and learn from them in order to pursue goals set for the growth of a company. Therefore, to take entrepreneurship outside the borders implies a growing demand, as well as an imminent risk for SMEs. Therefore, international entrepreneurship is conceptualized as the ability of a company to execute a successful export sales plan.

International entrepreneurship is framed into economic globalization, which means that it contributes to the generation of gross revenues for one or more economies to the new jobs for foreign markets and investing directly in these countries, and on the other hand generating profits for the domestic market with the revenue that cames from international markets in which the company invests.

The base of the increase in wealth of a country can be considered to be international trade. The place where the paradigm of efficiently marketing of goods-based economy was developed, was the European continent between the sixteenth and eighteenth centuries. At this time, the fundamental premise was to take into account the trade surplus as a privileged economic indicator. This is how priority was given to the export of goods before the domestic market as a source of income.

Trade liberation is attributed to Adam Smith, who pushed the theory of absolute advantage as an advocate and driving idea of international trade. Smith was convinced that once the borders were opened for products from foreign markets, the economy of the countries would benefit. So, once the country's economy adopted this theory, it would contribute to the formalization of international trade. Definitely no country could grow and develop alone. It is thanks to the export of merchandise that an entity or country creates relationships that lead it to form a commercially organized community with the rest of the world.

Once a country manages to form a commercial community with other countries and they achieve identity, specialization occurs creating a market relationship. Naturally, this relationship requests merchandise, which implies supply. Supply is generated by the demand for the goods that organizations, governments or individuals require from each other.

It is then established that the world's economies, regardless of the geographical zone in which they are, according to the liberal economic ideology are immersed in globalization.

The economic political paradigm that has prevailed over the last thirty years so far in Latin American countries is the neoliberal one, where these countries open their borders and cease to have customs as an import barrier to export management trading offices, such as economic development engine. That is why they are constantly fighting for the reduction of trade barriers. These countries are not interested in national protection but rather in the support for the free market.

The trade liberalization idea presented by Adam Smith, formulates the convenience of doing international trade between countries, based on their guarantees and profits. Smith's theory emphasizes the margin that the government must take in this process and encourages the country to specialize in production. These results must achieve overproduction by guaranteeing coverage considering the needs of other countries.

Therefore, it is recommended that each nation produce what it specializes on, to be able to buy other products to other countries at a lower cost. Concepts such as specialization, division of labor, value cataloging are products of Adam Smith's mind; as well as the subsequent emergence of the so-called serial production. We find John Stuart Mill, David Ricardo and Bertil Ohlin among others as thinkers who have enriched Smith's theory. As for Stuart Mill, he focused on dealing with the freedom of man in all aspects, including, of course, marketing and devoting himself to whatever is of greater value to his interests (Roldán, 2019).

In the case of David Ricardo (1772-1823), he wrote about the comparative advantage, starting from the labor cost and the relations between nations at the time of commercialization, taking into account the advantages of foreign trade (Selva, 2019). Those who improved the state of the art of international trade were Heckscher and Ohlin considering competitive advantage as a concept that does not lie between the differences in technology in different countries, but rather in the relativity of various factors.

Many authors now believe that the superiority of countries, from the perspective of new factors, is not determined by the natural resources of each country. Currently, the factors are related to the ability to innovate new products to offer them in the market, so they must be productive, competitive, flexible, even efficient, and they must also prepare the workforce with skills that promote the productivity of companies and the development of the same employees, and innovative entrepreneurs ready to present new products, because to catch the niches is required, as international changes and demand are changing.

Today, marketing has identified the need as the basis of any marketing process. That's why it is important to launch differentiated and competitive products and services.

Kotler and Armstrong (2007) say that business entrepreneurship aims to achieve a favorable negotiation, with full success and in turn break down an essential prior process into two major activities: firstly, the identification of the market segment with potential for attention and, after that, the completion of a market study. The objective of this process is to present the best offer as opposed to the other bidders.

INTERNATIONAL ENTREPRENEURSHIP: MEXICO IN THE WORLD

The Latin American market and especially SMEs is constantly motivated to potentialize themselves to undertake international trade. Amoros et al. (2012) were the first to detect and analyze this formally and to affirm the lack of entrepreneurial orientation towards the international market. Such guidance is decisive for small and restricted markets.

In 1986, Mexico decided to open up to international trade, approximately forty years after using an import substitution policy that aimed to protect the national business section. Immediately after that, Mexico directed its efforts towards trade opening, joining liberal economic countries as part of agreements taken before by the International Monetary Fund to recover from major economic crises. Upon entering the World Trade Organization (WTO), Mexico began a career in commercial treaty signatures.

With that antecedent, the historical stage known as neoliberal period was opened in Mexico. With this, Mexico took one of the most impactful decisions as a nation, joining the free market and therefore international business.

By 1986, when Mexico barely allowed import substitution, it exported 22 billion dollars; while for 2015, 380,772 billion dollars were exported (Secretaría de Economía, 2016). In that period, Mexico went from a petroleum economy (this commodity is still important for the Mexican economy) to a manufacturing economy, being a world leader in the automotive industry according to data from INEGI (2017).

Even so, the notion of an oil or intermediate goods economy still exists to this day because this has been the policy of transformation in recent decades. National companies do not represent yet a significant growth because, unlike export of products from companies that make up their products here, they are really scarce. Eight out of ten pesos exported correspond to large companies, according to data from the Expansión Magazine (2011). It is important to highlight the fact that every 8 of 10 products are exported to the United States despite so many signed treaties (Secretary of Economy, 2016).

THE ENTREPRENEUR'S PROFILE

The non-Anglo-Saxon entrepreneur profile has to be analyzed from its own historical and socio-cultural context rooted in pre-Columbian times. Particularly, to refer to the entrepreneur's profile, the term "business mentality" is used. In order to decipher and characterize these mental molds, an effort is needed in the construction of the recognition of one's own business culture not far from the desirable good practices of the global context but without leaving aside the Latin American businessman's own culture.

In these circumstances, we consider the following research topic: the profile of the Mexican businessman, who seeks the internationalization of his products through a high diversification of markets and exported products. It should be noted that the services are also exportable, although intangible, without leaving aside foreign direct investment by Mexican companies. Those who exports must establish precise objectives with attainable goals (Bancomext, 2015). Understanding these meanings of "international entrepreneurship" gives a basic guide to the vision of the international entrepreneur who not only needs capital, but must also have a culture of openness and negotiation skills.

It is in this context, international entrepreneurship walks between three different areas: in the first place, the business environment where the development of negotiation, leadership and alliance building skills is required; secondly, the national level, where the entrepreneur is in excessive competition; finally, we have the global scope, where the world entrepreneur must bring Mexican business culture and its values to an intricate global economy that is always being built and reformed between the homogenization of the global citizen and the richness of different cultures.

Globalization begins with trade and goes back to the Silk Road but is based on the economy. This is the cornerstone of international entrepreneurship that has placed a large part of the countries, co-participation in the delivery of values and products between nations, organizations and individuals. Currently, the task of the international entrepreneur is to participate in the collapse of trade barriers that currently threaten to rebuild where they had already been destroyed with the arrival of nationalist governments.

Countries compete with the entire world and Mexico is no exception. SMEs are competing with foreign companies with enormous advantages, which are "global", from China, Japan, Germany, USA, Colombia, Italy, Chile, and so on. Mexico is recognized for its potential commercial reach among world markets. Resulting from the signing of various alliances with blocks of countries such as the entire European continent, North America, Central America and countries of the Pacific Alliance (Colombia, Peru, and Chile). It is of utmost importance for the Mexican entrepreneurs to take advantage of these resources (not only NAFTA, now called T-MEC) that provide them with a competitive advantage in terms of the decrease or disappearance of tariffs that countries apply discriminately to "nearby" countries. Mexico has an advantage over many countries by being a leader in the signing of trade agreements although it currently misses them.

SUCCESSFUL ENTREPRENEURSHIP AND THE ENTREPRENEUR'S PROFILE

Carl Rogers (1902-1987) is an important name of the Humanist theory. He wroted about an actualizing tendency, that is to say, it is prone to improve or decrease but always changing and this is what makes it transform permanently. Rogers affirmed (1957), in one of his articles, published in the Journal of Counseling Psyhchology:

My experience is that man is a member of the human species, basically trustworthy and whose deepest characteristics tend towards development, differentiation, cooperative relationships; whose life tends fundamentally to move from dependence to independence; whose impulses naturally tend to harmonize in a complex and changing pattern of self-regulation; whose total character is such that it tends to be preserved and improved and to better preserve its species, and perhaps to lead it towards its wider evolution. In my experience, discovering that an individual is truly and deeply a unique member of the human species is not a discovery that arouses horror. Rather, I am inclined to believe that being human is to penetrate the complex process of being one of the creatures of this planet, more widely sensitive, responsive, creative and adaptable (Brazier, 1997, citing Rogers, 1957).

In another part of the article "The Humanist", originally published in 1957, he adds:

Therefore, the conduct of man is exquisitely rational, moves with orderly and insightful complexity towards the goals that your body strives to achieve. The tragedy for most of us is that our defenses prevent us from realizing this rationality, so that we consciously move in one direction while our organism is moving in another (Brazier, 1997, citing Rogers, 1957).

Looking for works on personality characteristics linked to corporate exports, we indirectly have the work of Alfred Adler (1870-1937). For him, "human beings are goal-oriented organisms" (Bottome, 1939).

Personal growth is the first object of study in the theory of human behavior. Not having a direction, an entrepreneur would lead a life without philosophy of desolate, nihilistic style. The personal growth of the international entrepreneur must be fed beyond economic growth and personal growth.

According to Bottome (1939), Adler pointed out the fact that it was imperative to maintain an objective view, attached to social events in the construction of the archetype of the employer. An entrepreneur with values and vision is not only a good person but a good leader. He clarifies that it would be necessary to study the personality of the individual for a better understanding of what is happening in the world. A world without values is the product of the personal growth of its inhabitants.

When the vision is directed by the superego of the person, this tends to get preeminent goals. In the absence of a balance between the ego and the superego, the business vision can be unbalanced and the desire for power increased. International entrepreneurship requires the use of empathy with others. Engler (1996) in this regard refers to the period of childhood, in a different way to Freudian, because he elaborates questions on how it is that what happens to us at a later age at the stages of psychosexual development. Engler mentions the inferiority that prevails in childhood and that if it is not attended to, it can lead the employer to anti-social, hedonistic and even autocratic conditions and actions, as compensatory measures.

The personality of the entrepreneur when he has the idea of exporting his products is part of Adler's individual psychology, which suggests that people have a life direction towards achieving their goals naturally. The social environment in which the individual is immersed during the development of his childhood and preteen life affects this process. The theory falls to entrepreneurship as an activity or conduct that results from the skills and beliefs of the individual in their personal growth to face challenges and fears, their ability to develop and train with time management skills and communicate effectively with social groups.

The ability to construct a self-image would be integral to balance the entrepreneur's capabilities and from then, to develop his and his company's growth with the relevant actors involved in the process. Entrepreneurship is difficult and requires effort and self-determination. With companies, this time I am referring to the definition that the Royal Spanish Academy makes to the word, not to its business project: action or task that involves difficulty and whose execution requires decision and effort. Entrepreneurship is difficult and requires efforts and strong self-determination.

STRATEGIC THINKING

Strategic thinking has its core in three big questions and the quality of the answers to them influence the design assertiveness strategies. These questions are: What is the current situation of the company? The answer to this question is based on a diagnosis involving substantial areas of the company and can be parametrically or through the analysis of internal and external environment of the organization. The second question is where the company needs to go? From the diagnosis and aligned to the vision, what stage or scenario should we consider to take the company in a given time horizon? The third question corresponds to what should do to get what is needed to reach and how visualize to get there?

The discipline of strategic thinking as a prior and needed exercise to address planning, action and strategic assessment has not received enough time (Garrido, 2007). Not only enough time but it has not received the importance that it has in the formation of the business directors, entrepreneurship and the training of those who already hold these positions. Policy analysis is desired to elaborate a protocol involving these three questions.

The suggested sequence is Vision, Diagnosis, Strategies, which are the answers to the questions of strategic thinking. A company that has a superior strategy is able to keep its customers satisfied for a

Figure 1. Strategic thinking

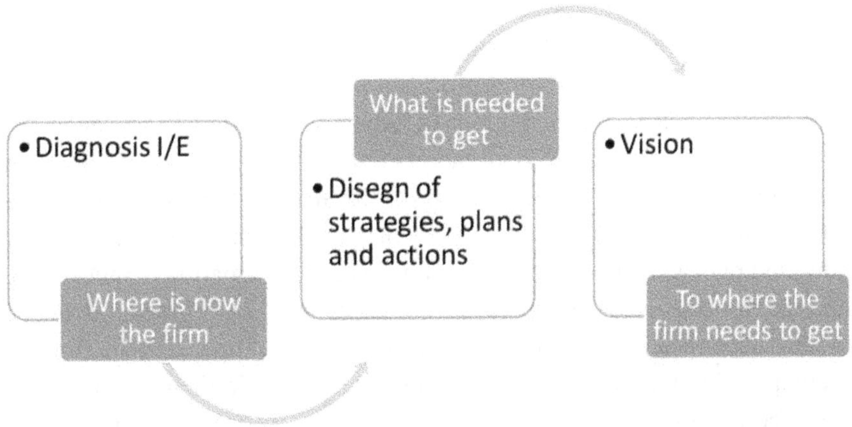

period of time and, continuously, to implement this strategy is necessary to move it to action, to create value for its shareholders, this being the ultimate goal of the strategy (Kluyver, 2001).

A CHALLENGE TO GENERATE INNOVATION ENVIRONMENTS IN THE COMPANIES OF THE 21ST CENTURY

The 21st century has a challenge for companies: taking innovation seriously, seen as appropriating innovation in all its forms in order to generate it. With this and for it, a particular and personalized mix of leadership, governance, knowledge of human capital and creation of collaborative networks is required. The above in such a way that ecosystems of innovation are created, where actors of the companies, collaborators, partners, competition and market form a synergistic system that promotes practices that lead to innovation.

Innovation in a global world is the common denominator towards success in the reality of the global economic environment of constant dynamism, which requires innovation as a fundamental idea for the holistic appropriation of innovation in companies. According to Drucker (1985), innovation is of vital strategic importance in management as a survival mechanism for corporations. Among the main factors for innovation, Whiting and Solomon (1989) emphasize the willingness to take risks, the generation of creative ideas, and the adaptability to entrepreneurial spirituality.

Taking into account the importance of innovation, it is worth mentioning that its impact is not only internal. Business innovation can come from: the introduction of a new good, the introduction of a new production method, the opening of a new market, the conquest of a new source of supply, and the implementation of a new structure in a market (Abbas & Asghar, 2010; Schumpeter, 1961)

Other very important characteristic recently mentioned for companies and their members are suggested by Livermore (2010) who comments only that culturally intelligent companies carry out the innovation, likewise the styles of leadership and administration, will generate a collective conscience tending to create environments of innovation. Leadership style is one of the most important factors to consider as the leaders are those individuals who establish the direction of the work and guide the collaborators in the direction of fulfilling the goals of the company by motivating each member who has gained their trust (Conger, 1992).

Among the factors that limit the development of nations are the lack of financing, difficulties to exploit technology, limited managerial skills, low productivity and regulatory burdens (Guellec & Potterie, 2000). In the present investigation, the limitations of managerial capacities as well as the difficulties to exploit the technology will be addressed; both factors related to a low knowledge of human capital as well as to the limited appropriation of innovation in all the areas of the company in a systemic way. In other words, the two limitations mentioned above prevent the appropriation of techniques, philosophy and styles of leadership and management of the company in favor of the creation of innovation environments.

To understand the importance of the elements of a company, Marvel et al. (2011) have established that an organization can be seen as a micro-environment, a cluster of open and limited sets and subsets in space and time, composed of individuals, positions and areas of work, their activities, capabilities and a variety of elements, both physical and of natural environment as well as cultural. The work environment is made up of general elements such as economic, social, and legal aspects, etc. Operational aspects such as customers, employees and suppliers and internal elements such as culture, organizational climate, processes, leadership styles, among others, are also critical.

There are indicators that reflect how well the resources of an economy are being used in production, that is, any company that has noticed deficiencies or underutilization of its resources and capacities can see the importance of improving processes and ways of doing things, being able to integrate the new highly technological companies and the constant innovation. Sar and Werneke (1984) refer to a relationship between the resources used and the products obtained and denotes the efficiency related to human resources, capital, knowledge, energy, etc. They are vital to produce goods and services in the market.

Now who carries out the innovation are the subjects that are involved in it, actors such as employees, directors, employees and investors, put their capabilities in favor of the objectives and the survival of the company. If a company had identified the best elements hypothetical greater competitive advantage would be achieved. To confirm the above, this research analyzes studies identifying the most important elements and features that facilitate innovation in each area of a company, people with characteristics and/or tending attributes to innovation in a visible way (Rubio & Baz, 2015). Researchers have proposed approaches with variable results: using demographic data and socioeconomic characteristics to identify the characteristics of subjects that facilitate the appropriation and creation of innovative environments, focusing on how to put into practice their capacity in favor of innovation.

Researchers such as Livermore (2010) have points of view based on their studies to culturally intelligent companies, which are responsible for the creation of innovation i.e. companies that have managed to understand the differences given by the environment and the culture obtain a clearer vision of the attitude and responses to ways of interacting within an organization.

Gloor (2006) defines collective intelligence as a set of self-motivated individuals with a collective vision, encouraged by collaborating in the search for a common goal, sharing ideas, information, work and therefore skills.

Livermore (2010) raises the cultural intelligence quotient as one that identifies the differences given by the environment to a subject and that can be a factor of innovation. This concept measures the skill and ability to function effectively in a variety of ways: organizational, national, political, cultural and ethnic scenarios. On the other hand, Livermore (2010) also mentions that cultural intelligence is an essential capacity in order to achieve business success. The well-identified elements that make up cultural intelligence are enthusiasm or motivation, knowledge, strategy, and action, adaptability of behavior to different cultures.

To improve the potential and skills of human capital, we highlight the points developed by the study of Chiavenato and Villamizar (2009), in which the authors pointed out that the survival of organizations depends on the appropriate use that is given to human capital and inherent to it especially its intellectual capital (knowledge, experiences and cognitive abilities). In this study, it is emphasized that the investment of a company must include the development of intellectual capital.

From another point of view, the most important aspects necessary to generate innovation environments include variables such as motivation, cognition, metacognition, and behaviors that are included in tools for the measurement of cognitive capacity (Zulma, 2006).

In terms of capital and cultural knowledge, Gillezeau (2011) analyzes certain elements that facilitate the skill or ability of companies to function effectively with people belonging to diverse environments and cultures, using their different skills, knowledge and abilities in an efficient manner to harmonize the relationship between the subjects within an organization and the organization itself, elements such as culture, attachments, nature, values, emotions, sense of equity of the environment, actions of collaborators, organization and processes.

Nowadays, not all the context of an organization involves its human or intellectual capital, the rules of the game and interaction are given by leadership styles. For it, Lyons (2011) highlights the capabilities that an innovative leader should have: ability to identify problems, recognize opportunities and know how to experiment, decision-making capacity, choice and assessment of ideas and mention the cognitive aspect of the leaders themselves that involves knowledge of models and risk selection. Finally, the leader must possess the ability to increase and manage the capacity of the organization through the use of influence without using authority, conflict management, the impulse of the creativity of his team and the use of adaptive governance.

One of the most recent terms is that of cultural intelligence itself that is described as the interest and confidence of the person to function effectively in culturally diverse environments. This term encompasses the person's knowledge, cognition, experiences and ideas on how the cultures are similar and different. It helps to improve judgments about one's own or others' thought processes, as well as the person's ability to adapt their behavior to different cultures. It requires having a flexible repertoire of responses to adapt to different situations, while remaining true to oneself, and is therefore an indispensable element of the leaders of the present to generate environments where there is equality and understanding of cultural differences (Depaula & Azzollini, 2012).

EVIDENCE: THE PROFILE OF THE GASTRONOMIC ENTREPRENEUR IN THE RESTAURANT BUSINESS

In this study, we analyze the profile of a gastronomic entrepreneur in the restaurant Los Mochis, Sin., based on the specific case of the Restaurant Metropizza. The entrepreneur has some traits, skills and characteristics in his personality that may allow him to be in a position to develop and operate a gastronomic project. Some qualities that he must have are desire to conquer, self-confidence, taking risks, flexibility to frustration, mercantile orientation in restaurants, orientation to success, control in his actions, overcoming ignorance, and of course bureaucracy.

Table 1. Comparison of management styles and leadership

Management styles and leadership	Authors	Theories
According to Mintzberg and McHugh (1985) it is a detailed monitoring system of actions very similar to an ideal. Organizations require articulated objectives, clear division of work, defined tasks, hierarchies, and formalized systems of control.	Mintzberg and McHugh (1985)	Adhocracy
This system promotes productivity, employee satisfaction, confidence, and stability in terms of employment. In addition, this theory is influenced by the Japanese management styles, where the most important element in companies is human resources.	Ouchi (1982)	Theory Z
Management is responsible for meeting, through good practices, the company goals taking into consideration social needs, the need of self-fulfillment, and the ego of subordinates. It places special emphasis on management as well as on the same motivational aspects that promote better conditions, self-regulated behavior, adequate work environment, and consequently better productivity results.	Mc Gregor (1960)	Theory Y
Managers control their performance, provide motivations, set performance objectives and define a broader vision. It also includes the "measurement" of good practices and their results. Standards of quality in processes are therefore important. This approach requires the subordinate to establish short-term performance objectives. On the other hand, management actively reflects and makes a careful assessment of the strengths and weaknesses of the company, inciting subordinates to propose specific plans to achieve their objectives.	Drucker (2007, 2013)	Management by objectives0
In this model, the process and consequences of the efforts to exert control and influence on decisions affects the functioning of the organization and the quality of life of the community. The value orientation of empowerment suggests goals, objectives, and strategies for implement change. Likewise, it provides principles and a framework to organize the activities of the company. Empowerment is visualized as an intentional and continuous process focused on the local community, which implies mutual respect, critical reflection, responsibility, loyalty, trust, caring, and group participation.	Zimmernan (2000)	Empowerment
It describes three levels of top, middle, and frontline management as defined degrees of power that expand leadership.		Leadership CANVAS

Source: (Author's elaboration)

Table 2. Important factors for generating innovation environment. Exploratory phase of the characteristics of leaders

Authors	Key factors
Gillezeau (2011)	Knowledge concerning culture, nature, values, emotions, feeling of equity in the environment, actions of collaborators, organization, and processes.
Prahalad and Hamel (1993)	When capacities are used more intensively, they become better. The use of those capacities stimulates creativity and innovation.
Lyons (2011)	Leaders of innovative environments should have: ability to identify opportunities and problems, know how to make experiments, ability to make decisions in contexts that involve risk.
Depaula and Azzollini (2012)	Cultural intelligence, values and motivation factors, ability to function effectively in a variety of national, ethnic and organizational environments.
Fontalvo (2017)	Leadership and behavior skills in pursuit of innovative strategic thinking.
Middlemist and Hitt (1981)	Positive and high influence on employees, know how to perform routine tasks, respectful and direct in its interactions, and personal relationships within the work.

Source: (Author's elaboration)

The factors the gastronomic entrepreneur at Metropizza counts on and take into account are the following ones: worrying about making money without being obsessed, cunning and idealistic; not being obsessed with power, rather being interested in autonomy, enjoying testing oneself, planning the project and facing risks; taste for showing himself what he knows, what he is worth and what he can; has the ability to work under pressure and visualize successful exits to the situations of operation and/or administration of the project, passion and affection in their undertaking. On many occasions, not everything is clear and he may be afraid, however he is encouraged to undertake; has the capacity to sacrifice for the project, always trying to offer a service or product of supreme quality, different and/or outstanding; he seeks to leave a mark on his endeavor to be convinced of success.

The gastronomic entrepreneur of Metropizza is aware that he can be wrong, but convinced that failure is not trying again. In addition to the above, the gastronomic entrepreneur must have capacity of interpersonal communication, sales and negotiation skills, ability to communicate to obtain correct information for the objectives of the project, as well as to generate collaboration from others. He also needs to have flexibility to frustration, i.e., do not be discouraged by the eventual partial failure of the project. This aspect is essential since it is almost normal that not everything goes well, but he must face obstacles, he must be persistent. Finally, he must assume risks, i.e., being prepared for situations of potential risk or uncertainty.

Entrepreneurship should not be random, as it involves analyzing the viability of the gastronomic business (product and/or service). The entrepreneur should be oriented to success, i.e., persistence in achieving goals and executing personal objectives, that is, starting the gastronomic business. He must have a clear idea about where he wants to go, being willing to do the best to achieve it. This aspect is related to will, enthusiasm and energy to reach the objectives set. The entrepreneur should also be self-confident, which is related to the personal ability to believe in himself, as well as the idea of achieving the proposed goals.

The gastronomic entrepreneur is expected to have complete confidence in his gastronomic project and gets the planning to carry it out, be aware that he will make decisions and must do it in fast way, not be afraid and trust himself, it is possible that, despite mistakes, it must persist. Confidence is extended to the team of collaborators.

CONCLUSION AND RECOMMENDATIONS

From the above mentioned perspectives, it is demonstrated that there is a relationship between successful profiles and products in entrepreneurship and innovative environments in international business. Of course, out of the qualities of personality in relation to the profile of the entrepreneur, the most outstanding thing is the desire to conquer, push, courage, overcome fear, overcome ignorance and of course, bureaucracy.

Concluding our analysis we refer to a phrase by Porter that mentions that nothing harms more than the words and behavior of important individuals being unconscious of their words and actions. The above is a reflection of the need to consciously involve the superiors of companies to achieve true changes. On the other hand, the changes will be impossible if the attitude of the collaborators are not consistent and congruent with the philosophy of the organization's interests and values.

Similarly, managerial styles cannot be exactly aligned with company ideals or leaders' beliefs due to the fact that intrinsic interests or beliefs are involved in most cases. The ethical components such as preferences and corruption that affect the acquisition of long-term innovation and the loyalty of employees are also involved in decision-making.

According to the results obtained in this study, co-responsibility between superiors and subordinates is necessary if the company is really considering this as an opportunity to continue growing and evolving.

The evidence and results show the effect of corporate culture on organizational performance, organizational commitment, job satisfaction, as well as the effect of managerial leadership style on organizational commitment, job satisfaction, etc.

In order to make recommendations for future research on the characterization of the Mexican international entrepreneur, we propose to examine a random sample in which various variables are evaluated, allowing to describe the object of study as the status of the entrepreneur in the organization; a second variable would be the reasons that entrepreneurs have to be a part of the business, are they intrinsic or extrinsic?

The intrinsic ones can become the self-determined motivation and openness that they have to the challenges, their personality traits, while extrinsic factors would be the social motivators such as the family, the schoolmates, the partners and friends, their romantic partner, in general, its social environment could be decisive in an entrepreneurial culture by looking at the individual within an ecosystem. Another research variable would be their attitudes and actions towards international entrepreneurship, in terms of personality such as chauvinism and nationalism or openness and respect for other cultures.

Previous experience can also be a fundamental variable to understand the international entrepreneur. Examining the difficulties that entrepreneurs have experienced starting and running their businesses and knowing the risks involved in entrepreneurship are research variables that could be related to the personality characteristics of entrepreneurs in terms of looking for the profile of an international entrepreneur.

In statistical terms, the correlation of several variables such as sex, education level and social class, using measures of central tendency, could help to create the profile of the international entrepreneur.

In conclusion, we believe that strategic thinking is a key factor that can influence the competitiveness of a company, generating strategies that are easily translated into action and ended saying to each executive think strategically and make the business competitive.

REFERENCES

Abbas, W., & Asghar, I. (2010). *The role of leadership in organizatinal change: Relating the successful organizational change with visionary and innovative leadership.* University of Gävle, Faculty of Engineering and Sustainable Development, Department of Industrial Development, IT and Land Management. Independent thesis Advanced level.

Amorós, J. E., Felzensztein, C., & Etchebarne, M. (2012). Emprendimiento internacional en Latinoamérica: Desafíos para el desarrollo. *Esic Market Economics and Business Journal, 43*(3), 513–529.

Bancomext. (2015). *Guía básica del exportador.* Banco Nacional de Comercio Exterior, S.N.C.

Bottome, P. (1939). *Alfred Adler: A biography.* Putnam.

Brazier, D. (1997). *Más allá de Carl Rogers.* Desclée de Brouwer Editorial.

Chiavenato, I. (2009). *Gestión del talento humano: El nuevo papel de los recursos humanos en las organizaciones*. McGraw-Hill.

Conger, J. A. (1992). *Reflections on leadership and spirit. Domingo Conference on Leadership and Spirit*, Boston, MA.

Depaula, P. D., & Azzollini, S. C. (2012). Inteligencia cultural, valores y motivación para el aprendizaje en estudiantes militares argentinos. *Revista de Psicología, 30*(1), 75–102. doi:10.18800/psico.201201.004

Drucker, P. F. (1985). The discipline of innovation. *Harvard Business Review, 63*(3), 67–72. PMID:10272260

Drucker, P. F. (2007). *Management challenges for the 21st century*. Routledge.

Drucker, P. F. (2013). *People and performance*. Harvard Business School Press. doi:10.4324/9780080938417

Engler, B. (1996). *Introducción a las teorías de la personalidad*. McGraw-Hill.

Expansión Magazine. (2011). *Exportación: Solo para grandes empresas*. Recovered from https://expansion.mx/manufactura/2011/10/12/exportacion-solo-para-grandes-empresas

Fontalvo, S. M. I. (2017). Habilidades de liderazgo para una cultura de innovación en la gerencia de las universidades del distrito de Santa Marta. *Academia y Virtualidad, 10*(1).

Garrido, F. J. (2007). *Pensamiento estrategico. La estrategia como centro neuralgico de la empresa*. Ediciones Deusto.

Gillezeau, P. (2011). La cultura organizacional en el desarrollo de empresas inteligentes. Fundamentos: Valores, Comunicación y Liderazgo. *Telos, 1*(2), 221–232.

Gloor, P. A. (2006). *Swarm creativity: Competitive advantage through collaborative innovation networks*. Oxford University Press. doi:10.1093/acprof:oso/9780195304121.001.0001

Guellec, D., & de la Potterie, B. V. P. (2000). *The impact of public R&D expenditure on business R&D*. OECD Publishing.

Hernández, S. R., Fernández, C. C., & Baptista, P. L. (2014). *Metodología de la investigación* (6th ed.). McGraw-Hill.

INEGI. (2017). *Resumen de balanza comercial de mercancías de México. Participación porcentual de las exportaciones petroleras y no petroleras*. Recovered from https://www.inegi.org.mx/programas/comext/

Kim, W. C., & Mauborgne, R. A. (2017). Blue Ocean Leadership. *Harvard Business Review, 11*(67), 23. PMID:24956870

Kluyver, C. A. (2001). *Pensamiento estratégico. Una perspectiva para los ejecutivos*. Prentice Hall.

Kotler, P., & Armstrong, G. (2007). *Marketing versión para Latinoamérica*. Pearson Editorial.

Livermore, D. (2010, Jan. 6). CQ: The test of your potential for cross-cultural success. *Revista Forbes*.

Lyons, R. (2011). Paths to innovative leadership. *BizEd Magazine, 10*(2), 32-38.

Marvel C. M., Rodríguez M., C., & Núñez B. M. A. (2011). La productividad desde una perspectiva humana: Dimensiones y factores. *Intangible Capital, 7*(2).

Masood, S. A., Dani, S. S., Burns, N. D., & Backhouse, C. J. (2006). Transformational leadership and organizational culture: The situational strength perspective. *Proceedings of the Institution of Mechanical Engineers. Part B, Journal of Engineering Manufacture, 220*(6), 941–949. doi:10.1243/09544054JEM499

McGregor, D. (1960). *The human side of enterprise*. McGraw-Hill.

Middlemist, R. D., & Hitt, M. (1981). *Organizational behavior: Applied concepts*. Science Research Associates.

Mintzberg, H., & McHugh, A. (1985). Strategy formation in an adhocracy. *Administrative Science Quarterly, 30*(2), 160–197. doi:10.2307/2393104

Ouchi, W. (1982). *Theory Z*. Avon books.

Oviatt, B. M., & McDougall, P. P. (2005). Defining international entrepreneurship and modeling the speed of internationalization. *Entrepreneurship Theory and Practice, 29*(5), 537–553. doi:10.1111/j.1540-6520.2005.00097.x

Pavón, L. (2010). *Financiamiento a las microempresas y las pymes en México (2000-2009)*. Cepal Editorial.

Prahalad, C. K., & Hamel, G. (1993). Stretch and leverage. *Harvard Business Review, 71*, 75–84. PMID:10124635

ProMéxico. (2018). *Pasos para Exportar*. Recovered from http://www.promexico.gob.mx/es/mx/pasos-exportar

Roldan, P. N. (2019). John Stuart Mill. *Economipedia*. Recovered from https://economipedia.com/historia/biografia/john-stuart-mill.html

Rubio, L., & Baz, V. (2015). *El poder de la competitividad*. Fondo de Cultura Economica.

Sar, L., & Werneke, D. (1984). *Productivity: Problems, prospects, and policies*. The Johns Hopkins University Press.

Schumpeter, J. A. (1961). *The theory of economic development*. Oxford University Press.

Secretaría de Economía. (2016). *Subsecretaria de Comercio Exterior, Total exports in Mexico*. Recovered from https://www.economia.gob.mx/files/comunidad_negocios/comercio_exterior/informacion_estadistica/anual_exporta.pdf

Selva, V. (2019). David Ricardo. *Economipedia*. Recovered from http://economipedia.com/?s=david+ricardo

Whiting, B. G., & Solomon, G. T. (1989). *Key issues in creativity, innovation & entrepreneurship*. Bearly.

Zimmerman, B. J. (2000). Attainment of self-regulation: A social cognitive perspective. In M. Boekaerts, P. Pintrich, & M. Zeidner (Eds.), *Handbook of self-regulation, research, and applications* (pp. 13–39). Academic Press. doi:10.1016/B978-012109890-2/50031-7

Zulma, M. (2006). Aprendizaje autorregulado: El lugar de la cognición, la metacognición y la motivación. *Estudios Pedagógicos (Valdivia)*, *32*(2), 121–132. doi:10.4067/S0718-07052006000200007

Chapter 17
The Impact of Entrepreneur Personal Characteristics on New Firm Growth:
The Case of Portugal

Vítor Hugo Santos Ferreira
https://orcid.org/0000-0003-3400-5996
Polytechnic Institute of Leiria, Portugal

Tomás Almeida Luís
Instituto Universitário de Lisboa, Portugal

ABSTRACT

Entrepreneurship has emerged as a key vector, introducing dynamism in stagnant markets, through technological change, innovation, and process restructuring. However, despite all the potential benefits, this is a very arduous and uncertain process, to the extent that many of the companies created end up failing in the first five years of activity. This chapter aims to study the entrepreneur as an individual, focusing on the analysis of their personal characteristics and their impact on the growth of the new created firm. A mixed methodology was developed to test which personal characteristics impact growth. A questionnaire was carried out on a sample of 87 Portuguese entrepreneurs and, additionally, 10 interviews were held with the purpose of complementing the information of the collected data with a qualitative approach and a more personal perspective. Finally, the results revealed that there are certain characteristics that enhance and influence the growth of startups, the most crucial being leadership, the need for achievement, proactivity, and resilience and adaptability.

DOI: 10.4018/978-1-7998-7568-0.ch017

INTRODUCTION

Entrepreneurship has emerged as a key vector, introducing dynamism in stagnant markets, through technological change, innovation, and process restructuring. In this way, the entrepreneurial activity allows the creation of new job opportunities and improved productivity, contributing strongly to socioeconomic development. According to Birley (1989), the creation of new companies proves to be an important strategic alternative for economic recovery and growth. Entrepreneurship seems to have a highly positive impact on competitiveness, in the promotion of new jobs and the attribution of new responses to existing needs (Birch, 1979).

However, the entrepreneurial activity varies in different countries, territories, and societies, being conditioned by several factors, such as motivations, beliefs, patterns of behavior, available resources, and norms installed in society. Thus, despite the high positive impact that the creation of new companies can have, this process proves to be quite adverse and uncertain, given that most companies end up ceasing in the first years of activity (Jones, 2009).

It is extremely important to analyze the various factors that impact the development of the entrepreneurial activity and their implications for the performance and achievement of the success of the created companies.

This chapter is based on the study of the entrepreneur as a unique individual, paying particular attention to the identification of the main characteristics common to successful entrepreneurs. Thus, the research question is: What is the impact of the learned characteristics of the entrepreneurs in guaranteeing the success of their organizations? This question is analyzed in the context of the Portuguese economy, through a mixed methodology, based on a survey and in-depth interviews.

In this sense, the present chapter has as main objective analyze the impact of entrepreneurs' personal characteristics on the growth of their startups.

LITERATURE SURVEY

Entrepreneurship: Evolution of the Concept

According to Mars and Rios-Aguilar (2010) the concept of entrepreneurship emerged during the 17th and 18th centuries. However, authors like Salim and Silva (2010) go further, arguing that entrepreneurship is an intrinsic process to the human being and, therefore, its origin dates back to the early human race. Similarly, Duarte and Esperança (2012) and Sarkar (2010) state that the concept of entrepreneurship has been referred to with different meanings over the several years. However it was in recent years that it has achieved greater recognition. According to Kuratko (2005), the phenomenon of entrepreneurship began in the last two decades, revealing itself to be a very dynamic process with strong economic potential.

Most economists and sociologists are unanimous in considering entrepreneurship as a process and not as a static phenomenon. Nazir and Ramzan (2012) state that the concept of entrepreneurship involves two determinants: on the one hand, innovation, resulting from the possible creations resulting from its process and, on the other hand, the risk, arising from the change and the impacts that these changes may bring. Thus, according to Bucha (2009), entrepreneurship should not only be mentioned as a business concept, but also as a concept of life, since its sphere of action is quite broad, impelling a set of changes that need to be addressed.

According to Galloway et al. (2005), better businesses, products and services can be generated through entrepreneurship, benefiting those who best adapt to the changes that have occurred. In this way, Heinonen and Poikkijoki (2006) refer to entrepreneurship as an innovative approach to problem solving, stimulating the development of characteristics such as proactivity, leadership, and creativity, which are essential for economic progress.

Entrepreneurship is, therefore, the "process of creating something new with value, dedicating the necessary time and effort, taking the corresponding financial, psychological and social risks and receiving the consequent rewards of satisfaction and financial and personal independence" (Hisrich et al., 2010, p. 30), involving the connection between two phenomena: the creation of lucrative opportunities and the presence of entrepreneurial individuals (Shane & Venkataraman, 2000).

The Entrepreneur

According to several authors, such as Hébert and Link (1989) and Arthur and Hisrich (2011), Richard Cantillon (1680-1734) was the first researcher to introduce the concept of "entrepreneur", through the work "Essay on the Nature of Commerce in General", in 1755, in which he defined entrepreneurs as the most daring individuals who stimulate economic progress by discovering new and better ways of doing things. This core notion has endured until today, even if other remarkable contributions have been added. In the work "A Treaty of Political Economy or the Production, Distribution and Consumption of Wealth", in the 19th century, Jean-Baptiste (1767-1832) referred to the entrepreneur as a leader or manager. Later, in the work "Principles of Political Economy". Mill (1848) introduced the notion of entrepreneurship to the element of uncertainty and risk, a concept that has been emphasized later by other authors such as Knight (1921) or Baptista et al. (2008).

In the 20th century, Joseph Schumpeter (1934) presented a modern definition of entrepreneur, integrating the concept of "creative destruction", where he identifies the entrepreneur as the individual who destroys order in the existing economy by introducing new products, services, new production methods and by creating new forms of organization or by exploring new raw materials. Furthermore, according to the same author, it is more likely that this destruction is caused by the creation of a new business, but also by the innovation of something that already exists.

According to Baumol (1993), there are two entrepreneur profiles. The first refers to the profile in which the entrepreneur creates, organizes and conducts the activity of a new company, regardless of the existence of something innovative. The second portrays the entrepreneur as someone capable of transforming inventions and ideas into economically viable entities, even though during the process there was not necessarily the creation of a company.

Finally, Dornelas (2008) states that the entrepreneur is the one who detects a business opportunity and creates a business to capitalize on it, assuming calculated risks for this. Thus, the discussion around the concept of entrepreneur leads many researchers to study the motives and reasons why individuals decide to become entrepreneurs.

Main Reasons and Motivations for Undertaking

The entrepreneurial motivations and intentions that may arise on the part of individuals are distinct as well as the concepts themselves, but can be linked as is defended by some authors.

Motivation

Motivation is one of the most studied variables to perceive the behavior of entrepreneurs, that is, it studies what leads individuals to create their own business (Valencia et al., 2014). For Zimmerer et al. (2008), motivation is a type of energy that will encourage an individual to do an activity that arise from present needs, contributing to their satisfaction of opening a company or business, thus reducing some existing imbalances. Entrepreneurial motivations are a self-incentive, resulting from internal or external factors, thus allowing the growth of entrepreneurial intentions (Guerrero et al., 2008).

The entrepreneurial process occurs mainly, because people are motivated to act, since the entrepreneur's own action is the result of a set of motivational factors (Hechavarria et al., 2011).

According to David McClelland, 1961, one of the motivations for an individual to become an entrepreneur is the need for achievement (McClelland, 1961), in which it is not inevitably innate in individuals, and can be developed over time, through education and even from the stimuli of society itself (Valencia et al., 2014). The connections that individuals create with their family and society are considered fundamental in the motivations for the creation and support of the new business. Almeida and Teixeira (2014) argue that individuals are primarily responsible for having the will to create entrepreneurial initiatives.

According to Locke (2000), motivation influences entrepreneurial behavior in three ways: it influences the choice of the individual, that is, the course of action; influences the intensity of the action, based on the value and importance that the action has for the individual and influences the persistence of the action, that is, the frequency with which the action is performed. Thus, according to Eccles, Wigfield and Schiefele (1998), there are several theories about motivation that intend to explore the way in which motivation is at the base of decisions, of consistency and of the commitment that individuals grant in certain activities.

Cassar (2007) points out as the main motivations the need for independence and self-realization, the desire to learn and grow as individuals, the desire to obtain financial success, the need to obtain recognition from society and peers, the opportunity to reach a position higher and more prestigious in society but emphasizes the fact that the motivations described above can change throughout the process of entrepreneurship.

The objective of the study by Barba-Sánchez and Atienza-Sahuquillo (2012) was to understand what motivates individuals to create their own businesses. This study concluded that the need for achievement, independence, affiliation, competence, power, the preference for innovation and finally the willingness to take risks and challenges, have a greater influence when starting a business, than for example, making a lot of money or being your own boss (Barba-Sánchez & Atienza-Sahuquillo, 2012).

Gilad and Levine (1986) advocated a theory that allows classifying motivations in two categories: push and pull (Segal et al. 2005). In this sense, there is a categorization regarding the source of these motivations, with the push being identified as a necessity and the pull as an opportunity (Kirkwood & Walton, 2010). In this logic, the push theory states that individuals are "pushed" into the entrepreneurship process due to negative factors (e.g., dismissal, divorce, or dissatisfaction with the job), while the pull theory assumes that individuals are "attracted" to entrepreneurship due to positive factors (e.g., self-realization, seeking independence, and recognition of an opportunity, among others). According to Segal (2005), the number of entrepreneurs motivated by pull factors is higher than the push factors, which is quite important given that entrepreneurs with this type of motivation are naturally more likely to succeed (Amit & Muller, 1995).

However, according to Ferreira et al. (2017), what motivates an individual to create a new business may come to suffer some changes throughout the process of entrepreneurship, as these individuals acquire experience or even the occurrence of some adverse factors that arise over time.

Intention

According to Bird (2015, p.143) intention is "a process, state, or act of wanting some experience in the present, making it true, realized, manifested or created in the future. Intentions can be to do, be or have".

Entrepreneurial intention can be defined as the desire to carry out activities in an effective way, which influence individuals to use and implement certain relevant new business concepts (Krueger et al., 2000). The intention is seen as a desire to start a business, being the characteristic that is most reflected in the entrepreneur's behavior (Liñán et al., 2011).

For Nwankwo et al. (2012) entrepreneurship education is a very effective tool that promotes and reinforces the interest in entrepreneurship, with some who defend that the social role that the entrepreneur has in society, as an important factor that motivates entrepreneurial intentions.

Reardon (1991) saw culture as a factor linked to entrepreneurial intentions Thins like family background, the neighborhood, the peer group and the general work situation can influence the choice as to whether or not to start a business (Curran et al., 1996).

In addition to the reasons mentioned, it is important to highlight the fact that different individuals have different motivations. It is in this context that motivation represents an important link between intention and action, presenting itself as a matrix force in the pursuit of the different objectives of human behavior, especially in entrepreneurial behavior (Carsrud & Brannback, 2011).

Characteristics of the Entrepreneur

The characteristics of successful entrepreneurs have, over time, been the target of analysis of several studies, in an attempt to develop a unique profile capable of aggregating the main characteristics responsible for success (Littunen, 2000; Luegler & Mugler, 2003; Moore et al. 2008; Nandram & Samson, 2000; Salim, 2004).

Timmons et al. (1985) state that there is no single set of characteristics capable of guaranteeing total success in all business opportunities. For this reason, the entrepreneur must seek to continuously develop his skills and level of knowledge, to be able to gather the necessary tools in the different situations he faces. Thus, the premise arises that the entrepreneur's chances of success can improve due to the elimination, acquisition, or improvement of certain characteristics.

Other authors, such as Nieman and Bennett (2002), refer that the characteristics can be innate or acquired through personal and professional experiences. They also argue that the entrepreneur should make use of all the characteristics that he has in the most diverse situations, given that the absence of any one of them can become a critical weakness in the entrepreneurial activity.

According to studies carried out by Bernadette and Travaglione (2003), some characteristics common among entrepreneurs, such as the propensity to take risk, creativity, persistence, capacity for innovation, awareness, adaptability, resilience, knowledge in the market and capacity in dealing with adversity.

Finally, Kourilsky and Walstad (1998) argue that entrepreneurial characteristics are universal and timeless and should be cultivated and developed in the early stages of life, namely through education.

In this sense, the individual characteristics can be characterized in three different ways: attributed characteristics, acquired characteristics and learned characteristics, which we will present further.

Attributed Features

According to Ferrante (2008), the attributed characteristics correspond to the personal traits that the individual has after being born, without having to make an effort to do so. Thus, they are attributes that people have after birth, that develop over time, or that are acquired without any intent, such as age, ethnicity, gender, socioeconomic origin, among others.

Acquired Features

According to Good (2003), the acquired characteristics correspond to the qualities that require a high degree of effort and learning such as specialization in a given scientific area. These characteristics are highly appreciated and desired as they can really enhance the success of any business opportunity.

Learned Characteristics

The learned characteristics correspond to the qualities that require a high degree of effort and learning such as specialization in a given scientific area. These characteristics are highly appreciated and desired since they can really enhance the success of any business opportunity (Good, 2003).

Need for Achievement

The need for achievement has been one of the most studied characteristics in the scope of entrepreneurship. McClelland (1961) defines the need for achievement as a measurable set of spontaneous thoughts among individuals driven by the intention to do something better than what already exists.

Chell (1991) states that individuals who have a high level of need for accomplishment tend to avoid characterizing tasks as easy or difficult, but rather to perceive them as necessary steps to achieve the proposed objectives or goals, thus creating a feeling of personal fulfillment and satisfaction. Similarly, Haworth and Brearley (1991) defend the need for achievement as a drive for excellence. Koh (1996) defines these individuals as extremely focused workers, with a great desire to be successful and, for that reason, more likely to embark on an entrepreneurial path. Thus, the author concludes that this is a fundamental characteristic for any entrepreneurial individual, and it can be acquired and developed over time.

Locus of Control

The concept of Locus of control was developed by Rotter (1966) and states that entrepreneurs' expectations are established and strengthened by their efforts and, therefore, are responsible for the results they obtain.

According to Henry (2003), the locus of control can be characterized in two different ways: locus of internal control and locus of external control. In this sense, he argues that individuals who have locus of internal control reveal a greater influence on their destinies and, for this reason, assume themselves as directly responsible for their successes or failures. On the other hand, individuals who have locus of external control tend to attribute the results of their lives to external factors, such as fate, luck, or other phenomena.

Stewart (2012) states that individuals with higher levels of locus of control are more capable of controlling not only their impulses, but also their environments, having the ability to discern information, focus on goals, exercise activities simultaneously, deal with frustration, lead and solve problems. This perspective intersects with Krueger's (1993) view, which states that the locus of control can be conceived as a catalyst for action.

Brockhaus (1975) found that students with entrepreneurial intentions had a high level of locus of control compared to others who did not intend to create a company. In this sense, entrepreneurs tend to have a high degree of locus of control in relation to the general population, due to the confidence they show in their own skills (Zinga, 2007).

Leadership

According to Greenberg and Baron (2000), leadership presents itself as a process in which individuals seek to influence others in order to achieve the proposed objectives and goals.

According to Surie and Ashley (2008), leadership is composed of three main characteristics: proactivity, innovation, and risk management. In this sense, the interpretation of future problems, the exploration of new opportunities, the ability to think creatively, the resolution of problems and the assumption of weighted and necessary risks for the development of the business are crucial for the leader.

Moore and Buttner (1997) argue that leadership takes on a fundamental role in entrepreneurial activity, proving to be a determinant in ensuring business success. In this sense, according to the authors, entrepreneurial leadership is the ability to build and share an entrepreneurial vision as well as to motivate individuals even in situations of greater tension or uncertainty. Timmons and Spinelli (2008) state that that leaders are honest, trustworthy, fair individuals, with a high level of experience, with deep knowledge of the market in which they operate and with the ability to explore opportunities in order to influence and lead the future.

Commitment and Determination

According to a study by Koh and Bhatia (2004), commitment and determination is an approach that can manifest itself in the face of an action, task or organization, since it reflects total loyalty towards the achievement of a certain objective, be it a lesser one or larger scale.

Baskerville and Flanagan (2002) defend commitment and determination as a crucial characteristic in the pursuit of entrepreneurial activities, as it allows individuals to overcome the different obstacles and challenges that may arise. For Collura and Applegate (2000), commitment and determination are defined as the unshakable will that entrepreneurs demonstrate in the incessant search for new opportunities. Similarly, Timmons and Spinelli (2008) argue that individuals with a high level of commitment and determination can overcome any obstacle as well as reinforce their weaknesses.

Hatch and Zweig (2000) reveal that most entrepreneurs demonstrate a high desire to achieve success, dispelling any obstacles or challenges that arise along the way.

Risk Propensity

Brockhaus (1980) defines risk propensity as the perception of the probability of receiving benefits associated with the success of an entrepreneurial action, instead of the consequences associated with the failure of the same action. In this sense, entrepreneurs tend to be less risk averse, which reveals a greater tolerance for the uncertain and, therefore, have a greater chance of success in situations of great change (Cunningham & O'Gorman, 1997).

Kuratko (2009) believes that these individuals take calculated risks even before entering any entrepreneurial activity in order to avoid unnecessary risks and maximize the chances of success. Likewise, Cunningham and Gorman (1997) state that entrepreneurs prone to risk taking are able to better deal with and manage situations of greater tension or uncertainty, which in turn makes them more apt to achieve success.

Several studies, such as Chell's (1991), consider the risk propensity as the main characteristic based on the construction of the entrepreneurial character. According to the author, entrepreneurs have a moderate degree of risk taking, and in situations of greater uncertainty they tend to choose scenarios whose probability of loss is not totally zero (maximizing the potential gain), nor of increasing risk (avoiding the risk factor), assuming, therefore, situations of considerable and predetermined risk.

On the other hand, Miner and Raju (2004) reveal some doubts regarding the fact that the risk propensity is perceived as an entrepreneurial characteristic. According to the authors, entrepreneurs, in certain situations, show less risk tolerance than their collaborators. Similarly, Hisrich and Peters (2002) argue that empirically there is no conclusive causal relationship between risk propensity and entrepreneurship. Finally, Deamer and Earle (2004) highlight the need for clarity of empirical facts regarding the risk propensity during entrepreneurial activities.

Proactivity

According to Venkatraman (1989), proactivity stands out as a process in which the individual anticipates and acts on future needs through the identification of opportunities that may or may not be related to the initial business. Likewise, Henry (2003) states that entrepreneurs are naturally enthusiastic people and, therefore, show a high spirit of initiative and tend to stimulate their business. For this reason, they are identified as proactive individuals with a constant desire to seek and find new opportunities.

According to Gorman and Cunningham (1997), proactive individuals maintain a high level of energy and interest in the idea of the product or business, even when progress is slow. According to a survey conducted by Mueller and Thomas (2001), several entrepreneurs do not achieve the success of their organizations since they are unable to prevail in the face of the fears and uncertainty inherent in the entrepreneurial process.

Tolerance of Ambiguity and Uncertainty

Teoh and Foo (1997) define tolerance for ambiguity and uncertainty as the ability to respond positively to unknown situations. Collura and Applegate (2000) state that individuals with this characteristic are more agile in dealing with and managing situations of great change, pressure, and conflict.

Schere (1982) identifies tolerance to ambiguity and uncertainty as one of the most important characteristics of the entrepreneurial universe, as it allows individuals to face different scenarios with optimism, which is crucial in the process of creating and developing companies.

According to Henry (2003), individuals capable of taking weighted risks are, in the majority, more determined and committed to the execution of tasks, even in the face of adverse situations. Similarly, Koh (1996) states that entrepreneurs tend to consider uncertain scenarios as a challenge and, therefore, identify it with a stimulus to overcome and develop their own performance. Thus, it is expected that entrepreneurs take on a set of challenges and changes along the way, considering them as necessary steps to achieve their goals (Good, 2003).

Spirit of Opportunity

Bygrave (2004) defines the spirit of opportunity as the relentless desire to take objectives and goals to the next level. In this sense, the author defends that it is one of the main tools to stimulate the creation of value.

According to Shane (2000) there are several ways to explore opportunities and create value, and this difference results from the fact that each individual has a set of characteristics and skills that make him / her distinct from others.

Longenecker (2006) states that entrepreneurs who have a high level of opportunity spirit seek to be systematically updated in relation to the needs of the market and the client, in order to find a possibility to build value. In contrast, Westhead and Wright (2001) claim that experience does not always represent a direct relationship with the ability to recognize opportunities. In this sense, they argue that experienced entrepreneurs tend to be overconfident and, for this reason, end up in a situation of illusion of control, which leads them to be less sensitive when decoding important aspects for the business, thus limiting the search for information.

Innovative Spirit

According to Schumpeter (1934), the entrepreneur is a catalyst for change capable of identifying new business opportunities. Thus, the capacity for innovation is a characteristic of entrepreneurs, standing out as the means for exploring changes and a major factor for the survival, development and success of any organization (Utterback, 1996).

Robinson et al. (2000) found that entrepreneurs have a greater capacity for innovation than non-entrepreneurs. In this sense, according to Morrison (2000), companies that run in the innovation hemisphere have higher success rates and more easily survive different changes. Mirela (2008) considers that for the realization of an innovation, the following conditions must be met: existence of a clear strategy, realistic assessment of the potential gain or benefit, detailed knowledge about the market, anticipation of future needs and identification of the necessary resources for the innovation.

Confidence

Trust has been identified as a fundamental characteristic in the universe of entrepreneurship, proving to be decisive in the achievement of business success (Ho, 1992). According to Koh (1996), entrepreneurial individuals show a higher level of self-confidence than non-entrepreneurs.

Robinson (1991) affirms that confidence is directly related to creativity and tolerance to ambiguity and, for this reason, it is essential that the individual is aware of his valences in order to build his self-esteem and enhance his effectiveness in solving organizational problems.

Bygrave (2004) argues that entrepreneurs who have a higher level of confidence blame their success or failure as a result of their effort and not due to external factors such as luck.

Resilience and Adaptability

Collura and Applegate (2000) define resilience and adaptability as the entrepreneur's ability to keep an open mind, adjust effectively to changes, learn quickly and develop new skills and perspectives.

Tichy (1990) highlights the importance of the characteristic of resilience and adaptability of entrepreneurs in the growth and guarantee of success of their organizations. In this sense, it is essential that companies promote the practice of activities capable of stimulating the development of these characteristics in employees, since they contribute positively to business excellence.

Rwigerma and Venter (2004) and Timmons and Spinelli (2010) argue that successful entrepreneurs believe in their control in the face of achievements and, therefore, reveal a high capacity for adaptability as well as commitment to the execution of their tasks.

Relationship Between the Individual's Characteristics and the New Firm Growth

Zhang and Bruning (2011) argue that the level of success of a startup depends strongly on the set of characteristics held by its owner. Additionally, he states that in order to achieve success, the entrepreneur must have a set of excellent and differentiating characteristics, capable of responding to the emergence of different needs and changes.

Thus, it is the entrepreneur as an individual that enables the company to innovate, embrace new business opportunities and respond to different adversities.

That said, since the bankruptcy rate of recent companies is quite high (the vast majority ends up ceasing in the first five years of activity), it becomes crucial for individuals to become aware of the impact that their characteristics reveal on performance in order to maximize their chances of success (Bannock, 2005).

METHODOLOGY AND RESEARCH MEANS

Model

Our model consists of an integrated system of relationships between the various characteristics previously presented and their venture success.

Thus, this chapter aims to validate the following hypothesis.

1. **H1:** The need for achievement positively impacts the growth of startups.
2. **H2:** The locus of control positively impacts the growth of startups.
3. **H3:** Leadership positively impacts the growth of startups.

Figure 1. Research model
Source: Self elaboration

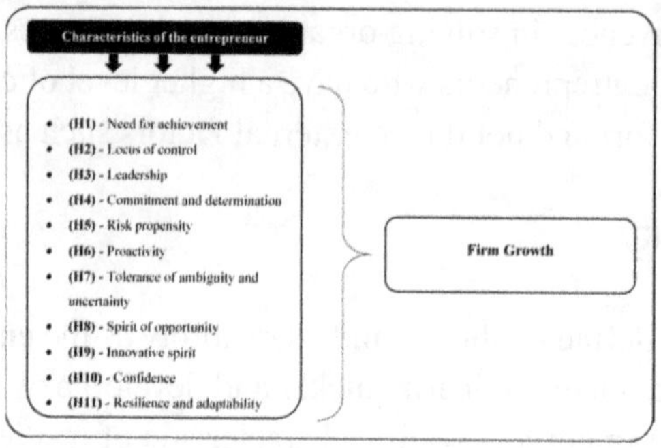

4. **H4:** Commitment and determination positively impacts the growth of startups.
5. **H5:** The risk propensity positively impacts the growth of startups.
6. **H6:** Proactivity positively impacts the growth of startups.
7. **H7:** Tolerance of ambiguity and uncertainty positively impacts the growth of startups.
8. **H8:** The spirit of opportunity positively impacts the growth of startups.
9. **H9:** The innovative spirit positively impacts the growth of startups.
10. **H10:** Trust positively impacts the growth of startups.
11. **H11:** Resilience and adaptability positively impacts the growth of startups.

MEANS OF RESEARCH

The present research adopts two types of instruments for data collection. For the first phase of the investigation, two questionnaires were applied and, for the second, 10 interviews were conducted. According to Malhotra (2004), the questionnaire is an aggregation of structured questions whose purpose is centered on the collection of information from respondents. Thus, in order to reach a considerable number of people, the language used must be objective and simple, ensuring the clarity of all questions for the interviewee. Thus, both questionnaires aimed to gather and consolidate information regarding the different characteristics of the stakeholders.

In the second phase, interviews were conducted with the aim of collecting more personal data, complementing the previously consolidated information. In this sense, the purpose was to explore a more personal and subjective aspect of certain individuals, seeking to understand in more detail their experiences, views and opinions regarding the subject under study.

Self-Administered Questionnaires

A questionnaire carried out was based on obtaining concrete data regarding the valences and characteristics of the individuals. In this sense, it intended to evaluate personal elements such as gender, age, marital status, educational qualifications, and previous experience in the company's activity sector.

Among the individual characteristics, the degree of leadership, commitment, determination, self-confidence, innovation, locus of control, risk aversion, adaptability, among others, were evaluated. Thus, in this questionnaire the seven-point Likert scale was used, seeking to identify the degree of agreement from 1 - strongly disagree to 7 - strongly agree according to the questions asked. These dimensions were measured based on Barbosa (2015) that builds on the theoretical base we previously presented.

Additionally, we include a 5 point Likert scale to measure sales growth in the past years, where 1 was negative growth, 2 - zero growth, 3 - 1% to 15% growth, 4 -16% to 34% growth and 5 - 35% or more growth.

Interviews

In addition to the questionnaire previously presented, interviews were conducted with a small group of entrepreneurs. This group is made up of entrepreneurs who in recent years have shown high levels of notoriety due to their performance, achievements, and uniqueness. For this reason, the main objective of the interviews focused on evaluating a more personal aspect of individuals, debating with several questions, such as: their path, the vision about entrepreneurship, the difficulties experienced during the development of their startup, among others.

Thus, the added value underlying the interviews carried out was based on the possibility of complementing the information collected from the questionnaires through the opinions, information and thoughts shared by the individuals. Thus, according to Guerra (2006), the use of the interview becomes essential since, through this method, the subjects start to have a status of privileged informants. That said, the in-depth understanding of the testimony of several individuals is guaranteed, fundamental in obtaining several complementary conclusions.

Data Analysis

Data analysis aims to collect information that helps to face and solve the problem under study. Therefore, for the proposed study, several factors were analyzed, such as the type of data, the research model and the premises presented in the questionnaires and interviews.

In this sense, some methods of analysis have been identified which, after research, have proved to be quite relevant for carrying out the investigation. Among the methods of data analysis, descriptive analysis, Cronbach's alpha, the correlation matrix, regressions, as well as the use of various statistics and tests were selected, namely the chi-square, ANOVA, the t test and Pearson's correlation. Statistical Package for the Social Sciences - SPSS was used to perform the statistics and tests. According to Coakes (2005), the SPSS has practically all the characteristics of available statistics, reason why it is frequently used by the researchers for the accomplishment of quantitative analyzes.

Sample

As part of the study, 94 responses to the questionnaire were collected. Thus, all responses were submitted to a process of analysis and elimination of cases that did not match the proposed requirements of the sample:

"Portuguese citizens, at least 18 years old and belonging to the NUTS II regions of Norte, Centro and Lisbon, who have created and managed for at least one year at least one startup".

In this sense, from the total data collected, seven responses were excluded from the study, six of which were due to the fact that the entrepreneurs had developed entrepreneurial initiatives for an insufficient period (less than one year) and the other because the completion was completed carried out at random which would end up making the study unfeasible.

That said, and in order to guarantee the exploration of diversified paths that could reflect the reality of the study, the objective of 80 responses was defined. Therefore, through the collaboration of different entrepreneurs, it was possible to exceed the defined objective, and 87 responses were considered for the study.

FINDINGS

Sample Characterization

The interviewees, that is, the entrepreneurs who answered the questionnaires, can be characterized according to the following variables: gender, age, marital status, educational qualifications and previous experience in the company's activity sector.

Regarding age, it was divided into five intervals (18 - 24; 25 - 30; 31 - 40; 41 - 54; > 55) in order to facilitate the analysis. Thus, in terms of distribution, respondents aged between 18 - 24 represent approximately 16% of the total sample, individuals aged between 25 - 30 represent 23%, individuals between 31 - 40 represent 26%, respondents aged 41 - 54 represent 21% and the remainder, aged over 54 years, represent 14% of the total sample.

According to the data obtained, we verified a relatively young sample, given that the majority of respondents are under 40 years old, being the most frequent age group from 31 to 40 years old. The male gender predominates, corresponding to 61% of the total respondents.

Regarding the respondents' marital status, according to the results, 47 are married and only 25 are single, which, for the sample in question, suggests a predominance of individuals living with their spouse or partner.

According to the study, according to educational qualifications, it appears that, in general, respondents show a high level of academic qualifications. In this sense, in terms of distribution, only 6 individuals out of 87 respondents have a level of education up to secondary level. On the other hand, individuals with a degree represent 20% of the total sample, followed by respondents with a graduate degree representing 32%. About the master's degree, 32 of the respondents present the conclusion of this degree, thus representing the largest percentage of the total sample, 37%. In addition, 4 respondents have completed their doctoral degree, which represents 5% of the total data collected.

Therefore, most entrepreneurs have training in addition to compulsory education, which reveals the concern to deepen studies and broaden the knowledge base.

Regarding experience, it is observed that of the total of 87 respondents, 62 already had previous experience in the activity sector before creating the company, representing 71% of the total sample. In addition, in relation to the others, only 25 of the individuals admitted to having created their own business even without having previous experience in the activity sector.

Consistency of Variables: Cronbach's Alpha

According to Vaskea (2017), Cronbach's Alpha is generally used in order to allow the assessment of the level of consistency and reliability associated with a set of variables, constructs or scales. In this way, the present metric can vary between 0 (if there is no consistency) and 1 (in case of total consistency). In practical terms, an alpha of 0.80 means that 80% of the data is reliable.

In addition, there may be a possibility that the metric reflects negative values, in which case it means an eventual non-correlation between the variables. According to several authors such as Sarstedt and Mooi (2014), the lower limit for the coefficient is 0.70, and values greater than 0.80 are considered quite satisfactory.

Table 1. *Cronbach's alpha of the variables* represents the average of the scores referring to Cronbach's Alpha for each of the characteristics used in the present study.

Table 1. Cronbach's alpha of the variables

Variable	No. of questions	Cronbach's alpha	Consistency	Conclusion
Need for achievement	4	0.942	94%	High consistency
Control locus	4	0.987	99%	High consistency
Leadership	4	0.841	84%	High consistency
Commitment and determination	4	0.980	98%	High consistency
Risk propensity	4	0.859	86%	High consistency
Proactivity	4	0.829	83%	High consistency
Tolerance of ambiguity and uncertainty	3	0.861	86%	High consistency
Spirit of opportunity	3	0.933	93%	High consistency
Innovative spirit	3	0.819	82%	High consistency
Confidence	3	0.865	87%	High consistency
Resilience and adaptability	3	0.900	90%	High consistency

Source: (Own elaboration)

The characteristics presented were determined using the 7-point Likert scale applied to the different questions for each of the variables. In this sense, according to the Cronbach's Alpha test carried out, it appears that all characteristics revealed values above the agreed limit of 0.70, which reflects a high rate of internal consistency for all items present in the model.

In this way, no changes were made to the variables since all data are considered reliable, the lowest value being 0.819 for the innovative spirit characteristic and the highest was 0.987 for the control locus characteristic. That said, it appears that the instruments used demonstrate a great deal of relevance and relevance for the measurement and preparation of the study.

Personal Characteristics

Regarding personal characteristics of the entrepreneurs, the questionnaire allowed to assess the levels associated with the need for achievement, locus of control, leadership, commitment and determination, risk propensity, proactivity, tolerance to ambiguity and uncertainty, spirit of opportunity, innovative spirit, confidence and resilience and adaptability. In this sense, the main objective of the questionnaire was to verify which of these characteristics had a greater impact or importance in the process of creation and development of startups.

Need for Achievement

Regarding the characteristic of the need for achievement, it appears that question 1.3 - I like to receive feedback on my performance -, is the one with the highest average, with a value of 6.52. At the same time, it is also the one with the smallest standard deviation, which means that there is less variability in the answers to this question. On the other hand, the question with the lowest average is 1.2 - I am open to new ideas and I prefer to work alone than in a team -, with 3.52. In addition, in terms of the standard deviation, it has a value of 1.914, which translates into greater variability in response among respondents.

Locus of Control

Regarding the characteristic of the locus of control, it appears that question 2.2 - I am willing to accept the consequences (positive or negative) arising from my decisions and actions -, is the one with the highest average, with a value of 6.66. However, it is also the one with the smallest standard deviation, which means that there is less variability in the answers to this question.

On the other hand, the question with the lowest average is 2.3 - I believe that success is the result of luck and faith and not of individual effort -, with 4.77 (readjusted in SPSS due to the fact that the scale is reversed). In addition, in terms of the standard deviation, it has a value of 1.578, which translates into greater variability in response among respondents.

Leadership

In global terms, this characteristic is highly valued, and two statements stand out whose average values are quite high. Therefore, question 3.1 - I try to build communication environments that promote the discussion of ideas and opinions -, and question 3.2 - I demonstrate to my colleagues that trust is the basis for successful collaboration -, they have an average value of 6, 57 and 6.48 respectively. In parallel, according to the data collected, the total standard deviation of the questions applied to the leadership characteristic is 0.927, which reveals a uniform and consensual opinion among the respondents.

Commitment and Determination

Regarding the characteristic of commitment and determination, it appears that most of the individuals showed a great commitment to solving problems and, for that reason, the question with the highest average (with a value of 6.38), was 4.2 - I am decided (a) and very persistent in solving problems. On the other hand, according to the respondents' answers, it appears that there is still some fear on the part of individuals to manage or perform new and different tasks, leading in many cases to end up losing motivation. For this reason, the question that presented a lower average was 4.4 - When I am confronted with new and different tasks, I am afraid and tend to lose motivation -, whose value is 4.19 (readjusted in SPSS due to the scale is reversed). In addition, in terms of the standard deviation, it has a value of 1.939, which reveals a high variability between respondents' responses.

Risk Propensity

Since the questions use the inverse Likert scale, that is, 1 - I totally agree with 7 - I totally disagree, these answers were adjusted in the SPSS in order to maintain the consistency of the measurement.

Therefore, among the questions presented, the one that revealed the greatest degree of agreement was question 5.3 - I am afraid to work on my own because I consider it to be a stable job, so, taking the reverse direction of the question, the individuals believe that this fear is easily overcome, with an average of 5.33 and a standard deviation of 0.856, which indicates a low variability of responses. On the other hand, according to the respondents, there is still a great fear of losing investment in case of failure, so this is one of the reasons that assumes a greater influence on the individual's decision to become an entrepreneur.

Proactivity

According to the characteristic of proactivity, it appears that, taking into account the respondents' answers, the questions that showed a higher average, and therefore represent a greater degree of agreement, were questions 6.1 - I am attentive to changes in the market -, and 6.4 - I am very participative in solving problems and looking for solutions -, with 6.24 and 6.19 respectively.

Conversely, even though it still presents a high average, the question that generated the least degree of agreement was 6.3 - I have ideas for new products / services that respond to needs that others have not thought of, with a value of 5.57 and a standard deviation of 1.434, which means that there is greater variability in the responses of individuals.

Tolerance to Ambiguity and Uncertainty

Regarding the characteristic of tolerance to ambiguity and uncertainty, it appears that question 7.3 - I believe that it is in moments of greatest uncertainty that the greatest opportunities arise. It is the one that presents the highest average, with a value of 5.76. However, it is the one with the highest standard deviation, which means that there is a greater variability in the answers to this question. On the other hand, the question with the lowest average is 7.2 - After setting goals, I work with consistency even when the results seem uncertain, with a value of 5.52. In this sense, although the value is significantly high, there is an inverse relationship between the uncertainty of the results and the consistency of the focus and the work, and in times of greater uncertainty the consistency of the work tends to be less.

Spirit of Opportunity

Regarding the characteristic of the spirit of opportunity, it appears that a large number of individuals reveal that they are market oriented and, for this reason, the issue with the highest average is 8.3 - I am highly market oriented (e.g. focused on the customer, trends, competition, etc.), with a value of 5.76.

However, it is also the one with the smallest standard deviation, which means that there is less variability in the answers to this question. Otherwise, the question that presented a lower average was 8.2 - I prefer to focus on new opportunities than on generating money -, whose value is 4.38. According to the value presented, it appears that most individuals assume a greater preference in exploring new opportunities than in generating money, however, in terms of the standard deviation, this presents the value of 1.532, which still reveals a high variability between respondents' responses.

Innovative Spirit

It appears that the respondents reveal a knowledge about the requirements, tastes and preferences of their customers. Therefore, question 9.1 - Do I know my clients and their requirements -, is the question with the highest average, with a value of 6.19. In parallel, according to the data collected, this is the question that has the lowest value regarding the standard deviation which translates into less variability in terms of the answers. In contrast, the question with the lowest average is 9.3 - I have the ability to anticipate changes and identify trends before they become evident to everyone -, with 5.38. In addition, in terms of the standard deviation, it has a value of 1.322, which reflects greater variability in response among respondents.

Trust

Regarding the characteristic of trust, it appears that question 10.3 - Even in the face of more adverse situations, I believe that my control and influence allow me to achieve the goals -, is the one with the highest average, with a value of 6.01. At the same time, it is also the one with the smallest standard deviation, which means that there is less variability in the answers to this question. On the other hand, the question with the lowest average is 10.2 - My success or failure does not depend on factors such as luck or fate -, with 5.10. In addition, in terms of the standard deviation, it has a value of 1.528, which reflects greater variability in response among respondents.

Resilience and Adaptability

It appears that most individuals assume that errors and failures are inherent in the entrepreneurial process and, therefore, necessary to achieve success. For this reason, the question with the highest average is 11.2 - I believe that mistakes and failures are necessary to achieve success -, with a value of 6.35. On the other hand, the remaining questions also present a high average, which means that for respondents this is a very important and valued feature. In this sense, in global terms, the average presented by the set of questions is 6.25 and the standard deviation is 0.821, which reflects a greater agreement in the responses between the different individuals.

Regression Analysis: Growth and Personal Characteristics

Following the completion of the present study, the analysis of the different hypotheses was carried out in order to effectively understand the impact of the personal characteristics considered in the model on startup growth. We regressed the dependent ordinal variable "Growth" on each one of the personal characteristics estimating the level of significance for each variable (for the analysis to be viable we considered p-values below 0.05, for the t-test). On the other hand, the coefficient of determination R^2 that indicates the amount of Y variability explained by X was also used, as well as the Durbin-Watson test to ascertain the existence of residues independence.

Following the regressions performed, it was possible to verify the degree of influence of each characteristic on the growth of startups. Therefore, it was found that the characteristics of need for achievement (R2 = 0.106), leadership (R2 = 0.152), and proactivity (R2 = 0.106) proved to be significantly impacting and determining the success of startups and, interpreting the previous values of R2, about 36% of the growth variable of startups is explained by these three characteristics. That said, it was possible to ascertain the validation of the hypotheses posed, so that, according to the investigation, 8 of the 11 hypotheses proved to be valid, allowing us to conclude that the need for achievement, leadership, commitment and determination, proactivity, the spirit of opportunity, innovative spirit, trust and resilience and adaptability positively impact the growth of startups. Table 2 – *Summary of Research Hypotheses* summarizes the results.

Table 2. Summary of research hypotheses

	Hypotheses	**Shelf life**
H1	The need for achievement positively impacts the growth of startups.	Valid
H2	The locus of control positively impacts the growth of startups.	Not valid
H3	Leadership positively impacts the growth of startups.	Valid
H4	Commitment and determination positively impact the growth of startups.	Valid
H5	The risk propensity positively impacts the growth of startups.	Not valid
H6	Proactivity positively impacts the growth of startups.	Valid
H7	Tolerance of ambiguity and uncertainty positively impacts the growth of startups.	Not valid
H8	The spirit of opportunity positively impacts the growth of startups.	Valid
H9	The innovative spirit positively impacts the growth of startups.	Valid
H10	Trust positively impacts the growth of startups.	Valid
H11	Resilience and adaptability positively impacts the growth of startups.	Valid

Analysis of the Interviews: "Being an Entrepreneur"

To complement the conclusions drawn following the data collected from the sample, 10 interviews were carried out in order to formulate a qualitative view on the topic under study. In this sense, the objective was to explore a more personal aspect of the stakeholders and collect the respective opinions, suggestions, visions, and beliefs collected through the path and experience of the entrepreneurs.

Thus, the interviews conducted were based on 8 central questions:

- Q1 How do you identify yourself as a person? What personal characteristics do you consider to be most important for your company?
- Q2 How did you come up with the idea of becoming an entrepreneur?
- Q3 How do you identify opportunities?

- Q4 How do you deal with failure?
- Q5 What importance do you give to the company's internal and external relations? Which actors do you consider to be most important (e.g. suppliers, customers, partners, investors, etc.)?
- Q6 Do you consider yourself a leader? What differentiates you from other people?
- Q7 What gives you the most pleasure in the entrepreneurial process?
- Q8 What do you consider to be the most important factor for your company's success?

In accordance with the theme that has been studied, one of the concerns of the study was, effectively, to understand how the personal characteristics of entrepreneurs affect the growth of startups and, of course, realize which of these have the greatest influence.

Thus, according to the first question posed in the interviews, most entrepreneurs were characterized as a very creative and organized person. Additionally, there was a real emphasis on the fact that individuals face entrepreneurship as an arduous path, which is why it is necessary to face it with a lot of determination, confidence and persistence, as pointed out by one of the interviewees: "(...) I consider the most determination, resilience, boldness and confidence are important".

In addition, it appears that one of the characteristics considered most important for the success of startups was the concern for others, as seen in the responses: "I identify myself as someone oriented to people and who always wants to develop and help others to develop in a genuine way" and "an enormous desire to help others", so there is a tendency to recognize stakeholders as a key factor for the company's sustainability.

Regarding the second question whose objective was to understand the reason why individuals decided to become entrepreneurs, it appears that the most common answer is related with the fact that they seek a professional situation that would make them feel fulfilled doing what they like and, simultaneously, allow them to have greater freedom. In this sense, one of the interviewees says: "It has always been a dream. To have my freedom "and another: "I always wanted to have my own business and I decided to undertake when I failed to see growth potential in the company I was in, I did not do what I love to do and I wanted more freedom of hours".

According to the third question, it was found that one of the principles that gathered the greatest consensus among entrepreneurs is that market analysis, systematic and consistent study of ideas and needs and contact with people in order to understand their concerns are the most widely used way to identify new opportunities. Therefore, several responses of this nature were collected to answer the third question as noted: "Through felt needs, which are lacking in the market. And market research", "(...) are identified through direct contact with people", "I regularly analyze the market, read a lot and make sharing calls every week", "I read a lot. I see what's going on outside. I listen to my customers. I see the pains I have in a certain situation".

The fourth question asked had as its main objective to understand how entrepreneurs dealt with failure. Thus, it was found that failure should be seen as part of the process, as stated by the vast majority of respondents: "It is a whole process", "It is part of progress", "It is natural. It is part of someone who is doing things differently". For this reason, according to the interviewees, the most important thing is to look at failures as a source of learning: "It is necessary to digest, learn from mistakes, and come back more strongly" and, finally, according to one of the interviewees: "The secret is how after that first moment we react and look at failure, and then I get up quickly. With calm eyes I look at what can be improved and I take the lessons to the future even more strongly!"

Regarding the fifth question, where we tried to understand the importance given to the company's internal and external relations, it was found that the most important player was the customer / user, as stated: "Customers are the most important. They are the ones that we have to satisfy and keep satisfied in order to continue to have a business", " Customers are essential "," (...) we focus more on the user ", as these are the ones that guarantee companies the necessary source of revenue for its sustainability. However, it is important to emphasize that all stakeholders play an important role in the organizational ecosystem: "They are all part of the ecosystem", so they must also be considered: "Everyone is fundamental! Relationships of any kind are crucial for growth in an organization".

Following the sixth question, whose purpose was to evaluate the leadership relationship as a characteristic of the individual and how he differs from the others, it was concluded that most entrepreneurs claimed to be a leader. Additionally, in relation to the second part of the question, it appears that individuals have differentiating skills and competences, which, to a certain extent, allows them to be successful entrepreneurs. Therefore, some of the testimonies given relate to skills such as: "Not being afraid to fail (...) and not being afraid to take risks", "Knowing how to deal with people from different cultures, education and ambition", "I am extremely organized and outline strategies and paths for everything" and "The genuine desire to listen to the others, understand their side and make room for their individuality".

According to the seventh question, a large part of the interviewees admitted that the part of creation was the one that gave the most pleasure in the entrepreneurial process: "Create again. The challenge of outlining a whole project and executing it", "Thinking about a product and defining how to promote it" and "Bringing something that people indicate: Wow this is really different from everything else and it makes perfect sense". In addition, the fact that it was an opportunity to do what one really likes, culminating in a sense of accomplishment, was highlighted: "Making my own schedules, being free, doing what I love to do and the pride of seeing the path I take. I'm on my way".

Finally, regarding the eighth question, whose main objective was to identify the most important factor for the success of the company, it was found that a large part of the entrepreneurs considered people as the key element: "My team and its strength", "The people. They are the ones who have the final contact with the customer, and they make all the difference for their satisfaction" and "Proximity to the customer, constant innovation". In this sense, according to the responses collected, the focus on people is extremely important given that in most cases these end up being the catalyst elements for change and, consequently, business success.

FINAL REMARKS

The present chapter had as main objective to analyze the impact of the personal characteristics of the entrepreneurs in the growth of the respective startups. In this sense, an in-depth literature review was carried out on the subject, with the main focus being the study of entrepreneurship as a phenomenon, of the entrepreneur as an individual and of personal characteristics as factors influencing the growth of organizations. In this way, based on the previous investigation, the conceptual model targeted by the study was built, as well as the formulation of the underlying hypotheses to enable the realization of the empirical analysis of the study.

The realization of the empirical analysis was based on two types of data collection methodology, quantitative and qualitative, with the purpose of ensuring the consistency of the data, as well as guaranteeing a solid analysis capable of reflecting concrete facts. In this sense, for the quantitative approach,

87 responses were obtained from entrepreneurs, and of the total there was a predominance of males among the respondents (62%).

According to the responses collected from the first applied questionnaire, it was found that the characteristics that were most relevant in the creation and development process of startups were leadership, resilience and adaptability and proactivity. In this sense, it is extremely important that throughout the life of individuals, they seek ways to foster and improve these skills more and more.

Therefore, according to Greenberg and Baron (2000), leadership corresponds to the process by which individuals influence others in order to achieve the defined objectives. Thus, the level of leadership is crucial in guaranteeing the success of the startup, given that, in more adverse situations, it is necessary for the entrepreneur to be able to rebuild the company's purpose and redirect his team according to the objectives set. At the same time, resilience and adaptability is a key feature for any individual wishing to become an entrepreneur. Therefore, according to Carrier and Verstraete (1999), entrepreneurs must have a high level of resilience in order to be able to survive and grow in a highly competitive and challenging business world. Finally, it turns out that proactivity stands out as one of the most important characteristics in the entrepreneurial process. In this sense, according to Penrose (1959), entrepreneurs are considered the fundamental pieces for the companies' performance due to their different capacities, namely the propagation of their vision and imagination necessary for the entry of companies in new business opportunities.

Through the conceptual model it is verified that the variables need for achievement, leadership, commitment and determination, proactivity, spirit of opportunity, innovative spirit, confidence and resilience and adaptability are statistically significant for the model. In addition, its measurement was based on a set of questions and the results reflected an excellent level of internal consistency, since all variables had values greater than 0.82.

The results of the interview allowed us to identify the reasons that tend to lead individuals to become entrepreneurs, namely the search for greater freedom, the possibility to cultivate their own ideas and, of course, to do what they really like and that gives them pleasure.

On the other hand, authenticity and altruism were considered essential characteristics for the practice of entrepreneurship, that is, to do things in a genuine way and try to help others, the management of priorities, trying to carry out and perform the tasks proposed in an efficient and timely way and, finally, confidence, in order to guarantee consistency and enthusiasm in the pursuit of the objectives and goals set.

It is possible to conclude, based on the answers, that for an individual to become an entrepreneur it is essential that he becomes aware of the intensity and difficulty that the process entails, and that is why it is essential that he is aware that mistakes are natural and necessary to reach of success. Additionally, there was a consensus among respondents regarding the importance of promoting a solid relationship with the organization's stakeholders, and it is strictly crucial to seek to satisfy customers and users as they are responsible for the consumption of goods and/or services.

Following the study, some limitations were observed that, to a certain extent, conditioned the results obtained. The first limitation identified is related to the subject under study, given that only the impact of the characteristics of entrepreneurs on the growth of startups was analyzed, however there are many other factors and conditions that also have influence and that for this investigation were not considered.

On the other hand, the sample collected was exclusively based on Portuguese entrepreneurs, so it was not analyzed how geography, culture or daily life in other regions of the world can change the perception of what organizational success is like differences in terms of the impact of personal characteristics.

In addition, taking into account the limitation of the present study, only eleven personal characteristics were considered, however there are many other characteristics that could also be considered.

Finally, there is a limitation in terms of statistical analysis. Despite the empirical approach used to analyze the results, it is important to highlight the fact that there are several analyzes that could also be applied and, for this reason, could complement the information or even present different results. However, all these limitations present suggestions for improvements for further studies or investigations.

REFERENCES

Almeida, F., & Teixeira, R. (2014). Influence of the family and of social networks on business creation by young entrepreneurs. *Pretexto*, *15*(2), 110–128.

Amit, R., & Muller, E. (1995). "Push" and "pull" entrepreneurship. *Journal of Small Business and Entrepreneurship*, *12*(4), 64–80. doi:10.1080/08276331.1995.10600505

Applegate, L. M., & Collura, M. (2000). *Emerging networked business models: lessons from the field.* Harvard Business School.

Arthur, S. J., & Hisrich, R. D. (2011). Entrepreneurship through the ages: Lessons learned. *Journal of Enterprising Culture*, *19*(01), 1–40. doi:10.1142/S0218495811000696

Bannock, G. (2005). *The economics and management of small business: An international perspective.* Psychology Press.

Baptista, R., Escária, V., & Madruga, P. (2008). Entrepreneurship, regional development and job creation: The case of Portugal. *Small Business Economics*, *30*(1), 49–58. doi:10.100711187-007-9055-0

Barba-Sánchez, V., & Atienza-Sahuquillo, C. (2012). Entrepreneurial behavior: Impact of motivation factors on decision to create a new venture. *European Research on Management and Business Economics*, *18*(1), 132–138.

Barbosa, P. (2015). *Determinantes do sucesso individual e da intenção empreendedora através da propensão empreendedora.* Dissertação de Mestrado em Gestão.

Baumol, W. J. (1993). Formal entrepreneurship theory in economics: Existence and bounds. *Journal of Business Venturing*, *8*(3), 197–210. doi:10.1016/0883-9026(93)90027-3

Birch, L. L. (1979). Preschool children's food preferences and consumption patterns. *Journal of Nutrition Education*, *11*(4), 189–192. doi:10.1016/S0022-3182(79)80025-4

Bird, B. (2015). Entrepreneurial intentions research: A Review and outlook. *International Review of Entrepreneurship*, *13*(3), 143–168.

Birley, S. (1989). Corporate strategy and the small firm. In D. C. Asch & C. Bowman (Eds.), *Readings in strategic management* (pp. 78–82). MacMillian Education. doi:10.1007/978-1-349-20317-8_6

Bucha, A. I. (2009). *Empreendedorismo, aprender a saber ser empreendedor.* Editora RH.

Buttner, E. H., & Moore, D. P. (1997). *Women entrepreneurs: Moving beyond the glass ceiling.* Sage.

Bygrave, W. D. (2004). The entrepreneurial process. In W. D. Bygrave & A. Zacharakis (Eds.), *The portable MBA in entrepreneurship* (p. 6). John Wiley & Sons.

Carsrud, A., & Brännback, M. (2011). Entrepreneurial motivations: What do we still need to know? *Journal of Small Business Management*, *49*(1), 9–26. doi:10.1111/j.1540-627X.2010.00312.x

Carter, S., Anderson, S., & Shaw, E. (2001). Women business ownership: A review of the academic, popular and internet literature. Report to the Small Business Service.

Cassar, G. (2007). Money, money, money? A longitudinal investigation of entrepreneur career reasons, growth preferences and achieved growth. *Entrepreneurship and Regional Development*, *19*(1), 89–107. doi:10.1080/08985620601002246

Chrisman, J. J., Chua, J. H., & Steier, L. P. (2002). The influence of national culture and family involvement on entrepreneurial perceptions and performance at the state level. *Entrepreneurship Theory and Practice*, *26*(4), 113–130. doi:10.1177/104225870202600407

Coakes, E., & Bradburn, A. (2005). What is the value of intellectual capital? *Knowledge Management Research and Practice*, *3*(2), 60–68. doi:10.1057/palgrave.kmrp.8500050

Curran, J., Blackburn, R., Kitching, J., & North, J. (1996). *Establishing small firms' training practices, needs, difficulties and use of industry training organizations*. HMSO.

Davey, T., Plewa, C., & Struwig, M. (2011). Entrepreneurship perceptions and career intentions of international students. *Education + Training*, *53*(5), 335–352. doi:10.1108/00400911111147677

Dollinger, S. C. (1995). Identity styles and the five-factor model of personality. *Journal of Research in Personality*, *29*(4), 475–479. doi:10.1006/jrpe.1995.1028

Dornelas, J. C. A. (2008). *Empreendedorismo*. Elsevier Brasil.

Du Rietz, A., & Henrekson, M. (2000). Testing the female underperformance hypothesis. *Small Business Economics*, *14*(1), 1–10. doi:10.1023/A:1008106215480

Duarte, C., & Esperança, J. P. (2012). *Empreendedorismo e planeamento financeiro*. Edições Sílabo.

Eccles, J. S., Wigfield, A., & Schiefele, U. (1998). Motivation to succeed. In W. Damon & N. Eisenberg (Eds.), Handbook of child psychology: Vol. 3. *Social, emotional, and personality development* (5th ed., pp. 1017–1095). Wiley.

Federici, D., Ferrante, F., & Vistocco, D. (2008). On the sources of entrepreneurial talent in Italy: Tacit vs. codified knowledge. *Journal of Knowledge Management*, *6*(6), 7–28.

Ferreira, A., Loiola, E., & Guedes Gondim, S. M. (2017). Motivations, business planning, and risk management: Entrepreneurship among university students. *Revista de Administração e Inovação*, *14*(2), 140–150. doi:10.1016/j.rai.2017.03.003

Galloway, L., Anderson, M., Brown, W., & Wilson, L. (2005). Enterprise skills for the economy. *Education + Training*, *47*(1), 7–17. doi:10.1108/00400910510580593

Gaspar, F. C. (2009). *O processo empreendedor e a criação de empresas de sucesso*. Edições Sílabo.

Gilad, B., & Levine, P. (1986). A behavioral model of entrepreneurial supply. *Journal of Small Business Management, 24*, 45.

Hair, J. F., Celsi, M., Ortinau, D. J., & Bush, R. P. (2010). *Essentials of marketing research* (Vol. 2). McGraw-Hill/Irwin.

Hébert, R. F., & Link, A. N. (1989). In search of the meaning of entrepreneurship. *Small Business Economics, 1*(1), 39–49. doi:10.1007/BF00389915

Hechavarria, D. M., Renko, M., & Matthews, C. H. (2011). The nascent entrepreneurship hub: Goals, entrepreneurial self-efficacy and start-up outcomes. *Small Business Economics, 39*(3), 685–701. doi:10.100711187-011-9355-2

Heinonen, J., & Poikkijoki, S. A. (2006). An entrepreneurial-directed approach to entrepreneurship education: Mission impossible? *Journal of Management Development, 25*(1), 80–94. doi:10.1108/02621710610637981

Hisrich, R. D., Peters, M. P., & Shepherd, D. A. (2010). *Entrepreneurship*. McGraw-Hill.

Jones, C., & Spicer, A. (2009). *Unmasking the entrepreneur*. Edward Elgar. doi:10.4337/9781781952689

Kirchhoff, B. A., & Phillips, B. D. (1988). The effect of firm formation and growth on job creation in the United States. *Journal of Business Venturing, 3*(4), 261–272. doi:10.1016/0883-9026(88)90008-0

Kirkwood, J., & Walton, S. (2010). What motivates ecopreneurs to start businesses? *International Journal of Entrepreneurial Behaviour & Research, 16*(3), 204–228. doi:10.1108/13552551011042799

Koh, H. C. (1996). Testing hypotheses of entrepreneurial characteristics. *Journal of Managerial Psychology, 11*(3), 12–25. doi:10.1108/02683949610113566

Kourilsky, M. L., & Walstad, W. B. (1998). Entrepreneurship and female youth: Knowledge, attitudes, gender differences, and educational practices. *Journal of Business Venturing, 13*(1), 77–88. doi:10.1016/S0883-9026(97)00032-3

Krueger, N. F., & Carsrud, A. L. (1993). Entrepreneurial intentions: Applying the theory of planned behaviour. *Entrepreneurship and Regional Development, 5*(4), 315–330. doi:10.1080/08985629300000020

Krueger, N. F. Jr, Reilly, M. D., & Carsrud, A. L. (2000). Competing Models of Entrepreneurial Intentions. *Journal of Business Venturing, 15*(5-6), 411–432. doi:10.1016/S0883-9026(98)00033-0

Kuratko, D. F. (2005). The emergence of entrepreneurship education: Development, trends, and challenges. *Entrepreneurship Theory and Practice, 29*(5), 577–597. doi:10.1111/j.1540-6520.2005.00099.x

Kuratko, D. F., & Audretsch, D. B. (2009). Strategic entrepreneurship: Exploring different perspectives of an emerging concept. *Entrepreneurship Theory and Practice, 33*(1), 1–17. doi:10.1111/j.1540-6520.2008.00278.x

Lee, D. Y., & Tsang, E. W. (2001). The effects of entrepreneurial personality, background and network activities on venture growth. *Journal of Management Studies, 38*(4), 583–602. doi:10.1111/1467-6486.00250

Liñán, F., Rodríguez-Cohard, J., & Rueda-Cantuche, J. (2011). Factors affecting entrepreneurial intention levels: A role for education. *The International Entrepreneurship and Management Journal, 7*(2), 195–218. doi:10.100711365-010-0154-z

Littunen, H. (2000). Entrepreneurship and the characteristics of the entrepreneurial personality. *International Journal of Entrepreneurial Behaviour & Research, 6*(6), 295–309. doi:10.1108/13552550010362741

Locke, E. (2000). Motivation, cognition, and action: An analysis of studies of task goals and knowledge. *Applied Psychology, 49*(3), 408–429. doi:10.1111/1464-0597.00023

Locke, E. A. (1991). The motivation sequence, the motivation hub and the motivation core. *Organizational Behavior and Human Decision Processes, 50*(2), 288–299. doi:10.1016/0749-5978(91)90023-M

Longenecker, J. G., Moore, C. W., Petty, J. W., Palich, L. E., & McKinney, J. A. (2006). Ethical attitudes in small businesses and large corporations: Theory and empirical findings from a tracking study spanning three decades. *Journal of Small Business Management, 44*(2), 167–183. doi:10.1111/j.1540-627X.2006.00162.x

Lumpkin, G. T., & Dess, G. G. (1996). Clarifying the entrepreneurial orientation construct and linking it to performance. *Academy of Management Review, 21*(1), 135–172. doi:10.5465/amr.1996.9602161568

Lussier, R. N., & Pfeifer, S. (2001). A crossnational prediction model for business success. *Journal of Small Business Management, 39*(3), 228–239. doi:10.1111/0447-2778.00021

Mars, M. M., & Rios-Aguilar, C. (2010). Academic entrepreneurship (re) defined: Significance and implications for the scholarship of higher education. *Higher Education, 59*(4), 441–460. doi:10.100710734-009-9258-1

McClelland, D. C. (1961). Achieving society (No. 15). Simon and Schuster.

Mill, J. S. (1848). *Principles of political economy with some of their applications*. Social Philosophy.

Mooi, E., & Sarstedt, M. (2014). *A concise guide to market research*. Springer.

Mueller, S. L., & Dato-on, M. C. (2008). Gender role orientation as a determinant of entrepreneurial self e efficacy. *Journal of Developmental Entrepreneurship, 13*(1), 3–20. doi:10.1142/S108494670800082X

Nazir, M. A., & Ramzan, M. (2012). Contribution on entrepreneurship in economic growth. *Interdisciplinary Journal of Contemporary Research in Business, Economics, and Finance, 4*(3), 273–294.

Neneh, B. N. (2011). *The impact of entrepreneurial characteristics and business practices on the long term survival of small and medium enterprises (SMEs)* (Doctoral dissertation). University of the Free State.

Nwankwo, B. E., Kanu, G. C., Marire, M. I., Balogun, S. K., & Uhiara, C. (2012). Gender-role orientation and self-efficacy as correlates of entrepreneurial intention. *European Journal of Business and Social Sciences, 1*(6), 9-26.

Parasuraman, S., Purohit, Y. S., Godshalk, V. M., & Beutell, N. J. (1996). Work and family variables, entrepreneurial career success, and psychological well-being. *Journal of Vocational Behavior, 48*(3), 275–300. doi:10.1006/jvbe.1996.0025

Portela, J., Hespanha, P., Nogueira, C., Teixeira, M., & Baptista, A. (2008). *Microempreendedorismo em Portugal: Experiências e perspectivas*. Lisboa: INscooP.

Reardon, K. K. (1991). *Persuasion in practice*. Sage Publications.

Reynolds, P. D. (1992). Sociology and entrepreneurship: Concepts and contributions. *Entrepreneurship Theory and Practice*, *16*(2), 47–70. doi:10.1177/104225879201600205

Sarkar, S. (2010). *Empreendedorismo e inovação*. Escolar Editora.

Schumpeter, J. A., & Nichol, A. J. (1934). Robinson's economics of imperfect competition. *Journal of Political Economy*, *42*(2), 249–259. doi:10.1086/254595

Segal, G., Borgia, D., & Schoenfeld, J. (2005). The motivation to become an entrepreneur. *International Journal of Entrepreneurial Behaviour & Research*, *11*(1), 42–57. doi:10.1108/13552550510580834

Shane, S., Locke, E. A., & Collins, C. J. (2003). Entrepreneurial motivation. *Human Resource Management Review*, *13*(2), 257–279. doi:10.1016/S1053-4822(03)00017-2

Shane, S., & Venkataraman, S. (2000). The promise of entrepreneurship as a field of research. *Academy of Management Review*, *25*(1), 217–226. doi:10.5465/amr.2000.2791611

Staw, B. M. (1991). Dressing up like an organization: When psychological theories can explain organizational action. *Journal of Management*, *17*(4), 805–819. doi:10.1177/014920639101700412

Stewart, A., & Cotton, J. (2013). Making sense of entrepreneurship journals: Journal Rankings and Strategy Choices. *International Journal of Entrepreneurial Behaviour & Research*, *19*(3), 303–323. doi:10.1108/13552551311330192

Surie, G., & Ashley, A. (2008). Integrating pragmatism and ethics in entrepreneurial leadership for sustainable value creation. *Journal of Business Ethics*, *81*(1), 235–246. doi:10.100710551-007-9491-4

Teoh, H. Y., & Foo, S. L. (1997). Moderating effects of tolerance for ambiguity and risk taking propensity on the role conflict-perceived performance relationship: Evidence from Singaporean entrepreneurs. *Journal of Business Venturing*, *12*(1), 67–81. doi:10.1016/S0883-9026(96)00035-3

Thompson, J. L. (2004). The facets of the entrepreneur: Identifying entrepreneurial potential. *Management Decision*, *42*(2), 243–258. doi:10.1108/00251740410515861

Timmons, J. A., & Bygrave, W. D. (1986). Venture capital's role in financing innovation for economic growth. *Journal of Business Venturing*, *1*(2), 161–176. doi:10.1016/0883-9026(86)90012-1

Valencia, F., Montoya, I., & Restrepo, J. (2014). Motivational theories in the study of entrepreneurship. *Pensamiento & Gestión*, *36*, 206–238.

Zimmerer, T. W., Scarborough, N. M., & Wilson, D. (2008). *Essentials of entrepreneurship and small business management* (5th ed.). Pearson/Prentice Hall.

Chapter 18
The Relationship Between Price Indices and Pricing Methods

Mikail Kar
Bursa Uludag University, Turkey

ABSTRACT

Incumbent firms, potential new entrants, policymakers, and regulatory authorities want to know the commonly used pricing method in the market to which they are associated to use in their decisions and strategies. The most widely used approach to determining the pricing method commonly used in a market in the literature is to analyze the causality relationship between producer and consumer prices. It is accepted that the demand-based pricing method is commonly used in the markets where the change in consumer prices leads the producer prices, and the cost-based pricing method is commonly used in the markets where the change in the producer prices leads the consumer prices. This study examines pricing methods and price indices and discusses the determination of the pricing method commonly used in a market based on the causality relationship between the producer and consumer price indices.

INTRODUCTION

Price, which is the value paid for the change of ownership in the purchase of a good or service, is considered as the factor that determines how much that goods or service will be produced, how much it will be consumed, and which firms will make this production for which consumers. Price is an economic variable of great importance for all market actors as the main determinant of consumer behavior, the source of firms' profit, and the factor that ensures the efficient distribution of resources in the economy. For this reason, pricing which refers to the process of determining the price as a result of the evaluation of the factors affecting the price has gained a very important place in the economic literature. If the markets operating in the economy fulfill the perfectly competitive market assumptions, the price will be taken as given from the market and there will be no such issue as pricing. However, in today's economies, as the imperfect competitive markets are common, each firm has more or less the power to set prices in the market and pricing becomes one of the most important decisions of the firms. Firms prefer various pricing methods in line with targets such as profit maximization, market growth, survival, and leadership

DOI: 10.4018/978-1-7998-7568-0.ch018

depending on multivariable factors such as the structure of the market, life of the goods, production costs, market power, demand for goods, price and demand in complementary and substitute product markets.

Firms mainly use three different pricing methods: cost-based, demand-based, and competition-based pricing. Incumbent firms operating in the markets, potential firms seeking entry, policymakers, and regulatory authorities closely follows the pricing methods used in the markets for their strategies and decisions. While not the pricing method used by each firm in the market, determining the pricing method commonly used in the market is very important for these market actors. There were two basic ways to determine the commonly used pricing method in a market. The first of these is to collect and analyze the private information of all firms in the market. This method is not useful and is not much preferred because the firms are reluctant to share their private data and because it is difficult and costly to compile and analyze the data to be obtained in markets where the number of firms is high. The second method is the determination of the commonly used pricing method in the market with the help of a causality relationship between producer and consumer prices. In the empirical analysis, price indices are used to represent producer and consumer prices. This method is very useful and highly preferred because the available data on the market is sufficient for analysis.

Price indices are the criteria used to analyze the changes in prices of selected goods and services and to compare the changes in average prices. Among price indices, the most used are the consumer prices index (CPI) and the producer prices index (PPI). The existence and direction of the causality relationship between PPI and CPI are highly controversial as empirical studies in the literature have yielded disparate results. There are four types of relationships that can be inferred from previous studies. The first is the one-way causality relationship from the CPI to the PPI, the second is the one-way causality relationship from the PPI to the CPI, the third is the two-way causality relationship between the PPI and the CPI, and the fourth is a state of independence, which means that there is no causality relationship between these two indices. At this point, the leading view is the supply-side approach. According to this approach, there is a causality relationship from producer prices to consumer prices, so producer prices determine consumer prices. On the other hand, it is argued that the demand-side approach may dominate the market. According to this approach, the causality relationship is from consumer prices to producer prices, and therefore consumer prices determine producer prices. Approaches that find the two-way causality relationship between the two indices argue that there are mutual interaction and producer prices and consumer prices cannot be evaluated independently. Studies, which argue that there is no causality relationship between the indices, emphasize that the indices act independently by drawing attention to the differences in the calculation methods. As a result, the causality relationship from producer prices to consumer prices indicates that the supply-side approach is dominant in the relevant market and that the cost-based pricing method is commonly used, if the causality relationship is from consumer prices to producer prices, it indicates that the demand-side approach is dominant and the demand-based pricing method is commonly used.

The aim of this study is to discuss the determination of the commonly used pricing method by firms in the whole economy or especially in a certain market with the help of a causality relationship between producer and consumer price indices. In the study, the meaning of causality between price indices is revealed in terms of the pricing method by drawing attention to supply-side and demand-side approaches. Although the causality relationship between CPI and PPI is analyzed for different purposes in the literature, the connection of this relationship with pricing methods is not discussed adequately. This study contributes to the elimination of this shortcoming in the literature. The study consists of four main sections. In the first part, price and pricing are generally examined and basic pricing methods are explained. In the second part, index and price indices are discussed and calculation methods and types of price indices are explained. In the third part, the relationship between price indices and pricing methods, methods of determination of this relationship, and evaluation of the results are discussed. In the fourth part, prominent empirical studies in the literature are shared and the results obtained from the studies are evaluated by considering the focus of this book chapter. In the conclusion part, a general evaluation is made taking into account the purpose of the book chapter.

PRICE AND PRICING

Firms make many important strategic decisions in the long and short term in order to achieve their goals of being in the market. One of the most prominent of these decisions is pricing. Price is the exchange value of goods or services in the most general sense and pricing is the process of determining the price as a result of evaluating the factors affecting the price. Price has different meanings for all actors of economic activities, but it is one of the most fundamental factors for all. Price is the main determinant of consumer behavior in the goal of benefit maximization, the most important criterion that shapes supply as a source of income for firms, and the basic organizer of the economic system that provides efficiency in resource distribution by balancing supply and demand. So whether it is handled with a macro perspective or evaluated with a micro approach, price is always one of the elements in the focus of economic analysis (Kar, 2019; Kotler & Armstrong, 2013; Nagle & Holden, 1995; Skouras et al., 2005).

When pricing, firms take into account many internal and external factors, that they can and cannot control, such as objectives, competitors, costs, consumers, the structure of the market in which they operate, the structure of the markets of substitution and complementary goods, the general economic situation and legal regulations. Pricing is a very complicated process as well as important. The pricing process includes six basic steps: selecting the pricing target, estimating the demand, calculating costs, analyzing the prices of competitors, choosing the pricing method, and ultimately determining the price (Dibb & Simkin, 2013; Kotler & Keller, 2013; Shipley & Jobber, 2001). A clear determination of the firm's position in the market and the purpose of its existence in the market is a prerequisite for the firm's success in its decisions. In other words, the firm should clarify what it wants to accomplish in the short and long term with its preferred pricing strategy. The objectives of the firms in pricing can be examined with five basic categories: profitability-related objectives, sales volume-related objectives, competition-related objectives, image-related objectives, and stability-related objectives. Firms that are able to successfully demonstrate their goals should then analyze the demand, costs, and competition situation in the market. The firm will be able to decide on the pricing method in line with the results obtained from these analyzes (Nagle & Hogan, 2010; Smith, 2012; Skouras et al., 2005).

There are three basic pricing methods in the literature: cost-based pricing, demand-based pricing, and competition-based pricing (Cunningham & Hornby, 1993; Kar, 2019; Kotler & Armstrong, 2013; Kotler & Keller, 2013; Nagle & Hogan, 2010).

Cost Based Pricing: In cost-based pricing, the price is determined based on fixed and variable costs in the production of the firm's goods and services. Cost-based pricing is one of the simplest, oldest, and most preferred pricing methods. This method is based on calculating all costs attributable to a product or service and adding a certain dividend to that cost. Cost-based pricing has advantages such as easy to apply, the required information is available in firm records, income and profit amount from sales are clear.

Demand Based Pricing: In this method, which is also called consumer-based pricing, the pricing process is based on estimating how much a consumer is willing to pay for a product that meets their wants and needs. The company wants to reduce the difference between the price that the consumer is willing to pay and the price that the consumer is actually paying. So this method is based on minimizing consumer surplus. However, it is a difficult task to determine the value consumers attribute to a good. Companies that use this method have to accurately demonstrate the price elasticity of consumers. The price is raised as the price elasticity of demand decreases, and the price is reduced as the price elasticity of demand increases.

Competition Based Pricing: In the competition-based pricing method, prices are determined based on the prices applied by competitors. In this method, the price reacts not to the cost and demand characteristics of the firm and consumers but to the price changes of the competitors. In this pricing method, which is observed extensively in markets where competition is intense, product differentiation is difficult and substitute products are widely used, competitors react to each other's price decisions and generally follow the market leader's prices. The most challenging decision of the company that wants to make pricing with this method is to determine who its main competitors are in the market.

All three pricing methods have their own unique advantages and disadvantages. The relationship between cost and demand is important for determining the lower and upper limits of the price of a good or service. Since the price of a good or service cannot be below costs in the long term, so the lower limit for the price is the costs. However, the upper limit for the price of a good or service is determined by demand. Therefore, in the long term, the price cannot be more than the value of the benefit provided to the buyer by the goods and services. Many firms prefer the cost-based pricing method because it is easy and the profit to be obtained from unit sales is certain. Competition-based pricing is an avoided approach in terms of causing price wars. Demand-based pricing is based on the value consumers place on a good or service, but due to the difficulty in determining this value, demand-based pricing is considered a more difficult approach than others. Apart from these, although there are many different pricing methods, each of them basically is based on the differentiated version of these three pricing methods or their common use with different weights. As stated above, which of these methods the firms will use depends on many factors (Kar, 2019; Kotler & Armstrong, 2013; Smith, 2012; Skouras et al., 2005).

INDEX AND PRICE INDICES

Index

Indices are indicators that show proportionally changes in the values of a statistical event for various time periods or different geographical regions. In other words, the index shows the proportional change in the time and space dimension in the numerical data of a particular event. They are statistical tools used to measure changes in data groups. Working with indices provides simplicity and ease of comparison in the evaluation of complex data, and since there is no unit of measure, it expands the use of values. Indices are formed by five basic elements: the base period, the items to be taken to the index account, the information of variables, weights, and the formula. How these elements are formed when the index is created depends on what purpose the index is used for. In the indices, the base period refers to the start period and the current period refers to the period when the change is measured. The base period is the period in which comparisons are made with other periods and the index value for this period is set to 100. If the index is greater than 100, there is an increase compared to the base period and if it is less than 100, there is a decrease compared to the base period (Akçay, 2011; Allen, 1949; Anggraeni & Irawan, 2018; Fisher & Shell, 1972; Gang et al., 2009).

Indices can be classified as place and time indices, fixed and variable based indices, simple and compound indices according to the type and scope of the index:

Place and Time Indices: Place and time indices measure the proportional change in data in terms of time and geographic region for a particular event. The place index gives a measure of the proportional change in the values of any variable such as population, production, price, etc. by a place such as region, province, county, continent. The time index, on the other hand, expresses the measure of the proportional change in the values of variables such as population, production, and price over time.

Fixed and Variable Based Indices: Fixed and variable based indices are calculated for time series. If the base period value is constant when calculating the number of each index, there is a fixed-based index, if the base period is the value of the previous period each time, it is called a variable-based index

Simple and Compound Indices: In its calculation, indices containing one item are called simple indices, indices that include two and more items are called compound indices.

Compound indices are also classified into three different groups: simple sum index, weightless average of simple indexes, and weighted average of simple indexes. The most commonly used compound index in economic index calculations is the weighted average of simple indexes. In calculating this method, there are three different index calculations, namely fixed weighted total index (Laspeyres index), variable weighted total index (Paasche index) and ideal index (Fisher index);

Fixed Weighted Total Index (Laspeyres Index): In the fixed weighted total index, which is the oldest index calculation method of the compound index group, the quantities of the base period are used as the weighted factor and the quantities of the base period are included in both the numerator and the denominator. So the Laspeyres index is a base period-weighted index. In this index, base year quantities are used when measuring the change of the current year value of a certain basket of goods and services according to the previous year's value.

Variable Weighted Total Index (Paasche Index): The Paasche index is the current period weighted. In other words, the period in which weights are referenced is the last period from the compared periods. In the Paasche index, when comparing the current year values with those of the previous period, the quantities of the year in which the index is calculated are taken and the amount of the current year is included in both the numerator and the denominator. In the Paasche index, items that exist in the base year but do not exist in the index year are not included in the index.

Ideal Index (Fisher Index): The Laspeyres index tends to show index increases more than they are, while the Paasche index tends to show less than it is. Fisher developed an index to eliminate the disadvantages of the Laspeyres and Paasche indices. The Fisher index, which is a cross-weighted index, is calculated by taking the geometric mean of the Laspeyres and Paasche indices, thus ensuring that weights belong to both of the periods compared. The main disadvantage of the ideal index is that the value of the index cannot be calculated before the end of the period due to the calculation of the Paasche index values only at the end of the period and therefore the estimated values are used.

Price Indices

While indices are defined as the tool that measures the proportional change of the variable belonging to a particular statistical event in terms of features such as time and place, price indices can be expressed as criteria that allow to analyze and compare the changes in average prices of selected goods and services over a given period of time. Price indices provide guidance on issues such as determining the economic structure of the country, making economic decisions, determining the purchasing power of the people, making new investment decisions, determining wages and determining social security payments by providing data on issues such as inflation, price movements, supply and demand relations, productivity level, investment efficiency, the real value of wages and cost of living levels (Anggraeni & Irawan, 2018; Caporale et al., 2002; Jones, 1986).

Price indices are calculated by the ratio of the value of a basket of goods and services calculated at current prices for a particular year to the value of the based year. In order to calculate a price index, four basic variables are required, namely goods and services basket, base year weights, base year prices, and current year prices. Since the prices of all goods and services will be difficult and inefficient to be used while calculating, the goods and services baskets are created according to certain criteria and changes in the value of this basket over time are tried to be measured. A simple average is not suitable because some goods have a larger weight in consumers' spending or budget. Items whose consumption or production is affected by months or seasons are included in the calculations as variable weighted, while unaffected items are treated as fixed weighted. The total expenditure required to purchase the specified basket of goods and services at the prices in the base year is determined by taking into account the weighting. The total expenditure to be made in order to purchase the same basket of goods in the current year is also calculated and its ratio with the base year total is taken. As mentioned before, various methods with different advantages and disadvantages are used in calculating price indices. Among these methods, Laspeyres index has been widely used in price index calculations for years in almost all countries due to its advantages such as data acquisition possibilities, calculation speed and ease (Anggraeni & Irawan, 2018; Gang et al., 2009; Tiwari, 2012; Tiwari & Shahbaz, 2010).

A wide variety of price indices such as consumer price index, producer price index, wholesale price index, construction cost index, foreign trade prices index, export prices index, import prices index, farmer's paid price index are calculated and named according to the markets where the prices are monitored. Among the price indices, the consumer price index (CPI) and the producer price index (PPI) are the most used. Since these indices come to the fore in this study, they are explained in detail below (Anggraeni & Irawan, 2018; Caporale et al., 2002; Gang et al., 2009; Tiwari, 2012; Tiwari & Shahbaz, 2010).

Consumer Price Index (CPI): The consumer price index (CPI) is calculated as a tool to measure the changes in the prices of goods and services purchased for consumption by households over time. In other words, the CPI shows the average change of the prices of goods and services used to satisfy the needs and wishes of the households between the two time periods. CPI demonstrates the difference in the amount of money that must be spent to maintain a defined standard of living by showing how the price of a basket of goods and services changes. The most important issue in the calculation of CPI is the determination of a sample group that will represent the overall community of the country at the highest possible level. After determining the sample group, it is calculated how much money this group spent on which goods and services during the year. According to the results of this calculation, the spending groups are given different weights within the index. Thus, goods and services that are consumed at a high rate are weighed higher, while those that are consumed less are weighed lower. Finally, CPI is calculated by measuring the prices of goods and services purchased from certain points of the country on certain days of the month during the year, according to the weights obtained. CPI, which is the most well-known among the price indices, is the main index closely monitored by market actors, government departments, and central banks because it is easy to calculate, can be monitored on a monthly basis, is easy to understand, and is the main indicator of inflation.

CPI has a wide variety of uses in economic life. These can be summarized under nine basic titles. First, it shows the level of inflation and provides information to the government, market actors, and consumers about the general price changes in the economy. Second, it allows to measure the performance and efficiency of economic policies. Third, it guides decision-makers in forward-looking economic decisions. Fourth, is used as a deflator, which allows the purification of economic data from inflation and enables more reliable analysis. Fifth, is used to adjust prices, wages, and rents. Sixth, is preferred as an indicator in national accounting accounts. Seventh, acts as a guide in creating a balance of supply and demand and making short and long term decisions. Eighth, allows for price analysis. Ninth, is used effectively in determining social security payments.

Producer Price Index (PPI): The Producer price index (PPI) is the price index that measures the price changes of the producer prices of the products produced in the country's economy in a certain reference period and subject to domestic sales. The prices included in the index are ex-works prices of goods and services sold by manufacturers, excluding taxes, transportation costs, and retail and wholesale trade share. In other words, it includes cash sales prices. While the CPI measures the change in retail prices, in PPI it is essential that prices are compiled especially from producers. In the PPI, the first-hand sales prices of the products offered by the producers operating in sectors such as agriculture, animal husbandry, forestry, mining, manufacturing industry, electricity, gas, and water are monitored. The basket, which is based on the calculation of the price index, can be defined as a basket consisting of intermediate goods and investment goods such as machinery and equipment. The scope and weights of the existing items are updated by taking into account the changes in the production structure in the country's economy. Determining the price movements and inflation in the economy, determining the policies to be implemented by the government, adjusting wages and prices, evaluating accounting accounts, making price analyses, and making investment decisions can be counted as the usage purposes of the producer price index.

An important issue to be mentioned when talking about the PPI is the wholesale price index (WPI). WPI indicates the change in the prices of products that are generally subject to wholesale. WPI measures the price change of the substances in the country's economy in the production activities by sectors. Although there is no significant difference between WPI and PPI, the main difference emerges in the compiled units. In PPI, it is essential that prices are compiled from producers. In WPI, price information is compiled from wholesale points, as well as producers. Domestic production and sales are taken into consideration in WPI calculations, imports are excluded. PPI and WPI are often used instead of each other in economic analysis depending on the purpose of the study and data access status. However, due to the desire to measure price changes during the direct production phase, the effectiveness of WPI has decreased in almost all countries and PPI usage has come to the fore.

THE RELATIONSHIP BETWEEN PRICE INDICES AND PRICING METHODS

As explained in detail in the previous titles, firms are pricing based on various internal and external factors. Firms prefer one of the cost-based pricing, demand-based pricing, and competition-based pricing methods for their goals. Incumbent and potential firms, policymakers and regulatory authorities involved in a market want to know the commonly used method in pricing in the relevant market. In the decisions to be taken and the strategies to be developed, it is more useful to determine the commonly used pricing method in the market instead of the pricing method preferred by each firm. Two ways are often used to determine the commonly used pricing methods by firms in a market. The first is to directly collect information about pricing methods from all firms in the market analyzed. The information obtained from the firms are compiled and the commonly used pricing method in the market is determined. This method is not useful and is not preferred because it is both reluctant to share the private data of firms and it is difficult and costly to compile and analyze the data to be obtained in the markets where the number of firms is high. The second way is to determine the commonly used pricing method in the sector under consideration by making use of the causality relationships between producer and consumer prices. For consumer and producer prices, the existence and direction of causality relationships are determined and evaluated by using CPI and PPI. This method is very useful and highly preferred because the producer and consumer price index data, which are ready data in the market, are sufficient (Anggraeni & Irawan, 2018; Blomberg & Haris, 1995; Caporale et al., 2002; Clark, 1995; Gang et al., 2009; Nagle & Hogan, 2010; Tiwari, 2012).

In the literature, the causality relationship between the PPI and CPI with two different approaches, supply-side and demand-side, provides information about the commonly used pricing method in a market. The common idea at this point is that the change in producer prices will direct consumer prices as a supply-side approach. In the demand-side approach, the change in the prices of consumer goods will affect producer prices. If the supply-side approach is valid, it is concluded that the commonly used pricing method in the market in question is the cost-based pricing method, and if the demand-side approach is valid, the demand-based pricing method is commonly used in the market in question. In other words, if firms use cost-based pricing in a market, it is said that producer prices in that market will direct consumer prices, that is, there will be a causality relationship from producer prices to consumer prices. On the contrary, when the demand-based pricing method is used commonly, it can be said that the consumer prices in that market will direct the producer prices. The fact that there is a two-way relationship between price indices or no relationship can be revealed is interpreted as the firms use competition-based pricing method or various mixed combinations of the three methods (Caporale et al., 2002; Clark, 1995; Cushing & McGarvey, 1990; Shahbaz et al., 2009; Shahbaz et al., 2012; Woo & Jia, 2013).

According to the supply-side approach, the change in producer prices in the markets where the cost-based pricing method is commonly used will change consumer prices in the same direction in the following periods. In the cost-based pricing method, it basically takes into account the factors that appear as fixed and variable costs in firm production. Therefore, a change in raw material prices will increase producer costs and thus producer prices. Consequently, this change in producer prices will increase the market price of the good or service, that is, the price that the consumer faces. It is already argued in the literature that changes in raw material prices are an indicator for future inflation rates. According to this supply-side approach, supply movements in the primary product's market affect producer prices and consumer prices with a certain delay. Because producer goods transactions occur before retail operations, the change in all wholesale prices will be reflected in the retail prices of the products within the distribution system (Anggraeni & Irawan, 2018; Belton & Reichert, 2007; Ghazali et al., 2008; Guthrie, 1981; Jones, 1986; Shahbaz et al., 2009; Woo & Jia, 2013).

According to the demand side approach, the change in consumer prices in the markets where the demand-based pricing method is commonly used will affect the producer prices in the same direction in the following periods. In the demand-side approach, a change in consumer demand will affect the supply of the producer. Changing the supply of the producer will change the demand of the input used by the producer and thus the price of the input. In other words, there will be interaction from consumer prices to producer prices. According to the derived demand analysis based on this view, developments in the industrial market are derived from changes in the consumer market. This idea is based on the change in demand for final products that will result in the demand change for primary products. Actually, the demand for primary products depends on the retailer's future demand, as well as its current and past demands. Therefore, the change in the demand and prices of final consumer goods may affect the input demand and the input price of the producers. Since the supply and demand in the end product market are determined from the end consumer behavior, the supply, demand, and price in the producer market that feeds the end market are also determined from the end consumer behavior (Akcay, 2011; Anggraeni & Irawan, 2018; Caporale et al., 2002; Colclough & Lange 1982; Cushing & McGarvey, 1990; Shahbaz et al., 2012).

The relationships between CPI and PPI can be analyzed in two different ways: graphical representation and econometric analysis. With the help of graphical representation, in analyzing the relationship between price indices, CPI and PPI values are shown together on a graph and the cause-effect relationship is tried to be observed. How they act as of the same periods and how they behave as for delayed periods are examined. In graphic representation, definitive expressions cannot be used, only basic evaluations are made for different period intervals. With the help of econometric analysis, the existence and direction of causality relationship between CPI and PPI are determined to depend on the time series. Depending on the reliability of the test and estimation methods used, it is possible to obtain more detailed and useful information.

Whether the changes in one variable cause changes in another variable is a frequently discussed issue in the economy. The relationships between inflation and interest rates, exports or imports, and economic growth are examples of this. So, causality research has an important place in the economic literature. If the change occurring in one case causes a change in another case, and this situation is continuous, the first of these cases is described as a cause and the other as a result, and it is said that they are in a causality relationship. Causality, which has been discussed and analyzed with its unique ways and methods in many disciplines, was first introduced to an econometric analysis by Granger (1969) with the article "Investigating causal relations by econometric models and cross-spectral methods" published in Econometrica. According to the causality analysis, the lagged values of a random variable, such as X, after all related factors and non-random data are evaluated, provides a more accurate prediction of the future of another random variable such as Y. The concept of causality, which explains the cause-effect connection between X and Y, is interpreted as X is the cause of Y, or the result of X is Y. Causality analysis between two variables can be obtained one-way, two-way or independently:

- *One-way causality:* While X causes Y, if Y doesn't cause X, causality is called one-way causality from X to Y.
- *Two-way causality:* The situation of causality relationship both from X to Y and from Y to X is expressed as two-way causality.
- *Independence:* The situation where X does not cause Y and Y does not cause X is expressed as independence.

As mentioned above, the most preferred method for determining the commonly used pricing method in a market is to look at the causality relationship between producer and consumer prices. At this point, the relationship between CPI and PPI is analyzed. The existence and direction of the causality relationship between PPI and CPI is a controversial issue in empirical studies in the literature since different results have been obtained in the studies. There are four types of relationships that can be drawn from previous studies. The first is a one-way relationship from CPI to PPI, the second is a one-way relationship from PPI to CPI, the third is a two-way relationship between PPI and CPI, and the fourth is a state of independence, which means that there is no causal relationship between these two indices. The relationship between PPI and CPI is viewed from two perspectives, the supply-side approach, and the demand-side approach. As a result, if the causality relationship is from PPI to CPI, it is interpreted that the supply-side approach is dominant in the relevant market and the cost-based pricing method is commonly used. On the contrary, if the causality relationship is from CPI to PPI, it indicates that the demand-side approach is dominant in the market and that the demand-based pricing method is commonly used. In addition, if the causality relationship between PPI and CPI for the market in question is a two-way relationship or no relationship can be revealed, it is interpreted that firms use competition-based pricing method or various mixed combinations of three methods in their pricing strategies (Anggraeni & Irawan, 2018; Caporale et al., 2002; Clark, 1995; Gang et al., 2009).

EMPIRICAL LITERATURE

Although the empirical literature examining the commonly use pricing method in the market is not rich, studies analyzing the relationship between producer and consumer prices are wide in the literature. The existence and direction of the causality relationship between CPI and PPI (sometimes WPI) reveal whether the dominant approach in the markets is the demand-side approach or supply-side approach. The determination of the commonly used pricing method is the evaluation and interpretation of the results obtained from these analyzes. Leading studies at this point consist of studies analyzing the US economy. Over time, these studies have become widespread for other countries and within the country groups as data sets are formed. The leading ones of these studies are summarized below and the results obtained from the studies are briefly shared. In addition, the results obtained from the shared studies have been briefly interpreted and evaluated in accordance with the purpose of this book chapter.

Silver and Wallace's (1980) study for the USA is one of the pioneering studies that analyze the relationship between consumer prices and producer prices. In their study, Silver and Wallace (1980) analyzed using the quarterly time series data between 1952: 01 and 1977: 04 using the Pearson method. In the study, the wholesale prices index, which was more widely used at the time, was used instead of PPI, and as a result, a one-way causality relationship was found from wholesale prices to consumer prices. According to the results, a shock of 1% in wholesale prices could affect consumer prices by 0.50%-0.55% in the same direction within four or five months. Based on the analysis results of Silver and Wallace (1980), it can be said that the supply-side approach for the US economy was dominant in the relevant period and the cost-based pricing method was commonly used.

Lamm and Westcott (1981) analyzed the relationship between producer prices and consumer prices in the US food industry using quarterly data from 1968: 02-1979: 04. The study, whose main purpose is to observe the reflections of changes in factor prices on retail, addresses the food price determination process with an econometric model with twenty linear equations following Popkin's approach to processing. In the study, in which all important inputs used in domestic food production in the USA are included in the analysis, it is revealed that a change in producer prices reflected on consumer prices in a short period of like two quarters. According to the results of the study, the existence of a supply-side approach in the US food market was revealed in the relevant period and it was determined that the cost-based pricing method was commonly used in pricing.

Guthrie (1981) in his study analyzed whether there is a relationship between producer prices and consumer prices in the USA using monthly data for the period 1947: 01-1975: 12. Assuming that the lag coefficients of the model follow a Pascal distribution, the author tested the overall approach, which argues that current changes in WPI are automatically followed by future changes in CPI. Although it is not strong at the end of the study, it supports the hypothesis that there is a relationship between the changes in the wholesale price index and the changes in the consumer price index. It also reveals that the relationship has grown stronger in the years to come, and the rate of reflection has increased. Depending on the results, it can be said that the supply-side approach was dominant for the US economy in the relevant period, and this dominance would increase over time and the cost-based pricing method was commonly used.

Jones (1986) analyzed the relationship between producer and consumer prices using Granger causality analysis using monthly data between the periods of 1947: 01-1983: 12 of the USA. In his study (1986), Jones divided the data set into two subgroups (1945: 01-1971: 05 and 1974: 05-1983: 12) and analyzed them separately, taking into consideration the possibility of a different structural relationship between consumer and wholesale prices for the periods before and after the wage and price controls were in force. According to the results obtained in the general analysis, it has been found that there is a two-way causality relationship between the PPI and the CPI in the USA as of the period analyzed. In other words, producer prices are effective in determining consumer prices, while consumer prices are effective in determining producer prices. In addition, as a result of the analysis made for the two sub-periods, it was revealed that wage and price controls did not constitute a structural change in this relationship between indices. Based on the results obtained from the study, it can be said that both the supply-side approach and the demand-side approach were effective and that mixed approaches were commonly used in pricing.

Cushing and McGarvey's (1990) study for the USA using monthly data between 1954 and 1987 is considered one of the main studies in this topic. In their study, Cushing and McGarvey (1990) analyze the criticisms of Silver and Wallace (1980) on their methods and results theoretically and empirically. As a result of their analysis, Cushing and McGarvey (1990) conclude that the demand for industrial goods is determined from the demand for final goods and services with a pro derived demand theory approach. As a result of their derived demand approach, they emphasize that as much as today's demand is taken into consideration, it is necessary to pay attention to today's demand, which is expected in the past. In their study, Cushing and McGarvey (1990) reveal that consumer prices depend on current demand, and producer prices depend on expected demand in the future. Depending on the results obtained, it can be said that consumer prices on a sectoral basis direct the producer prices that was, the demand-side approach was dominant, and therefore demand-based pricing was commonly used.

Clark (1995) in his study, which has an important place in the literature, examines whether there is a causal relationship from producer prices to consumer prices. As a result of regression and VAR analysis made with monthly data between the years 1977-1994 of the USA, it is said that price changes in the first stages of production did not cause a strong change in consumer prices. The author basically says that with a simple economic approach, changes in producer prices should affect consumer prices in accordance with the production chain, and therefore producer prices should be used to predict changes in consumer prices. Empirically analyzing whether this simple approach has a response in real markets, Clark (1995) found that consumer prices did not react significantly to the change in producer prices. In other words, producer prices are not always a good and sufficient determinant of consumer prices.

As a result, the author, who tested the dominance of the supply-side approach and the common use of cost-based pricing, could not find satisfactory evidence at this point.

Caporale et al. (2002) examined the causal relationship between producer and consumer prices for G7 countries, which consist of Canada, England, France, Germany, Italy, Japan, and the USA. In this study, in which data between 1976 and 1999 was used, Toda and Yamamato (1995) causality test method were preferred. Unlike other studies, this study also discussed the effect of the monetary transmission mechanism on this causality relationship. In the analysis, in which the monetary transmission mechanism is ignored, a two-way causality relationship between producer and consumer prices was revealed. However, considering the monetary transmission mechanism, a one-way causality relationship has been found from producer prices to consumer prices. According to the results, considering the monetary transmission mechanism, it can be said that the supply-side approach was dominant in G7 countries and cost-based pricing was commonly used.

Ghazali et al. (2008) analyzed the causal relationship between PPI and CPI for Malaysia using monthly data for the period 1986: 01-2007: 04. Using Angle-Granger and Johansen cointegration method and Toda-Yamamato causality test in their analysis, the authors found a long-term relationship and found a one-way causality from PPI to CPI. Based on these results, it can be said that the supply-side approach was dominant in Malaysia and the cost-based pricing method was commonly used in Malaysia.

Kwon and Koo (2009), using the data between 1985 and 2008, analyzed the transitivity between producer and consumer prices in food prices in the USA with the Toda-Yamamoto method. The authors analyzed and compared datasets by dividing into two subgroups, 1985-2001 and 2002-2008. As a result of the empirical analysis, the authors, who found a two-way relationship between the PPI and the CPI for the period 1985-2001, concluded that the demands and costs were effective in determining the prices. For the 2002-2008 range, they concluded that price transitivity is one-way from producer prices to consumer prices due to cost. According to the results obtained, while the supply-side approach and the demand-side approach were effective for the first period, the supply-side approach became dominant in the following period and cost-based pricing was commonly used.

Gang et al. (2009) analyzed the causality relationship between CPI and PPI in China with the help of monthly data between 2001:01 and 2008:08 and tried to determine whether costs or demand are more effective in pricing. As a result of the Granger causality analysis they applied, a one-way causality relationship from CPI to PPI was revealed. They determined that the changes in CPI changed PPI in the same direction with 1-3 month delays. The authors conclude that demand-side factors play an important role in price transitivity rather than supply-side factors in the Chinese economy. According to these results, it can be said that the demand-side approach was dominant and demand-based pricing was more commonly used in China for the relevant period.

Shahbaz et al. (2009) analyzed the relationship between producer and consumer prices for Pakistan. ARDL Bounds Testing Approach was preferred in the study where monthly data between 1992:01 and 2007:06 was used. Based on the empirical analysis, it was determined that producer and consumer prices move together in the long term and there is a two-way causality relationship between CPI and PPI in the short term. According to the results obtained from the study, supply-side approaches and demand-side approaches were effective together in the Pakistan economy and costs and demand were used together in determining the prices.

Tiwari and Shahbaz (2010) analyzed the causality between producer prices and consumer prices for India using the data set for the 1950-2009 period. The authors have applied the autoregressive distributed lag (ARDL) bounds testing approach, whose purpose is to reveal the static and dynamic causality between WPI and CPI for both long and short term. As a result of the empirical analysis, the authors found a two-way relationship between CPI and WPI in India for the period in question, both in the long and short term. According to these results, it can be said that both supply-side and demand-side approaches were effective in the Indian economy for the relevant period and mixed pricing methods were used instead of a commonly pricing strategy.

Akcay (2011) empirically analyzed the causality relationship between WPI and PPI for five European countries: Finland, France, Germany, Netherlands, and Sweden. Using the monthly data between 1995:08 and 2007:12, Akcay (2011) preferred the method of Toda–Yamamato (1995) and showed the results separately for the countries. Akcay (2011), which preferred countries with low inflation rates while making country choices, found one-way causality from producer prices to consumer prices in Finland and France, and two-way causality in Germany. For the Netherlands and Sweden, no causality relationship was detected between the two variables. According to these results, while the supply-side approach is dominant and cost-based pricing was commonly in Finland and France, both supply-side and demand-side approach efficient and mixed pricing methods were commonly used in Germany.

Abdioglu and Korkmaz (2012), using monthly data for the years 2003 to 2012, the relationship between the PPI and CPI in Turkey has analyzed both in general and in particular in the sub-sector. Abdioglu and Korkmaz (2012) analyzed the price transitivity between consumer and producer price indices and tried to determine whether the price increases were due to cost or demand. In addition, the sectoral transfer of price movements was analyzed by investigating causality relations in terms of sub-sectors such as food and soft drinks, education-communication-culture, housing, and clothing. As a result of the analysis made with general data, it was determined that there is a two-way causality relationship between CPI and PPI. As for the sub-sectors, it was determined that the two-way causality in question was provided only for the health sector. It has been determined that the direction of causality for other sectors other than education-communication-culture sectors is from consumer prices to producer prices. It is revealed that there is no relationship between producer and consumer prices for the food sector. The obtained results also proved that the effect of demand-side factors on price increases rather than supply-side factors is more important for sub-sectors such as clothing and housing, which have a significant weight in the general economy. When all the results are compiled, it can be said that both supply-side and demand-side approaches are effective for the overall economy and both cost-based and demand-based pricing methods are commonly used. While the health sector acts similarly to the general economy, it can be said that the demand-side approach was dominant in the clothing and housing sectors and the demand-based pricing method was commonly used.

Woo and Jia (2013) analyzed the causal relationship between PPI and CPI of countries with different economic characteristics, such as Australia, Canada, Denmark, Indonesia, Japan, Norway, Spain, Pakistan, Uruguay, and the USA. In order to make a comparative analysis, both linear cointegration Engle-Granger and nonlinear cointegration Enders-Siklos test were applied. In the study, as a result of the Enders-Granger cointegration analysis, co-integration between the CPI and PPI was determined only for Indonesia and Pakistan within the country group. In the Enders-Siklos test, the cointegration relationship for Canada, Denmark, Indonesia, Japan, Pakistan, Spain, and Uruguay was revealed. As a result of the causality analysis, while a two-way relationship has been revealed between the PPI and the CPI for Australia, Canada, Denmark, Indonesia, Japan, Norway, Pakistan, Uruguay, and the USA, a one-way relationship has been found for Spain from the CPI to the PPI. According to the results, the demand-side approach was dominant and demand-based pricing was common in Spain, whereas in other countries, both the supply and demand-side approach can be said to be effective.

Anggraeni and Irawan (2018) analyzed the causality relationship between the CPI and PPI for the case of Indonesia, both for the overall economy and for six different sub-sectors such as food, clothing, processed food, beverage, cigarette, and tobacco. VAR analysis was performed with the Granger causality test with the help of monthly time series data between 2010:01 and 2016:08. As a result of the analysis made with general data, a one-way causality relationship was determined from PPI to CPI. According to this result, it was emphasized that a shock to the PPI in the Indonesian economy will be the leading indicator of the same directional change in the CPI. In the analysis made with the data of the food sector, a two-way relationship between PPI and CPI was revealed. In the results of the analysis made for the clothing sector, a causality relationship from CPI to PPI was determined. In the analysis made for processed food, beverage, cigarette, and tobacco group, no causality relationship was found between PPI and CPI. When all the results obtained are evaluated in the focus of this study, it can be said that the supply-side approach was dominant in the Indonesian economy and cost-based pricing was commonly used. It can be said that the cost-based pricing strategy was commonly used in the food industry and the demand-based pricing method was commonly preferred in the clothing industry. It can be concluded that more mixed pricing methods were preferred in processed food, beverage, cigarette, and tobacco groups.

FUTURE RESEARCH DIRECTIONS

It is very important to be able to determine the pricing methods commonly used in the markets. This area requires studies and analyzes that are constantly updated and renewed. New and more specific studies should be carried out in the light of existing studies, taking into account the changing market conditions.

These studies can be developed with dynamic models that consider more different economic variables. In addition, the analyzes made for the general economy and for certain markets can be enriched by applying to specific products for which data can be obtained. For markets where the number of firms is small and private data can be collected, empirical results obtained from the causal relationship between CPI and PPI can be evaluated by comparing them with primary data from firms.

CONCLUSION

This study focuses on estimating the commonly used pricing method in the whole economy or especially in a certain market with the help of causality relationship between PPI and CPI. In the markets where the supply-side approach is dominant, a change in raw material prices will increase producer costs and thus producer prices, and it is assumed that the change in producer prices will eventually change consumer prices in the same direction. According to this situation where there is a causality relationship from producer prices to consumer prices, it is evaluated that cost-based pricing is commonly used in markets where the supply-side approach is dominant. Considering the demand-side approach, on the other hand, it is argued that a change in consumer demand will affect the supply of the producer, thereby changing the demand of the input used by the producer in production and, consequently, the price of the input. According to this situation where there is a causality relationship from consumer prices to producer prices, demand-based pricing is accepted to be commonly used in markets where the demand-side approach is dominant. The fact that there is a two-way relationship between the price indices or the failure to reveal any relationship between two variables means that one of the supply-side or demand-side approaches cannot be observed predominantly and it can be interpreted as suggesting that the firms use the competition-based pricing method or various mixed combinations of the three methods.

In the literature, the relationship between CPI and PPI has been examined with empirical analysis for various purposes, but the connection of this relationship with the pricing method has not been sufficiently discussed. This book chapter contributes to the elimination of this shortcoming in the literature. When the results of empirical studies in the literature are examined, different results were encountered in different studies in the causality relationship between CPI and PPI. In fact, different results have been achieved even from time to time, in studies covering the same countries and covering a similar period. There are several reasons for this situation. Firstly, differences arise because of the different methods and different data set used. Secondly, obtaining contradictory results, especially in the evaluations made for the general economy, may result from the fact that economies consist of various markets that have very different characteristics. Thirdly, in the analysis made for both a general and a certain market, failure to consider the input-output relationships between the markets may lead to inconsistent results. Fourthly, differences in CPI and PPI calculations may result in unexpected results from the analysis of the relationship. Fifthly, baskets used to calculate indices can vary considerably between countries. Especially in country comparative analysis, these situations may have misleading results. Sixthly, ignoring factors that directly or indirectly affect the prices of producers and consumers in the goods and services markets, such as interest rates and exchange rates, may lead to misleading results. As a result, it should be taken into consideration that the evaluations made for the commonly used pricing method, based on the causality relationship between the CPI and the PPI, constitute a general idea and do not express certainty.

REFERENCES

Abdioglu, Z., & Korkmaz, O. (2012). Tuketici ve uretici fiyat endekslerinde fiyat geciskenligi: Alt sektorler. *Cukurova Universitesi IIBF Dergisi*, *16*(2), 65–81.

Akçay, S. (2011). The causal relationship between producer price index and consumer price index: Empirical evidence from selected European countries. *International Journal of Economics and Finance*, *3*(6), 227–232. doi:10.5539/ijef.v3n6p227

Allen, R. G. D. (1949). The economic theory of index numbers. *Economica*, *16*(63), 197–203. doi:10.2307/2549677

Anggraeni, D., & Irawan, T. (2018). Causality analysis of producer price index (ppi) and consumer price index (cpi) in Indonesia. *Jurnal Ekonomi Dan Kebijakan Pembangunan*, *7*(1), 60–77. doi:10.29244/jekp.7.1.60-77

Belton, W. J., & Nair-Reichert, U. (2007). Inflation regimes, core inflation measures and the relationship between producer and consumer price inflation. *Applied Economics*, *39*(10), 1295–1305. doi:10.1080/00036840500447682

Blomberg S.B., & Harris, E.S. (1995). The commodity - consumer price connection: fact or fable. *Federal Reserve Bank of New York Economic Policy Review, 1*(3).

Caporale, G. M., Katsimi, M., & Pittis, N. (2002). Causality links between consumer and producer prices: Some empirical evidence. *Southern Economic Journal*, *68*(3), 703–711. doi:10.2307/1061728

Clark, T. F. (1995). Do producer prices lead consumer prices? *Federal Reserve Bank of Kansas City Economic Review, 80*(3), 25–39.

Colclough, W. G., & Lange, M. D. (1982). Empirical evidence of causality from consumer to wholesale prices. *Journal of Econometrics, 19*(2-3), 379–384. doi:10.1016/0304-4076(82)90012-4

Cunningham, D., & Hornby, W. (1993). Pricing decision in small firms: Theory and practice. *Management Decision, 31*(7), 46–55. doi:10.1108/00251749310046765

Cushing, M. J., & McGarvey, M. G. (1990). Feedback between wholesale and consumer price inflation: A reexamination of the evidence. *Southern Economic Journal, 56*(4), 1059–1072. doi:10.2307/1059891

Dibb, S., & Simkin, L. (2013). *Marketing essentials* (2nd ed.). Cengage Learning.

Fisher, F., & Shell, K. (1972). *The economic theory of price indexes.* Academic Press.

Fisher, I. (1921). The best form of index number. *Journal of the American Statistical Association, 17*, 533–537.

Gang, F., Liping, H., & Jiani, H. (2009). CPI vs. PPI: Which drives which? *Frontiers of Economics in China, 4*(3), 317–334. doi:10.100711459-009-0018-z

Ghazali, M. F., Yee, O. A., & Muhammad, M. Z. (2008). Do producer prices cause consumer prices? Some empirical evidence. *International Journal of Business and Management, 3*(11), 78–82.

Granger, C. W. J. (1969). Investigating causal relations by econometrics models and cross spectral methods. *Econometrica, 37*(3), 424–438. doi:10.2307/1912791

Guthrie, R. S. (1981). The relationship between wholesale and consumer prices. *Southern Economic Journal, 47*(4), 1046–1055. doi:10.2307/1058161

Jones, J. B. (1986). Consumer prices, wholesale prices, and causality. *Empirical Economics, 11*(1), 41–55. doi:10.1007/BF01978144

Kar, M. (2019). Pricing strategies in mobile telecommunications markets. *Social. Mentality and Researcher Thinkers Journal, 5*(16), 360–371. doi:10.31576mryj.240

Kotler, P., & Armstrong, G. (2013). *Principles of marketing*. Pearson Prentice-Hall.

Kotler, P., & Keller, K. (2013). *Marketing management.* Pearson Prentice-Hall.

Kwon, D., & Koo, W. (2009). Price transmission mechanism among disaggregated processing stages of food: demand-pull or cost-push? Paper Presented at the *Annual Meeting of the Agricultural and Applied Economics Associations*, Milwaukee, WI.

Lamm, R. M. Jr, & Westcott, P. C. (1981). The effects of changing input costs on food prices. *American Agricultural Economics Association, 63*(May), 187–196. doi:10.2307/1239554

Nagle, T. T., & Hogan, J. E. (2010). *The strategy and tactics of pricing* (4th ed.). Pearson Education.

Nagle, T. T., & Holden, R. K. (1995). *The strategy and tactics of pricing*. Prentice-Hall.

Shahbaz, M., Awan, R. U., & Nasir, N. M. (2009). Producer & consumer prices nexus: ARDL bounds testing approach. *International Journal of Marketing Studies, 1*(2), 78–86. doi:10.5539/ijms.v1n2p78

Shahbaz, M., Tiwari, A. K., & Tahir, M. I. (2012). Does CPI Granger-cause WPI? New extensions from frequency domain approach in Pakistan. *Economic Modelling, 29*(5), 1592–1597. doi:10.1016/j.econmod.2012.05.016

Shipley, D., & Jobber, D. (2001). Integrative pricing via the pricing wheel. *Industrial Marketing Management, 30*(3), 301–314. doi:10.1016/S0019-8501(99)00098-X

Silver, L., & Wallace, T. D. (1980). The lag relationship between wholesale and consumer prices. *Journal of Econometrics, 12*(3), 375–387. doi:10.1016/0304-4076(80)90063-9

Skouras, T., Avlonitis, G. J., & Indounas, K. A. (2005). Economics and marketing on pricing: How and why do they differ? *Journal of Product and Brand Management, 14*(6), 362–374. doi:10.1108/10610420510624512

Smith, T.J. (2012). *Pricing strategy*. South-Western Cengage Learning.

Tiwari, A., & Shahbaz, M. (2010). *Modelling the relationship between wholesale price and consumer price indices: Cointegration and causality for India.* Working Paper, ICFAI University, Tripura, Comsats Institute of Information Technology.

Tiwari, A. K. (2012). An empirical investigation of causality between producers' price and consumers' price indices in Australia in frequency domain. *Economic Modelling, 29*(5), 1571–1578. doi:10.1016/j.econmod.2012.05.010

Woo, K. Y., & Jia, L. X. (2013). *Threshold cointegration and causality between cpi and ppi in selected countries–some international evidence.* Working Paper Series August, Hong Kong Shue University.

ADDITIONAL READING

Akdi, Y., Berument, H., & Cilasun, S. Y. (2006). The relationship between different price indices: Evidence from Turkey. *Physica A, 360*(2), 483–492. doi:10.1016/j.physa.2005.05.037

Avlonitis, G. J., Indounas, K. A., & Gounaris, S. P. (2005). Pricing objectives over the service life cycle: Some empirical evidence. *European Journal of Marketing, 39*(5/6), 696–714. doi:10.1108/03090560510590773

Davidson, A., & Simonetto, M. (2005). Pricing strategy and execution: An overlooked way to increase revenues and profits. *Strategy and Leadership, 33*(6), 25–33. doi:10.1108/10878570510631639

Dolgui, A., & Proth, J. M. (2010). Pricing strategies and models. *Annual Reviews in Control, 34*(1), 101–110. doi:10.1016/j.arcontrol.2010.02.005

Dorestani, A., & Arjomand, L. H. (2006). An empirical study of the relationship between consumer and producer price index: A unit root test and test of cointegration. *The Coastal Business Journal, 5*(1), 33–38.

Hakimipoor, N., Alipour, M. S., & Akbaryan, H. (2016). Investigation on causality relationship between consumer price index and producer price index in Iran. *Reports on Economics and Finance*, *2*(1), 37–49. doi:10.12988/ref.2016.51113

Katsouli, A., Vogiatzis, A., & Manitsaris, A. (2002). Linking consumer prices to wholesale prices: Error correction models for the case of Greece. *Agricultural Economics Review*, *3*(1), 12–22.

Liping, H., Gang, F., & Jiani, H. (2008). CPI vs. PPI: Which drives which? *Economic Research Journal*, *11*, 16–26.

Martinez, W. O. R., Caicedo, E. G., & Tique, E. J. C. (2013). Exploring the relationship between the CPI and the PPI: The Colombian case. *International Journal of Business and Management*, *8*(17), 142–152.

Silver, L., & Wallace, T. D. (1980). The lag relationship between wholesale and consumer prices. *Journal of Econometrics*, *12*(3), 375–387. doi:10.1016/0304-4076(80)90063-9

KEY TERMS AND DEFINITIONS

Causality: The cause-effect connection between X and Y. While X causes Y, if Y doesn't cause X, causality is called one-way causality from X to Y. The situation of causality relationship both from X to Y and from Y to X is expressed as two-way causality. The situation where X does not cause Y and Y does not cause X is expressed as independence.

Competition-Based Pricing: In the competition-based pricing method, prices are determined based on the prices applied by competitors.

Consumer Price Index (CPI): CPI is calculated as a tool to measure the changes in the prices of goods and services purchased for consumption by households over time.

Cost-Based Pricing: The price is determined based on fixed and variable costs in the production of the firm's goods and services.

Demand-Based Pricing: The pricing process is based on estimating how much a consumer is willing to pay for a product that meets their wants and needs.

Index: Indicator that show proportionally changes in the values of a statistical event for various time periods or different geographical regions.

Price: The value paid for the change of ownership in the purchase of a good or service.

Price Indices: Criteria that allow to analyze and compare the changes in average prices of selected goods and services over a given period of time.

Pricing: The process of determining the price as a result of evaluating the factors affecting the price.

Producer Price Index (PPI): PPI is the price index that measures the price changes of the producer prices of the products produced in the country's economy in a certain reference period and subject to domestic sales.

Compilation of References

A.T. Kearney/Foreign Policy. (2001). Measuring globalization. *Foreign Policy, 122*, 56–65.

Abbas, W., & Asghar, I. (2010). *The role of leadership in organizatinal change: Relating the successful organizational change with visionary and innovative leadership*. University of Gävle, Faculty of Engineering and Sustainable Development, Department of Industrial Development, IT and Land Management. Independent thesis Advanced level.

Abbott, K. W., & Snidal, D. (1998). Why states act through formal international organizations. *The Journal of Conflict Resolution, 42*(1), 3–32. doi:10.1177/0022002798042001001

Abdioglu, Z., & Korkmaz, O. (2012). Tuketici ve uretici fiyat endekslerinde fiyat geciskenligi: Alt sektorler. *Cukurova Universitesi IIBF Dergisi, 16*(2), 65–81.

Acar, S., Söderholm, P., & Brännlund, R. (2018). Convergence of per capita carbon dioxide emissions: Implications and meta-analysis. *Climate Policy, 18*(4), 512–525. doi:10.1080/14693062.2017.1314244

Acemoglu, D., & Zilibotti, F. (1997). Was Prometheus unbound by chance? Risk, diversification, and growth. *Journal of Political Economy, 105*(4), 709–751. doi:10.1086/262091

Adeseyoju, A. (2001). *Attracting foreign investors to Nigeria*. Dailynews Paper n°31.

Agenor, P. R. (2004). Orderly exits from adjustable pegs and exchange rate bands. *The Journal of Policy Reform, 7*(2), 83–108. doi:10.1080/1384128002000242388

Aghion, P., & Howitt, P. (1990). A model of growth through creative destruction. *Econometrica, 60*(2), 323–351. doi:10.2307/2951599

Aghion, P., & Howitt, P. (2009). *The economics of growth*. The MIT Press. http://eprints.ucl.ac.uk/17829/

Agosin, M. R. (2009). Crecimiento y diversificación de exportaciones en economías emergentes. *Revista CEPAL, 97*(97), 117–134. doi:10.18356/0e25c429-es

Agosin, M. R., Alvarez, R., & Bravo-Ortega, C. (2012). Determinants of export diversification around the world: 1962-2000. *World Economy, 35*(3), 295–315. doi:10.1111/j.1467-9701.2011.01395.x

Ahmed, M., Khan, A. M., Bibi, S., & Zakaria, M. (2017). Convergence of per capita CO_2 emissions across the globe: Insights via wavelet analysis. *Renewable & Sustainable Energy Reviews, 75*, 86–97. doi:10.1016/j.rser.2016.10.053

Akçay, S. (2011). The causal relationship between producer price index and consumer price index: Empirical evidence from selected European countries. *International Journal of Economics and Finance, 3*(6), 227–232. doi:10.5539/ijef.v3n6p227

Akhtaruzzaman, M., Berg, N., & Christopher, H. (2017). *Expropriation risk and FDI in developing countries: Does return of capital dominate return on capital? Bank of Canada Staff Working, 9.* Bank of Canada.

Aldy, J. E. (2006). Per capita carbon dioxide emissions: Convergence or divergence? *Environmental and Resource Economics, 4*(33), 533–555. doi:10.100710640-005-6160-x

Alemu, A. M. (2009). Determinants of vertical and horizontal export diversification: Evidences from Sub-Saharan Africa and East Asia. *Ethiopian Journal of Economics, 17*(2), 1–56. doi:10.4314/eje.v17i2.47311

Alesina, A., & Perotti, R. (1995). The political economy of budget deficits. *IMF Staff Papers, 42*(1), 1–31. doi:10.2307/3867338

Alesina, A., & Perotti, R. (1996). Income distribution, political instability, and investment. *European Economic Review, 40*(6), 1203–1228. doi:10.1016/0014-2921(95)00030-5

Ali, A., Ibrahim, M., & Omar, Z. (2017). Impact of changes in the exchange rate on foreign direct investment: Evidence from Somalia. *African Journal of Economic and Sustainable Development, 8*(8), 27–54.

Alianza del Pacifico. El poder de la Integracion. (2020). [Pacific Alliance: The power of integration]. https://alianza-pacifico.net/

Allen, C. R., Angeler, D. G., Garmestani, A. S., Gunderson, L. H., & Holling, C. S. (2014). Panarchy: Theory and application. *Ecosystems (New York, N.Y.), 17*(4), 578–589. doi:10.100710021-013-9744-2

Allen, R. G. D. (1949). The economic theory of index numbers. *Economica, 16*(63), 197–203. doi:10.2307/2549677

Almeida, F., & Teixeira, R. (2014). Influence of the family and of social networks on business creation by young entrepreneurs. *Pretexto, 15*(2), 110–128.

Alobari, C., Paago, J., Igbare, F. N., & Emmah, D. (2016). Exchange rate and foreign direct investment. Implication for economic growth in Nigeria. *Equatorial Journal of Finance and Management Science, 1*(1), 10–23.

Alon, I., Zhang, W., & Lattermann, C. (2018). Introduction. In I. Alon, W. Zhang, & C. Lattermann (Eds.), *China's Belt and Road initiative: Changing the rules of globalization* (pp. 1–13). Palgrave. doi:10.1007/978-3-319-75435-2_1

Al-Rodhan, N. R., & Stoudmann, G. (2006). Definitions of globalization: A comprehensive overview and a proposed definition. *Program on the Geopolitical Implications of Globalization and Transnational Security, 6*, 1–21.

Alves, A. (2008). China lusophone connection. *China in Africa Report, 2.*

Amador, J., & Cabral, S. (2016). *Networks of value added trade.* ECB Working Paper No. 1931.

Amiti, M. (1999). Specialization patterns in Europe. *Weltwirtschaftliches Archiv, 135*(4), 573–593. doi:10.1007/BF02707385

Amit, R., & Muller, E. (1995). "Push" and "pull" entrepreneurship. *Journal of Small Business and Entrepreneurship, 12*(4), 64–80. doi:10.1080/08276331.1995.10600505

Amorós, J. E., Felzensztein, C., & Etchebarne, M. (2012). Emprendimiento internacional en Latinoamérica: Desafíos para el desarrollo. *Esic Market Economics and Business Journal, 43*(3), 513–529.

Amsler, C., & Lee, J. (1995). An LM test for a unit root in the presence of a structural change. *Econometric Theory, 11*(2), 359–368. doi:10.1017/S026646660000921X

Ancelovici, M. (2013). The origins of dynamic organizational resilience. In P. A. Hall & M. Lamont (Eds.), *Social resilience in the neoliberal era* (pp. 346–375). Cambridge University Press. doi:10.1017/CBO9781139542425.019

Anderson, D., Dennis, B., & Hunt, B. (2014). *Is Japan's population aging deflationary?* IMF Working Paper Series No. WP/14/139. Retrieved from https://www.imf.org/en/Publications/WP/Issues/2016/12/31/Is-Japans-Population-Aging-Deflationary-41812

Anderson, J., & van Wincoop, E. (2003). Gravity with gravitas: A solution to the border puzzle. *The American Economic Review, 93*(1), 170–192. doi:10.1257/000282803321455214

Ang, B. J. (2008). Determinants of foreign direct investment in Malaysia. *Journal of Policy Modeling, 30*(1), 185–189. doi:10.1016/j.jpolmod.2007.06.014

Anggraeni, D., & Irawan, T. (2018). Causality analysis of producer price index (ppi) and consumer price index (cpi) in Indonesia. *Jurnal Ekonomi Dan Kebijakan Pembangunan, 7*(1), 60–77. doi:10.29244/jekp.7.1.60-77

Antweiler, W., Copeland, B. R., & Taylor, M. S. (2001). Is free trade good for the environment? *The American Economic Review, 91*(4), 877–908. doi:10.1257/aer.91.4.877

Anwar, A. (2020). Report, South Asia and China's Belt and Road Initiative: Security implications and ways forward. In A. L. Vuving (Ed.), *Hindsight, insight, foresight: Thinking about security in the Indo-Pacific* (pp. 161–178). Daniel K. Inouye Asia-Pacific Center for Security Studies.

Anyanwu, J. C. (1998). An econometric investigation of the determinants of foreign direct investment in Nigeria. *Nigerian Economic Society Annual Conference Publication.*

Apergis, N., & Payne, J. E. (2020). NAFTA and the convergence of CO_2 emissions intensity and its determinants. *Inter Economics, 161*, 1–9. doi:10.1016/j.inteco.2019.10.002

Applegate, L. M., & Collura, M. (2000). *Emerging networked business models: lessons from the field.* Harvard Business School.

Arellano, M., & Bond, S. (1991). Some test of specification for panel data: Monte Carlo evidence and application to employment equations. *The Review of Economic Studies, 58*(2), 277–297. doi:10.2307/2297968

Aremu, J.A. (1997). Foreign private investment: Determinants, performance and promotion. *CBN Bulletin*, 108–112.

Aremu, J. A. (2005). *Attracting and negotiating foreign direct investment with transnational corporations in Nigeria.* Market Link Communications.

Arezki, R., & Nguyen, H. (2020). Novel coronavirus hurts the Middle East and North Africa through many channels. In R. Baldwin & B. W. di Mauro (Eds.), *Economics in the Time of COVID-19* (pp. 53–58). Centre for Economic Policy Research.

Arribas, I., Bensassi, S., & Tortosa-Ausina, E. (2020). Trade integration in the European Union: Openness, interconnectedness, and distance. *The North American Journal of Economics and Finance, 52*, 101167. doi:10.1016/j.najef.2020.101167

Arribas, I., Pérez, F., & Tortosa-Ausina, E. (2009). Measuring globalization of international trade: Theory and evidence. *World Development, 37*(1), 127–145. doi:10.1016/j.worlddev.2008.03.009

Arthur, S. J., & Hisrich, R. D. (2011). Entrepreneurship through the ages: Lessons learned. *Journal of Enterprising Culture, 19*(01), 1–40. doi:10.1142/S0218495811000696

Asia Pacific Economic Cooperation. (2020). *About APEC.* https://www.apec.org/About-Us/About-APEC

Asiedu, E. (2002). On the determinants of foreign direct investment to developing countries: Is Africa different? *World Development, 30*(1), 107–119. doi:10.1016/S0305-750X(01)00100-0

Asiedu, E. (2006). Foreign direct investment in Africa: The role of natural resources, market size, government policy, institutions and political instability. *World Economy, 29*(1), 63–77. doi:10.1111/j.1467-9701.2006.00758.x

Aslan, A. (2009). Kişi başına karbon dioksit emisyon yakınsama analizi: 1950-2004. *Ege Akademik Bakış, 9*(4), 1427–1427. doi:10.21121/eab.2009419683

Atkins, G. P. (2018). *Latin American and the Caribbean in the international system*. Routledge. doi:10.4324/9780429499395

Audley, J. J., Papademetriou, D., Polaski, S., & Vaughan, S. (2003). *La promesa y la realidad del TLCAN*. Lecciones de México para el Hemisferio.

Auerbach, A. J. (2014). Budget rules and fiscal policy: Ten lessons from theory and evidence. *German Economic Review, 15*(1), 84–99. doi:10.1111/geer.12023

Baharumshah, A. Z., Lau, E., & Khalid, A. M. (2006). Testing twin deficits hypothesis using VARs and variance decomposition. *Journal of the Asia Pacific Economy, 11*(3), 331–354. doi:10.1080/13547860600764245

Bahmani-Oskooee, M. (1995). The long-run determinants of the U.S. trade balance revisited. *Journal of Post Keynesian Economics, 17*(3), 457–465. doi:10.1080/01603477.1995.11490040

Balassa, B. (1965). Trade liberalisation and “revealed” comparative advantage 1. *Manchester School, 33*(2), 99–123. doi:10.1111/j.1467-9957.1965.tb00050.x

Baldwin, R. E. (1971). Determinants of the commodity structure of U.S. Trade. *The American Economic Review, 61*(1), 126–146.

Baldwin, R., & Evenett, S. J. (2020). *Covid-19 and trade policy: Why turning inward won’t work*. CEPR Press.

Baldwin, R., & Lopez-Gonzalez, J. (2015). Supply-chain trade: A portrait of global patterns and several testable hypotheses. *World Economy, 38*(11), 1682–1721. doi:10.1111/twec.12189

Baldwin, R., & Tomiura, E. (2020). Thinking ahead about the trade impact of COVID-19. In R. Baldwin & B. W. di Mauro (Eds.), *Economics in the Time of COVID-19* (pp. 59–71). Centre for Economic Policy Research.

Banco Mundial. (2010). *PIB y PIB per capita de México*. Banco Mundial.

Bancomext. (2015). *Guía básica del exportador*. Banco Nacional de Comercio Exterior, S.N.C.

Bandyopadhyay, S., Rao, A., & Sinha, B. (2011). *Models for social networks with statistical applications*. Sage. doi:10.4135/9781452226538

Bannock, G. (2005). *The economics and management of small business: An international perspective*. Psychology Press.

BANXICO. (2017). *Desarrollo económico mexicano*. Banco de México.

Baptista, R., Escária, V., & Madruga, P. (2008). Entrepreneurship, regional development and job creation: The case of Portugal. *Small Business Economics, 30*(1), 49–58. doi:10.100711187-007-9055-0

Barassi, M. R., Cole, M. A., & Elliott, R. J. (2008). Stochastic divergence or convergence of per capita carbon dioxide emissions: Re-examining the evidence. *Environmental and Resource Economics, 40*(1), 121–137. doi:10.100710640-007-9144-1

Barba-Sánchez, V., & Atienza-Sahuquillo, C. (2012). Entrepreneurial behavior: Impact of motivation factors on decision to create a new venture. *European Research on Management and Business Economics, 18*(1), 132–138.

Barbosa, P. (2015). *Determinantes do sucesso individual e da intenção empreendedora através da propensão empreendedora*. Dissertação de Mestrado em Gestão.

Barro, R. J. (1974). Are government bonds net wealth? *Journal of Political Economy*, *82*(6), 1095–1117. doi:10.1086/260266

Barro, R. J. (1989). The Ricardian approach to budget deficits. *The Journal of Economic Perspectives*, *3*(2), 37–54. doi:10.1257/jep.3.2.37

Baruah, D. M. (2018). *India's answer to the Belt and Road: A road map for South Asia* (Report). Carnegie Endowment for International Peace Working Paper.

Baruah, A. G., & Panda, J. P. (2019). Xi Jinping's authoritarianism, Chinese foreign policy and India. *Megatrend Review*, *16*(1), 151–172. doi:10.5937/MegRev1901151G

Battersby, B., & Ewing, R. (2005). *International trade performance: The gravity of Australia's remoteness*. Treasury Working Paper No. 2005-03.

Baum, C. F. (2001). Residual diagnostics for cross-section time series regression models. *The Stata Journal*, *1*(1), 101–104. doi:10.1177/1536867X0100100108

Baumol, W. J. (1993). Formal entrepreneurship theory in economics: Existence and bounds. *Journal of Business Venturing*, *8*(3), 197–210. doi:10.1016/0883-9026(93)90027-3

Beck, N., & Katz, J. N. (1995). What to do (and not to do) with time-series cross-section data. *The American Political Science Review*, *89*(3), 634–647. doi:10.2307/2082979

Belsley, D., Kuh, E., & Welsch, R. (1981). Regression diagnostics - identifying influential data and sources of collinearity. *The Journal of the Operational Research Society*, *32*(2), 157–158. doi:10.1057/jors.1981.33

Belton, W. J., & Nair-Reichert, U. (2007). Inflation regimes, core inflation measures and the relationship between producer and consumer price inflation. *Applied Economics*, *39*(10), 1295–1305. doi:10.1080/00036840500447682

Bernheim, B. D. (1989). A neoclassical perspective on budget deficits. *The Journal of Economic Perspectives*, *3*(2), 55–72. doi:10.1257/jep.3.2.55

Berthelon, M., & Freund, C. (2008). On the conservation of distance in international trade. *Journal of International Economics*, *75*(2), 310–320. doi:10.1016/j.jinteco.2007.12.005

Beule, D., Van, D., & Bulcke, D. (2012). Locational determinants of outward foreign direct investment: An analysis of Chinese and Indian Greenfield investments. *Transnational Corporations*, *21*(1), 1–34. doi:10.18356/66d08267-en

Bhagwati, J. (2008). *Termites in the trading system: How preferential agreements undermine free trade*. Oxford University Press. doi:10.1093/acprof:oso/9780195331653.001.0001

Bhardwaj, V., & Fairhurst, A. (2010). Fast fashion: Response to changes in the fashion industry. *International Review of Retail, Distribution and Consumer Research*, *20*(1), 165–173. doi:10.1080/09593960903498300

Bhattacharya, K., Mukherjee, G., Saramäki, J., Kashi, K., & Manna, S. (2008). The international trade network: Weighted network analysis and modelling. *Journal of Statistical Mechanics*, *2008*(02), 1–10. doi:10.1088/1742-5468/2008/02/P02002

Bilgili, F., & Ulucak, R. (2018). Is there deterministic, stochastic, and/or club convergence in ecological footprint indicator among G20 countries? *Environmental Science and Pollution Research International*, *25*(35), 35404–35419. doi:10.100711356-018-3457-1 PMID:30350136

Birch, L. L. (1979). Preschool children's food preferences and consumption patterns. *Journal of Nutrition Education, 11*(4), 189–192. doi:10.1016/S0022-3182(79)80025-4

Bird, B. (2015). Entrepreneurial intentions research: A Review and outlook. *International Review of Entrepreneurship, 13*(3), 143–168.

Birley, S. (1989). Corporate strategy and the small firm. In D. C. Asch & C. Bowman (Eds.), *Readings in strategic management* (pp. 78–82). MacMillian Education. doi:10.1007/978-1-349-20317-8_6

Bitzinger, R. (2011). Recent developments in naval and maritime modernization in the asia-pacific: implications for regional security. In P. C. Saunders, C. D. Yung, M. Swaine, & A. Yang (Eds.), *The Chinese navy: Expanding capabilities, evolving roles* (pp. 23–40). National Defense University Press for the Center for the Study of Chinese Military Affairs.

Blainey, G. (1966). *The tyranny of distance: How distance shaped Australia's history.* Sun Books.

Blank, S. (2018). Paradoxes abounding Russia and the South China Sea issue. In C. Anders (Ed.), Great powers, grand strategies: The new game in the South China Sea. Naval Institute Press.

Bloch, F., Jackson, M., & Tebaldi, P. (2017). *Centrality measures in networks.* arXiv:1608.05845v3. https://arxiv.org/pdf/1608.05845v3.pdf

Blomberg S.B., & Harris, E.S. (1995). The commodity - consumer price connection: fact or fable. *Federal Reserve Bank of New York Economic Policy Review, 1*(3).

Blonigen, B., & Piger, J. (2014). Determinants of foreign direct investment. *The Canadian Journal of Economics. Revue Canadienne d'Economique, 47*(3), 775–812. doi:10.1111/caje.12091

Bohl, M. T., Michaelis, P., & Siklos, P. L. (2016). Austerity and recovery: Exchange rate regime choice, economic growth, and financial crises. *Economic Modelling, 53*, 195–207. doi:10.1016/j.econmod.2015.11.017

Bordo, M. (2017). *The second era of globalization is not yet over: An historical perspective.* NBER Working Paper No. 23786.

Born, B., Juessen, F., & Müller, G. J. (2013). Exchange rate regimes and fiscal multipliers. *Journal of Economic Dynamics & Control, 37*(2), 446–465. doi:10.1016/j.jedc.2012.09.014

Bottome, P. (1939). *Alfred Adler: A biography.* Putnam.

Bourbeau, P. (2018). A genealogy of resilience. *International Political Sociology, 12*(1), 19–35. doi:10.1093/ips/olx026

Boussemart, J. P., Leleu, H., & Shen, Z. (2015). Environmental growth convergence among Chinese regions. *China Economic Review, 34*, 1–18. doi:10.1016/j.chieco.2015.03.003

Brasili, A., Epifani, P., & Helg, R. (2000). On the dynamics of trade patterns. *De Economist, 148*(2), 233–258. doi:10.1023/A:1004065229330

Brautigam, D. (2010). *The dragon's gift: The real story of China in Africa.* Oxford University Press.

Brazier, D. (1997). *Más allá de Carl Rogers.* Desclée de Brouwer Editorial.

Breitung, J., & Pesaran, M. H. (2008). Unit roots and cointegration in panels. In L. Matyas & P. Sevestre (Eds.), *The Econometrics of Panel Data Advanced Studies in Theoretical and Applied Econometrics* (pp. 279–322). Springer.

Breuer, J. (2017). *Two belts, one road? The role of Africa in China's Belt and Road Initiative.* BlickWechse.

Breusch, T. S., & Pagan, A. R. (1980). The Lagrange Multiplier test and its applications to model specification in econometrics. *The Review of Economic Studies*, *47*(1), 239–253. doi:10.2307/2297111

Briceño-Ruiz, J., & Morales, I. (2017). *Post-hegemonic regionalism in the Americas: Toward a Pacific–Atlantic divide?* Routledge. doi:10.4324/9781315601663

Brill, H. (1985). Political geography, geopolitics, and geostrategy: An attempt at systematization. *Strategic Studies*, *8*(2), 86–98.

Brock, W. A., & Taylor, M. S. (2010). The Green Solow model. *Journal of Economic Growth*, *15*(2), 127–153. doi:10.100710887-010-9051-0

Brülhart, M. (2001). Evolving geographical concentration of European manufacturing industries. *Weltwirtschaftliches Archiv*, *137*(2), 215–243. doi:10.1007/BF02707264

Brülhart, M. (2006). The fading attraction of central regions: An empirical note on core-periphery gradients in Western Europe. *Spatial Economic Analysis*, *1*(2), 227–235. doi:10.1080/17421770601009866

Brülhart, M., & Traeger, R. (2005). An account of geographic concentration patterns in Europe. *Regional Science and Urban Economics*, *35*(6), 597–624. doi:10.1016/j.regsciurbeco.2004.09.002

Bucha, A. I. (2009). *Empreendedorismo, aprender a saber ser empreendedor*. Editora RH.

Burger, M., Ianchovichina, E., & Rijkers, B. (2014). Risky business political instability and Greenfield foreign direct investment in the Arab world. *The World Bank Economic Review*, *30*(2), 306–331. doi:10.1093/wber/lhv030

Buttner, E. H., & Moore, D. P. (1997). *Women entrepreneurs: Moving beyond the glass ceiling*. Sage.

Bygrave, W. D. (2004). The entrepreneurial process. In W. D. Bygrave & A. Zacharakis (Eds.), *The portable MBA in entrepreneurship* (p. 6). John Wiley & Sons.

Caccia, F. C., Baleix, J. M., & Paniagua, J. (2018). Foreign direct investment in oil abundant countries: The role of institutions. *PLoS One*, *14*(4), e0215650. doi:10.1371/journal.pone.0215650 PMID:31013300

Cáceres, S. B. (2014). *China's strategic interests in the South China Sea: Power and resources*. Routledge.

Cadot, O., Carrere, C., & Strauss-Kahn, V. (2011). Export diversification: What's behind the hump? *The Review of Economics and Statistics*, *93*(2), 590–605. doi:10.1162/REST_a_00078

Calabrese, J. (2017). *China's role in post-hegemonic Middle East*. Middle East Institute.

Calabrese, L., & Can, C. (2016). *China-Africa: A maturing relationship? Growth, change and resilience*. DFID-ESRC Growth Research Programme.

Calder, K. E. (2012). *The new continentalism: Energy and twenty-first-century Eurasian geopolitics*. Yale University Press.

Calderóna, C. (2010). *Trade and economic growth: Evidence on the role of complementarities for CAFTA-DR countries*. The World Bank: Latin America and the Caribbean Region.

Callahan, W. A. (2016). China's "Asia Dream": The Belt Road Initiative and the new regional order. *Asian Journal of Comparative Politics*, *1*(3), 226–243. doi:10.1177/2057891116647806

Calpp, J. (2006). WTO Agriculture negotiations: Implications for the Global South. *Third World Quarterly*, *27*(4), 563–577. doi:10.1080/01436590600720728

Campante, F. R., & Chor, D. (2012). Why was the Arab world poised for revolution? Schooling, economic opportunities, and the Arab Spring. *The Journal of Economic Perspectives*, *26*(2), 167–187. doi:10.1257/jep.26.2.167

Candau, F. (2020). Trade, FDI and migration. *International Economic Journal*, *27*(3), 441–461. doi:10.1080/10168737.2012.676058

Caporale, G. M., Ciferri, D., & Girardi, A. (2011). Fiscal shocks and real exchange rate dynamics: Some evidence for Latin America. *Journal of International Money and Finance*, *30*(5), 709–723. doi:10.1016/j.jimonfin.2011.04.001

Caporale, G. M., Katsimi, M., & Pittis, N. (2002). Causality links between consumer and producer prices: Some empirical evidence. *Southern Economic Journal*, *68*(3), 703–711. doi:10.2307/1061728

Carlino, G. A., & Mills, L. O. (1993). Are U.S. regional incomes converging?: A time series analysis. *Journal of Monetary Economics*, *32*(2), 335–346. doi:10.1016/0304-3932(93)90009-5

Carranza, M. E. (2014). Resilient or declining? Latin American regional economic blocs in the postneoliberal era. *Latin American Politics and Society*, *56*(3), 163–172. doi:10.1111/j.1548-2456.2014.00244.x

Carranza, M. E. (2017). Resilient or declining? Mercosur and the future of post-neoliberal regionalism in Latin America. In J. Briceño-Ruiz & I. Morales (Eds.), *Post-hegemonic regionalism in the Americas* (pp. 125–140). Routledge. doi:10.4324/9781315601663-7

Carsrud, A., & Brännback, M. (2011). Entrepreneurial motivations: What do we still need to know? *Journal of Small Business Management*, *49*(1), 9–26. doi:10.1111/j.1540-627X.2010.00312.x

Carter, S., Anderson, S., & Shaw, E. (2001). Women business ownership: A review of the academic, popular and internet literature. Report to the Small Business Service.

Carvalho, M. I. V. (2010). Condicionantes internacionais e domésticos: O Brasil e o G-20 nas negociações agrícolas da Rodada Doha. *DADOS Revista de Ciências Sociais*, *53*(2), 405–438. doi:10.1590/S0011-52582010000200005

Casarini, N. (2015). *Is Europe to benefit from China's Belt and Road Initiative?* Istituto Affari Internazionali (IAI).

Caselli, F. (2005). Accounting for cross-country income differences. In P. Aghion & S. Durlauf (Eds.), *Handbook of Economic Growth* (pp. 679–741). North-Holland.

Cassar, G. (2007). Money, money, money? A longitudinal investigation of entrepreneur career reasons, growth preferences and achieved growth. *Entrepreneurship and Regional Development*, *19*(1), 89–107. doi:10.1080/08985620601002246

Castro A. (2008, June 15). Que es el tratado de libre comercio. *El Universal.*

Catão, L., & Obstfeld, M. (2019). Introduction. In L. Catão & M. Obstfeld (Eds.), *Meeting Globalization's Challenges: Policies to make Trade Work for All.* Princeton University Press. doi:10.2307/j.ctvh1dr13.6

Cavoli, T., Gopalan, S., & Rajan, R. S. (2019). Exchange rate policies in Asia in an era of financial globalisation: An empirical assessment. *World Economy*, *42*(6), 1774–1795. doi:10.1111/twec.12767

CEDRSSA (2020). *Reporte del sector agropecuario en México.* Centro de Estudios para el Desarrollo Rural Sustentable la Soberanía Alimentaria. Poder legislativo de San Lázaro, Cd. De México.

Çekin, S. E. (2018). Inflation targeting, fiscal policy, and the exchange rate regime. *Emerging Markets Finance & Trade*, *54*(9), 2093–2116. doi:10.1080/1540496X.2017.1358162

CEPAL. (2014). *Tratados de libre comercio, América Latina y el Caribe.* Comisión Económica para América Latina y el Caribe.

Chakrabarti, A. (2001). The determinants of foreign direct investments: Sensitivity analyses of cross-country regressions. *International Review of Social Sciences, 54*(1), 89–114. doi:10.1111/1467-6435.00142

Chakrabarti, A. S. (2018). Dispersion in macroeconomic volatility between the core and periphery of the international trade network. *Journal of Economic Dynamics & Control, 88*, 31–50. doi:10.1016/j.jedc.2018.01.019

Chakraborty, D., & Mukherjee, S. (2013). How do trade and investment flows affect environmental sustainability? Evidence from panel data. *Environmental Development, 6*, 34–47. doi:10.1016/j.envdev.2013.02.005

Chang, R., & Velasco, A. (2000). Financial fragility and the exchange rate regime. *Journal of Economic Theory, 92*(1), 1–34. doi:10.1006/jeth.1999.2621

Chase-Dunn, C., Kwon, R., Lawrence, K., & Inoue, H. (2011). Last of hegemons: U.S. decline and global governance. *International Review of Modern Sociology, 37*(1), 1–29.

Chauhan, P. (2019). Energy dimension of the Belt and Road Initiative. *Indian Journal of Asian Affairs, 32*(1/2), 119–115.

Chayawisan, N. (2015). The interaction between domestic and foreign direct investment in Thailand. *British Journal of Economics, 9*(2), 1–6. doi:10.9734/BJEMT/2015/19274

Chaziza, M. (2019). China's economic diplomacy approach in the Middle East conflicts. *China Report (New Delhi, India), 55*(1), 24–39. doi:10.1177/0009445518818210

Chen, S., & Ravallion, M. (2008). *The developing world is poorer than we thought, but no less successful in the fight against poverty.* The World Bank Policy Research Working Paper 4703.

Chen, D. H. C., & Chen, D. H. C. (2016). Population age structure and the budget deficit. *Journal of Insurance and Financial Management, 1*(4), 32–67.

Chen, N. (2004). Intra-national versus international trade in the European Union: Why do national borders matter? *Journal of International Economics, 63*(1), 93–118. doi:10.1016/S0022-1996(03)00042-4

Chen, X., & Fazilov, F. (2018). Re-centering Central Asia: China's "New Great Game" in the old Eurasian Heartland. *Palgrave Communications, 4*(71), 1–12. doi:10.105741599-018-0125-5

Chen, Z. (2016). China debates the non-interference principle. *The Chinese Journal of International Politics, 9*(9), 349–374.

Chen, Z. (2016). China, the European Union and the fragile world order. *Journal of Common Market Studies, 54*(4), 775–792. doi:10.1111/jcms.12383

Chen, Z., & Zhang, X. (2020). Chinese conception of the world order in a turbulent Trump era. *The Pacific Review, 33*(3-4), 1–31. doi:10.1080/09512748.2020.1728574

Chete, L. N. (1998). Determinants of foreign direct investment in Nigeria. Niser Monograph Series 7.

Chiavenato, I. (2009). *Gestión del talento humano: El nuevo papel de los recursos humanos en las organizaciones.* McGraw-Hill.

Chia, W.-M., Cheng, T., & Li, M. (2012). Exogenous shocks and exchange rate regimes. *World Economy, 35*(4), 444–460. doi:10.1111/j.1467-9701.2012.01445.x

Chihi, F., & Normandin, M. (2013). External and budget deficits in some developing countries. *Journal of International Money and Finance, 32*(1), 77–98. doi:10.1016/j.jimonfin.2012.03.002

Chinese Government. (2015). *Vision and actions on jointly building Silk Road Economic Belt and 21st Century Maritime Silk Road.* Academic Press.

Chiu, E. M. P., & Willett, T. D. (2009). The interactions of strength of governments and alternative exchange rate regimes in avoiding currency crises. *International Studies Quarterly, 53*(4), 1001–1025. doi:10.1111/j.1468-2478.2009.00566.x

Choi, I. (2001). Unit root tests for panel data. *Journal of International Money and Finance, 20*(2), 249–272. doi:10.1016/S0261-5606(00)00048-6

Chowdhury, M. T. H., Bhattacharya, P. S., Mallick, D., & Ulubaşoğlu, M. A. (2015). Persistence, capital account openness, and financial sector health in exchange rate regime choice. *The Economic Record, 91*(294), 279–299. doi:10.1111/1475-4932.12204

Chowdhury, M. T. H., Bhattacharya, P. S., Mallick, D., & Ulubaşoğlu, M. A. (2016). Exchange rate regimes and fiscal discipline: The role of trade openness. *International Review of Economics & Finance, 45*, 106–128. doi:10.1016/j.iref.2016.04.013

Chrisman, J. J., Chua, J. H., & Steier, L. P. (2002). The influence of national culture and family involvement on entrepreneurial perceptions and performance at the state level. *Entrepreneurship Theory and Practice, 26*(4), 113–130. doi:10.1177/104225870202600407

Christopherson, S., Garretsen, H., & Martin, R. (2008). The world is not flat: Putting globalization in its place. *Cambridge Journal of Regions, Economy and Society, 1*(3), 343–349. doi:10.1093/cjres/rsn023

Chudik, A., Mohaddes, K., Pesaran, M. H., & Raissi, M. (2013). *Debt, inflation and growth: Robust estimation of long-run effects in dynamic panel data models. Center for Applied Financial Economics.* CAFE.

Chudik, A., & Pesaran, M. H. (2015). Common correlated effects estimation of heterogeneous dynamic panel data models with weakly exogenous regressors. *Journal of Econometrics, 188*(2), 393–420. doi:10.1016/j.jeconom.2015.03.007

Chudik, A., Pesaran, M. H., & Tosetti, E. (2011). Weak and strong cross-section dependence and estimation of large panels. *The Econometrics Journal, 14*(1), C45–C90. doi:10.1111/j.1368-423X.2010.00330.x

Churchill, S. A., Inekwe, J., & Ivanovski, K. (2020). Stochastic convergence in per capita CO_2 emissions: Evidence from emerging economies, 1921-2014. *Energy Economics, 86*, 104659. doi:10.1016/j.eneco.2019.104659

Cingolani, I., Panzarasa, P., & Tajoli, L. (2017). Countries' positions in the international global value networks: Centrality and economic performance. *Applied Network Science, 2*(1), 2–21. doi:10.100741109-017-0041-4 PMID:30443576

Cirera, X., Willenbockel, D., & Lakshman, R. W. (2014). Evidence on the impact of tariff reductions on employment in developing countries: A systematic review. *Journal of Economic Surveys, 28*(3), 449–471. doi:10.1111/joes.12029

Clark, T. F. (1995). Do producer prices lead consumer prices? *Federal Reserve Bank of Kansas City Economic Review, 80*(3), 25–39.

Coakes, E., & Bradburn, A. (2005). What is the value of intellectual capital? *Knowledge Management Research and Practice, 3*(2), 60–68. doi:10.1057/palgrave.kmrp.8500050

CODESIN. (2017). *Las exportaciones en Sinaloa.* Consejo para el Desarrollo Económico de Sinaloa.

CODESIN. (2021). *Reporte 07 del 2021. Indicador trimestral de la actividad económica estatal (ITAEE) en Sinaloa.* Consejo para el Desarrollo Económico de Sinaloa.

Colclough, W. G., & Lange, M. D. (1982). Empirical evidence of causality from consumer to wholesale prices. *Journal of Econometrics, 19*(2-3), 379–384. doi:10.1016/0304-4076(82)90012-4

Cole, M. A., & Elliott, R. J. R. (2003). Determining the trade–environment composition effect: The role of capital, labor and environmental regulations. *Journal of Environmental Economics and Management*, *46*(3), 363–383. doi:10.1016/S0095-0696(03)00021-4

Coleman, G., Kalish, I., Konigsburg, D., & Sitao, X. (2014). *Competitiveness: Catching the next wave China*. Deloitte.

Combes, J. L., Minea, A., & Sow, M. (2016). Crises and exchange rate regimes: Time to break down the bipolar view? *Applied Economics*, *48*(46), 4393–4409. doi:10.1080/00036846.2016.1158917

Combes, J. L., & Saadi-Sedik, T. (2006). How does trade openness influence budget deficits in developing countries? *The Journal of Development Studies*, *42*(8), 1401–1416. doi:10.1080/00220380600930762

Comunidad Andina. (2020). http://www.comunidadandina.org

CONAPO. (2017). *Estadísticas de exportación*. Consejo Nacional de Población.

Conger, J. A. (1992). *Reflections on leadership and spirit. Domingo Conference on Leadership and Spirit*, Boston, MA.

Crespo, N., & Fontoura, M. (2006). Economic centrality, per capita income and human capital – some results at regional and local level in 275 counties of Portugal. *Regional and Sectoral Economic Studies, 6*.

Crespo, N., Fontoura, M., & Simões, N. (2015). Spatial centrality: An approach with sectoral linkages. *Applied Econometrics and International Development, 15*(1), 45-56.

Crump, L. (2006). Global trade policy development in a two-track system. *Journal of International Economic Law*, *9*(2), 487–510. doi:10.1093/jiel/jgl005

Crump, L. (2019). Trump on trade. *Negotiation Journal*, *35*(1), 141–145. doi:10.1111/nejo.12250

Crump, L., & Downie, C. (2018). The G20 chair and the case of the global *economic* steering committee. *Global Society*, *32*(1), 23–46. doi:10.1080/13600826.2017.1394818

Culem, G. C. (1988). The locational determinants of direct investments among industrialized countries. *European Economic Review*, *32*(4), 885–904. doi:10.1016/0014-2921(88)90051-7

Cunningham, D., & Hornby, W. (1993). Pricing decision in small firms: Theory and practice. *Management Decision*, *31*(7), 46–55. doi:10.1108/00251749310046765

Curran, J., Blackburn, R., Kitching, J., & North, J. (1996). *Establishing small firms' training practices, needs, difficulties and use of industry training organizations*. HMSO.

Cushing, M. J., & McGarvey, M. G. (1990). Feedback between wholesale and consumer price inflation: A reexamination of the evidence. *Southern Economic Journal*, *56*(4), 1059–1072. doi:10.2307/1059891

Dabene, O. (2009). *The politics of regional integration in Latin America: Theoretical and comparative exploration*. Palgrave Macmillan. doi:10.1057/9780230100749

Dabene, O. (2012). Consistency and resilience through cycles of repoliticization. In P. Riggirozzi & D. Tussie (Eds.), *The rise of post-hegemonic regionalism: The case of Latin America* (pp. 41–64). Springer. doi:10.1007/978-94-007-2694-9_3

Dahlman, C. J., & Aubert, J. E. (2001). *China and the knowledge economy: Seizing the 21st century*. World Bank Publications. doi:10.1596/0-8213-5005-6

Danner, L. K., & Martín, F. E. (2019). China's hegemonic intentions and trajectory: Will it opt for benevolent, coercive, or dutch-style hegemony? *Asia & the Pacific Policy Studies*, *6*(2), 186–207. doi:10.1002/app5.273

Das, P. (2019). *Econometrics in Theory and Practice*. Springer. doi:10.1007/978-981-32-9019-8

Daude, C., Nagengast, A., & Perea, J. R. (2016). Productive capabilities: An empirical analysis of their drivers. *The Journal of International Trade & Economic Development, 25*(4), 504–535. doi:10.1080/09638199.2015.1073342

Davey, T., Plewa, C., & Struwig, M. (2011). Entrepreneurship perceptions and career intentions of international students. *Education + Training, 53*(5), 335–352. doi:10.1108/00400911111147677

Davis, D. R., & Weinstein, D. E. (2001). An account of global factor trade. *The American Economic Review, 91*(5), 1423–1453. doi:10.1257/aer.91.5.1423

De Benedictis, L., Gallegati, M., & Tamberi, M. (2009). Overall trade specialization and economic development: Countries diversify. *Review of World Economics, 145*(1), 37–55. doi:10.100710290-009-0007-4

De Benedictis, L., Nenci, S., Santoni, G., Tajoli, L., & Vicarelli, C. (2014). Network analysis of world trade using the BACI-CEPII Dataset. *Global Economy Journal, 14*(03n04), 287–343. doi:10.1515/gej-2014-0032

De Benedictis, L., & Tajoli, L. (2011). The world trade network. *World Economy, 34*(8), 1417–1454. doi:10.1111/j.1467-9701.2011.01360.x

De Ferranti, D., Lederman, D., Maloney, W. E., & Perry, G. E. (2002). *From natural resources to the knowledge economy: Trade and job quality*. Wold Bank. *Latin American and Caribbean Ethnic Studies*. Advance online publication. doi:10.1596/0-8213-5009-9

De Haan, J., & Sturm, J. E. (1994). Political and institutional determinants of fiscal policy in the European Community. *Public Choice, 80*(1–2), 157–172. doi:10.1007/BF01047953

De Haan, J., & Sturm, J. E. (1997). Political and economic determinants of OECD budget deficits and government expenditures: A reinvestigation. *European Journal of Political Economy, 13*(4), 739–750. doi:10.1016/S0176-2680(97)00033-5

De Hoyos, R. E., & Sarafidis, V. (2006). Testing for cross-sectional dependence in panel-data models. *The Stata Journal, 6*(4), 482–496. doi:10.1177/1536867X0600600403

De Lombaerde, P., Iapadre, L., McCranie, A., & Tajoli, L. (2019). Using network analysis to study globalization, regionalization, and multi-polarity - Introduction to special section. *Network Science, 6*(4), 494–516. doi:10.1017/nws.2018.25

De Piñeres, S. A. G., & Ferrantino, M. (1997). Export diversification and structural dynamics in the growth process: The case of Chile. *Journal of Development Economics, 52*(2), 375–391. doi:10.1016/S0304-3878(96)00446-4

Deal, T., & Kennedy, A. (2000). *Corporate cultures: The rites and rituals of corporate life*. Perseus Book Publishing.

Declaration of Lima. (2011). [Declaracion de Lima: Alianza del Pacifico]. https://alianzapacifico.net/documentos-acuerdo-marco-de-la-alianza-del-pacifico/

Deng, Y. (2008). *China's struggle for status: The realignment of international relations*. Cambridge University Press. doi:10.1017/CBO9780511790768

Dennis, A., & Shepherd, B. (2011). Trade facilitation and export diversification. *World Economy, 34*(1), 101–122. doi:10.1111/j.1467-9701.2010.01303.x

Department of Defense. (2020). *Military and security developments involving the People's Republic of China*. Annual Report to Congress.

Depaula, P. D., & Azzollini, S. C. (2012). Inteligencia cultural, valores y motivación para el aprendizaje en estudiantes militares argentinos. *Revista de Psicología, 30*(1), 75–102. doi:10.18800/psico.201201.004

Dibb, P. (2018). The return of geography. In R. Glenn (Ed.), *New Directions in Strategic Thinking 2.0: ANU Strategic & Defence Studies Centre's Golden Anniversary Conference Proceedings* (pp. 91-104). Acton, Australia: ANU Press. 10.22459/NDST.07.2018.08

Dibb, S., & Simkin, L. (2013). *Marketing essentials* (2nd ed.). Cengage Learning.

Dickey, D. A., & Fuller, W. A. (1979). Distribution of the estimators for autoregressive time series with a unit root. *Journal of the American Statistical Association, 74*(366a), 427–431. doi:10.1080/01621459.1979.10482531

Dickey, D. A., & Fuller, W. A. (1981). Likelihood ratio statistics for autoregressive time series with a unit root. *Econometrica, 49*(4), 1057–1072. doi:10.2307/1912517

Diego-Fernández, M. (2008). Trade negotiations make strange bedfellows. *World Trade Review, 7*(2), 423–453. doi:10.1017/S1474745608003832

Dillon, J. (1991). *Bases teóricas y prácticas de los tratados de libre comercio*. Institution Ecumencial Coalition for Economic Toronto.

Disdier, A., & Head, K. (2008). The puzzling persistence of the distance effect on bilateral trade. *The Review of Economics and Statistics, 90*(1), 37–48. doi:10.1162/rest.90.1.37

Ditzen, J. (2019). *Estimating long-run effects in models with cross-sectional dependence using xtdcce2*. CEERP Working Paper Series 007, Centre for Energy Economics Research and Policy, Heriot-Watt University.

Doctor, M. (2015). Brazil's role in institutions of global economic governance: The WTO and G20. *Global Society, 29*(3), 286–300. doi:10.1080/13600826.2015.1025041

Dollinger, S. C. (1995). Identity styles and the five-factor model of personality. *Journal of Research in Personality, 29*(4), 475–479. doi:10.1006/jrpe.1995.1028

Dornelas, J. C. A. (2008). *Empreendedorismo*. Elsevier Brasil.

Dreher, A. (2006). Does globalization affect growth? Evidence from a New Index of Globalization. *Applied Economics, 38*(10), 1091–1110. doi:10.1080/00036840500392078

Driscoll, J. C., & Kraay, A. C. (1998). Consistent covariance matrix estimation with spatially dependent panel data. *The Review of Economics and Statistics, 80*(4), 549–559. doi:10.1162/003465398557825

Drucker, P. F. (1985). The discipline of innovation. *Harvard Business Review, 63*(3), 67–72. PMID:10272260

Drucker, P. F. (2007). *Management challenges for the 21st century*. Routledge.

Drucker, P. F. (2013). *People and performance*. Harvard Business School Press. doi:10.4324/9780080938417

Drukker, D. M. (2003). Testing for serial correlation in linear panel-data models. *The Stata Journal, 3*(2), 168–177. doi:10.1177/1536867X0300300206

Du Rietz, A., & Henrekson, M. (2000). Testing the female underperformance hypothesis. *Small Business Economics, 14*(1), 1–10. doi:10.1023/A:1008106215480

Duarte, C., & Esperança, J. P. (2012). *Empreendedorismo e planeamento financeiro*. Edições Sílabo.

Dylan, L. (2018). How Xi Jinping's 'Lifetime Presidency' could change China – for better or worse? *The Conversation, 2*.

Easterly, W., & Rebelo, S. (1993). Fiscal policy and economic growth. *Journal of Monetary Economics, 32*(3), 417–458. doi:10.1016/0304-3932(93)90025-B

Eccles, J. S., Wigfield, A., & Schiefele, U. (1998). Motivation to succeed. In W. Damon & N. Eisenberg (Eds.), Handbook of child psychology: Vol. 3. *Social, emotional, and personality development* (5th ed., pp. 1017–1095). Wiley.

Economy, E. (2010). The game changer: Coping with China's foreign policy revolution. *Foreign Affairs*, 1–10.

Edwards, L., & Lawrence, R. (2006). *South African trade policy matters: Trade performance and trade policy*. NBER Working Paper Series 12760. doi:10.1111/j.1468-0351.2008.00338.x

Edwards, S. (1990). *Capital flows, foreign direct investment, and dept - equity swaps in developing countries*. NBER Working Paper No. 3497.

Efstathopoulos, C. (2012). Leadership in the WTO: Brazil, India and the Doha development agenda. *Cambridge Review of International Affairs*, *25*(2), 269–293. doi:10.1080/09557571.2012.678294

Ekpo, A. H. (1995). Foreign direct investment in Nigeria: Evidence from time series data. *CBN Economic and Financial Review*, *35*(1), 59–78.

El Debate. (2017). *Exportaciones de Sinaloa (05.03.2017)*. El Debate.

El Financiero. (2017). El PIB de México en cinco gráficas. El financiero.

Eluwole, K. K., & Akadiri, A. A. (2019). Does the interaction between growth determinants a drive for global environmental sustainability? Evidence from world top 10 pollutant emissions countries. *The Science of the Total Environment*, 705.

Emmanuel, B., Criscent, I. E., & Alhasan, Y. (2018). Effect of exchange and interest rates on foreign direct investment in Nigeria 2006-2018. *International Journal of Contemporary Research and Review*, *10*(7), 21572–21585. doi:10.15520/ijcrr.v10i07.717

Enders, W., & Lee, J. (2012). A unit root test using a fourier series to approximate smooth breaks. *Oxford Bulletin of Economics and Statistics*, *74*(4), 574–599. doi:10.1111/j.1468-0084.2011.00662.x

Enderwick, P., & Buckley, P. (2020). Rising regionalization: Will the post-COVID-19 world see a retreat from globalization? *Transnational Corporations*, *27*(2), 99–112. doi:10.18356/8008753a-en

Engle, R. F., & Granger, C. W. J. (1987). Co-integration and error correction: Representation, estimation, and testing. *Econometrica*, *55*(2), 251–256. doi:10.2307/1913236

Engler, B. (1996). *Introducción a las teorías de la personalidad*. McGraw-Hill.

Erickson, A. S., Goldstein, L. J., & Li, N. (2010). *China, the United States, and 21st-Century Sea power: Defining a maritime security partnership*. Naval Institute Press.

Esperança, J. P., Reto, L. A., & Machado, F. L. (2017). Países de destino das multinacionais portuguesas: A importância da lusofonia. In N. Crespo & M. J. Tomás (Eds.), *A internacionalização da economia portuguesa, casos de sucesso empresarial* (pp. 71–89). Temas e Debates, Círculo de Leitores.

Estevadeordal, A., & Volpe Martincus, C. (2006). *Specialization and diverging manufacturing structures: The aftermath of trade policy reforms in developing countries*. Development Studies Working Papers 220.

Europa: Official Website of the European Union. (2020). https://europa.eu/european-union/index_en

Evans, P., & Stalling, B. (2016). Development studies: Enduring debates and possible trajectories. *Studies in Comparative International Development*, *51*(1), 1–31. doi:10.100712116-016-9223-9

Evenett, S. (2020). Sicken thy neighbour: The initial trade policy response to Covid-19. *World Economy*, *43*(4), 828–839. doi:10.1111/twec.12954

Expansión Magazine. (2011). *Exportación: Solo para grandes empresas*. Recovered from https://expansion.mx/manufactura/2011/10/12/exportacion-solo-para-grandes-empresas

Expansion. (2017). Economía internacional. *Expansión*.

Ezcurra, R. (2007). Is there cross-country convergence in carbon dioxide emissions? *Energy Policy, 35*(2), 1363–1372. doi:10.1016/j.enpol.2006.04.006

Faroh, A., & Shen, H. (2015). Impact of interest rates on foreign direct investment: Case study Sierra Leone economy. *International Journal of Business Management and Economic*, *6*(1), 124–132.

Federici, D., Ferrante, F., & Vistocco, D. (2008). On the sources of entrepreneurial talent in Italy: Tacit vs. codified knowledge. *Journal of Knowledge Management*, *6*(6), 7–28.

Feenstra, R. C., Lipsey, R. E., Deng, H., Ma, A. C., & Mo, H. (2005). *World Trade Flows: 1962-2000*. NBER Working Paper 11040. doi:10.3386/w11040

Feenstra, R. C., Inklaar, R., & Timmer, M. P. (2015). The next generation of the Penn World Table. *The American Economic Review*, *105*(10), 3150–3182. doi:10.1257/aer.20130954

Felix, A., & Watkins, K. (2013). *The impact of an aging U.S. population on state tax revenues*. https://www.kansascityfed.org/publicat/econrev/pdf/13q4Felix-Watkins.pdf

Ferreira, A., Loiola, E., & Guedes Gondim, S. M. (2017). Motivations, business planning, and risk management: Entrepreneurship among university students. *Revista de Administração e Inovação*, *14*(2), 140–150. doi:10.1016/j.rai.2017.03.003

Figge, L., & Martens, P. (2014). Globalisation continues: The Maastricht Globalisation Index revisited and updated. *Globalizations*, *11*(6), 875–893. doi:10.1080/14747731.2014.887389

Fiscal, C., Restrepo, B. L., & Rodríguez, H. (2017). Estructura productiva agrícola del estado de Sinaloa, México, y el tratado de libre comercio de América del Norte (TLCAN). *Chilean Journal of Agricultural & Animal Science*, *33*(1), 0. doi:10.4067/S0719-38902017005000102

Fischer, S. (2001). Exchange rate regimes: Is the bipolar view correct? *The Journal of Economic Perspectives*, *15*(2), 3–24. doi:10.1257/jep.15.2.3

Fisher, F., & Shell, K. (1972). *The economic theory of price indexes*. Academic Press.

Fisher, I. (1921). The best form of index number. *Journal of the American Statistical Association*, *17*, 533–537.

Flint, C., & Zhu, C. (2019). The geopolitics of connectivity, cooperation, and hegemonic competition: The Belt and Road Initiative. *Geoforum*, *99*, 95–101. doi:10.1016/j.geoforum.2018.12.008

Folke, C. (2006). Resilience: The emergence of a perspective for social-ecological systems analysis. *Global Environmental Change*, *16*(3), 253–267. doi:10.1016/j.gloenvcha.2006.04.002

Fonchamnyo, D. C., & Akame, A. (2017). Determinants of export diversification in Sub-Sahara African region: A fractionalized logit estimation model. *Journal of Economics and Finance*, *41*(2), 330–342. doi:10.100712197-016-9352-z

Fontalvo, S. M. I. (2017). Habilidades de liderazgo para una cultura de innovación en la gerencia de las universidades del distrito de Santa Marta. *Academia y Virtualidad*, *10*(1).

Forough, M. (2019). Intervention with Chinese characteristics: The Belt and Road Initiative reconfiguring (Afro-) Eurasian geo-economics. *Conflict Security and Development*, *19*(3), 275–281. doi:10.1080/14678802.2019.1608023

Framework Agreement of the Pacific Alliance. (2012). [Acuerdo Marco de la Alianza del Pacifico]. https://alianzapacifico.net/documentos-acuerdo-marco-de-la-alianza-del-pacifico/

Frees, E. W. (1995). Assessing cross-sectional correlation in panel data. *Journal of Econometrics*, *69*(2), 393–414. doi:10.1016/0304-4076(94)01658-M

Friedman, M. (1989). Quantity theory of money. In J. Eatwell, M. Milgate, & N. Peter (Eds.), *Money* (pp. 1–40). London: Palgrave Macmillan UK.

Friedman, M. (1937). The use of ranks to avoid the assumption of normality implicit in the analysis of variance. *Journal of the American Statistical Association*, *32*(200), 675–701. doi:10.1080/01621459.1937.10503522

Friedman, M. (1968). The role of monetary policy. *The American Economic Review*, *58*(1), 1–17. www.jstor.org/stable/1831652

Friedman, M. (1992). Do old fallacies ever die? *Journal of Economic Literature*, *30*(4), 2129–2132.

Friedman, T. (2005). *The world is flat: A brief history of the globalised world in the 21st century.* Allen Lane-Penguin Books.

Friedt, F. (2021). The triple effect of COVID-19 on Chinese exports: GVC contagion effects dominate export supply and import demand shocks. *VOX, CEPR Policy Portal.*

Friedt, F., & Zhang, K. (2020). The triple effect of Covid-19 on Chinese exports: First evidence of the export supply, import demand & Gvc contagion effects. *Covid Economics*, *53*, 72–109.

Froot, K. A., & Stein, J. C. (1991). Exchange rates and foreign direct investment: An imperfect capital markets approach. *The Quarterly Journal of Economics*, *106*(4), 1191–1217. doi:10.2307/2937961

Fujita, M., Krugman, P., & Venables, A. (1999). *The spatial economy: Cities, regions and international trade.* MIT Press. doi:10.7551/mitpress/6389.001.0001

Fukase, E., & Martin, W. (2016). The Economic Potential of an India-US Free Trade Agreement. *Journal of Economic Integration*, *31*(4), 774–816. doi:10.11130/jei.2016.31.4.774

GACPC - General Administration of Customs of People's Republic of China. (n.d.). http://english.customs.gov.cn/

Gala, P., Camargo, J., & Freitas, E. (2018). The Economic Commission for Latin America and the Caribbean (ECLAC) was right: Scale-free complex networks and core-periphery patterns in world trade. *Cambridge Journal of Economics*, *42*(3), 633–651. doi:10.1093/cje/bex057

Galeano, E. (1970). Las venas abiertas de América latina (Vol. 2). Montevideo, Uruguay: Siglo XXI Editores.

Gallant, A. R. (1981). On the bias in flexible functional forms and an essentially unbiased form: The fourier flexible form. *Journal of Econometrics*, *15*(2), 211–245. doi:10.1016/0304-4076(81)90115-9

Galloway, L., Anderson, M., Brown, W., & Wilson, L. (2005). Enterprise skills for the economy. *Education + Training*, *47*(1), 7–17. doi:10.1108/00400910510580593

Gang, F., Liping, H., & Jiani, H. (2009). CPI vs. PPI: Which drives which? *Frontiers of Economics in China*, *4*(3), 317–334. doi:10.100711459-009-0018-z

Garrett, C. (2018). Constructing narratives of global order: The Obama presidency, TPP, TTIP, and the contested politics of geoeconomics. *Atlantic Studies*, *16*(2), 261–281. doi:10.1080/14788810.2018.1434107

Garrido, F. J. (2007). *Pensamiento estrategico. La estrategia como centro neuralgico de la empresa.* Ediciones Deusto.

Gaspar, F. C. (2009). *O processo empreendedor e a criação de empresas de sucesso*. Edições Sílabo.

Gaur, P. (2020). India's withdrawal from RCEP: Neutralising national trade concerns. *Journal of the Asia Pacific Economy*, 1–19. doi:10.1080/13547860.2020.1809772

Gereffi, G. (1998). Commodity chains and regional divisions of labour in East Asia. In E. M. Kim (Ed.), *The Four Asian Tigers: Economic development and the global political economy* (pp. 93–124). Academic Press.

Gereffi, G., & Memedovic, O. (2003). *The global apparel value chain: What prospects for upgrading by developing countries. Sectoral Studies Series*. United Nations Industrial Development Organization.

Ghali, S., & Rezgui, S. (2011). FDI contribution to technical efficiency in the Tunisian manufacturing Sector: Evidence from Micro-Panel Data. *International Economic Journal*, *25*(2), 319–339. doi:10.1080/10168737.2010.504215

Ghani, E., Grover Goswami, A., & Kharas, H. (2012). *Service with a smile*. openknowledge.worldbank.org

Ghazali, M. F., Yee, O. A., & Muhammad, M. Z. (2008). Do producer prices cause consumer prices? Some empirical evidence. *International Journal of Business and Management*, *3*(11), 78–82.

Ghiasy, R. (2018). *China's Belt and Road Initiative: Security implications and ways forward for the European Union*. Stockholm International Peace Research Institute.

Ghiasy, R. (2021). The Belt and Road Initiative in South Asia: Regional impact and the evolution of perceptions and policy responses. In F. Schneider (Ed.), *Global perspectives on China's Belt and Road Initiative: Asserting agency through regional connectivity* (pp. 265–290). Amsterdam University Press.

Ghodsi, M. (2020). How do technical barriers to trade affect foreign direct investment? Tariff jumping versus regulation haven hypotheses. *Structural Change and Economic Dynamics*, *52*, 269–278. doi:10.1016/j.strueco.2019.11.008

Ghorbani Dastgerdi, H., Yusof, Z. B., & Shahbaz, M. (2018). Nexus between economic sanctions and inflation: A case study in Iran. *Applied Economics*, *50*(49), 5316–5334. doi:10.1080/00036846.2018.1486988

Gianinazzi, W. (2018). Penser global, agir local: Histoire d'une idée. *EcoRev*, *46*(1), 19–30. doi:10.3917/ecorev.046.0019

Gilad, B., & Levine, P. (1986). A behavioral model of entrepreneurial supply. *Journal of Small Business Management*, *24*, 45.

Gillezeau, P. (2011). La cultura organizacional en el desarrollo de empresas inteligentes. Fundamentos: Valores, Comunicación y Liderazgo. *Telos*, *1*(2), 221–232.

Gloor, P. A. (2006). *Swarm creativity: Competitive advantage through collaborative innovation networks*. Oxford University Press. doi:10.1093/acprof:oso/9780195304121.001.0001

Goldberg, P., & Pavcnik, N. (2007). Distributional effects of globalization in developing countries. *Journal of Economic Literature*, *45*(1), 39–82. doi:10.1257/jel.45.1.39

Gomez, M. B. (2013). *Coca Cola: International business strategy for globalization*. International Trade & Academic Research Conference.

Gomez-Mera, L. (2013). *Power and regionalism in Latin America: The politics of MERCOSUR*. University of Notre Dame Press. doi:10.2307/j.ctvpj7g3t

Gompert, D. (2013). *Sea power and American interests in the Western Pacific*. The Rand Corporation.

Gong, X. (2020). China's Belt and Road Initiative financing in Southeast Asia. *Southeast Asian Affairs*, 77-95.

Gorodnichenko, Y., Svejnar, J., & Terrell, K. (2020). Do foreign investment and trade spur innovation? *European Economic Review, 121*, 103343. doi:10.1016/j.euroecorev.2019.103343

Götz, E., & Merlen, C. R. (2019). Russia and the question of world order. *European Political Science*, *20*(2), 133–153.

Granger, C. W. J. (1969). Investigating causal relations by econometrics models and cross spectral methods. *Econometrica*, *37*(3), 424–438. doi:10.2307/1912791

Grant, R. (1994). The geography of international trade. *Progress in Human Geography*, *18*(3), 298–312. doi:10.1177/030913259401800302

Grauer, S. (1989). *Think globally, act locally: A Delphi Study of educational leadership through the development of international resources in the local community*. University of San Diego.

Gray, C. S. (1999). Inescapable geography. In C. S. Gray & G. Sloan (Eds.), *Geopolitics, geography and strategy* (pp. 161–177). Frank Cass Publishers.

Gray, J. (2018). Life, death, or zombie? The vitality of international organizations. *International Studies Quarterly*, *62*(1), 1–13. doi:10.1093/isqqx086

Greenaway, D., Hine, R., & Milner, C. (1995). Vertical and horizontal intra-industry trade: A cross industry analysis for the United Kingdom. *Economic Journal (London)*, *105*(433), 1505–1518. doi:10.2307/2235113

Greene, W. (2003). *Econometric analysis* (5th ed.). Prentice Hall.

Grossman, D. (2020). What China wants in South Asia. *ORF Issue Brief*, *368*, 1–16.

Grossman, G. M., & Helpman, E. (1991). Quality ladders in the theory of growth. *The Review of Economic Studies*, *58*(1), 43. doi:10.2307/2298044

Grugel, J., & Riggirozzi, R. (2019). Facing the future: The legacies of post-neoliberalism in Latin America – Introduction to development and change virtual issue. *Development and Change*, *0*(0), 1–17. doi:10.1111/dech.12508

Guellec, D., & de la Potterie, B. V. P. (2000). *The impact of public R&D expenditure on business R&D*. OECD Publishing.

Guha, N., Han, A., & Lin, A. (2016). Network analysis of global trade. *CS224W*, 1-8.

Gunter, B. G., & Wilcher, B. (2020). Three decades of globalisation: Which countries won, which lost? *World Economy*, *43*(4), 1076–1102. doi:10.1111/twec.12915

Gurevich, T., Herman, P., Abbyad, N., Demirkaya, M., Drenski, A., Horowitz, J., & Kenneally, K. (2018). *The Dynamic Gravity Dataset: 1948-2016*. Economics Working Paper 2018-02-A. U.S. International Trade Commission.

Guthrie, R. S. (1981). The relationship between wholesale and consumer prices. *Southern Economic Journal*, *47*(4), 1046–1055. doi:10.2307/1058161

Gutiérrez, J., & Urbano, P. (1996). Accessibility in the European Union: The impact of the trans-European road network. *Journal of Transport Geography*, *4*(1), 15–25. doi:10.1016/0966-6923(95)00042-9

Gygli, S., Haelg, F., Potrafke, N., & Sturm, J. (2019). The KOF Globalisation Index–Revisited. *The Review of International Organizations*, *14*(3), 543–574. doi:10.100711558-019-09344-2

Haddad, M., Jerome Lim, J., Pancaro, C., & Saborowski, C. (2013). Trade openness reduces growth volatility when countries are well diversified. *The Canadian Journal of Economics. Revue Canadienne d'Economique*, *46*(2), 765–790. doi:10.1111/caje.12031

Hair, J. F., Celsi, M., Ortinau, D. J., & Bush, R. P. (2010). *Essentials of marketing research* (Vol. 2). McGraw-Hill/Irwin.

Hall, P. A., & Lamont, M. (2013). *Social resilience in the neoliberal era.* Cambridge University Press. doi:10.1017/CBO9781139542425

Hamid, Z. (2010). Concentration of exports and patterns of trade: A time-series evidence of Malaysia. *Journal of Developing Areas, 43*(2), 255–270. doi:10.1353/jda.0.0065

Hammouda, H. B., Karingi, S., Njuguna, A., & Sadni Jallab, M. (2006). Diversification: Towards a new paradigm for Africa's development. Munich Personal RePEc Archive, 35.

Hansen, L. P. (1982). Large sample properties of generalized method of moments estimators. *Econometrica, 50*(4), 1029. doi:10.2307/1912775

Hans-Peter, B. (2013). *What is economic corridor development and what can it achieve in asia's subregions?* ADB Working Paper Series on Regional Economic Integration, No. 117, Asian Development Bank (ADB). http://hdl.handle.net/11540/2308

Harms, G., & Méon, P. (2018). Good and useless FDI: The growth effects of Greenfield investment and mergers and acquisitions. *Review of International Economics, 26*(1), 37–59. doi:10.1111/roie.12302

Hartmann, D., Guevara, M. R., Jara-Figueroa, C., Aristarán, M., & Hidalgo, C. A. (2017). Linking economic complexity, institutions, and income inequality. *World Development, 93*, 75–93. doi:10.1016/j.worlddev.2016.12.020

Hartnett, D. M., & Vellucci, F. (2011). Toward a maritime security strategy: An analysis of Chinese views since the early 1990s. In P. Saunders, C. Yung, M. Swaine, & A. Yang (Eds.), *The Chinese Navy: Expanding Capabilities, Evolving Roles* (pp. 81–108). National Defense University Press for the Center for the Study of Chinese Military Affairs.

Hattangadi, V. (2019). *Six dimensions to understand cultural differences in the world.* Financial Express.

Hausmann, R., & Hidalgo, C. A. (2011). *The Atlas of Economic Complexity - mapping paths to prosperity.* Massachusetts Institute of Technology. https://atlas.cid.harvard.edu/media/atlas/pdf/HarvardMIT_AtlasOfEconomicComplexity.pdf

Hausmann, R., & Klinger, B. (2007). *The structure of the product space and the evolution of comparative advantage.* CID Working Paper 146.

Hausmann, R., & Rodrik, D. (2002). *Economic development as self-discovery.* NBER Working Papers 8952. doi:10.3386/w8952

Hausmann, R., Hwang, J., & Rodrik, D. (2005). *What you export matters.* NBER Working Paper 11905. doi:10.3386/w11905

Hausmann, R., & Klinger, B. (2006). *Structural transformation and patterns of comparative advantage in the product space.* Center for International Development. doi:10.2139srn.939646

Head, K., & Mayer, T. (2002). *Illusory border effects: Distance mismeasurement inflates estimates of home bias in trade.* CEPII Working Papers No. 2002-01.

Head, K., & Mayer, T. (2000). Non-Europe: The magnitude and causes of market fragmentation in the EU. *Weltwirtschaftliches Archiv, 136*(2), 284–314. doi:10.1007/BF02707689

Head, K., & Mayer, T. (2004). Market potential and the location of Japanese investment in the European Union. *The Review of Economics and Statistics, 86*(4), 959–972. doi:10.1162/0034653043125257

Head, K., & Mayer, T. (2013). What separates us? Sources of resistance to globalization. *The Canadian Journal of Economics. Revue Canadienne d'Economique*, *46*(4), 1196–1231. doi:10.1111/caje.12055

Head, K., Mayer, T., & Ries, J. (2010). The erosion of colonial trade linkages after independence. *Journal of International Economics*, *81*(1), 1–14. doi:10.1016/j.jinteco.2010.01.002

Hébert, R. F., & Link, A. N. (1989). In search of the meaning of entrepreneurship. *Small Business Economics*, *1*(1), 39–49. doi:10.1007/BF00389915

Hechavarria, D. M., Renko, M., & Matthews, C. H. (2011). The nascent entrepreneurship hub: Goals, entrepreneurial self-efficacy and start-up outcomes. *Small Business Economics*, *39*(3), 685–701. doi:10.100711187-011-9355-2

Heinonen, J., & Poikkijoki, S. A. (2006). An entrepreneurial-directed approach to entrepreneurship education: Mission impossible? *Journal of Management Development*, *25*(1), 80–94. doi:10.1108/02621710610637981

Helliwell, J., & Verdier, G. (2001). Measuring internal trade distances: A new method applied to estimate provincial border effects in Canada. *The Canadian Journal of Economics. Revue Canadienne d'Economique*, *34*(4), 1024–1041. doi:10.1111/0008-4085.00111

Helmy, H. E. (2018). The twin deficit hypothesis in Egypt. *Journal of Policy Modeling*, *40*(2), 328–349. doi:10.1016/j.jpolmod.2018.01.009

Helpman, E., & Krugman, P. R. (1989). *Trade policy and market structure*. The MIT Press.

Herédia, M., Cabral, C., & Veiga, P. (2010). *Determinants of export diversification and sophistication in Sub-saharan Africa*. FEUNL Working Paper Series wp550.

Hernández, S. R., Fernández, C. C., & Baptista, P. L. (2014). *Metodología de la investigación* (6th ed.). McGraw-Hill.

Herrerias, M. J. (2013). The environmental convergence hypothesis: Carbon dioxide emissions according to the source of energy. *Energy Policy*, *61*, 1140–1150. doi:10.1016/j.enpol.2013.06.120

Herrero, A. G., & Xu, J. (2016). *China's Belt and Road Initiative: Can Europe expect trade gains?* Bruegel Working Paper Issue 5.

Hertel, T., Ivanic, M., Preckel, P., & Cranfield, J. (2003). *Trade liberalization and the structure of poverty in developing countries*. GTAP Working Paper 25.

Hertel, T., Powell, A., Frisvold, G., Gehlhar, M., Gray, D., Hanslow, K., Huff, K., Ianchovichina, E., Kuhn, B., Lanclos, D., MacLaren, D., Martin, W., McDonald, B., McDougall, R., Pearson, K., Perroni, C., Swaminathan, P., Tsigas, M., Tyers, R., . . . Young, L. (1997). *Global Trade Analysis: Modeling and Applications* (University of Cambridge). Purdue University, West Lafayette, IN: Global Trade Analysis Project (GTAP). Retrieved from https://www.gtap.agecon.purdue.edu/resources/res_display.asp?RecordID=4840

Hertel, T. W. (1996). *Global trade analysis: Modeling and applications*. Cambridge University Press. doi:10.1017/CBO9781139174688

Hidalgo, C. A., Klinger, B., Barabasi, A. L., & Hausmann, R. (2007). The product space conditions the development of nations. *Science*, *317*(5837), 482–487. doi:10.1126cience.1144581 PMID:17656717

Hillman, J.E. (2020). *China and Russia: Economic Unequals*. CSIS.

Hirschman, I. I. (1958). On multiplier transformations. United States Air Force, Office of Scientific Research.

Hisrich, R. D., Peters, M. P., & Shepherd, D. A. (2010). *Entrepreneurship*. McGraw-Hill.

Hofstede, G. (1991). *Cultures and organizations: Software of the Mind.* McGraw-Hill.

Hofstede, G. (1994). The business of international business is culture. *International Business Review, 3*(1), 1–14. doi:10.1016/0969-5931(94)90011-6

Hofstede, G. (2001). *Culture's consequences: Comparing values, behaviors, institutions and organizations across nations.* Sage Publications.

Ho, J., Poh, F., Zhou, J., & Zipser, D. (2019). *China consumer report 2020: The many faces of the Chinese consumer.* McKinsey & Company.

Hojman, D. A., & Szeidl, A. (2008). Core and periphery in networks. *Journal of Economic Theory, 139*(1), 295–309. doi:10.1016/j.jet.2007.07.007

Hondroyiannis, G., & Papapetrou, E. (2000). Do demographic changes affect fiscal developments? *Public Finance Review, 28*(5), 468–488. doi:10.1177/109114210002800505

Hood, N., & Young, S. (1979). *The economics of multinational enterprise.* Longman.

Hopewell, K. (2013). New protagonists in global economic governance: Brazilian agribusiness at the WTO. *New Political Economy, 18*(4), 603–623. doi:10.1080/13563467.2013.736957

Hoque, S. (2005). *The impact of tariff reduction on Bangladesh economy: a computable general equilibrium assessment. MPRA Paper 16246.* University Library of Munich.

Hori, M., & Wong, Y. C. (2013). Costs of Myanmar's multiple exchange-rate regime. *The Journal of International Trade & Economic Development, 22*(2), 209–233. doi:10.1080/09638199.2011.555561

HsiaoC.PesaranM. H.PickA. (2007). *Diagnostic tests of cross section independence for nonlinear panel data models.* IZA Discussion Paper / CESifo Working Paper Series / IEPR Working Paper No. 2756 / No. 1984 / No. 07.17.

Huang, C. H., & Yang, C. Y. (2015). European exchange rate regimes and purchasing power parity: An empirical study on eleven eurozone countries. *International Review of Economics & Finance, 35*, 100–109. doi:10.1016/j.iref.2014.09.008

Hugueney, C. (2004). *The G-20: Passing phenomenon or here to stay?* Dialogue on Globalization. Briefing Papers, Fes Berlin, March 2004.

Huiyun, F. (2009). Is China a revisionist power? *The Chinese Journal of International Politics, 2*(3), 313–334. doi:10.1093/cjip/pop003

Hummels, D., & Klenow, P. J. (2005). The variety and quality of a nation' s exports. *The American Economic Review, 95*(3), 704–723. doi:10.1257/0002828054201396

Hurley, J., S., & Portelance, G. (2018). *Examining the debt implications of the Belt and Road Initiative from a Policy Perspective.* Center for Global Development Policy Paper 121.

Hurlin, C., & Mignon, V. (2006). *Une synthèse des tests de cointégration sur données de panel.* halshs-00070887.

Hurrell, A., & Narlikar, A. (2006). A new politics of confrontation? Brazil and India in multilateral trade negotiations. *Global Society, 20*(4), 415–433. doi:10.1080/13600820600929762

Ikenberry, G. J. (2014). From hegemony to the balance of power: The rise of China and American grand strategy. *International Journal of Korean Unification Studies, 23*(2), 41–63.

Ilzetzki, E., & Reichardt, H. (2020). *Ramping up ventilator production: Lessons from WWII.* VoxEU. https://voxeu.org/article/ramping-ventilator-production-lessons-wwii

Ilzetzki, E., Mendoza, E. G., & Végh, C. A. (2013). How big (small?) are fiscal multipliers? *Journal of Monetary Economics*, *60*(2), 239–254. doi:10.1016/j.jmoneco.2012.10.011

Ilzetzki, E., Reinhart, C. M., & Rogoff, K. S. (2019). Exchange arrangements entering the twenty-first century: Which anchor will hold? *The Quarterly Journal of Economics*, *134*(2), 599–646. doi:10.1093/qje/qjy033

Imbs, J., & Wacziarg, R. (2003). Stages of diversification. *The American Economic Review*, *93*(1), 63–86. doi:10.1257/000282803321455160

Indian Council of World Affairs (ICWA). (2015). China Pakistan Economic Corridor (CPEC). *Issue Brief*, 1–15.

INEGI. (2017). *Resumen de balanza comercial de mercancías de México. Participación porcentual de las exportaciones petroleras y no petroleras.* Recovered from https://www.inegi.org.mx/programas/comext/

International Growth Center. (2010). *Economic growth and structural change in South Asia: Miracle or Mirage?* Working Papers 10/0859.

International Monetary Fund (IMF). (2020a). *Direction of Trade Statistics (DOTS).* Retrieved from https://data.imf.org/?sk=9D6028D4-F14A-464C-A2F2-59B2CD424B85

International Monetary Fund (IMF). (2020b). *World Economic Outlook Database (October 2019).* https://www.imf.org/external/pubs/ft/weo/2019/02/weodata/index.aspx

Jacob, T., Kattookaran, T., & Paul, S. (2019). Impact of exchange rate volatility on Foreign Direct Investment in India: An Empirical Analysis. *Journal of Management*, *8*(1), 13–22.

Jaffe, A. B. (1984). *The effects of market demand, technological opportunity and research spillovers on R&D intensity and productivity growth. NBER Working Paper 1432.* doi:10.3386/w1432

Jaiblai, P., & Shenai, P. (2019). The determinants of FDI in Sub-Saharan economies: A study of data from 1990–2017. *International Journal of Financial Studies*, *7*(43), 1–32. doi:10.3390/ijfs7030043

Jain, B. M. (2004). India–China relations: Issues and emerging trends. *The Round Table*, *93*(374), 374. doi:10.1080/00358530410001679602

Jalil, A., Tariq, R., & Bibi, N. (2014). Fiscal deficit and inflation: New evidences from Pakistan using a bounds testing approach. *Economic Modelling*, *37*, 120–126. doi:10.1016/j.econmod.2013.10.029

Jalles, J. T., Mulas-Granados, C., Tavares, J., & Correa Caro, C. (2018). Single currency and fiscal performance: The early Euro Area in perspective. *Applied Economics Letters*, *25*(6), 415–419. doi:10.1080/13504851.2017.1327119

Jaspersen, F., Aylward, A.H., & Knox, A.D. (2000). The effects of risks on private investment: Africa compared with other developing countries. *Investment and Risk in Africa*, 71–95.

Javetski, B. F. (1996). Old world, new investment. *Business Week*, 50-51.

Javorcik, B. (2020). Global supply chains will not be the same in the post Covid-19 World. In R. Baldwin & S. J. Evenett (Eds.), *Covid-19 and trade policy: Why turning inward won't work* (pp. 111–116). CEPR Press.

Javorcik, B. S., Lo Turco, A., & Maggioni, D. (2018). New and improved: Does FDI Boost production complexity in host countries? *Economic Journal (London)*, *128*(614), 2507–2537. doi:10.1111/ecoj.12530

Jenkins, C., & Thomas, L. (2002). *Foreign direct investment in Southern Africa: Determinants, characteristics and implications for economic growth and poverty alleviation.* https://www.csae.ox.ac.uk/reports

Jenkins, R. (2019). *How China is reshaping the global economy: Development impacts in Africa and Latin America.* Oxford University Press.

JetterM.HassanA. (2013). *The roots of export diversification.* Documentos de Trabajo 13–02. Medellín. doi:10.2139srn.2193650

Jetter, M., & Hassan, A. (2015). Want export diversification? Educate the kids first. *Economic Inquiry, 53*(4), 1765–1782. doi:10.1111/ecin.12213

Jobert, T., Karanfil, F., & Tykhonenko, A. (2010). Convergence of per capita carbon dioxide emissions in the EU: Legend or reality? *Energy Economics, 32*(6), 1364–1373. doi:10.1016/j.eneco.2010.03.005

Johansson, J. (2000). *Global marketing - Foreign entry, local marketing, and global management.* McGraw-Hill.

Jones, C., & Spicer, A. (2009). *Unmasking the entrepreneur.* Edward Elgar. doi:10.4337/9781781952689

Jones, J. B. (1986). Consumer prices, wholesale prices, and causality. *Empirical Economics, 11*(1), 41–55. doi:10.1007/BF01978144

Jordaan, J. C. (2004). *Foreign direct investment and neighbouring influences* (Unpublished doctoral thesis). University of Pretoria.

Jordaan, A. C. (2015). Choice of exchange rate regime in a selection of african countries. *Journal of African Business, 16*(3), 215–234. doi:10.1080/15228916.2015.1075645

Joseph, J. (2013). Resilience as embedded neoliberalism: A governmentality approach, *Resilience: International Policy, Practices and Discourse, 1*(1), 38–52. doi:10.1080/21693293.2013.765741

Joseph, J. (2018). *Varieties of resilience: Studies in governmentality.* Cambridge University Press. doi:10.1017/9781316551028

Kalemli-Ozcan, S., Sørensen, B. E., & Yosha, O. (2003). Risk sharing and industrial specialization: Regional and international evidence. *The American Economic Review, 93*(3), 903–918. doi:10.1257/000282803322157151

Kammoun, S., Romdhane, Y., & Fakhfakh, M. (2020). Effects of economic and political risks on Foreign Direct Investment: A panel data analysis in MENA region. In A. Prabhakar, T. Dutta, G. Kaur, V. Sarin, & V. Erokhin (Eds.), *Regional Trade and Development Strategies in the Era of Globalization.* doi:10.4018/978-1-7998-1730-7.ch012

Kano, L., & Oh, C. H. (2020). Global value chains in the post-COVID world: Governance for reliability. *Journal of Management Studies, 57*(8), 1773–1777. doi:10.1111/joms.12626

Kaplan, R. (2012). *The revenge of geography: What the map tells us about coming conflicts and the battle against fate.* Random House Publishing Group.

Kar, M. (2019). Pricing strategies in mobile telecommunications markets. *Social. Mentality and Researcher Thinkers Journal, 5*(16), 360–371. doi:10.31576mryj.240

Kassi, D. F., Sun, G., Ding, N., Rathnayake, D. N., & Assamoi, G. R. (2019). Asymmetry in exchange rate pass-through to consumer prices: Evidence from emerging and developing Asian countries. *Economic Analysis and Policy, 62*, 357–372. doi:10.1016/j.eap.2018.09.013

Kastner, S. L., & Saunders, P. C. (2012). Is China a status quo or revisionist state? Leadership travel as an empirical indicator of foreign policy priorities. *Studia Quaternaria, 56*, 163–177.

Kearney, A. T. (2007). *The Globalization Index 2007.* Accessed on: https://foreignpolicy.com/2009/10/12/the-globalization-index-2007/

Keating, D., Siddiqi, A., & Nguyen, Q. (2013). National differences in population health and development. In P. A. Hall & M. Lamont (Eds.), *Social resilience in the neoliberal era* (pp. 239–263). Cambridge University Press. doi:10.1017/CBO9781139542425.014

Keeble, D., Offord, J., & Walker, S. (1988). Peripheral regions in a community of twelve Member States. Report for the European Commission, Brussels.

Keeble, D., Owens, P., & Thompson, C. (1982). Regional accessibility and economic potential in the European Community. *Regional Studies, 16*(6), 419–432. doi:10.1080/09595238200185421

Keegan, W. (2002). *Global Marketing Management.* Pearson Education.

Keita, K., & Turcu, C. (2019). *On promoting fiscal discipline: The role of exchange rate regimes, fiscal rules and institutions.* Policy Research Working Papers. doi:10.1596/1813-9450-8964

Kimakova, A. (2008). The political economy of exchange rate regime determination: Theory and evidence. *Economic Systems, 32*(4), 354–371. doi:10.1016/j.ecosys.2008.04.001

Kim, J.-O., Traore, M. K., & Warfield, C. (2006). The textile and apparel industry in developing countries. *Textile Progress, 38*(3), 1–64. doi:10.1533/tepr.2006.0003

Kim, S. (1995). Expansion of markets and the geographic distribution of economic activities: The trends in US regional manufacturing structure, 1860–1987. *The Quarterly Journal of Economics, 110*(4), 881–908. doi:10.2307/2946643

Kim, S., & Roubini, N. (2008). Twin deficit or twin divergence? Fiscal policy, current account, and real exchange rate in the U.S. *Journal of International Economics, 74*(2), 362–383. doi:10.1016/j.jinteco.2007.05.012

Kimura, F., Thangavalu, S., Narzioko, D., & Findlay, C. (2020). Pandemic (COVID-19) policy, regional cooperation and the emerging global production network. *Asian Economic Journal, 34*(1), 3–27. doi:10.1111/asej.12198

Kim, W. (2003). Does capital account liberalization discipline budget deficit? *Review of International Economics, 11*(5), 830–844. doi:10.1046/j.1467-9396.2003.00420.x

Kim, W. C., & Mauborgne, R. A. (2017). Blue Ocean Leadership. *Harvard Business Review, 11*(67), 23. PMID:24956870

Kirchhoff, B. A., & Phillips, B. D. (1988). The effect of firm formation and growth on job creation in the United States. *Journal of Business Venturing, 3*(4), 261–272. doi:10.1016/0883-9026(88)90008-0

Kirkwood, J., & Walton, S. (2010). What motivates ecopreneurs to start businesses? *International Journal of Entrepreneurial Behaviour & Research, 16*(3), 204–228. doi:10.1108/13552551011042799

Klabbers, J., Castren, E., & Wallendahl, A. (2011). *Research Handbook on the law of international organizations.* Edward Elgar. doi:10.4337/9780857931290

Klinger, B., & Lederman, D. (2004). *Discovery and development: An empirical exploration of new products.* World Bank Policy Research Working Papers 2004-11. doi:10.1596/1813-9450-3450

Klinger, B., & Lederman, D. (2006). *Diversification, innovation, and imitation inside the global technological frontier.* Policy Research Working Papers 3872.

Kluge, F. A. (2013). The fiscal impact of population aging in Germany. *Public Finance Review, 41*(1), 37–63. doi:10.1177/1091142112439225

Kluyver, C. A. (2001). *Pensamiento estratégico. Una perspectiva para los ejecutivos.* Prentice Hall.

Koh, H. C. (1996). Testing hypotheses of entrepreneurial characteristics. *Journal of Managerial Psychology, 11*(3), 12–25. doi:10.1108/02683949610113566

Kojima, K. (1973). A macroeconomic approach to foreign investment. *Hitotsubashi Journal of Economics, 16*, 1–12.

Kojima, K. (1982). Macroeconomics versus international business approach to foreign direct investment. *Hitotsubashi Journal of Economics, 23*, 1–19.

Kojima, K., & Ozawa, T. (1984). Micro and macro economic models of direct foreign investment: Toward a synthesis. *Hitotsubashi Journal of Economics, 25*, 1–20.

Kolstad, I., & Wiig, A. (2012). What determines Chinese outward FDI? *Journal of World Business, 47*(1), 26–34. doi:10.1016/j.jwb.2010.10.017

Konings, J. (2018). Trade impacts of the Belt and Road Initiative. *ING, Economic & Financial Analysis*, 1-12.

Koremenos, B., Lipson, C., & Snidal, D. (2001). The rational design of international institutions. *International Organization, 55*(4), 761–799. doi:10.1162/002081801317193592

Koren, M., & Tenreyro, S. (2007). Volatility and development. *The Quarterly Journal of Economics, 122*(1), 243–287. doi:10.1162/qjec.122.1.243

Korolev, A. (2015). Russia's reorientation to Asia: Causes and strategic implications. *Pacific Affairs, 89*(1), 53–73. doi:10.5509/201689153

Kosekahyaoglu, L. (2006). A comparative analysis of FDI in Turkey and the CEECs: Is there any link between FDI and trade? *Journal of Business Economics and Management, 7*(4), 183–200. doi:10.3846/16111699.2006.9636140

Kotler, P., & Armstrong, G. (2007). *Marketing versión para Latinoamérica*. Pearson Editorial.

Kotler, P., & Armstrong, G. (2013). *Principles of marketing*. Pearson Prentice-Hall.

Kotler, P., & Keller, K. (2013). *Marketing management*. Pearson Prentice-Hall.

Kottaridia, C., Giakoulas, C., & Manolopoulos, D. (2019). Escapism FDI from developed economies: The role of regulatory context and corporate taxation. *International Business Review, 28*(1), 36–47.

Kourilsky, M. L., & Walstad, W. B. (1998). Entrepreneurship and female youth: Knowledge, attitudes, gender differences, and educational practices. *Journal of Business Venturing, 13*(1), 77–88. doi:10.1016/S0883-9026(97)00032-3

Kravis, L. B., & Lipsey, R. E. (1982). The location of overseas production and production for export by US multinational firms. *Journal of International Economics, 12*(3/4), 201–223.

Krueger, N. F., & Carsrud, A. L. (1993). Entrepreneurial intentions: Applying the theory of planned behaviour. *Entrepreneurship and Regional Development, 5*(4), 315–330. doi:10.1080/08985629300000020

Krueger, N. F. Jr, Reilly, M. D., & Carsrud, A. L. (2000). Competing Models of Entrepreneurial Intentions. *Journal of Business Venturing, 15*(5-6), 411–432. doi:10.1016/S0883-9026(98)00033-0

Krugman, P. (1993). First nature, second nature, and metropolitan location. *Journal of Regional Science, 33*(2), 129–144. doi:10.1111/j.1467-9787.1993.tb00217.x

Krugman, P. R., Obstfeld, M., & Melitz, M. J. (2006). *Economía internacional: Teoría y Política*. Pearson.

Kuratko, D. F. (2005). The emergence of entrepreneurship education: Development, trends, and challenges. *Entrepreneurship Theory and Practice, 29*(5), 577–597. doi:10.1111/j.1540-6520.2005.00099.x

Kuratko, D. F., & Audretsch, D. B. (2009). Strategic entrepreneurship: Exploring different perspectives of an emerging concept. *Entrepreneurship Theory and Practice*, *33*(1), 1–17. doi:10.1111/j.1540-6520.2008.00278.x

Kwon, D., & Koo, W. (2009). Price transmission mechanism among disaggregated processing stages of food: demand-pull or cost-push? Paper Presented at the *Annual Meeting of the Agricultural and Applied Economics Associations*, Milwaukee, WI.

Lai, D. (2011). The Power Transition Theory. In The United States and China in Power Transition. Strategic Studies Institute, US Army War College.

Lairson, T. D. (2018). *The global strategic environment of the BRI: Deep interdependence and structural power.* Academic Press.

Lamm, R. M. Jr, & Westcott, P. C. (1981). The effects of changing input costs on food prices. *American Agricultural Economics Association*, *63*(May), 187–196. doi:10.2307/1239554

Leachman, L. L., Rosas, G., Lange, P., & Bester, A. (2007). The political economy of budget deficits. *Economics and Politics*, *19*(3), 369–420. doi:10.1111/j.1468-0343.2007.00320.x

Lederman, D., & Maloney, W. F. (2003). *Trade structure and growth.* Policy Research Working Papers 3025. Washington, DC: The World Bank. doi:10.1596/1813-9450-3025

Lee, C.-C., Chang, C.-P., & Chen, P.-F. (2008). Do CO_2 emission levels converge among 21 OECD countries? New evidence from unit root structural break tests. *Applied Economics Letters*, *15*(7), 551–556. doi:10.1080/13504850500426236

Lee, D. Y., & Tsang, E. W. (2001). The effects of entrepreneurial personality, background and network activities on venture growth. *Journal of Management Studies*, *38*(4), 583–602. doi:10.1111/1467-6486.00250

Leeper, E. M. (1991). Equilibria under "active" and "passive" monetary and fiscal policies. *Journal of Monetary Economics*, *27*(1), 129–147. doi:10.1016/0304-3932(91)90007-B

Lemke, D., & Tammen, R. L. (2003). Power transition theory and the rise of China. *International Interactions*, *29*(4), 269–271. doi:10.1080/714950651

Leontief, W. (1953). Factor proportions and the structure of American trade: Further theoretical and empirical analysis. *The Review of Economics and Statistics*, *38*(4), 386–407. doi:10.2307/1926500

Levinson, M. (2006). *The box: How the shipping container made the world smaller and the world economy bigger.* Princeton University Press.

Levitt, T. (1983). The globalization of markets. *Harvard Business Review*, (May-June), 92–102.

Levy-Yeyati, E., & Sturzenegger, F. (2005). Classifying exchange rate regimes: Deeds vs. words. *European Economic Review*, *49*(6), 1603–1635. doi:10.1016/j.euroecorev.2004.01.001

Li, X., Meng, B., & Wang, Z. (2019). Recent patterns of global production and Gvc participation. In *Technological Innovation, Supply Chain Trade, and Workers in a Globalized World.* Geneva: Centre William Rappard.

Liangxiang, J., & Janardhan, N. (2020). Belt and Road Initiative: Opportunities and obstacles for the Gulf. In N. Janardhan (Ed.), *The Arab Gulf's Pivot to Asia: From Transactional to Strategic Partnerships* (pp. 35–48). Gerlach Press. doi:10.2307/j.ctv15r56r3.5

Lien, D., Selmier, W. T., & Oh, C. (2012). Confucius Institute effects on China's trade and FDI: Isn't it delightful when folks Afar Study Hanyu? *International Review of Economics & Finance*, *2*, 147–155.

Li, J., & Rajan, R. (2009). Foreign direct investment and technology transfer under uncertainty in a liberalizing host economy. *International Economic Journal*, *23*(1), 23–41. doi:10.1080/10168730802696483

Lim, J. J., & Saborowski, C. (2012). Export diversification in a transitioning economy: The case of syrialim and saborowski export diversification in Syria. *Economics of Transition*, *20*(2), 339–367. doi:10.1111/j.1468-0351.2011.00430.x

Liñán, F., Rodríguez-Cohard, J., & Rueda-Cantuche, J. (2011). Factors affecting entrepreneurial intention levels: A role for education. *The International Entrepreneurship and Management Journal*, *7*(2), 195–218. doi:10.100711365-010-0154-z

Links, S. (2021). Ascertaining agency Africa and the Belt and Road Initiative. In F. Schneider (Ed.), *Global perspectives on China's Belt and Road Initiative: Asserting agency through regional connectivity* (pp. 113–139). Amsterdam University Press.

Linneker, B., & Spence, N. (1996). Road transport infrastructure and regional economic development: The regional development effects of the M25 London Orbital Motorway. *Journal of Transport Geography*, *4*(2), 77–92. doi:10.1016/0966-6923(96)00001-4

Littunen, H. (2000). Entrepreneurship and the characteristics of the entrepreneurial personality. *International Journal of Entrepreneurial Behaviour & Research*, *6*(6), 295–309. doi:10.1108/13552550010362741

Liu, J., Wei, W., Shi, Y. B., & Chang, C. P. (2020). The nexus between country risk and exchange rate regimes: A global investigation. *The North American Journal of Economics and Finance*, *51*, 100842. doi:10.1016/j.najef.2018.08.025

Liu, W., & Dunford, M. (2019). Chinese perspectives on the Belt and Road Initiative. *Cambridge Journal of Regions, Economy and Society*, *12*(1), 145–167. doi:10.1093/cjres/rsy032

Livermore, D. (2010, Jan. 6). CQ: The test of your potential for cross-cultural success. *Revista Forbes*.

Livermore, D. (2015). *Leading with cultural intelligence: The real secret to success*. Amacom.

Li, Y. (2018). The greater Euroasian partnership and the Belt and Road Initiative: Can the two be linked? *Journal of Euroasian Studies*, *9*(2), 94–99. doi:10.1016/j.euras.2018.07.004

Li, Y. (2019). RMB exchange rate reforms and exchange rate preferences of domestic interest groups in China. *Economic and Political Studies*, *7*(4), 413–432. doi:10.1080/20954816.2019.1667601

Locke, E. (2000). Motivation, cognition, and action: An analysis of studies of task goals and knowledge. *Applied Psychology*, *49*(3), 408–429. doi:10.1111/1464-0597.00023

Locke, E. A. (1991). The motivation sequence, the motivation hub and the motivation core. *Organizational Behavior and Human Decision Processes*, *50*(2), 288–299. doi:10.1016/0749-5978(91)90023-M

Longenecker, J. G., Moore, C. W., Petty, J. W., Palich, L. E., & McKinney, J. A. (2006). Ethical attitudes in small businesses and large corporations: Theory and empirical findings from a tracking study spanning three decades. *Journal of Small Business Management*, *44*(2), 167–183. doi:10.1111/j.1540-627X.2006.00162.x

Lumpkin, G. T., & Dess, G. G. (1996). Clarifying the entrepreneurial orientation construct and linking it to performance. *Academy of Management Review*, *21*(1), 135–172. doi:10.5465/amr.1996.9602161568

Lussier, R. N., & Pfeifer, S. (2001). A crossnational prediction model for business success. *Journal of Small Business Management*, *39*(3), 228–239. doi:10.1111/0447-2778.00021

Lyons, R. (2011). Paths to innovative leadership. *BizEd Magazine*, *10*(2), 32-38.

Maddala, G. S., & Wu, S. (1999). A comparative study of unit root tests with panel data and a new simple test. *Oxford Bulletin of Economics and Statistics*, *61*, 631–652.

Mahbuba, T., & Jongwanich, J. (2019). Determinants of foreign direct investment (FDI) in the power sector: A case study of Bangladesh. *Energy Strategy Reviews*, *24*(1), 178–192.

Makhlouf, Y., Kellard, N. M., & Vinogradov, D. (2015). Trade openness, export diversification, and political regimes. *Economics Letters*, *136*, 25–27. doi:10.1016/j.econlet.2015.08.031

Mancini, C. (2010). O esforço do setor agrícola para influenciar a agenda brasileira na Rodada Doha. *Revista Administração em Diálogo*, *14*(1), 135–161. doi:10.20946/rad.v12i1.2939

Mariani, M. S., Vidmer, A., Medo, M., & Zhang, Y. C. (2015). Measuring economic complexity of countries and products: Which metric to use? *The European Physical Journal B*, *88*(11), 1–9. doi:10.1140/epjb/e2015-60298-7

Mariano, M. P., & Ramanzini, H. R. J. (2013). Brazil and the G-20: Domestic pressures and the construction of the negotiating position in the Doha Round of the WTO. *Journal of World Trade*, *47*(6), 1203–1224.

Markiewicz, A. (2006). Choice of exchange rate regime in transition economies: An empirical analysis. *Journal of Comparative Economics*, *34*(3), 484–498. doi:10.1016/j.jce.2006.06.004

Marques, A. C., & Fuinhas, J. A. (2012). Are public policies towards renewables successful? Evidence from European countries. *Renewable Energy*, *44*, 109–118. doi:10.1016/j.renene.2012.01.007

Márquez-Ramos, L., Florensa, L., & Recalde, M. (2015). Economic integration effects on trade margins: Sectoral evidence from Latin America. *Journal of Economic Integration*, *30*(2), 269–299. doi:10.11130/jei.2015.30.2.269

Marshal, M. G., & Elzinga-Marshal, G. (2017). *Global Report 2017: Conflict, Governance, and State Fragility*. http://www.systemicpeace.org/globalreport.html

Mars, M. M., & Rios-Aguilar, C. (2010). Academic entrepreneurship (re) defined: Significance and implications for the scholarship of higher education. *Higher Education*, *59*(4), 441–460. doi:10.100710734-009-9258-1

Martens, P., & Zywietz, D. (2006). Rethinking globalization: A modified Globalization Index. *Journal of International Development*, *18*(3), 331–350. doi:10.1002/jid.1223

Martin, A., & Mercurio, B. (2017). Doha dead and buried in Nairobi: Lessons for the WTO. *Journal of International Trade Law & Policy*, *16*(1), 49–66. doi:10.1108/JITLP-01-2017-0001

Martin-Mayoral, F., Morán Carofilis, G., & Cajas Guijarro, J. (2016). The effects of integration agreements in Western Hemisphere trade, 1970–2014. *The Journal of International Trade & Economic Development*, *25*(5), 724–756. doi:10.1080/09638199.2015.1125519

Marvel C. M., Rodríguez M., C., & Núñez B. M. A. (2011). La productividad desde una perspectiva humana: Dimensiones y factores. *Intangible Capital*, *7*(2).

Masood, S. A., Dani, S. S., Burns, N. D., & Backhouse, C. J. (2006). Transformational leadership and organizational culture: The situational strength perspective. *Proceedings of the Institution of Mechanical Engineers. Part B, Journal of Engineering Manufacture*, *220*(6), 941–949. doi:10.1243/09544054JEM499

Matsumura, M. A. (2019). A realist approach to Japan's free and open Indo-Pacific Strategy vs. China's Belt and Road Initiative: A propaganda rivalry. *International Journal of China Studies*, *10*(2), 131–154.

Mattis, J. (2018). *Summary of the 2018 national defense strategy of the United States of America*. US Department of Defense.

Mattli, W. (1999). *The logic of regional integration: Europe and beyond.* Cambridge University Press. doi:10.1017/CBO9780511756238

Mawejje, J., & Odhiambo, N. M. (2020). The determinants of fiscal deficits: A survey of literature. *International Review of Economics, 67*(3), 403–417. doi:10.100712232-020-00348-8

Mayer, T., & Zignago, S. (2011). *Notes on CEPII's distances measures: The Geodist Database.* CEPII Working Papers No. 2011-25.

McBride, S., Cohen, M., Dobuzinskis, L., & Busumtwi-Sam, J. (2002). Global instability: Uncertainty and new visions in political economy. In S. McBride, L. Dobuzinskis, M. Cohen, & J. Busumtwi-Sam (Eds.), *Global instability* (pp. 1–6). Social Indicators Research Series. Springer. doi:10.1007/978-94-010-0251-6_1

McCallum, B. T., & Nelson, E. (2005). Monetary and fiscal theories of the price level: The irreconcilable differences. *Oxford Review of Economic Policy, 21*(4), 565–583. doi:10.1093/oxrep/gri032

McClelland, D. C. (1961). Achieving society (No. 15). Simon and Schuster.

McGregor, D. (1960). *The human side of enterprise.* McGraw-Hill.

McKinsey Global Institute. (2019). *China and the world: Inside the dynamics of a changing relationship.* Author.

Mehmood, F., Fatima, N., & Ullah, K. (2019). Impact of China-Pakistan economic corridor on Pakistan's future energy consumption and energy saving potential: Evidence from sectoral time series analysis. *Energy Strategy Reviews, 25,* 34–46. doi:10.1016/j.esr.2019.04.015

Melitz, J. (2007). North, south and distance in the gravity model. *European Economic Review, 51*(4), 971–991. doi:10.1016/j.euroecorev.2006.07.001

Melitz, M. (2003). The impact of trade on intra-industry reallocations and aggregate industry productivity. *Econometrica, 71*(6), 1695–1725. doi:10.1111/1468-0262.00467

Middlemist, R. D., & Hitt, M. (1981). *Organizational behavior: Applied concepts.* Science Research Associates.

Mill, J. S. (1848). *Principles of political economy with some of their applications.* Social Philosophy.

Mina, W. (2020). Do GCC market-oriented labor policies encourage inward FDI flows? *Research in International Business and Finance, 5,* 101092.

Ministro de Asuntos Exteriores y de Cooperación. (2017). *Exteriores de gobierno.*

Mintzberg, H., & McHugh, A. (1985). Strategy formation in an adhocracy. *Administrative Science Quarterly, 30*(2), 160–197. doi:10.2307/2393104

Mishra, R. (2019). China's global maritime engagement and the Indian Ocean Region. In J. Wang & H. Boon (Eds.), *China's omnidirectional peripheral diplomacy* (pp. 281–316). World Scientific Publishing Co. doi:10.1142/9789813141797_0012

Mobley, T. (2019). The Belt and Road Initiative: Insights from China's backyard. *Strategic Studies Quarterly, 13*(3), 52–72.

Moghadam, A. T., Mazlan, N. S., Chin, L., & Ibrahim, S. (2019). Mergers and acquisitions and Greenfield foreign direct investment in selected ASEAN countries. *Journal of Economic Integration, 34*(4), 746–765.

Moller, J. O. (2021). Asia's transformation: From economic globalization to regionalization. ISEAS: Yusof Ishak Institute.

Montecinos, V. (1996). Ceremonial regionalism, institutions and integration in the Americas. *Studies in Comparative International Development, 31*(2), 110–123. doi:10.1007/BF02719330

Montiel, P., & Agenor, P. (2008). *Development macroeconomics* (3rd ed.). Princeton University Press.

Mooi, E., & Sarstedt, M. (2014). *A concise guide to market research.* Springer.

Moscone, F., & Tosetti, E. (2009). A review and comparison of tests of cross-section independence in panels. *Journal of Economic Surveys, 23*(3), 528–561. doi:10.1111/j.1467-6419.2008.00571.x

Mubeen, N., & Ahmad, N. (2016). Towards measurement and determinants of export diversification: An empirical analysis of Pakistan. *Pakistan Journal of Commerce and Social Sciences, 10*(3), 588–605.

Mueller, S. L., & Dato-on, M. C. (2008). Gender role orientation as a determinant of entrepreneurial self e efficacy. *Journal of Developmental Entrepreneurship, 13*(1), 3–20. doi:10.1142/S108494670800082X

Mypimes. (Ed.). (2017). *Libre comercio agrícola, teoría y realidade.* México: Mypimes.

NAFTA de hoy. (2014). Tratado de libre comercio de américa del norte. *TMEC de hoy.* https://www.sec-TMEC-mex.org/Inicio/Bienvenida

Nagle, T. T., & Hogan, J. E. (2010). *The strategy and tactics of pricing* (4th ed.). Pearson Education.

Naisbitt, J. (1982). *Megatrends: Ten new directions transforming our lives.* Warner Books.

Narlikar, A., & Tussie, D. (2004). The G-20 at the Cancun ministerial: Developing countries and their evolving coalitions in the WTO. *World Economy, 27*(7), 947–966. doi:10.1111/j.1467-9701.2004.00636.x

National Development and Reform Commission. (2015). *Vision and Actions on Jointly Building Silk Road Economic Belt and 21st Century Maritime Silk Road.* reconasia-production.s3.amazonaws.com

Nazir, M. A., & Ramzan, M. (2012). Contribution on entrepreneurship in economic growth. *Interdisciplinary Journal of Contemporary Research in Business, Economics, and Finance, 4*(3), 273–294.

Neaime, S., & Gaysset, I. (2017). Sustainability of macroeconomic policies in selected MENA countries: Post financial and debt crises. *Research in International Business and Finance, 40*, 129–140. doi:10.1016/j.ribaf.2017.01.001

Neneh, B. N. (2011). *The impact of entrepreneurial characteristics and business practices on the long term survival of small and medium enterprises (SMEs)* (Doctoral dissertation). University of the Free State.

Neto, P., Brandão, A., & Cerqueira, A. (2008). The impact of FDI, cross-border mergers and acquisitions, and Greenfield investments on economic growth. *The IUP Journal of Business Strategy,* 24–44.

Nguyen Van, P. (2005). Distribution dynamics of CO_2 emissions. *Environmental and Resource Economics, 32*(4), 495–508. doi:10.100710640-005-7687-6

Nitsch, V. (2000). National borders and international trade: Evidence from the European Union. *The Canadian Journal of Economics. Revue Canadienne d'Economique, 33*(4), 1091–1105. doi:10.1111/0008-4085.00055

Nohara, J. J. (2017). Sea power as a dominant paradigm: The rise of China's new strategic identity. *Journal of Contemporary East Asia Studies, 6*(2), 210–232. doi:10.1080/24761028.2017.1391623

Nourry, M. (2009). Re-examining the empirical evidence for stochastic convergence of two air pollutants with a pair-wise approach. *Environmental and Resource Economics, 44*(4), 555–570. doi:10.100710640-009-9301-9

Nwankwo, B. E., Kanu, G. C., Marire, M. I., Balogun, S. K., & Uhiara, C. (2012). Gender-role orientation and self-efficacy as correlates of entrepreneurial intention. *European Journal of Business and Social Sciences, 1*(6), 9-26.

O'Clery, N. (2015). A tale of two clusters: The evolution of Ireland's economic complexity since 1995. *Journal of the Statistical and Social Inquiry Society of Ireland, 45*(2009), 16–66.

O'Loughlin, J. (1994). *Dictionary of geopolitics*. Greenwood Press.

Obadan, M. I. (1982). Direct investment in Nigeria: An empirical analysis. *African Studies Review, 25*(1).

Oberhofer, W., & Kmenta, J. (1974). A general procedure for obtaining maximum likelihood estimates in generalized regression models. *Econometrica, 42*(3), 579–590. doi:10.2307/1911792

Obiamaka, P. E., Onwumere, J. U., & Okpara, G. C. (2011). Foreign direct investment and economic growth in Nigeria: A Granger causality analysis. *International Journal of Current Research, 3*(11), 225–232.

Odell, J. S. (2007). Growing power meets frustration in the Doha round's first four years. In L. Crump & J. Maswood (Eds.), *Developing countries and global trade negotiations* (pp. 7–40). Routledge.

Odozi, V. A. (1995). *An overview of foreign investment in Nigeria 1960–1995*. Central Bank of Nigeria Occasional Paper No. 11.

OEC - Data Sources. (n.d.). Author.

OECD. (2018). *China's Belt and Road Initiative in the global trade, investment and finance landscape*. OECD Business and Finance Outlook.

OECD. (2020a). *Shocks, risks and global value chains: Insights from the OECD METRO model*. http://www.oecd.org/trade/documents/shocks-risks-gvc-insights-oecd-metro-model.pdf

OECD. (2020b). *Trade interdependencies in Covid-19 goods*. http://oecd.org/coronavirus/policy-responses/trade-interdependencies-in-covid-19-goods-79aaa1d6/

Ohashi, H. (2018). The Belt and Road Initiative (BRI) in the context of China's opening-up policy. *Journal of Contemporary East Asia Studies, 7*(2), 85–103. doi:10.1080/24761028.2018.1564615

Oke, O. B., Ezike, E. J., & Ojogbo, E. S. (2012). Locational determinants of foreign direct investment in Nigeria. *International Business Research, 5*(4), 103.

Omankhanlen, A. E. (2011). The effect of exchange rate and inflation on foreign direct investment and its relationship with economic growth in Nigeria. *Economics and Applied Informatics, 1*, 5–16.

ORF (2020) Issue Brief, No. 395.

Osinubi, T., & Amaghionyeodiwe, L. A. (2010). Foreign private investment and economic growth in Nigeria. *Review of Economic Business Studies, 10*(2), 105–127.

Ottaviano, G. (2008). Infrastructure and economic geography: An overview of theory and evidence. *European Investment Bank Papers, 13*, 8–35.

Ouchi, W. (1982). *Theory Z*. Avon books.

Oviatt, B. M., & McDougall, P. P. (2005). Defining international entrepreneurship and modeling the speed of internationalization. *Entrepreneurship Theory and Practice, 29*(5), 537–553. doi:10.1111/j.1540-6520.2005.00097.x

Pacific Alliance. (2020). *What is the Pacific Alliance*. https://alianzapacifico.net/en/what-is-the-pacific-alliance/

Palacio, A. M. (2019). The Pacific Alliance: Building a pathway to the high-hanging fruit of deep integration. In P. Sauve, R. P. Lazo, & J. M. Alvarez Zarate (Eds.), *The Pacific Alliance in a world of preferential trade agreements* (pp. 3–27). Springer International. doi:10.1007/978-3-319-78464-9_1

Palangkaraya, A., & Waldkirch, A. (2008). Factor abundance and FDI factor intensity in developed countries. *International Economic Journal, 22*(4), 489–508.

Palan, N., Simoes, N., & Crespo, N. (2020). Measuring fifty years of trade globalization. *World Economy*, twec.13016. doi:10.1111/twec.13016

Panopoulou, E., & Pantelidis, T. (2009). Club convergence in carbon dioxide emissions. *Environmental and Resource Economics, 44*(1), 47–70. doi:10.100710640-008-9260-6

Parasuraman, S., Purohit, Y. S., Godshalk, V. M., & Beutell, N. J. (1996). Work and family variables, entrepreneurial career success, and psychological well-being. *Journal of Vocational Behavior, 48*(3), 275–300. doi:10.1006/jvbe.1996.0025

Parks, R. W. (1967). Efficient estimation of a system of regression equations when disturbances are both serially and contemporaneously correlated. *Journal of the American Statistical Association, 62*(318), 500–509. doi:10.1080/01621459.1967.10482923

Pärletun, J. (2008). *The determinants of foreign direct investment: A regional analysis with focus on Belarus.* http://biblioteket.ehl.lu.se/olle/papers/0002948.pdf

Parteka, A., & Tamberi, M. (2011). Export diversification and development: An empirical assessment. *Quaderni Di Ricerca, 359*, 1–38. doi:10.2139srn.1890767

Parteka, A., & Tamberi, M. (2013). What determines export diversification in the development process? Empirical assessment. *World Economy, 36*(6), 807–826. doi:10.1111/twec.12064

Paterson, S. (2018). *China, Trade and Power: Why the West's economic engagement has failed.* London Publishing Partnership.

Pavón, L. (2010). *Financiamiento a las microempresas y las pymes en México (2000-2009).* Cepal Editorial.

Payne, J. E. (2020). The convergence of carbon dioxide emissions: A survey of the empirical literature. *Journal of Economic Studies* (ahead-of-print). doi:10.1108/JES-12-2019-0548

Pearson, K., Horridge, M., & Corong, E. (2018). *Hands-on Computing with RunGTAP and WinGEM To Introduce GTAP and GEMPACK* (Center of Policies Studies). Purdue University, West Lafayette, IN: Global Trade Analysis Project (GTAP). Retrieved from https://www.gtap.agecon.purdue.edu/resources/res_display.asp?RecordID=1638

Pedroni, P. (1995). *Panel cointegration, asymptotic and Önite sample properties of pooled time series tests with an application to the PPP hypothesis.* Indiana University Working Paper in Economics 92–013.

Pedroni, P. (1996). *Fully modified OLS for heterogeneous cointegrated panels and the case of purchasing power parity.* Indiana University Working Paper in Economics.

Pedroni, P. (1999). Critical values for cointegration tests in heterogenous panels with multiple regressor. *Oxford Bulletin of Economics and Statistics, 61*, 653–670.

Pedroni, P. (2004). Panel cointegration: Asymptotic and finite sample properties of pooled time series tests with an application to the PPP hypothesis. *Econometric Theory, 20*(3), 597–625.

Pendall, R., Foster, K. A., & Cowell, M. (2010). Resilience and regions: Building understanding of the metaphor. *Cambridge Journal of Regions, Economy and Society, 3*(1), 71–84. doi:10.1093/cjres/rsp028

Perkins, R., & Neumayer, E. (2008). Fostering environment efficiency through transnational linkages? trajectories of CO_2 and SO_2, 1980–2000. *Environment and Planning A. Economy and Space*, *40*(12), 2970–2989. doi:10.1068/a4089

Perron, P. (1989). The great crash, the oil price shock, and the unit root hypothesis. *Econometrica*, *57*(6), 1361–1401. doi:10.2307/1913712

Pesaran, M. H. (2020). General diagnostic tests for cross-sectional dependence in panels. *Empirical Economics*, *60*(1), 1–38. doi:10.100700181-020-01875-7

Pesaran, M. H., Pesaran, M. H., Shin, Y., & Smith, R. P. (1999). Pooled mean group estimation of dynamic heterogeneous panels. *Journal of the American Statistical Association*, *94*(446), 621–634. doi:10.1080/01621459.1999.10474156

Petreski, M. (2012). Exchange-rate regime and economic growth: A review of the theoretical and empirical literature. Kiel Institute for the World Economy (IfW) Economics Discussion Papers No. 2009–31. doi:10.2139srn.1726732

Pettersson, F., Maddison, D., Acar, S., & Soderholm, P. (2014). Convergence of carbon dioxide emissions: A review of the literature. *International Review of Environmental and Resource Economics*, *7*(2), 141–178. doi:10.1561/101.00000059

Pfeffermann, G.P., & Madarassy, A. (1992). *Trends in private and investment in developing countries*. World Bank Paper 16.

Phelan, W. (2015). Enforcement and escape in the Andean Community: Why the Andean Community of nations is not a replica of the European Union. *Journal of Common Market Studies*, *53*(4), 840–856. doi:10.1111/jcms.12222

Phillips, P. C. B., & Perron, P. (1988). Testing for a unit root in time series regression. *Biometrika*, *75*(2), 335–346. doi:10.2307/2336182

Pike, A., Dawley, S., & Tomaney, J. (2010). Resilience, adaptation and adaptability. *Cambridge Journal of Regions, Economy and Society*, *3*(1), 59–70. doi:10.1093/cjres/rsq001

Portela, J., Hespanha, P., Nogueira, C., Teixeira, M., & Baptista, A. (2008). *Microempreendedorismo em Portugal: Experiências e perspectivas*. Lisboa: INscooP.

Prahalad, C. K., & Hamel, G. (1993). Stretch and leverage. *Harvard Business Review*, *71*, 75–84. PMID:10124635

Prakash, L., & Assaf, R. (2001). How beneficial is foreign direct investment for developing countries. *Finance & Development*, *38*(2), 7–9.

Prasad, P., & Prasad, A. (2006). Global transitions: The emerging new world order and its implications for business and management. *Business Renaissance Quarterly*, *1*, 91–113.

Presno, M. J., Landajo, M., & Fernández González, P. (2018). Stochastic convergence in per capita CO_2 emissions. An approach from nonlinear stationarity analysis. *Energy Economics*, *70*, 563–581. doi:10.1016/j.eneco.2015.10.001

ProMéxico. (2018). *Pasos para Exportar*. Recovered from http://www.promexico.gob.mx/es/mx/pasos-exportar

Proudman, J., & Redding, S. (2000). Evolving patterns of international trade. *Review of International Economics*, *8*(3), 373–396. doi:10.1111/1467-9396.00229

Qi, X., Erickson, A., & Goldstein, L. (2006). Maritime geostrategy and the development of the Chinese navy in the early twenty-first century. *Naval War College Review*, *59*(4), 46.

Quah, D. T. (1997). Empirics for growth and distribution: Stratification, polarization, and convergence clubs. *Journal of Economic Growth*, *2*(1), 27–59. doi:10.1023/A:1009781613339

Ramasamy, B., Yeung, M., Utoktham, C., & Duval, Y. (2017). *Trade and trade facilitation along the Belt and Road Initiative Corridors*. ARTNetT Working Paper Series No. 172.

Ratner, E. (2018). *Geostrategic and military drivers and implications of the Belt and Road Initiative*. Council on Foreign Relations.

Real Estate Market. (2017). Artículos, Infraestructura y construcción, puerta para la industria-mexicana. Market, Real estate, México.

Reardon, K. K. (1991). *Persuasion in practice*. Sage Publications.

Rebelo, S., & Végh, C. A. (2008). When is it optimal to abandon a fixed exchange rate? *The Review of Economic Studies*, *75*(3), 929–955. doi:10.1111/j.1467-937X.2008.00479.x

Redacción. (2020). *Gobierno de Sinaloa fortalece sectores primários (09.06.2020)*. El Economista.

Redding, S. (2002). Specialization dynamics. *Journal of International Economics*, *58*(2), 299–334. doi:10.1016/S0022-1996(01)00169-6

Redding, S., & Schott, P. (2003). Distance, skill deepening and development: Will peripheral countries ever get rich? *Journal of Development Economics*, *72*(2), 515–541. doi:10.1016/S0304-3878(03)00118-4

Redding, S., & Venables, A. (2004). Economic geography and international inequality. *Journal of International Economics*, *62*(1), 53–82. doi:10.1016/j.jinteco.2003.07.001

Reed, W. R., & Ye, H. (2011). Which panel data estimator should I use? *Applied Economics*, *43*(8), 985–1000. doi:10.1080/00036840802600087

Regilme, S. Jr. (2019). The decline of American power and Donald Trump: Reflections on human rights, neoliberalism, and the world order. *Geoforum*, *102*, 157–166. doi:10.1016/j.geoforum.2019.04.010

Reinhart, C. M., & Rogoff, K. S. (2004). The modern history of exchange rate arrangements: A reinterpretation. *The Quarterly Journal of Economics*, *119*(1), 1–48. doi:10.1162/003355304772839515

Rennen, W., & Martens, P. (2003). The globalisation timeline. *Integrated Assessment*, *4*(3), 137–144. doi:10.1076/iaij.4.3.137.23768

Reyes Rodríguez, E., & Quintero Reyes, G. (2020). *Agronegocios oportunidades de inversión en el sector agroalimentario en Sinaloa (02.04.2020)*. El Economista.

Reynolds, P. D. (1992). Sociology and entrepreneurship: Concepts and contributions. *Entrepreneurship Theory and Practice*, *16*(2), 47–70. doi:10.1177/104225879201600205

Riggirozzi, P., & Tussie, D. (2012). *The rise of post-hegemonic regionalism: The case of Latin America*. Springer. doi:10.1007/978-94-007-2694-9

Ritzer, E. M. (2001). *Globalization theory: Lessons from the exportation of McDonaldization and the new means of consumption*. Sage Publications.

Rivarola Puntigliano, A., & Briceño-Ruiz, J. (2013). *The resilience of regionalism in Latin America and the Caribbean: Development and autonomy*. Palgrave. doi:10.1057/9781137328373

Robalino-López, A., García-Ramos, J. E., Golpe, A. A., & Mena-Nieto, A. (2016). CO_2 emissions convergence among 10 South American countries. A study of Kaya components (1980–2010). *Carbon Management*, *7*(1–2), 1–12. doi:10.1080/17583004.2016.1151502

Rogers, J. (2011). A new geography of European power? (Rep.). Egmont Institute.

Roldan, P. N. (2019). John Stuart Mill. *Economipedia*. Recovered from https://economipedia.com/historia/biografia/john-stuart-mill.html

Romero-Ávila, D. (2008). Convergence in carbon dioxide emissions among industrialised countries revisited. *Energy Economics, 30*(5), 2265–2282. doi:10.1016/j.eneco.2007.06.003

Root, F. R. (1990). *International trade and investment*. South Western Publishing Co.

Rosenstein-Rodan, P. N. (1943). Problems of Industrialisation of Eastern and South-Eastern Europe. *Economic Journal (London), 53*(210/211), 202–211. doi:10.2307/2226317

Roubini, N. (1991). Economic and political determinants of budget deficits in developing countries. *Journal of International Money and Finance, 10*, S49–S72. doi:10.1016/0261-5606(91)90046-M

Roubini, N., & Sachs, J. D. (1989). Political and economic determinants of budget deficits in the industrial democracies. *European Economic Review, 33*(5), 903–933. doi:10.1016/0014-2921(89)90002-0

Rubio, L., & Baz, V. (2015). *El poder de la competitividad*. Fondo de Cultura Economica.

Runar, B., Amin, K., & Patrik, S. (2017). Convergence in carbon dioxide emissions and the role of growth and institutions: A parametric and non-parametric analysis. *Environmental Economics and Policy Studies, 19*(2), 359–390. doi:10.100710018-016-0162-5

Sakwa, R. (2008). New Cold War or twenty years crisis? Russia and international politics. *International Affairs, 84*(2), 241–267. doi:10.1111/j.1468-2346.2008.00702.x

Santana-Gallego, M., & Pérez-Rodríguez, J. V. (2019). International trade, exchange rate regimes, and financial crises. *The North American Journal of Economics and Finance, 47*, 85–95. doi:10.1016/j.najef.2018.11.009

Sarafidis, V., & Wansbeek, T. (2012). Cross-Sectional Dependence in Panel Data Analysis. *Econometric Reviews, 31*(5), 483–531. doi:10.1080/07474938.2011.611458

Sargent, T. J., & Wallace, N. (1981). Some unpleasant monetarist arithmetic. *Federal Reserve Bank of Minneapolis Quarterly Review, 5*(3), 1–17. doi:10.21034/qr.531

Sarkar, S. (2010). *Empreendedorismo e inovação*. Escolar Editora.

Sar, L., & Werneke, D. (1984). *Productivity: Problems, prospects, and policies*. The Johns Hopkins University Press.

Schlesinger, A. (1967). Origins of the Cold War. *Foreign Affairs, 46*(1), 22–52. doi:10.2307/20039280

Schmidt, P., & Phillips, P. (1992). LM tests for a unit root in the presence of deterministic trends. *Oxford Bulletin of Economics and Statistics, 54*(3), 257–287. doi:10.1111/j.1468-0084.1992.tb00002.x

Schmitz, A., & Jurg, B. (1972). EEC tariffs and U.S. direct investment. *European Economic Review, 3*(3), 259–270.

Schneider, F. (2021). Actors and agency in China's Belt and Road Initiative: An Introduction. In F. Schneider (Ed.), *Global perspectives on China's Belt and Road Initiative: Asserting agency through regional connectivity* (pp. 11–32). Amsterdam University Press.

Scholte, J. (2008). Defining globalisation. *World Economy, 31*, 1471–1502.

Schortgen, F. (2018). China and the twenty-first-century Silk Roads: A new era of global economic leadership? In China's Belt and Road Initiative: Changing the rules of globalization (pp. 17-33). Cham, Switzerland: Palgrave.

Schumpeter, J. A. (1961). *The theory of economic development*. Oxford University Press.

Schumpeter, J. A., & Nichol, A. J. (1934). Robinson's economics of imperfect competition. *Journal of Political Economy*, *42*(2), 249–259. doi:10.1086/254595

Schürmann, C., & Talaat, A. (2000). *Towards a European Peripherality Index*. Report for General Directorate XVI Regional Policy of the European Commission.

Schütz, M., & Palan, N. (2016). Restructuring of the international clothing and textile trade network: The Role of Italy and Portugal. *Journal of Economic Structures*, *5*(1), 1–29. doi:10.118640008-016-0046-7

Second protocol of amendment to the additional protocol of the framework agreement of the Pacific Alliance. (2016). [Alianza del Pacifico: Declaracion de Puerto Varas]. https://alianzapacifico.net/documentos-acuerdo-marco-de-la-alianza-del-pacifico/

Secretaría de Economía. (2016). *Subsecretaria de Comercio Exterior, Total exports in Mexico*. Recovered from https://www.economia.gob.mx/files/comunidad_negocios/comercio_exterior/informacion_estadistica/anual_exporta.pdf

Secretariado del TLCAN. (2017). NAFTA, Secretariado del TMEC.

Segal, G., Borgia, D., & Schoenfeld, J. (2005). The motivation to become an entrepreneur. *International Journal of Entrepreneurial Behaviour & Research*, *11*(1), 42–57. doi:10.1108/13552550510580834

Selva, V. (2019). David Ricardo. *Economipedia*. Recovered from http://economipedia.com/?s=david+ricardo

Sforza, A., & Steininger, M. (2020). *Globalization in the time of COVID-19*. CESifo Working Paper, No. 8184, Center for Economic Studies and ifo Institute (CESifo), Munich.

Shahbaz, M., Awan, R. U., & Nasir, N. M. (2009). Producer & consumer prices nexus: ARDL bounds testing approach. *International Journal of Marketing Studies*, *1*(2), 78–86. doi:10.5539/ijms.v1n2p78

Shahbaz, M., Tiwari, A. K., & Tahir, M. I. (2012). Does CPI Granger-cause WPI? New extensions from frequency domain approach in Pakistan. *Economic Modelling*, *29*(5), 1592–1597. doi:10.1016/j.econmod.2012.05.016

Shane, S., Locke, E. A., & Collins, C. J. (2003). Entrepreneurial motivation. *Human Resource Management Review*, *13*(2), 257–279. doi:10.1016/S1053-4822(03)00017-2

Shane, S., & Venkataraman, S. (2000). The promise of entrepreneurship as a field of research. *Academy of Management Review*, *25*(1), 217–226. doi:10.5465/amr.2000.2791611

Shepotylo, O. (2013). Export diversification across countries and products: Do Eastern European (EE) and Commonwealth of Independent States (CIS) countries diversify enough? *The Journal of International Trade & Economic Development*, *22*(4), 605–638. doi:10.1080/09638199.2011.577797

Shin, F. (2020). A financial alliance won't help China and Russia Dethrone the US Dollar. *The Diplomat, 26*.

Shipley, D., & Jobber, D. (2001). Integrative pricing via the pricing wheel. *Industrial Marketing Management*, *30*(3), 301–314. doi:10.1016/S0019-8501(99)00098-X

Shouyi, B. (1982). An outline history of China. Pequim: China Knowledge Series, Foreign Languages Press.

Silver, L., & Wallace, T. D. (1980). The lag relationship between wholesale and consumer prices. *Journal of Econometrics*, *12*(3), 375–387. doi:10.1016/0304-4076(80)90063-9

Simoes, N., Palan, N., & Crespo, N. (2020). Is the world flat or not (yet)? Trade globalization and digitalization. In Y. Bayar (Ed.), *Institutional, economic, and social impacts of globalization and liberalization*. IGI Global.

Sims, C. A. (1994). A simple model for study of the determination of the price level and the interaction of monetary and fiscal policy. *Economic Theory*, *4*(3), 381–399. doi:10.1007/BF01215378

Siriphattrasophon, S. (2012). Cross-cultural management of a multinational enterprise: A case of Thailand and Vietnam. *International Journal of Business and Management Studies*, *1*(3), 379–390.

Skouras, T., Avlonitis, G. J., & Indounas, K. A. (2005). Economics and marketing on pricing: How and why do they differ? *Journal of Product and Brand Management*, *14*(6), 362–374. doi:10.1108/10610420510624512

Sloan, G. (2017). *Geopolitics, geography and strategic history*. Routledge. doi:10.4324/9780203489482

Smith, T.J. (2012). *Pricing strategy*. South-Western Cengage Learning.

Solow, R. M. (1956). A contribution to the theory of economic growth. *The Quarterly Journal of Economics*, *70*(1), 65–94. doi:10.2307/1884513

Søndergaard, N. (2020). Food regime transformations and structural rebounding: Brazilian state–agribusiness relations. *Territory, Politics, Governance*, 1–20. doi:10.1080/21622671.2020.1786447

Søndergaard, N., & Dias da Silva, R. (2020). Reshaping the policy arena: How the agro-export policy network propelled Brazil within global agricultural governance. *World Trade Review*, *19*(4), 550–566. doi:10.1017/S1474745619000375

Song, Z., Che, S., & Yang, Y. (2018). The trade network of the Belt and Road Initiative and its topological relationship to the global trade network. *Journal of Geographical Sciences*, *28*(9), 1249–1262. doi:10.100711442-018-1523-8

Spencer-Oatey, H. (2008). *Culturally speaking: Culture, communication and politeness theory* (2nd ed.). Bloomsbury.

Spiekermann, K., & Neubauer, J. (2002). *European accessibility and peripherality: Concepts, models and indicators. Nordregio Working Paper No. 2002:9.*

Ssebulime, K., & Edward, B. (2019). Budget deficit and inflation nexus in Uganda 1980–2016: A cointegration and error correction modeling approach. *Journal of Economic Structures*, *8*(1), 1–14. doi:10.118640008-019-0136-4

Statista. (2020). *The Statistics Portal for Market Data, Market research and market data modelling*. Author.

Staw, B. M. (1991). Dressing up like an organization: When psychological theories can explain organizational action. *Journal of Management*, *17*(4), 805–819. doi:10.1177/014920639101700412

Stehrer, R., Ali-Yrkkö, J., Hanzl-Weiss, D., Foster, N., Rouvinen, P., Seppälä, T., Stöllinger, R., & Ylä-Anttila, P. (2011). *Trade in intermediate products and EU manufacturing supply chains.* WIIW Research Report No. 369. The Vienna Institute for International Economic Studies.

Stevens, C. E., Xie, E., & Peng, M. W. (2016). Toward a legitimacy-based view of political risk: The case of Google and Yahoo in China. *Strategic Management Journal*, *37*(5), 945–963.

Stewart, A., & Cotton, J. (2013). Making sense of entrepreneurship journals: Journal Rankings and Strategy Choices. *International Journal of Entrepreneurial Behaviour & Research*, *19*(3), 303–323. doi:10.1108/13552551311330192

Stojkoski, V., & Kocarev, L. (2017). *The relationship between growth and economic complexity: Evidence from South-eastern and Central Europe.* Munich Personal RePEc Archive, no. 77837. https://mpra.ub.uni-muenchen.de/77837/3/MPRA_paper_77837.pdf

Strazicich, M. C., & List, J. A. (2003). Are CO_2 emission levels converging among industrial countries? *Environmental and Resource Economics*, *24*(3), 263–271. doi:10.1023/A:1022910701857

Sturgeon, T., & Van Biesebroeck, J. (2011). Global value chains in the automotive industry: An enhanced role for developing countries? *International Journal of Technological Learning Innovation and Development*, *4*(1/2/3), 181–205. doi:10.1504/IJTLID.2011.041904

Sturgeon, T., Van Biesebroeck, J., & Gereffi, G. (2008). Value chains, networks, and clusters: Reframing the global automotive industry. *Journal of Economic Geography*, *8*(3), 297–321. doi:10.1093/jeg/lbn007

Subramanian, A., & Kessler, M. (2014). The hyperglobalization of trade and its future. In F. Allen, J. R. Behrman, N. Birdsall, S. Fardoust, D. Rodrik, A. Steer, & A. Subramanian (Eds.), *Towards a better global economy: Policy implications for citizens worldwide in the 21st century*. Oxford University Press. doi:10.1093/acprof:oso/9780198723455.003.0004

Summers, L. H. (1988). Tax policy and international competitiveness. In J. Frenkel (Ed.), *International Aspects of Fiscal Policies* (pp. 349–375). Chicago University Press.

Sun, J., Su, C.-W., & Shao, G. (2016). Is carbon dioxide emission convergence in the ten largest economies? *International Journal of Green Energy*, *13*(5), 454–461. doi:10.1080/15435075.2014.966373

Surie, G., & Ashley, A. (2008). Integrating pragmatism and ethics in entrepreneurial leadership for sustainable value creation. *Journal of Business Ethics*, *81*(1), 235–246. doi:10.100710551-007-9491-4

Swartz, P. M. (2011). Rising powers and naval power. In P. Saunders, C. Yung, M. Swaine, & A. Yang (Eds.), *The Chinese navy: Expanding capabilities, evolving roles* (pp. 1–21). National Defense University Press for the Center for the Study of Chinese Military Affairs.

Swidler, A. (2013). Cultural sources of institutional resilience. In P. A. Hall & M. Lamont (Eds.), *Social resilience in the neoliberal era* (pp. 319–345). Cambridge University Press. doi:10.1017/CBO9781139542425.018

Tacchella, A., Cristelli, M., Caldarelli, G., Gabrielli, A., & Pietronero, L. (2012). A new metrics for countries' fitness and products' complexity. *Scientific Reports*, *2*(1), 723. Advance online publication. doi:10.1038rep00723 PMID:23056915

Teoh, H. Y., & Foo, S. L. (1997). Moderating effects of tolerance for ambiguity and risk taking propensity on the role conflict-perceived performance relationship: Evidence from Singaporean entrepreneurs. *Journal of Business Venturing*, *12*(1), 67–81. doi:10.1016/S0883-9026(96)00035-3

Teorell, J., Dahlberg, S., Holmberg, S., Rothstein, B., Pachon, N. A., & Axelsson, S. (2020). *The Quality of Government Standard Dataset, version Jan20*. Retrieved from https://www.gu.se/en/quality-government/qog-data/data-downloads/standard-dataset

The Economist. (2019). *Slowbalisation. The steam has gone out of globalisation*. https://www.economist.com/leaders/2019/01/24/the-steam-has-gone-out-of-globalisation

The Growth Lab at Harvard University. (2019). International Trade Data (SITC, Rev. 2). Harvard Dataverse, 3166. doi:10.7910/DVN/H8SFD2

The World Bank. (2020a). *World Bank country and lending groups*. Retrieved from https://datahelpdesk.worldbank.org/knowledgebase/articles/906519-world-bank-country-and-lending-groups

The World Bank. (2020b). *World Development Indicators (WDI) Database*. The World Bank. Retrieved from https://data.worldbank.org/indicator

Thompson, J. L. (2004). The facets of the entrepreneur: Identifying entrepreneurial potential. *Management Decision*, *42*(2), 243–258. doi:10.1108/00251740410515861

Timmons, J. A., & Bygrave, W. D. (1986). Venture capital's role in financing innovation for economic growth. *Journal of Business Venturing*, *1*(2), 161–176. doi:10.1016/0883-9026(86)90012-1

Tiwari, A., & Shahbaz, M. (2010). *Modelling the relationship between wholesale price and consumer price indices: Cointegration and causality for India.* Working Paper, ICFAI University, Tripura, Comsats Institute of Information Technology.

Tiwari, A. K. (2012). An empirical investigation of causality between producers' price and consumers' price indices in Australia in frequency domain. *Economic Modelling*, *29*(5), 1571–1578. doi:10.1016/j.econmod.2012.05.010

Tobin, J. (1984). A Keynesian view of the budget deficit. *California Management Review*, *26*(2), 7–14. doi:10.2307/41165063

Tokatli, N. (2008). Global sourcing: Insights from the global clothing industry – the case of Zara, a fast fashion retailer. *Journal of Economic Geography*, *8*(1), 21–38. doi:10.1093/jeg/lbm035

Toledo, M. (2020). Sinaloa, en el primer lugar en exportación de productos cárnicos. *El Sol De Mazatlán.*

Tomás, M. J. (2013). *Da Primavera ao Inverno Árabe*. Temas e Debates, Círculo de Leitores.

Tomás, M. J. (2017). Os desafios culturais na internacionalização. In N. Crespo & M. J. Tomás (Eds.), *A Internacionalização da economia portuguesa, Casos de sucesso empresarial* (pp. 179–195). Temas e Debates, Círculo de Leitores.

Tornell, A., & Velasco, A. (1995). Fiscal discipline and the choice of exchange rate regime. *European Economic Review*, *39*(3–4), 759–770. doi:10.1016/0014-2921(94)00083-C

Tornell, A., & Velasco, A. (1998). Fiscal discipline and the choice of a nominal anchor in stabilization. *Journal of International Economics*, *46*(1), 1–30. doi:10.1016/S0022-1996(97)00039-1

Tornell, A., & Velasco, A. (2000). Fixed versus flexible exchange rates: Which provides more fiscal discipline. *Journal of Monetary Economics*, *45*(2), 399–436. doi:10.1016/S0304-3932(99)00057-4

Torres Y. (2017). 14-paises-abrieron-su-mercado-a-productos-mexicanos-en-2016. *El financiero*.

Tsai, P. (1994). Determinants of FDI and its impact on economic growth. *Journal of Economic Development*, *19*, 137–162.

Tsygankov, A. (2015). The Sino-Russian challenge to the World order: National identities, bilateral relations, and East versus West in the 2010s. *The Journal of Asian Studies*, *74*(3), 731–732. doi:10.1017/S0021911815000698

Umbach, F. (2019). *China's Belt and Road Initiative and its energy-security dimensions.* S. Rajaratnam School of International Studies, RSIS Working Paper, 320.

UNCTAD. (2015). *Tracing the value added in global value chains: Product-level case studies in China.* United Nations.

Uremadu, S. O. (2010). The impact of foreign private investment on capital formation in Nigeria, 1980 - 2004: An Empirical Analysis. *Lex et Scientia*, *XV*(2), 166–182.

US Government Services. (2020). *US history and historical documents.* https://www.usa.gov/history

Utkovski, Z., Pradier, M. F., Stojkoski, V., Perez-Cruz, F., & Kocarev, L. (2018). Economic complexity unfolded: Interpretable model for the productive structure of economies. *PLoS One*, *13*(8), 1–24. doi:10.1371/journal.pone.0200822 PMID:30086166

Valencia, F., Montoya, I., & Restrepo, J. (2014). Motivational theories in the study of entrepreneurship. *Pensamiento & Gestión*, *36*, 206–238.

Van Tongeren, F. (2020). *Shocks, risks and global value chains in a Covid-19 world.* https://oecdecoscope.blog/2020/08/25/shocks-risks-and-global-value-chains-in-a-covid-19-world

VanGrasstek, C. (2019). Concluding remarks: The Pacific Alliance – stocktaking and the way forward. In P. Sauve, R. P. Lazo, & J. M. Alvarez Zarate (Eds.), *The Pacific Alliance in a world of preferential trade agreements* (pp. 251–262). Springer International. doi:10.1007/978-3-319-78464-9_14

Vernon, R. (1966). International investment and international trade in the product life cycle. *The Quarterly Journal of Economics, 80*, 190–207.

Vettas, N. (2000). Investment dynamics in markets with endogenous demand. *The Journal of Industrial Economics, 48*(2), 189–203. doi:10.1111/1467-6451.00118

Vujakovic, P. (2010). *How to Measure Globalization? A New Globalization Index (NGI).* FIW Working Paper No. 46.

Walker, J. (2008). *China, U.S. and Africa: Competition or cooperation?* (Master Thesis). U.S. Army War College.

Wang, Y. (2016). Offensive for defensive: The Belt and Road Initiative and China's new grand strategy. *The Pacific Review, 29*(3), 455–463. doi:10.1080/09512748.2016.1154690

Wang, Z., & Sun, Z. (2020). From globalization to regionalization: The United States, China and the Post-Covid-19 world economic order. *Journal of Chinese Political Science, 28*(October). Advance online publication. doi:10.100711366-020-09706-3 PMID:33144822

Watkins, M. (2013). *Culture and society.* Harvard Business Review, Fontana Press.

Weinhardt, C., & Brink, T. (2020). Varieties of contestation: China's rise and the liberal trade order. *Review of International Political Economy, 27*(2), 258–280. doi:10.1080/09692290.2019.1699145

Westerlund, J., & Basher, S. A. (2008). Testing for convergence in carbon dioxide emissions using a century of panel data. *Environmental and Resource Economics, 40*(1), 109–120. doi:10.100710640-007-9143-2

Whiting, B. G., & Solomon, G. T. (1989). *Key issues in creativity, innovation & entrepreneurship.* Bearly.

Wolf, H. (1997). *Patterns of intra- and inter-state trade.* NBER Working Paper No. 5939.

Wolfe, D. A. (2010). The strategic management of core cities: Path dependency and economic adjustment in resilient regions. *Cambridge Journal of Regions, Economy and Society, 3*(1), 139–152. doi:10.1093/cjres/rsp032

Wolf, H. (2000). Intranational home bias in trade. *The Review of Economics and Statistics, 82*(4), 555–556. doi:10.1162/003465300559046

Woo, K. Y., & Jia, L. X. (2013). *Threshold cointegration and causality between cpi and ppi in selected countries–some international evidence.* Working Paper Series August, Hong Kong Shue University.

Woodford, M. (1994). Monetary policy and price level determinacy in a cash-in-advance economy. *Economic Theory, 4*(3), 345–380. doi:10.1007/BF01215377

Wooldridge, J. M. (2009). Introductory econometrics: A modern approach (4th ed.). Cengage Learning, George Mason University.

World Bank (2019a). *Three opportunities and three risks of the Belt and Road Initiative.* worldbank.org

World Bank. (2010). *World Development Indicators.* The World Bank.

World Bank. (2018). *Public procurement in the Belt and Road Initiative.* Author.

World Bank. (2019b). Belt and road economics: Opportunities and risks of transport corridors. Washington, DC: Author.

World Bank. (2020). East Asia and the Pacific economic update: From containment to recovery. Washington, DC: Author.

World Bank. (2021). Global Economic prospects, A World Bank Group Flagship Report. Washington, DC: Author.

WTO, IDE-JETRO, OECD, VIBE, & World Bank. (2019). *Technological Innovation, Supply Chain Trade, and Workers in a Globalized World.* Authors.

WTO. (1996). *International Trade*. Trends and Statistics.

Xaypanya, P., Rangkakulnuwat, P., & Paweenawat, P. S. (2015). The determinants of foreign direct investment in ASEAN: The first differencing panel data analysis. *International Journal of Social Economics*, *42*(3), 239–250.

Xi, J. (2017). *Secure a Decisive Victory in Building a Moderately Prosperous Society in all Respects and Strive for the Great Success of Socialism with Chinese Characteristics for a New Era.* Delivered at the 19th National Congress of the Communist Party of China.

Xi, J. (2017). *Work together to build the Silk Road economic Belt and the 21st Century Maritime Silk Road.* Full text of President Xi's speech at opening of Belt and Road forum.

Yang, J., Zhang, T., Sheng, P., & Shackman, J. D. (2016). Carbon dioxide emissions and interregional economic convergence in China. *Economic Modelling*, *52*, 672–680. doi:10.1016/j.econmod.2015.09.038

Yang, S. (2013). Power transition, balance of power, and the rise of China: A theoretical reflection about rising great powers. *China Review*, *13*(2), 35–66.

Yavuz, N. C., & Yilanci, V. (2013). Convergence in per capita carbon dioxide emissions among G7 countries: A TAR panel unit root approach. *Environmental and Resource Economics*, *54*(2), 283–291. doi:10.100710640-012-9595-x

Yoon, J.-W., Kim, J., & Lee, J. (2014). *Impact of demographic changes on inflation and the macroeconomy.* Working Paper Series No. WP/14/210. Retrieved from https://www.imf.org/en/Publications/WP/Issues/2016/12/31/Impact-of-Demographic-Changes-on-Inflation-and-the-Macroeconomy-42463

Younkins, E. (1998). *Individualism and freedom: Vital pillars of true communities*. Retrieved from https://fee.org/articles/individualism-and-freedom-vital-pillars-of-true-communities/

Zhang, B. (2014). Xi Jinping, 'Pragmatic' offensive realism and China's Rise. *Global Asia*, *9*(2), 71–79.

Zhang, J., & Luo, Y. (2017). Degree centrality, betweenness centrality, and closeness centrality in social network. *2nd International Conference on Modelling, Simulation and Applied Mathematics (MSAM)*, 300-303.

Zhang, Z. (2018). The Belt and Road Initiative: China's new geopolitical strategy? *China Quarterly of International Strategic Studies*, *4*(3), 327–343. doi:10.1142/S2377740018500240

Zhao, Y., de Haan, J., Scholtens, B., & Yang, H. (2014). Leading indicators of currency crises: Are they the same in different exchange rate regimes? *Open Economies Review*, *25*(5), 937–957. doi:10.100711079-014-9315-y

Zheng, Y. (2020). Rediscovering continentalism: The new geographic foundations of Chinese Power. *International Politics*, 1–35. doi:10.105741311-019-00206-7

Zhu, Z., Cesina, F., Chessa, A., Caldarelli, G., & Riccaboni, M. (2014). The rise of China in the international trade network: A community core detection approach. *PLoS One*, *9*(8), 1–8. doi:10.1371/journal.pone.0105496 PMID:25136895

Zicheng, Y. (2011). *Inside China's grand strategy: The perspective from the People's Republic*. University Press of Kentucky.

Ziegler, C. E. (2006). The energy factor in China's foreign policy. *Journal of Chinese Political Science*, *11*(1), 1–23. doi:10.1007/BF02877031

Zimmerer, T. W., Scarborough, N. M., & Wilson, D. (2008). *Essentials of entrepreneurship and small business management* (5th ed.). Pearson/Prentice Hall.

Zimmerman, B. J. (2000). Attainment of self-regulation: A social cognitive perspective. In M. Boekaerts, P. Pintrich, & M. Zeidner (Eds.), *Handbook of self-regulation, research, and applications* (pp. 13–39). Academic Press. doi:10.1016/B978-012109890-2/50031-7

Zokalj, M. (2016). The impact of population aging on public finance in the European Union. *Financial Theory and Practice*, *40*(4), 383–412. doi:10.3326/fintp.40.4.2

Zulma, M. (2006). Aprendizaje autorregulado: El lugar de la cognición, la metacognición y la motivación. *Estudios Pedagógicos (Valdivia)*, *32*(2), 121–132. doi:10.4067/S0718-07052006000200007

Zweig, D., & Jianhai, B. (2005). China's global hunt for energy. *Foreign Affairs*, *84*(5), 25–38. doi:10.2307/20031703

About the Contributors

Nuno Crespo holds a PhD in Economics and a Master degree in International Economics. He is the Director of the Master in Business Economics and Competition. In the most recent years, Nuno Crespo was Vice-Rector of ISCTE-IUL and assumed several other positions such as Director of the Department of Economics, Scientific Commission of the Department of Economics, and the coordenation of courses (Master in Portuguese Economy and International Integration and Master in Health Services Management). Researcher at Business Research Unit (BRU-IUL), he has several publications in scientific journals such as World Economy, World Development, Economics Letters, Review of World Economics, Journal of Common Market Studies, Journal of Economic Surveys, Empirical Economics, Papers in Regional Science, Tourism Analysis, Journal of Economics and Social Measurement, Telecommunications Policy, Journal of Informetrics, Scientometrics, International Review of Applied Economics, International Journal of Social Economics. Publications of books and book chapters in his areas of expertise. He is Co-Editor-in-Chief of the Academy of Entrepreneurship Journal and member of the editorial board of several international scientific journals (European Journal of International Management, International Journal of Trade and Global Markets, International Journal of Knowledge and Learning, Sustainability, and Tourism Analysis, among others). Editor of the MPRA. Member of the International Economics Advisory Board of the Cambridge Scholars Publishing. Member of the Global Partner of the National Economic Education Delegation (NEED). He integrates the board of the Portuguese Economists Association (Ordem dos Economistas).

Nadia Simoes holds a PhD in Economics and a Master degree in Economics from ISEG (Universidade de Lisboa). Started to teach in the Economics Department of ISCTE - Instituto Universitário de Lisboa in 2002. Director of the Bachelor Degree in Economics (Iscte - Instituto Universitário de Lisboa). Former Director of the Master in Business Economics and Competition for nine editions of the programme. Researcher of the Economics Group of the Business Research Unit (BRU-IUL). She has published paper articles in several journals such as Economics Letters, Journal of Economic Surveys, Empirical Economics, Acta Oeconomica, International Review of Applied Economics, Telecommunications Policy, Panoeconomicus, International Journal of Social Economics, Economics Bulletin, among others. Associate Editor of the journal International Journal of Education Economics and Development (SCOPUS Q4) and Editor of the journal Cogent Economics & Finance (SCOPUS Q3). Member of the Editorial Board of the following journals: Entrepreneurship and Sustainability Issues (SCOPUS Q1); Journal of Entrepreneurship Education (SCOPUS Q2); Panoeconomicus (SCOPUS Q2); Journal of Entrepreneurship in Emerging Economies (SCOPUS Q2); Academy of Entrepreneurship Journal (SCOPUS Q3); and of the International Journal of Entrepreneurship (SCOPUS Q3). NEP Editor for the area of

Education (nep-edu). Member of the Editorial Board of the European Training Foundation (European Union). She has participated in several research national and international research projects financed by public institutions (including two projects funded by FCT and a project funded by the Ministry of Employment). Expert for different national and international institutions such as the European Employment Observatory (European Commission), International Labour Organization, Cedefop, Eurofound, European Centre of Expertise, Portuguese Labour Ministry, and Portuguese Ministry of Education.

***

Naman Agrawal is a Senior Undergraduate in the Department of Economic Sciences of Indian Institute of Technology Kanpur. He is ranked 1st in his class and has consistently won Academic Excellence Awards for 2016-17 and 2018-19. Naman has also been involved in raising the Public Policy and Opinion Cell (formerly Students' Opinion Society) of IIT Kanpur from the founding days.

Sachin Angural has graduated from Indian Institute of Technology Kanpur with majors in Economic Sciences. He is currently working with a global investment bank as an analyst. He has worked in the field of quantitative finance for more than two years during his undergraduate program at IIT Kanpur. He has presented his works at various national and international conferences.

Larry Crump is Deputy Director of the APEC Study Centre at Griffith University (Australia) and Senior Fellow Alumni at the Centre for Global Cooperation Research (Germany). Each institution supported the development of this chapter. Larry teaches international negotiation at Griffith University, while devoting over 25 years to the study of negotiation complexity. Larry has examined negotiations involving the G20, UN climate change negotiations, the WTO, negotiations involving regional associations (APEC, EU, Mercosur, Pacific Alliance, TPP, Union for the Mediterranean) and many bilateral trade negotiations to extend theory on negotiation strategy, linkage dynamics, institutional structure, closure, turning points, framing and coalition building.

Iulia Monica Dumitrescu is a teaching assistant at "Babes-Bolyai" University in Cluj-Napoca, Romania. She is a PHD candidate developing her thesis in a joint collaboration between ISCTE-IUL, Lisbon, Portugal and "Babes-Bolyai" University on the topic of international trade. She also holds a masters degree in international business management.

Jorge Falcón Gómez has a Master Degree from the FLACSO-Ecuador. His areas of interest are Economic Growth, Foreign Trade and Public Economics. He has been undersecretary of fiscal relations and national director of spending quality in Ministry of Finance in Ecuador. In the private sector he has carried out numerous analysis and research for a public policy proposal from the Chamber of Industries and Production, as well as an independent consultant for different institutions. He has also several academic publication and research in progress.

Vítor Hugo Ferreira has received his PhD from Lisbon University (ISEG) in Entrepreneurship & Innovation, focusing the innovation dynamics and regional catching up. He was the Executive Director of Leiria Business School in Portugal until 2020. He is an associate professor of Polytechnic Institute of Leiria and has been collaborating with some European Business Schools in Finland, Holland, Hungary and France. Since his MSc which has focused Portugal Vs China: Strategies, Competences and Innovation, he has been working as consultant in entrepreneurship and innovation projects for many different companies and Business Associations, where he has also worked as a Business Consultant and taught courses for business owners. He was co-responsible for several important studies such as the comparison of the Portuguese mold industry with the Chinese, the evaluation the education needs of Leria's Region and the evaluation of a hydrogen-based industry in South Africa. He is author of many scientific published works, chair at GBATA (Global Business and Technology Association) and reviewer in many different conference and journals. He was also coordinator of the MSc in Management Control and co-founder of the company Look and Go. He is an invited professor at IBS - ISCTE in Lisbon and Feevale University in Brazil. He is co-founder of Plan4Sustain. Currently he is the General Manager at Startup Leiria. Specialties: Innovation, Creativity, Economics, Strategy.

Maria Paula Fontoura is Full Professor of Economics at ISEG- School of Economics and Management of the Universidade de Lisboa. Member of the Research Unit on Complexity and Economics/REM - Research in Economics and Mathematics, a research consortium of ISEG, makes research in the field of international trade. Has publications in scientific journals such as World Economy, World Development, Journal of Common Market Studies, Papers in Regional Science, Review of World Economics, Applied Econometrics and International Development, among others, and several book chapters.

Souhaila Kammoun is an assistant professor et the department of Economics at IHEC Sfax. She holds a PhD in Economics from the University of Social Sciences of Toulouse 1, France. She has taught Economics at the University of Social Sciences of Toulouse and in several university institutions in Tunisia. Her research interests focus on Innovation, Corporate Social Responsibility, Fintechs and FDI. She has published a number of research articles in international journals and collective books. She is currently an active member of the executive board of the Association Université Environnement, at the University of Sfax. She was a member of the PAQ-ES project committee, director of the Master's degree in Entrepreneurship and International Development (Tempus Project funded by the European Union) and member of the scientific council at IHEC of Sfax. She has held the positions of Head of the Department of Economics, Director of Studies and Vice-Director. She was also Director of IHEC of Sfax, Tunisia.

Mikail Kar is working as an academic at Bursa Uludag University, Department of Economics. He completed his undergraduate degree at Istanbul Marmara University, his master's degree at the State University of New York, and his PhD degree at Bursa Uludag University. He mainly works on economic theory, market analysis, methodological issues, economic policy, industrial economics. He has many book chapters and articles published in distinguished international publishing houses and journals in these fields of study. He is still continuing his academic studies at Bursa Uludag University and giving lectures in the field of economic theory.

Mustafa Kiziltan works at Department of Public Finance, Faculty of Economics and Administrative Sciences, Hacettepe University. He has a PhD degree in public finance field from the same university. His research interests are public finance, regional economics and spatial econometrics.

Youssra Ben Romdhane Loukil holds a PhD in Economics from the Faculty of Economics and Management in Sfax (FSEGS), Tunisia. She is a researcher at the laboratory of economics and development (LED). Her research focuses on the following topics: macroeconomic aggregates, political uncertainty, technology and FDI. She also have published many book chapters in IGI Global and some papers in international journals.

Fernando Martín Mayoral has a Doctorate Degree from the University of Salamanca and received the "Enrique Fuentes Quintana" National Award from the FUNCAS Foundation for the best doctoral thesis published in Spain in 2008. His areas of interest are Regional Economics, Economic Growth, Foreign Trade and Public Economics. He has been an undergraduate professor at the University of Salamanca (Spain) and at the Institute for the International Education of Students (IES-Abroad) and postgraduate professor at FLACSO-Ecuador. He was Coordinator of the Department of Development, Environment and Territory and is currently a research professor in the Department of Development, Environment and Territory at FLACSO and Head of the Development Economics Program. He is co-director of the Center for Development Studies and Applied Economics (CEDEA-FLACSO) where he participates in various research for international organizations such as the ILO, WFP or UNU Wider. He has also participated in numerous international events as a lecturer and speaker.

Guy-Maurille Massamba has an academic background in Political Science, International Political Economy, as well as Anthropology, and Philosophy, and has developed a professional background in academic research, university teaching, and international development. His research and publications deal with questions related to Africa's involvement in the global economy, and the impact of information technology on institutional development. He worked as Associate Faculty at Arizona State University. He also works as a contributor to the ongoing research and analysis of democracy in Africa through a comprehensive and extended study launched by the University of Gothenburg. As an International Development Analyst and professional, Dr. Massamba worked as a Consultant for the World Bank for over five years, giving training and advice in capacity building and Results-oriented Project Management methodology to African public institutions.

Somesh Kumar Mathur is a Professor in the Department of Economic Sciences at the Indian Institute of Technology (IIT) Kanpur. His specialization includes, efficiency and productivity analysis, new trade and growth theories, evaluating trade agreements, gravity analysis, convergence issues, spatial planning, CGE and SMART analysis, TRIPS and other WTO Issues, and econometric theory. His research interests are: testing of new trade theories, application of spatial regression, gravity modelling, trade growth accounting, frontier areas in trade, evaluation of regional trade agreements, and applied econometrics and growth.

Imen Ouerghi holds a Phd in Quantitative Methods, CAMPUS MANAR, Manar University. She is currently an Assistant Professor at the Ecole Supérieure de Commerce de Tunis (ESC) , University of Manouba, Tunisia. She is also a researcher at Quantitative Analysis Research Group (QuARG), University of Manouba, Tunisia.

Nicole Palan is a post-doc Researcher at the University of Graz. She has published on structural change, international trade and the impact of digitalization onjJob markets. In a current research project on inequality and digitalization, she analyzes how digitalization affects production and work in Austria as well as trade worldwide.

Niels Søndergaard is a research fellow at the Global Agribusiness Center at Insper, São Paulo. From 2018 to 2020, he was a postdoctoral researcher at the Institute for International Relations at the University of Brasilia. He holds a PhD in International Relations from the University of Brasilia, Brazil (2018), a Masters in Global Studies with major in Political Science from the University of Lund, Sweden (2014), and Bachelor in Global Studies and International Development from the University of Roskilde, Denmark (2011). His research focuses on agricultural production, trade, and governance.

Anusha Thakur has done B.Tech in "Electronics and Instrumentation Technology" from Tumkur, Karnataka, and Master's in Business Administration (MBA) in "International Business" from University of Petroleum & Energy Studies, (UPES) Dehradun. In addition to this, Anusha has also completed a Post-Graduation certification in "Market Research and Data Analytics" from MICA, Ahmedabad. Anusha has also few national and international publications. One of her published works includes chapter on "Market for Plant-Based Meat Alternatives" for the book "Environmental, Health, and Business Opportunities in the New Meat Alternatives Market" which has won accolades across the world. The book was considered #1 in the WORLD in the category of Vegetarian Writing. Further, the book was also announced as the national winner for Australia in the Vegetarian Writing Category. Further, she has a work experience of approximately 4 years in the Market Research industry. Her work primarily focuses, on the secondary research, market analysis, market sizing, interpretation, forecasting and report writing.

Maria João Tomás is an Associate Professor at Universidade Autónoma de Lisboa, Integrated Researcher Observare. PhD History- FCSH-UNL, MD History -FL-UL, Intenrships -University of Basel, UCLA.

José G. Vargas-Hernández, M.B.A., Ph.D., Member of the National System of Researchers of Mexico and a research professor at University Center for Economic and Managerial Sciences, University of Guadalajara. Professor Vargas-Hernández has a Ph. D. in Public Administration and a Ph.D. in Organizational Economics. He has undertaken studies in Organisational Behaviour and has a Master of Business Administration, published four books and more than 200 papers in international journals and reviews (some translated to English, French, German, Portuguese, Farsi, Chinese, etc.) and more than 300 essays in national journals and reviews. He has obtained several international Awards and recognition.

Furkan Yıldız is currently employed in Department of Economics at Kırklareli University, Turkey. He received his bachelor degree in economics from Marmara University in 2008 and MA degree in international trade and money management from Marmara University in 2012. He holds a Ph.D in economics from İstanbul University since 2017.

Index

E

F

G

I

M

N

P

R

S

T

U

V

W

www.ingramcontent.com/pod-product-compliance
Lightning Source LLC
LaVergne TN
LVHW062108300926
849161LV00010B/2403

* 9 7 8 1 7 9 9 8 7 5 6 8 0 *